Daniel Vaughan

Windows Phone 7.5

D1402183

UNLEASHED

 800 East 96th Street, Indianapolis, Indiana 46240 USA

Trademarks

All terms mentioned in this book that are known to be trademarks or service marks have been appropriately capitalized. Sams Publishing cannot attest to the accuracy of this information. Use of a term in this book should not be regarded as affecting the validity of any trademark or service mark.

Warning and Disclaimer

Every effort has been made to make this book as complete and as accurate as possible, but no warranty or fitness is implied. The information provided is on an "as is" basis. The author and the publisher shall have neither liability nor responsibility to any person or entity with respect to any loss or damages arising from the information contained in this book.

Bulk Sales

Sams Publishing offers excellent discounts on this book when ordered in quantity for bulk purchases or special sales. For more information, please contact

> **U.S. Corporate and Government Sales**
> **1-800-382-3419**
> **corpsales@pearsontechgroup.com**

For sales outside of the U.S., please contact

> **International Sales**
> **international@pearsoned.com**

Editor-in-Chief
Greg Wiegand

Executive Editor
Neil Rowe

Development Editor
Mark Renfrow

Managing Editor
Kristy Hart

Project Editor
Betsy Harris

Copy Editor
Geneil Breeze

Indexer
Heather McNeill

Proofreaders
Williams Woods Publishing
Jess DeGabriele

Technical Editor
J. Boyd Nolan

Publishing Coordinator
Cindy Teeters

Book Designer
Gary Adair

Compositor
Nonie Ratcliff

Contents at a Glance

Table of Contents

Foreword

Dear *Windows Phone 7.5 Unleashed* reader,

Welcome to the ranks of the many developers trying to achieve richness or fame in this new and exciting platform. It has been a year since Windows Phone 7 launched (and 1.5 years since it was announced). You are joining the ranks of thousands of registered developers who delivered more than 30,000 apps within the first year after launch. Windows Phone developers are having a lot fun because we have the best tools and, (especially) with this Windows Phone "Mango" release, one of the best platforms. Don't worry if you are just getting started; the business opportunity is still in its infancy. You are still on time (if you hurry), and you are in luck because you now have in your hands (or on your screen) one of the best tools for delivering compelling, well-architected, maintainable Windows Phone applications. That tool is this book: *Windows Phone 7.5 Unleashed*.

I have known Daniel, your author, for about four years. We first met as part of the WPF Disciples, an elite group of XAML experts that spent countless hours passionately discussing and sharing patterns and best practices for .NET and Silverlight application development. Within the group, Daniel is well respected for his knowledge and recognized for his always optimistic attitude toward raising the bar (both on quality and experience) on projects he works on. As usual, he has raised the bar with this epic 16-month writing effort.

Windows Phone 7.5 Unleashed is much more than a great introduction to Windows Phone development. Besides providing a comprehensive view of the platform, where this book excels is in striking the perfect balance between great samples, good and detailed explanations, insightful tips, and—most importantly—real-world experiences and real-world best practices. While other Windows Phone books simply introduce a concept like the application bar, Daniel provides great wrappers or abstractions to improve the development experience. Other books might oversimplify a sample to keep a chapter focused on the topic, but Daniel delivers a useful, real-world example that is more interesting and comprehensive. I can't say he keeps it short—at about 1,200 pages this is not a brief book—but it is an easy read because of its focus and carefully editorialized relevance. I could go on citing examples of Daniel's thoroughness (maybe one more since I am confident few books will have unit testing or input validation chapters), but instead I will let you get to the task at hand: building your Windows Phone apps.

Enjoy the journey!

Happy Windows Phone coding!

Jaime Rodriguez
Principal Evangelist, Microsoft

P.S. To Daniel (and the Sams team):

I know you spent more than a year writing this book and when facing tough decisions, such as what to cut or whether to hold off the book to cover Mango instead of releasing a book that was going to be out-of-date at print, you always made the right calls for the readers. The book shows it.

Congratulations!

Preface

Windows Phone OS is Microsoft's new mobile phone operating system. It is a substantial departure from Microsoft's previous Windows Mobile technology, as it provides the capability to develop applications for the mobile phone using either Silverlight or XNA. Silverlight, in particular, is a technology that has seen rapid adoption for multimedia web development and desktop line of business applications. Extending the Silverlight development experience to the phone was welcome news to many Silverlight developers because it opened up many exciting opportunities. Silverlight's key advantage is that it brings increased productivity to developers.

Windows Phone offers developers the opportunity not only to target the phone OS but also to build cross-platform games and applications that run on the desktop and in the browser: on Windows, Linux, and the Mac. In addition, Windows Phone supports integration with XBox Live and Zune services.

Many features make Windows Phone compelling, such as the phone's built-in services for geographic location, multitouch capabilities, and hubs, which combine both local and online content. Most importantly, the tooling and platform make it fun to develop for.

Windows Phone has a friendlier tiled interface than its predecessor and has been designed around the Metro UI philosophy. The Metro UI philosophy had its origins in the ill-fated Zune media devices. The large typography and fluid scrolling lists make Metro beautiful and highly suited to mobile devices. We now see the Metro language making it to the tablet and desktop environment with Windows 8. Likewise, the application marketplace paradigm will also accompany the release of Windows 8, and like Windows Phone, Windows 8 Metro apps will operate in a sandboxed environment, with fewer capabilities than their fully trusted desktop counterparts. The sandboxing of Windows Phone and Windows 8 Metro apps ensures that the user never has a bad experience with an app. What does this have to do with Windows Phone, you may ask. It is important to recognize the evolution of these various technologies, to have an eye on the future, and to prepare for the likely convergence of the technologies. A total convergence of Windows Phone and Windows desktop OSs may happen at some point. Yet, until it does, both OSs will continue to drive innovation in the other. New features of the Windows Metro UI will undoubtedly make their way to the phone OS over time, and vice-versa. There was, and continues to be, some uncertainty about Silverlight, especially on the browser. Silverlight on Windows Phone, however, is alive and well, and with the upcoming release of Windows 8 and the incorporation of the Metro UI in Windows 8, demand for developers with skills in this area is set to rise.

Over the course of writing this book I witnessed the initial release of the Windows Phone OS 7.0 and the subsequent release of Windows Phone OS 7.5 (Mango). Development of Windows Phone apps using Silverlight is a large topic, and one that increased broadly with version 7.5. Many new features (more than 500 according to Microsoft) were added to the OS, and these had to be covered for the release of the book, adding several more months of writing time. The new features of Mango are, however, compelling, and they unlock many new and exciting opportunities on the platform.

Scope of This Book

This book targets Windows Phone 7.5 Mango. While you see some examples incorporating XNA, this book's focus is squarely on Silverlight for Windows Phone. The book covers all main areas of the topic in a deep, yet easily comprehensible way, using practical examples with a real-world context. The goal is to provide you with the concepts and techniques that will help you to design and develop well-engineered and robust Windows Phone apps.

Throughout this book you see a small number of techniques and custom code applied to make developing phone apps easier. It is not the intention to make what you learn in the book harder to reach, but, on the contrary, the techniques are tried and tested approaches that, once familiar, will help you build more testable and maintainable apps. The competition between apps on the platform is set to intensify as the number of apps in the Windows Phone marketplace increases. This competition will not only bring a "long tail," where independent developers find evermore niche categories to create apps for, but will also require apps competing in the more popular categories to increase their feature sets. As apps become more complex, maintainability comes to the forefront, and greater attention to managing complexity is required.

This book is not a Silverlight beginner's book. Although there is considerable reference material for some essential Silverlight infrastructure, included within its chapters are also advanced topics such as the Model-View-ViewModel design pattern (MVVM). In fact, most sample apps follow the MVVM pattern. The concepts and techniques used throughout the book are described in Chapter 2, "Fundamental Concepts in Silverlight Development for Windows Phone." Do not worry if some of these approaches seem foreign to you; by the end of the book they will be second nature.

Wherever possible you are provided with tips and techniques that go beyond the topic, and you will frequently find content not easily found elsewhere. A lot of custom code is provided that extends the Windows Phone SDK to support real app scenarios.

Assumptions about the Reader

If you are an experienced developer who has basic experience in Silverlight or WPF concepts, looking to transfer your skills to Windows Phone, this book is for you. It is assumed that you are familiar with C#, XAML, and Visual Studio.

Book Structure

The book is divided into five parts:

- ▶ Part I, "Windows Phone App Development Fundamentals"
- ▶ Part II, "Essential Elements"
- ▶ Part III, "Windows Phone App Development"
- ▶ Part IV, "Building Windows Phone Data Driven Applications"
- ▶ Part V, "Multitasking"

Most chapters have sample apps. Chapter 2 is required reading to understand the techniques used throughout the book and the samples.

Some chapters, in particular Chapter 9, "Silverlight Toolkit Controls," are not intended to be read from end to end but rather are intended as references that you may refer back to when you need to learn about a particular topic within the chapter.

Code Samples

To demonstrate each concept, this book contains more than 100 samples. The sample code for this book can be downloaded from http://informit.com/title/9780672333484.

All code is in C#. The project structure is divided into topic areas. To view a particular sample, you can run the main solution and select the sample page from the index (see Figure P.1).

FIGURE P.1   The sample code index page

In the downloadable sample code there are several solutions. In most cases, the DanielVaughan.WindowsPhone7Unleashed.sln is used. Some topics, however, have been separated into separate solutions due to technical constraints.

Much of the infrastructure code presented in the book has been consolidated into the Calcium open-source project. You can find more information about the Calcium SDK at http://calciumsdk.net.

A note about the code snippets printed in the book: Occasionally, when a line runs too long for the printed page, a code-continuation arrow (➥) has been used to indicate the line continuation.

About the Author

Daniel Vaughan is cofounder and president of Outcoder, a Swiss software and consulting company dedicated to creating best-of-breed user experiences and leading-edge back-end solutions, using the Microsoft stack of technologies—in particular Silverlight, WPF, WinRT, and Windows Phone.

Daniel is a technical advisory board member of PebbleAge, a Swiss finance company specializing in business process management.

He is a Microsoft MVP for Client Application Development, with more than a decade of commercial experience across a wide range of industries including finance, e-commerce, and multimedia.

He is a Silverlight and WPF Insider, a member of the elite WPF Disciples group, and three-time CodeProject MVP. Daniel is also the creator of a number of open-source projects, including Calcium and Clog.

Daniel blogs at http://danielvaughan.org, where he publishes articles and software prototypes.

He has a degree in Computer Science from UNE, where he received various awards including the Thomas Arnold Burr Memorial Prize in Mathematics, and twice the annual School of Mathematics, Statistics and Computer Science Prize.

With his wife, Daniel runs the Windows Phone Experts group on LinkedIn at http://linkd.in/jnFoqE

Originally from Australia and the UK, Daniel is based in Zurich, Switzerland, where he lives with his wife, Katka.

Dedication

To my wonderful wife, Katka.

Acknowledgments

Brennon Williams, for first suggesting to Sams Publishing that I write the book and for his inspiration and encouragement along the way.

Jaime Rodriguez, for answering my numerous questions about the SDK and the future of the platform.

My friends Sacha Barber and Peter O'Hanlon, for technically reviewing some chapters.

Katka Vaughan, for endless advice, proofreading, and formatting. Your contribution and unending patience made this book possible.

Laurent Bugnion, for being my "author buddy" and for answering my numerous authoring-related questions.

The great folks at PebbleAge—in particular Olivier Parchet and Christian Kobel—for their encouragement and goodwill.

Microsoft, for answering questions and building great tools.

The terrific team at Sams, especially Neil Rowe, for guidance throughout the entire process, technical editor J. Boyd Nolan, for going over my code with a fine-toothed comb, and Mark Renfrow and Betsy Harris.

For inspiration and support (in no particular order):

David Anson, Cliff Simpkins, John Papa, Davide Zordan, Marlon Grech, Glenn Block, Charles Petzold, Erik Mork, Jeremy Likness, Rene Schulte, Josh Smith, Corrado Cavalli, Colin Eberhardt, Jeff Wilcox, all the WPF Disciples.

We Want to Hear from You!

As the reader of this book, *you* are our most important critic and commentator. We value your opinion and want to know what we're doing right, what we could do better, what areas you'd like to see us publish in, and any other words of wisdom you're willing to pass our way.

You can email or write me directly to let me know what you did or didn't like about this book—as well as what we can do to make our books stronger.

Please note that I cannot help you with technical problems related to the topic of this book, and that due to the high volume of mail I receive, I might not be able to reply to every message.

When you write, please be sure to include this book's title and author as well as your name and phone number or email address. I will carefully review your comments and share them with the author and editors who worked on the book.

E-mail: feedback@samspublishing.com

Mail: Neil Rowe
Executive Editor
Sams Publishing
800 East 96th Street
Indianapolis, IN 46240 USA

Reader Services

Visit our website and register this book at informit.com/register for convenient access to any updates, downloads, or errata that might be available for this book.

CHAPTER 1

Introduction to Windows Phone App Development

The mobile phone industry is highly competitive. After stiff competition from other mobile technologies, Microsoft has gone all out to reenter the mobile software market with a strong emphasis on software, hardware, and services. Windows Phone 7 represents a clean break from the past, and as a consequence Windows Mobile 6.5 applications are not compatible with Windows Phone 7.

Windows Phone provides developers with two powerful UI technologies for developing apps: Silverlight and XNA. While the focus of this book is Silverlight, it would not be complete without some coverage of XNA, since after all there is overlap between the two in the Windows Phone SDK, and, as you see in Chapter 20, "Incorporating XNA Graphics in Silverlight," it is even possible to combine the two!

Both technologies are fundamentally different; each was designed with a different set of goals in mind, and each has various pros and cons. Silverlight was designed for building rich Internet applications, and XNA was designed for simplifying game development and to enable cross-platform game development.

Silverlight is based on Windows Presentation Foundation (WPF) and was first released in 2007. Since then it has gone on to encompass not only the Web but also the desktop with out-of-browser applications (OOB), and even Linux, with the Moonlight project. Silverlight for Windows Phone is a close subset of Silverlight 4 for the browser, and some features, relating to the specific UI requirements of the phone, go beyond Silverlight for the browser.

XNA's goal is to free game developers from writing repetitive boilerplate code, and to combine various aspects of game development into a single system. XNA was first released in 2006 and includes an extensive set of class libraries, specific to game development.

Both technologies can utilize the rich development environment of Visual Studio 2010. In addition, the developer tools, which include Visual Studio Express 2010 and Expression Blend, are free!

This chapter provides a step-by-step guide to getting started with Silverlight and XNA for Windows Phone. The chapter looks at the installation of the Windows Phone development tools, examines the feature differences of Silverlight and XNA, and finally demonstrates how to create a simple app using either technology.

Installing the Windows Phone SDK

The Windows Phone SDK includes all the software required to get you started building Windows Phone apps. It can be downloaded from the App Hub developer site at http://create.msdn.com. Once you have downloaded and started the setup program, the setup automatically downloads and installs the required components. The SDK supports both the development of Silverlight and XNA apps.

The developer tools include the following items:

▶ Visual Studio Express 2010

▶ The Windows Phone Emulator, which allows you to debug your applications on the desktop

▶ Silverlight for Windows Phone

▶ Microsoft Expression Blend for Windows Phone

▶ XNA Game Studio 4.0

> **NOTE**
>
> During installation, if you have Visual Studio 2010 already installed, then the tools are integrated into the existing Visual Studio installation. If not, Visual Studio 2010 Express is installed.

Comparing XNA and Silverlight

The choice to use Silverlight or XNA as your primary UI technology for your app depends on a number of factors, including the platforms you intend to target (for example, Xbox, Web, and so on), the performance requirements of the graphics system, the skill set of the developer, and the number of business related features, such as input forms and dialogs.

Silverlight is the preferred technology for business apps on the phone, as it offers an event driven environment with a rich set of controls that can be used out-of-the-box to match the look and feel of the phone, and built-in layout and navigation systems.

Silverlight applications can be deployed to the Web, the Windows desktop (as out-of-browser applications), and, of course, to Windows Phone. For games, Silverlight provides support for vector graphics and GPU acceleration.

While Silverlight can be a good choice for both business applications and games, it lacks the raw performance of XNA. XNA offers a high performance 2D and 3D graphics system, with support for shaders, collision detection, and positional audio. XNA games can be deployed to Xbox 360, the Windows desktop, and Windows Phone.

At this time, C# and VB.NET are the supported development language for both Silverlight and XNA on the phone. Other .NET languages, such as F#, may be used for development, but be mindful of avoiding references to assemblies that use APIs not available on the phone. The Windows Phone SDK also does not include Visual Studio project templates for languages other than C# and VB.NET.

The key differences between Silverlight and XNA are listed in Table 1.1.

> **TIP**
>
> While the differences between Silverlight and XNA are considerable, keep in mind that if you are not planning on targeting a platform other than Windows Phone, there is no reason why Silverlight and XNA cannot be combined in the same app.

TABLE 1.1   Silverlight and XNA Feature Comparison

Feature	XNA	Silverlight
Web	X	✓
Desktop	✓	✓
Zune	✓	X
Xbox	✓	X*
2D	✓	✓
3D	✓	X**
Xbox LIVE	✓	X
Rich controls	X	✓
Web browser control	X	✓
Vector graphics	X	✓
Layout support	X	✓
Free design-time environment	X	✓
Advanced tools support (physics, shaders, collision detection, positional audio)	✓	X

TABLE 1.1   Continued

Data binding and styles	X	✓
GPU acceleration	✓	✓
Full screen video	✓	✓
Composite video	X	✓
Hardware keyboard support	✓	✓
Software keyboard support	X	✓

* While not currently supported, there are rumors that Silverlight will eventually make its way to the Xbox 360.

** Silverlight does not have native support for 3D, although a number of third party, open-source, frameworks exist; such as Balder (http://balder.codeplex.com/) and Kit3D (http://kit3d.codeplex.com/).

Creating Your First Silverlight for Windows Phone App

This section walks through the creation of a simple Silverlight for Windows Phone app using Visual Studio and looks at using the Windows Phone emulator to debug applications on the desktop.

To create a Silverlight project for Windows Phone, follow these steps:

1. From within Visual Studio 2010, select New Project from the File menu.

2. Select the Silverlight for Windows Phone node in the Installed Templates pane of the Add New Project dialog (see Figure 1.1).

3. Select Windows Phone Application.

4. Provide the project with a name and location.

5. Click OK.

6. A dialog is presented allowing you to select either the 7.0 or 7.1 (Mango) platform. Select Windows Phone OS 7.1 and click OK.

The Windows Phone Application template produces a project containing an App.xaml file, a MainPage.xaml, and their respective code-beside[1] files (see Figure 1.2).

---

1. *The term code-beside is analogous to code-behind, except that rather than the code-behind class being a subclass of the class generated from the markup file, the code-beside and the markup file are partial classes of the same class type.*

FIGURE 1.1   Creating a new Windows Phone Application project using the Add New Project dialog

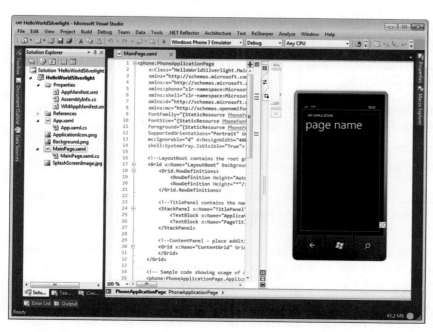

FIGURE 1.2   A newly created Windows Phone Silverlight project

TIP

The XAML design view within Visual Studio can take a few moments to render a page or control. To prevent the designer from automatically loading the design view, select Options from the Tools menu, locate the Text Editor/XAML/Miscellaneous node, and check the option Always Open Documents in Full XAML View.

Once the project has been created, it is ready to be run inside the emulator. Select Start Debugging from the Debug menu in Visual Studio or press F5 to launch the emulator and then the debugger. The first time the emulator starts, it presents the message "Windows Phone Emulator Loading..." and may take several seconds to initialize.

TIP

The Windows Phone emulator is a virtual machine containing the actual Windows Phone operating system (OS). Launching the emulator incurs a delay because the OS takes time to boot. If the emulator is left open between debugging sessions, the initial startup delay is minimized.

The emulator contains a floating menu that allows you to close or minimize the emulator, change the orientation of the display, change the display size of the emulated device, and open the Additional Tools window (see Figure 1.3).

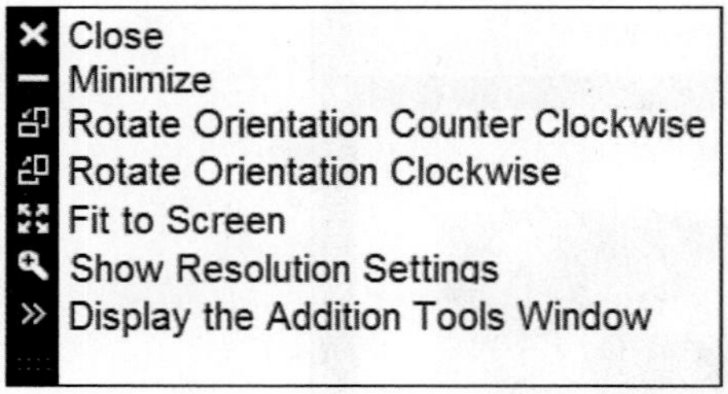

```
✕  Close
─  Minimize
⊞  Rotate Orientation Counter Clockwise
⊞  Rotate Orientation Clockwise
⛶  Fit to Screen
🔍  Show Resolution Settings
»  Display the Addition Tools Window
```

FIGURE 1.3   The Windows Phone emulator's floating menu

The Close button shuts down the Windows Phone emulator. It is best to refrain from using the Close button to end a debugging session for reasons explained in the previous tip.

The Minimize button works in the same manner as the Minimize button on a Windows desktop application. The emulator continues to run but is not visible on the desktop.

Rotate Orientation (Clockwise and Counter Clockwise) changes the display orientation from landscape to portrait or portrait to landscape. In Chapter 4, "Page Orientation," you see how changes to the orientation of a page can be monitored and controlled.

Fit to Screen scales the emulator display to fit about 80% of your smallest screen dimension.

Show Resolution Settings is used to display the Resolution Settings dialog, which is used to scale the display from 33% to 100%. The phone's screen has a pixel density of 262 DPI, which is more than twice as great as the default 96 DPI that Windows uses. This is why, at 100%, the emulator looks so large on the desktop.

> **NOTE**
>
> Using the Windows Phone emulator inside a virtual machine is not supported.

Once the emulator finishes loading, the newly created application launches, and the MainPage is displayed (see Figure 1.4).

FIGURE 1.4   A freshly created app running on the emulator

A new Silverlight for Windows Phone application project starts out with a PhoneApplicationPage called MainPage, set to a Portrait orientation. MainPage is the default starting page for the application.

> **NOTE**
>
> To change the application's startup page, expand the Properties node in the Solution Explorer, and open the file WMAppManifest.xml. Then modify the DefaultTask element, as shown in the following excerpt:
>
> ```
> <DefaultTask Name="_default" NavigationPage="YourPage.xaml" />
> ```

Right-clicking on the project node and selecting Properties opens the project's properties tab. From this tab, the deployment title can be customized, along with various other fields including the application's icon, its tile background image, the project's default namespace, and output file names (see Figure 1.5).

The deployment title and icon fields are used to distinguish the application from others on the phone's App List (see Figure 1.6). You can reach the App List from the phone's start page, known as the Start Experience.

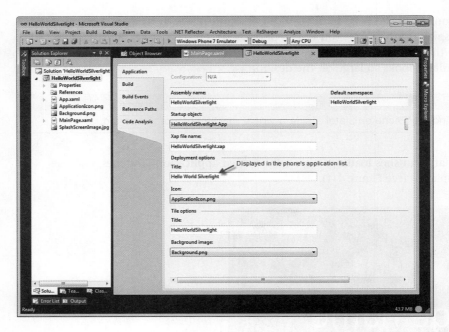

FIGURE 1.5   The project properties tab allows customization of the application's title.

FIGURE 1.6   The application's title is displayed on the App List.

The Tile options, including the Title and Background Image fields, are applied when the app is pinned to the Start Experience.

You explore tiles in greater detail in Chapter 13, "Push Notification."

After a debugging session has ended, despite the debugger being detached from the emulator the app is still deployed to the emulator and can be relaunched from the App List. Closing the emulator, however, removes the app from the App List and, in fact, resets the state of the emulator. Therefore, customization of an app within the emulator persists only while the emulator is running and is lost when the emulator is closed.

The Silverlight Application Class

Silverlight applications rely on an instance of the System.Windows.Application class to perform the startup activities of the app. Visual Studio's Silverlight Windows Phone Application template creates an App class that subclasses the Application class. The App class consists of an App.xaml.cs file (the code-beside) containing a partial class and an accompanying App.xaml XAML file. The App.xaml file allows for resources, such as styles, to be defined in XAML and used throughout your app (see Listing 1.1).

The App class is derived from the Application class by using the x:Class attribute in the Application element of the App.xaml file.

LISTING 1.1   App.xaml

```
<Application
x:Class="HelloWorldSilverlight.App"
xmlns="http://schemas.microsoft.com/winfx/2006/xaml/presentation"
xmlns:x="http://schemas.microsoft.com/winfx/2006/xaml"
xmlns:phone="clr-namespace:Microsoft.Phone.Controls;assembly=Microsoft.Phone"
xmlns:shell="clr-namespace:Microsoft.Phone.Shell;assembly=Microsoft.Phone">

    <!--Application Resources-->
    <Application.Resources>
    </Application.Resources>

    <Application.ApplicationLifetimeObjects>
        <!--Required object that handles lifetime events for the application-->
        <shell:PhoneApplicationService
        Launching="Application_Launching" Closing="Application_Closing"
        Activated="Application_Activated"
        Deactivated="Application_Deactivated"/>
    </Application.ApplicationLifetimeObjects>

</Application>
```

Within App.xaml, the PhoneApplicationService is used to subscribe to application lifetime events. You look at lifetime events in greater detail in Chapter 3, "Application Execution Model."

Event handlers for lifetime events are located in the App class. This class can be used to perform tasks before the UI is shown and is used to create the PhoneApplicationFrame instance, which plays host to the `MainPage`, and any other pages, at runtime. The `PhoneApplicationFrame` is analogous to a web browser in that it handles navigation to and from each `PhoneApplicationPage`.

The `App` class also includes an event handler for unhandled exceptions. If an exception is raised anywhere in the app from any thread and it is not handled, the `Application.UnhandledException` event is raised, affording your app the opportunity to log the error or warn the user that an error has occurred.

TIP

If there are multiple `Application` classes within a project, then the desired `Application` class can be specified using the project's properties tab, as shown in Figure 1.5.

Sometimes renaming a namespace can cause the project setting for the startup `Application` class to become invalid. If this occurs, the project properties tab can be used to correct the problem.

MainPage

The `MainPage` code-beside is shown in Listing 1.2. The using statements beginning with `System.Windows` are part of the Silverlight 4 Framework Class Library (FCL). The using statement for `Microsoft.Phone.Controls` is particular to Windows Phone and contains controls such as the `PhoneApplicationPage`.

TIP

The using statements are placed in the code-beside file as a convenience, to save you time when writing code. It is a good practice to remove any unused using statements from a class because it decreases clutter and eliminates unnecessary dependencies, which can sometimes prevent compilation when linking class files across different projects, where the namespaces are not present.

LISTING 1.2   MainPage.cs

```
using System;
using System.Collections.Generic;
using System.Linq;
using System.Net;
using System.Windows;
using System.Windows.Controls;
using System.Windows.Documents;
using System.Windows.Input;
using System.Windows.Media;
using System.Windows.Media.Animation;
using System.Windows.Shapes;
using Microsoft.Phone.Controls;
```

LISTING 1.2   Continued

```
namespace HelloWorldSilverlight
{
    public partial class MainPage : PhoneApplicationPage
    {
        // Constructor
        public MainPage()
        {
            InitializeComponent();
        }
    }
}
```

MainPage.xaml contains the initial layout, with a `Grid` as the root content, a child `StackPanel` containing the application title and page title, and another `Grid` to place the page's content (see Listing 1.3).

LISTING 1.3   MainPage.xaml

```xml
<phone:PhoneApplicationPage
    x:Class="HelloWorldSilverlight.MainPage"
    xmlns="http://schemas.microsoft.com/winfx/2006/xaml/presentation"
    xmlns:x="http://schemas.microsoft.com/winfx/2006/xaml"
    xmlns:phone="clr-namespace:Microsoft.Phone.Controls;assembly=Microsoft.Phone"
    xmlns:shell="clr-namespace:Microsoft.Phone.Shell;assembly=Microsoft.Phone"
    xmlns:d="http://schemas.microsoft.com/expression/blend/2008"
    xmlns:mc="http://schemas.openxmlformats.org/markup-compatibility/2006"
    FontFamily="{StaticResource PhoneFontFamilyNormal}"
    FontSize="{StaticResource PhoneFontSizeNormal}"
    Foreground="{StaticResource PhoneForegroundBrush}"
    SupportedOrientations="Portrait" Orientation="Portrait"
    mc:Ignorable="d" d:DesignWidth="480" d:DesignHeight="768"
    shell:SystemTray.IsVisible="True">

    <!--LayoutRoot contains the root grid where all other page content is placed-->
    <Grid x:Name="LayoutRoot" Background="Transparent">
        <Grid.RowDefinitions>
            <RowDefinition Height="Auto"/>
            <RowDefinition Height="*"/>
        </Grid.RowDefinitions>

        <!--TitlePanel contains the name of the application and page title-->
        <StackPanel x:Name="TitlePanel" Grid.Row="0" Margin="24,24,0,12">
            <TextBlock x:Name="ApplicationTitle"
                    Text="MY APPLICATION"
```

LISTING 1.3   Continued

```
                  Style="{StaticResource PhoneTextNormalStyle}"/>
          <TextBlock x:Name="PageTitle" Text="page name" Margin="-3,-8,0,0"
                  Style="{StaticResource PhoneTextTitle1Style}"/>
        </StackPanel>

        <!--ContentPanel - place additional content here-->
        <Grid x:Name="ContentGrid" Grid.Row="1">
        </Grid>
    </Grid>

</phone:PhoneApplicationPage>
```

The x:Class attribute indicates the code-beside type, which in this case is the HelloWorldSilverlight.MainPage class.

The mc:Ignorable="d" attribute is used to tell the compiler to ignore any elements or attributes that begin with d:. The two attributes d:DesignHeight and d:DesignWidth are used at design-time by Visual Studio and Expression Blend to render the page using the specified dimensions. In other words, these attributes are for your benefit and do not influence the page at runtime.

Various text related properties are set in the phone:PhoneApplicationPage element, specifically the FontFamily, FontSize, and Foreground properties. These indicate the default appearance of text in an element such as a TextBlock, when not specified on the element itself. This is an example of parent-child property value inheritance, where the child control uses the closest ancestor's property value if it does not define its own.

Styles are set to predefined StaticResources, and colors vary according to what theme the user selected for the phone device, either light or dark and the selected accent color. For a complete list of predefined styles see http://bit.ly/cUmhGi.

Creating a First Windows Phone XNA App

This section walks you through the creation of a simple XNA app that writes a message on the phone's display. As you see, unlike Silverlight, XNA requires some extra work before text can be used in the UI.

To create an XNA game project for Windows Phone, perform the following steps:

1. From within Visual Studio 2010, select New Project from the File menu.
2. Select the XNA Game Studio 4.0 node in the Installed Templates pane of the New Project dialog (see Figure 1.7).
3. Select Windows Phone Game.
4. Provide the project with a name and location.
5. Click OK.

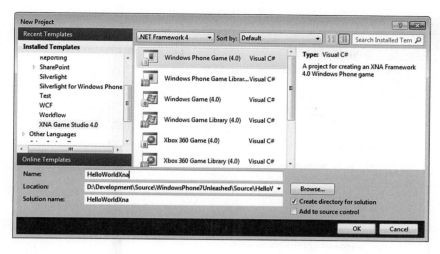

FIGURE 1.7   Creating a new XNA game using the New Project dialog

The Windows Phone Game (4.0) template produces two projects: an XNA Game Studio project and an empty content project that will later contain resources such as image and audio files (see Figure 1.8).

The Program.cs file is not used in the Windows Phone project. The class itself is wrapped in the preprocessor directive `#if WINDOWS || XBOX`. Thus, the code is not compiled because the conditional compilation symbols `WINDOWS` and `XBOX` are by default not defined for a Windows Phone project.

The properties tab for the game project can be opened by right-clicking on the project node and selecting Properties, or by pressing Alt+Enter (see Figure 1.9).

The Game Thumbnail defines the image that is used to represent the application on the phone's App List. The Tile Title and Tile Image define the default representation of the game when it is pinned to the Start Experience.

The Game Startup Type defaults to the `Game1` class if not set. Use this setting to distinguish between multiple game classes.

`Game1` is the entry point for the Windows Phone XNA application. It subclasses the `Microsoft.Xna.Framework.Game` class, which has various virtual methods for handling game execution events, and which are used for the loading of game content, processing of game logic, and for drawing graphics.

Game Execution

The execution model of XNA is fundamentally different than Silverlight. Silverlight is event driven; controls provide events that allow you to respond to user interaction, while the execution model of XNA is a more manual affair. Game execution in XNA involves the following:

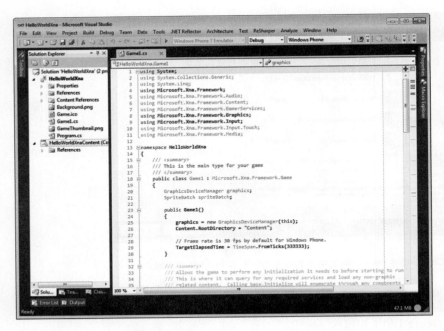

FIGURE 1.8   HelloWorldXna solution

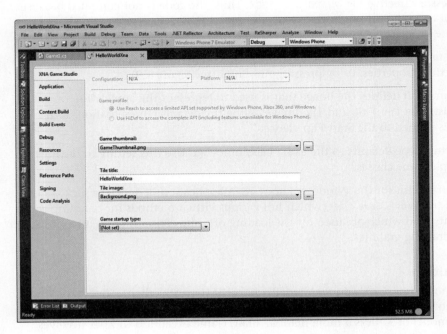

FIGURE 1.9   XNA Game Studio tab allows modification of the tile image and title.

- ▶ Initialization of graphics, sound, and input controllers.
- ▶ Loading resources that will be used for the game, such as sounds, images, and fonts.
- ▶ Periodically processing game logic and drawing graphics.
- ▶ Unloading of content before exiting the game.

Figure 1.10 depicts the game execution life cycle.

The processing of game logic and the drawing of graphics occurs within what is commonly known as the *game loop*.

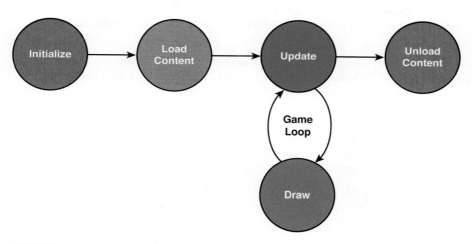

FIGURE 1.10   XNA game execution life cycle

The corresponding Game class methods for handling these events are as follows:

- ▶ Class Constructor
- ▶ Initialize
- ▶ LoadContent
- ▶ Update
- ▶ Draw
- ▶ UnloadContent

The Game1 class constructor, shown in the following excerpt, instantiates the GraphicsDeviceManager, which is later used in conjunction with a SpriteBatch object to draw text and 2D images:

```
public Game1()
{
    graphics = new GraphicsDeviceManager(this);
    Content.RootDirectory = "Content";

    // Frame rate is 30 fps by default for Windows Phone.
    TargetElapsedTime = TimeSpan.FromTicks(333333);
}
```

Content.RootDirectory

XNA uses a content pipeline to retrieve game content during game execution. All content (images, audio files, and so on) is ordinarily placed in a second Visual Studio content project.

The Content.RootDirectory tells XNA where to locate content within the content project. The root directory for the HelloWorldXnaContent project, in the downloadable sample code, is HelloWorldXna/bin/Windows Phone/Debug/Content.

Game.TargetElapsedTime

The default frame rate for Windows Phone is 30 frames/second (fps). The TargetElapsedTime property defines the period between calls to the Update method of the Game class and is measured in milliseconds.

The previous excerpt derives the period from 333333 ticks; where one tick is equal to 100 nanoseconds (ns). 333333 ticks is equal to 33333300 ns or 0.0333333 seconds (s), and thus 1 s / 0.0333333 s/f = 30 fps.

Game Loop

The Microsoft.Xna.Framework.Game class provides two virtual methods that are called as part of the game loop: Update and Draw. It is the task of the Update method to detect user input, process game logic, and test for end game conditions (see Figure 1.11).

The default behavior of the Update method is to test whether the user is pressing the phone's Back button. The phone's hardware back button corresponds to the Xbox 360's Back ButtonState. When it is detected, Exit is called, as shown in the following excerpt:

```
protected override void Update(GameTime gameTime)
{
    // Allows the game to exit
    if (GamePad.GetState(PlayerIndex.One).Buttons.Back == ButtonState.Pressed)
        this.Exit();

    // TODO: Add your update logic here

    base.Update(gameTime);
}
```

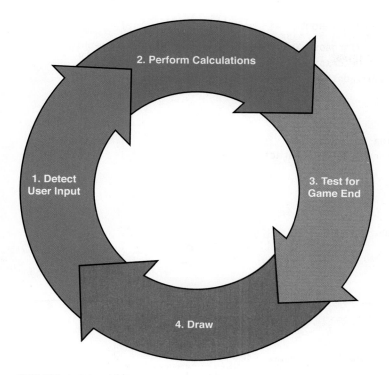

FIGURE 1.11   XNA game loop

Unlike Silverlight, a new generated XNA game does not display any text whatsoever. Launching the game results in a blank screen colored in cornflower blue. The next section looks at writing some text to the display.

Using Fonts in XNA

XNA does not have any built-in fonts of its own and, unlike Silverlight, does not allow the use of system fonts without defining them first. Fonts, like any other content, must be embedded as a resource and must accompany the game. In fact, while Silverlight allows you to use TrueType fonts, which are vector based, XNA requires those fonts to be converted to bitmaps. The process of conversion is, however, done automatically during compilation.

To enable the use of a font within an XNA app, a new Sprite Font must be added to the content project. This is done by right-clicking on the content project and selecting Add, and then New Item, or by using the keyboard shortcut Ctrl+Shift+A (see Figure 1.12).

The Sprite Font file is an XML file that specifies the name of the font, its display size, and various other properties (see Listing 1.4).

LISTING 1.4   NormalSpriteFont.spritefont

```
<XnaContent xmlns:Graphics="Microsoft.Xna.Framework.Content.Pipeline.Graphics">
  <Asset Type="Graphics:FontDescription">
    <FontName>Segoe UI Mono</FontName>
    <Size>30</Size>
    <Spacing>0</Spacing>
    <UseKerning>true</UseKerning>
    <Style>Regular</Style>
    <!-- <DefaultCharacter>*</DefaultCharacter> -->

    <CharacterRegions>
      <CharacterRegion>
        <Start>&#32;</Start>
        <End>&#126;</End>
      </CharacterRegion>
    </CharacterRegions>
  </Asset>
</XnaContent>
```

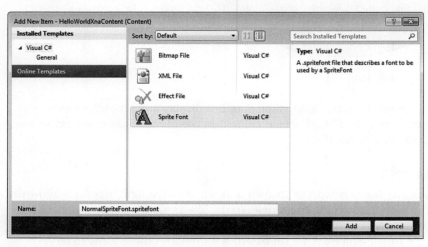

FIGURE 1.12   Adding a Sprite Font to display text

CAUTION

Fonts, as with all graphical assets, may be copyrighted. It is therefore important to ensure that you are legally able to use a particular font in your application. Most of the fonts that come with Windows are in fact copyrighted and therefore cannot be used. There is, however, a set of fonts that comes with XNA Game Studio 4.0 that is fine to use. Also numerous websites provide free and for-purchase fonts.

The official set of fonts that have been licensed by Microsoft from Ascender Corporation and that may be redistributed with your game are shown in Figure 1.13:

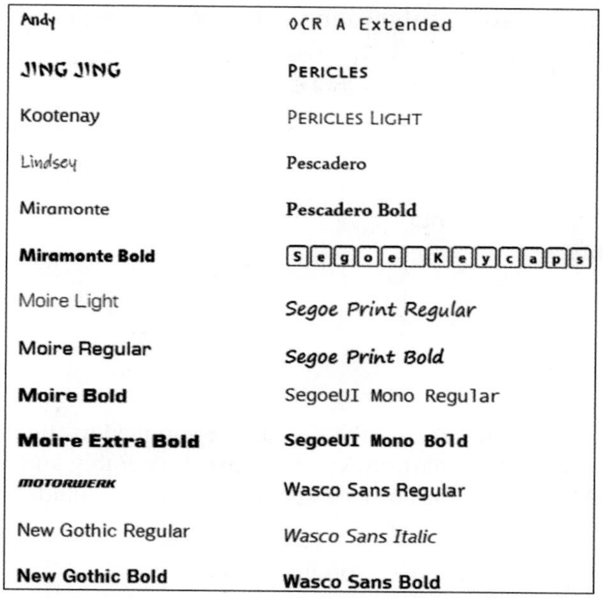

Andy	OCR A Extended
JING JING	PERICLES
Kootenay	PERICLES LIGHT
Lindsey	Pescadero
Miramonte	**Pescadero Bold**
Miramonte Bold	Segoe Keycaps
Moire Light	*Segoe Print Regular*
Moire Regular	*Segoe Print Bold*
Moire Bold	SegoeUI Mono Regular
Moire Extra Bold	**SegoeUI Mono Bold**
MOTORWERK	Wasco Sans Regular
New Gothic Regular	*Wasco Sans Italic*
New Gothic Bold	**Wasco Sans Bold**

FIGURE 1.13   The official set of fonts

To use the SpriteFont, a declaration is added to the Game1 class, as shown in the following excerpt:

```
public class Game1 : Microsoft.Xna.Framework.Game
{
    GraphicsDeviceManager graphics;
    SpriteBatch spriteBatch;

    SpriteFont normalFont;
//...
}
```

The LoadContent method sets up a SpriteBatch instance that can be used to load the SpriteFont from the Content Pipeline, as shown in the following excerpt:

```
protected override void LoadContent()
{
    // Create a new SpriteBatch, which can be used to draw textures.
    spriteBatch = new SpriteBatch(GraphicsDevice);

    normalFont = Content.Load<SpriteFont>("NormalSpriteFont");
}
```

A string can then be drawn, using the SpriteBatch, as shown in the following excerpt:

```
protected override void Draw(GameTime gameTime)
{
    GraphicsDevice.Clear(Color.CornflowerBlue);

    spriteBatch.Begin();
    spriteBatch.DrawString(normalFont, "Hello World!",
        new Vector2(50, 50), Color.Black);
    spriteBatch.End();

    base.Draw(gameTime);
}
```

The location of the string on the display is determined by the coordinate supplied in the Vector2 instance. Vector2 is a struct found in the Microsoft.Xna.Framework assembly and is used frequently not only within XNA, but in various other APIs for the phone, including the phone sensor APIs.

As can be seen in Figure 1.14, the top-left corner marks the origin (0, 0).

Screen coordinates correspond directly with screen resolution. This means that with the *large* screen hardware chassis, 800 by 480 pixels are available.

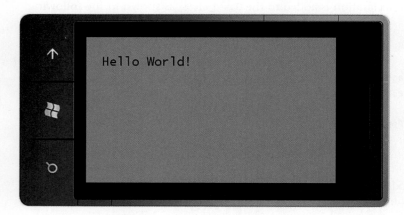

FIGURE 1.14   Displaying text using XNA for Windows Phone

Rotate the emulator's display by using the floating menu (refer to Figure 1.3). This presents the display in landscape mode.

Summary

This chapter provided a step-by-step guide to getting started with Silverlight and XNA. You looked at the installation of the Windows Phone development tools, examined the feature differences of Silverlight and XNA, and, finally, saw a demonstration of how to create a simple app using either technology.

1

CHAPTER 2

Fundamental Concepts in Silverlight Development for Windows Phone

This chapter provides an overview of some common pieces of phone infrastructure and describes various techniques that are useful when building Windows Phone apps.

This chapter begins with a look at the principal output of a Visual Studio Phone Application project: the XAP file. The chapter discusses its composition and shows how to deploy a XAP file to a developer unlocked device.

The chapter then looks at the security capability model of the phone and at how this model is used to notify the user of any potential dangers before downloading an app from the Windows Phone Marketplace. You also look at using the Marketplace Test Kit to determine the capability requirements of your app.

The chapter then examines the threading model of Silverlight for Windows Phone and examines various performance considerations when creating animations or hiding and showing visual elements. You see how the Windows Phone frame rate counter works and learn how to interpret each reading shown on the display.

The chapter then looks at the Windows Phone Performance Analysis tool. You see how to profile your app's performance and memory usage, improve the responsiveness of your app, and help ensure that your app passes the Windows Phone Marketplace certification requirements.

The chapter then turns to the custom code and commonly used techniques that you see frequently throughout the book and that underpin many of the examples in subsequent chapters.

It is not uncommon to have many pages in a Windows Phone app, and having a solid codebase that contains a common infrastructure and frequently used services can save a lot of time. In fact, with more than 100 examples included in the downloadable sample code, creating the code for this book would have taken considerably longer without it.

The techniques demonstrated are tried and tested approaches that will help you build more maintainable apps and by the end of the book will be exceedingly familiar to you if they are not so already.

The overview of the custom infrastructure begins with an exposé of the Model-View-ViewModel pattern, and you see how it is applied in the downloadable sample code. You then examine how property change notification is implemented and see techniques for improving the traditional implementation of INotifyPropertyChanged so that it works effortlessly with multithreaded apps.

The chapter then looks at the commanding infrastructure used throughout the book and examines a custom ICommand that allows you to specify handlers for command evaluation and execution. There is also a brief overview of the argument validation system commonly used in the sample code to validate method arguments.

Finally, you look at a custom dialog service that enables you to ask the user a question from your viewmodel, while remaining compatible with unit testing.

Understanding the Role of XAP Files

The output of a Visual Studio project normally consists of a multitude of files, which may include assemblies, images, config files, manifest files, and so forth. XAP (pronounced *zap*) files contain project output that has been bundled up, ready for deployment.

XAP files have been around since the early days of Silverlight 2 (beta 1) and allow developers to easily deploy an entire Silverlight application to a remote server. On the Windows Phone platform, they are used to deploy an app to the Windows Phone Marketplace or to a developer unlocked device.

A XAP file is a compressed zip file that contains your project assemblies and resources, along with two application manifest files: AppManifest.xml and WMAppManifest.xml, both of which are located in the Properties directory of the project.

NOTE

It is a Windows Phone Marketplace certification requirement that the XAP file contains both an AppManifest.xml file and a WMAppManifest.xml file. Both of these files are automatically generated when creating a new Windows Phone application from within Visual Studio. In nearly all cases, AppManifest.xml does not require changes by you. WMAppManifest.xml, however, may require editing depending on the capabilities supported by your app. This is discussed in the section "The Windows Phone Capabilities Model" later in the chapter.

When publishing to the Windows Phone Marketplace, your app's XAP file is submitted as part of the publishing process.

To obtain the XAP file for your app, perform a build using a Release build configuration. You can then find the XAP file located in your app's Bin/Release directory.

> **NOTE**
>
> When submitting your application to the Windows Phone Marketplace, the XAP file that you submit must be built using a release configuration or it may fail the certification process.

> **NOTE**
>
> The maximum allowed size of the XAP package file for Windows Phone Marketplace certification is 225MB.

The Application Deployment Tool

XAP files allow you to circulate your app to developers who have a developer unlocked device. This is done using the Application Deployment tool located in the Windows Start menu under the Windows Phone SDK. The tool allows you to navigate to select a XAP file and deploy it to a connected phone device (see Figure 2.1).

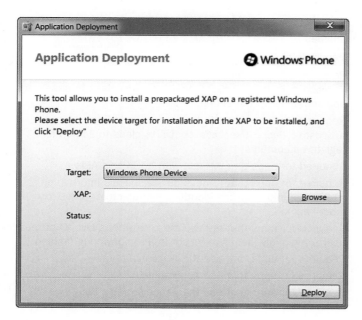

FIGURE 2.1   The Application Deployment tool

If you have not encountered XAP files before, they will certainly become relevant once you want to publish your first app to the Windows Phone Marketplace.

The Windows Phone Capabilities Model

Microsoft recognizes that making the user experience on the phone the best it can be helps to secure greater adoption of the platform. To this end, users should never regret installing an app, and one way to ensure this is by using a security model that requires users to opt-in to certain functionality within the app, called capabilities.

A capability is a phone resource that when used by your app may bring with it privacy or security concerns, or it may incur a cost that the user should be made aware of. Examples of capabilities include the camera, geographic location services, microphone, and SMS.

Capabilities are a way of disclosing to the user what an app is potentially able to do. Your app's capabilities are displayed to potential users, those considering downloading the app from the Windows Phone Marketplace. It is at the user's discretion whether to download your app; if a user does not want an app to have access to, for example, the phone's camera, then the user may decide not to download that app.

Capabilities are defined in your app's WMAppManifest.xml file. When a new Silverlight Windows Phone application is created, the full set of capabilities[1] is included by default in the manifest file. The Windows Phone operating system grants security permissions to the application according to the capabilities listed in the manifest file. See Table 2.1 for a list of these capabilities.

TABLE 2.1   Windows Phone Capabilities

Capability	Description
ID_CAP_APPOINTMENTS	Required for apps that use the `Microsoft.Phone.UserData.Appointments` class to search for appointments on the phone.
ID_CAP_CONTACTS	Required for apps that use the `Microsoft.Phone.UserData.Contacts` class to search for registered contacts.
ID_CAP_GAMERSERVICES	Required for apps that interact with XBOX Live APIs.
ID_CAP_IDENTITY_DEVICE	Required for apps that retrieve device-specific information such as a unique device identifier, manufacturer name, or model name.
ID_CAP_IDENTITY_USER	Required for apps that retrieve the anonymous Live ID of the user to uniquely identify the user in an anonymous fashion.
ID_CAP_ISV_CAMERA	Required for apps that use the device camera.
ID_CAP_LOCATION	Required for apps that use geographic location services.
ID_CAP_MEDIALIB	Required for apps that use the phone's media library.

---

1. *All apart from one capability, the ID_HW_FFCCAMERA (front facing camera) capability, are included.*

TABLE 2.1   Continued

Capability	Description
ID_CAP_MICROPHONE	Required for apps that use the phone device's microphone.
ID_CAP_NETWORKING	Using a data connection can incur a cost to the user, especially when the phone is roaming. Apps are required to disclose whether they perform any network access.
ID_CAP_PHONEDIALER	This capability is required to support tap-to-call features on click-through web pages.
ID_CAP_PUSH_NOTIFICATION	Required for apps that can receive push notifications from an Internet service. This must be disclosed because usage could incur roaming charges.
ID_CAP_SENSORS	Required for apps that use any of the Windows Phone sensors, including accelerometer, gyroscope, compass, and motion sensors.
ID_CAP_WEBBROWSERCOMPONENT	There can be risks when opening web pages that use JavaScript. This capability is therefore required when using the `WebBrowser` control in your app.
ID_HW_FFCCAMERA	This capability is not included by default. It allows access to the phone device's front facing camera if it is present.

When an app is submitted to the Windows Phone Marketplace, the XAP file is decompressed, validated, and repackaged. During this process the security capabilities of the app are discovered and written back to the WMAppManifest.xml file. As a result, if the manifest does not contain capabilities that are used by your app, these capabilities are inserted as part of the submission process.

> **NOTE**
>
> The capabilities specified in the WMAppManifest.xml file before submission are relevant only while debugging your app. By removing unneeded capabilities from the manifest you ensure that no unintended capabilities have crept in during development.
>
> Two capabilities, however, are exceptions to this process: ID_CAP_NETWORKING and ID_HW_FFCCAMERA.
>
> If the ID_CAP_NETWORKING (networking) capability is removed from your app's manifest, it will not be reinserted during the submission process; this enables you to prevent all network activity from your app if you want.
>
> If the ID_HW_FFCCAMERA (front facing camera) capability is specified in your manifest file, it is not automatically removed during the submission process.

> **NOTE**
>
> After submission to the Windows Phone Marketplace, and during the capability discovery process, the Microsoft Intermediate Language (MSIL) of the assemblies located in your XAP file are analyzed. If a phone API that requires a particular capability is detected, the capability is added to the WMAppManifest.xml file. This occurs even if the code is never called by your app at runtime. It is therefore important to be mindful that referencing other assemblies can inadvertently add security capabilities to your app if the other assemblies require capabilities. The security capability detection mechanism is not clever enough to walk your MSIL to discover whether it is actually used; it merely identifies the presence of the API.

> **NOTE**
>
> To pass Windows Phone Marketplace certification, apps are not allowed to use P/Invoke or COM Interop.

Determining App Capabilities Using the Marketplace Test Kit

The Windows Phone SDK includes a tool for analyzing the capabilities required for your app. To analyze your app's capability requirements, perform the following steps:

1. Build the app using a Release configuration.

2. Right-click on the launch project's node in the Visual Studio Solution Explorer and select Open Marketplace Test Kit. The Automated Tests tab includes a Capability Validation test whose Result Details column indicates the capabilities used by the app (see Figure 2.2).

3. Click the Run Tests button to begin the analysis process.

> **NOTE**
>
> The Iconography and Screenshots automated tests fail if you have not specified any icons or screenshots for your app. This is to be expected and does not affect the outcome of the Capability Validation test.

The Marketplace Test Kit is a recent addition to the Windows Phone SDK (it was not present in the first release of the SDK) and offers numerous tests that can assist you in ensuring that your app is Marketplace ready. It can also save you time and the frustration caused by failing the Marketplace submission requirements.

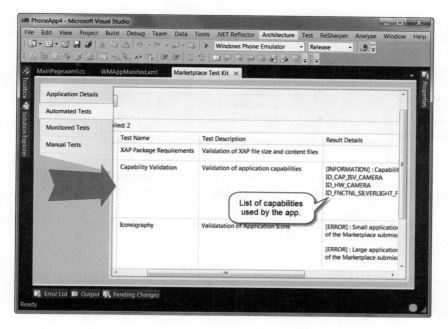

FIGURE 2.2   Viewing the list of required capabilities with the Marketplace Test Kit

The Threading Model for Silverlight Graphics and Animation in Windows Phone

Silverlight for Windows Phone uses two threads for graphics and animation: a UI thread and a composition thread. The composition thread was introduced with the second release (7.5) of the Windows Phone OS. The first release of the OS had issues with performance around user input. A single UI thread had been largely acceptable for Silverlight for the desktop and browser because both generally rely on the mouse for input. The phone, however, relies on touch, which, as it turns out, needs to be substantially more reactive to user input. When using a mouse, a slight delay does not unduly affect the user's perception of your app, but when using touch, a slight delay can make the user feel like the device is broken. Thus, the composition thread was introduced in Windows Phone 7.5[2] to assist in rendering visuals by offloading some of the work traditionally done by the UI thread.

The UI thread is the main thread in Silverlight for Windows Phone and handles user input, events, parsing and creation of objects from XAML, and the initial drawing of all visuals.

---

2. *The composition thread was also introduced to Silverlight for the browser with Silverlight 5 but still lacks the auto-caching capabilities present in Silverlight for Windows Phone. Auto-caching is described in a moment.*

The composition thread aides the UI thread in handling graphics and animation, freeing up the UI thread and making it more responsive to user input. Storyboard-driven animations that run on the composition thread are cached and handled by the device GPU in a process called auto-caching.

> **NOTE**
>
> While the composition thread frees the UI thread in some situations, the key to writing responsive applications is still making sure that the UI thread is not overloaded or blocked by user code, in event handlers for example. If you anticipate that a particular section of code will tie up the UI thread for a considerable amount of time, for more than, say, 50 milliseconds, then use a background thread to perform the activity. The web service APIs, for example, are all designed to be used asynchronously so that they do not block the UI thread.
>
> If you are not familiar with the various mechanisms for spawning background threads, do not worry; you see many examples throughout the book.

The composition thread is used for animations involving the `UIElement`'s `RenderTransform` and `Projection` properties. Typically these animations include the following from the `System.Windows.Media` namespace:

- ▶ `PlaneProjection`
- ▶ `RotateTransform`
- ▶ `ScaleTransform`
- ▶ `TranslateTransform`

> **NOTE**
>
> The composition thread is used only for scale transforms that are less than 50% of the original size. If the scale transform exceeds this amount, the UI thread performs the animation. In addition, the `UIElement.Opacity` and `UIElement.Clip` properties are handled by the composition thread. If an opacity mask or nonrectangular clip is used, however, the UI thread takes over.

Animations and Threads

The composition thread is ideal for handling storyboard animations because it is able to pass them to the device GPU for processing, even while the UI thread is busy. Code-driven animations, however, do not benefit from the composition thread as such animations are handled exclusively by the UI thread, frame by frame using a callback. They are, therefore, subject to slowdown depending on what else occupies the UI thread, and the animation will update only as fast as the frame rate of the UI thread.

Performance and Element Visibility

Silverlight provides two properties that allow you to hide or reveal UI elements: `UIElement.Visibility` and `UIElement.Opacity`—each of which has performance implications depending on how it is used.

The `UIElement.Visibility` property is handled by the UI thread. When an element's `Visibility` property is set to Collapsed, the visual tree must be redrawn. The upside is that when collapsed, the `UIElement` is not retained in visual memory, and thus decreases the amount of memory used by your app.

Conversely, controlling the visibility of an element using the `UIElement.Opacity` property allows the element to be bitmap cached; the element is stored as a simple bitmap image after the first render pass. Bitmap caching allows Silverlight to bypass the render phase for the cached element and to use the composition thread to display the bitmap instead, which can free up the UI thread considerably. By setting the opacity of a cached element to zero, you hide the element without requiring it to be redrawn later. This, however, does mean that, unlike the `Visibility` property, the element is still retained in visual memory.

> **NOTE**
>
> Avoid manipulating the `UIElement.Opacity` property without enabling bitmap caching. Set the `UIElement.CacheMode` property to BitmapCache, as shown in the following example:
>
> ```
> <Path CacheMode="BitmapCache" … />
> ```

Deciding Between Visibility and Opacity

Element opacity in conjunction with bitmap caching usually produces the best performance when hiding and revealing elements. There may be times, however, when the `UIElement.Visibility` property is better and is influenced by the number and complexity of the visual elements being rendered. In such cases it may require experimentation to determine the best approach.

Understanding the Frame Rate Counter

Developing for a mobile device requires particular attention to performance. Mobile devices have less computing power than desktop systems and are more susceptible to performance bottlenecks.

The Windows Phone SDK comes with a built-in control that allows you to monitor the performance of your app, including frames per second and memory usage.

By default, the frame rate counter is enabled in your app's App.xaml.cs file if a debugger is attached, as shown in the following excerpt:

```
if (System.Diagnostics.Debugger.IsAttached)
{
    // Display the current frame rate counters.
    Application.Current.Host.Settings.EnableFrameRateCounter = true;
...
}
```

> **NOTE**
>
> It is possible to enable or disable the frame rate counter programmatically at any time from your app.

The `EnableFrameRateCounter` property is somewhat of a misnomer, since the control also reports a number of other UI metrics, such as texture memory usage, as shown in Figure 2.3.

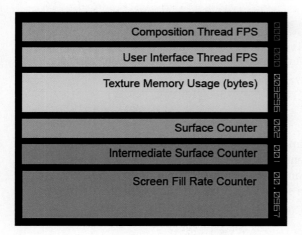

FIGURE 2.3   The Frame Rate Counter

Each field is updated periodically while the app is running. Table 2.2 describes each counter field.

TABLE 2.2   Frame Rate Counter Field Descriptions

Field	Description
Composition (Render) Thread Frame Rate (FPS)	The rate at which the screen is updated. It also represents how often supported animations driven by a storyboard are updated. This value should be as close to 60 as possible. Application performance begins to degrade when this value is below 30. The text in this counter is red when displaying a value below 30.

TABLE 2.2   Continued

Field	Description
User Interface Thread Frame Rate (FPS)	The rate at which the UI thread is running. The UI thread drives input, per-frame callbacks, and any other drawing not handled by the composition thread. The larger this value, the more responsive your application should be. Typically this value should be above 20 to provide an acceptable response time to user input. The text in this counter is red when displaying a value below 15.
Texture Memory Usage	The video memory and system memory copies of textures being used in the application. This is not a general memory counter for the application but represents only memory that surfaces use.
Surface Counter	The number of explicit surfaces being passed to the GPU for processing. The biggest contributor to this number is automatic or developer-cached elements.
Intermediate Surface Counter	The number of implicit surfaces generated as a result of cached surfaces. These surfaces are created in between UI elements so that the application can accurately maintain the Z-order of elements in the UI.
Screen Fill Rate Counter	The number of pixels being painted per frame in terms of screens. A value of 1 represents 480 x 800 pixels. The recommended value is about 2.5. The text in this counter turns red when displaying a value higher than 3.

Source: MSDN: http://bit.ly/l8i0z0

The frame rate counter is a valuable tool for identifying performance bottlenecks in your app. For more detailed performance metrics turn to the Performance Analysis tool, discussed next.

The Windows Phone Performance Analysis Tool

Not only is performance important in ensuring that your app provides an enjoyable experience for your users, but it is also important in a stricter sense: for meeting the certification requirements of the Windows Phone Marketplace. Marketplace certification includes a number of performance related criteria that your app must adhere to. The requirements are as follows:

▶ An application must not exceed 90MB of RAM usage, except on devices that have more than 256MB of memory. Note that even though this specification exists, the Windows Phone hardware specifications for phone manufacturers state that all devices must have at least 256MB of RAM.

▶ If an application performs an operation that causes the device to appear to be unresponsive for more than 3 seconds, such as downloading data over a network connection, the application must display a visual progress or busy indicator.

▶ An app must display the first screen within 5 seconds after launch. You see how to work around this requirement for slow loading apps by creating a splash screen in Chapter 3, "Application Execution Model."

▶ An app must be responsive to user input within 20 seconds after launch.

The Windows Phone Performance Analysis tool comes with the Windows Phone SDK and is integrated into Visual Studio, allowing you to analyze and improve the performance of your apps. The tool profiles your app during runtime to gather either execution metrics or memory usage information.

Execution profiling may include method call counts and visual profiling, allowing you to view the frame rate of your app over time, while memory profiling allows you to analyze your app's memory usage.

To launch the tool select Start Windows Phone Performance Analysis from the Debug menu in Visual Studio. The profiling type can then be selected along with other advanced metrics by expanding the Advanced Settings node, as shown in Figure 2.4.

To begin the profiling session, click the Launch Application link.

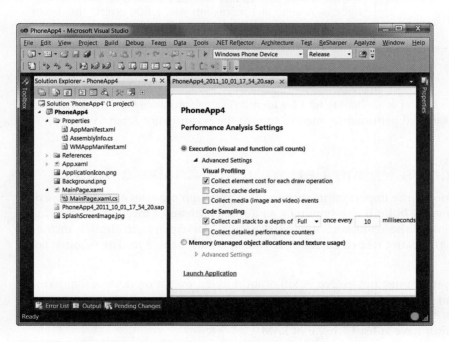

FIGURE 2.4   Configuring the Performance Analysis settings

Whenever the Performance Analysis tool runs, it creates a .sap file in the root directory of your project. A .sap file is an XML file that contains the profiling information gathered during a profiling session and can later be opened by the profiling analysis tools built into Visual Studio.

When done putting your app through its paces, click the Stop Profiling link, shown in Figure 2.5. You can, alternatively, use the device's hardware Back button to stop the profiling session.

> **NOTE**
>
> Avoid disconnecting the phone device to stop a profiling session, as this can lead to sampling errors. Instead always use the Stop Profiling link or the hardware Back button.

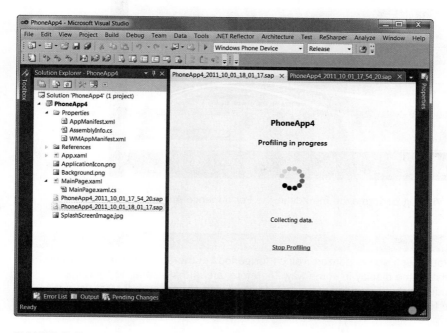

FIGURE 2.5   Profiling in progress with the Performance Analysis tool

Once stopped, the analysis tools automatically parse the .sap file and present the analyzed data in a graph (see Figure 2.6).

The .sap file can be reloaded into the analysis tools by double-clicking on the .sap file in the Visual Studio Solution Explorer.

Each section of the analysis tools view is discussed in the following sections.

Frame Rate Graph

The Frame Rate graph displays the number of screen redraws (in frames per second) that the app completed at the particular point in the timeline.

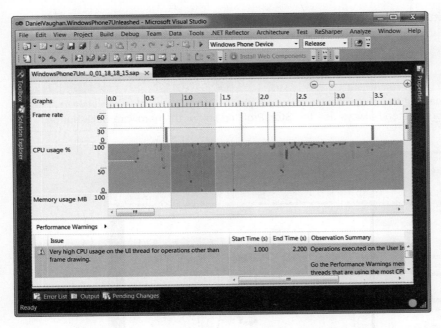

FIGURE 2.6   Viewing performance metrics in the Performance Analysis tool

> **NOTE**
>
> The Frame Rate graph shows nonzero values for periods in the timeline where the application was updating the display in some way. Therefore, areas that appear to have a zero frame rate indicate that no updating was taking place and not necessarily that your app was not able to render any frames.

> **NOTE**
>
> You should aim to have the frame rate value averaging between 30 and 60 fps.

CPU Usage Graph

The CPU Usage graph displays the activity of various threads using different colors, as described in Table 2.3.

TABLE 2.3   CPU Graph Colors

Color	Thread	Notes
Green	UI Thread	Green shading indicates screen updates and touch input. You should aim to keep the UI thread to less than 50% of CPU usage.
Purple	App Threads	Purple indicates application activity that is not on the UI thread. Activity can be from the composition thread or from your app's background threads, such as those used from the `AppPool`.
Grey	System Threads	Grey indicates activity that is independent of your app, such as background agent activity.
White	Idle Threads	White indicates the available CPU percentage. The higher the idle thread percentage, the more responsive the app should be.

Memory Usage MB Graph

Memory Usage MB shows the amount of RAM being consumed by your app in megabytes, at any point along the timeline. This graph allows you to identify excessive memory usage.

Storyboards

Storyboards are displayed as an S flag on the timeline to indicate the occurrence of a storyboard event, and typically indicate the start of an animation. There are two kinds of flags: A red flag indicates a storyboard that is CPU-bound; a purple flag indicates a storyboard that is not CPU bound.

Image Loads

When an image is loaded into memory, an I flag is displayed on the graph. While JPG and PNG files might have a small size when stored in isolated storage, when displayed using an Image control for example, images are expanded into bitmaps and consume a lot more memory. Use the image load flag to identify places in your app where excessive memory consumption is taking place.

GC Events

When the CLR performs garbage collection, a G flag is displayed on the graph. Garbage collection reclaims memory and ordinarily decreases the value shown in the Memory Usage MB graph.

Viewing Detailed Profiling Information

Within the analysis tool, a region can be selected within the graph to view detailed performance warnings for that period. Much like Visual Studio's Error List view, the Performance

Warnings view identifies three types of items: Information, Warning, and Error items (see Figure 2.7).

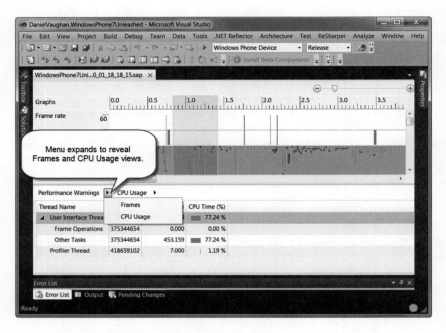

FIGURE 2.7   The Performance Warnings view

The Observation Summary provides advice on how to rectify each particular warning item.

The CPU Usage breadcrumb can also be expanded and allows you to view various other CPU related metrics, such as a function call tree.

The Performance Analysis tool provides detailed runtime performance metrics and allows you to identify the source of performance bottlenecks, enabling you to improve the responsiveness of your app and in turn the user experience for your app.

Device Status

The `Microsoft.Phone.Info.DeviceStatus` class is a static class used to retrieve information about the phone device, such as the device manufacturer, firmware version, and total memory available to your app.

Table 2.4 describes each property of the `DeviceStatus` class.

TABLE 2.4   DeviceStatus Properties

Name	Description
ApplicationCurrentMemoryUsage	The memory usage of the current application in bytes.
ApplicationMemoryUsageLimit	The maximum additional amount of memory, in bytes, that your application process can allocate.
ApplicationPeakMemoryUsage	The peak memory usage of the current application in bytes.
DeviceFirmwareVersion	The firmware version running on the device.
DeviceHardwareVersion	The hardware version running on the device.
DeviceManufacturer	The device manufacturer name.
DeviceName	The device name.
DeviceTotalMemory	The physical RAM size of the device in bytes.
IsKeyboardDeployed	If true the user has deployed the physical hardware keyboard of the device.
IsKeyboardPresent	If true the device contains a physical hardware keyboard.
PowerSource	Indicates if the device is currently running on battery power or is plugged in to an external power supply.

In the first release of the Windows Phone OS, the DeviceExtendedProperties class was used to retrieve many of the DeviceStatus property values. DeviceExtendedProperties has since been deprecated, and DeviceStatus takes its place for all but one piece of device information: the Windows Live anonymous id of the user, which is, in fact, the only value retrievable using the DeviceExtendedProperties class. Windows Live anonymous IDs are discussed in Chapter 28, "Background File Transfers."

The downloadable sample code contains a DeviceStatusView.xaml page, which displays each of the DeviceStatus properties. The memory related values have been converted to megabytes to make them more easily understandable (see Figure 2.8).

Calculating Available Memory

Windows Phone manufacturers are obligated to produce phones that have at least 256MB of RAM.

> **NOTE**
>
> While many phones have more than 256MB of RAM, be mindful of the minimum specification and aim to support the lowest common denominator. Do not assume your app will be running on a device with more than 256MB of RAM.

FIGURE 2.8   `DeviceStatusView` page

To determine how much memory your app has to work with, use the `DeviceStatus.ApplicationMemoryUsageLimit`.

For example, if a particular task is estimated at costing an additional 10MB of memory, then determining whether the task will exceed the memory usage limit can be calculated as follows:

```
long requiredBytesEstimate = 10 * 1048576; /* 1048576 bytes equals 1 megabyte. */
if (DeviceStatus.ApplicationMemoryUsageLimit
        >= DeviceStatus.ApplicationCurrentMemoryUsage + requiredBytesEstimate)
{
    /* Perform expensive task. */
}
```

> **NOTE**
>
> If your app attempts to allocate more memory than is available on the device—that is, if it exceeds the value of `DeviceStatus.ApplicationMemoryUsageLimit`, the application terminates with an `OutOfMemoryException`.

In addition to foreground app memory constraints, background tasks are limited to 6MB of memory. Background tasks and their memory usage requirements are discussed in Chapter 27, "Scheduled Actions."

DeviceStatus Events

While DeviceStatus allows you to retrieve device information, it also includes the following two events:

- ▶ KeyboardDeployedChanged
- ▶ PowerSourceChanged

If the phone device has a hardware keyboard, such as a sliding keyboard, the KeyboardDeployedChanged event allows you to detect when the keyboard is extended.

The KeyboardDeployedChanged event can be subscribed to as shown:

```
DeviceStatus.KeyboardDeployedChanged += HandleKeyboardDeployedChanged;
```

The event handler can be used to determine whether the keyboard is deployed using the DeviceStatus class, as shown:

```
void HandleKeyboardDeployedChanged(object sender, EventArgs e)
{
    bool keyboardDeployed = DeviceStatus.IsKeyboardDeployed;
...
}
```

PowerSourceChanged Event

When the phone device is connected to a user's computer, it may be a good time to perform some processor intensive task that could potentially consume a lot of power, which would otherwise flatten the user's battery. The PowerSourceChangedEvent allows you to detect when the user attaches or detaches an external power supply.

The PowerSourceChanged event can be subscribed to as shown:

```
DeviceStatus.PowerSourceChanged += HandlePowerSourceChanged;
```

The event handler can be used to retrieve the new PowerSource value from the DeviceStatus class, as shown:

```
void HandlePowerSourceChanged(object sender, EventArgs e)
{
    PowerSource powerSource = DeviceStatus.PowerSource;
...
}
```

> **NOTE**
>
> The DeviceStatus.PowerSourceChanged event is not raised on the app's UI thread. All updates to visual elements must, therefore, be invoked on the UI thread, either directly by using the app's global Dispatcher or indirectly via a custom property change notification system, discussed later in this chapter.

NOTE

Avoid using `DeviceState.PowerSource` for determining whether to use the phone's network connection to transfer a substantial amount of data. See Chapter 24, "Network Services," to learn how to monitor network connectivity and how to determine the type of network connection being used.

Applying the Model-View-ViewModel Pattern to a Windows Phone App

A dominant pattern that has emerged in XAML UI based technologies, in particular WPF and Silverlight, is the Model-View-ViewModel (MVVM) pattern. MVVM is an architectural pattern largely based on the Model-View-Controller (MVC) pattern, which like the MVC pattern serves to isolate the domain logic from the user interface logic. In addition, MVVM leverages the strong data binding capabilities of XAML based technologies, which allows loose coupling between the view and the viewmodel so that the viewmodel does not need to directly manipulate the view. This eliminates the need for almost all code-beside, which has a number of benefits, including freeing interactive designers from writing view specific code.

The following are the principal elements of the MVVM pattern:

- **Model**—The model is responsible for managing and delivering data.

- **View**—The view is responsible for displaying data. The view is ordinarily a UI element, and, in the case of Silverlight for Windows Phone apps, it is a `UserControl` such as a `PhoneApplicationPage`.

- **ViewModel**—A bridge or intermediary between the model and the view, which commonly retrieves model objects and exposes them to the view. Often the view-model is designed to respond to commands that are bound to UI elements in the view. The viewmodel can be thought of as the model of the view.

With the release of the Windows Phone 7.1 SDK came Silverlight 4 and support for `ICommand`s. The use of commands is discussed in the section "Using Commands" later in the chapter.

There are numerous benefits to using MVVM in your apps. MVVM can improve an app's testability because it is easier to test code from a unit test that does not rely on surfacing UI objects. Testing apps is discussed further in Chapter 22, "Unit Testing."

Placing application interaction logic in a viewmodel also makes it easier to redesign your app while reducing the need to refactor interaction logic. Occasionally you may like to reuse some of your UI logic in different apps or, to a lesser extent, on multiple platforms; for example, WPF and Silverlight. Decoupling interaction logic from any particular UI technology makes it easier to target multiple platforms.

Implementing the MVVM Pattern

There are two general approaches to MVVM viewmodel and view creation: view-first and viewmodel-first. The view-first approach sees the creation of the view before the view-model. Conversely, in the viewmodel-first approach, it is usually the viewmodel that creates the view. Both approaches have their pros and cons. Viewmodel-first potentially offers complete independence from the UI, allowing an app to be executed entirely without a UI; yet it suffers from various implementation challenges. View-first is far simpler to implement when page navigation is used, as is the case in a Silverlight for Windows Phone app.

In this book, the view-first approach is used exclusively.

MVVM in Silverlight relies on the assignment of a viewmodel to the view's `DataContext` property. There are a number of commonly used techniques for marrying a viewmodel to its view. Some offer a high degree of flexibility at the cost of greater complexity and decreased visibility. The technique employed throughout this book, and the one I find to be adequate in most cases, has the viewmodel instantiated in the view's constructor. In the following example a viewmodel is assigned to the view's `DataContext` property:

```
public partial class FooView : PhoneApplicationPage
{
    public FooView()
    {
        InitializeComponent();

        DataContext = new FooViewModel();
    }
    ...
}
```

With the `DataContext` set to the viewmodel, properties of the viewmodel can be used in data binding expression in the view's XAML.

ViewModelBase Class

Silverlight for Windows Phone apps often consist of many pages. As such, a likely candidate for sharing common infrastructure across all viewmodels in an app is a viewmodel base class.

In the samples throughout this book, every viewmodel subclasses a custom `ViewModelBase` class that provides, among other things, navigation support, error validation, state preservation, and property change notification (see Figure 2.9). Each of these capabilities along with specific related topics is discussed in subsequent chapters.

`ViewModelBase` inherits from a custom `NotifyPropertyChangeBase` class, which provides for property change notification, discussed in the next section.

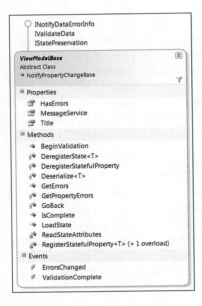

FIGURE 2.9   ViewModelBase class diagram

Property Change Notification

A key aspect of MVVM in Silverlight relating to data binding is property change notification. Property change notification allows an object (the source, for example, a viewmodel) to signal to a FrameworkElement (the target) that a value needs updating.

There are two ways to implement change notification in a source class: either using dependency properties or by implementing INotifyPropertyChanged, which is frequently referred to as INPC.

> **NOTE**
>
> The use of dependency properties is not recommended for viewmodels because it requires that the viewmodel class inherit from DependencyObject and that all property updates occur on the UI thread, which can lead to a lot of thread related plumbing code in the viewmodel and make your code less portable because of dependence on the Silverlight dependency property system.

Implementing INotifyPropertyChanged: The Traditional Approach

The INotifyPropertyChanged interface has a single event called PropertyChanged. The implementation of INotifyPropertyChanged ordinarily includes the following construct:

```
public event PropertyChangedEventHandler PropertyChanged;

protected virtual void OnPropertyChanged(string propertyName)
{
    PropertyChangedEventHandler tempEvent = PropertyChanged;
    if (tempEvent != null)
    {
        tempEvent(this, new PropertyChangedEventArgs(propertyName));
    }
}
```

> **NOTE**
>
> To determine whether the `PropertyChanged` event field has any subscribers, it is copied to a temporary local variable, which allows you to then test whether it is null in a thread safe manner. Without first obtaining a copy, another thread could potentially unsubscribe from the event after the null check but before the event is raised, which would inadvertently lead to a `NullReferenceException` being raised.
>
> An alternative that avoids the null check is to assign the event to an empty handler, as shown:
>
> ```
> public event PropertyChangingEventHandler PropertyChanging = delegate {};
> ```

A property is then able to signal to a subscriber of the event that a property value needs updating, like so:

```
string foo;

public string Foo
{
    get
    {
        return foo;
    }
    set
    {
        if (foo != value)
        {
            foo = value;
            OnPropertyChanged("Foo");
        }
    }
}
```

When setting a property that is the source property of a data binding, the update must occur on the UI thread or an `UnauthorizedAccessException` will ensue. Source properties can be set from non-UI threads using the application's `Dispatcher` as shown in the following excerpt:

```
Deployment.Current.Dispatcher.BeginInvoke(
    delegate
        {
            Foo = "bah";
        });
```

There are a number of reasons why peppering your code with `BeginInvoke` calls is not a good idea. First, it imposes an unnecessary threading model on your viewmodel code. Second, it can lead to code that need not be executed on the UI thread, creeping in to the handler. And, third, it is pretty ugly.

The next section looks at extracting INPC into a reusable and UI thread friendly class.

Implementing INotifyPropertyChanged: An Alternative Approach

While there is nothing manifestly wrong with adding the `OnPropertyChanged` method to every class that implements `INotifyPropertyChanged` (apart from violating the DRY principle), it makes sense to extract the change notification code into a reusable class, as this allows you to not only reduce boilerplate code but also to add other features to the event raising code, such as improving support for multithreaded apps and implementing `INotifyPropertyChanging` (as well as `INotifyPropertyChanged`).

The downloadable sample code includes such a class called `PropertyChangeNotifier`. The `ViewModelBase` class delegates change notification to a `PropertyChangeNotifier` instance.

Throughout this book you frequently see viewmodel properties (with backing fields) resembling the following:

```
string foo;

public string Foo
{
    get
    {
        return foo;
    }
    set
    {
        Assign(() => Foo, ref foo, value);
        // Or use the following for frequently assigned properties:
        // Assign("Foo", ref foo, value);
    }
}
```

Here, rather than passing the property name as a loosely typed string, a lambda expression allows the `Assign` method to extract the name of the property.

A reference to the field is passed to the `Assign` method along with the new value.

A call to the base class `Assign` method updates the field value, while also offering the following advantages:

- ▶ The application's `Dispatcher` is used to automatically raise the `PropertyChanged` event on the UI thread if called from a non-UI thread. This eliminates the need to add `Dispatcher.BeginInvoke` calls to a viewmodel to avoid cross thread errors.

- ▶ A lambda expression can be used, rather than a loosely typed string, to identify the property. This can help to prevent a property name mismatch if you forget to change the name string after renaming the property. While refactoring tools, such as Resharper, assist in detecting string name mismatches, mismatches can still be easily missed and often require careful attention during refactoring.

- ▶ A `PropertyChanging` event is also raised if there are any subscribers. `PropertyChangeNotifier` also implements the `INotifyPropertyChanging` interface as well as `INotifyPropertyChanged` and allows a subscriber to cancel an update if desired.

- ▶ `PropertyChangeNotifier` assists the viewmodel in remaining UI technology agnostic. For example, retrieving an application's `Dispatcher` in WPF is done differently in Silverlight.

- ▶ `PropertyChangeNotifier` uses a weak reference to its owner, thereby preventing memory leaks from occurring when targets fail to unsubscribe from events.

- ▶ The single line `Assign` method reduces the amount of boilerplate code in properties.

NOTE

Using a lambda expression to identify a property comes with a performance penalty, and for properties that are changed with high frequency, such as those responding to phone sensor events, it is recommended to use one of the other `Assign` method overloads that accept a string name instead.

The return value of the `Assign` method is an `AssignmentResult` enum value, whose values are described in the following list:

- ▶ **Success**—The assignment occurred and the field value now equals the new value.

- ▶ **Cancelled**—A subscriber to the `PropertyChanging` event cancelled the assignment. This relies on a custom extension to the `INotifyPropertyChanging` event.

- ▶ **AlreadyAssigned**—No assignment was made because the existing field value was already equal to the new value.

▶ **OwnerDisposed**—The `PropertyChangeNotifier` uses a weak reference to the object for which it is providing property changing monitoring. This value indicates that no assignment was performed because the owner object has been disposed.

Since property change notification is such a common requirement of model and view-model classes, for the sake of convenience a `NotifyPropertyChangeBase` class is also provided in the downloadable sample code. It leverages an instance of the `PropertyChangeNotifier`, and can be used as a base class for any class that needs `INotifyPropertyChanged` to be implemented.

The `ViewModelBase` class, in particular, inherits from this class (see Figure 2.10).

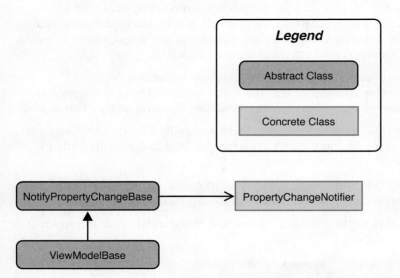

FIGURE 2.10   `ViewModelBase` inherits from `NotifyPropertyChangeBase`, which has a `PropertyChangeNotifier`.

The implementation details of the `PropertyChangeNotifier` are lengthy and are not included here. Instead, however, an article already covers the topic at http://daniel-vaughan.org/post/Property-Change-Notification-using-a-Weak-Referencing-Strategy.aspx.

Before moving on to commanding, I must affirm that you do not need to use the property notification system presented here in your own projects. If you are happy using the traditional approach to INPC, that is perfectly fine. Be mindful, however, that a lot of the phone SDK APIs have events that do not always return on the UI thread, and you may need to rely more heavily on the `Dispatcher` to prevent cross thread errors.

Using Commands

Silverlight for Windows Phone supports the `ICommand` interface for buttons and various other controls. Commands are useful because when exposed from a viewmodel they allow your view to bind to them just like other properties; when the user interacts with the visual element, the command is executed. This enables you to move your UI logic from event handlers to higher level classes.

The `ICommand` interface defines the following three members:

- ▶ **CanExecute(object)**—A method called by the Silverlight commanding infrastructure, which automatically sets the enabled state of the target control
- ▶ **Execute(object)**—A method that performs the logic of the command
- ▶ **CanExecuteChanged**—An event that signals that the Silverlight commanding infrastructure should reevaluate the executable state of the command by calling its `CanExecute` method

Within the downloadable sample code there is a default implementation of the `ICommand` interface called `DelegateCommand<T>`. This class has features such as object parameter type coercion, which, for example, enables you to use strings to represent enum values in binding expressions, which are automatically converted to the appropriate enum type.

In this book you commonly see commands defined as read only fields exposed using a property get accessor, as this excerpt from the `MediaViewModel` in Chapter 7, "Media and Web Elements," shows:

```
readonly DelegateCommand playCommand;

public ICommand PlayCommand
{
    get
    {
        return playCommand;
    }
}
```

Most often you see commands instantiated in the viewmodels constructor.

The `DelegateCommand` constructor accepts an `Action` argument, which is carried out when the command is executed. In the following excerpt you see the instantiation of a command called `playCommand` that when executed sets a number of viewmodel properties:

```
public MediaViewModel()
{
    playCommand = new DelegateCommand(
        obj =>
        {
            PlayerState = PlayerState.Playing;
            CanPlay = false;
            CanPause = true;
        });
...
}
```

DelegateCommand along with its generic counterpart DelegateCommand<T> also allow you to specify an Action that is used to evaluate whether the command is able to be executed.

Ordinarily the Silverlight commanding infrastructure is only supported on buttons (ButtonBase) and a couple of specialized controls. Some extra capabilities are provided in the ICommand implementation that allow you to wire the command to any FrameworkElement, such as in the following example, which shows a Silverlight Image element that when tapped causes an ICommand to be executed:

```
<Image Source="/Foo.png"
        c:Commanding.Command="{Binding ViewCommand}"
        c:Commanding.CommandParameter="{Binding FullScreen}" />
```

> **NOTE**
>
> The event used to trigger command execution can be specified by using the Commanding.Event attached property. In subsequent chapters you see several examples of using these custom commanding attached properties.

Argument Validation

The book sample code commonly uses a custom ArgumentValidator class to ensure that method arguments are not null. You frequently see statements like the following at the beginning of a method:

```
string PerformSomeAction(string value)
{
    stringField = ArgumentValidator.AssertNotNull(value, "value");
...
}
```

Here, if value is null, then an ArgumentNullException is raised. If not null, then the stringField field is set to the value in a fluent manner.

> **NOTE**
>
> Microsoft has a far more feature rich argument validation tool called Code Contracts, which integrates into Visual Studio and can provide static checking as well as runtime checking, along with documentation generation. See http://bit.ly/10zWtK.

All the ArgumentValidator methods are fluent; they return the value passed to them so that they can be assigned to local variables or fields in a single statement.

The `ArgumentValidator.AssertNotNull` method is as follows:

```
public static T AssertNotNull<T>(T value, string parameterName) where T : class
{
    if (value == null)
    {
        throw new ArgumentNullException(parameterName);
    }

    return value;
}
```

`ArgumentValidator` contains various other assertion methods for strings and numeric values, some of which are briefly discussed.

`ArgumentValidator` allows you to assert that an argument falls within a particular range. The following `AssertLessThan` method ensures that the value is less than a certain value:

```
public static double AssertLessThan(
    double comparisonValue, double value, string parameterName)
{
    if (value >= comparisonValue)
    {
        throw new ArgumentOutOfRangeException(
            "Parameter should be less than "
            + comparisonValue, parameterName);
    }
    return value;
}
```

This then allows you to validate that a numeric value is less than, for example, 1:

```
ArgumentValidator.AssertLessThan(1, value, "value");
```

Other methods, such as `AssertNotNullAndOfType`, allow you to raise an exception if an argument is null or not of the expected type, and `AssertNotNullOrWhiteSpace` accepts a string and raises an `ArgumentException` if `string.IsNullOrWhiteSpace(value)` returns true.

A Platform Agnostic Dialog Service

Over the last few years, I have found myself doing a lot of cross-platform development, in particular Silverlight for the browser, WPF, and now Windows Phone development. Being able to abstract common tasks away from technology specific types, such as displaying simple dialogs, has made reusing code far easier. In addition, mocking certain types, which would otherwise cause a unit test to fail on a build server, such as displaying a message box, has proven invaluable.

In several places throughout the book you see the use of an `IMessageService`, which is used to display message dialogs to the user. The `ViewModelBase` class exposes the `IMessageService` as a `MessageService` property, and you see calls like the following:

```
MessageService.ShowMessage("Hi from Windows Phone!");
```

If you are itching to sink your teeth into more phone specific content, feel free to skip this section and return to it later.

The `IMessageService` interface describes a class that is able to display messages to the user, and to ask the user questions (see Figure 2.11).

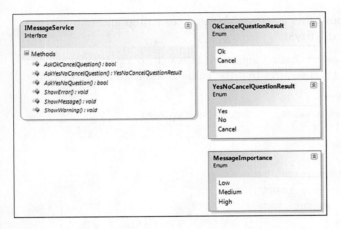

FIGURE 2.11   `IMessageService` class diagram

There are various parameters for specifying captions and so forth, along with the ability to provide a message importance threshold value, so that the user can nominate to have messages filtered based on importance.

There are differences between the built-in dialog related enums in Silverlight and WPF. Hence, these types have been replaced with the technology agnostic enum types shown in Figure 2.11.

The Windows Phone implementation of the `IMessageService` is done by extending a single class, the `MessageServiceBase` class, and by overriding two abstract methods: one called `ShowCustomDialog`, the other `AskQuestion` (see Figure 2.12).

The `ShowCustomDialog` method uses the `Dispatcher` to display the dialog on the UI thread (see Listing 2.1). Extension methods are used to convert the native Silverlight `MessageBoxButton` enum values and `MessageBoxResult` enum values to the technology agnostic enum values.

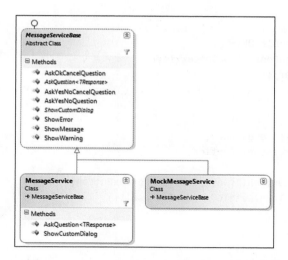

FIGURE 2.12 MessageService extends MessageServiceBase.

LISTING 2.1 MessageService Class (excerpt)

```csharp
public partial class MessageService : MessageServiceBase
{
    public override MessageResult ShowCustomDialog(
        string message,
        string caption,
        MessageButton messageButton,
        MessageImage messageImage,
        MessageImportance? importanceThreshold,
        string details)
    {
        /* If the importance threshold has been specified
         * and it's less than the minimum level required (the filter level)
         * then we don't show the message. */
        if (importanceThreshold.HasValue
                && importanceThreshold.Value < MinumumImportance)
        {
            return MessageResult.Ok;
        }

        if (Deployment.Current.Dispatcher.CheckAccess())
        {   /* We are on the UI thread,
                and hence no need to invoke the call.*/
            var messageBoxResult = MessageBox.Show(message, caption,
                messageButton.TranslateToMessageBoxButton());
            return messageBoxResult.TranslateToMessageBoxResult();
        }
```

LISTING 2.1   Continued

```
        MessageResult result = MessageResult.Ok;
        var context = new DispatcherSynchronizationContext(
            Deployment.Current.Dispatcher);
        context.Send(
            delegate
            {
                var messageBoxResult = MessageBox.Show(
                                    message, caption,

                            messageButton.TranslateToMessageBoxButton());
                result = messageBoxResult.TranslateToMessageBoxResult();
            }, null);

        return result;
    }


    /* Content omitted. */
}
```

The downloadable sample code also contains a `MockMessageService` class that also inherits from `MessageService` and is designed to be used for unit testing purposes. It allows you to verify that code correctly displayed a message or asked a question. The absence of a mocking framework for Windows Phone makes it especially useful.

The `MessageService` can be used to display a message, or ask the user a question, from any viewmodel (see Figure 2.13).

You see how to use the `IMessageService` in greater detail in the next chapter.

FIGURE 2.13   Using the `MessageService` to display a message

By using an interface based approach, it affords the opportunity to substitute the `IMessageService` implementation for a mock implementation, or to even change the behavior of the `IMessageService` entirely.

These classes are, of course, included in the downloadable sample code. Yet, they also reside in the Calcium SDK repository at http://calciumsdk.com, where you can always find the most up-to-date code, freely available for use in your projects.

Summary

This chapter provided an overview of some common pieces of phone infrastructure and described various techniques that are useful when building Windows Phone apps.

The chapter began with a discussion of the deployment and composition of XAP files. The security capability model of the phone was then discussed, and you learned how to use the Marketplace Test Kit to determine the capability requirements of your app.

The chapter then examined the threading model of Silverlight for Windows Phone and you saw how the Windows Phone frame rate counter works.

You then learned about the Windows Phone Performance Analysis tool and saw how to profile your app's performance and memory usage.

The chapter then turned to the custom code and commonly used techniques that you see used in subsequent chapters.

The overview of the custom infrastructure began with an exposé of the Model-View-ViewModel pattern, and you saw how it is applied in the downloadable sample code. How property change notification is implemented was discussed, and you saw techniques for improving the traditional implementation of INotifyPropertyChanged so that it works effortlessly with multithreaded apps.

The chapter then looked at the commanding infrastructure used throughout the book and gave a brief overview of the argument validation system commonly used in the sample code to validate method arguments.

Finally, you looked at a custom dialog service that enables you to ask the user a question from your viewmodel while remaining compatible with unit testing.

Application Execution Model

Understanding the events within the life cycle of a Windows Phone application is critical to providing an optimal user experience on the phone. The phone's single application process model means that your app may be interrupted and terminated at any time. It is your responsibility to maintain the appearance of continuity across interruptions, to save your app's state whenever an interruption occurs, and, if necessary, restore the state when the user returns to your app.

While the 7.5 release of Windows Phone OS includes support for *fast application switching*, where your app is kept in memory and its threads suspended, you still need to preserve the state of your app because there are no guarantees that an app will not be terminated if the device memory runs low.

Like localizability, app state preservation is an aspect of development that should not be deferred and is likely one of the biggest challenges you will face as a Windows Phone developer.

Traditionally, developers of Windows desktop applications have not been overly concerned with persisting runtime state. There is usually no need to maintain state for a desktop application, since the application remains in execution and resident in memory while it is open. This is in stark contrast to Windows Phone apps, where an application may be stopped and started many times during a single session.

Seasoned ASP.NET developers who recall the days before AJAX may feel slightly more at home developing for Windows Phone, with ASP.NET's reliance on view state to overcome the transient nature of page state in which the lifespan of a web page is limited to the period before a postback occurs. This is not too dissimilar to the state model of the phone, although Silverlight has nothing like the view state system built into ASP.NET. For that you need to roll your own, and you see how to build an automated state preservation system in Chapter 25, "Isolated Storage and State Preservation."

There is no doubt that the single application process model of the phone presents some challenge for developers, but it may also lead to better designed and more robust applications, with an emphasis on decoupling visual elements from their state so that it can be more readily preserved.

This chapter begins with an overview of the application execution model and examines the various application life cycle events, which are used to coordinate state persistence and restoration.

You see how to enable an app to run under the lock screen. You also look at page navigation and how to optimize the user experience by using a splash screen or a loading indicator.

Finally, the chapter delves into the sample application and looks at image caching, design-time data, and consuming a simple WCF service.

Exploring the Execution Model

The execution model of Windows Phone is designed to make the phone as responsive as possible and to maximize the battery life of the device. One way that this is achieved is by limiting the phone to a single running application. Multiple applications running in the background risk slowing the foreground application and may tie up the processor and cause the phone to consume more power.

> **NOTE**
>
> While the phone's execution model is limited to a single app being in execution at any time, Windows Phone allows the use of background tasks, which run periodically and are independent of your foreground app. These are explored in Chapter 27, "Scheduled Actions."

In addition to greater responsiveness and extended battery life, the execution model provides users with a consistent navigation experience between applications. On Windows Phone, users are able to launch applications from the App List screen or from a tile on the Start Experience. The hardware Back button allows users to navigate backward, through the pages of a running application or through the stack of previously running applications.

The goal of transient state preservation and restoration is to provide the user with a simulated multiple application experience, where it seems to the user that your application was left running in the background, even though it may have been terminated by the operating system.

Application State

There are two types of application state: persistent and transient. Persistent state exists when an application launches. It is saved to a private storage area called isolated storage and may include data such as configurable settings or files.

Transient state is discarded when an application is closed. It is stored at the application level in the `Microsoft.Phone.Shell.PhoneApplicationService.State` dictionary or at the page level in the `PhoneApplicationPage.State` dictionary.

There is a single `PhoneApplicationService` instance for the entire app, and its state dictionary should be used only by objects running in the context of the application as a whole. A unique state dictionary is created for each page in your app, and you should use it rather than the `PhoneApplicationService.State` dictionary whenever possible.

> **NOTE**
>
> The `PhoneApplicationPage.State` dictionary is accessible only during or after the `OnNavigatedTo` method is called, or during or before the `OnNavigatedFrom` method is called. If you attempt to access it too early or too late an exception is raised.
>
> The `PhoneApplicationPage.State` dictionary is limited to 2MB for each page and 4MB for the entire app. You should, therefore, not use it for excessive storage.

Transient state may include results from web service calls, or data from partially completed forms (see Figure 3.1).

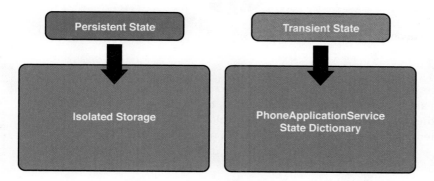

FIGURE 3.1   Persistent state and transient state storage locations

Life Cycle Events

The `Microsoft.Phone.Shell.PhoneApplicationService` exposes four life cycle related CLR events, which provide an application with the opportunity to save or load state (see Figure 3.2).

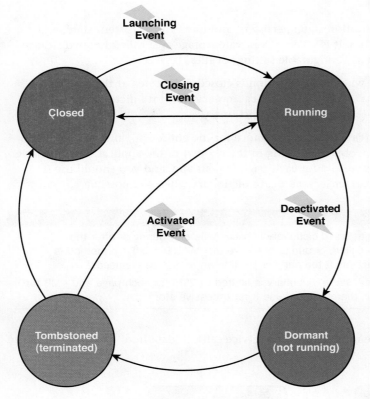

FIGURE 3.2   Application life cycle

Launching Event

When a user selects an application from the App List screen, or from a tile on the Start Experience, or when the application is being debugged, the application moves from the stopped state, to the running state. This represents a cold start. Use the `Launching` event to restore any persistent state from isolated storage that is not page specific. This event occurs after the `App` class is instantiated, but before the main page of an application is created.

> **NOTE**
>
> The Windows Phone 7 Certification Requirements state that an application must render the first screen within 5 seconds after launch and activation, and be fully responsive within 20 seconds. A splash screen can be used to offset startup delay. Later in this chapter you see how to create a splash screen for an application.

The `Launching` and `Activated` events are mutually exclusive. That is, exactly one of these two events occurs when the application is being started. Likewise, the `Deactivated` and

`Closing` events are also mutually exclusive; only one of these events occurs when the application is exiting.

Subscribing to Life Cycle Events Using the `PhoneApplicationService`

The `PhoneApplicationService` allows your app to be notified of the various life cycle events. The `PhoneApplicationService` is, by default, initialized in XAML by the application's `App` instance, as shown in the following example:

```
<Application.ApplicationLifetimeObjects>
    <!--Required object that handles lifetime events for the application-->
    <shell:PhoneApplicationService
        Launching="Application_Launching" Closing="Application_Closing"
        Activated="Application_Activated" Deactivated="Application_Deactivated"/>
</Application.ApplicationLifetimeObjects>
```

The `PhoneApplicationService` is a singleton class, which exposes an instance of the class via a static property called `Current`. Code to handle the `Launching`, `Closing`, `Activated`, and `Deactivated` events can be placed in the `App` class, for which handlers are created when a new project is created, or directly in code by using the `Current` property of the `PhoneApplicationService`.

NOTE

Subscription to the `PhoneApplicationService.Activated` event must occur via the `App` class. If subscription to the event is done in a UI element, the handler will not be called. This is because the `PhoneApplicationService` itself subscribes to the `System.Windows.Application.Current`'s `Startup` event. When the application raises the `Startup` event, the `PhoneApplicationService` notifies the operating system that it is ready to receive execution model events (that is, `Launching`, `Closing`, `Activated`, and `Deactivated`). This causes the `PhoneApplicationService.Activated` event (or the `Launched` event in the case of a non-tombstoned application) to occur almost immediately. Therefore, subscription to the event after this point has no effect. Moreover, event subscription is lost when an application is tombstoned; the application has, after all, terminated at that point. Thus, subscription to the `Activated` or `Launching` events from, for example, the MainPage constructor, will occur after the event has already been raised.

There may be times when it is tempting to promote certain kinds of transient state to persistent state. When launching your app, however, the user should feel like he is not resuming your app, but rather that it is indeed a new instance, a clean slate.

Persistent state is stored in isolated storage, while transient state is stored in the `PhoneApplicationService.State` dictionary, an `IDictionary<string, object>` that is maintained while the application is tombstoned, but abandoned when the application moves from the tombstoned state to the not running state.

Deactivation Event and Tombstoning

On entering the running state, an application must contend with being interrupted. Each interruption causes the `PhoneApplicationService.Deactivated` event to be raised. The app is then placed in a dormant state, where it remains in memory but its threads are suspended.

If an app is reactivated after being in the dormant state, there is no need for your app to restore its transient state, reducing its load time.

Detecting whether an app is returning from a dormant state can be done within the `PhoneApplicationService.Activated` event handler using the `IsApplicationInstancePreserved` property of the `ActivatedEventArgs`, as shown in the following excerpt:

```
void Application_Activated(object sender, ActivatedEventArgs e)
{
    if (e.IsApplicationInstancePreserved)
    {
        /* Application was placed in the dormant state. */
    }
    else
    {
        /* Application state should be restored manually. */
    }
}
```

When the device's memory usage reaches a minimum threshold, the operating system may decide to tombstone your app.

> **NOTE**
>
> When an application is tombstoned, it is terminated.

When tombstoned, the operating system is aware that the application may be reactivated. If an application moves from being tombstoned back to the running state, it will be from a cold start, and all objects must be instantiated and persistent and transient state must be restored. The only differences between the tombstoned state and the closed state are that when tombstoned, the operating system retains the transient state dictionary for the app along with an identifier for the app, so that if activated, chooser and launcher events can be resubscribed. Launchers and choosers perform common tasks, such as sending email. You learn more about choosers and launchers in Chapter 12, "Launchers and Choosers."

An application is deactivated when it is no longer the foreground application. The following is a list of causes for deactivation:

▶ The user presses the start button.

▶ The phone's lock screen is engaged without having enabled running under the lock screen. Enabling your app to run under the lock screen is discussed in the section "Running Under the Lock Screen" later in the chapter.

- ▶ A launcher or a chooser is shown.
- ▶ The user selects a toast notification, which launches another application.

Saving Transient State

The `Deactivated` event provides an application with the opportunity to save its transient and persistent state.

NOTE

Saving the transient state of a `PhoneApplicationPage` should be performed in its `OnNavigatedFrom` method, as you see later in the chapter.

The goal is to enable restoration of the application to its prior state before being tombstoned. It should be assumed, however, that when the `Deactivated` event occurs, the application is going to be closed, moving to the closed state. The user may, after all, opt not to resume the application, or may use the Start Experience to relaunch the application, rather than using the hardware Back button to return to the application. Moreover, if the user launches many other apps, your app may get bumped off the end of the Back button application stack.

The Visual Studio new project templates place an empty handler for the `Deactivated` event in the `App` class. See the following excerpt:

```
void Application_Deactivated(object sender, DeactivatedEventArgs e)
{
    /* Save transient state like so:
     * PhoneApplicationService.Current.State["DataContractKey"]
     *       = DataContract;
     */

    /* Save persistent state like so:
     * IsolatedStorageSettings.ApplicationSettings["Key"] = someObject; */
}
```

You can also subscribe to the `Deactivated` event elsewhere, in the following manner:

```
PhoneApplicationService.Current.Deactivated += OnDeactivated;

void OnDeactivated(object o, DeactivatedEventArgs args)
{
    ...
}
```

> **CAUTION**
>
> The operating system gives an app 10 seconds when the `PhoneApplicationService.` `Closing` event occurs, before it is forcibly terminated. If the time required to save your app's state exceeds this amount, then its state should be saved periodically, and perhaps incrementally, while it is running.

> **NOTE**
>
> The Windows Phone emulator terminates an application if it takes longer than 10 seconds to display its first visual. Therefore, when debugging an `Activated` or `Launched` event, if this time is exceeded the application exits and the debugger detaches before any UI elements can be shown.

Transient State Requirements

All objects to be stored in the `PhoneApplicationService.State` property must meet one of the following requirements:

- ▶ It is a primitive type.

- ▶ It is a known serializable reference type including `decimal`, `string`, or `DateTime`, with a matching `System.Convert.ToString` method signature.

- ▶ It is capable of being serialized using a `DataContractSerializer`. To achieve this, it must be decorated with a `System.Runtime.Serialization.DataContract` attribute. Each property or field intended for serialization must be decorated with the `DataMember` attribute, and in turn each serializable property or field type must be decorated with the `DataContract` attribute.

Storing an application's transient state can be difficult because objects containing state often have event subscriptions to or from other objects that are not serialized. Also, types from third-party libraries are usually not decorated with the `DataContract` attribute, preventing serialization.

Restoring Transient State

When an app transitions from being tombstoned or dormant, back to the running state, the `PhoneApplicationService.Activated` event is raised. This provides an opportunity to restore the transient and persistent state of the app.

> **NOTE**
>
> Restoring the transient state of a `PhoneApplicationPage` should be performed in its `OnNavigatedTo` method, as you see later in the chapter.

Restoring the transient state involves taking the user to the point where she was when the `Deactivated` event occurred, and may involve restoring the positions of UI elements, repopulating viewmodel properties, and so on. The goal is to provide the user with a seamless experience, and to emulate a multiple application-like environment, so that to the user the application appears as though it was left running in the background.

The following code demonstrates handling of the `PhoneApplicationService.Activated` event, to restore transient and persistent state:

```
void Application_Activated(object sender, ActivatedEventArgs e)
{
    /* Restore persistent state like so: */
    someObject = IsolatedStorageSettings.ApplicationSettings["Key"];

    /* Restore transient state like so: */
    DataContract = PhoneApplicationService.Current.State["DataContractKey"];
}
```

Saving Persistent State

Persistent state is usually stored whenever transient state is stored. In addition, your app should save its persistent state when it is closing, by subscription to the `PhoneApplicationService.Closing` event. Persistent state may include files or application settings, as shown in the following excerpt from the App class:

```
void Application_Closing(object sender, ClosingEventArgs e)
{
    System.IO.IsolatedStorage
        .IsolatedStorageSettings.ApplicationSettings["someObject Key"]
            = someObject;
}
```

NOTE

Transient state should not be retained when the Closing event occurs.

Running Under the Lock Screen

Users expect some kinds of apps to run under a lock screen. These apps include music players, mapping apps, stop watches, and so on.

In the first release of the Windows Phone OS, running under the lock screen was favorable to apps that wanted to avoid being tombstoned. These were apps that were slow to load or relied on complex state models. This was alleviated, however, with the introduction of fast application switching in Windows Phone 7.5. Now apps are placed in a dormant state and remain in memory.

> **NOTE**
>
> Running under the lock screen is not an alternative to implementing efficient transient state persistency. Recall that an app may still be tombstoned if the phone runs low on memory.

The following steps outline how to enable your app to run under the lock screen:

1. Set `PhoneApplicationService.Current.ApplicationIdleDetectionMode = IdleDetectionMode.Disabled`.

2. Detect when the lock screen is engaged, or disengaged, by handling the `PhoneApplicationFrame.Obscured` and `Unobscured` events, respectively.

3. When the lock screen is engaged your app should reduce its processing to a bare minimum to minimize CPU usage and thus battery consumption.

4. When the lock screen is disengaged your app should resume from where it left off.

5. Optionally, you should prompt the user to allow him or her to opt-in to running under the lock screen, and/or provide an options setting for enabling or disabling running under the lock screen.

Lock Screen Management

I created a reusable class called `LockScreenManager` that makes it easy to manage your app's lock screen policy. The class implements a custom `ILockScreenManager` interface that has the following three properties:

▶ **RunningUnderLockScreen**—Gets a value indicating whether the app is running under the lock screen

▶ **RunningUnderLockScreenEnabled**—Allows you to set whether the app is allowed to run under the lock screen

▶ **UserPrompted**—Allows your app to remember whether the user has been prompted to allow running under the lock screen

At your app's first launch you query the `UserPrompted` property. If false, you present a dialog asking the user whether it is okay to run under the lock screen, and you set the `RunningUnderLockScreenEnabled` property accordingly. You subscribe to the `PropertyChanged` event of the `LockScreenManager`, and when the `RunningUnderLockScreen` property changes, it indicates that the lock screen has been either engaged or disengaged. `LockScreenManager` is a singleton and subclasses `NotifyPropertyChangeBase` for property change notification (see Listing 3.1). The private constructor attempts to retrieve the `UserPrompted` and `RunningUnderLockScreenEnabled` property values from isolated storage settings. It then subscribes to the `PhoneApplicationFrame.Obscured` and `Unobscured` events.

When the `Obscured` event is raised the `RunningUnderLockScreen` property is set.

The LockScreenManager class is located in the Shell directory of the
WindowsPhone7Unleashed project.

LISTING 3.1   LockScreenManager Class (excerpt)

```
public class LockScreenManager : NotifyPropertyChangeBase, ILockScreenManager
{
    static readonly string promptedKey
            = "UserPromptedToAllowRunningUnderLockScreen";
    static readonly string runningEnabledKey = "RunningUnderLockScreenEnabled";

    LockScreenManager()
    {
        IsolatedStorageSettings settings
            = IsolatedStorageSettings.ApplicationSettings;
        bool prompted;
        if (settings.TryGetValue(promptedKey, out prompted))
        {
            UserPrompted = prompted;
        }

        bool enabledValue;
        if (settings.TryGetValue(runningEnabledKey, out enabledValue))
        {
            RunningUnderLockScreenEnabled = enabledValue;
        }

        var frame = (PhoneApplicationFrame)Application.Current.RootVisual;
        frame.Obscured += (o, args) => RunningUnderLockScreen = args.IsLocked;
        frame.Unobscured += (o, args) => RunningUnderLockScreen = false;
    }
    ...
}
```

When either of the UserPrompted or RunningUnderLockScreenEnabled properties is set, its
new value is saved to isolated storage settings using a SaveSetting method, as shown:

```
void SaveSetting(string key, object value)
{
    IsolatedStorageSettings settings
        = IsolatedStorageSettings.ApplicationSettings;
    settings[key] = value;
    settings.Save();
}
```

When the `RunningUnderLockScreenEnabled` property is enabled the idle detection mode is disabled, which allows the app to run under the lock screen. If disabled, the app must be restarted or deactivated before the idle detection mode can be enabled or an `InvalidOperationException` is raised. This is a limitation of the phone OS. See the following excerpt:

```
public bool RunningUnderLockScreenEnabled
{
    get
    {
        return runningUnderLockScreenEnabled;
    }
    set
    {
        var result = Assign(() => RunningUnderLockScreenEnabled,
                        ref runningUnderLockScreenEnabled, value);

        if (result == AssignmentResult.Success)
        {
            if (runningUnderLockScreenEnabled)
            {
                PhoneApplicationService.Current.ApplicationIdleDetectionMode
                    = IdleDetectionMode.Disabled;
            }
            /* Idle detection mode cannot be enabled
               until the application is restarted. */

            SaveSetting(runningEnabledKey, runningUnderLockScreenEnabled);
        }
    }
}
```

The `LockScreenView` page and its associated `LockScreenViewModel` class demonstrate the use of the `LockScreenManager`, and are located in the ExecutionModel directory of the WindowsPhone7Unleashed.Examples project. The `LockScreenViewModel` uses the `MessageService` to ask the user whether she wants to opt-in to running under the lock screen. When the manager's `RunningUnderLockScreen` property changes, a string is written to the Visual Studio Output view (see Listing 3.2).

LISTING 3.2   `LockScreenViewModel` Class

```
public class LockScreenViewModel : ViewModelBase
{
    public LockScreenViewModel() : base("lock screen settings")
    {
        LockScreenManager manager = LockScreenManager.Instance;
```

LISTING 3.2   Continued

```
            if (!manager.UserPrompted)
            {
                bool allow = MessageService.AskYesNoQuestion(
                    "Is it OK to run under the phone's lock screen?");
                manager.RunningUnderLockScreenEnabled = allow;
                manager.UserPrompted = true;
            }

            manager.PropertyChanged
                += (o, args) =>
                {
                    if (args.PropertyName == "RunningUnderLockScreen")
                    {
                        Debug.WriteLine("RunningUnderLockScreen: "
                                            + manager.RunningUnderLockScreen);
                    }
                };
        }

        public bool RunningUnderLockScreenEnabled
        {
            get
            {
                return LockScreenManager.Instance.RunningUnderLockScreenEnabled;
            }
            set
            {
                LockScreenManager.Instance.RunningUnderLockScreenEnabled = value;
            }
        }
    }
}
```

The `LockScreenView` XAML has a Silverlight Toolkit `ToggleSwitch` control that is bound to the `RunningUnderLockScreenEnabled` viewmodel property, as shown in the following excerpt:

```
<StackPanel x:Name="ContentPanel">
    <toolkit:ToggleSwitch
        Header="run under lock screen"
        IsChecked="{Binding RunningUnderLockScreenEnabled, Mode=TwoWay}" />
</StackPanel>
```

Figure 3.3 shows the `ToggleSwitch` located on the `LockScreenView` page with the Run Under Lock Screen setting enabled.

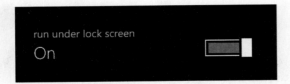

FIGURE 3.3   `LockScreenView` page

Running under the lock screen is the only way to allow your foreground app to run while the phone is idle. It should, however, be used with caution, because if an app continues to consume the device CPU, it may rapidly flatten the device battery.

Page Navigation

Windows Phone navigation in Silverlight is based on the Silverlight for the browser navigation model. The navigation class model looks a little different in the phone SDK however. Rather than Silverlight 4's `Frame` and `Page` controls, Silverlight for Windows Phone apps use the subclasses `PhoneApplicationFrame` and the `PhoneApplicationPage` (see Figure 3.4).

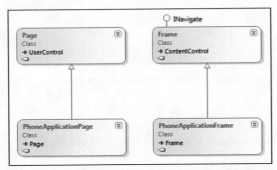

FIGURE 3.4   The `PhoneApplicationFrame` and `PhoneApplicationPage` classes are derived from the `Frame` and `Page` classes, respectively.

> **NOTE**
>
> `Frame` and `Page` must not be used directly in your app. They are prohibited because of underlying differences in the way the Silverlight infrastructure interacts with the OS within the constrained environment of the phone.

Page navigation in Silverlight for Windows Phone works in much the same way as page navigation in a web browser. `PhoneApplicationFrame` is analogous to the web browser, coordinating page transitions within your app.

Figure 3.5 depicts the display elements of a Silverlight for Windows Phone app.

FIGURE 3.5   Display elements of a Silverlight for Windows Phone app

The `PhoneApplicationFrame` is the host for `PhoneApplicationPages` and reserves space for the system tray and the application bar. The `PhoneApplicationPage` consumes all remaining space after the system tray and the application bar.

> **NOTE**
>
> There can be only one `PhoneApplicationFrame` for an application. Attempting to place a `PhoneApplicationFrame` within a `PhoneApplicationPage` causes the content to become infinitely nested at runtime, as the page will be forced inside the frame, the frame inside the page, and so on.

Navigation Using Unmapped URIs

There are numerous ways of allowing the user to perform page navigation. This section looks at using `Buttons` with code-beside to open external URLs, and at `HyperlinkButtons`, which can rely solely on XAML. In subsequent chapters you explore other techniques to perform navigation including the use of commands and a custom navigation service.

Internal URIs

When navigating to `PhoneApplicationPages` within an application, URIs either must be relative to the root directory of the project, and use the relative path syntax, as shown in the following excerpt:

```
Uri uri = new Uri("/DirectoryName/PageName.xaml", UriKind.Relative);
```

or they must use the relative component URI format, such as that used in the following example:

```
Uri uri = new Uri("/AssemblyName;component/PageName.xaml", UriKind.Relative);
```

The assembly name segment must be the name of an assembly that is locatable at runtime. The name of a project's output assembly can be found in the project properties editor by right-clicking on the project node in the Solution Explorer and selecting Properties, or by pressing Alt+Enter.

The HyperlinkButton control can be used to allow the user to navigate directly to a page within your application, as shown:

```
<HyperlinkButton NavigateUri="/Directory/PageName.xaml" Content="Internal Page" />
```

External Navigation Using the Button Control

The Button control is a flexible way for determining user intent. A Button can be used for navigation by subscribing to its Click event, as shown in the following excerpt from the ProductDetailsView.xaml in the downloadable sample code:

```
<Button Click="Button_ExternalLink_Click"
        Tag="{Binding Product.ExternalUrl}"
        Content="External Page" />
```

The WebBrowserTask allows you to navigate to external URIs using the phone's built-in web browser: Internet Explorer. This causes your app to be deactivated while the user views the page. You explore tasks in more detail in Chapter 12.

To provide the WebBrowserTask with the location of the web page, use the button's Tag property. The Click event handler, which initiates the WebBrowserTask, is shown in the following excerpt:

```
void Button_ExternalLink_Click(object sender, RoutedEventArgs e)
{
    FrameworkElement button = sender as FrameworkElement;
    if (button == null || button.Tag == null)
    {
        return;
    }
    WebBrowserTask task = new WebBrowserTask
    {
        URL = button.Tag.ToString()
    };
    task.Show();
}
```

External Navigation Using the `HyperlinkButton` Control

The disadvantage of using a `Button` control for links to external content is that it does not provide the familiar look and feel of a hyperlink. The `HyperlinkButton` control provides an easier way for navigating to pages within an application. There is a trick to using the `HyperlinkButton` with external URIs. Set its `TargetName` property to `_blank`, as shown in the following example:

```
<HyperlinkButton TargetName="_blank" NavigateUri="http://create.msdn.com"
                 Content="http://create.msdn.com" />
```

> **NOTE**
>
> Failing to set the `HyperlinkButton.TargetName` to `_blank`, when using an external URI, raises the `Frame.NavigationFailed` event when the button is tapped.

Hosting Web Content Within an App

An alternative to using the phone's built-in Internet Explorer app is to host the content in a `Microsoft.Phone.Controls.WebBrowser` control.

The following excerpt from the `WebBrowserView.xaml` page, in the downloadable sample code, shows a `WebBrowser` placed within the main content grid of a page:

```
<Grid x:Name="ContentGrid" Grid.Row="1">
    <phone:WebBrowser Source="{Binding Url}"/>
</Grid>
```

Here, the `Source` property of the `WebBrowser` is bound to the `Url` property of the view-model. The `WebBrowser` control is discussed in greater detail in Chapter 7, "Media and Web Elements."

A dedicated web browser page can be used in your app to host all external content. To launch the dedicated web browser page, a relative URI can be constructed using the `Binding.StringFormat` property, as shown in the following excerpt:

```
<HyperlinkButton
    NavigateUri="{Binding ExternalUrl, StringFormat=/WebBrowser/\{0\}}"
    Content="External Page" />
```

Backslashes are used to escape the curly brackets in the `StringFormat` value.

The `StringFormat` property transforms the `HyperlinkButton`'s binding expression into the following:

```
string.Format("/WebBrowser/{0}", ExternalUrl);
```

URI mapping is used to pass the external URL as a query string parameter. This is explored further in a later section.

Passing Page Arguments Using Query Strings

Query strings allow for key value pairs to be embedded in a URL and passed to a page. Just like HTML web applications, Silverlight uses query string parameters for interpage communication.

The PhoneApplicationPage.NavigationContext property, which is initialized after the page is created, is used to retrieve the query string. Its QueryString property is an IDictionary of string key and value pairs. The following excerpt from the WebBrowserView.xaml, in the downloadable sample code, demonstrates how to retrieve a query string value:

```
void OnLoaded(object sender, RoutedEventArgs e)
{
    string url;
    if (NavigationContext.QueryString.TryGetValue("url", out url))
    {
        ViewModel.LoadPage(url);
    }
}
```

Navigation History Stack

The Silverlight navigation infrastructure maintains a history of pages that have been loaded. Each time an app navigates to a different page, the current page's OnNavigatedFrom method is called and the page is placed on the history stack (see Figure 3.6).

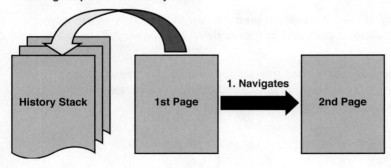

FIGURE 3.6   Pages are placed on the history stack.

While on the history stack, the page remains in memory unless the application is tombstoned or closed. This means that subscribing to the PhoneApplicationService. Deactivated event provides the page with the opportunity to save its transient state. It is, however, preferable to use the page's OnNavigatedFrom method for the saving of page state.

Using the Deactivate event to save page state runs the risk of slowing down deactivation when all pages on the history stack are saving their state simultaneously.

BEST PRACTICE

Use the `OnNavigatedFrom` and `OnNavigatedTo` methods of `PhoneApplicationPage` to save both transient and persistent state.

NOTE

Unlike Silverlight for the browser, in Windows Phone the page's `NavigationCacheMode` property is not assignable, and it is set to `Disabled` by default. This means that internal caching of pages does not occur, and when navigating to a page that does not exist on the history stack, the page is always instantiated.

Restoration of transient state should occur with the page's `OnNavigatedTo` method. The `OnNavigatedTo` method is called when the `PhoneApplicationFrame` navigates to the page. This is triggered by the following actions:

▶ Navigation to a specified page URI occurs using one of various navigation methods such as the `PhoneApplicationFrame.Navigate` method.

▶ The `NavigationService.GoBack` method is called.

▶ The user presses the hardware Back button.

▶ The page is the current page when the app moves from the tombstoned or dormant state to the running state.

▶ The page is the app's start page and the app is launched.

NOTE

When an application is activated, the frame navigates to the page that was active when the phone was dormant or tombstoned. The `NavigationContext.QueryString` is preserved, which means that there is no need to store this in the `PhoneApplicationService.State` dictionary.

URI Mapping

Relying on URIs that include the full path to each page in your app can make your app brittle and makes it harder to change the physical location of individual pages. If a page is moved, all references to that file must be updated. This can lead to maintainability issues as the size of the project grows.

The URI mapping system of Silverlight allows requests for a URI to be routed to another URI, and uses a single configuration point for the management of page URIs. Mapped URIs can be made shorter and are, thus, less subject to typographical errors. They also allow the exclusion of technology specific information, such as the .xaml page file extension, making it easier to retarget business logic for different platforms.

To use URI mapping, you must assign a System.Windows.Navigation.UriMapper instance to the UriMapper property of an app's PhoneApplicationFrame. This can be done in XAML, as shown in the following excerpt from the App.xaml file in the downloadable sample code:

```
<Application
    x:Class="DanielVaughan.WindowsPhone7Unleashed.Examples.App"
    xmlns="http://schemas.microsoft.com/winfx/2006/xaml/presentation"
    xmlns:x="http://schemas.microsoft.com/winfx/2006/xaml">

        <Application.RootVisual>
            <phone:PhoneApplicationFrame x:Name="RootFrame">
                <phone:PhoneApplicationFrame.UriMapper>
                    <navigation:UriMapper>
                        <navigation:UriMapper.UriMappings>
                            <navigation:UriMapping
                              Uri="/ProductDetails/{productId}"
        MappedUri="/Navigation/ProductDetailsView.xaml?productId={productId}" />
                            <navigation:UriMapping Uri="/WebBrowser/{url}"
                        MappedUri="/WebBrowser/WebBrowserView.xaml?url={url}" />
                        </navigation:UriMapper.UriMappings>
                    </navigation:UriMapper>
                </phone:PhoneApplicationFrame.UriMapper>
            </phone:PhoneApplicationFrame>
        </Application.RootVisual>

        <!-- Content omitted. -->
</Application>
```

The UriMapping class contains a Uri property and a MappedUri property. When navigation is requested from the Uri value, it is rerouted to the MappedUri property.

By using the curly brace syntax, as shown in the previous excerpt, a substring of the requested URI can be transplanted into the rerouted MappedUri value. This is especially useful when you want to target the same page using different URIs and allows the query string to be used to convey the action to be undertaken by the page.

In the previous excerpt you see a UriMapping for the ProductDetailsView page. The ProductDetailsView displays detailed information for a particular product, identified by a query string parameter. When navigating to the ProductDetails page, if the requested URL is /ProductDetails/2, this is rerouted to /Navigation/ProductDetailsView.xaml?productId=2.

If you were to request the ProductDetailsView page using the NavigationService, as shown in the following example, the request would be rerouted accordingly:

```
NavigationService.Source = new Uri("/ProductDetails/2", UriKind.Relative);
```

The product to be displayed can then be determined in the ProductsDetailsView by reading the productId query string parameter, as demonstrated in the following excerpt:

```
protected override void OnNavigatedTo(NavigationEventArgs e)
{
    base.OnNavigatedTo(e);
    string productIdString = NavigationContext.QueryString["productId"];
    int productId = int.Parse(productIdString);
    ViewModel.LoadProduct(productId);
}
```

You see later in this chapter how the viewmodel uses the product ID to retrieve the product information from a WCF service.

Navigation Using the NavigationService

The PhoneApplicationPage class exposes a public NavigationService property, which allows direct control over navigation.

> **NOTE**
>
> The NavigationService cannot be used to launch Internet Explorer to view an external URL. Instead, use either the WebBrowserTask, or open the page within the app using the WebBrowserControl. See the previous sections on external navigation using the Button and HyperlinkButton controls.

The NavigationService.Navigate method causes the frame to load the specified PhoneApplicationPage, like so:

```
NavigationService.Navigate(
    new Uri("/DirectoryName/PageName.xaml", UriKind.Relative));
```

The URI must be either a path relative to the project's root directory, as shown in the previous example, or a relative component URI such as in the following example:

```
NavigationService.Navigate(
        new Uri("/AssemblyName;component/PageName.xaml", UriKind.Relative));
```

> **TIP**
>
> The NavigationService cannot be used within the constructor of the PhoneApplicationPage because it is assigned after the page's constructor has been called. Therefore, wait until the page's OnNavigatedTo method is called or the Loaded event has occurred before using the NavigationService.

The NavigationService.Source property allows you to retrieve the URI of the current page. Setting the Source property performs the same action as using the Navigate method; the frame loads the page at the specified URI. See the following example:

```
NavigationService.Source = new Uri(
        "/DirectoryName/PageName.xaml", UriKind.Relative);
```

Routing is also enabled for the NavigationService, which means that mapped URIs can be used instead of relative URIs.

If you examine the API of the NavigationService, you will likely wonder what the difference is between the CurrentSource property and the Source property. The answer is that the CurrentSource property does not change until navigation has completed. Conversely, the Source property changes as soon as navigation is initiated.

Backward Navigation

The NavigationService maintains the app's navigation history, via an internal Journal instance. This allows the GoBack method of the NavigationService to move to the previous page in the history stack.

> **NOTE**
>
> If the GoBack method is called, and the history stack is empty because the current page is the app's start page, then an InvalidOperationException is raised. To determine whether the NavigationService is able to go back, query its CanGoBack property.

Forward Navigation

Unlike Silverlight for the browser, the GoForward method of the NavigationService does not allow forward navigation and raises an InvalidOperationException when called. Consequently, the CanGoForward property always returns false.

> **NOTE**
>
> Forward navigation using the NavigationService is not supported.

Handling Page Navigation

The PhoneApplicationPage extends the System.Windows.Controls.Page class, which has a number of virtual methods called when the page is brought into view or removed from view by the PhoneApplicationFrame (see Figure 3.7).

The OnNavigatingFrom method is called before a page is removed from view by the PhoneApplicationFrame, and the OnNavigatedFrom method is called after navigation occurs. Conversely, the OnNavigatedTo method is called when the frame brings the page into view.

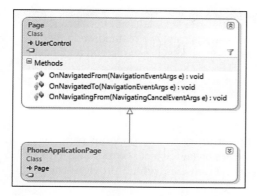

FIGURE 3.7   `PhoneApplicationPage` inherits `Page` navigation methods.

Cancelling Navigation

The `OnNavigatingFrom` method offers the opportunity to cancel navigation using the `NavigatingCancelEventArgs` parameter.

`NavigatingCancelEventArgs` has the following properties:

▶ **NavigationMode**—An enum value that indicates the type of navigation. This value may be Back, Forward, New, or Refresh.

▶ **Uri**—The destination URI.

▶ **Cancel**—Setting this value to true cancels the navigation.

The `NavigationCancelEventArgs` class subclasses `CancelEventArgs`, which provides the `Cancel` property. By setting this property to `true`, the page can prevent the navigation from occurring, as shown in the following excerpt:

```
protected override void OnNavigatingFrom(
    System.Windows.Navigation.NavigatingCancelEventArgs e)
{
    base.OnNavigatingFrom(e);
    MessageBoxResult boxResult = MessageBox.Show(
        "Leave this page?", "Question", MessageBoxButton.OKCancel);
    if (boxResult != MessageBoxResult.OK)
    {
        e.Cancel = true;
    }
}
```

> **NOTE**
>
> You should not attempt to cancel navigation in the `OnNavigatingFrom` method when the hardware Back button is pressed. Instead, override the `OnBackKeyPress` method to cancel the back key, which prevents navigation.

Cross-Page Communication

Once navigation has occurred, there remains an opportunity for the previous page to interact with the current page from the previous page's `OnNavigatedFrom` method. This is achieved using the `Content` property of the `NavigationEventArgs`, which provides the destination `PhoneApplicationPage` object.

To see this in action, place a breakpoint in the `OnNavigatedFrom` method. When the breakpoint is hit, notice that the page being navigated to has already been instantiated and is provided in the `Content` property of the `NavigationEventArgs` (see Figure 3.8).

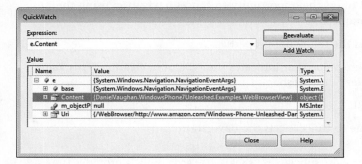

FIGURE 3.8   The `Content` property of the `NavigationEventArgs` contains the page being navigated to.

The `Uri` property of the `NavigationEventArgs` contains the URI of the destination page, including any query string that may be present.

> **NOTE**
>
> If navigating to an external URI, or when the app is being deactivated, the `Uri` property of the `OnNavigatedFrom` method's `NavigationEventArgs` is equal to app://external/.

Page Redirection

The `OnNavigatingFrom` method allows you to intercept a navigation event and to even cancel the navigation if needed. Additionally, there may be times when you want to redirect the user to a different URI based on some conditional logic.

The NavigationService, however, does not support overlapping navigation. That is, you are unable to cancel an existing navigation and immediately commence another.

You can, however, cancel navigation and schedule navigation to a different Uri using the page's Dispatcher property, as shown in the following excerpt:

```
protected override void OnNavigatingFrom(NavigatingCancelEventArgs e)
{
    if (e.Uri.ToString().Contains("RequestedUrl"))
    {
        e.Cancel = true;
        /* Perform the redirect on the UI thread. */
        Dispatcher.BeginInvoke(() => NavigationService.Navigate(
            new Uri("RedirectUrl", UriKind.Relative)));
    }

    base.OnNavigatingFrom(e);
}
```

By using the Dispatcher to invoke the lambda expression, which performs the call to the NavigationService, you allow the current navigation to complete first. This works because the UI thread can be thought of as a queue of prioritized delegates, all waiting in turn to be executed. Once all the Navigating event handlers have been serviced, the delegate represented by the lambda expression will be taken out of the queue and performed by the UI thread. This technique, of using the Dispatcher to enqueue an action, is also useful when working with some UI controls, whose event handlers may be called before the control is finished reacting to a user action.

Hardware Back Button

The hardware Back button is analogous to the Back button on a web browser. However, when the user presses the Back button, past the first page of a phone app, the app is closed. This is in contrast to the phone's hardware start button, which merely causes an app to be deactivated.

> **NOTE**
>
> The hardware Back button should not be used for application-specific behavior. It is only for navigation, and if used otherwise, may cause your app to fail Windows Phone Marketplace certification.

To determine whether navigation is occurring because the hardware Back button was pressed or the navigation was initiated by a call to NavigationService.GoBack, use the NavigatingEventArgs.NavigationMode property as shown:

```
protected override void OnNavigatedFrom(NavigationEventArgs e)
{
    base.OnNavigatedFrom(e);
```

```
    if (e.NavigationMode == NavigationMode.Back)
    {
        // Back button pressed.
    }
}
```

The Back key button can also be cancelled by overriding the
`PhoneApplicationPage.OnBackKeyPress`, as shown in the following excerpt:

```
protected override void OnBackKeyPress(CancelEventArgs e)
{
    base.OnBackKeyPress(e);

    e.Cancel = true;
}
```

`OnBackKeyPress` is called before `OnNavigatedFrom`, and if the Back button is cancelled, then
`OnNavigatedFrom` is not called at all.

NOTE

The Windows Phone Marketplace certification requirements forbid cancelling the Back
button in most cases. To maintain a consistent user experience, the Back button must
only be used for backward navigation in the application. The following four certification
requirements relate to use of the Back button:

▶ Pressing the Back button must return the application to the previous page or return
   to any previous page within the back stack.

▶ Pressing the Back button from the first screen of an application must close the
   application.

▶ If the current page displays a context menu or a dialog, the pressing of the Back
   button must close the menu or dialog and return the user to the screen where the
   context menu or dialog box was opened.

▶ For games, when the Back button is pressed during gameplay, the game can choose
   to present a pause context menu or dialog or navigate the user to the prior menu
   screen. Pressing the Back button again while in a paused context menu or dialog
   closes the menu or dialog.

For more information see section 5.2.4 of the Technical Certification Requirements at
http://bit.ly/lYcurV.

Creating an Application Splash Screen

Windows Phone Silverlight projects have baked-in support for application splash screens.
To create a splash screen it is simply a matter of placing a jpg image called
SplashScreenImage.jpg, with the dimensions of 480 by 800 pixels, in the root directory of
your project. Ensure that its Build Action is set to Content (see Figure 3.9).

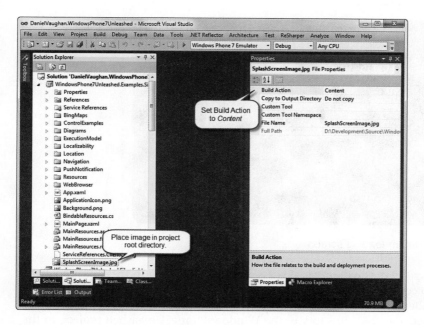

FIGURE 3.9   Creating an application splash screen

Using an image for a splash screen does not, however, prevent an application from being closed by the OS if the first page takes longer than 10 seconds to load. If your application's first page takes longer than this to load, it is best to overlay the content with a loading indicator and perform the time consuming initialization on a background thread. Once loading is complete, the indicator can be dismissed.

The `ProductsView` and `ProductsViewModel` classes, located in the Navigation directory of the WindowsPhone7Unleashed.Examples project in the downloadable sample code, demonstrate this principle (see Figure 3.10).

The `ProductsView` page uses a `StackPanel` to present an indeterminate progress bar to the user while the viewmodel is loading, as shown in the following excerpt:

```
<StackPanel Grid.Row="1"
            Visibility="{Binding Loaded,
            Converter={StaticResource BooleanToVisibilityConverter},
            ConverterParameter=Collapsed}"
            Height="150" >
    <TextBlock Text="Loading..." Style="{StaticResource PhoneTextTitle2Style}"
            HorizontalAlignment="Center" Margin="20"/>
    <toolkit:PerformanceProgressBar IsIndeterminate="True" />
</StackPanel>
```

FIGURE 3.10   A custom loading screen

The Visibility property of the StackPanel is assigned via a binding to the viewmodel's Loaded property. To convert the boolean Loaded property to a Visibility type, a custom IValueConverter called BooleanToVisibilityConverter is used (see Listing 3.3). The class is located in the ValueConverters directory of the WindowsPhone7Unleashed project, in the downloadable sample code.

LISTING 3.3   BooleanToVisibility Class

```
public class BooleanToVisibilityConverter : IValueConverter
{
    public object Convert(object value, Type targetType,
        object parameter, CultureInfo culture)
    {
        string paramValue = (string)parameter;

        if (value == null || (bool)value)
        {
            return paramValue == "Collapsed"
                ? Visibility.Collapsed : Visibility.Visible;
        }

        return paramValue == "Collapsed"
            ? Visibility.Visible : Visibility.Collapsed;
    }

    public object ConvertBack(object value, Type targetType,
        object parameter, CultureInfo culture)
    {
        string paramValue = (string)parameter;
        if (value == null || (Visibility)value == Visibility.Visible)
```

LISTING 3.3   Continued

```
        {
            return paramValue != "Collapsed";
        }

        return paramValue == "Collapsed";
    }
}
```

The `ConverterParameter` attribute determines what value to assign to the `Visibility` property if the binding value is `true`. If the `Loaded` property of the viewmodel is `true`, then the `Visibility` property will set to `Visibility.Visible`.

To hide the rest of the content during loading, the same technique is employed for the main content control.

```
<StackPanel Grid.Row="1" Margin="10"
                Visibility="{Binding Loaded,
                    Converter={StaticResource BooleanToVisibilityConverter},
                    ConverterParameter=Visible}">
    <ScrollViewer>
        <!-- Content omitted. -->
    <ScrollViewer>
</StackPanel>
```

Here the `ConverterParameter` attribute is set to `Visible`, so that its `Visibility` is set to `Visible` when the viewmodel's `Loaded` property is `true` and `Collapsed` when it is `false`.

The code listings for the `ProductsView` page and associated files are provided in the following section.

Walking Through the Bookshop Sample Application

This chapter's sample app provides the beginnings of a simple data driven e-commerce app that demonstrates the use of navigation, transient and persistent state, image caching, and WCF services. It allows the user to select from a list of books, retrieved from a WCF service, and to view each item's details on a separate details page.

The `ProductsViewModel` class retrieves a list of `Product` objects from a WCF service. Each product has various properties such as a description, price, and an image URI.

The `ProductsViewModel` saves and restores its own transient state consisting of the list of products it retrieves from the WCF service (see Listing 3.4).

The code for this section resides in the Navigation directory of the WindowsPhone7Unleashed.Examples project in the downloadable sample code.

The viewmodel's constructor determines whether transient state exists for itself. If so, it restores the list of `Products` or else it requests the list of products from the WCF using the `BookshopServiceClient`. The call occurs asynchronously, and the products list is populated once the call completes.

The `ViewModelBase` class subclasses the `NotifyPropertyChangeBase` class, which implements `INotifyPropertyChanged`. The source for `NotifyPropertyChangeBase` is located in the downloadable sample code, and was discussed in Chapter 2, "Fundamental Concepts in Silverlight Development for Windows Phone."

LISTING 3.4   `ProductsViewModel` Class (excerpt)

```
public class ProductsViewModel : ViewModelBase
{
    readonly IDictionary<string, object> transientStateDictionary;
    const string transientStateKey = "ProductsViewModel_Products";

    public ProductsViewModel(
        IDictionary<string, object> transientStateDictionary)
    {
        this.transientStateDictionary = ArgumentValidator.AssertNotNull(
                transientStateDictionary, "transientStateDictionary");

        LoadTransientState();
        if (products != null)
        {
            return;
        }

        BookshopServiceClient client = new BookshopServiceClient();
        client.GetProductsCompleted += (sender, args) =>
        {
            if (args.Error != null)
            {
                MessageService.ShowError("Unable to retrieve products.");
                return;
            }

            Products = args.Result;
            Loaded = true;
        };
        client.GetProductsAsync();
    }

    ObservableCollection<Product> products;
```

LISTING 3.4   Continued

```csharp
    public ObservableCollection<Product> Products
    {
        get
        {
            return products;
        }
        private set
        {
            Assign(() => Products, ref products, value);
        }
    }

    bool loaded;

    public bool Loaded
    {
        get
        {
            return loaded;
        }
        private set
        {
            Assign(() => Loaded, ref loaded, value);
        }
    }

    public void SaveTransientState()
    {
        transientStateDictionary[transientStateKey] = products;
    }

    public void LoadTransientState()
    {
        object transientState;
        if (transientStateDictionary.TryGetValue(
                transientStateKey, out transientState))
        {
            products = transientState as ObservableCollection<Product>;
            if (products != null)
            {
                Loaded = true;
            }
        }
    }
}
```

Within the OnNavigatingTo method of the ProductsView page, a ProductsViewModel is instantiated and assigned to the page's DataContext. The ProductsViewModel is passed the transient state dictionary for the page (see Listing 3.5).

The OnNavigatingTo and OnNavigatedFrom methods are used to inform the viewmodel when to save its state.

LISTING 3.5   ProductsView Class

```csharp
public partial class ProductsView : PhoneApplicationPage
{
    public ProductsView()
    {
        InitializeComponent();
    }

    ProductsViewModel ViewModel
    {
        get
        {
            return (ProductsViewModel)DataContext;
        }
    }

    bool loaded;

    protected override void OnNavigatedTo(NavigationEventArgs e)
    {
        Debug.WriteLine("ProductsView OnNavigatedTo");
        base.OnNavigatedTo(e);

        if (!loaded)
        {
            DataContext = new ProductsViewModel(State);
            loaded = true;
        }

        ViewModel.LoadTransientState();
    }

    protected override void OnNavigatedFrom(NavigationEventArgs e)
    {
        base.OnNavigatedFrom(e);
        Debug.WriteLine("ProductsView OnNavigatedFrom");
        ViewModel.SaveTransientState();
    }
}
```

Displaying the Product List

The list of products exposed by the `ProductsViewModel.Products` property is displayed using a `ListBox` control in the `ProductsView` page. The `ListBox`'s `ItemTemplate` has various controls that are used to display the details of each `Product`, as shown in the following excerpt:

```xml
<StackPanel Grid.Row="1" Margin="10"
            Visibility="{Binding Loaded,
                Converter={StaticResource BooleanToVisibilityConverter},
                ConverterParameter=Visible}">
    <ScrollViewer>
        <ListBox ItemsSource="{Binding Products}" Height="610">
            <ListBox.ItemTemplate>
                <DataTemplate>
                    <StackPanel Orientation="Horizontal">
                        <Image Source="{Binding SmallImageUri}"
                               MaxWidth="150" MaxHeight="150"
                               Margin="0,0,10,10" />
                        <StackPanel Margin="5">
                            <TextBlock Text="{Binding Title}"
                                       TextWrapping="Wrap" />
                            <TextBlock Text="{Binding Price,
                                           StringFormat=\{0:C\}}" />
                            <HyperlinkButton
                                NavigateUri="{Binding Id,
                                    StringFormat=/ProductDetails/\{0\}}"
                                Content="View Details"
                                HorizontalAlignment="Left" Margin="0,10,0,0" />
                        </StackPanel>
                    </StackPanel>
                </DataTemplate>
            </ListBox.ItemTemplate>
        </ListBox>
    </ScrollViewer>
</StackPanel>
```

An `Image` control displays a thumbnail of the product, using the `SmallImageUri` property of the `Product`.

A string format is used to convert the `Price` property, which is a double value, to a currency formatted string using the format `{0:C}`. Similarly, a link is provided for the product details page, using the format `/ProductDetails/{0}`, and the value of the `Product`'s `Id` is substituted for the `{0}` placeholder. The `UriMapping` for this product details URI causes the application to reroute to the full URI of the `ProductDetailsView.xaml` page and includes the productId query string parameter.

Figure 3.11 shows the `ProductsView` displaying a list of books.

FIGURE 3.11   Products View

When the user presses the `HyperlinkButton`, he is directed to the `ProductDetailsView.xaml` page. This page displays the various properties of the product and includes a link for an external website, where the user can find more information about the product (see Figure 3.12).

When navigating to the `ProductDetailsView` the page attempts to retrieve the productId query string parameter from the `NavigationContext` (see Listing 3.6).

LISTING 3.6   `ProductDetailsView` Class (excerpt)

```
public partial class ProductDetailsView : PhoneApplicationPage
{
    public ProductDetailsView()
    {
        InitializeComponent();

        DataContext = new ProductDetailsViewModel(
            PhoneApplicationService.Current.State);
    }

    ProductDetailsViewModel ViewModel
    {
        get
        {
            return (ProductDetailsViewModel)DataContext;
        }
```

LISTING 3.6   Continued

```
    }

    protected override void OnNavigatedTo(NavigationEventArgs e)
    {        base.OnNavigatedTo(e);
        string productIdString = NavigationContext.QueryString["productId"];
        int productId = int.Parse(productIdString);
        ViewModel.LoadProduct(productId);
    }

    protected override void OnNavigatedFrom(NavigationEventArgs e)
    {        ViewModel.SaveTransientState();
        base.OnNavigatedFrom(e);
    }
}
```

FIGURE 3.12   View a product's details.

The view then passes the parameter along to the `ProductDetailsViewModel` class, which handles the loading of the specified product (see Listing 3.7). The `LoadProduct` method first tests for the existence of the product in transient state. If not present, it retrieves the product using the service client.

LISTING 3.7   `ProductDetailsViewModel` Class (excerpt)

```
public class ProductDetailsViewModel : ViewModelBase
{
    const string transientStateKey = "ProductDetailsViewModel_Product";
    readonly IDictionary<string, object> transientStateDictionary;
    public ProductDetailsViewModel(
        IDictionary<string, object> transientStateDictionary)
    {
        this.transientStateDictionary = ArgumentValidator.AssertNotNull(
            transientStateDictionary, "transientStateDictionary");
    }

    public void LoadProduct(int productId)
    {
        object transientState;
        if (PhoneApplicationService.Current.State.TryGetValue(
                transientStateKey, out transientState))
        {
            product = transientState as Product;
            if (product != null && product.Id == productId)
            {
                return;
            }
        }

        BookshopServiceClient client = new BookshopServiceClient();
        client.GetProductByIdCompleted += (sender, args) =>
        {
            if (args.Error != null)
            {
                throw args.Error;
            }
            Product = args.Result;
        };
        client.GetProductByIdAsync(productId);
    }

    Product product;

    public Product Product
    {
        get
        {
            return product;
        }
```

LISTING 3.7   Continued

```
    /* Setter is not private to enable sample data.
     * See ProductDetailsViewSampleData.xaml */
    internal set
    {
        product = value;
        OnPropertyChanged("Product");
    }
}

public void SaveTransientState()
{        transientStateDictionary[transientStateKey] = product;
}
}
```

When navigating away from the page, the viewmodel's `SaveTransientState` method is called, which places the product in the state dictionary.

The `ProductDetailsView.xaml` page presents the product details via the viewmodel's `Product` property (see Listing 3.8).

LISTING 3.8   ProductDetailsView.xaml (excerpt)

```xml
<StackPanel Grid.Row="1"
    Style="{StaticResource PageContentPanelStyle}"
    d:DataContext="{d:DesignData Source=ProductDetailsViewSampleData.xaml}">

    <TextBlock Text="{Binding Product.Title}" TextWrapping="Wrap"
            Style="{StaticResource PhoneTextTitle2Style}"/>
    <StackPanel Orientation="Horizontal">
        <Image Source="{Binding Product.LargeImageUri,
                Converter={StaticResource ImageCacheConverter}}"
                MaxWidth="250" MaxHeight="250" Margin="10,10,0,10" />
        <StackPanel>
            <TextBlock Text="{Binding Product.Author}" TextWrapping="Wrap"
                    Style="{StaticResource PhoneTextTitle3Style}"/>
            <TextBlock Text="{Binding Product.Price, StringFormat=\{0:C\}}"
                    Style="{StaticResource PhoneTextTitle3Style}"/>
            <StackPanel Orientation="Horizontal">
                <TextBlock Text="ISBN"
                        Style="{StaticResource PhoneTextTitle3Style}" />
                <TextBlock Text="{Binding Product.Isbn13}"
                        TextWrapping="Wrap"
                        Style="{StaticResource PhoneTextNormalStyle}" />
            </StackPanel>
```

LISTING 3.8   Continued

```
        <HyperlinkButton
            NavigateUri="{Binding Product.ExternalUrl,
                            StringFormat=/WebBrowser/\{0\}}"
            Content="External Page"
            Margin="0,10,0,0" HorizontalAlignment="Left" />
      </StackPanel>
    </StackPanel>
    <TextBlock Text="{Binding Product.Description}"
            Margin="10,20,0,10" TextWrapping="Wrap" />
</StackPanel>
```

The StackPanel includes a d:DataContext attribute that defines a design-time data context object, discussed in the next section.

Design-Time Data

It can be difficult and time consuming constructing a page or control without knowing how the content will appear at runtime. The dimensions of images can disturb the layout, as can the length of text and text wrapping settings. The d:DataContext markup extension, which exists in the http://schemas.microsoft.com/expression/blend/2008 namespace, allows you to simulate the runtime DataContext of a control with a design-time object (see Figure 3.13).

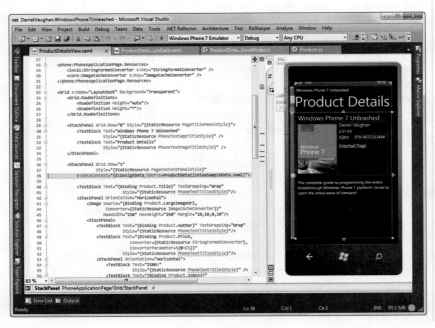

FIGURE 3.13   The d:DataContext markup extension provides for design-time sample data.

Here a design-time instance of the `ProductDetailsViewModel` class presents some sample data to improve the design-time experience of the developer or designer.

The content `StackPanel` includes a `d:DataContext` attribute, which causes a `ProductDetailsViewModel` instance to be loaded from a sample data file, as shown in the following excerpt:

```
<StackPanel Grid.Row="1"
    Style="{StaticResource PageContentPanelStyle}"
    d:DataContext="{d:DesignData Source=ProductDetailsViewSampleData.xaml}">
    ...
</StackPanel>
```

You can see that the `d:DesignData` markup extension has its `Source` property set to the location of a sample data file, ProductDetailsViewSampleData.xaml. The sample data file defines the property values of the viewmodel (see Listing 3.9). The design-time environment of Visual Studio or Expression Blend instantiates the sample viewmodel at design-time.

LISTING 3.9   ProductDetailsViewSampleData.xaml

```
<local:ProductDetailsViewModel
        xmlns:local="clr-namespace:DanielVaughan.WindowsPhone7Unleashed
            .Examples.Navigation"
        xmlns="http://schemas.microsoft.com/winfx/2006/xaml/presentation"
        xmlns:BookshopServiceReference="clr-namespace:DanielVaughan
            .WindowsPhone7Unleashed.Examples.BookshopServiceReference">
    <local:ProductDetailsViewModel.Product>
        <BookshopServiceReference:Product
            Id="1"
            Title="Windows Phone 7 Unleashed"
            Author="Daniel Vaughan"
            Description="The complete guide to programming..."
            Price="31.49"
            Isbn10="0672333481"
            Isbn13="978-0672333484"
            SmallImageUri="/DanielVaughan.WindowsPhone7Unleashed
                .Examples.Silverlight;component/
➥Navigation/Images/Product01Small.jpg"
            LargeImageUri="/DanielVaughan.WindowsPhone7Unleashed
                .Examples.Silverlight;component/
➥Navigation/Images/Product01Large.jpg"
            ExternalUrl="
                http://www.amazon.com/Windows-Phone-Unleashed-
➥Daniel-Vaughan/dp/0672333481/"
            />
    </local:ProductDetailsViewModel.Product>
</local:ProductDetailsViewModel>
```

Notice the relative component URIs of the images. The design-time environment will fail to resolve the image location unless relative component URIs are used and the Build Action of the image is set to Resource.

Image Caching

While the viewmodel saves the result of the WCF service call, which allows the app to restore its state after being tombstoned, downloaded images are not saved in the state dictionary, but rather, the app relies on some custom image caching.

A custom `IValueConverter`, called `ImageCacheConverter`, is used to download the image from the specified image URI, as shown in the following excerpt:

```
<Image Source="{Binding Product.LargeImageUri,
        Converter={StaticResource ImageCacheConverter}}" />
```

By using the `ImageCacheConverter`, images can be downloaded once and stored in isolated storage for an arbitrary period. Once that period has elapsed, the image will be downloaded again. This allows the application to work offline (see Listing 3.10).

LISTING 3.10   ImageCacheConverter Class

```csharp
public class ImageCacheConverter : IValueConverter
{
    public object Convert(object value, Type targetType,
        object parameter, CultureInfo culture)
    {
        if (EnvironmentValues.DesignTime)
        {
            return value;
        }

        string url = value as string;
        if (url != null)
        {
            try
            {
                return ImageCache.GetImage(new BitmapImage(new Uri(url)));
            }
            catch (IsolatedStorageException e)
            {
                Console.WriteLine(e);
                return value;
            }
        }

        BitmapImage bitmapImage = value as BitmapImage;
        if (bitmapImage != null)
```

LISTING 3.10   Continued

```
        {
            return ImageCache.GetImage(bitmapImage);
        }
        return value;
    }

    public object ConvertBack(object value, Type targetType,
        object parameter, CultureInfo culture)
    {
        throw new NotImplementedException();
    }
}
```

The `ImageCacheConverter` can be used in conjunction with a URL or a `BitMapImage`. In the sample code, it is used with a URL, supplied by the product's `SmallImageUri` and `LargeImageUri` properties. The `ImageCache` class maintains a dictionary of URI keyed cached images. It stores the dictionary in isolated storage, and when an image is requested, it attempts to locate it in the dictionary. If found it checks to ensure that the image has not expired, and then returns the image.

Many thanks to Peter Nowak (http://winphonedev.de/) for his image cache code, which I have adapted, with his permission, for use in the downloadable sample code.

The `ImageCache` class, in the downloadable sample code, maintains a list of `ImageCacheItem` objects, which represent cached images. The `ImageCache.GetImage` method is used to retrieve an image from the cache. If the image is not located in the cache, it is scheduled to be downloaded by the static `ImageDownloader` class.

The `ImageDownloader` coordinates an asynchronous download of the image file. It uses an `HttpWebRequest` to retrieve the image from a remote server, and then stores the downloaded file in isolated storage. Once downloaded, the `Source` property of the original image is assigned, which means that, if it is present in the UI, the image will appear (see the `ImageDownloader` class, located in the Data/ImageCache directory of the WindowsPhone7Unleashed project, in the downloadable sample code, for details).

Overview of the Sample Bookshop WCF Service

The Bookshop demo application includes a server-side component, which is used by both the `ProductsViewModel` and `ProductDetailsViewModel` classes, providing the application with a set of products to display. The server-side component is fairly arbitrary and is presented here merely for the sake of completeness.

The WCF service is called `BookshopService` and resides in the WindowsPhone7Unleashed. Web project of the downloadable sample code (see Listing 3.11).

LISTING 3.11   BookshopService Class

```
[AspNetCompatibilityRequirements(
    RequirementsMode = AspNetCompatibilityRequirementsMode.Allowed)]
public class BookshopService : IBookshopService
{
    public IEnumerable<Product> GetProducts()
    {
        return ProductManager.Products;
    }

    public Product GetProductById(int productId)
    {
        return ProductManager.GetProductById(productId);
    }
}
```

The BookshopService exposes static methods of the ProductManager class, shown in Listing 3.12. The ProductManager class creates an XDocument instance, using an XML file, to populate a list of Products.

LISTING 3.12   ProductManager Class

```
public static class ProductManager
{
    static readonly List<Product> products = new List<Product>();

    public static IEnumerable<Product> Products
    {
        get
        {
            return products;
        }
    }

    static ProductManager()
    {
        string path = HttpContext.Current.Server.MapPath(
            "~/Services/Bookshop/Products.xml");
        XDocument document = XDocument.Load(path);
        foreach (XElement element in
            document.Element("Products").Elements("Product"))
        {
            var product = new Product(element);
            product.SmallImageUri
                = ServerUtility.ResolveServerUrl(product.SmallImageUri);
```

LISTING 3.12   Continued

```
            product.LargeImageUri
                = ServerUtility.ResolveServerUrl(product.LargeImageUri);
            products.Add(product);
        }
    }

    public static Product GetProductById(int id)
    {
        if (id < 0 || id > products.Count)
        {
            throw new ArgumentOutOfRangeException("id");
        }
        return products[id - 1];
    }
}
```

The Product class contains the properties that are used to display each book's details, such as Title and Author. The Product class also knows how to populate itself from an XElement. The explicit casting operators of the XElement class make it easy to extract the values to the Product properties, as can be seen in the following excerpt from the Product class:

```
public Product(XElement element)
{
    if (element == null)
    {
        throw new ArgumentNullException("element");
    }
    Id = (int)element.Element("Id");
    Title = (string)element.Element("Title");
    Author = (string)element.Element("Author");
    Description = (string)element.Element("Description");
    SmallImageUri = (string)element.Element("SmallImageUri");
    LargeImageUri = (string)element.Element("LargeImageUri");
    Price = (double)element.Element("Price");
    Isbn10 = (string)element.Element("ISBN-10");
    Isbn13 = (string)element.Element("ISBN-13");
    ExternalUrl = (string)element.Element("ExternalUrl");
}
```

Summary

Maintaining the appearance of continuity after an application has been tombstoned is one of the key challenges facing Windows Phone developers.

There are two types of application state: persistent and transient. Persistent state exists across application launches and is saved using isolated storage. Transient state is discarded when an application is closed and is stored in the `Microsoft.Phone.Shell.PhoneApplicationService.State` dictionary.

Transient page state should be stored when the `Page.OnNavigatedFrom` method is called and restored when the `OnNavigatedTo` method is called. Transient application state can be stored when the `PhoneApplicationService.Deactivated` event occurs and restored when the `PhoneApplicationService.Activated` event occurs.

Persistent state should be saved when transient state is saved and also when the application is closing using the `PhoneApplicationService.Closing` event.

In this chapter you saw an overview of the application execution model and examined the various application life cycle events, which are used to coordinate state persistence and restoration.

You saw how to enable an app to run under the lock screen and then looked at page navigation and how to optimize the user experience by using a splash screen or a loading indicator.

Finally, the chapter delved into the sample application and discussed image caching, design-time data, and consuming a simple WCF service.

Page Orientation

P ages in Silverlight for Windows Phone apps can support either the landscape or portrait orientation, or both. When creating a page that supports both orientations, it is prudent to define the UI in XAML in such a way that it produces the layout you want in either orientation without relying on code-beside. Fortunately, Silverlight's dynamic layout system makes it easy to build pages that can support both orientations. The Grid and StackPanel elements, for example, resize themselves to inhabit available space when the page orientation changes and the dimensions of the page change.

This chapter begins by exploring the properties and events that govern page orientation. You look at using a custom IValueConverter to hide and display page elements based on the page orientation and at setting the orientation of a page programmatically.

The chapter then looks at animating UI elements when the page orientation changes using the VisualStateManager and examines how to substitute an application's RootVisual with a custom PhoneApplicationFrame to animate the entire page when the orientation changes.

Finally, the chapter looks at animating page transition using the Silverlight Toolkit.

Orientation and the PhoneApplicationPage Class

The PhoneApplicationPage class includes two orientation related properties: SupportedOrientations and Orientation.

The SupportedOrientations attribute allows you to restrict the orientation of the page and, if set to either Portrait or Landscape, prevent the orientation from being changed when the device is rotated. If the page has been designed to support both portrait and landscape, set SupportedOrientation to PortraitOrLandscape, which allows the orientation to be switched automatically when the device is rotated.

The Orientation property indicates the actual orientation of the page and can be set only at design-time. The Orientation property is discussed in greater detail later in the chapter.

When you create a new PhoneApplicationPage within Visual Studio, both SupportedOrientations and Orientation are set, by default, to Portrait in XAML.

OrientationChanged Event

Both the PhoneApplicationFrame and PhoneApplicationPage include an OrientationChanged event that allows you to detect when the orientation of the page changes. In addition, the PhoneApplicationPage includes an OnOrientationChanged virtual method. When the page orientation changes, the method is called, allowing you to update the UI, trigger animations, and so forth. See the following excerpt:

```
protected override void OnOrientationChanged(
                        OrientationChangedEventArgs e)
{
    base.OnOrientationChanged(e);
    /* Update UI, trigger animations etc. */
}
```

The OnOrientationChanged method is called before other OrientationChanged event handlers.

NOTE

The ActualWidth and ActualHeight of the page are not changed until after the OrientationChanged event has been raised.

To change the size of a UI element based on the dimensions of the page after the orientation change occurs use the Dispatcher.

By using the Dispatcher to invoke layout changes, the correct height and width of the page can be determined after the OrientationChanged event has been handled, as shown in the following excerpt:

```
protected override void OnOrientationChanged(OrientationChangedEventArgs e)
{
    Debug.WriteLine("Orientation changed to " + e.Orientation.ToString("G"));

    Dispatcher.BeginInvoke(
        delegate
        {
            Debug.WriteLine(string.Format(
                "Using dispatcher: ActualWidth: {0}, ActualHeight: {1}",
```

```
                ActualWidth, ActualHeight));
        });

    Debug.WriteLine(string.Format(
        "Without dispatcher: ActualWidth: {0}, ActualHeight: {1}",
        ActualWidth, ActualHeight));

    base.OnOrientationChanged(e);
}
```

The following is the output when switching orientations:

```
Orientation changed to LandscapeLeft
Without dispatcher: ActualWidth: 0, ActualHeight: 0
Using dispatcher: ActualWidth: 800, ActualHeight: 480
Orientation changed to PortraitUp
Without dispatcher: ActualWidth: 800, ActualHeight: 480
Using dispatcher: ActualWidth: 480, ActualHeight: 800
```

The `OrientionChanged` event is always raised before the page is loaded. This explains the zero values for the `ActualWidth` and `ActualHeight` in the previous output. The `Dispatcher` allows the correct width and height values to be obtained because by the time each value is read, the page has already loaded and the properties are populated with the correct values.

The `OrientationChangedEventArgs` class contains an `Orientation` property, which is an enum of type `PageOrientation`, indicating the new page orientation. `PageOrientation` has the following values:

- ▶ Landscape

- ▶ LandscapeLeft

- ▶ LandscapeRight

- ▶ None

- ▶ Portrait

- ▶ PortraitDown

- ▶ PortraitUp

The only values you will ever see in the `OrientationChangedEventArgs` are, however, `LandscapeLeft`, `LandscapeRight`, and `PortraitUp`. These values indicate the location of the display in relation to the phone hardware buttons (see Figure 4.1).

While `PortraitDown` exists as an enum value, at the time of writing, no device supports this orientation, nor does the emulator.

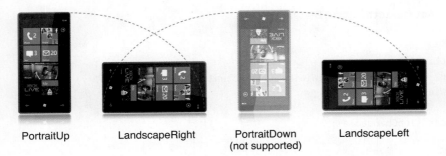

PortraitUp   LandscapeRight   PortraitDown   LandscapeLeft
                                            (not supported)

FIGURE 4.1   Device orientations

To determine whether the `OrientationChangedEventArgs.Orientation` value is either landscape or portrait, the value can be ANDed with the `PageOrientation.Landscape` or
`PageOrientation.Portrait` values, respectively. The `PageOrientationExtensions` class in the
downloadable sample code includes two extension methods for performing this directly
on a `PageOrientation` value (see Listing 4.1).

LISTING 4.1   `PageOrientationExtensions` Class

```
public static class PageOrientationExtensions
{
    public static bool IsLandscape(this PageOrientation pageOrientation)
    {
        return (pageOrientation & PageOrientation.Landscape) != 0;
    }

    public static bool IsPortrait(this PageOrientation pageOrientation)
    {
        return (pageOrientation & PageOrientation.Portrait) != 0;
    }
}
```

PhoneApplicationPage Orientation Property

The `PhoneApplicationPage` includes an `Orientation` dependency property, which is shown
in the following excerpt (take note of the set accessor):

```
public PageOrientation Orientation
{
    get
    {
        return (PageOrientation)base.GetValue(OrientationProperty);
    }
    [EditorBrowsable(EditorBrowsableState.Never)]
    set
```

```
    {
        if (Frame.IsInDesignMode())
        {
            base.SetValue(OrientationProperty, value);
        }
    }
}
```

You see that changing the page orientation at runtime is not as straightforward as it might first appear. The `Orientation` property's set accessor has an effect only at design-time and not at runtime. At runtime, the `Orientation` property indicates the physical orientation of the device, or the orientation of the emulator window. Setting the dependency property directly is also futile and has no effect on runtime page orientation either. A technique to set page orientation programmatically is discussed in the following section, "Setting Page Orientation at Runtime."

The `Orientation` property can be used in data binding expressions and allows you to adjust the layout depending on the availability of space. You can maximize space utilization by hiding or revealing content when the orientation changes. For example, when changing to a landscape orientation where horizontal space is more abundant, a `TextBlock` can be shown in the title section of an application. Conversely, in portrait mode, the `TextBlock` can be hidden to conserve space. See the following excerpt:

```
<TextBlock Text="Application Title"
            Visibility="{Binding ElementName=Page, Path=Orientation,
            Converter={StaticResource PageOrientationToVisibilityConverter},
            ConverterParameter=Landscape}" />
```

You can see that the `Orientation` property of the `PhoneApplicationPage` is used to set the `Visibility` property of the `TextBlock` using a custom `IValueConverter` called `PageOrientationToVisibilityConverter` (see Listing 4.2).

The converter's `ConvertTo` method translates the `PageOrientation` enum value to a `System.Windows.Visibility` enum value. The `ConverterParameter` from the previous excerpt indicates when to show the `UIElement`. If the `PageOrientation` value is a portrait orientation for example, and the `ConverterParameter` is equal to Portrait, then `Visibility.Visible` is returned.

LISTING 4.2   `PageOrientationToVisibilityConverter` Class

```
public class PageOrientationToVisibilityConverter : IValueConverter
{
    public object Convert(object value, Type targetType,
        object parameter, CultureInfo culture)
    {
        var orientation = (PageOrientation)value;
        string showWhenOrientation
            = ArgumentValidator.AssertNotNullAndOfType<string>(
```

LISTING 4.2   Continued

```
                    parameter, "parameter").ToLower();

    if (showWhenOrientation != "portrait"
        && showWhenOrientation != "landscape")
    {
        throw new ArgumentException(
            "ConverterParameter must be either Portrait or Landscape.");
    }

    bool show;
    switch (orientation)
    {
        case PageOrientation.Portrait:
        case PageOrientation.PortraitDown:
        case PageOrientation.PortraitUp:
            show = showWhenOrientation == "portrait";
            break;
        case PageOrientation.Landscape:
        case PageOrientation.LandscapeLeft:
        case PageOrientation.LandscapeRight:
            show = showWhenOrientation == "landscape";
            break;
        default:
            throw new ArgumentException("Unknown orientation: "
                + orientation);
    }

    return show ? Visibility.Visible : Visibility.Collapsed;
}

public object ConvertBack(object value, Type targetType,
    object parameter, CultureInfo culture)
{
    throw new NotImplementedException();
}
}
```

Setting Page Orientation at Runtime

As you saw in the previous section, the Orientation property of the PhoneApplicationPage class cannot be assigned at runtime. Another approach is required to change the page orientation. For this, turn to the SupportedOrientations property, which is assignable at runtime.

To recap, the SupportedOrientations property defines the allowed orientation or orientations of the page, which can be Portrait, Landscape, or PortraitOrLandscape.

Setting the SupportedOrientations property to the desired orientation forces the page to be shown in that orientation. For example, if the page is being viewed in portrait orientation, and you want to change the page orientation to landscape, then you can set the SupportedOrientations to Landscape, thereby restricting the allowed orientation to landscape and forcing the frame to change the orientation to landscape.

This technique is demonstrated in the OrientationView page in the downloadable sample code (see Figure 4.2).

FIGURE 4.2   Forcing the orientation of a page

The OrientationView class's Switch Supported Orientation button alternates between the three different SupportedPageOrientation values. This is performed in the button's Tap event handler, demonstrating how the orientation can be forcibly set by restricting the orientation, as shown in the following excerpt:

```
void Button_Tap(object sender, GestureEventArgs e)
{
    switch (SupportedOrientations)
    {
        case SupportedPageOrientation.Landscape:
            SupportedOrientations = SupportedPageOrientation.Portrait;
            break;
```

```
        case SupportedPageOrientation.Portrait:
            SupportedOrientations = SupportedPageOrientation.PortraitOrLandscape;
            break;
        default:
            SupportedOrientations = SupportedPageOrientation.Landscape;
            break;
    }
}
```

Animating Page Elements When the Page Orientation Changes

The `VisualStateManager` can be used to animate `UIElements` when the page orientation changes. This can be done by defining a set of `VisualStateGroups` corresponding to the `PageOrientation` values.

Each `VisualStateGroup` contains a collection of `VisualState` objects, each containing a collection of `Storyboard` objects that specify how an element's properties change when the control is placed in a particular visual state.

In Listing 4.3, you see how the `LandscapeRight` `VisualState` includes a set of `DoubleAnimations`, which move various `TextBlocks` on the page to new positions when the page orientation changes.

LISTING 4.3   OrientationView.xaml (excerpt)

```xml
<Grid x:Name="LayoutRoot">
    <VisualStateManager.VisualStateGroups>
        <VisualStateGroup x:Name="OrientationStates">
            <!--Portrait up is the default state-->
            <VisualState x:Name="PortraitUp">
                <Storyboard />
            </VisualState>

            <VisualState x:Name="LandscapeRight">
                <Storyboard>
                    <DoubleAnimation Storyboard.TargetName="topLeft"
                        Storyboard.TargetProperty="
                            (UIElement.RenderTransform).(TranslateTransform.X)"
                        To="650" />
                    <!-- Content omitted. -->
                </Storyboard>
            </VisualState>
            <!-- Content omitted. -->
        </VisualStateGroup>
    </VisualStateManager.VisualStateGroups>

    <!-- Content omitted. -->
```

LISTING 4.3   Continued

```
    <Grid x:Name="ContentGrid" Grid.Row="1">
        <TextBlock Text="Top-left corner" x:Name="topLeft"
               HorizontalAlignment="Left" VerticalAlignment="Top">
        <TextBlock.RenderTransform>
            <TranslateTransform/>
        </TextBlock.RenderTransform>
        </TextBlock>
        <!-- Content omitted. -->
    </Grid>
</Grid>
```

We subscribe to OrientationChanged event within the view's constructor, as shown in the
following excerpt:

```
OrientationChanged += (sender, args) => VisualStateManager.GoToState(
                            this, args.Orientation.ToString(), true);
```

When the OrientationChanged event is raised, the VisualStateManager is directed to the
state identified by the Orientation property of the OrientationChangedEventArgs (see
Figure 4.3).

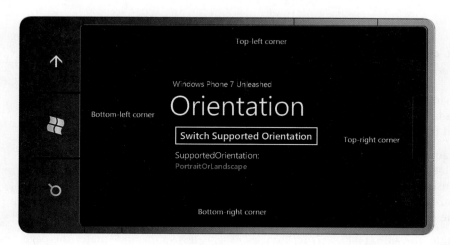

FIGURE 4.3   TextBlocks are animated into position when page orientation changes.

Animating the Entire Page When Orientation Changes

While animating UIElements is performed within the page, to animate the page itself
requires implementation of a custom PhoneApplicationFrame. This is achieved by subclassing the PhoneApplicationFrame class, and then subscribing to the frame's
OrientationChanged event to initiate the animation.

To replace your application's standard `PhoneApplicationFrame` with a custom frame, modify the `App` class, either in XAML or in the code-beside, to use the custom frame as the application's `RootVisual`.

The following excerpt shows how the App.xaml file can be modified to use a custom `PhoneApplicationFrame`:

```xml
<Application.RootVisual>
    <unleashed:AnimateOrientationChangesFrame x:Name="RootFrame">
        <!-- Content omitted. -->
    </unleashed:CustomFrame>
</Application.RootVisual>
```

If the `RootVisual` is assigned in the App.xaml.cs file, as is the case by default, modify the `InitializedPhoneApplication` method to assign a custom frame, as shown in the following excerpt:

```csharp
void InitializePhoneApplication()
{
    if (phoneApplicationInitialized)
    {
        return;
    }

    RootFrame = new AnimateOrientationChangesFrame();

    // Content omitted.
}
```

Microsoft's David Anson has written two custom `PhoneApplicationFrames` that perform rotation and fade animation when an orientation change occurs. With David's permission I have included them in the downloadable sample code.

The first is a frame that fades in content, called `FadeOrientationChangesFrame`. This class uses a `WriteableBitmap` to create an image overlay, which animates the `Opacity` property of the image. By using a `WriteableBitmap` to capture the screen, the performance of the transition is optimized and is unaffected by the page composition, that is, more controls won't risk slowing the animation.

The second frame, the `AnimateOrientationChangesFrame`, is less subtle and rotates the page when the orientation changes (see Figure 4.4).

To modify the default behavior of either the `FadeOrientationChangesFrame` or `AnimateOrientationChangesFrame`, use the `AnimationEnabled`, `Duration`, and `EasingFunction` properties.

`AnimationEnabled` allows you to turn off the animation at runtime.

FIGURE 4.4   The `AnimateOrientationChangesFrame` class rotates content when the page orientation changes.

The `Duration` property dictates how long the animation will take to complete, which if made too long, more than half a second, risks frustrating the user.

The `EasingFunction` property is used to control the speed of the animation. With easing, you can create a more realistic rate of acceleration and deceleration, such as when creating a bounce effect, or control other types of motion.

The following is a list of the various `IEasingFunction` available in the Windows Phone FCL (Framework Class Library), located in the `System.Windows.Media.Animation` namespace of the System.Windows assembly:

▶ **BackEase**—Retracts the motion of an animation slightly before it begins to animate along the path.

▶ **BounceEase**—Creates an animated bouncing effect.

▶ **CircleEase**—Creates an animation that accelerates and/or decelerates using a circular function.

▶ **CubicEase**—Creates an animation that accelerates and/or decelerates using the formula f(t) = t3.

▶ **ElasticEase**—Creates an animation that resembles a spring oscillating back and forth until it comes to rest.

▶ **ExponentialEase**—Creates an animation that accelerates and/or decelerates using an exponential formula.

▶ **PowerEase**—Creates an animation that accelerates and/or decelerates using the formula f(t) = tp, where p is equal to the Power property.

▶ **QuadraticEase**—Creates an animation that accelerates and/or decelerates using the formula f(t) = t2. This is the default `IEasingFunction` of the `FadeOrientationChangesFrame` class.

▶ **QuarticEase**—Creates an animation that accelerates and/or decelerates using the formula f(t) = t4. This is the default `IEasingFunction` for the `AnimateOrientationChangesFrame` class.

▶ **QuinticEase**—Creates an animation that accelerates and/or decelerates using the formula f(t) = t5.

▶ **SineEase**—Creates an animation that accelerates and/or decelerates using a sine formula.

Silverlight Toolkit Animated Page Transitions

Adding animated page transitions to your app can help it look more polished and, when used modestly, can increase the user's perception of the quality of your app.

The Silverlight Toolkit includes a set of classes that make it easy to add animated page transitions. The Toolkit is discussed in depth in Chapter 9, "Silverlight Toolkit Controls."

Within the Toolkit, transitions are defined by assigning a transition effect represented by `TransitionElement` objects such as `TurnstileTransition` to various transition events. These events occur during navigation and indicate the direction of the navigation (see Figure 4.5).

Forward in navigation occurs when the page is first navigated to; *forward out* occurs when navigating to a new page. *Backward in* and *backward out* occur when a backward navigation takes place, such as when the user taps the hardware Back button.

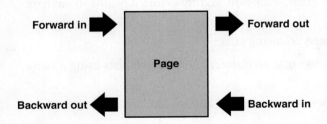

FIGURE 4.5   Transition navigation events

Navigation events are married with `TransitionElements`. The Silverlight Toolkit comes with the following five built-in `TransitionElements`:

▶ `RollTransition`

▶ `RotateTransition`

▶ `SlideTransition`

▶ SwivelTransition

▶ TurnstileTransition

In the next section you see how to add animated page transitions to an app, and how to specify the type of transition for each navigation event.

Using Silverlight Toolkit Transitions

The following steps outline how to add page transitions to your app:

1. Download and install the latest version of the Silverlight for Windows Phone Toolkit from http://silverlight.codeplex.com. Once installed, add a reference to the `Microsoft.Phone.Controls.Toolkit.dll` assembly.

2. Replace the default `PhoneApplicationFrame` with a `TransitionFrame` from the Silverlight Toolkit. To replace your app's standard `PhoneApplicationFrame`, modify the `App` class, either in XAML or in the code-beside, and set the custom frame as the application's `RootVisual`.

   The following excerpt shows how the App.xaml file can be modified to use a Silverlight Toolkit `TransitionFrame`:

```
<Application.RootVisual>
    <toolkit:TransitionFrame x:Name="RootFrame"
                        Navigated="RootFrame_Navigated"
                        Navigating="RootFrame_Navigating"
                        NavigationFailed="RootFrame_NavigationFailed">
        <!-- Content omitted. -->
    </toolkit:TransitionFrame>
    <!-- Content omitted. -->
</Application.RootVisual>
```

   If the `RootVisual` is assigned in the App.xaml.cs file, as is the case by default, modify the `InitializedPhoneApplication` method to assign the `TransitionFrame`, as shown in the following excerpt:

```
void InitializePhoneApplication()
{
    if (phoneApplicationInitialized)
    {
        return;
    }

    RootFrame = new TransitionFrame();

    // Content omitted.
}
```

3. In the page that you want to add a transition effect, add the toolkit namespace definition as shown:

```
xmlns:toolkit="clr-namespace:Microsoft.Phone.Controls;
➥assembly=Microsoft.Phone.Controls.Toolkit"
```

4. Associate a transition with each navigation event by adding the TransitionService.NavigationInTransition and NavigationOutTransition attached properties to the page, as shown in the following excerpt:

```
<phone:PhoneApplicationPage
    …
    xmlns:toolkit="clr-namespace:Microsoft.Phone.Controls;
➥assembly=Microsoft.Phone.Controls.Toolkit">

    <toolkit:TransitionService.NavigationInTransition>
        <toolkit:NavigationInTransition>
            <toolkit:NavigationInTransition.Backward>
                <toolkit:TurnstileTransition Mode="BackwardIn"/>
            </toolkit:NavigationInTransition.Backward>
            <toolkit:NavigationInTransition.Forward>
                <toolkit:TurnstileTransition Mode="ForwardIn"/>
            </toolkit:NavigationInTransition.Forward>
        </toolkit:NavigationInTransition>
    </toolkit:TransitionService.NavigationInTransition>
    <toolkit:TransitionService.NavigationOutTransition>
        <toolkit:NavigationOutTransition>
            <toolkit:NavigationOutTransition.Backward>
                <toolkit:TurnstileTransition Mode="BackwardOut"/>
            </toolkit:NavigationOutTransition.Backward>
            <toolkit:NavigationOutTransition.Forward>
                <toolkit:TurnstileTransition Mode="ForwardOut"/>
            </toolkit:NavigationOutTransition.Forward>
        </toolkit:NavigationOutTransition>
    </toolkit:TransitionService.NavigationOutTransition>

    <!-- Content omitted. -->

</phone:PhoneApplicationPage>
```

At this point, a turnstile animation will be applied to the page when navigating to and from the page.

You can view the transition effect by uncommenting the toolkit:TransitionFrame element in the App.xaml file in the WindowsPhone7Unleashed.Examples project. Then launch the downloadable sample, and tap the TransitionPage1 page in the PageOrientation section.

Reusing the Transition Attached Properties

The transition attached properties are rather verbose, and adding them to every page in your app adds a substantial amount of duplication. Fortunately you can create a reusable style that can be applied to each page.

Listing 4.4 shows a style called TransitionPageStyle, whose TargetType is of PhoneApplicationPage. The transition properties are placed within the style, so that when the style is applied to a page, so too are the navigation transition properties.

LISTING 4.4   TransitionPageStyle in App.xaml

```xml
<Application.Resources>

    <Style x:Key="TransitionPageStyle" TargetType="phone:PhoneApplicationPage">
        <Setter Property="toolkit:TransitionService.NavigationInTransition">
            <Setter.Value>
                <toolkit:NavigationInTransition>
                    <toolkit:NavigationInTransition.Backward>
                        <toolkit:TurnstileTransition Mode="BackwardIn"/>
                    </toolkit:NavigationInTransition.Backward>
                    <toolkit:NavigationInTransition.Forward>
                        <toolkit:TurnstileTransition Mode="ForwardIn"/>
                    </toolkit:NavigationInTransition.Forward>
                </toolkit:NavigationInTransition>
            </Setter.Value>
        </Setter>
        <Setter Property="toolkit:TransitionService.NavigationOutTransition">
            <Setter.Value>
                <toolkit:NavigationOutTransition>
                    <toolkit:NavigationOutTransition.Backward>
                        <toolkit:TurnstileTransition Mode="BackwardOut"/>
                    </toolkit:NavigationOutTransition.Backward>
                    <toolkit:NavigationOutTransition.Forward>
                        <toolkit:TurnstileTransition Mode="ForwardOut"/>
                    </toolkit:NavigationOutTransition.Forward>
                </toolkit:NavigationOutTransition>
            </Setter.Value>
        </Setter>
    </Style>

</Application.Resources>
```

The style can then be applied to each page in your app, like so:

```
<phone:PhoneApplicationPage

…

    Style="{StaticResource TransitionPageStyle}">

…

</phone:PhoneApplicationPage>
```

Silverlight Toolkit transitions come with several out-of-the-box transitions that can immediately add pizzazz to your app.

Summary

This chapter began by exploring the properties and events that govern page orientation. The `PhoneApplicationPage.Orientation` property only affects orientation at design-time. The `PhoneApplicationPage.SupportedOrientations` property is used to change the orientation at runtime.

The chapter then looked at using a custom `IValueConverter` to hide and display page elements depending on the page's orientation. You then saw how to animate page elements using the `VisualStateManager`, and how to substitute an application's `RootVisual` with a custom `PhoneApplicationFrame` to animate the entire page when the orientation changes.

Finally, the chapter looked at animating page transitions using the Silverlight Toolkit.

CHAPTER 5

Content Controls, Items Controls, and Range Controls

Silverlight for Windows Phone provides an extraordinarily diverse and rich set of controls, from layout to media controls, form elements suitable for line of business applications, to even multiscale image support (a.k.a. Deep Zoom). This was made possible by leveraging the existing controls and platform maturity of Silverlight for the browser.

Yet, bringing Silverlight to the phone was no mean feat, and meant that the Microsoft Silverlight team faced the challenge of adapting an existing set of controls, designed for the most part with a web browser experience in mind, to the mobile platform, where it was necessary to contend with differences in display size and resolution, touch support, and so on. Fortunately Silverlight itself has been designed with a seemingly remarkable level of foresight, allowing many controls to be dropped in to the Windows Phone Silverlight Framework Class Library (FCL) with only minor control template changes.

Accompanying this set of adapted controls are several new controls designed specifically for the phone, including the Panorama and Pivot (covered in Chapter 10, "Pivot and Panorama").

Additionally, Microsoft provides a third set of controls, which are located in the Silverlight for Windows Phone Toolkit (covered in Chapter 9, "Silverlight Toolkit Controls"). It includes controls like the ListPicker, seen in some of the phone's built-in apps, and providing increased usability and behavior in harmony with the Windows Phone Metro design philosophy.

This chapter begins by providing an overview of the elements available in the Silverlight for FCL. It then focuses on the three base control types: ContentControl, ItemsControl, and RangeBase. It examines the various subclasses of these controls, accompanied with practical examples. It looks at how ContentControls are able to host a single item of content and at the differences between the various button controls, including the HyperlinkButton, RepeatButton, and ToggleButton, and at how each is used. The chapter then ventures into some more advanced topics, such as binding CheckBox and RadioButton controls to view-model collections, and shows how to bind to the ListBox.SelectedItems property, a feat not readily achievable with Silverlight out-of-the-box!

Finally, the chapter explores the RangeBase controls: the Slider and ProgressBar and demonstrates how to provide feedback to a user during asynchronous activities carried out by a BackgroundWorker.

The majority of the source code for this chapter is located in the ControlExamples directory of the WindowsPhone7Unleashed project, in the downloadable sample code.

Control Type Taxonomy

Having a solid grasp of the class hierarchy of any library that you regularly use helps to improve your productivity and provides a good starting point to gaining a deeper understanding of how a framework is designed to work. It gives you a shortcut for determining what can and cannot be done with a particular type based on its inherited members and whether commonly named members from two different classes are from a shared superclass or have nothing to do with one another. In essence it allows you to better assess what you can achieve using the building blocks and how to avoid making poor design decisions. On that note, this section begins with an overview of the Silverlight control class hierarchy.

The title of this part of the book is "Essential Elements," and we begin with the class FrameworkElement. The FrameworkElement provides a set of common APIs for objects that participate in Silverlight layout. FrameworkElement also defines members related to data binding, the visual tree, and object lifetime feature areas in Silverlight. It is also the superclass for most of the types presented in this part of the book (see Figure 5.1).

The focus of this chapter is on types that derive from Control (see Figure 5.2), specifically ContentControl, ItemsControl, and RangeBase and their subclasses. The rest are explored in subsequent chapters.

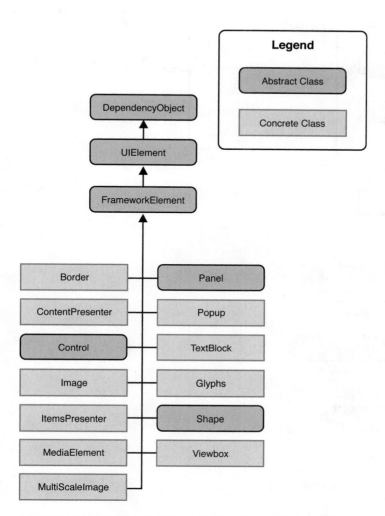

FIGURE 5.1   Top level elements of the Silverlight for Windows Phone FCL

Identifying Controls Not Supported or Absent in Silverlight for Windows Phone

Some controls that are present in Silverlight for Windows Phone are not shown in the Visual Studio Toolbox or are not recommended for use due to platform differences or design constraints. These platform differences are mostly related to the phone's touch driven UI and reduced display size.

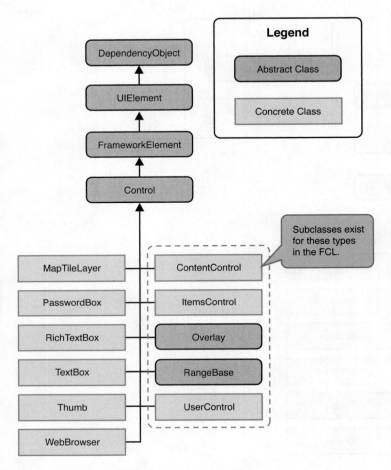

FIGURE 5.2   Control types within the FCL

In addition, the following Silverlight 4 controls do not exist in the Silverlight for Windows Phone FCL:

- ▶ `DataGrid`
- ▶ `DatePicker` (present in the Silverlight for Windows Phone Toolkit)
- ▶ `OpenFileDialog`
- ▶ `SaveFileDialog`
- ▶ `Label`
- ▶ `GridSplitter`
- ▶ `TabControl`
- ▶ `TreeView`

Some controls exist but are not supported. The following controls should not be used directly:

▶ **Calendar**

▶ **Frame**—Use the PhoneApplicationFrame instead.

▶ **Page**—Use the PhoneApplicationPage instead.

▶ **ScrollBar**—Used by the ScrollViewer.

Content Controls

Controls that are derived from ContentControl are able to host a single object. ContentControls include Buttons, ListBoxItems, and containers such as the PhoneApplicationFrame and the ScrollViewer control (see Figure 5.3).

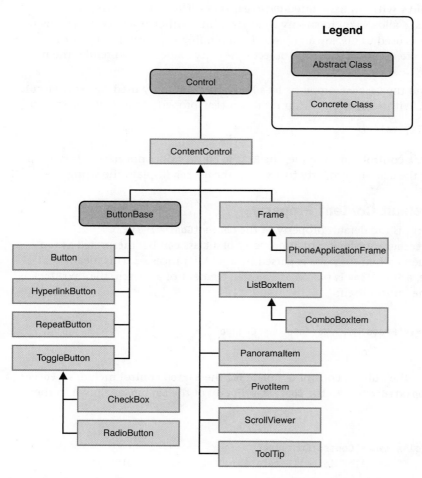

FIGURE 5.3   Content controls (excludes some mapping related types)

This chapter does not cover the `Frame` and its derived classes. For information on the `Frame` class see Chapter 3, "Application Execution Model." Nor does this chapter cover the `PanoramaItem` and `PivotItem` classes, which are discussed in Chapter 10.

`ContenControl` has a `Content` property, whose value can be of any type. The way content is presented in the UI, however, depends on its type and whether a `DataTemplate` is associated with the `ContentControl`. The following lists the three ways in which content is presented:

- ▶ **UIElements**—If the object derives from `UIElement`, then the object will be rendered.

- ▶ **Non-UIElements**—If the object does not derive from `UIElement` then its `ToString` method is used to retrieve a textual representation of the object. If the `ToString` method has not been overridden, then the result is the fully qualified class name of the object.

- ▶ **Non-UIElements with an associated `DataTemplate`**—The `ContentControl.ContentTemplate` allows you to specify a `DataTemplate`, either as a `StaticResource` or inline, which is used to display an object. Data binding expressions within the `DataTemplate` are used to extract the object's property values and to render them.

To better understand the `Content` property, let's look at a commonly used `ContentControl`: the `Button` control. With a `Button`, you can set its `Content` property to a string, as shown:

```
<Button Content="Tap me!" />
```

Unlike the `TextBlock` control, for example, the `Button` control does not have a `Text` property, yet by setting the `Content` property to a string, the `Button` displays the string.

Defining the Default Content Property

The `Content` property is the default property of the `ContentControl`. The `ContentPropertyAttribute` specifies which property of a class can be interpreted as the main content property when the class is parsed by a XAML processor. This means that when, for example, a `TextBlock` is placed as a nested element of a `Button`, the `TextBlock` is rendered within the button itself:

```
<Button>
    <TextBlock Text="Press me!" Foreground="Orange" />
</Button>
```

To further illustrate, the built-in control template for the `Button` control includes a `Border` that contains a `TemplateBinding` to the `Content` property of the `Button`, as shown in the following excerpt:

```
<Border>
    <ContentControl x:Name="ContentContainer"
                    ContentTemplate="{TemplateBinding ContentTemplate}"
```

```
                Content="{TemplateBinding Content}" />
</Border>
```

When the `Button` is rendered using its built-in style, the `Content` value, whatever it may be, is placed within a `Border`.

If you examine the source code for the `ContentControl` using Reflector, you see that a `ContentPropertyAttribute` is used to indicate to the Silverlight infrastructure that the `Content` property is the default property:

```
[ContentProperty("Content", true)]
public class ContentControl : Control
{ ... }
```

When creating your own custom controls, you can decorate a class with a `ContentPropertyAttribute` to specify a different default property.

Buttons

In most Silverlight for Windows Phone apps, buttons are the most commonly used element for receiving user input. Ordinarily, a button initiates an action when a user taps it. Unlike Silverlight for the browser, the minimum size of the `Button` has been increased, making it more amenable to touch. The shape is usually rectangular, and the standard layout allows for either text or an image to be displayed as content. `Buttons` support three visibility states: rest (the default state), pressed, and disabled. Unlike Silverlight for the browser, however, there is no visible focus state.

The inherited `FrameworkElement.HorizonalAlignment` and `VerticalAlignment` properties both default to `Stretch`. The `Button`'s `Horizontal` and `Vertical` size, therefore, depends on its parent's size; the bigger the parent `ContentControl` the bigger the button. By placing a `Button` in a `Grid`, the `Button` is free to expand to inhabit the entirety of the space provided by the `Grid` (see Figure 5.4).

If the parent `ContentControl` happens to be a `StackPanel`, the button will not expand farther than the space allowed. By default, the `StackPanel` arranges its child controls vertically. The `StackPanel` inhabits the entire width of its parent control, but only uses as much vertical space as it needs (see Figure 5.5).

To constrain the button size to the size of its content, set its `HorizontalAlignment` and `VerticalAlignment` properties to something other than `Stretch`. An effective way to do this is by using a style, as shown in the following example:

```
<Style x:Key="ButtonStyle" TargetType="ButtonBase">
    <Setter Property="HorizontalAlignment" Value="Left" />
    <Setter Property="VerticalAlignment" Value="Top" />
</Style>
```

FIGURE 5.4   By default a `Button` will expand to inhabit its parent.

FIGURE 5.5   `Button` conforms to the vertical size constraints afforded by the `StackPanel`.

The style can then be applied like so:

```
<Button Content="Press me!" Style="{StaticResource ButtonStyle}" />
```

Tap and Click Events

With the release of the Windows Phone 7.1 SDK, the `Click` event of the `ButtonBase` class has been superseded by a `UIElement` event named `Tap`. The `Tap` event is designed for touch input, while the `Click` event relies on legacy code that handles mouse state.

> **NOTE**
>
> While the `ButtonBase Click` event is still present in the SDK, unless your UI code needs to be shared with Silverlight for the browser projects, use the `Tap` event.

The following is an example of a `UIElement.Tap` event handler.

```
void Button_Tap(object sender, System.Windows.Input.GestureEventArgs e)
{
...
}
```

> **NOTE**
>
> There is another public `GestureEventArgs` class residing in the Silverlight Toolkit that is unfortunately located in the Microsoft.Phone.Controls namespace. If you are using the Silverlight Toolkit, be mindful that the correct type needs to be specified or a runtime exception will be raised.
>
> Either use the namespace qualified type name, as shown in the previous example, or add a type alias to the top of your class file, like so:
>
> ```
> using GestureEventArgs = System.Windows.Input.GestureEventArgs;
> ```

Button Click Mode

If you need to use the `Button.Click` event, rather than the `Tap` event for whatever reason, you can tailor the type of user interaction that is required to raise the `Button`'s `Click` event using the `Button.ClickMode` property.

The following is a list of the three possible `ClickMode` values:

- ▶ **Press**—The `Click` event is raised as soon as the user touches the button.

- ▶ **Release**—The `Click` event is not raised until the user lifts his finger off the button. This is the default value.

- ▶ **Hover**—Has the same effect as `Press`. As there is currently no support for detecting when the user hovers over a control on a Windows Phone device, this value serves no purpose and exists to maintain compatibility with Silverlight for the browser.

Hyperlink Button

The `HyperlinkButton` allows you to embed hypertext links in a page.

As previously stated, all `UIElements` have a `Tap` event, which can be used to perform navigation within an event handler. Performing navigation in this manner, however, can be cumbersome, and the `HyperlinkButton` provides an easier way to navigate to pages within your app without having to subscribe to an event or use an `ICommand`.

The `HyperlinkButton` includes a `NavigateUri` property. When a user presses the `HyperlinkButton`, the button takes care of performing the navigation.

The default appearance of the `HyperlinkButton` does not resemble a button at all. In fact, the default style of a `HyperlinkButton` is underlined text, not unlike an HTML hyperlink.

For more information on using the `HyperlinkButton` and page navigation, see Chapter 3.

Repeat and Toggle Buttons

Neither the `RepeatButton` nor the `ToggleButton` controls are abstract. Yet both reside in the System.Windows.Controls.Primitives namespace, not in the System.Windows.Controls namespace, indicating that these two controls are not intended to be used in day-to-day page code.

Repeat Button

The `RepeatButton` behaves the same as the `Button` control; however, the `RepeatButton`'s `Tap` event is raised repeatedly while it is being pressed, whereas the `Button` control raises its `Tap` event once for each user press.

The `RepeatButton` is used as part of the `ScrollBar` control, which itself is part of the `ScrollViewer` control. Unlike Silverlight for the browser, however, which uses the `RepeatButton` to incrementally scroll content when pressed, the `RepeatButton` in the `ScrollBar` serves little purpose on the phone because the `ScrollBar` is for display purposes only.

The `RepeatButton` has two main properties:

▶ **Interval**—The duration between events, measured in milliseconds. The default value is 250 ms.

▶ **Delay**—The duration before the event is raised, measured in milliseconds. The default value is 250 ms.

The `RepeatButton` can be placed in XAML like so:

```
<RepeatButton Content="Press me!" Interval="200" Delay="500"
              Tap="RepeatButton_Tap" />
```

Sample Overview

An example for the RepeatButton control can be found in the ButtonExampleView page and the ButtonExampleViewModel in the downloadable sample code. The ButtonExampleView has a RepeatButton that is used to execute the RepeatCommand in the viewmodel, as shown:

```
<RepeatButton Content="{Binding RepeatCount}" Interval="200" Delay="500"
              Command="{Binding RepeatCommand}" />
```

The Content property of the RepeatButton is populated using a data binding to the RepeatCount property in the viewmodel:

```
int repeatCount;

public int RepeatCount
{
    get
    {
        return repeatCount;
    }
    private set
    {
        Assign(() => RepeatCount, ref repeatCount, value);
    }
}
```

Tapping the RepeatButton causes the RepeatCommand to execute. The RepeatCommand is a public property of the viewmodel, defined as shown:

```
readonly DelegateCommand repeatCommand;

public ICommand RepeatCommand
{
    get
    {
        return repeatCommand;
    }
}
```

The repeatCommand is instantiated in the viewmodel constructor. When executed, the command increments the RepeatCount property, which updates the RepeatButton's Content property:

```
public ButtonExampleViewModel() : base("Buttons")
{
    repeatCommand = new DelegateCommand(obj => RepeatCount++);
}
```

When the button is pressed and held, it causes the RepeatCount to increment periodically, which updates the content of the button (see Figure 5.6).

FIGURE 5.6   Pressing and holding the RepeatButton causes a counter to increment.

Toggle Button

The ToggleButton can visually represent two states: pressed or not pressed. When the user taps a ToggleButton, it switches state and stays in that state until tapped again. The ToggleButton is the base class for the CheckBox and RadioButton controls and, as such, is actually able to represent three states, which includes a third, indeterminate, state.

> **NOTE**
>
> The terms *pressed* and *not pressed* are more readily understandable when talking about the ToggleButton. The ToggleButton, however, contains an IsChecked property that is used to identify the state of the button. So checked and unchecked, pressed and not pressed, are used interchangeably throughout this section.

While the ToggleButton inherits the Tap event from the UIElement class, it has other events that are raised when the state of the button is changed.

The following shows how to create a ToggleButton in XAML:

```
<ToggleButton Content="ToggleButton"
              Checked="ToggleButton_Checked"
              Unchecked="ToggleButton_Unchecked" />
```

Depending on the state of the ToggleButton, one of two events: Checked or Unchecked, is raised when the user presses the ToggleButton.

Setting the ToggleButton.IsThreeState property to true allows the user to set the indeterminate state by tapping the button. If set to false, the only way to return to the indeterminate state is via code.

> **NOTE**
>
> The name of the ToggleButton.IsThreeState property can be confusing. Even though IsThreeState may be set to false, you can still set the indeterminate state in code. A better name might have been something like UserCanSetIndeterminateState.

The following is an example of a three-state `ToggleButton`:

```
<ToggleButton Content="ToggleButton" IsThreeState="True"
              Checked="ToggleButton_Checked"
              Unchecked="ToggleButton_Unchecked"
              Indeterminate="ToggleButton_Indeterminate" />
```

The `ToggleButton.IsChecked` property is a nullable Boolean, with `true` representing checked, `false` representing unchecked, and `null` representing its indeterminate state.

While the `ToggleButton` can be used to allow the user to cycle through three states, it makes little sense unless you are providing a custom template to visually represent the third indeterminate state. The `CheckBox` and `RadioButton` controls do provide a representation of each of the three states, as you see later in the chapter.

> **NOTE**
>
> The `ToggleButton` indeterminate state can be specified in XAML by setting the `IsChecked` property like so:
>
> ```
> <ToggleButton Content="ToggleButton" IsChecked="{x:Null}" />
> ```

The `Checked`, `Unchecked`, and `Indeterminate` events detect when the button is tapped and has transitioned to a new state.

> **TIP**
>
> Rather than using the `Checked`, `Unchecked`, and `Indeterminate` events, use the `Tap` event to consolidate the logic for all three state changes. It is usually easier to handle all three state changes in the same place.

The state of the `ToggleButton` can be determined in a `Tap` event handler using the `ToggleButton.IsChecked` property, as shown in the following excerpt:

```
void ToggleButton_Tap(object sender, GestureEventArgs e)
{
    ToggleButton button = (ToggleButton)sender;
    Debug.WriteLine("IsChecked:"
        + (button.IsChecked.HasValue
            ? button.IsChecked.ToString() : "indeterminate"));
}
```

Radio Button

The `RadioButton` is a subclass of the `ToggleButton` class and offers the same events, such as `Checked`, `Unchecked`, and `Indeterminate`, and properties, such as `IsChecked`. A radio button is used to represent a set of related but mutually exclusive choices. The user taps on the radio button description text or glyph to select the control. Only one option from a particular group may be selected at a time.

RadioButtons that reside in the same container control automatically share the same group. In addition, the RadioButton has a GroupName property, which allows you to override the default behavior and to enforce mutual exclusivity explicitly by restricting those RadioButtons that share the same GroupName to no more than one being checked at a time. This is useful when multiple RadioButtons are placed in different containers but reside in the same logical group, or when multiple RadioButtons reside in the same container but reside in different logical groups. The GroupName property allows you to control the associations between the controls. Consider the following example:

```
<StackPanel>
    <RadioButton Content="RadioButton 1 (group 1)" GroupName="group1" />
    <RadioButton Content="RadioButton 2 (group 1)" GroupName="group1" />
    <RadioButton Content="RadioButton 3 (group 2)" GroupName="group2" />
    <RadioButton Content="RadioButton 4 (group 2)" GroupName="group2" />
</StackPanel>
```

By specifying the GroupName, you can have the RadioButtons reside in the same ContentControl, yet still operate as two distinct groups.

Data Binding Radio Button Controls to a ViewModel Collection

This example looks at data binding a ListBox.ItemsSource property to a collection of objects in a viewmodel, and you see how to represent each item in the collection as a RadioButton in the view. You also see how to synchronize the IsChecked property of a RadioButton with the ListBoxItem.IsSelected property.

The sample is located in the ButtonExampleView page and the ButtonExampleViewModel in the downloadable sample code. The viewmodel contains an ObservableCollection of a custom DataItem class, as shown:

```
readonly ObservableCollection<DataItem> radioItems
    = new ObservableCollection<DataItem>
    {
        new DataItem(0, "Item 1"),
        new DataItem(1, "Item 2"),
        new DataItem(2, "Item 3")
    };

public IEnumerable<DataItem> RadioItems
{
    get
    {
        return radioItems;
    }
}
```

The `DataItem` class is simply a container to hold an object value and an associated piece of text (see Listing 5.1).

Each `DataItem` object is represented as a `RadioButton` in the view. The `DataItem`'s `ToString` method override allows you to display the object easily in the view without requiring an explicit data binding path expression to the `DataItem.Text` property.

LISTING 5.1   DataItem Class

```
public class DataItem : NotifyPropertyChangeBase
{
    object itemValue;

    public object Value
    {
        get
        {
            return itemValue;
        }
        set
        {
            Assign("Value", ref itemValue, value);
        }
    }

    object text;

    public object Text
    {
        get
        {
            return text;
        }
        set
        {
            Assign("Text", ref text, value);
        }
    }

    public DataItem(object value, object text)
    {
        itemValue = ArgumentValidator.AssertNotNull(value, "value");
        this.text = ArgumentValidator.AssertNotNull(text, "text");
    }
}
```

LISTING 5.1   Continued

```
    public override string ToString()
    {
        return text != null ? text.ToString() : base.ToString();
    }
}
```

The collection of `DataItem` objects is displayed in the `ButtonExampleView` using a `ListBox`. The `ListBox.ItemsSource` is bound to the collection, as shown in the following excerpt:

```
<ListBox ItemsSource="{Binding RadioItems}"
    SelectedItem="{Binding SelectedRadioItem, Mode=TwoWay}"
    ItemContainerStyle="{StaticResource RadioButtonListItemStyle}"/>
```

By binding to the `SelectedRadioItem` property, the viewmodel is able to monitor and even to set the `IsChecked` property of any or all of the `RadioButton` controls.

To display each item in the collection as a `RadioButton`, we use a custom `ItemContainerStyle` called `RadioButtonListItemStyle`, which is located in the `phone:PhoneApplicationPage.Resources` element of the `ButtonExampleView.xaml` page. This style defines the `ControlTemplate` for a `ListBoxItem`, as shown in the following excerpt:

```
<Style x:Key="RadioButtonListItemStyle" TargetType="ListBoxItem">
    <Setter Property="VerticalContentAlignment" Value="Top" />
    <Setter Property="Template">
        <Setter.Value>
            <ControlTemplate TargetType="ListBoxItem">
                <Grid Background="{TemplateBinding Background}">
                    <RadioButton Content="{TemplateBinding Content}"
                    IsChecked="{Binding Path=IsSelected,
                    RelativeSource={RelativeSource TemplatedParent},
                        Mode=TwoWay}" />
                </Grid>
            </ControlTemplate>
        </Setter.Value>
    </Setter>
</Style>
```

The `IsChecked` property is assigned using a binding to the `ListBoxItem.IsSelected` property. In addition, `BindingMode` is set to `TwoWay`, so that when the item is checked it will be selected in the `ListBox`. Conversely, when unchecked by the user or from code in the viewmodel the items will be unselected in the `ListBox`.

The `Content` property of the `RadioButton` is assigned using a `TemplateBinding` to the `Content` property of the `ListBoxItem`. This causes the `DataItem` in the collection to be assigned to the `Content` property of the `RadioButton`. Because the `DataItem` does not derive from `UIElement`, the `RadioButton` renders the `DataItem` using the `ToString` method override of the `DataItem` class (see Figure 5.7).

FIGURE 5.7   The `DataItem` collection is displayed using `RadioButton` controls.

When a `RadioButton` is selected, it is assigned to the `SelectedRadioItem` property in the viewmodel.

Finally, the selected item is displayed using a `TextBlock`, as shown:

```
<TextBlock Text="{Binding SelectedRadioItem}"
           Style="{StaticResource ValueTextStyle}" />
```

Check Box

The `CheckBox` control is used to define a binary state and can be used in groups to display multiple choices from which the user can select one or more choices. A user can either tap a check box or the associated label text to select an option.

The `CheckBox` uses an alternative visual representation than its base class `ToggleButton` control, though it contains no new members.

`CheckBox` supports three visible states: rest, press, and disabled for both checked and unchecked settings. There is, however, no visible focus state. In addition to visible states, the `CheckBox` control is capable of representing three settings: checked, unchecked, or indeterminate, along with a disabled visual state for each (see Figure 5.8). The state of the `CheckBox` can be retrieved using its nullable Boolean `IsChecked` property.

The indeterminate state of the `CheckBox` is commonly used to show that the user has not set the state of the control, or that some data anomaly has been detected.

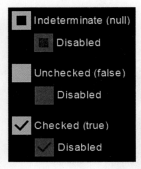

FIGURE 5.8   The CheckBox control checked states

Sample Overview

An example for the CheckBox control can be found in the ButtonExampleView page and the ButtonExampleViewModel, in the downloadable sample code. The ButtonExampleView has a CheckBox that has a two-way data binding to the Checked property of the viewmodel, as shown:

```
<CheckBox Content="{Binding Checked}" IsChecked="{Binding Checked, Mode=TwoWay}"
    IsThreeState="True" />
```

The viewmodel's Checked property is a nullable Boolean:

```
bool? isChecked;

public bool? Checked
{
    get
    {
        return isChecked;
    }
    set
    {
        Assign(() => Checked, ref isChecked, value);
    }
}
```

When the user taps the CheckBox, it transitions to the next state and updates the view-model's Checked property (see Figure 5.9).

Data Binding Check Boxes to a ViewModel Collection

This example looks at data binding a ListBox.ItemsSource property to a collection of objects in a viewmodel, and you see how to represent each item in the collection as a CheckBox in the view. You also see how to synchronize the IsChecked property of a

CheckBox with the `ListBoxItem.IsSelected` property. Finally, you investigate how to bind to the `ListBox.SelectedItems` property, which is not readily achievable with Silverlight out-of-the-box!

FIGURE 5.9   A `CheckBox` control, with its `IsChecked` property set to `true`

The sample for this section is located in the `ButtonExampleView` page and the `ButtonExampleViewModel`, in the downloadable sample code. Once again, the viewmodel contains an `ObservableCollection` of a custom `DataItem` class:

```
readonly ObservableCollection<DataItem> checkBoxItems
    = new ObservableCollection<DataItem>
        {
            new DataItem(0, "Item 1"),
            new DataItem(1, "Item 2"),
            new DataItem(2, "Item 3")
        };

public IEnumerable<DataItem> CheckBoxItems
{
    get
    {
        return checkBoxItems;
    }
}
```

The collection of `DataItems` is displayed in the `ButtonExampleView` using a `ListBox`. Each `DataItem` is represented as a `CheckBox`. The `ListBox.ItemsSource` is databound to the collection, as shown in the following excerpt:

```
<ListBox ItemsSource="{Binding CheckBoxItems}"
        SelectionMode="Multiple"
        ItemContainerStyle="{StaticResource CheckBoxListItemStyle}"
        unleashed:SelectedItems.Items="{Binding SelectedCheckBoxItems}" />
```

To allow multiple `CheckBox` controls to be checked simultaneously, the `ListBox.SelectionMode` property of the `ListBox` is set to `Multiple`.

We cannot bind to the `ListBox.SelectedItems` property because it is not a `DependencyProperty`. As a workaround, the attached property `SelectedItems.Items` is used to bind to the SelectedCheckBoxItems property of the viewmodel. The SelectedItems. Items attached property is discussed in the next section "Data Binding to ListBox.SelectedItems."

By binding to the SelectedCheckBoxItems property, you can monitor and set the IsChecked property of any or all of the CheckBox controls in the view.

To display each item in the collection as a CheckBox you use a custom ItemContainerStyle called CheckBoxListItemStyle, which is located in the phone:PhoneApplicationPage. Resources element of the ButtonExampleView.xaml page. This style defines the ControlTemplate for a ListBoxItem, as shown in the following excerpt:

```
<Style x:Key="CheckBoxListItemStyle" TargetType="ListBoxItem">
    <Setter Property="VerticalContentAlignment" Value="Top" />
    <Setter Property="Template">
        <Setter.Value>
            <ControlTemplate TargetType="ListBoxItem">
                <Grid Background="{TemplateBinding Background}">
                    <CheckBox Content="{TemplateBinding Content}"
                    IsChecked="{Binding Path=IsSelected,
                    RelativeSource={RelativeSource TemplatedParent},
                    Mode=TwoWay}" />
                </Grid>
            </ControlTemplate>
        </Setter.Value>
    </Setter>
</Style>
```

The IsChecked property is assigned using a binding to the ListBoxItem.IsSelected property. In addition, the BindingMode is set to TwoWay, so that when the item is checked it is selected in the ListBox. Conversely, when unchecked by the user or from code in the viewmodel the items will be unselected in the ListBox.

The Content property of the CheckBox is assigned using a TemplateBinding to the Content property of the ListBoxItem. This causes the DataItem in the collection to be assigned to the Content property of the CheckBox. Because the DataItem does not derive from UIElement, the CheckBox renders the DataItem using the ToString method override of the DataItem class (see Figure 5.10).

When a CheckBox is checked or unchecked, it is added to or removed from the list of SelectedCheckBoxItems property in the viewmodel:

```
readonly ObservableCollection<DataItem> selectedCheckBoxItems
    = new ObservableCollection<DataItem>();

public ObservableCollection<DataItem> SelectedCheckBoxItems
{
    get
    {
```

```
        return selectedCheckBoxItems;
    }
}
```

FIGURE 5.10   `DataItem` collection is displayed using `CheckBox` controls.

Finally, the selected items are, once again, displayed in a `ListBox` in the view. This time, however, they are displayed not with a `CheckBox`, but a `TextBlock`; as shown:

```
<ListBox ItemsSource="{Binding SelectedCheckBoxItems}">
    <ListBox.ItemTemplate>
        <DataTemplate>
            <TextBlock Text="{Binding}"
                Style="{StaticResource NormalTextStyle}" />
        </DataTemplate>
    </ListBox.ItemTemplate>
</ListBox>
```

> **NOTE**
>
> The `TextBlock.Text` data binding expression `{Binding}` indicates that value of the `Text` property is set to the result of calling the `ToString` method of the `DataItem`.

Data Binding to `ListBox.SelectedItems`

Recall that the previous example used the `SelectedItems.Items` attached property to enable data binding to the `SelectedItems` property of the `ListBox` control. We do this because the `ListBox.SelectedItems` property is not a `DependencyProperty`, which means it cannot be the target of a data binding.

The downloadable sample code contains a `SelectedItems` class, which enables data binding to the `ListBox.SelectedItems` property (see Listing 5.2).

The `SelectedItems` class contains two dependency properties: an `ItemsProperty` and a `SelectedItemsBehaviorProperty`. The `ItemsProperty` is used to specify the source property of the `DataContext` and is used to assign the selected items to the `ListBox`'s `DataContext`. When the `SelectionChanged` event of the `ListBox` is raised, the `DataContext`'s property is updated.

The `SelectedItemsBehavior` class contains the logic for updating the list of selected items, which also relies on the `DataContextChangedListener` class that raises an event when the `DataContext` of the `ListBox` changes. For more information on the `DataContextChangedListener`, see Chapter 23, "Input Validation."

An instance of the `SelectedItemsBehavior` is associated with the `ListBox` using the `SelectedItemsBehaviorProperty`.

LISTING 5.2   SelectedItems Class

```
public static class SelectedItems
{
    public static readonly DependencyProperty ItemsProperty
        = DependencyProperty.RegisterAttached(
            "Items",
            typeof(IList),
            typeof(SelectedItems),
            new PropertyMetadata(null, ItemsPropertyChanged));

    public static void SetItems(ListBox listBox, IList list)
    {
        listBox.SetValue(ItemsProperty, list);
    }

    public static IList GetItems(ListBox listBox)
    {
        return (IList)listBox.GetValue(ItemsProperty);
    }

    static readonly DependencyProperty SelectedItemsBehaviorProperty
        = DependencyProperty.RegisterAttached(
            "SelectedItemsBehavior",
```

LISTING 5.2   Continued

```
            typeof(SelectedItemsBehavior),
            typeof(ListBox), null);

    static void ItemsPropertyChanged(
        DependencyObject d, DependencyPropertyChangedEventArgs e)
    {
        var target = d as ListBox;
        if (target != null)
        {
            GetOrCreateBehavior(target, (IList)e.NewValue);
        }
    }

    static SelectedItemsBehavior GetOrCreateBehavior(
        ListBox listBox, IList list)
    {
        var behavior = (SelectedItemsBehavior)listBox.GetValue(
                                    SelectedItemsBehaviorProperty);
        if (behavior == null)
        {
            behavior = new SelectedItemsBehavior(listBox, list);
            listBox.SetValue(SelectedItemsBehaviorProperty, behavior);
        }

        return behavior;
    }

    class SelectedItemsBehavior
    {
        readonly ListBox listBox;
        readonly IList sourceList;

        public SelectedItemsBehavior(ListBox listBox, IList sourceList)
        {
            this.listBox = ArgumentValidator.AssertNotNull(listBox, "listBox");
            this.sourceList = ArgumentValidator.AssertNotNull(
                                        sourceList, "sourceList");
            this.listBox.SelectionChanged += OnSelectionChanged;
            DataContextChangedListener.Subscribe(
                        listBox, OnDataContextChanged);
        }

        void OnDataContextChanged(
            DependencyObject d, DependencyPropertyChangedEventArgs e)
```

LISTING 5.2   Continued

```
    {
        UpdateList();
    }

    void OnSelectionChanged(object sender, SelectionChangedEventArgs e)
    {
        UpdateList();
    }

    void UpdateList()
    {
        sourceList.Clear();

        foreach (object item in listBox.SelectedItems)
        {
            sourceList.Add(item);
        }
    }
  }
}
```

Tool Tip

The ToolTip control is present in the Windows Phone FCL, yet it serves no real purpose because it is a control designed to work with a pointing device such as a mouse and relies on hovering the mouse over the control. Hover events, which ordinarily dictate when a ToolTip is displayed, do not exist in the realm of the phone, making the ToolTip redundant unless used in an unorthodox way.

Perhaps future displays will have the ability to sense finger display proximity. Then, no doubt, the ToolTip will make it to the Windows Phone platform.

Items Controls

Just as the ContentControl plays host to a single child control, the ItemsControl can have many children. Controls that can contain more than one child usually derive from the ItemsControl class; these include the ComboBox control and, most notably, the ListBox control (see Figure 5.11).

An ItemsControl allows you to populate its children either directly in XAML or in code using the ItemsControl.Items property, or indirectly using a data binding and the ItemsControl.ItemsSource property.

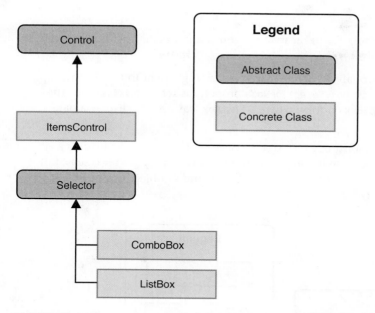

FIGURE 5.11   ComboBox and ListBox are derived from ItemsControl.

The Selector class extends the ItemsControl to provide the properties and events shown in Table 5.1.

TABLE 5.1   Selector Members

Name	Description
IsSynchronizedWithCurrentItem	Indicates that when the selected item in a collection changes, all the Selector controls that use the collection as their ItemsSource must be notified. This can be handy when you want to keep the selected item in several controls in synchronization without using code-beside or a secondary viewmodel property.
SelectedIndex	The zero based index of the selected item in the control.
SelectedItem	The content of the selected item in the control. If using the ItemsSource property, SelectedItem will resolve the object associated with the selected item's content, ordinarily its DataContext.
SelectionChanged	An event that is raised when the SelectedItem has changed.

ListBox

The `ListBox` is an items control, which means that you can populate it with items that contain text or other controls.

By default, the `ListBox` control allows the user to select a single item in the list. Multiple items can be selected if the `ListBox.SelectionMode` property is set to `Multiple` (see the previous section on the `CheckBox` control, where a `ListBox` was used to display a data bound collection).

The `ListBox` control contains a list of `ListBoxItem` controls. The `ListBox` control is a remarkably flexible control because it allows you to not only display `ListBoxItems`, but because the `ListBoxItem` control is a `ContentControl` any kind of object can be placed in a `ListBox` (see Figure 5.12).

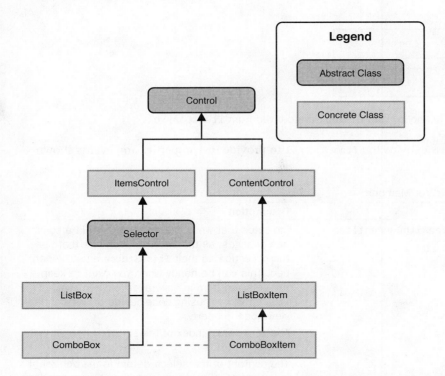

FIGURE 5.12   `ListBoxItem` and `ComboBoxItem` are derived from `ContentControl`.

In addition, it is unnecessary to wrap content in a `ListBoxItem` control, as shown in the following excerpt:

```
<ListBox>
    <ListBoxItem>
        <TextBlock Text="Item 1" Style="{StaticResource NormalTextStyle}" />
    </ListBoxItem>
    <ListBoxItem>
```

```
        <TextBlock Text="Item 2" Style="{StaticResource NormalTextStyle}" />
    </ListBoxItem>
</ListBox>
```

`ListBoxItems` are created implicitly for each element, making the previous excerpt equivalent to the following:

```
<ListBox>
    <TextBlock Text="Item 1" Style="{StaticResource NormalTextStyle}" />
    <TextBlock Text="Item 2" Style="{StaticResource NormalTextStyle}" />
</ListBox>
```

The example depicted in Figure 5.13 demonstrates that placing a `TextBlock`, implicitly or explicitly, in a `ListBoxItem` yields the same results.

FIGURE 5.13   ListBox with implicit and explicit `ListBoxItems`

This works because the `ListBoxItem` `ControlTemplate` uses a `TemplateBinding` to the `Content` and `ContentTemplate` properties of the item control. When an item is being displayed, the `ControlTemplate` places it in a `ContentControl`, as this excerpt from the built-in `ListBoxItem` `ControlTemplate` shows:

```
<ControlTemplate TargetType="ListBoxItem">
    <Border x:Name="LayoutRoot">
        <ContentControl x:Name="ContentContainer"
                    ContentTemplate="{TemplateBinding ContentTemplate}"
                    Content="{TemplateBinding Content}" />
    </Border>
</ControlTemplate>
```

The `ListBox` control inherits the `Selector.SelectedItem` and `SelectedIndex` properties together with a `SelectionChanged` event, which allow you to detect when the user selects or deselects an item.

> **NOTE**
>
> The `SelectedItem` property is the value of the content item and not the `ListBoxItem` itself. It is the `Content` property of the `ListBoxItem` that is used to resolve the value.

For an example of how to consume the `ItemsSource` property using a data binding, see the previous sections on the `CheckBox` and `RadioButton` controls.

In addition to the selection related properties provided by the `Selector` class, the `ListBox` also provides a `SelectedItems` property, which can be used when using the multiple `SelectionMode`. The `SelectedItems` property is, however, not a `DependencyProperty`, and this means that it is not available for data binding. See the previous section on the `CheckBox` control for a solution.

ComboBox

While the `ComboBox` control exists in the FCL, it is not suitable for use in most cases. The `ComboBox` has its origins in desktop UI and is more suited to a mouse-driven UI, where the user can rely on a high level of precision manipulating the control using a mouse. The `ComboBox` is not suited to touch input, and there are alternative superior controls, such as the `ListPicker` control provided in the Silverlight for Windows Phone Toolkit, which is examined in Chapter 9.

For this reason, the `ComboBox` does not appear in the Visual Studio Toolbox, and the built-in styles for the `ComboBox` do not reflect the light and dark themes of the phone.

Range Controls

The `RangeBase` control is an abstract class that represents a control that oversees a numeric value that falls between a minimum and a maximum value. Silverlight for Windows Phone provides three `RangeBase` controls: the `ProgressBar`, `ScrollBar`, and `Slider` (see Figure 5.14).

The `RangeBase` control provides various range related properties and events for monitoring its `Value` property (see Table 5.2).

TABLE 5.2   Properties of the `RangeBase` Class

Name	Description
Value	A `double` value that indicates the selected value within the control. This value should fall between the `Minimum` and `Maximum` values.
Minimum	A `double` value indicating the lower limit of the range. The default value is 0.0.
Maximum	A `double` value indicating the upper limit of the range. The default value is 10.0.

TABLE 5.2   Continued

Name	Description
SmallChange	A `double` value that specifies by how much the `Value` property should be increased, or decreased, when the user performs a *small action*. The small action depends on the kind of control. `SmallChange` does not affect the user experience for the `ProgressBar`, `ScrollBar`, or the `Slider`, but is present for use in custom controls. The default value is 0.1.
LargeChange	A `double` value that specifies by how much the `Value` property should be increased, or decreased, when the user performs a *large action*. As with the `SmallChange` property, the large action depends on the kind of control. For example, when using a `Slider` control, a large action occurs when the user presses the `Slider`'s track. The default value is 1.0.
ValueChanged	A routed event that is raised when the `Value` property has changed. The data type is `RoutedPropertyChangedEventHandler<double>`.

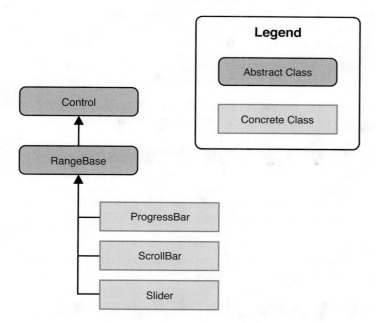

FIGURE 5.14   RangeBase controls

NOTE

If the `Value` property is set to a value outside the range defined by the `Minimum` and `Maximum` properties, no `Exception` is raised. Instead the `Value` property is coerced and set to either the `Minimum` or `Maximum` value.

However, setting `Minimum`, `Maximum`, `Value`, `SmallChange`, or `LargeChange` to NaN, NegativeInfinity, or PositiveInfinity raises an `ArgumentException`. In addition, setting `SmallChange` or `LargeChange` to a value less than zero raises an `ArgumentException`.

ProgressBar

During time-consuming operations, it is important to provide an indication to the user that your application is busy, while still remaining responsive. The `ProgressBar` serves this purpose. It is not interactive; the user cannot modify it directly, and it is able to work in two modes: determinate and indeterminate.

Determinate mode allows you to display a value indicating the amount of work completed relative to the amount of work remaining, allowing the user to estimate how long the remainder of the operation will take. If the `IsIndeterminate` property is not specified, the control defaults to determinate.

Progress is displayed by setting the `Value` property of the control to the amount of work completed, and the `Maximum` property to the total amount of work to be performed. There is also a `Minimum` property that allows you to set a base point and can be useful when a portion of the work has already been completed.

The noninteractive nature of the control means that the `Value` property is updated from code, or via a data binding, while performing a background operation.

Alternatively, when progress of an operation cannot be monitored, or the total duration of an operation is unknown, then the `ProgressBar`'s indeterminate mode can be engaged.

> **BEST PRACTICE**
>
> If the total amount of work required by an activity is known and progress can be periodically determined, avoid using an indeterminate `ProgressBar`. Use instead a determinate `ProgressBar`. Providing clear feedback about how long a user can expect to wait for completion of an operation improves the user's experience.

When using the indeterminate mode by setting the `IsIndeterminate` property to `true`, the control is displayed as a series of animated dots.

> **CAUTION**
>
> The `ProgressBar` has a performance issue caused by its built-in control template in Silverlight for Windows Phone. The template has a negative performance cost in *indeterminate* mode. This performance cost is present even when the `ProgressBar` is hidden.
>
> As a workaround, the `IsIndeterminate` property should be set to `false` when the control is not visible.

Alternatively, the Silverlight Toolkit's `PerformanceProgressBar` can be used in place of the FCL's `ProgressBar`. For more information on the `PerformanceProgressBar`, see Chapter 9.

In addition, the next section looks at the `PerformanceIndicator`, which leverages the native progress indicator in the phone's status bar.

Progress Indicator

In the initial release of the Windows Phone OS, there was no way to control the native progress bar located in the status bar of the phone. Fortunately, with Windows Phone 7.5, you now can with the new `ProgressIndicator` class.

`ProgressIndicator` is a subclass of the `DependencyObject` class and provides the following bindable properties:

- ▶ **IsIndeterminate**—A bool value that allows you to enable or disable the indeterminate state of the indicator.

- ▶ **IsVisible**—A bool value that allows you to show or hide the `ProgressIndicator`.

- ▶ **Text**—A string that is displayed beneath the indicator.

- ▶ **Value**—A double value between 0.0 and 1.0 that allows you to set the length of the progress bar when in determinate mode, that is, when `IsIndeterminate` is set to false.

> **NOTE**
>
> The default value of `ProgressIndicator.IsVisible` is false. You must set `IsVisible` to true, either explicitly or via a data binding for the control to be displayed.

A `ProgressIndicator` may be either defined in XAML or in code. The following example demonstrates adding a `ProgressIndicator` to a page's XAML file:

```
<phone:PhoneApplicationPage
...
    shell:SystemTray.IsVisible="True">

    <shell:SystemTray.ProgressIndicator>
        <shell:ProgressIndicator IsVisible="True"
                                 IsIndeterminate="False"
                                 Value="0.9"
                                 Text="{Binding Message}" />
    </shell:SystemTray.ProgressIndicator>
...
</phone:PhoneApplicationPage>
```

> **NOTE**
>
> `SystemTray.IsVisible` must be set to true for the `ProgressIndicator` to be displayed.

Adding a `ProgressIndicator` to a page must occur after the page has been initialized. This can be done by attaching the `ProgressIndicator` to the page within a `Loaded` event handler.

The `ProgressIndicator` instance may be retained as a field in the page and used directly, or data bindings can be established when the `ProgressIndicator` is instantiated, as demonstrated in Listing 5.3.

LISTING 5.3   Initializing a `ProgressIndicator` in Code

```
public partial class ExampleView : PhoneApplicationPage
{
    public ExampleView()
    {
        InitializeComponent();
        DataContext = new ExampleViewModel();
        Loaded += HandleLoaded;
    }

    void HandleLoaded(object sender, RoutedEventArgs e)
    {
        var progressIndicator = SystemTray.ProgressIndicator;
        if (progressIndicator != null)
        {
            return;
        }

        progressIndicator = new ProgressIndicator();

        SystemTray.SetProgressIndicator(this, progressIndicator);

        Binding binding = new Binding("Busy") { Source = ViewModel };
        BindingOperations.SetBinding(
            progressIndicator, ProgressIndicator.IsVisibleProperty, binding);

        binding = new Binding("Busy") { Source = ViewModel };
        BindingOperations.SetBinding(
            progressIndicator,
            ProgressIndicator.IsIndeterminateProperty,
            binding);
```

LISTING 5.3   Continued

```
        binding = new Binding("Message") { Source = ViewModel };
        BindingOperations.SetBinding(
            progressIndicator, ProgressIndicator.TextProperty, binding);
    }
    ...
}
```

Chapter 26, "Local Databases," uses the ProgressIndicator to display the progress of retrieving a live Twitter feed.

BEST PRACTICE

Performing time-consuming operations, such as downloads and database queries, on the UI thread is bad practice, as it locks the user interface making it unresponsive. Therefore, always perform any potentially long-running operation using a background thread.

Using a BackgroundWorker to Update the ProgressBar

The BackgroundWorker class allows you to run an operation on a separate, dedicated thread. When you want a responsive user interface and you must perform time-consuming operations, the BackgroundWorker class provides a convenient solution.

The BackgroundWorker class has events that are automatically raised on the UI thread, giving you the opportunity to update UIElements without risking cross-thread access exceptions. You can listen for events that report the progress of an operation and signal when the operation is completed. The following section uses a BackgroundWorker to perform an arbitrary time-consuming operation during which a ProgressBar is periodically notified of the progress.

ProgressBar and BackgroundWorker Sample Code

An example for the ProgressBar can be found in the ControlExamplesView page and the ControlExamplesViewModel class in the downloadable sample code.

The viewmodel contains a BackgroundWorker field. In the viewmodel's constructor, the BackgroundWorker.WorkerReportsProgress property is set to true. This causes the BackgroundWorker to raise an event when its ReportProgress method is called. We then subscribe to three events: the DoWork event, which is raised when the RunWorkerAsync method is called; the ProgressChanged event, which is called when the BackgroundWorker ReportProgress method is called; and the RunWorkerCompleted, which is raised when the backgroundWorker_DoWork method completes (see Listing 5.4).

LISTING 5.4   ControlExamplesViewModel Class (excerpt)

```
public class ControlExamplesViewModel : ViewModelBase
{
    readonly BackgroundWorker backgroundWorker = new BackgroundWorker();
```

LISTING 5.4   Continued

```
public ControlExamplesViewModel()
    : base("Controls")
{
    backgroundWorker.WorkerReportsProgress = true;
    backgroundWorker.DoWork
        += new DoWorkEventHandler(backgroundWorker_DoWork);
    backgroundWorker.ProgressChanged
        += new ProgressChangedEventHandler(
                    backgroundWorker_ProgressChanged);
    backgroundWorker.RunWorkerCompleted
        += new RunWorkerCompletedEventHandler(
            backgroundWorker_RunWorkerCompleted);

    backgroundWorker.WorkerSupportsCancellation = true;
    cancelProgressCommand = new DelegateCommand(
        obj => backgroundWorker.CancelAsync());

    backgroundWorker.RunWorkerAsync();
    Message = "BackgroundWorker performing task.";
}

void backgroundWorker_ProgressChanged(
        object sender, ProgressChangedEventArgs e)
{
    ProgressPercent = e.ProgressPercentage;
}

void backgroundWorker_DoWork(object sender, DoWorkEventArgs e)
{
    BackgroundWorker worker = (BackgroundWorker)sender;
    for (int i = 0; i < 100; i++)
    {
        if (worker.CancellationPending)
        {
            e.Cancel = true;
            return;
        }
        Wait(300);
        worker.ReportProgress(i);
    }
}

void backgroundWorker_RunWorkerCompleted(
        object sender, RunWorkerCompletedEventArgs e)
```

LISTING 5.4   Continued

```
    {
        Message = e.Cancelled
            ? "Background worker cancelled."
            : "Background worker completed.";
    }

    int progressPercent;

    public int ProgressPercent
    {
        get
        {
            return progressPercent;
        }
        private set
        {
            Assign("ProgressPercent", ref progressPercent, value);
        }
    }

    bool cancelProgress;
    DelegateCommand cancelProgressCommand;

    public ICommand CancelProgressCommand
    {
        get
        {
            return cancelProgressCommand;
        }
    }

    string message;

    public string Message
    {
        get
        {
            return message;
        }
        set
        {
            Assign(() => Message, ref message, value);
        }
    }
```

LISTING 5.4   Continued

```
    static readonly object waitLock = new object();

    static void Wait(int delayMs)
    {
        if (delayMs > 0)
        {
            lock (waitLock)
            {
                Monitor.Wait(waitLock, delayMs);
            }
        }
    }
}
```

While running, the worker thread repeatedly sleeps, using the viewmodel's Wait method, and then signals that the progress has changed.

> **NOTE**
>
> If the BackgroundWorker.WorkerReportsUpdates property is set to false and the BackgroundWorker ReportProgress method is called, an InvalidOperationException will be thrown.

The following excerpt shows the view's XAML for the relevant controls:

```
<TextBlock Text="ProgressBar" />
<ProgressBar Value="{Binding ProgressPercent}"
        Minimum="0" Maximum="100" />
<Button Content="Cancel Progress"
        Command="{Binding CancelProgressCommand}" />
<TextBlock Text="Message" />
<TextBlock Text="{Binding Message}" Height="80" />
```

On completion of the backgroundWorker_DoWork method, the backgroundWorker_RunWorkerCompleted method is called, and the viewmodel's MessageProperty is updated (see Figure 5.15).

The BackgroundWorker class also supports operation cancellation. By pressing the Cancel Progress button, the CancelProgressCommand is executed, which, in turn, calls the backgroundWorker's CancelAsync method. This is then detected in the backgroundWorker_DoWork method, which sets the Cancel property of the DoWorkEventArgs.

Although cancelled, the BackgroundWorker.RunWorkCompleted event is still raised, and the backgroundWorker_RunWorkerCompleted handler is still called; however, the RunWorkerCompletedEventArgs.Cancelled property allows you to determine whether the operation was cancelled.

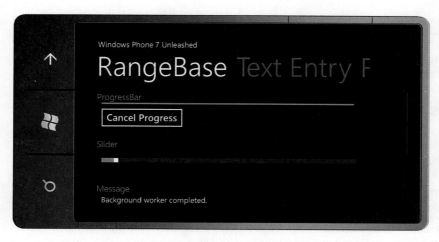

FIGURE 5.15   Updating the UI using a `BackgroundWorker`

> **NOTE**
>
> The `NotifyPropertyChangeBase` class in the downloadable sample code, which is the base class of the `ViewModelBase` class, automatically raises `INotifyPropertyChanged`. `PropertyChanged` events on the UI thread (one of its many benefits). Therefore, you could achieve the same thing shown in the example by replacing the `BackgroundWorker` with a thread from, for example, the `ThreadPool`, and by including two Boolean `cancel` and `cancelled` fields. It would make for a simpler implementation with fewer event subscriptions.

Slider

The `Slider` is an interactive control that allows the user to set its `Value` property by dragging or pressing the `Slider` track. It is ideal for values that do not require a high level of precision, such as the volume setting for music in a game.

The following demonstrates how to define a `Slider` in XAML:

```
<Slider Value="5" Minimum="0" Maximum="100" LargeChange="20" />
```

The `Value`, `Minimum`, and `Maximum` properties are described in the previous section on the `RangeBase` control.

When the user taps the `Slider` track, the `Value` property is incremented or decremented by the value of the `LargeChange` property.

The default orientation of the `Slider` is horizontal. The orientation can be changed by setting the `Orientation` property to `Vertical`.

The `Slider` is an especially useful control on the Windows Phone platform, since the use of touch makes the slider easier to control than it would otherwise be with the mouse.

> **NOTE**
>
> The built-in `Slider` control is, however, somewhat cumbersome to use. The control template for the `Slider` was built for Silverlight for the browser, where mice are better at hitting small targets. A number of custom templates are available on the Web that provide better usability. Dave Relyea, the lead developer of the Silverlight Toolkit team, provides an improved `Slider` control. See http://bit.ly/bOYtQj for more information.

Further examples of the `Slider` control can be found throughout this book, such as in the section "Selecting a Photo from the Photo Hub Using the `PhotoChooserTask`" in Chapter 12, "Launchers and Choosers," and the section "Displaying Location Using the `GeoPositionView` Page" in Chapter 15, "Geographic Location."

> **BEST PRACTICE**
>
> Do not place a horizontal `Slider` control on a `Pivot` or `Panorama` control. Doing so may interfere with a user's ability to move between items, or it may prevent a user from manipulating the `Slider` without moving between `Panorama` or `Pivot` items. This also applies to other controls like the Bing Maps control, which rely on the user performing a drag gesture.
>
> You learn more about the `Pivot` or `Panorama` in Chapter 10.
>
> Note that you may see a `Slider` placed in a `Pivot` in the sample code. This has been done for the sake of convenience and should not be taken as guidance.

ScrollBar

`ScrollBar` is a control that has a sliding thumb whose position corresponds to a value. The `ScrollBar` class provides a `ViewportSize` property, which determines the amount of scrollable content that is visible and an `Orientation` property, which can be either `Horizontal` or `Vertical`.

It is rare to see the `ScrollBar` used directly. It is more commonly used within other controls such as the `ScrollViewer` or in custom controls.

Summary

This chapter began by providing an overview of the elements available in the Silverlight for Windows Phone FCL. It then focused on the three control types: `ContentControls`, `ItemsControls`, and `RangeControls`. It showed the various subclasses of these controls, accompanied with practical examples.

The chapter examined how `ContentControls` can host a single element and the differences between the various buttons such as the `HyperlinkButton`, `RepeatButton`, and `ToggleButton`.

It also demonstrated how to bind `CheckBox` and `RadioButton` controls to viewmodel collections, and you saw how to bind to the `ListBox.SelectedItems` property, which is not readily achievable with Silverlight out-of-the-box.

Finally, the chapter explored the `RangeBase` controls: the `Slider` and `ProgressBar`, and demonstrated how to provide feedback to a user during asynchronous activities carried out by a `BackgroundWorker`.

5

CHAPTER 6

Text Elements

Text plays a key role in the design philosophy behind the Windows Phone UI. Metro, Microsoft's internal name for the design of the Windows Phone UI, places emphasis on text as a primary design element. Metro is about content, readability, and clarity, and less about chrome (colored backgrounds, borders, and so on).

This chapter begins by looking at the various types used for displaying and entering text in Silverlight for Windows Phone, in particular the TextBlock, TextBox, PasswordBox, and RichTextBox. It then explores each of these elements in greater depth, starting with the TextBlock, where you see how to create multiline text using Run and LineBreak objects. It then looks at font support, including the built-in fonts, and demonstrates techniques for providing custom fonts in your application using font embedding, or via a font data Stream. It also examines the Software Input Panel (SIP) and shows how to customize the onscreen keyboard using input scopes.

Also included in this chapter is a useful sample page that allows you to preview the various input scopes.

The chapter then looks at the PasswordBox and demonstrates how to bind the password string property to a view-model property. You then learn about the RichTextBox, which allows you to blend text and rich content such as hyperlinks, images, and other UI elements.

Finally, the chapter looks at the clipboard, and you see how to set the clipboard text and how to detect whether text is present on the clipboard.

Text Element Types

Within the Silverlight for Windows Phone Framework Class Library (FCL), there are some types, which, on first appearances, you could be forgiven for thinking that API similarities are the result of common ancestry. The `TextBlock` and `TextBox` elements, for example, have numerous similarly named text and font related properties, yet both have their own distinct API and their closest ancestor is `FrameworkElement` (see Figure 6.1).

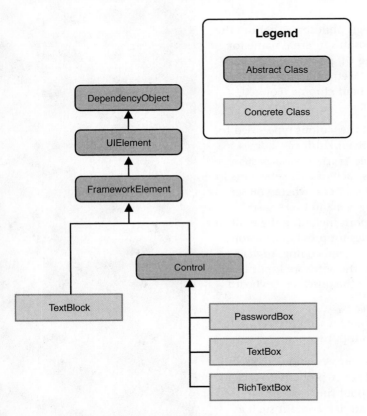

FIGURE 6.1   Text related framework elements

The `TextBox` and `PasswordBox` are derived from the `System.Windows.Control` class. The `Control` class is the base class for UI elements that use a `ControlTemplate` to define their appearance. And while the `TextBlock` lives in the `System.Controls` namespace, it is not a `Control`, making it impossible to drastically change its appearance. Those familiar with WPF will know that WPF has the `Label` class, which is derived from `Control` and which fills this gap. There is, however, no such control in Silverlight.

The similarities between the `TextBlock` and `TextBox` APIs do mean, however, that the elements can be styled in much the same manner; the characteristics of most font and layout related properties apply equally to all three text elements.

TextBlock

The TextBlock is an essential element in most Silverlight applications. It represents a section of text and is normally used to label controls or control groups. The TextBlock supports word wrapping, so that long runs of text are not hidden when they exceed the width of the control. The following code shows how to create a TextBlock in XAML, using the built-in PhoneTextNormalStyle:

```
<TextBlock Text="Windows Phone 7 Unleashed"
    Style="{StaticResource PhoneTextNormalStyle}" />
```

Alternatively, the TextBlock also allows you to nest content within the TextBlock element, like so:

```
<TextBlock Style="{StaticResource LabelTextStyle}">
    Windows Phone 7 Unleashed
</TextBlock>
```

Using the Run and LineBreak Objects

In XAML, white space is interpreted in the same way as in XML. White space is collapsed, leading and trailing white space is removed, and multiple lines are placed on the same line. The LineBreak class represents an explicit new line in a TextBlock. To create a multi-line TextBlock, use the LineBreak element within the content, as shown:

```
<TextBlock Style="{StaticResource LabelTextStyle}">
    You are reading<LineBreak />
    Windows Phone 7.5 Unleashed!
</TextBlock>
```

> **NOTE**
>
> The XML-like format of XAML does not allow you to use the greater than > or less than < symbols within XAML. This is because the symbols are interpreted as being part of an element. Instead, use the character entity references: > and <. These are translated to the greater than and less than characters at runtime.

Run elements can be embedded within the TextBlock content so that different font formatting can be applied to different parts of the text. LineBreak elements are generally used to delimit surrounding Run elements.

LineBreak and Run are derived from System.Windows.Documents.Inline. The TextBlock class contains a strongly typed InlineCollection called Inlines, which contains the items to be displayed (see Figure 6.2).

Inlines is the XAML content property of the TextBlock class. Thus, to specify items in the TextBlock, you specify various Run and LineBreak elements as child elements of the TextBlock.

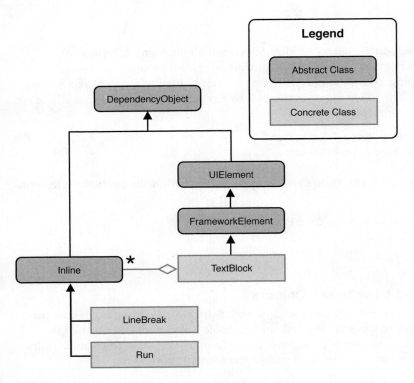

FIGURE 6.2   The `TextBlock` has a collection of `Inline` objects.

The following example shows how to display several strings of differing format in a `TextBlock` using `Run` elements separated with `LineBreak` elements.

```
<TextBlock>
    <Run Foreground="Blue" FontFamily="Courier New"
        FontSize="18">You are reading</Run><LineBreak/>
    <Run Foreground="Teal" FontFamily="Times New Roman"
        FontSize="24" FontStyle="Italic">Windows Phone 7 Unleashed!</Run>
</TextBlock>
```

The result is shown in Figure 6.3.

NOTE

Unfortunately the `Run.Text` property is not a `DependencyProperty`, which prevents using data binding with the property. If you attempt to place a binding on the `Text` property in XAML, a difficult to diagnose error will be raised at runtime.

A solution that allows you to display a mixture of static text and text populated via data bindings is to use multiple `TextBlock` elements within a `StackPanel`, with the `StackPanel` element's `Orientation` set to `Horizontal`.

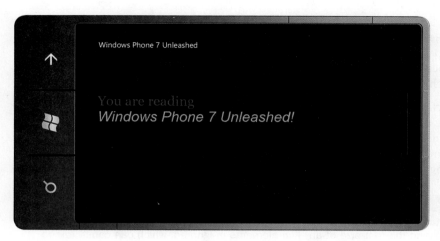

FIGURE 6.3   Using `Run` and `LineBreak` objects within a `TextBlock`

NOTE

When attempting to provide different formatting for a contiguous string of text, in XAML, `Run` elements should be placed side by side without separating whitespace because even though they appear to be properly laid out in the Visual Studio designer, at runtime white space can appear between the `Run` elements.

`LineBreak` forces the text in each `Run` to display on a separate line. Without the `LineBreak`, the text in each `Run` would be displayed on the same line. This can cause the text to be clipped if it exceeds the `TextBlock` width or the width of the parent container.

To avoid the clipping without using a `LineBreak`, set the `TextBlock` `TextWrapping` to `Wrap`, like so:

```
<TextBlock TextWrapping="Wrap" />
```

Better still, create a reusable `Style` for your `TextBlock`, like so:

```
<Style x:Key="NormalTextStyle" TargetType="TextBlock"
        BasedOn="{StaticResource PhoneTextNormalStyle}">
    <Setter Property="TextWrapping" Value="Wrap" />
</Style>
```

The `Style` can be placed in the Resources element of your page or app.xaml file.

Multiline `TextBlock` Text

As you have seen, `TextBlock` supports multiline text, either by setting `TextWrapping` to `Wrap` or by using `LineBreak` instances within the content.

Two properties, LineHeight and LineStackingStrategy, affect how multiline text is displayed. LineHeight determines the height of every line of text in the TextBlock. If LineHeight is set to a smaller value than the FontSize property, it may cause text to be vertically cropped. Typically, you leave LineHeight unset and rely on the default text rendering, which calculates the line height using FontSize plus an internal padding value.

The TextBlock class's LineStackingStrategy property determines the algorithm that is used to calculate line height. The LineStackingStrategy is an enum value, which can be either MaxHeight or BlockLineHeight. MaxHeight, the default strategy, calculates line height using the maximum height of any character in the font, whereas BlockLineHeight calculates the line height using the *block* font design measure stored as a value in the font.

> **NOTE**
>
> If the BlockLineHeight strategy is used, line height is calculated using the default font for the TextBlock and the font size of any Run elements is ignored, which can cause text to be squashed together.

Font Properties

The TextBlock and TextBox classes rely on various font related dependency properties, which specify how text is displayed. The list of font related properties is presented in Table 6.1.

TABLE 6.1   Font Related Properties of the TextBlock and TextBox Classes

Property	Description
FontFamily	The preferred top-level font family for the text content. There are many built-in fonts to choose from. These are described in the following section "Built-In Fonts."
	Custom fonts can also be used by including them in your app's XAP file (see the following section "Font Embedding").
FontSize	The size of the font in pixels. The default value is 11 pixels. This value indicates the size of the text from top to bottom. If you specify a FontSize of, for example, 16, the text will have a height of 16 pixels. The size of the TextBlock, however, will usually exceed this amount by approximately 33%, due to an area of space that is set aside to prevent text from sitting too close to other text.
	The default font size of 11 pixels, which is more suited to Silverlight for the browser, is far too small to be used as the default font size on Windows Phone. The Windows Phone device display resolution is about 250% that of the conventional Windows desktop display resolution. It is, therefore, important to use the built-in set of text related styles, which have higher FontSize values. See http://bit.ly/xC8vgo for the list of built-in styles and theme resources.

TABLE 6.1   Continued

Property	Description
FontSource	Allows a `Stream` containing font data to be used for rendering text. See the following section "Leveraging `FontSource` to Assign a Font Using a `Stream`."
FontStretch	OpenType fonts are able to be stretched or contracted by using this property. No fonts present on the phone, however, are OpenType, and setting this value has no effect for built-in fonts. The `FontStretch` value is obtained from one of the preset `System.Windows.FontStretches` properties, which include the following: ▶ `Condensed` ▶ `Expanded` ▶ `ExtraCondensed` ▶ `ExtraExpanded` ▶ `Normal` ▶ `SemiCondensed` ▶ `SemiExpanded` ▶ `UltraCondensed` ▶ `UltraExpanded`
FontStyle	Can be either Normal or Italic. The `FontStyle` value is obtained from one of the preset `System.Windows.FontStyles` properties.
FontWeight	The thickness or heaviness of the text. This value is retrieved from a set of presets in the `System.Windows.FontWeights` class. This property can be either Black, Bold, ExtraBlack, ExtraBold, ExtraLight, Light, Medium, Normal, SemiBold, or Thin. The default value is Normal. When setting a font to a variant that does not exist natively, such as Bold, Silverlight simulates the font weight by drawing around the text.

BEST PRACTICE

Avoid using a font size less than 15 points. Text that is smaller than 15 points in size can be hard to read and is likely too small to be an adequate touch target.

When using colored fonts, use high-contrast colors at smaller point sizes to enhance readability. Test colors against both themes and all accent colors.

Built-In Fonts

The Unicode font Segoe WP is the Windows Phone system font. It has kern pairing, which defines the distance between each character pair combination. It does not have font hinting. It is natively available in the following five styles:

▶ Regular

▶ Bold

▶ Semi-bold

▶ Semi-light

▶ Black

The Silverlight for Windows Phone standard fonts all have at least native variants for bold and italic. The following example, located in the `ControlExamplesView.xaml` page in the downloadable sample code, displays the list of standard fonts used by Latin, Cyrillic, and Greek-based languages. A `Run` is used to display each font with the font name as example text. See the following excerpt:

```
<TextBlock>
    <Run FontFamily="Arial">Arial</Run><LineBreak />
    <Run FontFamily="Arial Black">Arial Black</Run><LineBreak />
    <Run FontFamily="Calibri">Calibri</Run><LineBreak />
    <Run FontFamily="Comic Sans MS">Comic Sans MS</Run><LineBreak />
    <Run FontFamily="Courier New">Courier New</Run><LineBreak />
    <Run FontFamily="Georgia">Georgia</Run><LineBreak />
    <Run FontFamily="Lucida Sans Unicode">Lucida Sans Unicode</Run><LineBreak />
    <Run FontFamily="Portable User Interface">Portable User Interface</Run>
        <LineBreak />
    <Run FontFamily="Segoe WP">Segoe WP</Run><LineBreak />
    <Run FontFamily="Segoe WP Black">Segoe WP Black</Run><LineBreak />
    <Run FontFamily="Segoe WP Bold">Segoe WP Bold</Run><LineBreak />
    <Run FontFamily="Segoe WP Light">Segoe WP Light</Run><LineBreak />
    <Run FontFamily="Segoe WP Semibold">Segoe WP Semibold</Run><LineBreak />
    <Run FontFamily="Segoe WP SemiLight">Segoe WP SemiLight</Run><LineBreak />
    <Run FontFamily="Tahoma">Tahoma</Run><LineBreak />
    <Run FontFamily="Times New Roman">Times New Roman</Run><LineBreak />
    <Run FontFamily="Trebuchet MS">Trebuchet MS</Run><LineBreak />
    <Run FontFamily="Verdana">Verdana</Run><LineBreak />
    <Run FontFamily="Webdings">Webdings</Run> (Webdings)
</TextBlock>
```

The result is shown in Figure 6.4.

The following East Asian languages are also supported:

- **Japanese**—Meiryo UI

- **Simplified Chinese**—Microsoft YaHei

- **Simplified Chinese**—SimSum. This font is included only on devices that have the Chinese (Simplified) display language.

- **Korean**—Malgun Gothic

TIP

Since the Segoe font is such an integral part of the Metro UI experience, use alternative fonts sparingly.

FIGURE 6.4   Built-in font families

All fonts in the list of built-in fonts are free to use in your applications. There are, however, times when you may want to customize the font used to make your application stand out from the crowd. Fortunately, this is possible in Silverlight for Windows Phone using font embedding.

Font Embedding

Font embedding allows you to place a third-party font into your application. Numerous websites offer fonts for purchase, and some even offer free fonts.

> **NOTE**
>
> Like all media sourced from external sources, be sure that you are legally entitled to redistribute fonts that have been embedded in your application. Be aware that the licensing restrictions of some fonts allow you to create graphics with the font but not to redistribute the font itself.

To embed a font, include it in your Visual Studio project. Set the Build Action in the Visual Studio Properties pane to Content (see Figure 6.5). This causes the font file to be placed in the XAP file when the project is built.

FIGURE 6.5   For embedded fonts, set the file's Build Action to Content.

NOTE

The difference between the Content Build Action and the Resource Build Action is that the Resource option causes files to be placed in the project assembly, whereas Content files are not placed into an assembly but rather sit independently from the assembly inside the XAP file. This is important for performance reasons, because minimizing the assembly size causes it to load faster and ultimately improves the startup time of your app.

Embedding the font allows you to set the `FontFamily` of text controls by providing the path to the font file, as shown in the following example:

```
<TextBlock Text="Embedded Font"
           FontFamily="/ControlExamples/Fonts/orbitron-medium.ttf#Orbitron" />
```

Notice that the format for the path ends in a hash followed with the name of the font. This value allows Silverlight to find the font within the font file, as some font files may contain more than one font. To determine the name of the font in Windows 7, double-click on the font to open the Windows Font Preview tool (see Figure 6.6). For other operating systems, you might need to download a third-party font viewer.

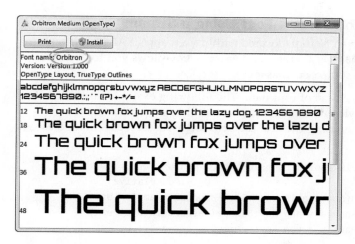

FIGURE 6.6   The Windows Font Preview tool indicates the name of the font.

Defining the FontFamily for each control used within your project is not a sound practice, because if the font is moved, or you later decide to use a different font, it will require updating the property across your project. Instead, define the FontFamily in the application's Resources and include a Style for TextBlocks that will use the FontFamily like so:

```
<Application.Resources>
    <FontFamily x:Key="EmbeddedFont">
        /ControlExamples/Fonts/orbitron-medium.ttf#Orbitron
    </FontFamily>
    <Style x:Key="EmbeddedTextStyle" TargetType="TextBlock"
            BasedOn="{StaticResource PhoneTextNormalStyle}">
        <Setter Property="FontFamily"
            Value="{StaticResource EmbeddedFont}" />
    </Style>
</Application.Resources>
```

It can then be used throughout your application in the following manner:

```
<TextBlock Text="Embedded font defined in app Resources
            Style="{StaticResource EmbeddedTextStyle}"/>
```

> **NOTE**
>
> The license terms of the Segoe WP fonts do not allow redistribution. This means packaging them within your application's XAP file is not allowed. Of course, you can still use the font in your app without embedding it.

Leveraging FontSource to Assign a Font Using a Stream

While font embedding is restricted to fonts located within your app's XAP file, the FontSource property of the TextBlock, TextBox, and PasswordBox allows you to download the font using an external data source, such as a cloud service.

The FontSource class requires a Stream of font data. The following example takes the same embedded font used in the previous example and provides it to a TextBlock object's FontSource property via a Stream, using the Application.GetResourceStream method as shown:

```
Uri fontUri = new Uri("ControlExamples/Fonts/orbitron-medium.ttf",
                                              UriKind.Relative);

StreamResourceInfo resourceInfo = Application.GetResourceStream(fontUri);
textBlockWithFontSource.FontSource = new FontSource(resourceInfo.Stream);
textBlockWithFontSource.FontFamily = new FontFamily("Orbitron");
```

The origin of the font file is arbitrary and could have just as easily been supplied via a web service.

While this approach offers a great deal of flexibility, ordinarily it would only be useful for a highly specialized perhaps font related app. If the font can be determined at development time, it is best to use embedding rather than the FontSource property to decrease the dependency on network services.

TextBox

Silverlight for Windows Phone includes three controls designed for text entry: TextBox, PasswordBox, and RichTextBox. Text can be entered either by using the onscreen keyboard known as the Software Input Panel (SIP) or by using the hardware keyboard if the phone has one.

The TextBox control displays content as well as allowing the user to type or edit content. A TextBox can display text on a single line, or on multiple lines. A multiline TextBox wraps text to the width of the control.

Text is stored as a System.String, using the TextBox.Text property. The alignment of the text can be changed using the TextAlignment property. Text is displayed according to various font related properties, shown earlier in Table 6.1.

Software Input Panel

The Software Input Panel (SIP) appears automatically when focus is set to an editable control unless the device has a hardware keyboard ready to receive input, such as when a sliding keyboard is in its extended position. When the control loses focus because the user taps outside the edit control, scrolls a list, or presses the hardware Back button, the SIP is closed by sliding down off the bottom of the screen. If a phone has a hardware keyboard, and it is deployed, the SIP closes automatically.

Table 6.2 shows the 10 most commonly used context-specific SIP keyboard layouts. Input Scope is an `InputScopeNameValue` enumeration value described in the next section.

TABLE 6.2   SIP Keyboard Layouts

Keyboard	Input Scope	Keyboard Layout
Default	Default and other standard input scope values	Standard QWERTY/QWERTZ/AZERTY etc., depending on the phone locale setting
Text	Text	Standard layout with ASCII based emoticons
Email Address	EmailSmtpAddress	Standard layout with .com and @ keys
Email Name or Address	EmailNameOrAddress	Standard layout with .com and @ key, and easy access to phone number layout
Phone Number	TelephoneNumber	Typical 12-key layout
Web Address	Url	Standard layout with .com key and customized Enter key
Maps	Maps	Standard layout with a customized Enter key
Search	Search	Semitransparent layout with a Search and .com key
SMS Address	NameOrPhoneNumber	Standard layout with easy access to phone number layout
Chat	Chat	Text input with emoticons

SIP Dimensions

The onscreen keyboard is 336 pixels tall in portrait view and 256 pixels tall in landscape view. The text suggestion window, which appears above the keyboard, is 65 pixels tall in both page orientations.

> **NOTE**
>
> It is your responsibility to ensure that the control, where text is being entered, is above the SIP and in view.

While it is not possible to define your own keyboard types or modify existing ones, you can switch the keyboard scheme of the SIP by using the `TextBox.InputScope` property. `InputScope` is discussed again in a moment.

Opening the SIP Programmatically

The SIP appears whenever a `TextBox` or `PasswordBox` gains focus. The SIP can, therefore, be opened programmatically by calling the `Focus` method of the control.

In some circumstances, such as when the primary purpose of a page is to allow the user to enter one or two pieces of information, it makes sense to open the SIP as soon as the page loads. This can be done by subscribing to the `PhoneApplicationPage.Loaded` event and calling the `Focus` method of the control, as shown in the following excerpt:

```
public partial class ExamplesView : PhoneApplicationPage
{
    public ExamplesView()
    {
        InitializeComponent();
        Loaded += new RoutedEventHandler(ExamplesView_Loaded);
    }

    void ExamplesView_Loaded(object sender, RoutedEventArgs e)
    {
        autoFocussedTextBox.Focus();
    }
}
```

> **BEST PRACTICE**
>
> Only expand the SIP automatically if the application page has no more than two editable controls and the first editable control is a single-line edit box. Likewise, do not automatically expand the SIP if the page has content or controls that would be obscured behind the keyboard.

Dismissing the SIP Programmatically

If the `TextBox` loses focus (the user taps the display outside the `TextBox`, for example) the SIP is closed. To dismiss the SIP programmatically, however, you must shift focus to another control on the page. An elegant way of achieving this, and one that does not rely on another arbitrary control, is to focus the main content container of your page.

The following example shows the main content `Grid` for a page. The `Grid` contains a single `TextBox` as shown:

```
<Grid x:Name="ContentGrid" Grid.Row="1"
      IsTabStop="True">
    <TextBox x:Name="TextBox_Input" KeyUp="TextBox_KeyUp"  />
</Grid>
```

To allow the user to dismiss the SIP via the SIP Enter key, you can subscribe to the `TextBox.KeyUp` event. When the Enter key is detected, the SIP is dismissed by focusing the container. See the following excerpt:

```
void TextBox_KeyUp(object sender, KeyEventArgs e)
{
    if (e.Key == Key.Enter)
    {
        this.Focus();
    }
}
```

> **NOTE**
>
> Make sure that the control to which you are shifting focus has its `IsTabStop` property set to true. When `IsTabStop` is false, the control is unable to receive focus, and hence will not cause the SIP to be closed. Most controls use true as the default `IsTabStop` value.

Input Scope

The `InputScope` property determines the set of keys and layout provided on the SIP. This value allows you to provide the user with a specialized keyboard, particular to the data that is being entered.

The following code demonstrates how to change the default alphanumeric SIP to one containing telephone digits, suitable for allowing the user to enter a telephone number:

```
<TextBox InputScope="TelephoneNumber" />
```

The `InputScope` is specified using one of the values from the `InputScopeNameValue` enum (see Table 6.3).

Most of the `InputScopeNameValue` enum values are mapped to a particular keyboard layout from Table 6.2.

TABLE 6.3   `InputScopeNameValue` Enum Values

InputScope	InputScope	InputScope
AddressCity	EmailNameOrAddress	PersonalNamePrefix
AddressCountryName	EmailSmtpAddress	PersonalNameSuffix
AddressCountryShortName	EmailUserName	PersonalSurname
AddressStateOrProvince	EnumString*	PhraseList*
AddressStreet	FileName	PostalAddress
AlphanumericFullWidth	Levels	PostalCode
AlphanumericHalfWidth	FullFilePath	Private
ApplicationEnd	Hanja	RegularExpression*
Bopomofo	Hiragana	Search
Chat	KatakanaFullWidth	Srgs*
CurrencyAmount	KatakanaHalfWidth	TelephoneAreaCode
CurrencyAmountAndSymbol	LogOnName	TelephoneCountryCode
CurrencyChinese	Maps	TelephoneLocalNumber
Date	NameOrPhoneNumber	TelephoneNumber
DateDay	Number	Text
DateDayName	NumberFullWidth	Time
DateMonth	OneChar	TimeHour
DateMonthName	Password	TimeMinorSec
DateYear	PersonalFullName	Url
Default	PersonalGivenName	Xml*
Digits	PersonalMiddleName	Yomi

At this time the value is not a valid InputScope. If used in XAML it will have no effect and the InputScope will fall back to the default value. Conversely, if set in code, an Exception is raised at runtime.

Word Prediction

Windows Phone has built-in support for word prediction while the user is entering text into a `TextBox`. To enable this feature, set the `InputScope` to either Text or Chat, as shown in the following example:

```
<TextBox InputScope="Text" />
```

Intellisense Support for the `InputScope` Property

When populating the `InputScope` property in XAML, you will notice that there is no intellisense support. This makes selecting the `InputScopeNameValue` rather difficult, as there are quite a few of them. To regain intellisense, use the more verbose element syntax to specify the `InputScope` property, like so:

```
<TextBox>
    <TextBox.InputScope>
        <InputScope>
```

```
            <InputScopeName NameValue="TelephoneNumber" />
        </InputScope>
    </TextBox.InputScope>
</TextBox>
```

Input Scope Sample Overview

To provide you with an opportunity to explore the various SIP layouts, I have created a sample view that allows you to switch the InputScope for a TextBox at runtime. The sample is located in the ControlExampleView page and the ControlExampleViewModel class in the downloadable sample code.

The viewmodel exposes a list of InputScopeNameValues, shown in the following excerpt, which is consumed in the view via a data binding to a Silverlight Toolkit ListPicker control. For more information on the Silverlight Toolkit and the controls contained therein, see Chapter 9, "Silverlight Toolkit Controls."

```
readonly IEnumerable<InputScopeNameValue> inputScopeNameValues
                    = EnumUtility.CreateEnumValueList<InputScopeNameValue>()
                            .OrderBy(nameValue => nameValue.ToString());


public IEnumerable<InputScopeNameValue> InputScopeNameValues
{
    get
    {
        return inputScopeNameValues;
    }
}
```

The System.Enum.GetNames method present in the .NET Desktop FCL is notably absent in Silverlight. To retrieve the enum values as a list of strings, we retrieve its field values, using a custom class called EnumUtility (see Listing 6.1).

The CreateEnumValueList<TEnum> method uses reflection to extract the names of each enum value.

LISTING 6.1   EnumUtility Class

```
public static class EnumUtility
{
    public static IEnumerable<TEnum> CreateEnumValueList<TEnum>()
    {
        Type enumType = typeof(TEnum);
        IEnumerable<FieldInfo> fieldInfos
            = enumType.GetFields().Where(x => enumType.Equals(x.FieldType));
        return fieldInfos.Select(
```

LISTING 6.1   Continued

```
            fieldInfo => (TEnum)Enum.Parse(
                        enumType, fieldInfo.Name, true)).ToList();
    }
}
```

The viewmodel tracks the `InputScopeNameValue` that is selected by the user using a `ListPicker` control.

```
InputScopeNameValue inputScopeNameValue = InputScopeNameValue.Default;

public InputScopeNameValue InputScopeNameValue
{
    get
    {
        return inputScopeNameValue;
    }
    set
    {
        Assign(() => InputScopeNameValue, ref inputScopeNameValue, value);
    }
}
```

The view binds to the viewmodel properties in its `TextBox` and `ListPicker` controls, as shown:

```
<TextBlock Text="Single-line TextBox"
    Style="{StaticResource LabelTextStyle}" />
<TextBox InputScope="{Binding InputScopeNameValue,
    Converter={StaticResource InputScopeValueConverter}}" />

<toolkit:ListPicker Header="InputScope"
    ItemsSource="{Binding InputScopeNameValues}"
    SelectedItem="{Binding InputScopeNameValue, Mode=TwoWay}">
</toolkit:ListPicker>
```

Changing the `ListPicker`'s selected item updates the viewmodel's `InputScopeNameValue` property. This, in turn, causes the `TextBox.InputScope` property to be updated.

A custom `IValueConverter` is used to convert the `InputScopeNameValue` property, which is an enum value, to an actual `InputScope`, which is a `DependencyObject` (see Listing 6.2).

LISTING 6.2   InputScopeValueConverter Class

```csharp
public class InputScopeValueConverter : IValueConverter
{
    public object Convert(
        object value, Type targetType, object parameter, CultureInfo culture)
    {
        if (value == null)
        {
            return null;
        }
        string scopeString = value.ToString();
        InputScope inputScope = new InputScope();
        var enumValue = (InputScopeNameValue)Enum.Parse(
            typeof(InputScopeNameValue), scopeString, true);
        inputScope.Names.Add(new InputScopeName { NameValue = enumValue });
        return inputScope;
    }

    public object ConvertBack(
        object value, Type targetType, object parameter, CultureInfo culture)
    {
        InputScope inputScope = value as InputScope;
        if (inputScope == null)
        {
            return null;
        }

        if (inputScope.Names.Count > 0)
        {
            InputScopeName scopeName = inputScope.Names[0] as InputScopeName;
            if (scopeName != null)
            {
                return scopeName.NameValue;
            }
        }
        return null;
    }
}
```

The InputScopeValueConverter is defined as a resource in the view, as shown:

```xml
<phone:PhoneApplicationPage.Resources>
    <Examples:InputScopeValueConverter x:Key="InputScopeValueConverter" />
</phone:PhoneApplicationPage.Resources>
```

The view is initially presented with the Default `InputScope` selected. This is equivalent to leaving the `TextBox.InputScope` property unset.

Figure 6.7 depicts the view with a single-line and a multiline `TextBox` each with its `InputScope` property bound to the `InputScopeNameValue` viewmodel property.

FIGURE 6.7　Text entry sample view

When either `TextBox` is selected, the SIP is displayed. See Figure 6.8, which shows the SIP displayed with the Default `InputScope`.

The Silverlight Toolkit `ListPicker` control is used to select the active `InputScope` (see Figure 6.9).

When an item is selected, the viewmodel's `InputScopeNameValue` property is updated, which causes the `InputScope` of both `TextBox` controls to be updated. In Figure 6.10, you see that by selecting the `TelephoneNumber` option, the SIP switches to a set of digits.

FIGURE 6.8   SIP displayed with default `InputScope`

FIGURE 6.9   The Silverlight Toolkit `ListPicker` control displays the list of `InputScopeNameValues`.

FIGURE 6.10   The SIP is displayed using the `TelephoneNumber` input scope.

PasswordBox

`PasswordBox` works in much the same way as the `TextBox`, allowing the user to type or edit its contents. Each character entered into a `PasswordBox`, however, appears briefly, for two seconds or until another character is entered, whichever is shorter, and is then changed to an *obscurity character*. The obscurity character is a bullet character by default.

The obscurity character can be customized using the `PasswordChar` property. For example, to use a question mark instead of the default obscurity character, the following can be used:

```
<PasswordBox PasswordChar="?" />
```

The `PasswordBox` does not contain a `Text` property, but rather a `Password` property, which is used to retrieve (or set) the password string.

Likewise, there is no `TextChanged` event, but rather a `PasswordChanged` event, which can be used to monitor when the user has finished entering a password.

Rather than relying on the `PasswordChanged` event, the `PasswordBox.Password` property can be bound to a viewmodel property, like the one shown in the following excerpt:

```
string password;

public string Password
{
    get
    {
        return password;
    }
    set
    {
        Assign(() => Password, ref password, value);
    }
}
```

A TwoWay binding expression allows the PasswordBox to update the viewmodel when the password text changes, as the following excerpt demonstrates:

```
<PasswordBox PasswordChar="?" Password="{Binding Password, Mode=TwoWay}" />
```

RichTextBox

RichTextBox is a control that enables you to intermingle rich content, including hyperlinks and inline images, with text. UIElements can also be embedded alongside other content, allowing you to display buttons and other interactive controls directly within the RichTextBox content.

Unlike Silverlight for the browser, however, the RichTextBox control for Windows Phone is not editable. Its IsReadOnly property is always true and cannot be set to false.

> **NOTE**
>
> If you attempt to set IsReadOnly to true in XAML a XamlParseException is raised; when done in code, a NotSupportedException is raised.

RichTextBox contains a collection of Paragraph elements. Within a Paragraph object are placed text and various Inline elements. See the following example:

```
<RichTextBox>
    <Paragraph>
        Hi from <Underline><Bold>Windows Phone</Bold>!</Underline>
    </Paragraph>
    <Paragraph>
        Paragraph 2
    </Paragraph>
</RichTextBox>
```

While more verbose, creating a RichTextBox can also be done in code, as shown:

```
void CreateRichTextBox()
{
    RichTextBox richTextBox = new RichTextBox();

    /* Create a Run of plain text and some underlined bold text. */
    Run run1 = new Run {Text = "Hi from "};
    Underline underline = new Underline();
    Bold bold = new Bold();
    bold.Inlines.Add("Windows Phone");
    underline.Inlines.Add(bold);
    Run run2 = new Run {Text = "!"};

    /* Place the inlines in a paragraph. */
    Paragraph paragraph = new Paragraph();
    paragraph.Inlines.Add(run1);
    paragraph.Inlines.Add(underline);
    paragraph.Inlines.Add(run2);

    richTextBox.Blocks.Add(paragraph);

    ContentPanel.Children.Add(richTextBox);
}
```

Within each Paragraph can be placed the following Inline elements:

- ▶ Span
- ▶ Bold
- ▶ Italic
- ▶ Underline
- ▶ Hyperlink
- ▶ InlineUIContainer
- ▶ Run

Span, Bold, Italic, and Underline are able to nest other Inline elements.

The Hyperlink element is used to embed a hyperlink within paragraph content. It behaves in much the same way as a Silverlight HyperlinkButton, and its NavigateUri property is assumed to be a relative URI of a page in the app. If the URI is external then the TargetName property must be set to _blank, as shown in the following excerpt:

```
<RichTextBox>
    <Paragraph>
```

```
        This is a
        <Hyperlink NavigateUri=http://danielvaughan.org
                   TargetName="_blank">Hyperlink</Hyperlink>.
    </Paragraph>
</RichTextBox>
```

To embed a UIElement within the RichTextBox use the InlineUIContainer. In the following example, an Image control is used to display an inline image, and a Button control is placed alongside:

```
<RichTextBox>
    <Paragraph>
        <InlineUIContainer>
            <Image Source="/Images/WindowsPhoneLogo.png"
                   Height="100" Width="100" />
        </InlineUIContainer>
        <InlineUIContainer>
            <Button>button</Button>
        </InlineUIContainer>
    </Paragraph>
</RichTextBox>
```

Formatting Text at Runtime

You can format text in a RichTextBox at the paragraph-level and inline-level at runtime. The following example shows how you can right-align the entire contents of the RichTextBox within a Button.Tap event handler:

```
void Button_Tap(object sender, System.Windows.Input.GestureEventArgs e)
{
    foreach (Block block in richTextBox1.Blocks)
    {
        block.TextAlignment = TextAlignment.Right;
    }
}
```

Figure 6.11 shows the contents of a RichTextBox after it has been right-aligned via a Button placed within the Paragraph.

The source for this section is located in the RichTextBoxView page in the ControlExamples directory of the WindowsPhone7Unleashed.Examples project in the downloadable sample code.

While the RichTextBox control for Windows Phone lacks the ability to be edited by the user, it does allow you to blend text and rich content in a way that is easier than, for example, nesting TextBlocks and other elements within a StackPanel.

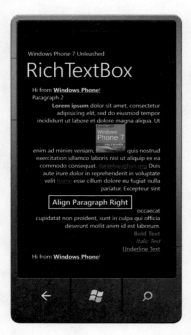

FIGURE 6.11   Tapping an inline `Button` causes the `Paragraph` to be right-aligned.

Further Reading

An MSDN article that includes an overview of the `RichTextBox` content model is located at http://bit.ly/nmazA0.

Clipboard

The static `System.Windows.Clipboard` class allows you to place text on the system-wide clipboard, or to detect whether any text exists on the clipboard.

> **NOTE**
>
> You cannot retrieve the clipboard text from a Windows Phone app, only set it. Calling the `GetText` method raises a `SecurityException`.

`Clipboard` contains the following three methods:

- ▶ **`ContainsText()`**—Queries the clipboard for the presence of text. Returns true if text is present; otherwise, false.

- ▶ **`SetText(string text)`**—Places text in the clipboard.

- ▶ **`GetText()`**—Raises a `SecurityException` on the Windows Phone platform.

Placing a Unicode string on the clipboard can be performed as shown:

```
Clipboard.SetText("foo");
```

The following example shows how to detect whether text is present on the clipboard:

```
bool clipBoardHasText = Clipboard.ContainsText();
```

If the `ContainsText` method returns true it indicates that the clipboard button will be visible when the SIP is displayed (see Figure 6.12).

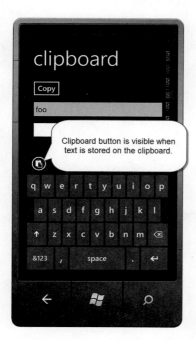

FIGURE 6.12   Text on the clipboard causes the SIP to display the clipboard button.

Summary

This chapter began by looking at the various types used for displaying and entering text in Silverlight for Windows Phone, in particular the `TextBlock`, `TextBox`, `PasswordBox`, and `RichTextBox`. It then explored each of these elements in greater depth, starting with the `TextBlock`, where it showed how to create multiline text using `Run` and `LineBreak` objects. It then looked at font support, including the built-in fonts, and demonstrated techniques for providing custom fonts in your application using font embedding, or the `FontSource` property using a `Stream`. It also examined the SIP, and how to customize the onscreen keyboard using input scopes.

Also included in this chapter was a useful sample page that allows you to preview the various input scopes.

The chapter then looked at the `PasswordBox` and demonstrated how to bind the password string property to a viewmodel property. It then examined the `RichTextBox`, which allows you to blend text and rich content such as hyperlinks, images, and other UI elements.

Finally, the chapter looked at the clipboard, and you learned how to set the clipboard text and how to detect whether text is present on the clipboard.

CHAPTER 7

Media and Web Elements

Silverlight for Windows Phone leverages a mature set of web and media related elements. This chapter explores some of the most feature-rich controls present in the Silverlight toolbox.

This chapter is jam-packed full of examples and begins by looking in depth at the `Image` element. The `InkPresenter` is discussed, and you see how to create a simple sketch app.

The `MediaElement` is also discussed and you see how it is used to play audio and video files stored locally on the phone, or streamed over the Internet. This chapter also examines a sample app that provides you with a test bed for experimenting with the `MediaElement`'s main properties.

The chapter looks at leveraging XNA within your Silverlight app to play sound effects more efficiently and then explores Deep Zoom to see how the `MultiScaleImage` element is used to provide stunning visual experiences, while making efficient use of your users' bandwidth. We delve into a sample client and server application that allows the user to select and manipulate a Deep Zoom image.

Finally, the chapter explores the `WebBrowser` control, and you see how to communicate to a web page from your Silverlight for Windows Phone app and vice versa. You also discover how to execute arbitrary JavaScript on a web page to modify page content or to attach new behaviors, and how to store and browse offline content to decrease network usage.

Displaying Images with the `Image` Element

The `Image` element is a `FrameworkElement` that makes it easy to display both local or remote images on the phone.

The `Image` element supports two image formats: PNG and JPEG, and displays indexed images with 1, 4, or 8 bit color-depth, or true color images with 24 or 32 bit color-depth.

The `Image.Source` property is used to set the URI of the image file location. This value can be either an absolute or relative URI. A URI can be used to specify a source file from a variety of locations, including the following:

- The current assembly
- A referenced assembly
- The XAP file
- An external network, such as an image on the Web

Relative URIs are the most common way to identify local images in Silverlight for Windows Phone apps. The following example demonstrates how to display an image called Book.jpg, which is located in the root directory of a project, and which has its Build Action set to Content:

```
<Image Source="/Book.jpg" />
```

> **NOTE**
>
> When the Build Action of an image file is set to Content, its path is relative to the root of the project. Conversely, when the Build Action is set to Resource, its path is relative to the directory in which it is located.

If the image were located in a subdirectory of the project, for example, a directory called *Images*, then the `Image` element would be as follows:

```
<Image Source="/Images/Book.jpg" />
```

The trailing slash is required when referring to images with a Build Action set to Content. If using a Build Action of Resource, a trailing slash cannot be used:

```
<Image Source="Images/BookAsResource.png" />
```

> **TIP**
>
> Avoid setting the Build Action of images to Resource. Instead use the Content Build Action because this will reduce the size of your project's assembly, thus reducing the time the CLR takes to load it.
>
> One caveat, however, is that it takes longer for the CLR to fetch a file that is content than it does to fetch a file that is a resource. This is because the image file data becomes

present in memory as soon as the assembly is loaded. So, the Content Build Action, while reducing the startup time of your app, may lead to some images being displayed after the rest of the UI has been displayed. This is especially important for background images, whose momentary absence will be glaringly evident. The rule of thumb: If you need an image to be loaded immediately because it is the background for a page, for example, use the Resource Build Action; otherwise, use the Content Build Action.

An absolute URI, which targets an image in the same or another assembly, can be specified using the Relative Component URI scheme, as the following example demonstrates:

```
<Image Source="/AssemblyNameWithoutTheDllExtension;component/Images/Book.png" />
```

The URL of an image located on the Web can also be specified as shown:

```
<Image Source="http://www.example.com/Images/Book.jpg" />
```

> **TIP**
>
> Try to limit the number of images in your app. Even if your image happens to be a 30KB compressed JPEG image, at runtime that image becomes an uncompressed surface that may take several MBs of memory. In most cases an application must never consume more than 90MB of RAM, unless it has more than 256MB of total memory; otherwise it will fail Windows Phone Marketplace certification.
>
> For more information on measuring the memory available to your app see the section "Device Status," in Chapter 2, "Fundamental Concepts in Silverlight Development for Windows Phone."

Working examples for each of these cases are located in the `MediaExamplesView.xaml` page in the downloadable sample code.

There are numerous examples of using the `Image` control throughout this book; you see how to implement image localizability, image caching, and in Chapter 12, "Launchers and Choosers," you see how to data bind the `Image.Source` property to a viewmodel property.

Image Sizing

The size of an image control either can be set explicitly using its `Width` and `Height` properties, or the image can depend on its container to determine its size. If the container is a simple container such as a `Canvas`, the `Image` will be displayed using the native dimensions defined in the image file. The `Image.Stretch` property is used to control the sizing behavior of the `Image` when its size differs from its native image size. The `Stretch` property is of type `System.Windows.Media.Stretch`, whose values are described in Table 7.1.

TABLE 7.1   Stretch Enum Values and Their Effect on Image Sizing

Name	Description
None	The image is displayed using its native dimensions.
Fill	The image is stretched to inhabit the entirety of the Image control, while not obeying the aspect ratio of the native image.
Uniform	The default value. The image is given the largest size available within the Image control, while still adhering to the aspect ratio of the native image.
UniformToFill	The aspect ratio of the native image is maintained. The native image is expanded to fill the Image control in both dimensions. This may result in the image being clipped.

The effects of each of these enum values on image sizing are depicted in Figure 7.1.

The source for this section is located on the MediaExamplesView.xaml page in the ControlExamples directory of the WindowsPhone7Unleashed.Examples project in the downloadable sample code.

FIGURE 7.1   The Image.Stretch property determines how an image is sized.

Providing a Drawing Surface with the InkPresenter Element

InkPresenter provides a primitive drawing surface to collect strokes or Bézier curves within a Canvas control. The InkPresenter is derived from the Canvas class and includes the addition of a single property called Strokes, which is a collection of Stroke objects. A Stroke represents a line segment and is comprised of a collection of StylusPoints.

The behavior of the `InkPresenter` can be likened to that of a pen and paper. When the pen makes contact with the paper, you begin a `Stroke`. As the pen moves on the paper, the `Stroke` is constructed using `StylusPoints`. When the pen leaves the paper, the `Stroke` is complete.

The appearance of a `Stroke` can be defined by using its `DrawingAttributes` property. This includes its color, height, outline, and width (see Figure 7.2).

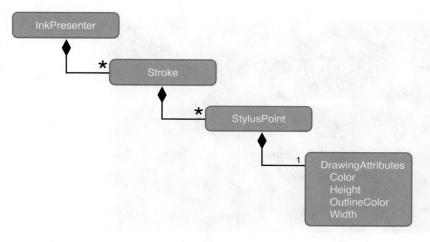

FIGURE 7.2   A `Stroke` consists of many `StylusPoint` objects.

The `InkPresenter` does not provide any specialized support for capturing touch input. Instead, `Strokes` are created either in code by subscribing to the various touch related events, which you see later in the section, or by defining a `StrokeCollection` directly in XAML, as shown:

```
<InkPresenter VerticalAlignment="Stretch">
    <InkPresenter.Strokes>
        <StrokeCollection>
            <Stroke>
                <Stroke.DrawingAttributes>
                    <DrawingAttributes Color="White"
                        OutlineColor="Yellow"
                        Width="20" Height="10" />
                </Stroke.DrawingAttributes>
                <Stroke.StylusPoints>
                    <StylusPoint X="118" Y="141" />

                    ...
                    <StylusPoint X="202" Y="383" />
                </Stroke.StylusPoints>
            </Stroke>
```

```
        </StrokeCollection>
    </InkPresenter.Strokes>
</InkPresenter>
```

In this excerpt, the single `Stroke` present in the `StrokeCollection` is styled using the `DrawingAttribute` element. The `OutlineColor` property is used to create a border around the `Stroke` (see Figure 7.3).

FIGURE 7.3   `InkPresenter` with a `StrokeCollection` defined in XAML

Capturing User Input

The touch related events, `MouseLeftButtonDown`, `MouseMove`, and `MouseLeftButtonUp`, are used to collect and display strokes in the `InkPresenter` while the user interacts with the control. The following excerpt shows an `InkPresenter` with subscriptions to the three mouse events:

```
<Grid x:Name="ContentPanel" Grid.Row="1">
    <InkPresenter Strokes="{Binding Strokes}"
        VerticalAlignment="Stretch"
        Background="Black"
        MouseMove="InkPresenter_MouseMove"
        MouseLeftButtonDown="InkPresenter_MouseLeftButtonDown"
        MouseLeftButtonUp="InkPresenter_MouseLeftButtonUp" />
</Grid>
```

> **NOTE**
>
> The `Background` property of the `InkPresenter` must be assigned to register Mouse events.

Listing 7.1 shows how the mouse event handlers are used to add `Stroke` objects to the `InkPresenter` element's `Strokes` collection. When the user touches the display, the `MouseLeftButtonDown` event is raised; at which time a new `Stroke` is created and added to the `Strokes` collection. When the user moves her finger, the `MouseMove` event is raised and the handler adds new `StylusPoints` to the `Stroke`. The stylus points are accessed through the `MouseEventArgs` of both the `MouseLeftButtonDown` and `MouseMove` events. When the user lifts her finger of the display, the `MouseLeftButtonUp` handler completes the current `Stroke` by setting it to null.

LISTING 7.1   InkPresenterView Class—Non-MVVM (excerpt)

```
public partial class InkPresenterView : PhoneApplicationPage
{
    public InkPresenterView()
    {
        InitializeComponent();
    }

    readonly StrokeCollection strokes = new StrokeCollection();
    Stroke stroke;

    void InkPresenter_MouseLeftButtonDown(object sender, MouseButtonEventArgs e)
    {
        InkPresenter inkPresenter = (InkPresenter)sender;
        stroke = new Stroke();
        StylusPointCollection points
            = e.StylusDevice.GetStylusPoints(inkPresenter);
        stroke.StylusPoints.Add(points);
        stroke.DrawingAttributes.Color = Colors.White;
        strokes.Add(stroke);
        inkPresenter.Strokes = strokes;
    }

    void InkPresenter_MouseMove(object sender, MouseEventArgs e)
    {
        InkPresenter inkPresenter = (InkPresenter)sender;
        if (stroke != null)
        {
            stroke.StylusPoints.Add(e.StylusDevice.GetStylusPoints(inkPresenter));
        }
    }

    void InkPresenter_MouseLeftButtonUp(object sender, MouseButtonEventArgs e)
    {
        stroke = null;
    }
}
```

7

InkPresenter Sample Code

The sample for this section is a simple sketch page that allows the user to draw a picture, undo and redo sketch lines, and clear the page using an application bar menu item (see Figure 7.4). The code presented in this section elaborates on the previous example and takes a more MVVM-centric approach.

FIGURE 7.4   InkPresenter sample app

The code for this sample is located in the `InkPresenterView` page and the `InkPresenterViewModel` class in the downloadable sample code.

An `InkPresenter` in the view is bound to the viewmodel's `StrokeCollection`. As the user interacts with the view, viewmodel commands populate the `StrokeCollection` with `Stroke` objects.

Each command is instantiated in the viewmodel's constructor. When executed, the `beginStrokeCommand` creates a new `Stroke` representing the beginning of a line drawn by the user. As the user moves a finger across the `InkPresenter`, the `setStrokePointCommand` is executed, which adds a new `StylusPoint` to the list of points for the current `Stroke`. Finally, when the user takes his finger off the display, the `endStrokeCommand` is executed setting the current `Stroke` to null (see Listing 7.2).

The viewmodel maintains a `Stack` of `Strokes`, called `undoneStrokes`, which contains strokes that have been undone by the user. The `undoCommand` pushes the last `Stroke` in the

StrokeCollection onto undoneStrokes and then removes it from the StrokesCollection. Conversely, the redoCommand pops the top Stroke from undoneStrokes and places it back in the StrokesCollection.

LISTING 7.2   InkPresenterViewModel Class (excerpt)

```
public InkPresenterViewModel() : base("InkPresenter")
{
    beginStrokeCommand = new DelegateCommand<Point>(
        point =>
            {
                stroke = new Stroke();
                stroke.StylusPoints.Add(ConvertToStylusPoint(point));
                stroke.DrawingAttributes.Color = stylusColor;
                strokes.Add(stroke);
            });

    setStrokePointCommand = new DelegateCommand<Point>(
        point =>
            {
                if (stroke != null)
                {
                    stroke.StylusPoints.Add(ConvertToStylusPoint(point));
                }
            });

    endStrokeCommand = new DelegateCommand(obj => stroke = null);

    clearCommand = new DelegateCommand(obj => strokes.Clear());

    undoCommand = new DelegateCommand(
        delegate
            {
                if (strokes.Count > 0)
                {
                    undoneStrokes.Push(strokes.Last());
                    strokes.RemoveAt(strokes.Count - 1);
                }
            });

    redoCommand = new DelegateCommand(
        delegate
            {
                if (undoneStrokes.Count > 0)
                {
```

LISTING 7.2   Continued

```
                strokes.Add(undoneStrokes.Pop());
            }
        });
}
```

The BeginStrokeCommand, SetStrokePointCommand, and EndStrokeCommand are executed when
the InkPresenters element's MouseLeftButtonDown, MouseMove, and MouseLeftButtonUp
events are raised, respectively (see Listing 7.3).

LISTING 7.3   InkPresenterView Class

```csharp
public partial class InkPresenterView : PhoneApplicationPage
{
    public InkPresenterView()
    {
        InitializeComponent();
        DataContext = new InkPresenterViewModel();
    }

    InkPresenterViewModel ViewModel
    {
        get
        {
            return (InkPresenterViewModel)DataContext;
        }
    }

    void InkPresenter_MouseMove(object sender, MouseEventArgs e)
    {
        InkPresenter inkPresenter = (InkPresenter)sender;
        ViewModel.SetStrokePointCommand.Execute(e.GetPosition(inkPresenter));
    }

    void InkPresenter_MouseLeftButtonDown(
            object sender, MouseButtonEventArgs e)
    {
        InkPresenter inkPresenter = (InkPresenter)sender;
        ViewModel.BeginStrokeCommand.Execute(e.GetPosition(inkPresenter));
    }

    void InkPresenter_MouseLeftButtonUp(object sender, MouseButtonEventArgs e)
    {
        ViewModel.EndStrokeCommand.Execute(null);
    }
}
```

The three commands UndoCommand, RedoCommand, and ClearCommand are executed via the custom ApplicationBar wrapper AppBar in the view. The AppBar is discussed further in Chapter 8, "Taming the Application Bar."

```
<u:AppBar IsEnabled="True" IsVisible="True" IsMenuEnabled="True">
    <u:AppBarIconButton
        Command="{Binding UndoCommand}"
        Text="Undo"
        IconUri="/ControlExamples/Images/AppBarArrowUndo.png" />
    <u:AppBarIconButton
        Command="{Binding RedoCommand}"
        Text="Redo"
        IconUri="/ControlExamples/Images/AppBarArrowRedo.png" />
    <u:AppBar.MenuItems>
        <u:AppBarMenuItem
            Command="{Binding ClearCommand}"
            Text="Clear" />
    </u:AppBar.MenuItems>
</u:AppBar>
```

When the Undo or Redo buttons is pressed, the associated viewmodel command is executed. In addition, when the user taps the Clear button in the application bar menu the ClearCommand is executed, removing all items from the StrokeCollection in the viewmodel.

Playing Audio and Video with the MediaElement

MediaElement allows you to play audio and video from a file located in the app's XAP file, from isolated storage, or by streaming it from a remote location. MediaElement is a FrameworkElement that provides a rectangular region used for displaying video on its surface.

To show video content in your app, place the MediaElement markup where you want the video to be displayed, as shown in the following example:

```
<MediaElement Source="http://www.example.net/Video.wmv" />
```

Once the MediaElement is loaded, it begins to download and play the content.

> **NOTE**
>
> The XNA SoundEffect class is better suited to playing short sound effects. There can be a slight delay when first playing a sound using the MediaElement class, which the SoundEffect class does not suffer from. The SoundEffect class also does not need to reside in your page's visual tree. See later in this chapter for an overview of the SoundEffect class.

The Source property indicates the location of the media file or stream and functions in the same manner as the Image element's Source property (see the previous "Displaying Images with the Image Element" section).

By default, the MediaElement begins playback as soon as it loads. To prevent this, set its AutoPlay property to false. Playback will then not occur until the MediaElement's Play method is called. Two other methods provide playback control: Pause and Stop.

Controlling Audio Output

The MediaElement allows control of audio output, via its IsMuted, Volume, and Balance properties.

The Volume property, a double value with a range between 0 and 1, allows control of the audio volume level.

Balance, a double value with a range between -1 and 1, allows control over the output to the left or right speaker. Its default value, 0, represents the center balance.

Streaming Content

For content located on a remote server, the DownloadProgress property indicates the proportion of the download completed. The range of this property is between 0 and 1, inclusively. Multiply this value by 100 to calculate the percentage. When the DownloadProgress property is changed, the DownloadProgressChanged event is raised.

The Position property is used to move to a location within a file or stream during playback. When a user skips to a location ahead of what has already been downloaded (for example, 5 minutes into a video), the DownloadProgressOffset property is set to this value.

The BufferingProgress property indicates the proportion of the stream that has been downloaded in relation to the minimum buffering time. This property also has a range between 0 and 1. When the value changes by more than 0.05, or a value of 1 is reached, the BufferingProgressChanged event is raised.

The buffering time is specified using the BufferingTime property, which has a default value of 5 seconds.

The MediaElement control has several read-only properties, such as the BufferingProgress property, which makes data binding to them difficult. Fortunately there are events that provide the opportunity to update viewmodel or code-beside properties.

MediaElement Sample Code

The sample for this section is a media viewer page, which allows you to specify a URL of a media file, and view and/or listen to the file. This sample demonstrates the main features of the MediaElement, and gives you a test bed for exploring the MediaElement's main properties and methods.

The sample code is located in the MediaView page and MediaViewModel class in the downloadable sample code.

The MediaViewModel class uses four commands to toggle the playback state of the MediaElement and to mute and unmute audio. When the PlayCommand is executed, it updates the PlayerState property, signaling to the view to begin playback. Likewise, the PauseCommand signals to the view that playback should be paused, as shown in the following excerpt:

```
public MediaViewModel() : base("Media View")
{
    playCommand = new DelegateCommand(
        obj =>
        {
                PlayerState = PlayerState.Playing;
                CanPlay = false;
                CanPause = true;
        });

    pauseCommand = new DelegateCommand(
        obj =>
        {
            PlayerState = PlayerState.Paused;
            CanPause = false;
            CanPlay = true;
        });

    muteCommand = new DelegateCommand(obj => Muted = true);

    unMuteCommand = new DelegateCommand(obj => Muted = false);
}
```

This example uses the PropertyChanged event of the viewmodel to signal that the MediaElement should pause or resume playback.

The MediaViewModel contains numerous properties that are consumed by the MediaElement in the view and that for the sake of brevity are not shown.

Much of the code in the view serves to update viewmodel properties when MediaElement events are raised. For example, when the DownloadProgressChanged event is raised, the viewmodel's DownloadProgress and DownloadProgressOffset properties are updated (see Listing 7.4).

LISTING 7.4   MediaView Class (excerpt)

```
public partial class MediaView : PhoneApplicationPage
{
    public MediaView()
    {
        InitializeComponent();
        MediaViewModel viewModel = new MediaViewModel();
```

LISTING 7.4   Continued

```csharp
        DataContext = viewModel;
        viewModel.PropertyChanged += viewModel_PropertyChanged;
    }

    void viewModel_PropertyChanged(object sender, PropertyChangedEventArgs e)
    {
        if (e.PropertyName == "PlayerState")
        {
            switch (ViewModel.PlayerState)
            {
                case PlayerState.Stopped:
                    mediaElement.Stop();
                    break;
                case PlayerState.Playing:
                    mediaElement.Play();
                    break;
                case PlayerState.Paused:
                    mediaElement.Pause();
                    break;
            }
        }
    }

    void mediaElement_DownloadProgressChanged(object sender, RoutedEventArgs e)
    {
        MediaElement element = (MediaElement)sender;
        ViewModel.DownloadProgress = element.DownloadProgress;
        ViewModel.DownloadProgressOffset = element.DownloadProgressOffset;
    }

    void mediaElement_BufferingProgressChanged(
            object sender, RoutedEventArgs e)
    {
        MediaElement element = (MediaElement)sender;
        ViewModel.BufferingProgress = element.BufferingProgress;
        ViewModel.DownloadProgressOffset = element.DownloadProgressOffset;
    }

    void mediaElement_MediaOpened(object sender, RoutedEventArgs e)
    {
        MediaElement element = (MediaElement)sender;
        ViewModel.PlayLength = element.NaturalDuration.TimeSpan;
    }
```

LISTING 7.4   Continued

```
void mediaElement_CurrentStateChanged(object sender, RoutedEventArgs e)
{
    MediaElement element = (MediaElement)sender;
    ViewModel.MediaElementState = element.CurrentState;
    ViewModel.CanSeek = element.CanSeek;
    ViewModel.CanPause = element.CanPause;
}

void mediaElement_MediaFailed(object sender, ExceptionRoutedEventArgs e)
{
    ViewModel.HandleMediaFailed(e.ErrorException);
}
}
```

When a command, such as the PlayCommand, is executed via a button in the view, the viewmodel causes the MediaElement to play by updating its PlayerState property, which then raises the PropertyChanged event, handled in the view.

Various MediaElement properties are bound to the viewmodel, as shown:

```
<MediaElement x:Name="mediaElement" Grid.Row="1"
            DownloadProgressChanged="mediaElement_DownloadProgressChanged"
            BufferingProgressChanged="mediaElement_BufferingProgressChanged"
            Source="{Binding MediaUri, Mode=TwoWay}"
            Position="{Binding Position, Mode=TwoWay}"
            MediaOpened="mediaElement_MediaOpened"
            CurrentStateChanged="mediaElement_CurrentStateChanged"
            AutoPlay="{Binding AutoPlay}"
            BufferingTime="{Binding BufferingTime, Mode=TwoWay}"
            IsMuted="{Binding Muted}"
            Volume="{Binding Volume}"
            Balance="{Binding Balance}"
            MediaFailed="mediaElement_MediaFailed" />
```

Two viewmodel properties are employed to track and control the position of the current media file: Position and SliderPosition.

> **NOTE**
>
> Avoid placing a two-way data binding on the MediaElement.Position property to a source object that raises a PropertyChanged event. Doing so causes the MediaElement to stutter as it continually tries to return to the Position at the time when the event was raised.

The view contains two sections. The upper section holds the MediaElement, while the lower holds various controls for modifying the MediaElement properties, for monitoring download progress, and so forth. There is a position Slider that tracks the position of the media and allows the user to move to a different position. Moving the position Slider causes the download and buffer related progress bars to provide feedback to the user (see Figure 7.5).

FIGURE 7.5   Playing a video in the MediaView

The lower section of the view contains a ScrollViewer, allowing access, for example, to the auto play CheckBox (see Listing 7.5).

LISTING 7.5   MediaView.xaml ScrollViewer (styling removed)

```
<ScrollViewer Height="400" Grid.Row="1"
        VerticalScrollBarVisibility="Visible">
    <StackPanel Margin="12,0,12,0">
        <TextBlock Text="Position" />
        <TextBlock Text="{Binding SliderPosition}" />
        <Slider Value="{Binding SliderPosition, Mode=TwoWay,
                    Converter={StaticResource TimespanToDoubleConverter}}"
            Maximum="{Binding PlayLength,
            Converter={StaticResource TimespanToDoubleConverter}}"
            IsEnabled="{Binding CanSeek}" />
```

LISTING 7.5   Continued

```xml
            <TextBlock Text="{Binding MediaElementState}" />

            <TextBlock Text="{Binding Message}" />

            <TextBlock Text="Download Progress" />
            <ProgressBar Value="{Binding DownloadProgress}"
                Minimum="0" Maximum="1" />

            <TextBlock Text="Download Progress Offset" />
            <ProgressBar Value="{Binding DownloadProgressOffset}"
                Minimum="0" Maximum="1" />

            <TextBlock Text="Buffer Progress" />
            <ProgressBar Value="{Binding BufferingProgress}"
                Minimum="0" Maximum="1" />

            <TextBlock Text="Volume" />
            <Slider Value="{Binding Volume, Mode=TwoWay}"
                Maximum="1" LargeChange=".1" />

            <TextBlock Text="Balance" />
            <Slider Value="{Binding Balance, Mode=TwoWay}"
                Minimum="-1" Maximum="1" LargeChange=".1" />

            <TextBlock Text="Buffering Time" />
            <TextBlock Text="{Binding BufferingTime}" />
            <Slider Value="{Binding BufferingTime, Mode=TwoWay,
                Converter={StaticResource TimespanToDoubleConverter}}"
                Maximum="60000" LargeChange="10000" />

            <CheckBox IsChecked="{Binding AutoPlay, Mode=TwoWay}"
                Content="Auto Play" />
        </StackPanel>
</ScrollViewer>
```

An AppBar control is used in the sample page, which provides data binding and commanding support. A custom AppBarToggleButton allows the use of two commands in conjunction with a Toggled property, which allows one of the commands to be enabled depending on the value of the property. If the Toggled property is false, then Command1, Text1, and Icon1Uri are used; if set to true the second set is used. For more information regarding the ApplicationBar, and the custom AppBar control used here, see Chapter 8.

PlayCommand becomes active if the CanPlay property of the viewmodel is true; when the
CanPlay property evaluates to false, the button text is replaced along with its icon, and the
PauseCommand becomes active (see Listing 7.6).

LISTING 7.6   MediaView.xaml AppBar

```
<u:AppBar IsEnabled="True"
        IsVisible="True"
        IsMenuEnabled="True">
    <u:AppBarToggleButton
        Command1="{Binding PauseCommand}"
        Text1="Pause"
        Icon1Uri="/ControlExamples/MediaView/Images/Pause.png"
        Command2="{Binding PlayCommand}"
        Text2="Play"
        Icon2Uri="/ControlExamples/MediaView/Images/Play.png"
        Toggled="{Binding CanPlay}" />
    <u:AppBarToggleButton
        x:Name="button_Mute"
        Command1="{Binding MuteCommand}"
        Text1="Mute"
        Icon1Uri="/ControlExamples/MediaView/Images/Speaker.png"
        Command2="{Binding UnMuteCommand}"
        Text2="Un-Mute"
        Icon2Uri="/ControlExamples/MediaView/Images/Mute.png"
        Toggled="{Binding Muted}" />
</u:AppBar>
```

Tapping the mute button executes the MuteCommand, which updates the Muted property in
the viewmodel, updating the MediaElement control via a data binding. When muted, the
property changed event for the Muted property indicates to the AppBarToggleButton that
Command2, Text2, and Icon2Uri should be used (see Figure 7.6).

XNA SoundEffect Class

Sometimes being a Windows Phone developer means being spoiled for choice. The XNA
FCL contains various classes that you can harness in your Silverlight apps, and vice versa.
One such class is the SoundEffect class, which is a lightweight class that allows you to
specify an audio file and to play it from code without relying on, for example, the
MediaElement control.

The SoundEffect class works well for short samples, where instant playback is required.
SoundEffect provides support for controlling volume, panning, looping, and pitch of the
audio, and even allows you to apply 3D audio effects. Be warned, however, that it is fussy

about the format of the audio. I found that only PCM format wav files are supported. I recommend using a tool like GoldWave (http://www.goldwave.com/) to save all audio to a PCM format. For longer clips, it makes more sense to use a more space efficient format, such as MP3, but for this you need to use the MediaElement control.

FIGURE 7.6   Scrolling to the bottom of the view reveals the Balance, Buffering Time, and Auto Play settings.

To use the SoundEffect class, add a reference to the Microsoft.Xna.Framework.dll assembly.

The Build Action of all audio files that you intend to be played by the XNA framework must be set as Content.

A sound effect can be defined in your page code-beside, as demonstrated:

```
readonly SoundEffect footstepSoundEffect
    = SoundEffect.FromStream(TitleContainer.OpenStream("Audio/Footstep.wav"));
```

The SoundEffect can then be played like so:

```
FrameworkDispatcher.Update();
footstepSoundEffect.Play();
```

> **NOTE**
>
> Calling `FrameworkDispatcher.Update` regularly is necessary for the XNA infrastructure to function correctly and for fire and forget sound effects to function correctly. If not called, an `InvalidOperationException` will be thrown.
>
> Configuring a Silverlight app to work correctly with the XNA framework is discussed in Chapter 20, "Incorporating XNA Graphics in Silverlight."

Behind the scenes a `SoundEffectInstance` object is automatically created from the `SoundEffect` class as soon as the `Play` method is called. You can create multiple `SoundEffectInstance` objects and play them from a single `SoundEffect`. The benefit of using `SoundEffectInstances` is that these objects share the resources of their parent `SoundEffect`, and a `SoundEffect` object can be used to control all its `SoundEffectInstance` sounds. The `SoundEffect.MasterVolume` property, for example, can be used to modulate the volume of all child `SoundEffectInstances`.

Use the `CreateInstance` method of the `SoundEffect` class to create a new `SoundEffectInstance`, as shown:

```
SoundEffectInstance instance = footStepSoundEffect.CreateInstance();
```

> **NOTE**
>
> A maximum of 16 `SoundEffectInstance` instances can be playing at one time, combined across all loaded `SoundEffect` objects. Attempting to play more than 16 has no effect.

> **NOTE**
>
> A `SoundEffect` continues to hold its memory resources throughout its lifetime. All `SoundEffectInstance` objects created from a `SoundEffect` share memory resources. When a `SoundEffect` object is destroyed, all `SoundEffectInstance` objects previously created by that `SoundEffect` will stop playing and become invalid.
>
> Both the `SoundEffect` class and the `SoundEffectInstance` class implement `IDisposable`. When you are finished using an instance of either type, be sure to call its `Dispose` method to free valuable resources.

Viewing High-Resolution Images with the `MultiScaleImage` Element

Providing web content optimized for mobile devices is an important challenge facing developers today. The high cost of data plans and relatively low connection speeds provided by many telcos mean phone app developers need to be mindful of techniques that can minimize network usage.

The `MultiScaleImage` class is one of the key elements of Silverlight's Deep Zoom technology. Deep Zoom allows an application to interactively view high-resolution images and to limit the download of image content to portions of an image that are being viewed on the screen and at a resolution appropriate to the scale of the image at the time.

Downloading only part of an image can vastly decrease the time it takes to present the initial view of the image, and it unlocks user exploration of high resolution images, which would otherwise consume too much bandwidth.

`MultiScaleImage` works well on the phone and is more suited to the phone than to the browser or desktop because of Windows Phone's touch capabilities, allowing the user to pinch to zoom into an image, for example.

Potential uses of Deep Zoom technology include mapping, photo galleries, high-resolution images, and interactive ads.

`MultiScaleImage` is modeled after `MediaElement` and allows a user to open a multiresolution image or collection of images. Multiresolution images can be created using a free tool provided by Microsoft called the *Deep Zoom Composer*.

When a Deep Zoom image is first viewed, it is normally presented in its entirety scaled-up at a low resolution and allowing the user to drill down into the image. When drilling down, higher resolution sub-images (or tiles) are retrieved, which blend with the larger and lower resolution portion of the image.

> **NOTE**
>
> An image that is loaded by the `MultiScaleImage` control zooms out (expands) when first loaded. This behavior can be disabled by setting the `UseSprings` property to false.

As the user explores the image by panning and zooming, higher detail tile images are downloaded and blended in. This is like the interlacing feature of the gif image format. At first the image appears to be fuzzy and blurry, but as more information is downloaded from the server, the image becomes more crisp. As a result, Deep Zoom images can be opened faster, regardless of file size, as they do not require a substantial part of the image to be downloaded before being displayed.

> **NOTE**
>
> Deep Zoom incurs an overall download penalty of approximately 33% in the worst-case scenario, which occurs if all the sub-images are downloaded.

A compelling feature in Deep Zoom is that multiple images can be used to compose a scene, and they can be optimized individually, while still maintaining the overall appearance of the image. Collections of images can also be manipulated programmatically.

Image Tiling

When exporting an image from Deep Zoom Composer at design-time, each image in the composition is partitioned (or sliced) into tiles. During the tiling process, an image pyramid is created of various resolutions. At the base of the pyramid sits the highest-resolution image, composed of multiple tiles, while at the top of the pyramid is a single tile, the lowest resolution image (see Figure 7.7).

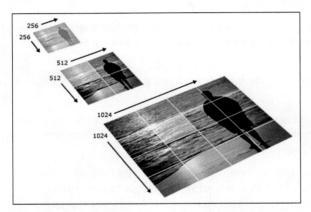

FIGURE 7.7   Image tiling (Image from MSDN. Used with permission from Microsoft.)

The tiles produced by Deep Zoom Composer are supposed to be 256 by 256 pixels. I found, however, that the nominal tile size is 258 by 258 pixels. Each zoom level is scaled by a factor of two compared to the level above. Of course, most images won't come in multiples of 258 pixels, and the resulting tile sets will usually contain many tiles with fewer than 258 pixels in width or height.

Creating a Deep Zoom Image

To begin creating your own Deep Zoom image, download and install the Deep Zoom Composer from Microsoft.com at http://bit.ly/hwf8Wp.

The Deep Zoom Composer has a built-in user guide. To view it, within Deep Zoom Composer press F1, or select the User Guide menu item from the Help menu. The user guide provides a good overview of using the tool, as well as some more advanced concepts that are not covered here, such as creating panoramic images and image hotspots.

In the example for this chapter, I created a Deep Zoom image composed of two images: a wide shot, and a zoomed in close-up. To do this, I created a new project (select File, New Project) within Deep Zoom Composer. I then used the Add Image button, located on the Import tab, to insert the images.

Composing the Deep Zoom image involved resizing and positioning the close-up shot, so that it blended into the wide shot (see Figure 7.8).

FIGURE 7.8   Composing a Deep Zoom image within Deep Zoom Composer

When I was happy with the composition, I switched to the Export tab.

There are various options for outputting the Deep Zoom image. For hosting on your own website, select the Silverlight Deep Zoom radio button. The generated output includes Visual Studio projects that you probably will not need, so select an output location that is independent from your Windows Phone app (see Figure 7.9).

Once the exporting process is complete, the Deep Zoom image files are located at \DeepZoomProjectSite\ClientBin\GeneratedImages in the output directory. This directory can be placed in a web application that will be accessible to your Windows Phone app.

The filename of the generated Deep Zoom image, and to which you point the `MultiScaleImage`, is dzc_output.xml. It contains references to other image definition files in subdirectories, along with image metadata.

FIGURE 7.9   Exporting a Deep Zoom image from Deep Zoom Composer

Exploring the `MultiScaleImage` API

Before diving into the sample code for this section, let's look at some of the key features of the `MultiScaleImage` API.

Instantiating a `MultiScaleImage` can be done in XAML, as shown:

```
<MultiScaleImage Source="http://www.example.com/dzc_output.xml" />
```

Or in code:

```
MultiScaleImage multiScaleImage = new MultiScaleImage();
multiScaleImage.Source = new DeepZoomImageTileSource(
        new Uri("http://www.example.com/dzc_output.xml"));
```

Source Property

When set in XAML, the `Source` property of the `MultiScaleImage` indicates the URL of the Deep Zoom image definition file, an XML file containing image metadata and paths to sub-image definition files. The `Source` property type is, however, an abstract class called `MultiScaleTileSource`, with an abstract method `GetTileLayers`. This offers an extensibility point for generating dynamic Deep Zoom images, though that is beyond the scope of this book.

Logical and Element Coordinates

As you see, some properties and methods of the MultiScaleImage rely on logical coordinates rather than element coordinates. Logical coordinates (also known as normalized coordinates) are points whose X and Y axis values are between 0 and 1. The methods ElementToLogicalPoint and LogicalToElementPoint are used to convert to and from both coordinate types. For example, calling ElementToLogicalPoint with a touch Point at the center of the control, returns a Point with X and Y coordinates of 0.5. Conversely, calling LogicalToElementPoint, with a Point(0.5, 0.5) and where the control measures 200 by 200 pixels, returns a Point with X and Y coordinates of 100.

SubImages Property

The SubImages property provides access to a collection of MultiScaleSubImage objects, which is populated if the Deep Zoom image is composed of multiple images, rather than a single high-resolution image. This is useful if you want to programmatically move individual images around the screen, or filter your images.

ViewportOrigin and ViewportWidth Properties

The ViewportOrigin and ViewportWidth properties are both Point objects that use logical coordinates. They work in conjunction to determine the zoom level of the image and the visible area of the image. The ViewportOrigin specifies the position of the image and is the location of the top-left corner of the image, while the ViewportWidth is how wide the viewport window is relative to the entire image. In other words, ViewportWidth is the fraction of the width of the image that is visible. The following is a list of ViewportWidth values and their effects:

▶ **ViewportWidth = 1**—When equal to one, the entire image is displayed. This is the default value.

▶ **ViewportWidth < 1**—When less than 1, the image is zoomed in. The closer you get to zero, the more zoomed in the image appears. Zero is completely zoomed in and the user cannot see the image at all.

▶ **ViewportWidth > 1**—When greater than 1, the image is zoomed out, and the value indicates the number of times that the viewport is larger than the image.

The width of the viewport specifies by how much to zoom in or out of the image, but it does not specify where on the image the viewport is positioned. To specify the viewport position, use the ViewportOrigin.

ZoomAboutLogicalPoint Method

This method enables zooming and panning on the MultiScaleImage, relative to a specified logical coordinate. This method takes a zoomIncrementFactor, a double that indicates by how much to change the existing zoom level.

UseSprings Property

The UseSprings property is used to enable or disable the animations that occur transitioning to a new zoom level or panning, such as when ZoomAboutLogicalPoint is called. The default value is true.

AllowDownloading Property

The `AllowDownloading` property can be used to halt downloading of image data at any time. This can be useful for halting bandwidth usage when leaving a WiFi connected area.

MotionFinished Event

The `MotionFinished` event is raised when a zoom or pan animation ends. This event can be used as an alternative to data binding to the `ViewportOrigin` and/or `ViewportWidth` properties because sometimes change events fail to be raised when using these properties.

Deep Zoom Viewer Sample Code

The sample code for this section is located in the `DeepZoomView` page and `DeepZoomViewModel` class, in the downloadable sample code.

The sample allows the selection of a Deep Zoom image, via a `ListPicker` control. The interface harnesses touch for zooming and panning of the `MultiScaleImage` control (see Figure 7.10).

FIGURE 7.10   Selecting a Deep Zoom image to explore

For information on the `ListPicker` control, see Chapter 9, "Silverlight Toolkit Controls." For information on touch, see Chapter 11, "Touch."

The view contains a grid with a `ListPicker`, which is data bound to an `ObservableCollection` of custom `DeepZoomSource` objects. Each `DeepZoomSource` holds the name and URL of a Deep Zoom image. When the user selects a different item from the

ListPicker, the `SelectedItem` property of the `ListPicker` is updated, which updates the `DeepZoomSource` viewmodel property. See the following excerpt:

```xml
<Grid Grid.Row="1">
    <toolkit:ListPicker ItemsSource="{Binding DeepZoomSources}"
        SelectedItem="{Binding DeepZoomSource, Mode=TwoWay}">
        <toolkit:ListPicker.ItemTemplate>
            <DataTemplate>
                <TextBlock Text="{Binding Name}"
                Style="{StaticResource PhoneTextTitle2Style}"
                Foreground="{StaticResource PhoneContrastForegroundBrush}"
                Margin="12, 10, 12, 10" />
            </DataTemplate>
        </toolkit:ListPicker.ItemTemplate>
    </toolkit:ListPicker>
</Grid>
```

The `MultiScaleImage` is located in a second `Grid` and has its `Source` property bound to the `Url` property of the viewmodel's `DeepZoomSource` property. Thus, changing the item in the `ListPicker` switches the Deep Zoom image.

For the sake of simplicity, the logic for zooming and dragging is placed in the view codebeside. A Silverlight Toolkit `GestureListener` is placed in the `Grid` as shown to monitor touch gestures, so that we can respond by zooming and dragging the `MultiScaleImage`:

```xml
<Grid x:Name="ContentPanel" Grid.Row="2">
    <toolkit:GestureService.GestureListener>
        <toolkit:GestureListener
        PinchStarted="OnPinchStarted"
        PinchDelta="OnPinchDelta"
        DragStarted="OnDragStarted"
        DragDelta="OnDragDelta" />
    </toolkit:GestureService.GestureListener>
    <MultiScaleImage x:Name="multiScaleImage"
        Source="{Binding DeepZoomSource.Url}" />
</Grid>
```

The view contains a method called `Zoom`, which uses the `MultiScaleImage`. `ZoomAboutLogicalPoint` to zoom in or out of the image. We constrain the zoom level to be greater than, or equal to, half the initial size of the image, as shown:

```csharp
double zoomLevel = 1;

void Zoom(double level, Point point)
{
    const double minimumZoomLevel = 0.5;
    if (level < minimumZoomLevel)
    {
```

```
        level = minimumZoomLevel;
    }

    multiScaleImage.ZoomAboutLogicalPoint(
        level / zoomLevel, point.X, point.Y);

    zoomLevel = level;
}
```

When the user performs a pinch gesture, it is handled in the view by recording the current zoom level of the `MultiScaleImage` control. The center position of the touch gesture is determined relative to the `MultiScaleImage`. The center point is calculated automatically using the two touch points involved in the pinch gesture. We then convert this pixel location to a logical location, which results in a value between 0 and 1. See the following excerpt:

```
void OnPinchStarted(object sender, PinchStartedGestureEventArgs e)
{
    pinchStartLevel = zoomLevel;
    Point pinchStartPoint = e.GetPosition(multiScaleImage);
    pinchLogicalStartPoint
        = multiScaleImage.ElementToLogicalPoint(pinchStartPoint);
}
```

When the user moves his fingers together or apart, the `OnPinchDelta` handler is called. We then call the `Zoom` method, passing it the new zoom level and the gesture reference point, like so:

```
void OnPinchDelta(object sender, PinchGestureEventArgs e)
{
    Zoom(e.DistanceRatio * pinchStartLevel, pinchLogicalStartPoint);
}
```

To allow the user to drag the image, we respond to the `DragStarted` and `DragDelta` events of the Toolkit's `GestureListener`. This involves recording the touch location relative to the `MultiScaleImage` and the location of the top-left corner of the control, the `ViewportOrigin`:

```
void OnDragStarted(object sender, DragStartedGestureEventArgs e)
{
    dragStartPoint = e.GetPosition(multiScaleImage);
    dragStartViewportOrigin = multiScaleImage.ViewportOrigin;
}
```

As the user performs a drag motion, the OnDragDelta handler is called. Here we determine the relative distance from the initial touch point to the current touch location and reposition the MultiScaleImage using its ViewportOrigin property. The ViewportWidth property is a logical property with a value between 0 and 1:

```
void OnDragDelta(object sender, DragDeltaGestureEventArgs e)
{
    Point touchPoint = e.GetPosition(multiScaleImage);
    double visibleSize
        = multiScaleImage.ActualWidth / multiScaleImage.ViewportWidth;
    Point newPoint = dragStartViewportOrigin;
    newPoint.X += (dragStartPoint.X - touchPoint.X) / visibleSize;
    newPoint.Y += (dragStartPoint.Y - touchPoint.Y) / visibleSize;
    multiScaleImage.ViewportOrigin = newPoint;
}
```

The sample allows the user to zoom-in via a double tap. To achieve this, we subscribe to the DoubleTap event of the Toolkit's GestureListener. In the handler, the location of the touch point relative to the MultiScaleImage is calculated. This point is then translated to a logical point, which acts as a reference point to perform the zoom. The zoom level is set to twice the existing zoom level, as shown:

```
void OnDoubleTap(object sender, GestureEventArgs e)
{
    Point tapPoint = e.GetPosition(multiScaleImage);
    Point logicalPoint = multiScaleImage.ElementToLogicalPoint(tapPoint);
    Zoom(zoomLevel * 2, logicalPoint);
}
```

Figure 7.11 shows the MultiScaleImage displaying the Deep Zoom image generated at the beginning of this section.

By performing a pinch gesture, or by double tapping, the user is able to zoom in to explore the image in greater detail (see Figure 7.12).

Deep Zoom technology on the phone makes viewing high resolution imagery viable and allows you to leverage the built-in touch support of the phone to unlock exploration of visually rich content.

7

FIGURE 7.11   Viewing a Deep Zoom image from the sample app

FIGURE 7.12   Zooming in on a composite Deep Zoom image

Displaying Web Content with the `WebBrowser` Element

While the phone's built-in web browser can be launched from your app to view content on an external website, the `WebBrowser` control allows the user to view content directly from your app.

The `WebBrowser` control also allows you to host HTML content within your app, something the built-in web browser does not. It provides for static content loaded from a string or via a relative URI to a page located in isolated storage, or for live content from the Web, using an absolute URI. You can generate HTML and pass it to the `WebBrowser` control at runtime, and you can download content, save it to isolated storage, and display it later. The control responds to touch: a double tap zooms in, and the pinch gesture is also supported.

To have the `WebBrowser` load content, set the `Source` property of the URI to the location of the content as demonstrated in the following examples:

```
<phone:WebBrowser Source="http://www.example.com" />
<phone:WebBrowser Source="{Binding Url}" />
```

Alternatively, use the `WebBrowser`'s `Navigate` method, as shown:

```
webBrowser.Navigate(
    new Uri("http://www.example.com", UriKind.Absolute));
```

The `Navigate` method has an overload that allows you to specify options for including posted form data and HTTP headers.

Loading a page from a string containing HTML is also possible using the `NavigateToString` method, as shown:

```
webBrowser.NavigateToString(
    "<html><head /><body>Windows Phone 7 Unleashed</body></html>");
```

The markup for the page loaded in the `WebBrowser` can be retrieved at runtime using the `WebBrowser.SaveToString` method.

Monitoring and Cancelling Navigation

The `WebBrowser` control allows in-place navigation. Users may click on a link to change the page displayed in the control, and in addition, client-side JavaScript may assign the `window.location.href` property to navigate to a new location, which requires that the `WebBrowser.IsScriptEnabled` property be set to true.

Allowing the user free rein over navigation may not always be desirable, and you may want to monitor or even cancel the navigation of a web page programmatically. Fortunately the `Navigating` event of the `WebBrowser` can be cancelled. This is done by subscription to the event in code, or in XAML as shown:

```
<phone:WebBrowser Navigating="webBrowser_Navigating"/>
```

When the `WebBrowser` begins navigating to a new web page, the event is raised, at which time you can examine the URL and determine whether to allow the navigation:

```
void webBrowser_Navigating(object sender, NavigatingEventArgs e)
{
    if (e.Uri.ToString().IndexOf("www.example.com",
        StringComparison.CurrentCultureIgnoreCase) != -1)
    {
        e.Cancel = true;
    }
}
```

Communicating with a Web Page

The `WebBrowser.InvokeScript` method allows you to call JavaScript functions on a web page, and unlike Silverlight for the desktop, it is not restricted to scripts loaded from the same site as the XAP package. This method allows you to pass the JavaScript function an array of string parameters and is useful when you want to interact with the page, such as by highlighting text, changing the visibility of particular elements, or by adding behavior to a page through subscription to existing client-side events.

Conversely, a web page is able to send messages to your Silverlight application using the client-side JavaScript method `window.external.Notify`, which raises the `WebBrowser.ScriptNotify` event, passing a single string argument.

The example for this section looks at both methods of communication. You see how to pass a string to Silverlight via an HTML button and how to modify the content of a web page via Silverlight.

The sample code for this section is located in the `WebBrowser` directory of the WindowsPhone7Unleashed.Examples.Silverlight project in the downloadable sample code, and includes the following files:

► `Webpage.html`

► `WebBrowserWithScriptingView.xaml`

► `WebBrowserWithScriptingView.xaml.cs`

We start by looking at the web page, which is loaded into the `WebBrowser` control at runtime (see Listing 7.7). This web page contains three key elements:

► A JavaScript function, called `Populate`, in its head element. We use `InvokeScript` to call this function from Silverlight.

► An HTML `div` element named `textDiv`, which is populated using the JavaScript `Populate` method.

► An HTML `input` button, which is used to send the content of the `textToSend` HTML text box to the Silverlight application.

LISTING 7.7   Webpage.html

```html
<!DOCTYPE html PUBLIC "-//W3C//DTD XHTML 1.0 Transitional//EN"
 "http://www.w3.org/TR/xhtml1/DTD/xhtml1-transitional.dtd">
<html xmlns="http://www.w3.org/1999/xhtml">
<head>
    <meta name="mobileoptimized" content="480" />
    <title>Windows Phone 7 Unleashed</title>
    <style type="text/css"> h1 {color:red}
        div { margin-bottom: 30px; padding: 5px }
        div.received
        {
            border: thin solid #000000;
            font-size: x-large;
            font-weight: bold;
            color: Blue; }
    </style>
    <script type="text/javascript">
        function Populate(input) {
            textDiv.innerHTML = input;
            return true;
        }
    </script>
</head>
<body>
    <div>
        <input name="textToSend" type="text" value="Hi from Page!" />
        <br />
        <input type="button"
               value="Send to Silverlight"
               onclick="window.external.Notify(textToSend.value)"/>
    </div>
    <div>Value received from Silverlight:
        <div id="textDiv" class="received" />
    </div>
    <a href="#dummy">A Link</a>
</body>
</html>
```

The PhoneApplicationPage, WebBrowserWithScriptingView.xaml, contains a WebBrowser
control with its IsScriptEnabled property set to true, as shown in the following excerpt:

```xml
<Grid x:Name="ContentGrid" Grid.Row="1">
    <Grid.RowDefinitions>
        <RowDefinition Height="Auto" />
        <RowDefinition Height="*" />
```

```
    </Grid.RowDefinitions>
    <StackPanel>
        <TextBox x:Name="textBox" Text="Hi from Silverlight!" />
        <Button Content="Send to Page"
                Click="Button_Click"
                Style="{StaticResource ButtonStyle}" />
    </StackPanel>
    <phone:WebBrowser x:Name="webBrowser"
        ScriptNotify="WebBrowser_ScriptNotify"
        IsScriptEnabled="True"  Grid.Row="1" />
</Grid>
```

By default, IsScriptEnabled is false.

The PhoneApplicationPage also contains a TextBox and a button that causes the content of the TextBox to be sent to the web page and placed into an HTML div element.

For the sake of simplicity, the logic for this example is placed in the XAML's code-beside file (see Listing 7.8). This file loads the web page, which is stored as content within the project and is tasked with calling the WebBrowser's InvokeScript method when the Send to Page button is tapped, and with responding to the JavaScript window.external.Notify by displaying a message box.

LISTING 7.8   WebBrowserWithScriptingView.xaml.cs

```
public partial class WebBrowserWithScriptingView : PhoneApplicationPage
{
    public WebBrowserWithScriptingView()
    {
        InitializeComponent();
    }

    void WebBrowser_ScriptNotify(object sender, NotifyEventArgs e)
    {
        MessageBox.Show(e.Value, "Received Value", MessageBoxButton.OK);
    }

    protected override void OnNavigatedTo(NavigationEventArgs e)
    {
        base.OnNavigatedTo(e);

        StreamResourceInfo streamResourceInfo = Application.GetResourceStream(
            new Uri("WebBrowser/Webpage.html", UriKind.Relative));
```

LISTING 7.8   Continued

```
    string html;
    using (StreamReader reader
              = new StreamReader(streamResourceInfo.Stream))
    {
        html = reader.ReadToEnd();
    }
    webBrowser.NavigateToString(html);
}

void Button_Click(object sender, RoutedEventArgs e)
{
    webBrowser.InvokeScript("Populate", textBox.Text);
}
}
```

The PhoneApplicationPage uses the WebBrowser's NavigateToString method to push the loaded HTML into the control.

> **NOTE**
>
> Calls to NavigateToString must occur after the WebBrowser control is in the Visual Tree. Trying to call NavigateToString in your page constructor raises an InvalidOperationException.

Figure 7.13 shows that when a user taps the Send to Page button, the content of the Silverlight TextBox control is sent to the web page.

Conversely, when the user taps the Send to Silverlight HTML button, the text located in the HTML input text control is sent to the Silverlight app (see Figure 7.14).

Injecting Web Page Behavior

On occasion you may want to invoke some JavaScript on a third-party web page, in which case relying on a named JavaScript function becomes impossible. Fortunately JavaScript's eval function gives us the power to execute arbitrary JavaScript.

> **NOTE**
>
> Be aware that it is possible to override the JavaScript eval function, which may result in less than complete reliability for the technique presented in this section. Overriding eval is, however, rare, and web pages that do, do not comply with the ECMAScript 5 specification.

FIGURE 7.13   Sending a string to a web page from Silverlight

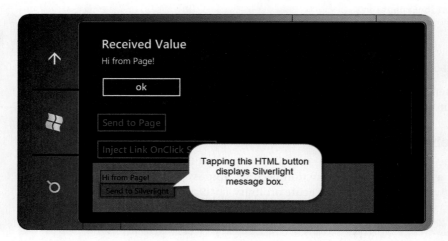

FIGURE 7.14   Receiving a message from a web page within a Silverlight for Windows Phone app

To demonstrate the execution of arbitrary JavaScript, another button has been added to the `WebBrowserWithScriptingView.xaml` page. Clicking on the button causes a script to be invoked on the web page, which identifies all the hyperlinks on the page and attaches a client-side event handler to each anchor's `onclick` event, as shown in the following excerpt:

```
void Button_InjectScript_Click(object sender, RoutedEventArgs e)
{
    webBrowser.InvokeScript("eval", evalScript);
}

const string evalScript
    = @"var anchors = document.getElementsByTagName('a');
    for(var i = 0; i < anchors.length; i++)
    {
        var anchor = anchors[i];
        anchor.attachEvent('onclick', function()
            {
                anchor.innerHTML = 'This text was changed by attaching'
                            + ' an event handler from Silverlight!';
            });
    }";
```

This script executes client-side, after which, when the user clicks on a link, the link's text is changed. It is a wacky example, yet we see that the `eval` function gives us the power to manipulate any part of the web page's Document Object Model (DOM). It could be used, for example, to highlight keywords on a web page or modify styles on a web page that you did not create.

Figure 7.15 shows the updated `PhoneApplication` page and the ordered steps for executing the JavaScript.

Once the script is invoked, clicking on the link causes an event handler to be called within the web page, where the style of the link is modified (see Figure 7.16).

Storing and Browsing Content in Isolated Storage

There may be times when you want to allow an app to download content, perhaps modify it, and store it for later viewing. Fortunately the `WebBrowser` has built-in capability for browsing offline content located in isolated storage. There is, however, no automatic way to store such content. It is your responsibility to place whatever content needs to be available for offline browsing in isolated storage.

CAUTION

Content loaded from the network has cross-site restrictions, which ordinarily prevents a web page from communicating with sites other than its site-of-origin. Content loaded from isolated storage, or by using the `NavigateToString` method, however, has no such restrictions on cross-site access. Therefore, be mindful of unwittingly compromising the privacy of your users.

FIGURE 7.15   Injecting web page behavior at runtime from Silverlight

FIGURE 7.16   The anchor style is modified via an injected JavaScript event handler.

The example for this section looks at storing a web page and a referenced image in isolated storage and then directing a WebBrowser to read the content directly from isolated storage. The sample code for this section is located in the WebBrowserIsolatedStorageView page, in the downloadable sample code.

WebBrowserIsolatedStorageView

The OnNavigatedTo method of the WebBrowserIsolatedStorageView saves some example content to isolated storage. Once the content has been stored, the WebBrowser's Base property is assigned to the isolated storage directory containing the web page; this is then used by the WebBrowser to locate HTML content (see Listing 7.9).

The Base property should point to an isolated storage directory and is used by the WebBrowser to resolve relative references. This includes the Uri Source property and references to images within the HTML document.

LISTING 7.9   WebBrowserIsolatedStorageView Class

```
public partial class WebBrowserIsolatedStorageView : PhoneApplicationPage
{
    public WebBrowserIsolatedStorageView()
    {
        InitializeComponent();
    }

    protected override void OnNavigatedTo(NavigationEventArgs e)
    {
        base.OnNavigatedTo(e);
        SaveHtmlToIsolatedStorage();
        webBrowser.Base = "WebContent";
        webBrowser.Source = new Uri(@"Webpage.html", UriKind.Relative);
    }
...
}
```

When the WebBrowser attempts to load the URL Webpage.html, it uses the base directory of WebContent to load all relative content (see Figure 7.17).

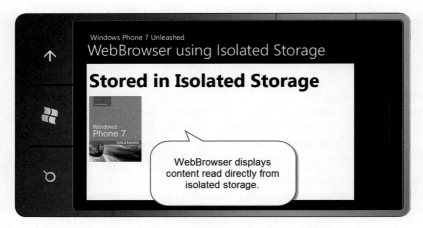

FIGURE 7.17   Viewing a page from isolated storage

Storing the Sample Web Content

Saving the web page and the image to isolated storage is done by retrieving the
`IsolatedStorageFile` for the app and creating a directory called *WebContent* in which the
content is placed. A simple document is written to a file in the directory, as shown in
Listing 7.10.

LISTING 7.10   SaveHtmlToIsolatedStorage Method

```
void SaveHtmlToIsolatedStorage()
{
    using (IsolatedStorageFile isolatedStorageFile
        = IsolatedStorageFile.GetUserStoreForApplication())
    {
        if (!isolatedStorageFile.DirectoryExists("WebContent"))
        {
            isolatedStorageFile.CreateDirectory("WebContent");
        }


        using (IsolatedStorageFileStream isolatedStorageFileStream
            = isolatedStorageFile.OpenFile(
                @"WebContent\Webpage.html", FileMode.Create))
        {
        using (StreamWriter streamWriter
            = new StreamWriter(isolatedStorageFileStream))
        {
            streamWriter.Write(@"<html><head></head><body>
            <h2>Stored in Isolated Storage</h2>
            <p><img src=""Images/Book.jpg"" /></p>
                    </body></html>");
        }
```

LISTING 7.10   Continued

```
        }

        if (!isolatedStorageFile.DirectoryExists("WebContent/Images"))
        {
            isolatedStorageFile.CreateDirectory("WebContent/Images");
        }

        StreamResourceInfo resourceInfo = Application.GetResourceStream(
            new Uri("WebBrowser/ImagePlacedInIsolatedStorage"
                    + "/WP7Unleashed200x.jpg",
                    UriKind.Relative));

        using (IsolatedStorageFileStream writeStream
            = new IsolatedStorageFileStream(
                    @"WebContent/Images/Book.jpg",
                    FileMode.Create, isolatedStorageFile))
        {
            CopyStreamBytes(resourceInfo.Stream, writeStream);
        }
    }
}
```

The image, which is referenced by the img element in the HTML document, is a project item with its Build Action set to Content. This image file is first opened using the static method GetResourceStream of the Application class. It is then converted to a byte array and saved in isolated storage. For the sake of completeness, the Stream related methods are shown in Listing 7.11.

LISTING 7.11   CopyStreamBytes and ReadStreamBytes Methods

```
void CopyStreamBytes(
    Stream fromStream, Stream toStream, bool closeToStream = true)
{
    if (toStream.CanWrite)
    {
        byte[] fileBytes = ReadStreamBytes(fromStream);
        toStream.Write(fileBytes, 0, fileBytes.Length);
        if (closeToStream)
        {
            toStream.Close();
        }
    }
}

byte[] ReadStreamBytes(Stream fileStream)
{
    /* Read the source file into a byte array. */
```

LISTING 7.11   Continued

```
    byte[] bytes = new byte[fileStream.Length];
    int readLength = (int)fileStream.Length;
    int bytesRead = 0;
    while (readLength > 0)
    {
        /* Read may return anything from 0 to readLength. */
        int read = fileStream.Read(bytes, bytesRead, readLength);

        /* When no bytes left to read it is the end of the file. */
        if (read == 0)
        {
            break;
        }

        bytesRead += read;
        readLength -= read;
    }
    return bytes;
}
```

Summary

This chapter began by looking at the Image element, how to reference image files, and the effect on sizing by the Image.Stretch property. Setting Visual Studio's Build Action for a file to Resource causes it to be placed in the assembly, whereas setting it to Content means it will sit outside the assembly in the application's XAP file.

The chapter then explored the InkPresenter and demonstrated how to create a simple sketch app. You saw how the Background property of the InkPresenter must be assigned to register touch events.

It then moved to the MediaElement, and you saw how audio and video files can be played from the phone or streamed via the Internet. The XNA SoundEffect class is better suited to playing short sound effects.

Deep Zoom and the MultiScaleImage element were discussed, including how they can be used to provide a stunning visual experience while making efficient use of your users' bandwidth. You saw how to allow the user to manipulate the Deep Zoom image using touch.

Finally, the chapter examined the WebBrowser control, and you saw how to communicate to a web page from Silverlight and vice versa. You also saw how to execute arbitrary JavaScript on a web page to modify page content or to attach new behaviors. You then looked at storing and browsing offline content to decrease network usage.

CHAPTER 8

Taming the Application Bar

The Windows Phone application bar provides a standard way of accessing common tasks within your app, and makes it easier for users to use your app by leveraging existing familiarity with a control that is used across all apps. Users are able to focus on content, rather than being distracted by having to learn an entirely new interface for each new app. The existence of the application bar also means that you as a developer do not have to reinvent the wheel every time you create a new app.

The application bar plays the same role as a combined toolbar and menu in a desktop or web application. It allows you to define a set of buttons and/or menu items that raise events when a user taps them.

This chapter explores the built-in application bar and its associated button and menu item classes. Most of this chapter is, however, devoted to a custom application bar, which is a wrapper for the built-in application bar and overcomes many of the built-in application bar's inherent limitations. The custom application bar improves on its built-in counterpart by providing support for data binding, commanding, toggle and hyperlink buttons, and controlling the visibility of menu items and buttons at runtime. Moreover, it is more compatible with design patterns like MVVM that rely on data binding.

Exploring the Built-In Application Bar

The phone's application bar API is somewhat of a conundrum. It has several serious limitations that make it difficult to work with, and considering that the application bar is such a fundamental element of most phone apps, it is odd that its API did not receive more care and attention during the development of Silverlight for Windows Phone.

The `ApplicationBar` class uses an interop wrapper to communicate with the phone's native application bar. The `ApplicationBar` is not a `UIElement`, nor is it a `DependencyObject`; in fact, it does not reside in the usual Silverlight UI class hierarchy at all. Furthermore, at runtime, the `ApplicationBar` exists outside the visual tree of your root visual, making interaction with it awkward.

Several features to which Silverlight developers have grown accustomed are also missing from the `ApplicationBar`, such as being able to control a button or menu item's visibility.

Using the ApplicationBar

Visual Studio provides you with a starting point by placing the markup for an `ApplicationBar` in a comment block when you create a new Windows Phone Portrait Page, a Windows Phone Landscape Page, and various Windows Phone projects using the Add New Item and New Project dialogs.

The `ApplicationBar` requires a namespace alias at the top of your page or control, as shown:

```
xmlns:shell="clr-namespace:Microsoft.Phone.Shell;assembly=Microsoft.Phone"
```

The markup for an `ApplicationBar` element is placed in the page's `phone:PhoneApplicationPage` element. Placed within it are `ApplicationBarIconButton` elements and a `MenuItems` element containing `ApplicationBarMenuItem` elements, as shown in the following example:

```
<phone:PhoneApplicationPage.ApplicationBar>
    <shell:ApplicationBar IsVisible="True" IsMenuEnabled="True">
        <shell:ApplicationBarIconButton
                        IconUri="/Images/appbar_button1.png"
                        Text="Button 1"/>
        <shell:ApplicationBarIconButton
                        IconUri="/Images/appbar_button2.png"
                        Text="Button 2"/>
        <shell:ApplicationBar.MenuItems>
            <shell:ApplicationBarMenuItem Text="MenuItem 1"/>
            <shell:ApplicationBarMenuItem Text="MenuItem 2"/>
        </shell:ApplicationBar.MenuItems>
    </shell:ApplicationBar>
</phone:PhoneApplicationPage.ApplicationBar>
```

> **NOTE**
>
> The application bar can contain up to four buttons, and up to 50 menu items.

BEST PRACTICE

Avoid placing more than six menu items in the application bar. Doing so decreases the usability of your page, forcing the user to scroll down a long list to find the menu item that she is seeking.

When your `PhoneApplicationPage` is created, its `ApplicationBar` property is automatically assigned to the `ApplicationBar` instance if it exists.

The `ApplicationBar` consists of two collections of items, each with a corresponding `ApplicationBar` property: `Buttons` and `MenuItems`. The `Buttons` property is the `ApplicationBar`'s Content property, which means that in XAML any items located directly as child elements of the `ApplicationBar` element must be `ApplicationBarIconButtons` and are placed in the `ApplicationBar.Buttons` collection automatically.

Figure 8.1 shows an example of an application bar in its expanded state.

FIGURE 8.1   Expanding the application bar reveals its menu items.

To prevent the menu section from being expanded, set the `ApplicationBar.IsMenuEnabled` property to `false`. To hide the application bar entirely, set the `ApplicationBar.IsVisible` property to `false`.

Minimizing the Icon Button Tray

With the release of Windows Phone 7.1 SDK you are now able to minimize the application bar so that just the bar's ellipsis is shown. This is controlled by the `Mode` property of the `ApplicationBar`, which can be either Default or Minimized.

Application Bar and System Tray Dimensions

In portrait mode the height of the application bar is fixed at 72 pixels. In landscape mode its width is also fixed at 72 pixels. When minimized, the application bar's icon buttons are not shown, and the height of the icon button tray is reduced from 72 pixels to 30 pixels.

The system tray is 32 pixels high in portrait mode and 72 pixels wide in landscape mode. It always extends to the edge of the screen.

Modifying the Application Bar's Appearance

The `ApplicationBar`'s foreground (text and icon color) can be modified using its `ForegroundColor` property. By default this value is set to the PhoneForegroundColor application resource. For more information on built-in color styles, see http://bit.ly/xC8vgo.

The `Background` color property determines the background of the entire control. By default this value is set to the PhoneChromeColor application resource.

The `Opacity` property determines the level of transparency of the application bar's background. It does not affect the foreground, nor any icons present. Its value can range from 0 to 1, with 1 being completely opaque (the default value), and 0 being completely transparent.

The sample for this chapter, presented in a later section, provides a page to experiment with these properties.

Icon Button and Menu Item

The `ApplicationBarIconButton` and `ApplicationBarMenuItem` classes have many things in common. Apart from the `ApplicationBarIconButton` class's `IconUri` property, both `ApplicationBarIconButton` and `ApplicationBarMenuItem` classes contain the same set of identically named properties.

Both `ApplicationBarIconButton` and `ApplicationBarMenuItem` classes have a `Text` property, which is displayed on the application bar. At runtime the text for both menu items and icon buttons is transformed to lowercase to conform to the Metro aesthetic.

Icon button text is displayed beneath the icon when the user expands the application bar. If the length of the string exceeds 7 to 13 characters, depending on the width of the characters that make up the string, it is clipped.

Menu item text does not wrap and should be limited to 14 to 20 characters in length, depending on the width of the characters.

Many languages use different amounts of space to convey the same meaning. Therefore, when choosing menu item or button text, consider the different lengths of the text strings for the language your app will be in. Assume that an average of 30% more space will be required for any text. Depending on the language and the phrase, the localized string might even require twice as much space.

The `ApplicationBarIconButton.IconUri` is used to specify the location of the icon image. This value must be a relative URI, pointing to either a JPG or PNG image in the same project.

When including an icon image in your project, be sure to set its Build Action to Content. Icon images must have a Build Action set to Content. If an image's Build Action is set to Resource, the image will not be resolved at runtime, and a default broken icon will be displayed in its place.

To disable a menu item or button set its `IsEnabled` property to `false`.

Both `ApplicationBarIconButton` and `ApplicationBarMenuItem` have a `Click` event, allowing you to place a handler in your code-beside.

If the `NavigationService` reports that navigation is in progress, `Click` events will not be raised by your menu items or buttons. This prevents event handlers from interfering with your control or page during navigation, when it may be in an inconsistent state.

Icon Button Image

The Windows Phone SDK comes with a set of icons that you can use freely in your app. The default location of the icon images is C:\Program Files (x86)\Microsoft SDKs\ Windows Phone\v7.1\Icons\. Other free icon packs are also available online, such as those at http://bit.ly/b1BvgG.

The icon image, for the `ApplicationBarIconButton`, should measure 48 by 48 pixels, but with a central area of 26 by 26 pixels. All content should be placed within a 26*26 square pixel area to ensure that it does not overlap the automatic circular button frame. Images that are other sizes will be scaled to fit, but image quality will be lower as a consequence.

The circle displayed on each icon button is automatically generated by the application bar, and therefore should not be included in the source image.

The application bar automatically modifies the tone of your icon depending on the theme being used. This is to allow a single icon image to be used for both the light and dark phone themes.

Although icon button images can be either in PNG or JPG format, avoid using JPG as this format does not support transparency and does not work well with the automatic tone conversion. All white pixels in a JPG image are replaced with the application bar's foreground color.

> **NOTE**
>
> The `ApplicationBarIconButton.IconUri` is limited to relative URIs. Relative component URIs are not supported, nor are images located on the Web. Attempting to use an absolute URI will cause an `ArgumentException` to be thrown at runtime.

Retrieving a Button or Menu Item at Runtime

While the built-in application bar allows you to assign names to buttons and menu items in XAML using the `x:Name` attribute, the CLR runs into trouble resolving items by name at runtime. Consider the following example:

```xml
<phoneNavigation:PhoneApplicationPage.ApplicationBar>
    <shell:ApplicationBar>
        <shell:ApplicationBar.Buttons>
            <shell:ApplicationBarIconButton
                IconUri="/Images/Play.png"
                Click="OnPlayButtonClick" />
            <shell:ApplicationBarIconButton
                x:Name="PauseButton"
                IconUri="/Images/Pause.png"
                Click="OnPlayButtonClick"
                IsEnabled="True" />
        </shell:ApplicationBar.Buttons>
    </shell:ApplicationBar>
</phoneNavigation:PhoneApplicationPage.ApplicationBar>
```

When the `PlayButton` is tapped, it raises the `Click` event, calling the `OnPlayButtonClick` method:

```csharp
void PlayButtonClick(object sender, EventArgs e)
{
    PauseButton.IsEnabled = true; /* Fails, PauseButton is always null */
}
```

This, however, raises a `NullReferenceException` because the named `PauseButton` is always null. This occurs despite Visual Studio providing intellisense for the named item. Thus, you cannot refer to an `ApplicationBarIconButton` or an `ApplicationBarMenuItem` by name in the code-beside. Instead, the `ApplicationBar.Buttons` property must be used to resolve a button, as shown:

```
void PlayButtonClick(object sender, EventArgs e)
{
    ApplicationBar.Buttons[1].IsEnabled = true;
}
```

This example highlights an earlier point regarding difficulties associated with the `ApplicationBar` being outside the Silverlight visual tree. It is an awkward class to develop with, and it has various limitations that make it a likely candidate for improvement in the future. In the meantime, however, I have created a wrapper for the class that behaves more as you would expect, yet possesses an almost identical API as the built-in `ApplicationBar`. The name of this custom wrapper class is `AppBar`, and it is the focus of the rest of this chapter.

Introducing the Custom `AppBar`

So far in this chapter we have examined the `ApplicationBar` and seen its limitations. This section examines a custom application bar called `AppBar`, which is an `ItemsControl` that wraps the built-in `ApplicationBar` class to provide support for data binding, button and menu item visibility, and commanding. `AppBar` also provides various extended buttons and menu items, such as a toggle button, which allows you to bind to multiple commands.

In this section you see how it is possible to bind to the various application bar, icon button, and menu item properties.

In Chapter 10, "Pivot and Panorama," you see how to leverage some additional features of the `AppBar` to assign a different application bar for each `PivotItem` in a `Pivot` control.

`AppBar` and associated classes are available in the downloadable sample code but are maintained within the Calcium project at http://www.calciumsdk.com. I recommend downloading the maintained version.

AppBar **Buttons and Menu Items**

`AppBar` is accompanied by the following list of button and menu item controls:

▶ **`AppBarIconButton`**—Provides the same functionality as the built-in `ApplicationBarIconButton`, but with added support for data binding and commanding.

▶ **`AppBarMenuItem`**—Provides the same functionality as the built-in `ApplicationBarMenuItem`, but with added support for data binding and commanding.

▶ **`AppBarToggleButton` and `AppBarToggleMenuItem`**—Adds support for dual states, each containing a separate `Text` value, `Command`, `CommandParameter`, and in the case of the `AppBarToggleButton`, dual `IconUri` properties.

▶ **AppBarHyperlinkButton** and **AppBarHyperlinkMenuItem**—Allows you to launch a local or external URL directly from the button and provides a bindable NavigateUri property.

Button and Menu Item Visibility

AppBar brings some extended features, including the ability to show or hide a button or menu item using its Visibility property. This is not easily achievable with the built-in ApplicationBar class, because to hide an item in the application bar requires the item's removal from the ApplicationBar. AppBar takes care of this automatically by repopulating the application bar when the visibility of an item changes.

Sample Code

The sample code for this section is located in the ApplicationBarView and ApplicationBarViewModel classes in the downloadable sample code. This sample presents a simple interface for demonstrating various application bar properties. The following is a list of items demonstrated in the sample:

▶ Data binding AppBar menu items and buttons to viewmodel commands

▶ Modifying the foreground, background, and opacity of the application bar via data binding

▶ Using a toggle button within the AppBar to modify the ApplicationBarIconButton's icon, text, and behavior based on a toggle state value

▶ Using a toggle menu item in the AppBar to modify the ApplicationBarMenuItem's text and behavior based on a toggle state value

▶ Using the menu item's Click event

▶ Using a hyperlink button and menu item to navigate to internal and external URIs

The ApplicationBarViewModel class contains several commands that are used by the buttons and menu items in the view. These commands modify the state of the viewmodel, which in turn changes the application bar, system tray, and layout within the view.

The viewmodel's Colors property allows you to experiment with the background and foreground colors of the application bar. The colors collection is populated using reflection to obtain the Color values from the System.Windows.Media.Colors class, as shown:

```
static IEnumerable<Color> GetColors()
{
    /* Use reflection to get known colors. */
    Type colorsType = typeof(Colors);
    PropertyInfo[] propertyInfos = colorsType.GetProperties(
        BindingFlags.Public | BindingFlags.Static);
```

```
    List<Color> knownColors = new List<Color>();
    foreach (PropertyInfo propertyInfo in propertyInfos)
    {
        try
        {
            Color color = (Color)propertyInfo.GetValue(null, null);
            knownColors.Add(color);
        }
        catch (Exception ex)
        {
            continue;
        }
    }

    return knownColors;
}

public void AddKnownColor(Color color)
{
    colors.Add(color);
}
```

The AddKnownColor method is used by the view to provide the viewmodel with some default colors, as shown in the following excerpt:

```
public ApplicationBarView()
{
    InitializeComponent();
    ApplicationBarViewModel viewModel = new ApplicationBarViewModel();
    DataContext = viewModel;

    /* Let the viewmodel know what the foreground
     * and background colors are for the application bar. */
    Color foregroundColor = ((SolidColorBrush)Foreground).Color;
    Color backgroundColor = (Color)Resources["PhoneChromeColor"];
    viewModel.AddKnownColor(foregroundColor);
    viewModel.AddKnownColor(backgroundColor);
    viewModel.BackgroundColor = backgroundColor;
    viewModel.ForegroundColor = foregroundColor;
}
```

The AppBar is instantiated in the view via XAML (see Listing 8.1). Data bindings are used to set various properties of the AppBar.

The first AppBarIconButton executes the viewmodel's SimpleCommand.

The AppBarToggleButton uses the Muted property of the viewmodel to determine which command is active, and which text and icon to display. When the viewmodel's Muted property is false, it indicates that the button is not toggled, and Text1 and Icon1Uri are displayed, and Command1 becomes active. Conversely, when Muted is true it indicates that the button is toggled, and Text2 and Icon2Uri are displayed. A second command can be specified if necessary. If a secondary property is not specified, then the control falls back to the primary (non-toggled property). For example, if Text2 is not specified, and the Toggled property is true, then Text1 is used.

AppBarToggleMenuItem works in the same manner as AppBarToggleButton but lacks the icon URI properties as the built-in application bar does not support icons in menu items.

An AppBarHyperlinkButton is used to navigate to an external URL. The AppBarHyperlinkButton uses a WebBrowserTask to launch the phone's built-in web browser. The WebBrowserTask is discussed further in Chapter 12, "Launchers and Choosers."

An AppBarHyperlinkMenuItem is used to navigate to a relative URL to the main page of the phone app.

LISTING 8.1   ApplicationBarView.xaml AppBar

```xml
<u:AppBar IsVisible="{Binding ApplicationBarVisible}"
          IsMenuEnabled="{Binding MenuEnabled}"
          BarOpacity="{Binding BarOpacity}"
          BackgroundColor="{Binding BackgroundColor}"
          ForegroundColor="{Binding ForegroundColor}"
          Mode="{Binding Mode}">

    <u:AppBarIconButton
        Command="{Binding SimpleCommand}"
                            CommandParameter="Rewind"
        Text="Rewind"
        IconUri="/ControlExamples/MediaView/Images/Rewind.png"
        Visibility="{Binding FirstButtonVisible, Mode=TwoWay,
                    Converter={StaticResource BooleanToVisibilityConverter}}"/>

    <u:AppBarToggleButton
        x:Name="button_Mute"
        Command1="{Binding ToggleMuteCommand}"
        Text1="Mute"
        Icon1Uri="/ControlExamples/MediaView/Images/Speaker.png"
        Text2="Un-Mute"
        Icon2Uri="/ControlExamples/MediaView/Images/Mute.png"
        Toggled="{Binding Muted}" />

    <u:AppBarHyperlinkButton
        IconUri="/ControlExamples/Images/appbar.upload.rest.png"
        Text="blog"
```

LISTING 8.1   Continued

```
            NavigateUri="http://danielvaughan.org" />

    <u:AppBar.MenuItems>

        <u:AppBarMenuItem Text="MenuItem with Click Handler"
                          Click="AppBarMenuItem_Click" />

        <u:AppBarMenuItem Text="MenuItem with Command"
                          Command="{Binding SimpleCommand}"
                          CommandParameter="This custom AppBar rocks!" />

        <u:AppBarMenuItem Text="FullScreen"
                          Command="{Binding FullScreenCommand}"
                          CommandParameter="true" />

        <u:AppBarToggleMenuItem
            Command1="{Binding ToggleMuteCommand}"
            Text1="Mute"
            Text2="Unmute"
            Toggled="{Binding Muted}" />

        <u:AppBarHyperlinkMenuItem Text="Main Page"
                                   NavigateUri="/MainPage.xaml" />

    </u:AppBar.MenuItems>
</u:AppBar>
```

The `ApplicationBarView` page uses a `CheckBox` to toggle the `AppBar.IsMenuEnabled` property, a `Slider` for the `AppBar.BarOpacity` property, and two Silverlight Toolkit `ListPicker` controls to change the background and foreground colors of the application bar (see Figure 8.2).

Although `AppBar` menu items and icon buttons support `ICommand`s, they also still support `Click` events. Tapping the first menu item causes an event hander to be called in the code-beside:

```
void AppBarMenuItem_Click(object sender, System.EventArgs e)
{
    ViewModel.Message = "Click event raised.";
}
```

> **NOTE**
>
> The `Click` event is raised regardless of whether a command has been specified for the button or menu item.

FIGURE 8.2   The sample application bar view

Disabling the Application Bar Menu

The view contains a check box that is bound to the viewmodel's `MenuEnabled` property:

```
<CheckBox IsChecked="{Binding MenuEnabled, Mode=TwoWay}"
          Content="Application Bar Menu Enabled" />
```

The `AppBar IsMenuEnabled` property is also bound to the viewmodel's `MenuEnabled` property, so that when the check box is checked or unchecked, the menu is enabled or disabled, respectively. By unchecking the check box, the application bar will not expand the menu when the expand button is tapped.

Minimizing the Icon Button Tray

Recall that the `Mode` property is used to minimize the application bar so that just the bar's ellipsis is shown.

In the sample, a custom `IValueConverter` called `ApplicationBarModeToBooleanConverter` converts the viewmodel's `Mode` property, which is of type `ApplicationBarMode`, to a Boolean value (see Listing 8.2).

LISTING 8.2   `ApplicationBarModeToBooleanConverter` Class

```
public class ApplicationBarModeToBooleanConverter : IValueConverter
{
    public object Convert(
```

LISTING 8.2   Continued

```
        object value, Type targetType, object parameter, CultureInfo culture)
    {
        ApplicationBarMode mode = (ApplicationBarMode)value;
        return mode != ApplicationBarMode.Default;
    }

    public object ConvertBack(
        object value, Type targetType, object parameter, CultureInfo culture)
    {
        bool minimized = (bool)value;
        return minimized
                ? ApplicationBarMode.Minimized : ApplicationBarMode.Default;
    }
}
```

The IValueConverter is defined as a page level resource.

The view contains a minimized CheckBox that is bound to the mode property, as shown:

```
<CheckBox IsChecked="{Binding Mode,
    Converter={StaticResource ApplicationBarModeToBooleanConverter}, Mode=TwoWay}"
    Content="minimized" />
```

The custom AppBar allows you to bind the Mode property of the application bar, which is demonstrated in the sample using the minimized button (see Figure 8.3).

Changing the Opacity of the Application Bar

To change the opacity of the application bar move the *application bar opacity* slider. The Slider is bound to the viewmodel's BarOpacity property, as shown:

```
<Slider Value="{Binding BarOpacity, Mode=TwoWay}"
        Maximum="1"
        LargeChange=".1" />
```

Changing the viewmodel's BarOpacity causes the AppBar.BarOpacity to be updated. Positioning the Slider all the way to the left causes the application bar background to be completely transparent.

Switching to Full-Screen

Switching to full-screen implies hiding the system tray and the application bar in its entirety. The early official Windows Phone architecture documents mention a supposed FullScreen property. Yet, in the final version of the SDK, no such property existed. No matter, because going full-screen involves simply hiding the system tray and the application bar. This is made rather easy by using the data binding capabilities of the custom

AppBar class. Fortunately the system tray's visibility is specified using a Boolean attached property called SystemTray.IsVisible. As a consequence, in the view, we are able to bind this property to a viewmodel property, like so:

```
shell:SystemTray.IsVisible="{Binding SystemTrayVisible}"
```

FIGURE 8.3   Checking the minimized button causes the icon button tray to collapse.

A menu item is used to execute a viewmodel command called FullScreenCommand, which sets the viewmodel's SystemTrayVisible and ApplicationBarVisible properties to false, effectively hiding both items (see Figure 8.4).

A simple Ellipse element is provided to allow the user to return from full-screen mode. The ellipse markup makes use of the custom commanding infrastructure.

The Ellipse class does not provide a Tap event, and so a non-default event MouseLeftButtonUp is specified using the Commanding.Event attached property, as shown:

```
<Ellipse dv:Commanding.Command="{Binding FullScreenCommand}"
        dv:Commanding.CommandParameter="false"
        dv:Commanding.Event="MouseLeftButtonUp"
        Visibility="{Binding ApplicationBarVisible,
            Converter={StaticResource BooleanToVisibilityConverter},
            ConverterParameter=Collapsed}"
        Fill="{StaticResource PhoneAccentBrush}"
        Width="50"
```

```
Height="15"
HorizontalAlignment="Right"
VerticalAlignment="Bottom" />
```

FIGURE 8.4   Full-screen mode is achieved by hiding the system tray and application bar.

The custom `BooleanToVisibilityConverter` is used to hide or show the ellipse depending on the value of the viewmodel's `ApplicationBarVisible` property.

Modifying the Application Bar's Foreground and Background Colors

Two Silverlight Toolkit `ListPicker` controls are populated with a collection of colors, allowing you to try out variations of the application bar's foreground (text and icon) color and background color. Selecting a color from either `ListPicker` changes the corresponding viewmodel `Color` property, which changes the appearance of the application bar.

For more information on the Silverlight Toolkit `ListPicker` control, see Chapter 9, "Silverlight Toolkit Controls."

A custom `IValueConverter` is used to convert to and from a `Color` value and a `SolidColorBrush`, allowing color bands to be rendered in the `ListPicker` (see Listing 8.3).

LISTING 8.3   ColorToBrushConverter Class

```
public class ColorToBrushConverter : IValueConverter
{
    public object Convert(
```

LISTING 8.3   Continued

```
        object value, Type targetType, object parameter, CultureInfo culture)
    {
        if (value == null)
        {
            return null;
        }
        return new SolidColorBrush((Color)value);
    }

    public object ConvertBack(
        object value, Type targetType, object parameter, CultureInfo culture)
    {
        if (value == null)
        {
            return null;
        }
        return ((SolidColorBrush)value).Color;
    }
}
```

Each ListPicker is populated via a binding to the Colors property of the viewmodel. A DataTemplate, defined as a page resource named ColorPickerItemTemplate, determines how each Color is rendered within the ListPicker:

```
<phone:PhoneApplicationPage.Resources>
    <ValueConverters:ColorToBrushConverter x:Key="ColorToBrushConverter" />
    <l:ApplicationBarModeToBooleanConverter
            x:Key="ApplicationBarModeToBooleanConverter" />

    <DataTemplate x:Name="ColorPickerItemTemplate">
        <Rectangle
            Fill="{Binding .,
                    Converter={StaticResource ColorToBrushConverter}}"
            Width="400" Height="20" Margin="0,10,0,10" />
    </DataTemplate>
</phone:PhoneApplicationPage.Resources>
```

When the user selects a color, a property is updated in the viewmodel via the SelectedItem property of the ListPicker, as shown:

```
<toolkit:ListPicker Header="application bar background color"
    ItemsSource="{Binding Colors}"
    SelectedItem="{Binding BackgroundColor, Mode=TwoWay}"
    ItemTemplate="{StaticResource ColorPickerItemTemplate}"
    FullModeItemTemplate="{StaticResource ColorPickerItemTemplate}" />
```

Customizing the Appearance of the System Tray

Unlike the `ApplicationBar`, the `SystemTray` class uses dependency properties, making it compatible with Silverlight's data binding infrastructure. `SystemTray` has the following four display related properties:

- ► `BackgroundColor`

- ► `ForegroundColor`

- ► `Opacity`

- ► `IsVisible`

Each of these properties coincides with the `ApplicationBar` properties. In the sample, the `SystemTray` is bound to the same viewmodel properties as the `AppBar`, as shown:

```
<phone:PhoneApplicationPage
...
    shell:SystemTray.IsVisible="{Binding SystemTrayVisible}"
    shell:SystemTray.BackgroundColor="{Binding BackgroundColor}"
    shell:SystemTray.ForegroundColor="{Binding ForegroundColor}"
    shell:SystemTray.Opacity="{Binding BarOpacity}">
...
</phone:PhoneApplicationPage>
```

Thus, when you alter the appearance of the application bar, the changes are also applied to the system tray.

Inside the AppBar Control

`AppBar` is a custom `ItemsControl` that wraps a `Microsoft.Phone.Shell.ApplicationBar`. As it is an `ItemsControl`, it enables you to add buttons and menu items to it, either in code or in XAML, in a manner not unlike the built-in `ApplicationBar`.

When the `AppBar` control is first loaded, it sets the host page's `ApplicationBar` to its own `ApplicationBar` field.

The `AppBar.Build` method is used to populate the `ApplicationBar` and is called in the following situations:

- ► When its `Loaded` event is raised

- ► When its collection of buttons or menu items changes

- ► When a button or menu item's visibility changes

The `Build` method calls the `BuildAux` method and prevents cycles from occurring while building is taking place, as shown:

```
bool building;

void Build()
{
    if (building)
    {
        return;
    }

    try
    {
        building = true;
        BuildAux();
    }
    finally
    {
        building = false;
    }
}
```

After requesting notification of button and menu item visibility changes, discussed in a moment, the `Build` method collects the members of its `ItemCollection` and, depending on their type, adds them to the `ApplicationBar`'s `Buttons` or `MenuItems` collection (see Listing 8.4).

LISTING 8.4   AppBar.BuildAux Method

```
void BuildAux()
{
    applicationBar.Buttons.Clear();
    applicationBar.MenuItems.Clear();

    foreach (FrameworkElement item in Items.OfType<FrameworkElement>())
    {
        RegisterForNotification("Visibility", item);
    }

    var buttonList = (from button in Items.Where(notUIElementOrVisibleFunc)
                            .OfType<IApplicationBarIconButtonProvider>()
                    select button.Button).ToList();

    if (buttonList.Count > 4)
    {
        buttonList = buttonList.Take(4).ToList();
    }
```

LISTING 8.4   Continued

```
    applicationBar.Buttons.AddRange(buttonList);

    var menuItemList = (from item in Items.Where(notUIElementOrVisibleFunc)
                        .OfType<IApplicationBarMenuItemProvider>()
                    select item.MenuItem).ToList();

    applicationBar.MenuItems.AddRange(menuItemList);
}
```

Two classes, AppBarIconButtonBase and AppBarMenuItemBase, provide an extensibility point that allows you to create your own custom application bar buttons or menu items. If they do not suit your needs, however, you can opt to implement IApplicationBarIconButton Provider and IApplicationBarMenuItemProvider instead.

The task of the custom AppBar items, such as the AppBarIconButton and the AppBarMenuItem, is to wrap an instance of the corresponding built-in ApplicationBar IconButton or ApplicationBarMenuItem, and to expose the wrapped item's properties as dependency properties.

Both IApplicationBarIconButtonProvider and IApplicationBarMenuItemProvider have a single property that is used to retrieve the actual ApplicationBarIconButton or ApplicationBarMenuItem.

During population of the ApplicationBar's Buttons and MenuItems properties within the AppBar.BuildAux method, a Func named notUIElementOrVisibleFunc is used to determine the visibility of an item, as shown:

```
readonly Func<object, bool> notUIElementOrVisibleFunc
    = x =>
    {
        var element = x as UIElement;
        return element == null || element.Visibility == Visibility.Visible;
    };
```

Monitoring Item Visibility

No built-in event exists to monitor the Visibility property of UIElements. Therefore, to be notified when a button or menu item's visibility changes, we rely on an attached property and a custom AppBar method called RegisterForNotification, which uses a Binding to listen for button and menu item visibility changes. See the following excerpt:

```
void RegisterForNotification(
    string propertyName,
    FrameworkElement element)
```

```
{
    BindingExpression expression
        = element.GetBindingExpression(ItemVisibilityProperty);
    if (expression == null)
    {
        Binding binding = new Binding(propertyName) { Source = element };
        element.SetBinding(ItemVisibilityProperty, binding);
    }
}
```

Extending the Icon and Menu Item Base Classes

AppBarHyperlinkButton subclasses AppBarIconButtonBase to provide support for page navigation and navigation to external resources (see Listing 8.5).

When the base class's Click event is raised, the PhoneApplicationFrame navigates to the NavigateUri property. If the Uri is an external resource, then the WebBrowserTask is used instead.

LISTING 8.5   AppBarHyperlinkButton Class

```
public class AppBarHyperlinkButton : AppBarIconButtonBase
{
    public static readonly DependencyProperty NavigateUriProperty
        = DependencyProperty.RegisterAttached(
            "NavigateUri",
            typeof(Uri),
            typeof(AppBarHyperlinkButton),
            null);

    public Uri NavigateUri
    {
        get
        {
            return (Uri)GetValue(NavigateUriProperty);
        }
        set
        {
            SetValue(NavigateUriProperty, value);
        }
    }

    protected override void OnClick(EventArgs e)
    {
        base.OnClick(e);
        Navigate();
    }
```

LISTING 8.5   Continued

```
void Navigate()
{
    Uri uri = NavigateUri;
    if (uri == null)
    {
        return;
    }

    if (uri.IsAbsoluteUri)
    {
        WebBrowserTask task = new WebBrowserTask { Uri = uri };
        task.Show();
        return;
    }

    var frame = Application.Current.RootVisual as PhoneApplicationFrame;
    if (frame == null)
    {
        return;
    }

    frame.Navigate(uri);
}
}
```

Several `AppBar` items are in the downloadable sample code, which you are free to use in your own code. If you spend time using the built-in `ApplicationBar` I am certain you will appreciate the benefits of wrapping it in a more developer friendly class like the `AppBar`.

Summary

This chapter explored the built-in application bar and its associated button and menu item classes. The application bar can contain up to 4 icon buttons and up to 50 menu items. For reasons of usability, the number of menu items should be restricted to 6 or fewer.

This chapter was mostly devoted to a custom application bar, which is a wrapper for the built-in application bar, and which overcomes many of the built-in application bar's inherent limitations. The custom `AppBar` class improves on its built-in counterpart by providing support for data binding, `ICommands`, toggle buttons, hyperlink buttons, and controlling the visibility of menu items and buttons at runtime. Moreover, it is more compatible with design patterns like MVVM, which rely on data binding.

`AppBarToggleButton` and `AppBarToggleMenuItem` allow you to define two sets of properties that become active depending on the state of a bindable `Toggle` property.

`AppBarHyperlinkButton` and `AppBarHyperlinkMenuItem` have a bindable `NavigateUri` property that allows you to navigate to a local or external URI.

CHAPTER 9

Silverlight Toolkit Controls

The Silverlight for Windows Phone Toolkit (henceforth referred to as just *Toolkit*) is a Microsoft open-source project that offers developers an additional set of components designed to match the rich user experience of Windows Phone and the Metro design aesthetic.

The Toolkit continues to enlarge Microsoft's offering beyond the official Phone Developer Tools. Over time, new components have been added to the Toolkit, and because the Toolkit has a shorter iteration cycle than the Windows Phone Developer Tools, it means that Microsoft is able to introduce new components more quickly and respond faster to the developer community.

One example of a control that benefited from the shorter release cycle is the progress bar control. After the first release of the `ProgressBar` as part of the FCL, it was found to be deficient in the area of performance, subsequently an alternative progress bar was introduced into the Toolkit.

The downside of the Toolkit is that components may not necessarily undergo as much scrutiny before they are released as those in the framework class library (FCL), and therefore may not be as polished as those that eventually make it into the FCL.

The Toolkit provides components that are fundamental to development on the platform. If you are doing Windows Phone development, then you should be using it.

This chapter begins with a short getting started guide, which shows how to obtain and reference the Toolkit. It then explores each Toolkit component.

This chapter is a long one. Please do not feel obligated to read it from start to end. Feel free to skip through, and refer back to it when you need to.

Getting Started with the Toolkit

The Toolkit is hosted on CodePlex.com. CodePlex is a site dedicated to open-source software. Projects hosted on CodePlex must include source code. This means that, unlike the rest of the Windows Phone FCL, the Toolkit source code is freely available and can even be modified by you under the MSPL license.

Download and install the latest release of the Silverlight for Windows Phone Toolkit from http://silverlight.codeplex.com.

To use the Toolkit in your project, add a reference to the Microsoft.Phone.Controls. Toolkit.dll assembly (see Figure 9.1).

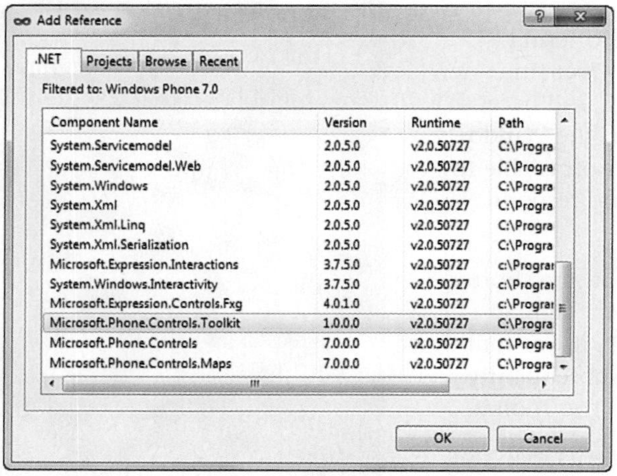

FIGURE 9.1   Adding a reference to the Toolkit assembly

Accompanying the Toolkit download are a myriad of examples that you may find worthwhile exploring. The Toolkit and samples get updated frequently so be sure to get the latest version from CodePlex.

This chapter also provides examples for each control, but often with a twist, and most examples seen here employ the MVVM pattern when demonstrating the functionality of each component.

To use components of the Toolkit in XAML add the following namespace definition to the top of your XAML file:

```
xmlns:toolkit="clr-namespace:
    Microsoft.Phone.Controls;assembly=Microsoft.Phone.Controls.Toolkit"
```

Subsequent sections look at each of the following components within the Toolkit (excluding those that have been described elsewhere in other chapters):

- ▶ ListPicker

- ▶ AutoCompleteBox

- ▶ ContextMenu

- ▶ DatePicker and TimePicker

- ▶ LoopingSelector

- ▶ LongListSelector

- ▶ Page transitions (presented in Chapter 4, "Page Orientation")

- ▶ PerformanceProgressBar

- ▶ TiltEffect

- ▶ ToggleSwitch

- ▶ WrapPanel

- ▶ GestureService (presented in Chapter 11, "Touch")

- ▶ GestureListener (presented in Chapter 11)

ListPicker

Due to the relatively small screen size of the phone, it can be awkward displaying a large number of options to the user without resorting to the use of a second page. At development time, you may not know the number of options that will be displayed, making the choice of using an in-place selection mechanism such as a ListBox or a dedicated option selection page difficult. Moreover, navigating to a page to retrieve a response from a user is cumbersome and entails handling navigation events and so forth.

Fortunately, the ListPicker solves this problem by enabling the user to select from a list of options, either with an expandable in-place picker (if the number of items is small) or with a full-screen picker (if the number of items is large). The ListPicker allows you to tailor the number of items that can be displayed using the expandable picker, according to the design and space requirements of your UI.

ListPicker is an invaluable control for Windows Phone development. It is also highly customizable; through the use of custom data templates, you can change the way the in-place and full-screen pickers are displayed.

ListPicker is most appropriate where the user has several options, and where it makes sense to display only one option while the control does not have focus, such as on a settings page. Conversely, ListPicker is not appropriate for displaying long lists of data, where the user is more likely to prefer viewing all options in-place; scenarios like the built-in People or Marketplace applications are better served by a `ListBox` or the Toolkit's `LongListSelector`, presented later in this chapter.

Display Modes

`ListPicker` is displayed in three modes: normal, expanded, and full-screen.

When in normal mode, the `ListPicker` is inactive and does not have focus, and displays its selected item while hiding the rest.

In expanded mode, the `ListPicker` resizes itself to display all items. This works best when there are only a few items to display. Page content is positioned to accommodate the size of the expanded `ListPicker`, and then is repositioned when the `ListPicker` contracts when an item is selected (see Figure 9.2).

FIGURE 9.2   `ListPicker` in expanded mode

When in full-screen mode, the `ListPicker` presents options using a pop-up, which hides the rest of the page content. Full-screen mode is appropriate when the number of options to choose from is large (see Figure 9.3).

The `ListPicker.ItemCountThreshold` property determines the maximum number of items for which expanded mode is used. If the number of items exceeds this value, full-screen mode is used instead of expanded mode. `ItemCountThreshold` default value is five.

FIGURE 9.3   ListPicker in full-screen mode

You can determine the current state of a `ListPicker` via its `ListPickerMode` property. `ListPickerMode` may be one of the following values:

- ▶ **Normal**—Only the selected value is visible.
- ▶ **Expanded**—The `ListPicker` is displaying all of its items by expanding inline and displacing other page content.
- ▶ **Full**—A dedicated pop-up displays all items.

The `ListPicker` sample uses the MVVM pattern. The `ListPickerViewModel` creates and exposes a list of `City` objects, which is then presented using a `ListPicker` in the view.

The `City` class has a `Name` and a `Description` property (see Listing 9.1).

LISTING 9.1   City Class

```
public class City
{
    public string Name { get; private set; }
    public string Description { get; private set; }

    public City(string name, string description)
    {
        Name = name;
        Description = description;
    }
}
```

The viewmodel creates several `City` objects as shown:

```
readonly IEnumerable<City> cities = new List<City>
    {
        new City("Prague", "Capital of the Czech Republic."),
        /* Removed for brevity. */
        new City("Los Angeles", "Most populous city in California.")
    };

public IEnumerable<City> Cities
{
    get
    {
        return cities;
    }
}
```

The second task of the viewmodel is to keep track of the currently selected `City`, using a property named `City`.

The view contains a `ListPicker` whose `ItemsSource` property is bound to the viewmodel's `Cities` property. In addition, the `ListPicker.SelectedItem` property uses a two-way data binding to the `City` property, so that when the user selects an item in the `ListPicker`, the `City` property is set to the selected value. See the following excerpt:

```
<toolkit:ListPicker ItemsSource="{Binding Cities}"
            ItemCountThreshold="20"
            SelectedItem="{Binding City, Mode=TwoWay}"
            Header="city"
            FullModeHeader="city">
    <toolkit:ListPicker.FullModeItemTemplate>
        <DataTemplate>
            <StackPanel>
                <TextBlock Text="{Binding Name}"
                    FontSize="{StaticResource PhoneFontSizeNormal}" />
                <TextBlock Text="{Binding Description}"
                    FontSize="{StaticResource PhoneFontSizeSmall}"
                    Foreground="#ff666666" />
            </StackPanel>
        </DataTemplate>
    </toolkit:ListPicker.FullModeItemTemplate>
    <toolkit:ListPicker.ItemTemplate>
        <DataTemplate>
            <StackPanel>
                <TextBlock Text="{Binding Name}"
                    FontSize="{StaticResource PhoneFontSizeNormal}" />
                <TextBlock Text="{Binding Description}"
```

```
                    FontSize="{StaticResource PhoneFontSizeSmall}"
                    Foreground="#ff666666" />
        </StackPanel>
      </DataTemplate>
    </toolkit:ListPicker.ItemTemplate>
</toolkit:ListPicker>
```

You see that a custom `DataTemplate` is defined for both the Expanded and Full `ListPickerMode` values. If the `ListPicker` is populated with a list of strings (or objects whose `ToString` method affords an appropriate representation of the object), then providing a custom `DataTemplate` for each of these modes is in most cases not necessary, as the built-in templates suffice.

The `FullModeHeader` property defines the content placed at the top of the item list when the `ListPickerMode` is equal to Full. The `FullModeHeader` property can be defined not only as a string, but also using a `DataTemplate`, much like the `ItemTemplate` and `FullModeItemTemplate`. The `FullModeHeader` property is not required (see Figure 9.4).

FIGURE 9.4   `ListPicker` with a custom `ItemTemplate`

AutoCompleteBox

The `AutoCompleteBox` displays suggestions in a drop-down list as the user enters text into a text box. The `AutoCompleteBox` control is composed of a `TextBox` and a `ListBox` that is made visible when the `TextBox` has focus.

The `TextBox` on which `AutoCompleteBox` relies is part of its default template. The `AutoCompleteBox` shares many of the `TextBox` control's characteristics, including a `Text` property, which allows you to set the text displayed.

Moreover, the `AutoCompleteBox` contains an `InputScope` property that allows you to set the keyboard shown on the Software Input Panel (SIP). For more information on `InputScope`, see Chapter 6, "Text Elements."

TIP

The `TextBox` control has built-in suggestion support using word completion when its `InputScope` is set to Text. If you do not need to customize the style or list of possible suggestions, then the `TextBox` may be preferable.

The simplest way to have an `AutoCompleteBox` display suggestions is to assign it a predefined list of strings. Place an `AutoCompleteBox` on a page, like so:

```
<toolkit:AutoCompleteBox x:Name="autoCompleteBox" />
```

Then, set its `ItemsSource` property to the list, as shown:

```
List<string> suggestions = new List<string>
                {
                        "Prague",
                        "Geneva",
                        "Canberra",
                        ...

                };

autoCompleteBox.ItemsSource = cities;
```

When the user enters text into the `AutoCompleteBox`, list items that begin with the string are displayed as suggestions (see Figure 9.5).

NOTE

At the time of writing the `AutoCompleteBox` has a bug that prevents the suggestion list from being displayed correctly when the control is placed within a `Pivot` or `Panorama`. This can be remedied by applying a custom template as documented on the blog of Jeff Wilcox, http://bit.ly/ecLlo1.

Using AutoCompleteBox with MVVM

This section looks at controlling an `AutoCompleteBox` from a viewmodel. The example code for this section is located in the `AutoCompleteBoxView` and `AutoCompleteBoxViewModel` in the downloadable sample code.

`AutoCompleteBox` provides various ways for selecting the items to be displayed in the suggestion list. The `AutoCompleteBox.FilterMode` property allows you to specify how entered text is matched with items in the suggestion list. When a match occurs, the item is displayed in the selection list. If `AutoCompleteFilterMode` is not specified then the StartsWith filter mode is used, which is a case-insensitive filter where the returned items start with the entered text. Table 9.1 lists the `FilterMode` values.

FIGURE 9.5   `AutoCompleteBox` displays a list of suggestions as the user enters text.

TABLE 9.1   `AutoCompleteFilterMode` Enum Values

Enum Value	Description
Contains	Specifies a culture-sensitive, case-insensitive filter where the returned items contain the specified text.
ContainsCaseSensitive	Specifies a culture-sensitive, case-sensitive filter where the returned items contain the specified text.
ContainsOrdinal	Specifies an ordinal, case-insensitive filter where the returned items contain the specified text.
ContainsOrdinalCaseSensitive	Specifies an ordinal, case-sensitive filter where the returned items contain the specified text.
Custom	Specifies that a custom filter is used. This mode is used when the `System.Windows.Controls.` `AutoCompleteBox.TextFilter` or `System.Windows.Controls.AutoCompleteBox.` `ItemFilter` properties are set. This filter mode is explored later in the chapter.

6

TABLE 9.1   Continued

Enum Value	Description
Equals	Specifies a culture-sensitive, case-insensitive filter, where the returned items equal the specified text. The filter uses the `System.String.Equals(System.String,System.StringComparison)` method, specifying `System.StringComparer.CurrentCultureIgnoreCase` as the search comparison criteria.
EqualsCaseSensitive	Specifies a culture-sensitive, case-sensitive filter where the returned items equal the specified text. The filter uses the `System.String.Equals(System.String,System.StringComparison)` method, specifying `System.StringComparer.CurrentCulture` as the string comparison criteria.
EqualsOrdinal	Specifies an ordinal, case-insensitive filter where the returned items equal the specified text. The filter uses the `System.String.Equals(System.String,System.StringComparison)` method, specifying `System.StringComparer.OrdinalIgnoreCase` as the string comparison criteria.
EqualsOrdinalCaseSensitive	Specifies an ordinal, case-sensitive filter where the returned items equal the specified text. The filter uses the `System.String.Equals(System.String,System.StringComparison)` method, specifying `System.StringComparer.Ordinal` as the string comparison criteria.
None	Specifies that no filter is used. All items are returned.
StartsWith	This is the default `ItemFilter` value. Specifies a culture-sensitive, case-insensitive filter where the returned items start with the specified text. The filter uses the `System.String.StartsWith(System.String,System.StringComparison)` method, specifying `System.StringComparer.CurrentCultureIgnoreCase` as the string comparison criteria.
StartsWithCaseSensitive	Specifies a culture-sensitive, case-sensitive filter where the returned items start with the specified text. The filter uses the `System.String.StartsWith(System.String,System.StringComparison)` method, specifying `System.StringComparer.CurrentCulture` as the string comparison criteria.
StartsWithOrdinal	Specifies an ordinal, case-insensitive filter where the returned items start with the specified text. The filter uses the `System.String.StartsWith(System.String,System.StringComparison)` method, specifying `System.StringComparer.OrdinalIgnoreCase` as the string comparison criteria.

TABLE 9.1   Continued

Enum Value	Description
StartsWithOrdinalCaseSensitive	Specifies an ordinal, case-sensitive filter where the returned items start with the specified text. The filter uses the System.String.StartsWith(System.String,System.StringComparison) method, specifying System.StringComparer.Ordinal as the string comparison criteria.

To demonstrate the FilterMode, we place a FilterMode property in the viewmodel and then bind the AutoCompleteBox.FilterMode property to it. The viewmodel's FilterMode property is shown in the following excerpt:

```
AutoCompleteFilterMode filterMode;

public AutoCompleteFilterMode FilterMode
{
    get
    {
        return filterMode;
    }
    set
    {
        Assign(() => FilterMode, ref filterMode, value);
    }
}
```

We bind the ItemsSource property of the AutoCompleteBox to the Suggestions property of the viewmodel. A two-way data binding is used to allow the AutoCompleteBox to update the FilterMode when a custom filter is supplied:

```
<toolkit:AutoCompleteBox ItemsSource="{Binding Suggestions}"
                FilterMode="{Binding FilterMode, Mode=TwoWay}" />
```

The viewmodel also exposes a list of available FilterModes, as shown:

```
readonly List<AutoCompleteFilterMode> filterModes
    = new List<AutoCompleteFilterMode>
            {
                AutoCompleteFilterMode.Contains,
                AutoCompleteFilterMode.ContainsCaseSensitive,
                /* Enum values removed for brevity. */
                AutoCompleteFilterMode.StartsWithOrdinalCaseSensitive,
            };

public IEnumerable<AutoCompleteFilterMode> FilterModes
{
```

```
    get
    {
        return filterModes;
    }
}
```

This list is used by a ListPicker, which enables the user to select the filter mode to use. The ItemsSource of the ListPicker is bound to the FilterModes property, and its SelectedItem property uses a two-way data binding to the viewmodel's FilterMode property:

```
<toolkit:ListPicker ItemsSource="{Binding FilterModes}"
                    SelectedItem="{Binding FilterMode, Mode=TwoWay}" />
```

Selecting an alternate filter mode via the ListPicker changes the filtering behavior of the AutoCompleteBox (see Figure 9.6).

FIGURE 9.6   AutoCompleteBox with FilterMode set to StartsWithCaseSensitive

Defining a Custom Filter Using the ItemFilter Property

If none of the predefined filters suit your needs, the ItemFilter property of the AutoCompleteBox allows you to define a custom method for determining whether a suggestion item matches the entered text. This works well in conjunction with the MVVM pattern, as you see in this section.

To add custom filtering to an `AutoCompleteBox`, you first create a method that conforms to the `AutoCompleteFilterPredicate` delegate, shown here:

```
bool AutoCompleteFilterPredicate<T>(string search, T item)
```

Your custom filter method must accept a search string (the text entered by the user) and an item from the list of suggestions (usually defined by the `ItemsSource` property of the `AutoCompleteBox`), and it must return a Boolean value indicating whether to display the item in the suggestion list.

The sample code located in the `AutoCompleteBoxViewModel` class contains a custom filter method called `FilterOnLastLetter`. This custom filter method determines whether the suggestion item ends with the entered text. See the following excerpt:

```
static bool FilterOnLastLetter(string enteredText, object suggestionItem)
{
    if (suggestionItem != null
        && suggestionItem.ToString().ToLower().EndsWith(enteredText))
    {
        return true;
    }

    return false;
}
```

To allow an `AutoCompleteBox` to use this method, a public property called `ItemFilter` is placed in the viewmodel. The `FilterOnLastLetter` is declared as a static method so that it can be assigned to the `itemFilter` field from outside the viewmodel's constructor, as shown:

```
AutoCompleteFilterPredicate<object> itemFilter = FilterOnLastLetter;

public AutoCompleteFilterPredicate<object> ItemFilter
{
    get
    {
        return itemFilter;
    }
    private set
    {
        Assign(() => ItemFilter, ref itemFilter, value);
    }
}
```

With the `ItemFilter` property in place, the `AutoCompleteBox` is able to bind to the property like so:

```
<toolkit:AutoCompleteBox ItemsSource="{Binding Suggestions}"
                         FilterMode="{Binding FilterMode, Mode=TwoWay}"
                         ItemFilter="{Binding ItemFilter}" />
```

When a user enters text into the `AutoCompleteBox`, the custom filter method
(`FilterOnLastLetter`) is called for each item in the data bound `Cities` property. Only those
items ending with the entered text are displayed (see Figure 9.7).

FIGURE 9.7   An `AutoCompleteBox` with custom filtering

NOTE

When using custom filtering, the `AutoCompleteBox.FilterMode` property is automatically
set to Custom.

Dynamic Population of the Suggestion List

Until now you have looked at using only predefined suggestion lists. There are times,
however, when you may want to change the contents of the suggestion list based on
what the user has entered. One example is performing a web search for the entered text
and using the search results as the suggestion list. The user enters some text, and you call
a website to get a list of suggestions. Once the call completes you populate the
`ItemsSource` property of the `AutoCompleteBox`. This entails an asynchronous operation,

which means you need some way of telling the `AutoCompleteBox` to dispense with filtering until the result of the asynchronous call is obtained. Fortunately, the `AutoCompleteBox` contains a built-in mechanism for doing just this. By using the `AutoCompleteBox.Populating` event, you can safely coordinate the population of its suggestion list.

The following steps outline how to provide a dynamic list of suggestions as the user enters text.

1. Subscribe to the `Populating` event of the `AutoCompleteBox`.

2. When the event handler is called, set the `Cancel` property of the `PopulatingEventArgs` to true.

3. Populate the `ItemsSource` property of the `AutoCompleteBox`.

4. Call the `PopulateComplete` method of the `AutoCompleteBox` to signal that the `ItemsSource` property has been populated and can be filtered.

Let's walk through these steps. The `AutoCompleteBoxView`, in the downloadable sample code, contains an event handler for the `AutoCompleteBox Populating` event. When the handler is called, it cancels the event and calls the viewmodel's `Populate` method. When the viewmodel is finished retrieving the suggestions, perhaps from a web service, it calls the `AutoCompleteBox.PopulateComplete` method, which is provided as an `Action` parameter:

```
void AutoCompleteBox_Populating(object sender, PopulatingEventArgs e)
{
    e.Cancel = true;
    AutoCompleteBox box = (AutoCompleteBox)sender;
    ViewModel.Populate(e.Parameter, box.PopulateComplete);
}
```

The `Populate` method is designed to show how the population of a list might take place, though it does not perform an asynchronous operation. All that is done is to replace the suggestion list with another. We could, however, be using Bing or Google, for example, to perform a search. See the following excerpt:

```
public void Populate(string text, Action completeAction)
{
    Suggestions = new List<string>
                    {
                        "Daniel", "Sacha", "Marlon", "Pete",
                        "Josh", "Jaime", "Laurent", "Katka"
                    };
    if (completeAction != null)
    {
        completeAction();
    }
}
```

The specified `completeAction` eventually calls the `PopulateComplete` method of the `AutoCompleteBox`, at which point filtering is reengaged.

Upon setting the `FilterMode` of the `AutoCompleteBox` to Contains and entering a single character, the suggestion list is populated as shown in Figure 9.8.

FIGURE 9.8   The suggestion list is populated when the `AutoCompleteBox` text changes.

Styling the Suggestion List

`AutoCompleteBox` allows you to customize the presentation of suggestion items using its `ItemTemplate` property.

Sample code for this section is located in the `AutoCompleteBoxTemplatedView` and `AutoCompleteBoxTemplatedViewModel`.

So far a string has been used to represent suggestion items. This section uses a custom `SuggestionItem` class to demonstrate more complex data binding and styling features (see Listing 9.2).

LISTING 9.2   `SuggestionItem` Class

```
public class SuggestionItem
{
    public string Name { get; private set; }
    public string Description { get; private set; }
```

LISTING 9.2   Continued

```
    public SuggestionItem(string name, string description)
    {
        Name = name;
        Description = description;
    }
}
```

Within the viewmodel is defined a list of `SuggestionItem` objects as shown:

```
IEnumerable<SuggestionItem> suggestions = new List<SuggestionItem>
    {
        new SuggestionItem("Prague", "Capital of the Czech Republic."),
        new SuggestionItem("Geneva", "Swiss city."),
        new SuggestionItem("Canberra", "Capital of Australia."),
        ...

    };
```

To have the `AutoCompleteBox` function correctly with a complex object, such as the custom `SuggestionItem` class, you need to inform it of which property to use for filtering. This is done using the `AutoCompleteBox.ValueMemberPath` property. The following excerpt shows how the `Name` property of the `SuggestionItem` class is designated as the filter property. You also see how a `DataTemplate` is used to present the `Name` and `Description` of each `SuggestionItem` object:

```
<toolkit:AutoCompleteBox
    ItemsSource="{Binding Suggestions}"
    ValueMemberPath="Name"
    FontFamily="{StaticResource PhoneFontFamilySemiBold}"
    FontSize="{StaticResource PhoneFontSizeSmall}"
    VerticalAlignment="Top">
    <toolkit:AutoCompleteBox.ItemTemplate>
        <DataTemplate>
            <StackPanel>
                <TextBlock Text="{Binding Name}"
                    FontSize="{StaticResource PhoneFontSizeNormal}" />
                <TextBlock Text="{Binding Description}"
                    FontSize="{StaticResource PhoneFontSizeSmall}"
                    Foreground="#ff666666" />
            </StackPanel>
        </DataTemplate>
    </toolkit:AutoCompleteBox.ItemTemplate>
</toolkit:AutoCompleteBox>
```

9

When the suggestion list is displayed, each `SuggestionItem` is presented using the `DataTemplate`, as shown in Figure 9.9.

FIGURE 9.9   A custom `ItemTemplate` displays each city's name and description.

TIP

If you want to programmatically collapse the suggestion list, set the `AutoCompleteBox.IsDropDownOpen` property to false.

Data Binding and the `AutoCompleteBox.Text` Property

Populating the `Text` property of the `AutoCompleteBox` via a data binding can be problematic, since when a suggestion is chosen the binding is effectively removed and therefore needs to be restored.

You can reapply a binding by subscribing to the `SelectionChanged` event of the `AutoCompleteBox`.

```
void AutoCompleteBox_SelectionChanged(
            object sender, SelectionChangedEventArgs e)
{
    AutoCompleteBox autoCompleteBox = (AutoCompleteBox)sender;
    Dispatcher.BeginInvoke(delegate
```

```
    {
        Binding binding = new Binding("YourViewModelTextProperty");
        binding.Source = autoCompleteBox.DataContext;
        autoCompleteBox.SetBinding(AutoCompleteBox.TextProperty, binding);
    });
}
```

When the `AutoCompleteBox.IsTextCompletionEnabled` property is set to true, the `AutoCompleteBox.KeyUp` event can be used instead of the `SelectionChanged` event to ensure that the binding is restored regardless of whether a selection is made.

ContextMenu

`ContextMenu` is an expanding menu control that is displayed when a host `FrameworkElement` is tapped and held. A `ContextMenu` can be added to any `FrameworkElement` using the `ContextMenuService.ContextMenu` attached property. The following excerpt shows a `Button` that has a context menu assigned to it, displaying three menu items:

```
<Button Margin="0,12" VerticalAlignment="Center" Padding="16"
        Content="Using Click Events">
    <toolkit:ContextMenuService.ContextMenu>
        <toolkit:ContextMenu>
            <toolkit:MenuItem
                Header="option 1"
                Click="MenuItem_Click"/>
            <toolkit:MenuItem
                Header="option 2"
                Click="MenuItem_Click"/>
            <toolkit:MenuItem
                Header="option 3"
                Click="MenuItem_Click"/>
        </toolkit:ContextMenu>
    </toolkit:ContextMenuService.ContextMenu>
</Button>
```

When the button is tapped and held, the page content is zoomed out and the list of menu items is displayed (see Figure 9.10).

In this example the event handler for each `MenuItem.Click` event is the same. The handler retrieves the `Header` text of the selected `MenuItem` and displays it in a `TextBlock`, like so:

```
void MenuItem_Click(object sender, RoutedEventArgs e)
{
    TextBlock_LastSelectedMenuItem.Text = (string)((MenuItem)sender).Header;
}
```

FIGURE 9.10   A `Button` plays host to a `ContextMenu`.

By default, when shown, the `ContextMenu` reduces the scale of all other elements on the page, giving the context menu center stage. Internally the `ContextMenu` does this by creating a `WriteableBitmap` containing an image of the page. A `ScaleTransform` is then applied to the `WriteableBitmap`, which is placed above the page content but below `ContextMenu` host. This is a nice little trick, used often in the Toolkit. One downside of this approach, however, and one that you may become more aware of as you find yourself progressing with the `ContextMenu`, is that the snapshot taken of the page content, captures buttons in their pressed state, which may or may not be what you want. Notice, in Figure 9.10, that the background of the button is white, which interferes with the highlighting of the menu items.

To prevent the background from being scaled when the context menu is shown, set the `ContextMenu.IsZoomEnabled` property to false, as shown:

```
<Button Margin="0,12" VerticalAlignment="Center" Padding="16"
        Content="Using IsZoomEnabled=false">
    <toolkit:ContextMenuService.ContextMenu>
        <toolkit:ContextMenu IsZoomEnabled="false">
            <toolkit:MenuItem Header="option 1" Click="MenuItem_Click"/>
            <toolkit:MenuItem Header="option 2" Click="MenuItem_Click"/>
            <toolkit:MenuItem Header="option 3" Click="MenuItem_Click"/>
        </toolkit:ContextMenu>
    </toolkit:ContextMenuService.ContextMenu>
</Button>
```

With `IsZoomEnabled` set to false, an image of the page content is not used, and the actual page elements are displayed and continue to show animation. Consequently, a button control is able to transition out of its pressed state when the menu is shown (see Figure 9.11).

FIGURE 9.11   Displaying a `ContextMenu` with `IsZoomEnabled` set to false

ContextMenu and MVVM

So far you have seen the `ContextMenu` employed with hardwired `MenuItems` and `Click` events. This approach is adequate for simple apps. Yet, the `MenuItem` class supports `ICommands` out of the box. And, with this, you can bind a viewmodel's `ICommand` to a `MenuItem`, removing the need for `Click` event handlers in the code-beside.

To demonstrate, we bind a viewmodel command to a `MenuItem`, which displays a message to the user. The `ContextMenuViewModel` class, in the downloadable sample code, contains a `ShowMessageCommand` property, declared as shown:

```
readonly DelegateCommand showMessageCommand;

public ICommand ShowMessageCommand
{
    get
```

```
    {
        return showMessageCommand;
    }
}
```

The task of the `ShowMessageCommand` is to display a message using the custom `IMessageService`. For more information regarding the `ImessageService`, see Chapter 2, "Fundamental Concepts in Silverlight Development for Windows Phone." The `ShowMessageCommand` is initialized within the viewmodel's constructor. When the command executes, it presents the command parameter using the message service, as shown in the following excerpt:

```
public ContextMenuViewModel()
{
    showMessageCommand = new DelegateCommand(
        parameter =>
        {
            var messageService = Dependency.Resolve<IMessageService>();
            messageService.ShowMessage(parameter + " clicked!");
        });

    /* Content omitted. */
}
```

As with most examples in this book, the viewmodel is initialized and assigned to the view's `DataContext` property like so:

```
public ContextMenuView()
{
    InitializeComponent();
    DataContext = new ContextMenuViewModel();
}
```

With the viewmodel and command in place, `MenuItems` are able to bind to the command in the view XAML. In the following excerpt you see three `MenuItem` controls, each bound to the `ShowMessageCommand`. The first uses a string as its command parameter. The second and third use the `RelativeSource` markup extension to bind to their own `Header` properties. See the following excerpt:

```
<Button Margin="0,12" VerticalAlignment="Center" Padding="16"
    Content="Using ICommands">
    <toolkit:ContextMenuService.ContextMenu>
        <toolkit:ContextMenu>
            <toolkit:MenuItem
                Header="option 1"
                Command="{Binding ShowMessageCommand}"
                CommandParameter="option 1" />
```

```
          ...

        </toolkit:ContextMenu>
    </toolkit:ContextMenuService.ContextMenu>
</Button>
```

When a `MenuItem` is tapped, a message box is displayed with the `MenuItem`'s `Header` (see Figure 9.12).

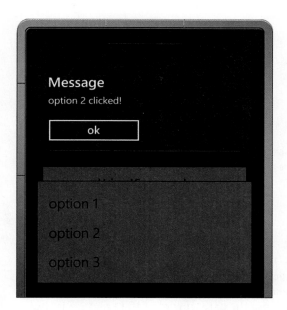

FIGURE 9.12   Tapping a `MenuItem` causes a message box to be displayed.

Hosting a `ContextMenu` in a `ListBoxItem`

Sometimes the need arises to provide a context menu for dynamically generated elements, such as those presented using a data bound `ItemsControl`. The following example demonstrates how to host a context menu for each item in a `ListBox`.

The `ContextMenuViewModel` contains an `ObservableCollection` of strings, declared as shown:

```
readonly ObservableCollection<string> items
                = new ObservableCollection<string>();

public IEnumerable<string> Items
{
    get
    {
```

```
        return items;
    }
}
```

The `items` collection is populated within the viewmodel constructor. In addition, a new command, named `DeleteCommand`, is placed in the viewmodel. When the command is executed, it removes the item, passed as a command parameter, from the `items` collection. See the following excerpt:

```csharp
public ContextMenuViewModel()
{
    IEnumerable<string> temp = from int i in Enumerable.Range(1, 5)
                                    select "Item " + i;
    foreach (var itemName in temp)
    {
        items.Add(itemName);
    }

    deleteCommand = new DelegateCommand<string>(
        itemName => items.Remove(itemName));

    /* Content omitted. */
}
```

A `ListBox` is placed on the page. Its `ItemTemplate` is defined, and a `TextBlock` is used to display each item in the list. The `TextBlock.Text` property is bound to the current item using the expression `{Binding}`. The `TextBlock` plays host to a `ContextMenu` onto which a single `MenuItem` is placed. Notice that the `MenuItem` is bound to the `DeleteCommand` using the `DataContext` property of the page. This is because the `DataContext` of the `MenuItem` is the string item and not the page, and therefore we specify the source explicitly using the `ElementName` binding property. See the following excerpt:

```xml
<ListBox ItemsSource="{Binding Items}" Height="200" Margin="12">
    <ListBox.ItemTemplate>
        <DataTemplate>
            <TextBlock Text="{Binding}" Margin="20">
            <toolkit:ContextMenuService.ContextMenu>
                <toolkit:ContextMenu IsZoomEnabled="false">
                    <toolkit:MenuItem
                        Header="Delete"
                        Command="{Binding DataContext.DeleteCommand,
                                        ElementName=page}"
                        CommandParameter="{Binding}" />
                </toolkit:ContextMenu>
            </toolkit:ContextMenuService.ContextMenu>
            </TextBlock>
```

```
      </DataTemplate>
    </ListBox.ItemTemplate>
</ListBox>
```

Tapping and holding an item in the list causes the `ContextMenu` for that item to be displayed. The `DeleteCommand` accepts a single parameter, which is the item string (see Figure 9.13). When executed, the item is removed from the list as expected.

FIGURE 9.13   The `ListBoxItem` plays host to a `ContextMenu` with a delete button.

DatePicker **and** TimePicker

Entering a date or time on the phone would be an otherwise cumbersome task if it relied solely on the phone SIP (Software Input Panel) or hardware keyboard. `DatePicker` and `TimePicker` conform to the Metro language of the phone and provide an interface that makes selecting a date or time easy.

Both the `DatePicker` and `TimePicker` use a `TextBox` to display a date or time value (see Figure 9.14).

When the user taps the `TextBox`, a form is presented that allows the user to specify the date or time using a set of infinitely scrollable controls (see Figure 9.15).

The `DatePicker` and `TimePicker` inherit from the same base class, which is `DateTimePickerBase`. The `DateTimePickerBase` class contains a `Value` property of type nullable `DateTime`. The `DatePicker` and `TimePicker` share the same public API, which is provided entirely by the base class. The `DatePicker` deals with the date segment of the `DateTime` value; the `TimePicker`, the time segment.

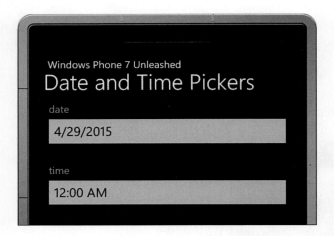

FIGURE 9.14   `DatePicker` and `TimePicker` controls

FIGURE 9.15   `DatePicker` while in selection mode

There are two main differences between the `DatePicker` and `TimePicker`. The first is the string pattern used to present the `DataTime` value. The `DatePicker` presents the `DateTime` value using the short date pattern, such that a date value of 6/1/2015 1:45:30 PM is presented as 6/1/2015. Conversely, the `TimePicker` presents the `DateTime` value using the short time pattern, such that a date value of 6/1/2015 1:45:30 PM is presented as 1:45 PM. You look at customizing the value format for both controls in a later section.

The second difference is the type of the associated `PhoneApplicationPage` for each control. `DatePicker` and `TimePicker` each rely on a particular `PhoneApplicationPage` for allowing the user to select the `DateTime` value. When the user taps the `DatePicker`, the control navigates to the built-in `DatePickerPage`. Conversely, when the user taps the `TimePicker`, the control navigates to the built-in `TimePickerPage`.

Using the DatePicker and TimePicker

When building small and simple apps, you may choose to give your `DatePicker` or `TimePicker` a name and respond to its `ValueChanged` event in your page code-beside file. The following excerpt shows a `ValueChanged` event handler. `DateTimeValueChanged` `EventArgs` contains both the value before being modified by the user, and the value after being modified:

```
void DatePicker_ValueChanged(object sender, DateTimeValueChangedEventArgs e)
{
    DateTime? oldDataValue = e.OldDateTime;
    DateTime? newDateValue = e.NewDateTime;
}
```

Alternatively, you may choose to rely on data binding and bind your control to a view-model property, as shown:

```
<toolkit:DatePicker Value="{Binding Date, Mode=TwoWay}"
                    Header="date"
                    ValueChanged="DatePicker_ValueChanged" />
```

In either case, tapping the control navigates to a particular `PhoneApplicationPage`, allowing the user to set the `DateTime` value. The two pages, `DatePickerPage` and `TimePickerPage`, both rely on two icons that must be placed in your project. The icons are used to confirm or cancel the `DateTime` selection operation. Without these icons, the OK and Cancel `ApplicationBarIconButtons` are not displayed correctly (see Figure 9.16).

For each `ApplicationBarIconButton` to be displayed correctly, images for the buttons must be placed in your project. The image icons should be placed in a directory called Toolkit.Content, in the root directory of your project. The images should be named ApplicationBar.Cancel.png and ApplicationBar.Check.png, and their Build Action should be set to Content (see Figure 9.17).

Once in place, the images are automatically used by the `DatePicker` and `TimePicker`.

FIGURE 9.16   Without correct inclusion of PNG images, icon buttons are displayed using a broken icon.

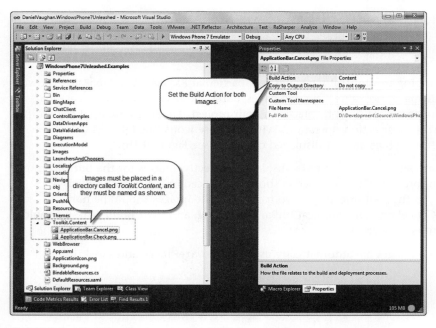

FIGURE 9.17   Set the icon image Build Action using the Properties pane.

Adding a Control Header

Many of the Toolkit controls allow you to customize the title text displayed above the control using a `Header` property. In addition, the `HeaderTemplate` property allows you to customize how the `Header` content is displayed. The following example provides a custom header template for a `TimePicker`:

```
<toolkit:TimePicker Value="{Binding Time, Mode=TwoWay}"
        Header="time">
    <toolkit:TimePicker.HeaderTemplate>
        <DataTemplate>
            <Border BorderThickness="2" BorderBrush="Yellow" Padding="10">
                <TextBlock Text="{Binding}" />
            </Border>
        </DataTemplate>
    </toolkit:TimePicker.HeaderTemplate>
</toolkit:TimePicker>
```

The `DataTemplate` places the `Header` text in a `TextBlock`, which is wrapped in a yellow border (see Figure 9.18).

FIGURE 9.18   `TimePicker` with a custom `HeaderTemplate`

Customizing the Value Format

The format of the `DateTime` value can be specified by setting the `DatePicker` or `TimePicker` `ValueStringFormat` property. For example, to present the `DateTime` value of a `TimePicker` using a long time format, the `ValueStringFormat` is set to {0:T}. Because curly brackets are treated as special characters in XAML, they must be escaped. This is done by prefixing {} to the format string, as shown in the following excerpt:

```
<toolkit:TimePicker x:Name="timePicker"
                    Value="{Binding Time, Mode=TwoWay}"
                    Header="time with custom format"
                    ValueStringFormat="{}{0:T}"/>
```

Alternatively, to set the format in the code-beside, you could use the following:

```
timePicker.ValueStringFormat = "{0:T}";
```

Figure 9.19 shows a `TimePicker` with the `ValueStringFormat` set to a long time format. You see that, unlike the default short time format, the seconds position is displayed.

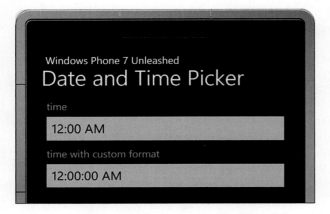

FIGURE 9.19   `TimePicker` with a custom format

> **NOTE**
>
> By changing the `ValueStringFormat` and the `PickerPageUri` (discussed in the next section), you can effectively change a `DatePicker` into a `TimePicker`, and vice versa. This, however, would make little sense, yet it illustrates the similarity and the flexibility of both controls.

The `DateTimePickerBase.ValueString` property allows you to retrieve the string that is presented in the `TextBox` after the format has been applied.

Customizing the Full-Screen Picker Page

Both the `DatePicker` and `TimePicker` allow you to change the full-screen picker page using the `DateTimePickerBase.PickerPageUri` property. This property is normally specified using a component URI, with the assembly and path to the `PhoneApplicationPage`. In the following example a `DatePicker` uses a custom picker page, located in an Examples assembly:

```
<toolkit:DatePicker Value="{Binding Date, Mode=TwoWay}"
                    Header="date with custom picker"
            PickerPageUri="/Examples;component/CustomDatePickerView.xaml" />
```

The task of the picker page is to allow the user to select a `DateTime` value, and then to use the `NavigationService` to navigate back to the original page. A picker page must implement the IDateTimePickerPage interface. This interface consists of a single nullable DateTime property called Value.

A custom picker page called CustomDatePickerView is located in the ControlExamples/SilverlightToolkit/DateAndTimePickers directory in the downloadable sample code. The sample allows the user to select from an arbitrary list of DateTime values.

The viewmodel consists of a list of DateTime values that the user selects from, a single DateTime property that tracks the selected date, and a command that is used to set the selected date value from buttons in the view.

The list of dates is defined in the viewmodel like so:

```
readonly List<DateTime> dates = new List<DateTime>();

public IEnumerable<DateTime> Dates
{
    get
    {
        return dates;
    }
}
```

The list is populated with five DateTime values, within the viewmodel constructor:

```
for (int i = 1; i < 6; i++)
{
    dates.Add(DateTime.Now.AddYears(i));
}
```

Each DateTime value in the list is presented as a button in the view.

Within the viewmodel, a property called Date holds the selected date:

```
DateTime? date = DateTime.Now;

public DateTime? Date
{
    get
    {
        return date;
    }
    set
    {
        Assign(() => Date, ref date, value);
    }
}
```

An ICommand is used to set the Date property via buttons in the view. The ICommand is shown in the following excerpt:

```
readonly DelegateCommand<DateTime?> setDateCommand;

public DelegateCommand<DateTime?> SetDateCommand
{
    get
    {
        return setDateCommand;
    }
}
```

The setDateCommand is initialized in the viewmodel constructor. The constructor accepts an Action parameter that is used during execution of the SetDateCommand to call the NavigationService.GoBack method, once a DateTime value has been selected by the user. The constructor is shown in full in the following excerpt:

```
public CustomDatePickerViewModel(Action completeAction)
{
    for (int i = 1; i < 6; i++)
    {
        dates.Add(DateTime.Now.AddYears(i));
    }

    setDateCommand = new DelegateCommand<DateTime?>(
        dateTime =>
            {
                if (dateTime == null)
                {
                    return;
                }

                Date = dateTime;

                if (completeAction != null)
                {
                    completeAction();
                }
            });
}
```

The custom picker view initializes its viewmodel, passing it a lambda expression, which allows the viewmodel to return to the calling page.

> **NOTE**
>
> As an alternative to passing the viewmodel a lambda expression, you may want to consider using a dedicated INavigationService for your app. Such a service is discussed in Chapter 26, "Local Databases," and exists as part of the Calcium framework for Windows Phone http://calciumsdk.com.
>
> Passing a reference to a page property, as shown in this example, causes the page to remain alive, ineligible for garbage collection, for the lifetime of the viewmodel. If the viewmodel does not share the same lifetime as the view, then a memory leak may ensue. In this example, the lifetime of the viewmodel is the same as the view's, and hence it is not an issue.

When the viewmodel determines that a DateTime value has been acquired, it invokes the specified Action, and the page with the DatePicker retrieves the DateTime value from the page's Value property (see Listing 9.3).

LISTING 9.3   CustomDatePickerView Class

```
public partial class CustomDatePickerView
    : PhoneApplicationPage, IDateTimePickerPage
{
    public CustomDatePickerView()
    {
        InitializeComponent();
        DataContext = new CustomDatePickerViewModel(
            () => NavigationService.GoBack());
    }

    CustomDatePickerViewModel ViewModel
    {
        get
        {
            return (CustomDatePickerViewModel)DataContext;
        }
    }

    public DateTime? Value
    {
        get
        {
            return ViewModel.Date;
        }
        set
        {
```

LISTING 9.3   Continued

```
            ViewModel.Date = value;
        }
    }
}
```

The XAML for the view contains a `ListBox` that is bound to the list of `DateTime` values. A `DataTemplate` is used to present each `DateTime` as a button. Each button is bound to the `SetDateCommand` of the viewmodel, as shown in the following excerpt:

```
<StackPanel x:Name="ContentPanel" Grid.Row="1">
    <ListBox ItemsSource="{Binding Dates}"
            SelectedItem="{Binding Date}">
        <ListBox.ItemTemplate>
            <DataTemplate>
                <Button Content="{Binding}"
                    Command="{Binding DataContext.SetDateCommand,
                    ElementName=page}"
                    CommandParameter="{Binding}" />
            </DataTemplate>
        </ListBox.ItemTemplate>
    </ListBox>
</StackPanel>
```

When visible, the custom picker page presents the five `DateTime` values, as shown in Figure 9.20.

FIGURE 9.20   The custom date/time picker page

LoopingSelector

The previous section looked at the DatePicker and TimePicker controls, whose base class, DateTimePickerBase, relies on a simpler control called LoopingSelector to display date and time values.

LoopingSelector provides all the functionality for an infinitely looping list of values.

LoopingSelector is not intended to be used day-to-day like other controls presented in this chapter, and as a result it resides in the Microsoft.Phone.Controls.Primitives namespace. Nonetheless, it is a useful control.

To use the control you must define a data source, which can be any object that implements ILoopingSelectorDataSource. The ILoopingSelectorDataSource interface defines the following four members:

- ▶ GetPrevious(object relativeTo) method
- ▶ GetNext(object relativeTo⑩ method
- ▶ SelectedItem property
- ▶ SelectionChanged event

GetPrevious and GetNext allow you to define the order of the data provided to the control. SelectedItem is used to keep track of the currently selected item in the control. The SelectionChanged event allows you to programmatically change the selected item in the control, which is normally done via the SelectedItem property.

To present a selectable list of numeric values to the user, we create an ILoopingSelectorDataSource called NumericDataSource (see Listing 9.4).

NumericDataSource allows you to define a range of integers using two properties: Minimum and Maximum.

LISTING 9.4   NumericDataSource Class

```
public class NumericDataSource : ILoopingSelectorDataSource
{
    public event EventHandler<SelectionChangedEventArgs> SelectionChanged;

    protected virtual void OnSelectionChanged(SelectionChangedEventArgs e)
    {
        EventHandler<SelectionChangedEventArgs> tempEvent = SelectionChanged;
        if (tempEvent != null)
        {
            tempEvent(this, e);
        }
    }
```

6

LISTING 9.4   Continued

```csharp
public object GetNext(object relativeTo)
{
    int nextValue = (int)relativeTo + 1;

    return nextValue <= Maximum ? nextValue : Minimum;
}

public object GetPrevious(object relativeTo)
{
    int previousValue = (int)relativeTo - 1;

    return previousValue >= Minimum ? previousValue : Maximum;
}

int selectedItem = 1;

public object SelectedItem
{
    get
    {
        return selectedItem;
    }
    set
    {
        int newValue = (int)value;

        if (selectedItem == newValue)
        {
            return;
        }

        int oldValue = selectedItem;
        selectedItem = newValue;

        OnSelectionChanged(new SelectionChangedEventArgs(
                            new[] {oldValue}, new[] {newValue}));
    }
}

public int SelectedNumber
{
    get
    {
        return (int)SelectedItem;
    }
```

LISTING 9.4   Continued

```csharp
        set
        {
            SelectedItem = value;
        }
    }

    int minimum = 1;

    public int Minimum
    {
        get
        {
            return minimum;
        }
        set
        {
            minimum = value;

            if (selectedItem < minimum)
            {
                SelectedItem = value;
            }
        }
    }

    int maximum = 100;

    public int Maximum
    {
        get
        {
            return maximum;
        }
        set
        {
            maximum = value;

            if (selectedItem > maximum)
            {
                SelectedItem = value;
            }
        }
    }
}
```

To use the NumericDataSource, we expose an instance via a property in a viewmodel, like so:

```
NumericDataSource numericDataSource
  = new NumericDataSource { Minimum = 0, Maximum = 10, SelectedNumber = 5 };

public NumericDataSource NumericDataSource
{
    get
    {
        return numericDataSource;
    }
}
```

A LoopingSelector can be data bound to the NumericDataSource property in the viewmodel. Its ItemTemplate defines the appearance of each item retrieved from the data source. See the following example:

```
<toolkitPrimitives:LoopingSelector
    DataSource="{Binding NumericDataSource}"
    Margin="12" Width="200" Height="500" ItemSize="128,128">
    <toolkitPrimitives:LoopingSelector.ItemTemplate>
        <DataTemplate>
            <Grid>
                <TextBlock Text="{Binding}" FontSize="54"
                    FontFamily="{StaticResource PhoneFontFamilySemiBold}"
                    HorizontalAlignment="Center" VerticalAlignment="Center" />
            </Grid>
        </DataTemplate>
    </toolkitPrimitives:LoopingSelector.ItemTemplate>
</toolkitPrimitives:LoopingSelector>
```

It is critical to assign values to the LoopingSelector element's Width, Height, and ItemSize properties.

Figure 9.21 shows the LoopingSelector after it has gained focus.

LoopingSelector is a control ideally suited to the touch-centric environment of the phone.

In Chapter 21, "Microphone and FM Radio," you see how two LoopingSelector controls are used to allow the user to select a radio frequency for the phone's FM Radio.

FIGURE 9.21   LoopingSelector example

LongListSelector

LongListSelector is like a ListBox that allows you to group items together. It is effective for large lists because it allows the user to more easily navigate through items by group.

LongListSelector supports full data and UI virtualization, and can display flat lists and grouped lists. When using grouped lists, the user is able to jump between groups using a group picker interface, which overlays the list.

LongListSelector may be used in place of a ListBox for displaying flat lists. To use it as an advanced ListBox with grouped lists, its ItemsSource property is normally assigned a list of lists (or rather an IEnumerable<IEnumerable<TItem>>).

Visual Structure

The LongListSelector includes several regions that you may customize using DataTemplates. Each group item is presented between a group header and footer. The entire list is placed between a list header and footer (see Figure 9.22).

When the group header is tapped, the GroupItemsPanel is presented, which allows the user to jump to a specific group. The GroupItemsPanel is discussed in greater detail later in the chapter.

FIGURE 9.22   Visual structure of the LongListSelector

Presenting Flat Lists

Presenting a list of non-grouped items is done by setting the LongListSelector's IsFlatList property to true. When presenting a flat list, there is little difference between a LongListSelector and a regular ListBox control, apart from the added header and footer of the LongListSelector.

To demonstrate how to display a flat list in a LongListSelector, we populate a LongListSelector with a list of custom City objects. The City class was presented earlier in this chapter (for a review of the City class see Listing 9.1).

The main differences between the LongListSelector examples downloaded with the Toolkit and those presented in this chapter are that the examples presented here mostly employ the MVVM pattern and rely on LINQ to a greater extent.

The FlatListViewModel in the downloadable sample code exposes a list of cities (see Listing 9.5).

LISTING 9.5   FlatListViewModel Class

```
public class FlatListViewModel : ViewModelBase
{
    readonly IEnumerable<City> cities = new List<City>
        {
            new City("Prague", "Capital of the Czech Republic."),
            new City("Geneva", "Swiss city."),
```

LISTING 9.5   *Continued*

```
            new City("Canberra", "Capital of Australia."),
            new City("Palma", "Major city of Mallorca."),
            new City("New York", "Most populous city in the USA."),
        };

    public IEnumerable<City> Cities
    {
        get
        {
            return cities;
        }
    }
}
```

The view XAML uses a `LongListSelector` with the `LongListSelector.IsFlatList` property set to true. The `LongListSelector.ItemsSource` property is bound to the `Cities` property of the viewmodel. A header and footer are provided, and the `ItemTemplate` is responsible for presenting each `City` object. See the following excerpt:

```xml
<toolkit:LongListSelector ItemsSource="{Binding Cities}"
                    IsFlatList="True"
                    Background="Transparent">

    <toolkit:LongListSelector.ListHeader>
        <TextBlock Text="ListHeader"
            Style="{StaticResource PhoneTextTitle1Style}"/>
    </toolkit:LongListSelector.ListHeader>

    <toolkit:LongListSelector.ItemTemplate>
        <DataTemplate>
            <StackPanel Margin="{StaticResource PhoneMargin}">
                <TextBlock Text="{Binding Name}"
                    Style="{StaticResource PhoneTextLargeStyle}" />
                <TextBlock Text="{Binding Description}"
                    Style="{StaticResource PhoneTextNormalStyle}" />
            </StackPanel>
        </DataTemplate>
    </toolkit:LongListSelector.ItemTemplate>

    <toolkit:LongListSelector.ListFooter>
        <TextBlock Text="ListFooter"
            Style="{StaticResource PhoneTextTitle1Style}"/>
    </toolkit:LongListSelector.ListFooter>

</toolkit:LongListSelector>
```

In addition to the `ListHeader` and `ListFooter` properties, the `LongListSelector` also includes a `ListHeaderTemplate` and `ListFooterTemplate`, which are used to modify the way the header and footer content is presented (see Figure 9.23).

NOTE

When setting the `ItemsSource` of the `LongListSelector` to a flat list, that is, a collection whose items do not implement `IEnumerable<IEnumerable<TItem>>`, then you must set the `LongListSelector.IsFlatList` property to true; otherwise, an `InvalidCastException` is raised at runtime.

FIGURE 9.23   `LongListSelector` displaying a flat list of cities

Presenting Grouped Lists

Presenting grouped, or composite, lists of items is where the `LongListSelector` shines. This section looks at two examples. The first example uses a `LongListSelector` to present a grouped list of Windows Phone Marketplace apps; the second example presents a grouped list of user contacts and demonstrates how to customize the `GroupItemsPanel`.

Marketplace App List Sample

The built-in Marketplace app presents apps in a flat list. This example groups a set of mock items using a `LongListSelector`.

The example code for this section is located in the WindowsPhone7Unleashed.Examples project, within the ControlExamples/SilverlightToolkit/LongListSelector/ MarketplaceAppList directory.

The custom `MarketplaceApp` class defines an app as having a name, description, image, price, and marketplace category. The marketplace category and its price are used to group a list of randomly generated `MarketplaceApp` objects. First the example briefly looks at the `MarketplaceApp` class and at how to generate a list of `MarketplaceApp` objects; this will increase your understanding as you move further through the example.

`MarketplaceApp` defines an array of hard-coded categories and prices. The array of category names is called *categories* and is defined as follows:

```
static readonly string[] categories
    = { "Games", "Photo", "Social", "Business", "Tools", "Travel" };
```

The array of prices is defined as shown:

```
static readonly double[] prices
    = { 0.99, 1.99, 2.99, 5.99 };
```

A category and price are randomly selected for each new `MarketplacApp` using a `System.Random`.

The `MarketplaceApp` class includes a static method called `CreateRandomApp` that instantiates a `MarketplaceApp` and populates it with random data. The `LoremIpsumGenerator` class, borrowed from the Toolkit examples, produces random text. The `LoremIpsumGenerator` code is not covered in this book, but the code is available in the downloadable sample code for this book.

```
public static MarketplaceApp CreateRandomApp()
{
    string name = LoremIpsumGenerator.GetWords(
                    random.Next(1, 5),
                    LoremIpsumGenerator.Capitalization.AllWords);
    string description = LoremIpsumGenerator.GetParagraph(random.Next(3, 7));
    string category = categories[random.Next(6)];
    double price = prices[random.Next(4)];
    MarketplaceApp result = new MarketplaceApp(
        name, description, category, price,
        "/ControlExamples/SilverlightToolkit/LongListSelector/
➥MarketplaceAppList/Images/MarketplaceAppIcon.png");
    return result;
}
```

To generate more than one `MarketplaceApp` object at a time, another static method called `CreateRandomApps` accepts an integer value and returns the specified number of instances. While fairly arbitrary, this method is shown in the following excerpt since it is referred to later in this section:

```
public static IEnumerable<MarketplaceApp> CreateRandomApps(int numberToCreate)
{
    ArgumentValidator.AssertGreaterThan(0, numberToCreate, "numberToCreate");
    for (int i = 0; i < numberToCreate; i++)
    {
        yield return CreateRandomApp();
    }
}
```

The viewmodel for this sample is called AppListViewModel. It contains a list of grouped MarketplaceApp objects.

When presenting grouped items, the LongListSelector depends on each item in the source collection implementing IEnumerable<TItem>. You could, therefore, simply place each MarketplaceApp object in a List<MarketplaceApp>, and the LongListSelector would happily display them. However, doing so would not provide a means of displaying a group title for each group within the LongListSelector; you need a way to associate a name with each group. For this we turn to the System.Linq.IGrouping interface. The IGrouping interface has just what you need; it is IEnumerable<TItem> and contains a Key property that you can use as each group's title by binding to it in XAML (see Figure 9.24).

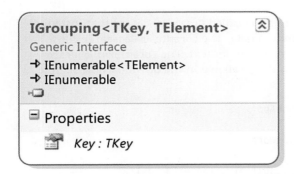

FIGURE 9.24   The IGrouping<TKey, TElement> interface extends IEnumerable interfaces.

The sample contains an implementation of IGrouping called CustomGrouping (see Listing 9.6). Rather than passing through a generic attribute for the IGrouping TKey attribute, the key type is defined as object to allow greater flexibility when switching collections within the viewmodel.

LISTING 9.6   CustomGrouping Class

```
public class CustomGrouping<TElement> : IGrouping<object, TElement>
{
    readonly IEnumerable<TElement> items;
    readonly object key;
```

LISTING 9.6   Continued

```csharp
    public CustomGrouping(object key, IEnumerable<TElement> items)
    {
        this.key = ArgumentValidator.AssertNotNull(key, "key");
        this.items = ArgumentValidator.AssertNotNull(items, "items");
    }

    public object Key
    {
        get
        {
            return key;
        }
    }

    public IEnumerator<TElement> GetEnumerator()
    {
        return items.GetEnumerator();
    }

    IEnumerator IEnumerable.GetEnumerator()
    {
        return items.GetEnumerator();
    }

    public bool HasItems
    {
        get
        {
            return items.Any();
        }
    }

    public override bool Equals(object obj)
    {
        var otherGrouping = obj as CustomGrouping<TElement>;
        return otherGrouping != null && Key.Equals(otherGrouping.Key);
    }

    public override int GetHashCode()
    {
        return Key.GetHashCode();
    }
}
```

The `AppListViewModel` contains a list of `CustomGrouping` objects, as shown:

```
IEnumerable<CustomGrouping<MarketplaceApp>> appGroupings;

public IEnumerable<CustomGrouping<MarketplaceApp>> AppGroupings
{
    get
    {
        return appGroupings;
    }
    private set
    {
        Assign(() => AppGroupings, ref appGroupings, value);
    }
}
```

LINQ is used to populate `AppGroupings`. The `MarketplaceApp.CreateRandomApps` method generates many `MarketplaceApp` objects, which are then grouped by the `MarketplaceApp.Category` property, as shown:

```
void GroupByCategory()
{
    AppGroupings = (from app in MarketplaceApp.CreateRandomApps(appCount)
            group app by app.Category into grouping
            select new CustomGrouping<MarketplaceApp>(
                grouping.Key, grouping.AsEnumerable())).ToList();
}
```

> **NOTE**
>
> Conversion of the resulting `IEnumerable<T>` to a `List<T>` is done to avoid deferred execution, which would otherwise produce incorrect ordering and behavior.

The viewmodel allows the marketplace apps to be sorted either by category or by price. When sorted by price, the LINQ expression relies on the fact that the `CustomGrouping.Key` property is of type object, allowing you to reassign the `AppGrouping` property despite using the `MarketplaceApp.Price` property, which is of a different type to the `MarketplaceApp.Category`.

Grouping items by price is performed by the `GroupByPrice` method, shown in the following excerpt:

```
void GroupByPrice()
{
    AppGroupings = (from app in MarketplaceApp.CreateRandomApps(appCount)
            group app by app.Price into grouping orderby grouping.Key
            select new CustomGrouping<MarketplaceApp>(
                grouping.Key, grouping.AsEnumerable())).ToList();
}
```

To allow the user to specify how items are grouped, the viewmodel includes a list of valid AppGroups:

```
readonly static IEnumerable<AppGroup> appGroups = new List<AppGroup>
                                        {
                                            AppGroup.Category,
                                            AppGroup.Price
                                        };

public IEnumerable<AppGroup> AppGroups
{
    get
    {
        return appGroups;
    }
}
```

How the items are grouped is determined by the viewmodel's GroupBy property. In the following excerpt, if the base class Assign method succeeds in setting the field value, then depending on the new value, the GroupByPrice or GroupByCategory method is called:

```
AppGroup groupBy = appGroups.First();

public AppGroup GroupBy
{
    get
    {
        return groupBy;
    }
    set
    {
        if (Assign(() => GroupBy, ref groupBy, value)
                == AssignmentResult.Success)
        {
            switch (value)
            {
                case AppGroup.Price:
                    GroupByPrice();
                    break;
                default:
                    GroupByCategory();
                    break;
            }
        }

    }
}
```

For more information regarding the custom `ViewModelBase.Assign` method see Chapter 2.

The view XAML contains a `ListPicker` that allows the user to switch how items are grouped. The `ListPicker`'s `ItemsSource` property is bound to the viewmodel's `AppGroups` property. The `ListPicker.SelectedItem` property has a two-way data binding to the viewmodel's `GroupBy` property:

```
<toolkit:ListPicker
    Header="group by"
    ItemsSource="{Binding AppGroups}"
    SelectedItem="{Binding GroupBy, Mode=TwoWay}" />
```

When the user selects an item from the `ListPicker`, the viewmodel's `GroupBy` property is updated, which in turn calls one of the group by methods (see Figure 9.25).

FIGURE 9.25   The group by property is able to be changed via a `ListPicker`.

The `LongListSelector.ItemsSource` property is bound to the `AppGroupings` property of the viewmodel.

The `LongListSelector` includes a `ListHeader`, `GroupHeaderTemplate`, `GroupItemTemplate`, and an `ItemTemplate`. The `ItemTemplate` presents each `MarketplaceApp` object. See the following excerpt:

```xml
<toolkit:LongListSelector ItemsSource="{Binding AppGroupings}" Grid.Row="1">

    <toolkit:LongListSelector.ListHeader>
        <TextBlock Text="latest apps"
            Style="{StaticResource PhoneTextTitle1Style}"/>
    </toolkit:LongListSelector.ListHeader>

    <toolkit:LongListSelector.GroupHeaderTemplate>
        <DataTemplate>
            <Border Background="{StaticResource PhoneAccentBrush}"
                    Margin="{StaticResource PhoneTouchTargetOverhang}"
                    Padding="{StaticResource PhoneTouchTargetOverhang}">
                <TextBlock Text="{Binding Key}"/>
            </Border>
        </DataTemplate>
    </toolkit:LongListSelector.GroupHeaderTemplate>

    <toolkit:LongListSelector.GroupItemTemplate>
        <DataTemplate>
            <Border Background="{StaticResource PhoneAccentBrush}"
                    Margin="{StaticResource PhoneTouchTargetOverhang}"
                    Padding="{StaticResource PhoneTouchTargetOverhang}">
                <TextBlock Text="{Binding Key}"
                    Style="{StaticResource PhoneTextLargeStyle}"/>
            </Border>
        </DataTemplate>
    </toolkit:LongListSelector.GroupItemTemplate>

    <toolkit:LongListSelector.ItemTemplate>
        <DataTemplate>
            <Grid Margin="{StaticResource PhoneTouchTargetOverhang}">
                <Grid.ColumnDefinitions>
                    <ColumnDefinition Width="Auto"/>
                    <ColumnDefinition Width="*"/>
                </Grid.ColumnDefinitions>
                <Image Source="{Binding ImageUrl}"
                    Width="110" Height="150"
                    VerticalAlignment="Top"/>
                <StackPanel Grid.Column="1" VerticalAlignment="Top">
                    <TextBlock Text="{Binding Name}"
                        Style="{StaticResource PhoneTextLargeStyle}"
                        FontFamily="{StaticResource PhoneFontFamilySemiBold}"
                        TextWrapping="Wrap" Margin="12,-12,12,6" />
                    <TextBlock Text="{Binding Description}"
                        Style="{StaticResource PhoneTextNormalStyle}"
                        TextWrapping="Wrap"
```

6

```
                    FontFamily="{StaticResource PhoneFontFamilySemiLight}"/>
            </StackPanel>
        </Grid>
    </DataTemplate>
</toolkit:LongListSelector.ItemTemplate>
</toolkit:LongListSelector>
```

When the user taps a group header, each grouping key is presented using the
`GroupItemTemplate`. With Category selected as the group by property, each category is
presented, allowing the user to jump to a specific category (see Figure 9.26).

FIGURE 9.26   `LongListSelector` displaying the group picker when grouped by category

With price selected as the group by property, the groups are presented from lowest to
highest (see Figure 9.27). Tapping on a price takes the user to the list of apps of that price.

Displaying a List of Contacts Using the `LongListSelector`

This second example looks at presenting a list of contacts, which represent people in a
custom address book. This example demonstrates some more advanced concepts, such as
customizing the group picker using a custom `GroupItemsPanel`.

FIGURE 9.27   LongListSelector displaying the group picker when grouped by price

Each contact is represented by a custom `Contact` class. The `Contact` class includes the following properties:

- ▶ `Id`
- ▶ `FirstName`
- ▶ `LastName`
- ▶ `EmailAddress`
- ▶ `HomeNumber`
- ▶ `MobileNumber`
- ▶ `ImageUrl`

Like the `MarketplaceApp` class from the first example, the `Contact` class includes a static `GetRandomContacts` method that generates a specified number of `Contact` objects, randomly selected from a set of predefined names in the `RandomContactGenerator` class.

The viewmodel for this section, called `ContactListViewModel`, includes a list of grouped `Contact` objects called `ContactGroupings`, shown in the following excerpt:

```
IEnumerable<CustomGrouping<Contact>> contactGroupings;

public IEnumerable<CustomGrouping<Contact>> ContactGroupings
{
    get
    {
        return contactGroupings;
    }
```

```
    private set
    {
        Assign(() => ContactGroupings, ref contactGroupings, value);
    }
}
```

`ContactGroupings` is initialized in the viewmodel constructor. A constant, called `contactCount`, determines how many `Contact` objects are generated:

```
const int contactCount = 35;
```

LINQ is used within the viewmodel constructor to build the list of grouped contacts. We first use the `Contact` class to generate a list of random contacts ordered by last name and then first name. The first letter of each contact's last name is used as the grouping key. The LINQ expression groups each contact by this key, creating a `CustomGrouping` object for each group. See the following excerpt:

```
List<CustomGrouping<Contact>> groupings
    = (from contact in Contact.GetRandomContacts(contactCount)
        orderby contact.LastName orderby contact.FirstName
        group contact by Char.ToLower(contact.LastName.First()) into grouping
        select new CustomGrouping<Contact>(
            grouping.Key, grouping.AsEnumerable())).ToList();
```

The result of this expression is a set of groups, one for each unique first character. At this point, however, the result does not contain groups for letters of the alphabet not present in the list. This is not what you want because the `LongListSelector` would be unable to display a list of all letters. To remedy this situation, create another set of groupings, one for each letter of the alphabet and each containing an empty list of contacts:

```
const string groupCharacters = "abcdefghijklmnopqrstuvwxyz";
List<Contact> emptyList = new List<Contact>();
var allGroupings = from character in groupCharacters
                   where !groupings.Any(x => character.Equals(x.Key))
                   select new CustomGrouping<Contact>(character, emptyList);
```

The two sets of groupings are then merged to create a single set of groupings, with each letter of the alphabet properly represented:

```
contactGroupings = groupings.Union(allGroupings).OrderBy(x => x.Key);
```

The `LongListSelector` in the view binds to the `ContactGroupings` property. `Contact` groups are presented in the same manner as were the `MarketplaceApps` in the previous section; the `ItemTemplate` specifies how each `Contact` object is presented.

This example differs from the Marketplace App List example in that here we replace the default items panel with a Toolkit `WrapPanel`. Using a `WrapPanel` causes each group header to be placed side by side, and then dropped to a new line once they exceed the width of

the container (see Listing 9.7). Pay particular attention to the
`LongListSelector.GroupItemTemplate`, which is used to present each group when the
`LongListSelector` is in the full-screen group selection mode.

LISTING 9.7   Contacts `LongListSelector` (excerpt from `LongListSelectorView.xaml`)

```xml
<toolkit:LongListSelector Background="Transparent"
        ItemsSource="{Binding ContactGroupings}">

    <toolkit:LongListSelector.ListHeader>
        <TextBlock Text="ListHeader"
            Style="{StaticResource PhoneTextTitle1Style}" />
    </toolkit:LongListSelector.ListHeader>

    <toolkit:LongListSelector.GroupItemsPanel>
        <ItemsPanelTemplate>
            <toolkit:WrapPanel Orientation="Horizontal"/>
        </ItemsPanelTemplate>
    </toolkit:LongListSelector.GroupItemsPanel>

    <toolkit:LongListSelector.GroupHeaderTemplate>
        <DataTemplate>
            <Border Background="Transparent">
                <Border Background="{StaticResource PhoneAccentBrush}"
                    Width="75" Height="75" HorizontalAlignment="Left">
                    <TextBlock Text="{Binding Key}"
                        Foreground="{StaticResource PhoneForegroundBrush}"
                        Style="{StaticResource PhoneTextExtraLargeStyle}"
                        VerticalAlignment="Bottom"/>
                </Border>
            </Border>
        </DataTemplate>
    </toolkit:LongListSelector.GroupHeaderTemplate>

    <toolkit:LongListSelector.ItemTemplate>
        <DataTemplate>
            <Grid Margin="{StaticResource PhoneTouchTargetOverhang}">
                <Grid.ColumnDefinitions>
                    <ColumnDefinition Width="Auto"/>
                    <ColumnDefinition Width="*"/>
                </Grid.ColumnDefinitions>

                <Image Source="{Binding ImageUrl}"
                    Width="110" Height="150"  VerticalAlignment="Top" />

                <StackPanel Grid.Column="1" VerticalAlignment="Top">
```

LISTING 9.7   Continued

```xml
                        <TextBlock Text="{Binding FullName}"
                            Style="{StaticResource PhoneTextLargeStyle}"
                            FontFamily="{StaticResource PhoneFontFamilySemiBold}"
                            Margin="12,-12,12,6" />
                        <TextBlock Text="{Binding EmailAddress}"
                            Style="{StaticResource PhoneTextNormalStyle}"
                            TextWrapping="Wrap"
                        FontFamily="{StaticResource PhoneFontFamilySemiBold}" />
                        <StackPanel Orientation="Horizontal">
                            <TextBlock Text="mobile"
                                Style="{StaticResource PhoneTextSmallStyle}" />
                            <TextBlock Text="{Binding MobileNumber}"
                            Style="{StaticResource PhoneTextSmallStyle}"
                        FontFamily="{StaticResource PhoneFontFamilySemiBold}" />
                        </StackPanel>
                        <StackPanel Orientation="Horizontal">
                            <TextBlock Text="home"
                                Style="{StaticResource PhoneTextSmallStyle}" />
                            <TextBlock Text="{Binding HomeNumber}"
                                Style="{StaticResource PhoneTextSmallStyle}"
                          FontFamily="{StaticResource PhoneFontFamilySemiBold}" />
                        </StackPanel>
                    </StackPanel>
                </Grid>
            </DataTemplate>
    </toolkit:LongListSelector.ItemTemplate>

    <toolkit:LongListSelector.GroupItemTemplate>
        <DataTemplate>
            <Border IsHitTestVisible="{Binding HasItems}"
                    Background="{Binding HasItems,
                    Converter={StaticResource BooleanToBrushConverter}}"
                    Width="99" Height="99" Margin="6">
                <TextBlock Text="{Binding Key}"
                    FontFamily="{StaticResource PhoneFontFamilySemiBold}"
                    FontSize="36"
                    Margin="{StaticResource PhoneTouchTargetOverhang}"
                    Foreground="{StaticResource PhoneForegroundBrush}"
                    VerticalAlignment="Bottom"/>
            </Border>
        </DataTemplate>
    </toolkit:LongListSelector.GroupItemTemplate>
```

LISTING 9.7   Continued

```
<toolkit:LongListSelector.GroupFooterTemplate>
    <DataTemplate>
        <Border Margin="{StaticResource PhoneTouchTargetOverhang}"
                Padding="{StaticResource PhoneTouchTargetOverhang}">
            <TextBlock Text="Group Footer"
                Style="{StaticResource PhoneTextExtraLargeStyle}" />
        </Border>
    </DataTemplate>
</toolkit:LongListSelector.GroupFooterTemplate>

<toolkit:LongListSelector.ListFooter>
    <TextBlock Text="ListFooter"
        Style="{StaticResource PhoneTextTitle1Style}" />
</toolkit:LongListSelector.ListFooter>

</toolkit:LongListSelector>
```

Figure 9.28 shows the contacts list, presented with the LongListSelector.

FIGURE 9.28   LongListSelector displaying the contact list

When the user taps a group header, the LongListSelector presents all groups as a jump list. Examining the GroupItemTemplate in more detail you see that each header is presented within a Border that only responds to a tap if the CustomGrouping.HasItems property is true. In addition, the background of the Border is set to a different brush according to the HasItems property value. Switching the Border background is done via a custom IValueConverter called BooleanToBrushConverter, which turns a Boolean value into one of two specified brushes (see Listing 9.8).

LISTING 9.8   BooleanToBrushConverter Class

```
public class BooleanToBrushConverter : IValueConverter
{
    public Brush BrushIfFalse { get; set; }
    public Brush BrushIfTrue { get; set; }

    public object Convert(
        object value, Type targetType, object parameter, CultureInfo culture)
    {
        return value != null && (bool)value ? BrushIfTrue : BrushIfFalse;
    }

    public object ConvertBack(
        object value, Type targetType, object parameter, CultureInfo culture)
    {
        throw new NotImplementedException("Only supports a one way binding");
    }
}
```

BooleanToBrushConverter is defined as a resource in the page resources like so:

```
<phone:PhoneApplicationPage.Resources>
    <ValueConverters:BooleanToBrushConverter x:Name="BooleanToBrushConverter"
        BrushIfFalse="{StaticResource PhoneChromeBrush}"
        BrushIfTrue="{StaticResource PhoneAccentBrush}" />
</phone:PhoneApplicationPage.Resources>
```

Thus, when a CustomGrouping HasItems property evaluates to true, the PhoneAccentBrush is used for the header background; otherwise, the PhoneChromeBrush is used. Figure 9.29 shows the LongListSelector presenting the Contact headers using a WrapPanel.

FIGURE 9.29   `GroupItemsPanel` allows the user to jump to a group.

Other Important `LongListSelector` Members

This section describes other important properties, events, and methods of the
`LongListSelector`. Table 9.2, Table 9.3, and Table 9.4, list the notable properties, events,
and methods, respectively.

TABLE 9.2   `LongListSelector` Notable Properties

Name	Description
BufferSize	BufferSize is a dependency property of type double. It allows you to specify the number of screens (as defined by the ActualHeight of the LongListSelector) above and below the visible items in the list that are filled with items. The default value is 1.0
DisplayAllGroups	DisplayAllGroups is a dependency property of type bool. Setting this property to true causes each group to be displayed whether or not the group has items. The default is false.
IsBouncy	IsBouncy is a dependency property of type bool. It controls whether the list can be (temporarily) scrolled past the end or beginning.
IsScrolling	IsScrolling is a read-only dependency property of type bool. It is true if the user is manipulating the list, or if an inertial animation is taking place.
MaximumFlickVelocity	MaximumFlickVelocity is a dependency property of type double. It determines the maximum velocity for flicks in pixels per second. The default value is 4000.0.
SelectedItem	Gets or sets the selected item.

TABLE 9.2   Continued

Name	Description
ShowListFooter	ShowListFooter is a dependency property of type bool. It controls whether the ListFooter is shown. The default is true.
ShowListHeader	ShowListHeader is a dependency property of type bool. It controls whether the ListHeader is shown. The default is true.

TABLE 9.3   LongListSelector Notable Events

Name	Description
Link	Virtualization may defer the loading of content. This event indicates that the ContentPresenter with the item is about to be realized.
Unlink	Indicates that the ContentPresenter with the item is being recycled and is becoming unrealized.
SelectionChanged	Indicates that the SelectedItem has changed to a different item or is now null.
ScrollingCompleted	Raised when the user has finished a drag or a flick completes.
ScrollingStarted	Raised when the user is manipulating the list.
StretchingBottom	Raised when IsBouncy is true and the user has dragged the items up from the bottom as far as they can go.
StretchingCompleted	Raised when the user is no longer stretching.
StretchingTop	Raised when IsBouncy is true and the user has dragged the items down from the top as far as they can go.

TABLE 9.4   LongListSelector Notable Methods

Name	Description
AnimateTo	Animate the scrolling of the list to the specified item. Scrolling speed is capped by MaximumFlickVelocity.
ScrollTo	Instantly jump to the specified item.
DisplayGroupView	Invokes the group picker if a GroupItemTemplate has been defined.
GetItemsInView	Returns all the items currently in view. Items that have associated visual elements are not necessarily returned, as they may be offscreen. Calling this method may result in an empty list if scrolling is happening too quickly.

PerformanceProgressBar

`PerformanceProgressBar` is an animated indeterminate progress bar that overcomes performance issues present in the `PerformanceBar` located in the FCL. For more information on the `ProgressBar` see Chapter 5, "Content Controls, Items Controls, and Range Controls."

> **NOTE**
>
> `PerformanceProgressBar` is for displaying indeterminate progress only. `PerformanceProgressBar` is not capable of displaying determinate progress, as it does not include a `Value` property, and its control template only contains visual states for representing the `IsIndeterminate` state. Use the FCL's `ProgressBar` for displaying determinate progress. In determinate mode, there is no advantage to using the `PerformanceProgressBar` instead of the built-in FCL's `ProgressBar`.

The Toolkits `PerformanceProgressBar` differs from the FCL's `ProgressBar`, in that there is an unfortunate performance issue with the control template of the `ProgressBar`. Both the `ProgressBar` and the `PerformanceProgressBar` represent indeterminate progress using five dots that move from left to right. To achieve the dot animation effect, the FCL's `ProgressBar` uses five slider controls, with each slider's thumb styled as a dot. This produces a lot of work for the UI thread. Conversely, the `PerformanceProgressBar` uses the compositor thread exclusively for animation, instead of the UI thread. This frees the UI thread for things like layout passes and application logic, and noticeably improves the responsiveness of the UI while the progress bar is displayed.

Using the PerformanceProgressBar

When the `PerformanceProgressBar.IsIndeterminate` property is set to true, the dot animation takes place. If you place a `PerformanceProgressBar` on a page and forget to set its `IsIndeterminate` property, nothing is displayed. The following is an example of a `PerformanceProgressBar` declared in XAML:

```
<toolkit:PerformanceProgressBar IsIndeterminate="True" />
```

A viewmodel can be used to control the visibility of a `PerformanceProgressBar` via a bound property. This is done by binding the `PerformanceProgressBar.IsIndeterminate` property to a Boolean viewmodel property. The `PerformanceProgressBarViewModel` class, in the downloadable sample code, contains such a property:

```
bool busy;

public bool Busy
{
    get
    {
        return busy;
    }
    private set
```

```
    {
        Assign(() => Busy, ref busy, value);
    }
}
```

To demonstrate the effect of changing the property value at runtime, the class simulates a background process that periodically inverts the busy value using a System.Threading.Timer, as shown:

```
Timer retryTimer;
int timerPeriod = 4 * 1000; /* 4 seconds. */

public PerformanceProgressBarViewModel()
{
    retryTimer = new Timer(o => Busy = !Busy, null, timerPeriod, timerPeriod);
}
```

The PerformanceProgressBar is bound to the viewmodel Busy property, so that when the Busy property is true, the animation effect is displayed; when false the bar is collapsed, as shown:

```
<toolkit:PerformanceProgressBar IsIndeterminate="true"
    Visibility="{Binding Busy,
        Converter={StaticResource BooleanToVisibilityConverter},
        ConverterParameter=Collapsed}"/>
```

The Visibility property binding uses a BooleanToVisibility converter, defined as a page resource, to convert the Boolean Busy property to a Visibility enum value. For more information on the BooleanToVisibility converter, see Chapter 3, "Application Execution Model."

See Chapter 3 for a demonstration of the PerformanceProgressBar in a custom application loading screen.

TiltEffect

In an environment whose primary input method is touch, providing feedback when a user interacts with UI elements helps to engage the user and improves the perceived responsiveness of the UI. On the desktop, a pointer indicates the location of the mouse, and hover events are used to provide different states for interactive controls. On the phone, however, there is no mouse, and no way of knowing when a user's finger is above an element if screen contact is not made. The TiltEffect component provides feedback to the user when she taps and holds an element. It is simple to set up and has out-of-the-box support for many of the built-in controls (see Figure 9.30).

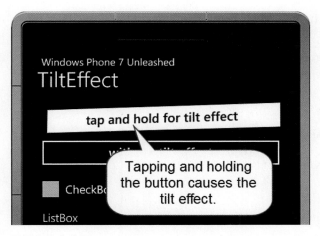

FIGURE 9.30   With the tilt effect enabled, a button tilts when it is tapped and held.

To use `TiltEffect` on your page, set the `IsTiltEnabled` attached property of the `TiltEffect` class to true within the `PhoneApplicationPage` element, like so:

```
<phone:PhoneApplicationPage
    ...
    toolkit:TiltEffect.IsTiltEnabled="True">
```

To prevent the tilt effect from being applied to a particular element on your page, set the `TiltEffect.SuppressTilt` attached property to True, as shown:

```
<Button Content="without tilt effect"
        toolkit:TiltEffect.SuppressTilt="True" />
```

Out of the box, `TiltEffect` supports two base control types: `ButtonBase` and `ListBoxItem`. The tilt effect is automatically applied to any classes deriving from `ButtonBase` or `ListBoxItem`, or indeed `ListBoxItem` itself.

Supporting Other Controls

Some controls may benefit from the tilt effect, yet may not necessarily derive from `ButtonBase` or `ListBoxItem`. To enable `TiltEffect` on an alternate `UIElement` type, such as on context menu items, add the element `Type` to the `TitleEffect`'s list of supported types via the `TiltEffect.TiltableItems` collection.

TIP

As `TiltEffect.TiltableItems` is a static property and global to your app, where possible populate it from a centralized location such as your `App` class, rather than in an ad hoc fashion from, for example, your page classes. This can help to reduce duplication, and allows you to manage type registrations in one location.

The following excerpt demonstrates how to add tilt effect support for the Toolkit's context menu `MenuItem` class:

```
public partial class App : Application
{

    public App()
    {
        /* Content omitted for clarity. */

        TiltEffect.TiltableItems.Add(typeof(MenuItem));
    }
//...
}
```

To enable the tilt effect on `MenuItem` elements, you must explicitly set the `IsTiltEnabled` attached property to true, as demonstrated in the following excerpt:

```
<Border Padding="10" BorderThickness="2" BorderBrush="White">
    <TextBlock Text="tilt effect applied to context menu" />
    <toolkit:ContextMenuService.ContextMenu>
        <toolkit:ContextMenu >
            <toolkit:MenuItem Header="item 1"
                toolkit:TiltEffect.IsTiltEnabled="true" />
            <toolkit:MenuItem Header="item 2"
                toolkit:TiltEffect.IsTiltEnabled="true" />
        </toolkit:ContextMenu>
    </toolkit:ContextMenuService.ContextMenu>
</Border>
```

> **NOTE**
>
> Regardless of whether the `TiltEffect.IsTiltEnabled` property is set to true, if the `TiltEffect.TiltableItems` collection does not contain the element type (or that of its ancestor), then the tilt effect is *not* applied.

Applying the tilt effect to a context menu item causes it to be indented slightly (see Figure 9.31).

Applied judiciously, `TiltEffect` can subtly enhance your UI, increasing its perceived responsiveness and making it stand out from the crowd.

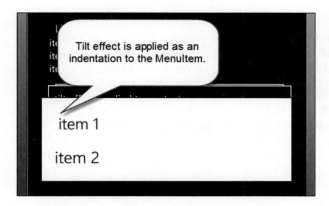

FIGURE 9.31   TiltEffect applied to a MenuItem

ToggleSwitch

ToggleSwitch enables the user to turn something on or off. It is much like the built-in CheckBox control, yet more compatible with the Metro design aesthetic of the phone. ToggleSwitch presents a large, touch friendly switch that users can alternate between two states (see Figure 9.32).

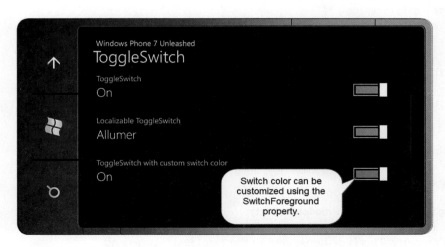

FIGURE 9.32   ToggleSwitch can be localized and its switch color modified.

While ToggleSwitch does not inherit from any built-in button related controls, such as ButtonBase, but rather from ContentControl, it behaves much like the built-in ToggleButton control in the FCL of which the built-in RadioButton and CheckBox controls are derived. In fact, internally the ToggleSwitch uses a ToggleButton to provide its functionality.

Using the `ToggleSwitch`

Like the `ToggleButton`, `ToggleSwitch` uses a nullable Boolean value to represent its state. In its On position, its `IsChecked` property is true. In the Off position, `IsChecked` is false. If the `IsChecked` property is `null`, the `ToggleSwitch` is displayed using its Off position.

You can use the `ToggleSwitch` by either binding its `IsChecked` property to a property in your viewmodel, or by responding to its `Checked` and `Unchecked` events in your code-beside. The latter approach involves subscribing to the `ToggleSwitch.Checked` and `Unchecked` events, as shown:

```
<toolkit:ToggleSwitch
        Header="ToggleSwitch"
        IsChecked="true"
        Checked="ToggleSwitch_Checked"
        Unchecked="ToggleSwitch_Unchecked"/>
```

Both the `Checked` and `Unchecked` events are `RoutedEvents`. The following excerpt shows what event handlers for these events might look like:

```
void ToggleSwitch_Checked(object sender, RoutedEventArgs e)
{
    ToggleSwitch toggleSwitch = (ToggleSwitch)sender;
    bool? isChecked = toggleSwitch.IsChecked;
    /* Do something with value. */
    MessageBox.Show("Checked!");
}

void ToggleSwitch_Unchecked(object sender, RoutedEventArgs e)
{
    MessageBox.Show("Unchecked!");
}
```

`ToggleSwitch` allows customization of its header using its `Header` and `HeaderTemplate` properties. For more information on creating a custom header for the control see the previous section "Adding a Control Header."

Binding the `ToggleSwitch` to a Viewmodel Property

Rather than placing UI logic in the code-beside, an alternative is to bind the `ToggleSwitch` to a viewmodel property. This is demonstrated in the `ToggleSwitchView` and `ToggleSwitchViewModel`, in the downloadable sample code.

The viewmodel contains a `ToggleOn` property, as shown:

```
bool? toggleOn;

public bool? ToggleOn
{
    get
```

```
    {
        return toggleOn;
    }
    set
    {
        Assign(() => ToggleOn, ref toggleOn, value);
    }
}
```

Consuming this property in the view is a `ToggleSwitch`, whose `IsChecked` property has a two-way data binding to the `ToggleOn` property of the viewmodel:

```
<toolkit:ToggleSwitch
    Header="ToggleSwitch"
    IsChecked="{Binding ToggleOn, Mode=TwoWay}" />
```

Thus, when the user taps the `ToggleSwitch`, the `ToggleOn` property of the viewmodel is inverted.

Localizing the `ToggleSwitch`

Unlike controls located in the FCL, the Toolkit does not ship with localized resources. In the case of the `ToggleSwitch`, it is something to be mindful of because of the default `Header` values: Off and On, which must be localized if you want to support other languages.

You could take the Toolkit source code and provide a localized resource dictionary for each language you want to support. This, however, would leave you having to update each new version of the Toolkit with your custom dictionaries—not the best approach.

An alternative approach is to use a custom `IValueConverter` to populate the `Content` property of the `ToggleSwitch` based on the value of its `IsChecked` property. Depending on the value of its `IsChecked` property, we display a particular localized string from a resource dictionary (see Listing 9.9).

For more information on localizing Windows Phone apps, see Chapter 17, "Internationalization."

LISTING 9.9   LocalizedToggleSwitchConverter Class

```
public class LocalizedToggleSwitchConverter : IValueConverter
{
    public object Convert(
        object value, Type targetType, object parameter, CultureInfo culture)
    {
        bool? toggleOn = (bool?)value;
        return toggleOn.HasValue && toggleOn.Value
                ? MainResources.ToggleSwitch_Checked
                : MainResources.ToggleSwitch_Unchecked;
```

LISTING 9.9   Continued

```
    }

    public object ConvertBack(
        object value, Type targetType, object parameter, CultureInfo culture)
    {
        throw new NotImplementedException();
    }
}
```

The IValueConverter can be declared as an application resource by placing it in your app's App.xaml file or in a referenced ResourceDictionary. This allows it to be used throughout your app. Alternatively, it can be defined within your page, as shown:

```
<phone:PhoneApplicationPage.Resources>
    <e:LocalizedToggleSwitchConverter
        x:Name="LocalizedToggleSwitchConverter" />
</phone:PhoneApplicationPage.Resources>
```

Once in place, a ToggleSwitch can bind to the viewmodel value representing the checked state and use the IValueConverter to populate the Content property, as shown:

```
<toolkit:ToggleSwitch
    Header="Localizable ToggleSwitch"
    IsChecked="{Binding ToggleOn, Mode=TwoWay}"
    Content="{Binding ToggleOn,
    Converter={StaticResource LocalizedToggleSwitchConverter}}" />
```

Just as the HeaderTemplate property is used to customize how the control's header is displayed, the ContentTemplate is used to customize how the Content property is displayed.

Changing the Switch Color

By default, the ToggleSwitch control template presents the On state using the phone's theme color. You can explicitly set the ToggleSwitch color using its SwitchForeground property, as shown in the following excerpt:

```
<toolkit:ToggleSwitch
        Header="ToggleSwitch with custom switch color"
        IsChecked="true"
        SwitchForeground="Red"/>
```

In most cases, ToggleSwitch makes for a better choice than the standard CheckBox control. And once you start using it, it becomes almost as ubiquitous as the Button control.

WrapPanel

WrapPanel is a flexible container that is ideally suited to the limited display size of the phone because it allows your UI elements to use space more efficiently. The WrapPanel positions child elements sequentially, from left to right or from top to bottom. When elements extend beyond the panel edge, they are positioned in the next row or column. WrapPanel can operate in one of two layout modes. The Orientation property of the WrapPanel determines its layout mode, either Horizontal (the default value) or Vertical. Figure 9.33 portrays how the WrapPanel positions its children when using a horizontal orientation.

WrapPanel

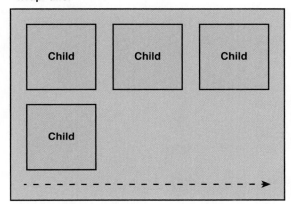

FIGURE 9.33   WrapPanel positions child elements sequentially from left to right (as shown), or from top to bottom.

Child Element Spacing

The ItemHeight and ItemWidth properties of the WrapPanel determine the amount of space that each child element is allocated. If the actual size of the element exceeds this amount, then the element is clipped.

Sample Overview

The WrapPanel sample is located within the ControlExamples/SilverlightToolkit/WrapPanel directory in the WindowsPhone7Unleashed.Examples project in the downloadable sample code.

The WrapPanelView.xaml presents two WrapPanels, one with the default horizontal orientation, the other with a vertical orientation. Each WrapPanel contains five TextBox child elements, as shown in the following excerpt:

```xml
<StackPanel x:Name="ContentPanel" Grid.Row="1">
    <TextBlock Text="horizontal wrap panel"
        Style="{StaticResource LabelTextIndentedStyle}" />
    <toolkit:WrapPanel ItemHeight="120" ItemWidth="120" Height="280"
            Background="DimGray">
        <TextBox Text="1" Background="Blue"
            Style="{StaticResource WrapPanelItem}" />
        <TextBox Text="2" Background="Red"
            Style="{StaticResource WrapPanelItem}" />
        <TextBox Text="3" Background="Orange"
            Style="{StaticResource WrapPanelItem}" />
        <TextBox Text="4" Background="Purple"
            Style="{StaticResource WrapPanelItem}" />
        <TextBox Text="5" Background="Green"
            Style="{StaticResource WrapPanelItem}" />
    </toolkit:WrapPanel>

    <TextBlock Text="vertical wrap panel"
        Style="{StaticResource LabelTextIndentedStyle}"
        Margin="12,30,0,0"/>
    <toolkit:WrapPanel Orientation="Vertical"
            ItemHeight="120" ItemWidth="120" Height="280"
            Background="DimGray">
        <TextBox Text="1" Background="Blue"
            Style="{StaticResource WrapPanelItem}" />
        <TextBox Text="2" Background="Red"
            Style="{StaticResource WrapPanelItem}" />
        <TextBox Text="3" Background="Orange"
            Style="{StaticResource WrapPanelItem}" />
        <TextBox Text="4" Background="Purple"
            Style="{StaticResource WrapPanelItem}" />
        <TextBox Text="5" Background="Green"
            Style="{StaticResource WrapPanelItem}" />
    </toolkit:WrapPanel>
</StackPanel>
```

Each `TextBox` is presented using a custom `ControlTemplate`, which places the `TextBox.Text` in a `TextBlock`. A `TextBox` was chosen because it allows you to create a template binding to its `Text` property. See the following excerpt:

```xml
<phone:PhoneApplicationPage.Resources>
    <Style x:Name="WrapPanelItem" TargetType="TextBox">
        <Setter Property="Width" Value="100" />
        <Setter Property="Height" Value="100" />
        <Setter Property="Template">
            <Setter.Value>
```

```
<ControlTemplate TargetType="TextBox">
    <Border Background="{TemplateBinding Background}">
        <TextBlock Text="{TemplateBinding Text}"
        VerticalAlignment="Center"
        HorizontalAlignment="Center"
        FontSize="50"
        Foreground="White" />
    </Border>
</ControlTemplate>
                </Setter.Value>
            </Setter>
        </Style>
</phone:PhoneApplicationPage.Resources>
```

Each `TextBox` is presented as a `TextBlock` wrapped in a `Border`. The horizontal wrap panel illustrates how the child elements are displayed from left to right, while the vertical wrap panel illustrates the vertical layout (see Figure 9.34).

FIGURE 9.34   A vertical and horizontal `WrapPanel`

Using a `WrapPanel` in Conjunction with a `ListBox`

`WrapPanel` is useful to present a list of items using XAML. However, using a `WrapPanel` to present a bound list of values located in a viewmodel can be best achieved by supplanting the `ItemsPanelTemplate` of a `ListBox` with a `WrapPanel`.

This technique is demonstrated in the downloadable sample code. The WrapPanelViewModel class contains a list of strings, representing the numbers 1 to 5, which we use as the source collection for a ListBox control. The list of strings is generated using the LINQ Range and Select methods. See the following excerpt:

```
readonly IEnumerable<string> items
    = Enumerable.Range(1, 5).Select(x => x.ToString());

public IEnumerable<string> Items
{
    get
    {
        return items;
    }
}
```

The view contains a ListsBox with its ItemsSource property bound to the viewmodel's Items property. We redefine the ItemsPanel of the ListBox and use a WrapPanel to host the child elements.

The ItemTemplate of the ListBox is also defined so that each item is presented in a TextBox, which is compatible with the custom WrapPanelItem template:

```
<ListBox ItemsSource="{Binding Items}">
    <ListBox.ItemsPanel>
        <ItemsPanelTemplate>
            <toolkit:WrapPanel
                ItemHeight="120" ItemWidth="120" Height="280"
                Background="DimGray"/>
        </ItemsPanelTemplate>
    </ListBox.ItemsPanel>
    <ListBox.ItemTemplate>
        <DataTemplate>
            <TextBox Text="{Binding}" Background="Blue"
            Style="{StaticResource WrapPanelItem}" />
        </DataTemplate>
    </ListBox.ItemTemplate>
</ListBox>
```

You see in Figure 9.35, that each item in the list is presented in a similar manner as the statically defined items presented earlier in this section.

Another example of presenting a list of items using a WrapPanel in conjunction with a ListBox can be found in Chapter 10, "Pivot and Panorama."

FIGURE 9.35   A `WrapPanel` is used to display the items in a `ListBox`.

Summary

This chapter began with a short getting started guide that showed how to obtain and reference the Toolkit. It then explored each Toolkit component starting with the `ListPicker`, which allows you to display a large number of options using an expandable or full-screen option picker. You saw how to bind a `ListPicker` to a viewmodel collection and how to customize the way items are displayed.

The chapter then looked at the `AutoCompleteBox`, which provides suggestions for the user in a drop-down list. You saw how to use the `AutoCompleteBox` from code-beside and via data binding to a viewmodel. You looked at dynamically changing the way the `AutoCompleteBox` filters items, at creating a custom filter, and at dynamic population of the suggestion list. How to overcome a limitation to allow binding from the `AutoCompleteBox.Text` property was also discussed.

The chapter looked at the `ContextMenu`, which is an expanding menu control that you can use to emulate the familiar right-click menu in Windows desktop applications. You saw how to consume the various `ContextMenu` events and how to use the `ContextMenu` in conjunction with the MVVM pattern. You also looked at hosting a `ContextMenu` in a `ListBoxItem`.

The `DatePicker` and `TimePicker`, which allow the user to select a date or time using infinitely scrollable lists, were discussed. You learned how to customize the `Value` format of the controls and how to create a custom full-screen picker page. You also learned how to use the lesser known `LoopingSelector` to allow the user to select a numeric value from an infinitely scrolling list.

9

The chapter then examined the `LongListSelector`, which is just like the `ListBox` control, yet allows you to group items and provides built-in virtualization for efficiently handling long lists of objects. Flat lists as well as grouped lists were discussed, and you saw two sample applications: one that displays a list of Windows Phone Marketplace apps and a second that displays a grouped list of user contacts. You saw how to dynamically switch the group by property, how to change the group picker panel, and also how to create a `BooleanToBrush` converter, so as to switch a background color depending on a bound Boolean value.

The `PerformanceProgressBar`, which is an animated progress bar that overcomes some performance issues with the FCL's `ProgressBar`, was then discussed along with the `TiltEffect` component, which allows you to add a subtle rotation effect to other controls when the user interacts with them, and which helps to engage the user and improve the perceived responsiveness of the UI. You also saw how to suppress the tilt effect on particular controls and how to add new control types to the list of tiltable control types.

The chapter then looked at the `ToggleSwitch`, which serves as a replacement for the `CheckBox` control in some scenarios. You saw how to respond to the `Checked` and `Unchecked` events of the `ToggleSwitch`, and at binding the `ToggleSwitch` to a viewmodel property. You looked at localizing the `ToggleSwitch` header text, allowing it to be used when the display language of the phone is not English, and also how to change the switch color using the `ToggleSwitch.SwitchForeground` property.

Finally, the chapter discussed the `WrapPanel`, which is a flexible container that positions items sequentially and is ideally suited to the limited display size of the phone. You learned how to use the `WrapPanel` in conjunction with a `ListBox`, to enable binding to a viewmodel collection.

CHAPTER 10

Pivot and Panorama

In the past, Silverlight applications that needed to present a large amount of information have usually done so by splitting the information across multiple Silverlight page elements. The Pivot and Panorama controls complement the existing page navigation infrastructure to provide the ability to present a large amount of information on a single page.

Pivot and Panorama are new controls and at the time of writing are unique to the phone. Both controls are fundamental to the visual user experience on the phone, and the phone's built-in apps use them extensively. You will, therefore, probably find yourself using them a lot, although they are not necessarily a suitable choice for every app.

This chapter begins by looking at both controls, their differences and similarities. It then looks at the anatomy of the Pivot and how to create a simple Pivot driven page. You see how to use the Pivot load events, allowing you to load content on demand. You explore a novel approach that allows you to associate a different application bar with each PivotItem using a custom AppBar control, which is not readily achievable with the built-in ApplicationBar! Putting it all together, you learn how to create a Pivot driven chat app, which is then augmented to demonstrate implicit PivotItem generation and data templating.

The second part of this chapter explores the Panorama. Again you look at the anatomy of the Panorama and discuss how to get the most out of the control. You learn how to create a simple bookshop app that uses a WCF service to retrieve a list of products displayed within a Panorama, and the chapter concludes by looking at some of the things to avoid when using a Pivot or Panorama.

Pivot and Panorama Differences and Similarities

The `Pivot` and `Panorama` are layout controls that help you display data in a unique way. They have several things in common. They both hold a number of horizontally arranged sections (items). They are visually similar; both show a segment of the offscreen content, have titles, and have section titles.

Both controls have built-in touch navigation. It is, therefore, not necessary to implement any special gesture functionality in your app, as it is already built-in. The touch support allows the user to navigate left to right between the different sections using the pan and flick touch-gestures.

Horizontal navigation is cyclical; after navigating past the last section, the first section appears.

Also, both the `Pivot` and `Panorama` allow complete customization of the title and headers.

While both controls have many similarities, they also have some fundamental differences, as each control is designed to serve a different purpose. The `Pivot` is designed to be more task-oriented; it is about getting something done. It has greater emphasis on each individual section within the control, and section content is confined to the width of the screen, whereas the `Panorama` has sections that span over screen boundaries and is designed to entice the user to explore all sections.

> **TIP**
>
> A page with a `Pivot` is a suitable candidate for an application bar, whereas one with a `Panorama` is not. If your page needs an application bar, use a `Pivot` not a `Panorama`.

There are also performance differences between the two controls. When a `Panorama` loads, all `Panorama` items go through a render pass. Conversely, items within a `Pivot` are loaded incrementally for each neighboring item. Thus, the `Pivot` generally offers a faster start time.

> **TIP**
>
> Regardless of whether you use a `Pivot` or `Panorama`, try to limit the number of `Panorama` or `Pivot` items. Memory usage expands rapidly when there are a lot of views and images. Moreover, if the user navigates to another page, the current page stays in memory. Therefore, complex `Pivot` or `Panorama` pages will also remain in memory unless explicitly discarded.

Style Assumptions

`Panorama` and `Pivot` items are styled under the assumption that most of their content has a 12-pixel margin on the left and right. The built-in styles include this margin by default. Therefore, if you place a control into a `Pivot` or `Panorama` that has a margin of less than 12 it may make your interface layout look incorrect.

Introduction to the `Pivot` Control

The `Pivot` may be regarded as the tab control for the phone. The control places individual views horizontally next to each other and manages left and right navigation. Flicking or panning horizontally on the page cycles between pivot items.

Unlike the `Panorama`, where content may exceed screen boundaries, `Pivot` content is confined to the screen's width. Where the `Panorama` displays a few pixels of content of the next section, the `Pivot` does not, but instead relies on section titles to give the user an indication of neighboring sections.

The `Pivot` is designed to represent data or items of a similar type. For example, a `Pivot` can be used as activities for similar content around the same task flow. A good example of using a `Pivot` in this manner is the built-in Email app, which shows all emails in one view, flagged emails in another, unread email in another, and so on.

The `Pivot` plays host to a secondary control called a `PivotItem`. The `PivotItem` serves as a container that hosts other content and controls, such as grids, lists, and buttons.

BEST PRACTICE

Try to limit the number of `Pivot` items to seven. This ensures that users are able to visualize a mental map of the `Pivot` sections and to comprehend what is being presented.

Introduction to the `Panorama` Control

The `Panorama` is a wide horizontal canvas that spans over screen boundaries. The canvas is partitioned into several different sections. The `Panorama` is designed to be a starting place and is normally used as the top layer to other pages. Ordinarily, page content is designed to fit within the confines of the phone display; the `Panorama`, however, offers a unique way to view controls and data by using the long horizontal canvas that extends beyond the confines of the display. Layered animations are used to smoothly pan content at different speeds, providing a parallax effect.

Like the `Pivot`, the `Panorama` also uses a secondary control called a `PanoramaItem`, which serves as a container that hosts other content and controls, such as grids, lists, and buttons.

As the `Panorama` is intended to coax the user to explore, it should show content that is interesting and specific to the user. The user should also not be overloaded with too much content; think *white space* and not *loads of data*. The `Panorama` should be thought of as a starting place, containing data and links that take the user to more detailed pages of content, pages that may include a `Pivot` for example. The user is then able to leave the exploratory style of the `Panorama` for the more focused style of the `Pivot`.

BEST PRACTICE

For the sake of usability and performance, try to limit the number of `Panorama` sections to four.

10

Unlike the `Pivot`, the `Panorama` is designed to be explorative; it is not about completing a task and should not show an application bar.

A page with a `Panorama` should offer a visually appealing experience. This can be achieved with an attractive background. A `Panorama` background can be either a single color or a background image. The image size should be 800 pixels high and 480 to 1000 pixels wide, depending on the number of sections to be displayed. It is possible to use an image with a width exceeding 1000 pixels, but more than 2000 pixels and the image will be clipped.

> **NOTE**
>
> An image with a height of less than 800 pixels is stretched to that height without constraining its proportions. This is important if you want to maintain the aspect ratio of your image.

Pivot and Panorama Placement in the FCL

`Pivot` and `Panorama` controls reside in the Microsoft.Phone.Controls assembly. Both the `Pivot` and the `Panorama` inherit from the `TemplatedItemsControl` (see Figure 10.1). The `TemplatedItemsControl`'s generic type parameter is specified as either a `PivotItem` for the `Pivot` class or a `PanoramaItem` by `Panorama` class.

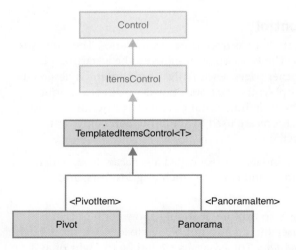

FIGURE 10.1   `Pivot` and `Panorama` inherit from `TemplatedItemsControl`.

The main role of the `TemplatedItemsControl` is the implicit creation of `PivotItems` and `PanoramaItems` when using the superclass `ItemsControl.ItemsSource` property to populate a `Pivot` or `Panorama`.

Using the `Pivot` Control

The `Pivot` can be used for displaying combinations of controls, user controls, and even other pages. The `Pivot` plays host to individual pages of content called `PivotItems`. A `PivotItem` control is analogous to an individual tab and is responsible for displaying the content within a page. Only one `PivotItem` is displayed at a time. Flicking or panning left to right on the page, or tapping a `PivotItem`'s header, advances to the next page of content.

The `Pivot` supports the following gestures and navigational effects:

▶ **Horizontal pan**—This is done by dragging a `PivotItem` or its header, from left to right, or right to left.

▶ **Horizontal flick**—This is done by a quick swipe, either left to right, or right to left.

▶ **Tap**—Tapping a `PivotItem`'s header transitions to that `PivotItem`.

Placing a `Pivot` on a Page

The following items describe the ways in which to surface a `Pivot` on a page within Visual Studio:

▶ Using the Windows Phone Pivot Application template, which can be selected when creating a new project. This template generates a Windows Phone application project, with the main page prepopulated with a `Pivot`.

▶ Using the Windows Phone Pivot Page template from the Visual Studio Add New Item dialog.

▶ The `Pivot` control can be added to the Toolbox in Visual Studio and can then be dropped onto the design surface of your page or onto the XAML editor.

▶ The `Pivot` control can be simply added to an existing page by removing the title panel of a page and adding the `Pivot` XAML.

To use a `Pivot` on an existing page, remove the title panel on the page and add a `Pivot` element in XAML, like so:

```
<Grid x:Name="LayoutRoot" Background="Transparent">

    <controls:Pivot Title="Windows Phone 7 Unleashed">
        <controls:PivotItem Header="first">
            <TextBlock Text="Lorem ipsum dolor sit amet, consectetur..."
                TextWrapping="Wrap"
                Style="{StaticResource PhoneTextSubtleStyle}"/>
        </controls:PivotItem>

        <controls:PivotItem Header="second">
            <TextBlock Text="Lorem ipsum dolor sit amet, consectetur..."
```

10

```
            TextWrapping="Wrap"
            Style="{StaticResource PhoneTextSubtleStyle}"/>
    </controls:PivotItem>

    <controls:PivotItem Header="third">
        <TextBlock Text="Lorem ipsum dolor sit amet, consectetur..."
            TextWrapping="Wrap"
            Style="{StaticResource PhoneTextSubtleStyle}"/>
    </controls:PivotItem>
</controls:Pivot>

</Grid>
```

The `Pivot` has Visual Studio design-time support. The Visual Studio Silverlight designer automatically shifts to the active `PivotItem` when the cursor is placed with the `PivotItems` element in the XAML view.

When the app is launched, you see the result shown in Figure 10.2.

FIGURE 10.2   A page with a `Pivot` containing three `PivotItems`

The usual page and application title panel should be omitted from any pages containing a `Pivot` or `Panorama`, because the `Pivot` and the `Panorama` take care of displaying that information.

Creating a Pivot Application with the Visual Studio New Project Dialog

The Visual Studio New Project dialog can also be used to generate an entire application along with a page surfacing a `Pivot` or `Panorama` control (see Figure 10.3).

FIGURE 10.3   Using the New Project dialog to create a Windows Phone pivot application

The *Pivot Application* project template produces a `PhoneApplicationPage` (MainPage.xaml) containing a `Pivot`. The template produces a `Pivot` with two `PivotItems`, and each item contains a `ListBox`.

Pivot Anatomy

The `Pivot` is comprised of two distinct sections: a header list and a `PivotItem` presenter (see Figure 10.4).

The `Pivot` headers are displayed using a `PivotHeadersControl`. The active `PivotItem` has its header highlighted. Inactive `PivotItems` have their headers displayed until the headers exceed the width of the control. If there are too few headers to take up the full width of the control, the headers do not loop, and each header is displayed only once.

`PivotItems` are displayed using an `ItemsPresenter`. `PivotItem` is a `ContentControl` playing host to a single item of content. A `ContentPresenter` is used to display the content of the `PivotItem`.

Only `PivotItem` controls can be defined within the `Pivot` control. If you attempt to place another element type directly within the `Pivot` control, in XAML, an `InvalidOperationException` is thrown when the `Pivot` is initialized. This is contrary to the official Microsoft documentation on MSDN, which states that an element other than a `PivotItem` is implicitly wrapped into a `PivotItem` control.

10

FIGURE 10.4   Anatomy of the `Pivot`

The contents of a `PivotItem` control can either be specified in XAML, or added programmatically through the `PivotItem`'s `Content` property.

Setting the Active `PivotItem`

The `SelectedItem` or `SelectedIndex` can be used to shift to a particular `PivotItem` within the `Pivot`. If the `Pivot` is populated using its `ItemsSource` property, then the `SelectedItem` retrieves the data object rather than the actual `PivotItem` control.

NOTE

Setting a `Pivot`'s `SelectedIndex` before it has loaded raises an exception. This can be prevented by suppressing the `Exception` by wrapping the assignment in a try/catch block, or by performing the assignment in a `Loaded` event handler.

Pivot Load Events

`Pivot` raises various events to indicate when a `PivotItem` is being brought into view and when it is being moved out of view.

BEST PRACTICE

To improve the performance of your app, use the `LoadingPivotItem` event to load content on demand. One approach is to convert the content of each `PivotItem` into a `UserControl`. You can then subscribe to the `LoadingPivotItem` event on the `Pivot`, and then when the event is raised instantiate the `UserControl` and set it as the `PivotItem`'s content.

The `UnloadedPivotItem` event also provides the opportunity to clean up any unneeded resources.

When the user switches from one `PivotItem` to another, events are raised in the following order:

1. The `UnloadingPivotItem` event is raised for the first `PivotItem`.

2. The `LoadingPivotItem` event is raised for the second `PivotItem`.

3. The `UnloadedPivotItem` event is raised for the first `PivotItem`.

4. The `LoadedPivotItem` event is raised for the second `PivotItem`.

These events are not cancellable. That is, they are not designed to allow for preventing or returning the `Pivot` to the previously active `PivotItem`. It is possible, however, to queue a change back to the previously active `PivotItem`. Queuing an index change in one of the load event handlers has to be performed after the current `PivotItem` change has finished; otherwise, the `Pivot` will get out of sync. This can be done by using the `Dispatcher` to invoke the change, which means it occurs after the current UI thread task completes. The following example demonstrates how to use the `Dispatcher` to lock the `Pivot` to the first `PivotItem`:

```
void Pivot_LoadingPivotItem(object sender, PivotItemEventArgs e)
{
    Dispatcher.BeginInvoke(delegate { pivot.SelectedIndex = 0; });
}
```

Hosting Multiple Application Bars with the `Pivot`

Particular `PivotItems` within your `Pivot` may require differing capabilities with separate sets of application bar menu items and buttons. The ability to associate a different application bar with each `PivotItem` is not natively supported by the Windows Phone FCL. You can, however, achieve this by using the custom `AppBar` control (discussed in Chapter 8, "Taming the Application Bar").

This section looks at the relevant changes made to the `AppBar` that have been made to support this capability, and then at an example of creating a page containing a `Pivot`, whose items each contain an independent application bar that is swapped into place when the `PivotItem` becomes active.

10

Code has been added to the AppBar's Attach method, which detects whether the AppBar is located within a Pivot. This method is called when AppBar is first loaded and is shown in the following excerpt:

```
public void Attach()
{
    var page = this.GetVisualAncestors<PhoneApplicationPage>()
                                    .FirstOrDefault();

    var pivot = this.GetVisualAncestors<Pivot>().FirstOrDefault();
    if (pivot != null)
    {
        pivot.SelectionChanged -= pivot_SelectionChanged;
        pivot.SelectionChanged += pivot_SelectionChanged;
        UpdateApplicationBar(pivot);
    }
    else if (page != null)
    {
        page.ApplicationBar = applicationBar;
        Build();
    }
}
```

If the AppBar is located within a Pivot, each time a different PivotItem is displayed within the Pivot, the SelectionChanged event is raised, which in turn calls the UpdateApplicationBar method, shown here:

```
protected virtual void UpdateApplicationBar(Pivot pivot)
{
    var page = this.GetVisualAncestors<PhoneApplicationPage>()
                                        .FirstOrDefault();

    if (pivot == null || page == null)
    {
        return;
    }

    bool assignBar = false;

    if (pivot.SelectedItem == DataContext)
    {
        assignBar = true;
    }
    else
    {
```

```
        var frameworkElement = pivot.SelectedItem as FrameworkElement;
        if (frameworkElement != null
                && frameworkElement.DataContext == DataContext)
        {
            assignBar = true;
        }
    }

    if (assignBar)
    {
        page.ApplicationBar = applicationBar;
        Build();
    }
    else if (page.ApplicationBar == applicationBar)
    {
        page.ApplicationBar = null;
    }
}
```

A custom extension method called `GetVisualAncestors` (located in the `VisualTree` class) is used to locate the parent page.

We then determine whether the `AppBar` is located in the currently selected `PivotItem`. This is done by either comparing the `Pivot`'s `SelectedItem` or the `DataContext` of the `SelectedItem` with the `DataContext` of the `AppBar`. If equal then you know that the `AppBar` should be shown.

> **NOTE**
>
> When a `Pivot`'s `ItemsSource` is used to populate the `Pivot`, `PivotItems` are generated implicitly, much like `ListBoxItems` are for the `ListBox` (see Chapter 5, "Content Controls, Items Controls, and Range Controls").

With these changes in place you can display a different application bar depending on the selected `PivotItem`. To demonstrate its use, the following example creates a simple messaging app that allows the user to send a message via one `PivotItem` and view received messages via another.

The example code for this section is located in the `PivotView.xaml` page and the `PivotViewModel` class in the downloadable sample code.

The `PivotViewModel` class bootstraps two other viewmodels: `SendMessageViewModel` and `MessagesViewModel`, both of which become the viewmodels for two different `PivotItems` in the `PivotView` page (see Listing 10.1).

10

LISTING 10.1   PivotViewModel Class

```
public class PivotViewModel : ViewModelBase
{
    public PivotViewModel() : base("Pivot")
    {
        MockChatService chatService = new MockChatService();
        sendMessageViewModel = new SendMessageViewModel(chatService);
        messagesViewModel = new MessagesViewModel(chatService);
    }

    SendMessageViewModel sendMessageViewModel;

    public SendMessageViewModel SendMessageViewModel
    {
        get
        {
            return sendMessageViewModel;
        }
        private set
        {
            Assign("SendMessageViewModel", ref sendMessageViewModel, value);
        }
    }

    MessagesViewModel messagesViewModel;

    public MessagesViewModel MessagesViewModel
    {
        get
        {
            return messagesViewModel;
        }
        private set
        {
            Assign("MessagesViewModel", ref messagesViewModel, value);
        }
    }
}
```

A class implementing the custom IChatService allows messages to be sent and received. The MockChatService class implements the custom IChatService, which has two members:

▶ **SendMessage**—A method that accepts a single string parameter and sends the message to all subscribers

▶ **MessageReceived**—An event that is raised when the chat service receives a message

For the purposes of the demonstration, a simple loopback implementation of the
IChatService is used; when the SendMessage method is called, the MessageReceived event
is raised.

The SendMessageViewModel uses the IChatService to send messages via the SendCommand (see
Listing 10.2). When the messageBody field has been populated, the
IChatService.SendMessage method is called.

Listing 10.2   SendMessageViewModel Class

```
public class SendMessageViewModel : ViewModelBase
{
    public SendMessageViewModel(IChatService chatService) : base("Send")
    {
        ArgumentValidator.AssertNotNull(chatService, "chatService");

        sendCommand = new DelegateCommand(
            obj =>
            {
                if (!string.IsNullOrEmpty(messageBody))
                {
                    chatService.SendMessage(messageBody);
                    MessageBody = null;
                    Feedback = "Message sent";
                }
            });
    }

    string emailAddress = "John@example.com";

    public string EmailAddress
    {
        get
        {
            return emailAddress;
        }
        set
        {
            Assign("EmailAddress", ref emailAddress, value);
        }
    }

    string messageBody = "Sample message";

    public string MessageBody
    {
        get
```

LISTING 10.2   Continued

```
        {
            return messageBody;
        }
        set
        {
            Assign("MessageBody", ref messageBody, value);
        }
    }

    readonly DelegateCommand sendCommand;

    public ICommand SendCommand
    {
        get
        {
            return sendCommand;
        }
    }

    string feedback;

    public string Feedback
    {
        get
        {
            return feedback;
        }
        private set
        {
            Assign("Feedback", ref feedback, value);
        }
    }
}
```

The purpose of the MessagesViewModel class is to listen for the MessageReceived event of the IChatService and to place incoming messages into an ObservableCollection, which is displayed in the view (see Listing 10.3). The RefreshCommand merely emulates a refresh by populating its Feedback property.

Listing 10.3   MessagesViewModel Class

```
public class MessagesViewModel : ViewModelBase
{
    public MessagesViewModel(IChatService chatService): base("Received")
```

LISTING 10.3   Continued

```csharp
{
    ArgumentValidator.AssertNotNull(chatService, "chatService");
    chatService.MessageReceived
        += (sender, args) =>
            {
                if (args == null)
                {
                    return;
                }
                messageItems.Add(new MessageItem(args.Message));
                Feedback = "Message received.";
            };

    refreshCommand = new DelegateCommand(
        obj =>
        {
            Feedback = "Refresh command executed.";
        });
}

ObservableCollection<MessageItem> messageItems
    = new ObservableCollection<MessageItem>();

public ObservableCollection<MessageItem> MessageItems
{
    get
    {
        return messageItems;
    }
    internal set
    {
        Assign("MessageItems", ref messageItems, value);
    }
}

string feedback;

public string Feedback
{
    get
    {
        return feedback;
    }
    private set
```

10

LISTING 10.3   Continued

```
        {
            Assign("Feedback", ref feedback, value);
        }
    }

    readonly DelegateCommand refreshCommand;

    public ICommand RefreshCommand
    {
        get
        {
            return refreshCommand;
        }
    }
}
```

The PivotView page instantiates the PivotViewModel, assigning it to its own DataContext:

```
public partial class PivotView : PhoneApplicationPage
{
    public PivotView()
    {
        InitializeComponent();
        DataContext = new PivotViewModel();
    }
}
```

The view's XAML contains a Pivot with two PivotItems: one for allowing the user to send messages using the SendMessageViewModel, the other for viewing received messages using the MessagesViewModel.

An independent AppBar is present in both PivotItems. The PivotItem showing the received messages allows the user to refresh the list using the viewmodel's RefreshCommand via its AppBar, while the PivotItem for sending a message allows the user to dispatch a message using a SendCommand via a different AppBar. Listing 10.4 shows an excerpt from the PivotView.xaml page containing the Pivot.

Listing 10.4   PivotView.xaml (excerpt)

```
<Grid x:Name="LayoutRoot" Background="Transparent">

    <controls:Pivot x:Name="pivot"
            Title="Windows Phone 7 Unleashed">
        <controls:Pivot.Background>
            <ImageBrush ImageSource="../../../Images/PivotBackground.png"/>
```

LISTING 10.4   Continued

```xml
        </controls:Pivot.Background>
        <controls:PivotItem DataContext="{Binding MessagesViewModel}"
                Header="{Binding Title}">
            <StackPanel>
                <u:AppBar>
                    <u:AppBarIconButton
                        Command="{Binding RefreshCommand}"
                        Text="Refresh"
                    IconUri="/Images/ApplicationBarIcons/AppBarRefresh.png" />
                </u:AppBar>
                <ListBox ItemsSource="{Binding MessageItems}">
                    <ListBox.ItemTemplate>
                        <DataTemplate>
                            <TextBlock Text="{Binding Body}"
                            Style="{StaticResource PhoneTextNormalStyle}" />
                        </DataTemplate>
                    </ListBox.ItemTemplate>
                </ListBox>
                <TextBlock Text="{Binding Feedback}"
                    Style="{StaticResource PhoneTextAccentStyle}"
                    Margin="12,30,12,0" />
            </StackPanel>
        </controls:PivotItem>
        <controls:PivotItem DataContext="{Binding SendMessageViewModel}"
                Header="{Binding Title}">
            <StackPanel>
                <u:AppBar>
                    <u:AppBarIconButton
                    Command="{Binding SendCommand}"
                    Text="Send"
                IconUri="/Images/ApplicationBarIcons/AppBarMessageSend.png"/>
                </u:AppBar>
                <TextBlock Text="user"
                    Style="{StaticResource PhoneTextTitle3Style}" />
                <TextBox InputScope="EmailSmtpAddress"
                    Text="{Binding EmailAddress, Mode=TwoWay}" />
                <TextBlock Text="message"
                    Style="{StaticResource PhoneTextTitle3Style}" />
                <TextBox Text="{Binding MessageBody, Mode=TwoWay}"
                    TextWrapping="Wrap"
                    Height="140" />
                <TextBlock Text="{Binding Feedback}"
                    Style="{StaticResource PhoneTextAccentStyle}"
                    Margin="12,30,12,0" />
```

10

LISTING 10.4   Continued

```
            </StackPanel>
        </controls:PivotItem>
    </controls:Pivot>
</Grid>
```

An image is used as the background for the `Pivot`. It is usually recommended to set the Build Action of image files to Content so as to minimize the size of the assembly and thereby decrease your app's startup time. This is not the case with `Pivot` and `Panorama`.

> **NOTE**
>
> If you use a background image in a `Pivot` or `Panorama` control, set its Build Action to Resource to ensure that it is shown as soon as the control is shown. When the Build Action is set to Content, it causes the image to be loaded asynchronously, and may leave your `Pivot` or `Panorama` momentarily sitting on a plain white or black background.

The `DataContext` of each `PivotItem` is set to a different property in the viewmodel. The `Header` for each `PivotItem` is then resolved to the `Title` property of the `ViewModelBase` class.

As an aside, while the `PivotItem.Header` property can be specified using either property attribute syntax, assigning it to a simple string; or property element syntax, assigning to a nested element, it can also be specified by using a `DataTemplate` defined at the `Pivot` element level, as shown in the following sample:

```
<controls:Pivot Title="Windows Phone 7 Unleashed">
    <controls:Pivot.HeaderTemplate>
        <DataTemplate>
            <TextBlock Text="{Binding Title}"
                    Style="{StaticResource PhoneTextTitle2Style}" />
        </DataTemplate>
    </controls:Pivot.HeaderTemplate>
    <controls:PivotItem DataContext="{Binding MessagesViewModel}">
        <!--Content omitted. -->
    </controls:PivotItem>
    <controls:PivotItem DataContext="{Binding SendMessageViewModel}">
        <!-- Content omitted. -->
    </controls:PivotItem>
</controls:Pivot>
```

Continuing with the example, when the Received `PivotItem` is active the Refresh button allows the user to simulate refreshing the data source (see Figure 10.5).

FIGURE 10.5   Received view in the sample app

Conversely, when the *Send* `PivotItem` is active, the user can enter a message and use the Send button to dispatch the message (see Figure 10.6).

FIGURE 10.6   Dispatching a message via the Send `PivotItem`

When the Send button is tapped, the `SendMessageViewModel`'s `SendCommand` is executed and the message is passed to the `IChatService` using its `SendMessage` method. On receipt, the chat service merely raises its `MessageReceived` event. Recall that the `MessagesViewModel` subscribes to this event. When it is raised, the new message is added to its `MessageItems` `ObservableCollection`, which causes the Received `PivotItem` to be updated with the new message (see Figure 10.7).

FIGURE 10.7   The message is received and displayed on the Received `PivotItem`.

Populating a `Pivot` Via a Data Bound Collection

This second example looks at using a collection of viewmodels to dynamically populate a `Pivot` using a `DataTemplate`. The result of this example is the same as the previous example, except in this case the `PivotItems` are dynamically created based on their data type. This provides some added flexibility that can be useful in larger apps.

The example code for this section is located in the files `DataboundPivotView.xaml`, `DataboundPivotView.xaml.cs`, and `DataboundPivotViewModel.cs` in the downloadable sample code.

In this example the viewmodel has been changed from exposing two child viewmodel properties to a collection of viewmodels (see Listing 10.5).

Listing 10.5   `DataboundPivotViewModel` Class

```
public class DataboundPivotViewModel : ViewModelBase
{
    public DataboundPivotViewModel() : base("Databound Pivot")
    {
        MockChatService chatService = new MockChatService();
        items.Add(new MessagesViewModel(chatService));
        items.Add(new SendMessageViewModel(chatService));
    }

    readonly ObservableCollection<ViewModelBase> items
        = new ObservableCollection<ViewModelBase>();

    public ObservableCollection<ViewModelBase> Items
    {
        get
        {
```

LISTING 10.5   Continued

```
            return items;
        }
    }
}
```

By using this approach you can dynamically add and remove content via the main view-model. Depending on the data type of the viewmodel, a particular `DataTemplate` is resolved from the application's `Resources` collection. This is done using a custom `ContentControl` called `TypeTemplateSelector` (see Listing 10.6).

Listing 10.6   TypeTemplateSelector Class

```
public class TypeTemplateSelector : ContentControl
{
    protected override void OnContentChanged(
            object oldContent, object newContent)
    {
        base.OnContentChanged(oldContent, newContent);
        if (newContent == null)
        {
            return;
        }
        Type newContentType = newContent.GetType();
        ContentTemplate = Application.Current.Resources[
            newContentType.Name + "Template"] as DataTemplate;
    }
}
```

The `TypeTemplateSelector` attempts to resolve the `DataTemplate` for the viewmodels by applying the naming convention *[data type]Template*. This simplifies our main view, whose XAML is shown in Listing 10.7.

Listing 10.7   Data BoundPivotView.xaml (excerpt)

```
<Grid x:Name="LayoutRoot" Background="Transparent">

    <controls:Pivot Title="Windows Phone 7 Unleashed"
            ItemsSource="{Binding Items}">
        <controls:Pivot.Background>
            <ImageBrush ImageSource="../../../Images/PivotBackground.png"/>
        </controls:Pivot.Background>
        <controls:Pivot.HeaderTemplate>
            <DataTemplate>
                <TextBlock Text="{Binding Title}" />
```

LISTING 10.7   Continued

```
              </DataTemplate>
          </controls:Pivot.HeaderTemplate>
          <controls:Pivot.ItemTemplate>
              <DataTemplate>
                  <p:TypeTemplateSelector Content="{Binding}"
                      VerticalAlignment="Top"
                      HorizontalAlignment="Left" />
              </DataTemplate>
          </controls:Pivot.ItemTemplate>
      </controls:Pivot>

</Grid>
```

The `DataTemplates` are placed in the application resources using the App.xaml file. Contained within the App.xaml file is the `SendMessageViewModelTemplate`, which is used to present the `SendMessageViewModel`, shown in the following excerpt:

```
<DataTemplate x:Key="SendMessageViewModelTemplate">
    <StackPanel Width="400">
        <u:AppBar>
            <u:AppBarIconButton
                Command="{Binding SendCommand}"
                Text="Send"
                IconUri="/Images/ApplicationBarIcons/AppBarMessageSend.png"/>
        </u:AppBar>
        <TextBlock Text="user"
            Style="{StaticResource PhoneTextTitle3Style}" />
        <TextBox InputScope="EmailSmtpAddress"
            Text="{Binding EmailAddress, Mode=TwoWay}" />
        <TextBlock Text="message"
            Style="{StaticResource PhoneTextTitle3Style}" />
        <TextBox Text="{Binding MessageBody, Mode=TwoWay}"
            TextWrapping="Wrap"
            Height="300" />
        <TextBlock Text="{Binding Feedback}"
            Style="{StaticResource PhoneTextAccentStyle}"
            Margin="12,30,12,0" />
    </StackPanel>
</DataTemplate>
```

In addition, the `MessageViewModel` is presented using the MessageViewModelTemplate:

```
<DataTemplate x:Key="MessagesViewModelTemplate">
    <StackPanel>
        <u:AppBar>
```

```
            <u:AppBarIconButton
                Command="{Binding RefreshCommand}"
                Text="Refresh"
            IconUri="/Images/ApplicationBarIcons/AppBarRefresh.png"/>
        </u:AppBar>
        <ListBox ItemsSource="{Binding MessageItems}">
            <ListBox.ItemTemplate>
                <DataTemplate>
                    <TextBlock Text="{Binding Body}"
                    Style="{StaticResource PhoneTextNormalStyle}"/>
                </DataTemplate>
            </ListBox.ItemTemplate>
        </ListBox>
        <TextBlock Text="{Binding Feedback}"
            Style="{StaticResource PhoneTextAccentStyle}"
            Margin="12,30,12,0" />
    </StackPanel>
</DataTemplate>
```

Using the Panorama Control

Working with the Panorama control is much like working with the Pivot. You can create a Panorama in the same way as a Pivot, either by using the built-in project or application template, or by manually adding the Panorama XAML to an existing page. The XAML for a Panorama usually looks something like this:

```
<controls:Panorama Title="an application">

    <controls:PanoramaItem Header="item1">
        <!-- Place content here. -->
    </controls:PanoramaItem>

    <controls:PanoramaItem Header="item2">
        <!-- Place content here. -->
    </controls:PanoramaItem>

</controls:Panorama>
```

The PanoramaItem controls host the panoramic content, and these represent the sections displayed within the control.

Panorama Anatomy

The Panorama is comprised of three different layers:

- ▶ Background layer
- ▶ Title layer
- ▶ Items layer

Each layer is contained within a Grid control that serves as the layout root for the Panorama control (see Figure 10.8).

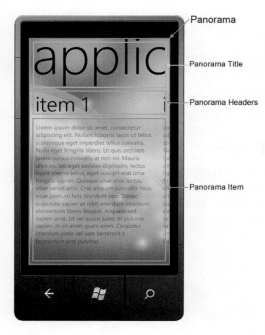

FIGURE 10.8   The Panorama control anatomy

Background Layer

The background represents the bottom layer of the Panorama, with sections sitting above. The background layer is represented by a PanningBackgroundLayer within the Panorama class. This layer is set with the Background property on the Panorama control.

You can set the background of the Panorama to an image using an ImageBrush. Alternatively, a color or gradient can be used by assigning the Background property to a SolidColorBrush or GradientBrush.

NOTE

You should not set a `Panorama` control's `Background` to null. If it is set to null, gesture response is unreliable. The `Background` is set to Transparent by default in the default template.

The background is stretched vertically to fill the height of the `Panorama`. The `ImageBrush` retains the width of the `ImageSource`, while the `GradientBrush` is stretched to fill the width of the items.

NOTE

The default template for the `Panorama` uses bitmap caching for the `Panorama`'s `Background` property. Clipping occurs for UI elements with bitmap caching enabled if they exceed 2000 by 2000 pixels. Therefore, restrict the size of your background image to less than this size.

Bitmap caching helps to improve performance by storing visual elements as bitmaps after the first time they are rendered. Once an element has been cached as a bitmap, it no longer needs to be included as part of the render phase when the UI refreshes. This means less processing needs to be done, as just the cached bitmap is rendered. Cached bitmaps can take advantage of hardware acceleration using the phone's GPU, which has the potential of yielding significant performance improvements in some situations.

TIP

Avoid positioning the background according to the content position. The `Panorama` title moves at a different rate than its section titles, as the user moves across the `Panorama`.

Title Layer

The title layer is represented by a `PanningTitleLayer` within the `Panorama` class. This layer presents the title of the app and is assigned using the `Panorama.Title` property.

The `Panorama Title` can be specified as text; however, there is also a `TitleTemplate` property, which allows you to completely customize the appearance of the `Title`.

The vertical height of this layer remains constant and is unaffected by oversized content or the absence of content. The layer does not wrap back on itself but rather animates back to the starting position when you pan past the final section.

BEST PRACTICE

Avoid animating the `Panorama` title or dynamically changing its size after it has loaded. Doing so can interfere with the `Panorama`'s built-in animations.

10

Items Layer

The items layer is represented by a `PanningLayer` within the `Panorama` class. This layer contains the content of the `PanoramaItem` controls. A pan gesture causes this layer to move at the same rate. Therefore, the content beneath the finger at the beginning of the pan gesture remains beneath the finger until the finger leaves the display.

`PanoramaItem` Control

Each `PanoramaItem` control represents individual sections of content. The `PanoramaItem` is itself comprised of two parts: a header part and a content part. Each part is contained within a `Grid` that serves as the layout root for the `PanoramaItem` control.

The contents of a `PanoramaItem` can either be specified in XAML, or added programmatically using its `Content` property.

The headers of all `PanoramaItems` can be uniformly customized by using the `Panorama`'s `HeaderTemplate` property. This works in the same manner as the example for the `Pivot` in the previous section.

You can hide a `PanoramaItem` by setting its `Visibility` property to Collapsed. This can be useful when you need to conceal an item before it has loaded some other resource.

TIP

As mentioned earlier in the chapter, when a `Panorama` loads, all `Panorama` items undergo a render pass. Thus, a `Panorama` with too many items may take a long time to load. Alternatively, to improve performance, where reducing the number of items is not an option, consider delay loading controls and content. Unlike the `Pivot`, however, the `Panorama` does not have load events (such as the `LoadingPivotItem` event), which further underscores the differences between the purpose and nature of the two controls. If you find that the `Panorama`'s performance is not up to scratch, then it may indicate that your content is not suited to the `Panorama` and that a different control or approach is needed.

`PanoramaItem` Orientation

The `Orientation` property of the `PanoramaItem` affects how content is snapped into place during a pan gesture. The default value of the `Orientation` property is Vertical. By setting the property to `Horizontal`, the user is able to pan around the content without snapping a `PanoramaItem` into place. A horizontal orientation also allows for the content to be placed off the screen instead of being clipped. This reinforces the panoramic nature of the control.

Sample `Panorama` Application

The sample for this section makes use of the WCF Bookshop Service, which was detailed in Chapter 3, "Application Execution Model." This service is used to retrieve a list of products and present them within a `Panorama`.

The code is located in the files `PanoramaView.xaml`, `PanoramaView.xaml.cs`, and `PanoramaViewModel.cs` in the downloadable sample code.

The viewmodel, for this example, exposes a collection of Product objects, which are retrieved from the Bookshop Service when the viewmodel is instantiated, and a single *featured* product, which is simply the first member of the collection (see Listing 10.8).

LISTING 10.8   PanoramaViewModel Class

```csharp
public class PanoramaViewModel : ViewModelBase
{
    public PanoramaViewModel()
    {
        BookshopServiceClient client = new BookshopServiceClient();
        client.GetProductsCompleted
            += (sender, args) =>
                {
                    if (args.Error != null)
                    {
                        throw args.Error;
                    }

                    Products = args.Result;
                    FeaturedProduct = args.Result.FirstOrDefault();
                };
        client.GetProductsAsync();
    }

    ObservableCollection<Product> products;

    public ObservableCollection<Product> Products
    {
        get
        {
            return products;
        }
        private set
        {
            Assign("Products", ref products, value);
        }
    }

    Product featuredProduct;

    public Product FeaturedProduct
    {
        get
        {
            return featuredProduct;
```

LISTING 10.8   Continued

```
        }
        private set
        {
            Assign("FeaturedProduct", ref featuredProduct, value);
        }
    }
}
```

The `PanoramaView` code-beside is used to instantiate an instance of the `PanoramaViewModel`, which is assigned to `PanoramaView`'s `DataContext` (see Listing 10.9).

LISTING 10.9   PanoramaView Class

```
public partial class PanoramaView : PhoneApplicationPage
{
    public PanoramaView()
    {
        InitializeComponent();
        DataContext = new PanoramaViewModel();
    }
}
```

The view contains two `PanoramaItems`. The first displays the list of products and is titled Best Picks. A Silverlight Toolkit `WrapPanel` control is used to display the Product images thumbs (see Listing 10.10). For more information on the `WrapPanel` control, see Chapter 9, "Silverlight Toolkit Controls."

The second `PanoramaItem` presents the details of the featured product; a larger image is displayed for the product, and a `HyperlinkButton` allows you to open the built-in web browser application.

LISTING 10.10   PanoramaView.xaml (excerpt)

```
<Grid x:Name="LayoutRoot" Background="Transparent">
    <controls:Panorama x:Name="Panorama"
        Title="Bookshop">
        <controls:Panorama.Background>
            <ImageBrush ImageSource="../../../Images/PanoramaBackground.png" />
        </controls:Panorama.Background>

        <controls:PanoramaItem Header="Best Picks">
            <ListBox ItemsSource="{Binding Products}">
                <ListBox.ItemsPanel>
                    <ItemsPanelTemplate>
                        <toolkit:WrapPanel x:Name="wrapPanel"  />
```

LISTING 10.10   Continued

```
                </ItemsPanelTemplate>
            </ListBox.ItemsPanel>
            <ListBox.ItemTemplate>
                <DataTemplate>
                    <Image Source="{Binding SmallImageUri}"
                        MaxWidth="150" MaxHeight="150"
                        Margin="10" />
                </DataTemplate>
            </ListBox.ItemTemplate>
        </ListBox>
</controls:PanoramaItem>

<controls:PanoramaItem Header="Featured"
            DataContext="{Binding FeaturedProduct}">
    <StackPanel>
        <TextBlock Text="{Binding Product.Title}"
        TextWrapping="Wrap"
        Style="{StaticResource PhoneTextTitle2Style}"/>
        <StackPanel Orientation="Horizontal">
            <Image Source="{Binding LargeImageUri}"
                MaxWidth="250" MaxHeight="250"
                Margin="10,10,0,10"/>
            <StackPanel>
                <TextBlock Text="{Binding Author}"
                TextWrapping="Wrap"
                Style="{StaticResource PhoneTextTitle3Style}"/>
                <TextBlock Text="{Binding Price,
                Converter={StaticResource StringFormatConverter},
                ConverterParameter=\{0:C\}}"
                Style="{StaticResource PhoneTextTitle3Style}"/>
                <StackPanel Orientation="Horizontal">
                    <TextBlock Text="ISBN"
                    Style="{StaticResource PhoneTextTitle3Style}"/>
                    <TextBlock Text="{Binding Isbn13}"
                    TextWrapping="Wrap"
                    Style="{StaticResource PhoneTextNormalStyle}"/>
                </StackPanel>

                <HyperlinkButton
                    NavigateUri="{Binding ExternalUrl}"
                    TargetName="_blank"
                    Content="External Page"
                    Margin="0,10,0,0"
                    HorizontalAlignment="Left" />
```

10

LISTING 10.10   Continued

```
                    </StackPanel>
                </StackPanel>
            </StackPanel>
        </controls:PanoramaItem>

    </controls:Panorama>
</Grid>
```

Figure 10.9 shows the `Panorama` presenting the first `PanoramaItem`. Notice that the second `PanoramaItem` is partially displayed. This helps to improve the user's awareness of neighboring content.

FIGURE 10.9   The first `PanoramaItem` presents a list of `Products` in a `WrapPanel`.

Figure 10.10 shows the second `PanoramaItem` selected. Here the title and background have been scrolled horizontally.

FIGURE 10.10   The second `PanoramaItem` presents the featured product.

Things to Avoid When Using the `Panorama` and `Pivot`

The following is a list of things that should be avoided when using the `Pivot` and `Panorama`:

▶ Do not place a `Pivot` inside a `Panorama`, or nest `Pivots`.

▶ Do not attempt to use either the `Pivot` or `Panorama` for creating a wizard flow. The user sees the `Pivot` and `Panorama` as distinct areas of data, and not as a flow to be stepped through. For a wizard, use a page flow instead.

▶ Using a control that relies on horizontal touch gestures, such as a map control, inside a `Pivot` or `Panorama` is not recommended, as it interferes with horizontal navigation within the `Pivot` or `Panorama`.

▶ Avoid animating the `Panorama` title or section titles as they change position when the user moves across the control.

▶ Avoid dynamically changing the `Panorama` title.

▶ Do not override the horizontal pan and flick functionality of the controls because it may interfere with the built-in touch support.

10

▶ Keep to the recommended number of views, seven for the Pivot and four for the Panorama. The user should never lose his place inside the Panorama.

▶ Avoid making your Panorama overly complex, for example, where every link on the Panorama takes the user to a Pivot.

Silverlight Toolkit Lockable Pivot

The Silverlight Toolkit contains a LockablePivot control that allows a PivotItem to be locked in place so that navigation to other PivotItems is disabled. This allows you to host content, such as a Slider control, that would otherwise be unsuitable for a Pivot due to the Pivot control's reliance on horizontal panning gestures.

LockablePivot extends Pivot and provides a single public property named IsLocked. When set to true from your code, this property prevents navigation to other PivotItems and hides the adjacent pivot item names within the header.

Summary

This chapter began by looking at the differences and similarities of the Pivot and Panorama. You saw how the Pivot is designed to be used for completing a task, whereas the Panorama is designed to entice the user to explore.

The chapter then looked at the anatomy of the Pivot and how to create a simple Pivot driven page. You saw how to use the Pivot load events, allowing you to load content on demand, and you explored a novel approach that allows you to associate a different application bar with each PivotItem using a custom AppBar control. You then learned how to create a Pivot driven chat app, which was augmented to demonstrate implicit PivotItem generation and templating. By generating PivotItems by assigning the Pivot.ItemsSource property, the Pivot can be dynamically populated at runtime.

The second part of this chapter focused on the Panorama. You saw how to create a simple bookshop app that uses a WCF service to retrieve a list of products displayed within a Panorama.

Finally, the chapter concluded by looking at some things to avoid when using a Pivot or Panorama.

CHAPTER 11

Touch

Windows Phone devices come equipped with capacitive touch screens that offer a smooth, accurate, multitouch enabled experience. By adding touch and gesture support to your apps, you can greatly enhance user experience.

You can handle touch input in your Silverlight for Windows Phone app in a number of ways, including the following:

▶ Mouse events

▶ TouchPoint class

▶ Manipulation events

▶ UIElement gesture events

▶ Silverlight Toolkit for Windows Phone gestures

Mouse events are an easy way to get basic touch support, and allow you to detect simple, one-finger gestures such as tap and double tap.

The TouchPoint class provides a low-level input system that you can use to respond to all touch activity in the UI. The TouchPoint class is used by the higher-level touch input systems.

Manipulation events are UIElement events used to handle more complex gestures, such as multitouch gestures and gestures that use inertia and velocity data.

UIElement and Toolkit gestures further consolidate the low-level touch API into a set of gesture-specific events and make it easy to handle complex single and multitouch gestures.

This chapter explores each of these four approaches in detail. The chapter presents an example app demonstrating how to move, resize, rotate, and animate a UIElement using gestures and concludes by looking at the best practices for optimizing your user interfaces for touch input.

> **NOTE**
>
> The Windows Phone Emulator does not support multitouch input using the mouse, therefore multitouch apps must be tested on a development computer that supports touch input, or on an actual phone device.

Handling Touch with Mouse Events

Silverlight mouse events can be used to detect a simple, one-finger gesture. Mouse event handlers can be quickly added to your app and provide an easy way to get basic touch support.

For more complex gestures, additional code is required to translate manipulation values to detect the actual gesture type. As you see in later sections of this chapter, there are easier higher-level APIs for handling more complex gestures.

In this chapter, the term *touch point* is used to describe the point of contact between a finger and the device screen.

The UIElement class includes the following mouse events:

- ▶ **MouseEnter**—Raised when a touch point enters the bounding area of a UIElement.

- ▶ **MouseLeave**—Raised when the user taps and moves his finger outside the bounding area of the UIElement.

- ▶ **MouseLeftButtonDown**—Raised when the user touches a UIElement.

- ▶ **MouseLeftButtonUp**—Raised when a touch point is removed from the screen while it is over a UIElement (or while a UIElement holds mouse capture).

- ▶ **MouseMove**—Raised when the coordinate position of the touch point changes while over a UIElement (or while a UIElement holds mouse capture).

- ▶ **MouseWheel**—This event is unutilized on a touch-driven UI.

The following example responds to the MouseLeftButtonDown, MouseLeftButtonUp, and MouseLeave events to change the background color of a Border control. See the following excerpt from the MouseEventsView.xaml file:

```
<Grid x:Name="ContentPanel" Grid.Row="1" Margin="12,0,12,0">
    <Border
        Tap="HandleTap"
        MouseLeftButtonDown="HandleLeftButtonDown"
        MouseLeftButtonUp="HandleLeftButtonUp"
        MouseLeave="HandleMouseLeave"
```

```
            Height="100"
            Width="200"
            Background="{StaticResource PhoneAccentBrush}" />
</Grid>
```

The event handlers in the code-beside change the color of the Border (see Listing 11.1).

LISTING 11.1   MouseEventsView Class

```
public partial class MouseEventsView : PhoneApplicationPage
{
    readonly SolidColorBrush dragBrush = new SolidColorBrush(Colors.Orange);
    readonly SolidColorBrush normalBrush;

    public MouseEventsView()
    {
        InitializeComponent();

        normalBrush = (SolidColorBrush)Resources["PhoneAccentBrush"];
    }

    void HandleLeftButtonDown(object sender, MouseButtonEventArgs e)
    {
        Border border = (Border)sender;
        border.Background = dragBrush;
    }

    void HandleLeftButtonUp(object sender, MouseButtonEventArgs e)
    {
        Border border = (Border)sender;
        border.Background = normalBrush;
    }

    void HandleMouseLeave(object sender, MouseEventArgs e)
    {
        Border border = (Border)sender;
        border.Background = normalBrush;
    }
}
```

The MouseButtonEventArgs class derives from MouseEventArgs. MouseEventArgs is a RoutedEvent, which is discussed in more detail later in this chapter.

While mouse events provide a simple way to respond to touch in your app, they do not come equipped to support complex gestures or multitouch, nor do they provide any built-in means for ascertaining more detailed touch information, such as touch velocity.

Fortunately, as you see later in the chapter, a number of alternative touch APIs do just that. For now though, turn your attention to the `Touch` and `TouchPoint` classes that represent the low-level touch API.

Touch and TouchPoint Classes

The low-level interface for touch in Silverlight is the `TouchPoint` class. Unlike mouse events, the `TouchPoint` class is designed exclusively for touch without a pointing device in mind. A `TouchPoint` instance represents a finger touching the screen.

`TouchPoint` has four read-only properties, described in the following list:

▶ **Action**—Represents the type of manipulation and can have one of the three following values:

  ▶ **Down**—Indicates that the user has made contact with the screen.

  ▶ **Move**—Indicates that the touch point has changed position.

  ▶ **Up**—Indicates that the touch point has been removed.

▶ **Position**—Retrieves the X and Y coordinate position of the touch point, as a `System.Windows.Point`. This point is relative to the top-left corner of the element beneath the touch point.

▶ **Size**—This is supposed to get the rectangular area that is reported as the touch-point contact area. The value reported on Windows Phone, however, always has a width and height of 1, making it of no use on the phone.

▶ **TouchDevice**—Retrieves the specific device type that produced the touch point. This property allows you to retrieve the `UIElement` beneath the touch point via its `TouchDevice.DirectlyOver` property. The `TouchDevice.Id` property allows you to distinguish between fingers touching the display.

The `Touch` class is an application-level service used to register for touch events. It contains a single *public static* member, the `FrameReported` event. This event is global for your app and is raised whenever a touch event occurs.

To register for touch notifications, you subscribe to the `Touch.FrameReported` event like so:

```
Touch.FrameReported += HandleFrameReported;
```

A handler for the `FrameReported` event accepts a `TouchFrameEventArgs` argument, as shown:

```
void HandleFrameReported(object sender, TouchFrameEventArgs args)
{
.../* method body */
}
```

A *frame* is a time slice where one or more touch events have occurred. When the `FrameReported` event is raised, there may be up to four `TouchPoint` objects.

`TouchFrameEventArgs` contains four public members, which are described in the following list:

► **TimeStamp property**—An `int` value that indicates when the touch event occurred.

► **GetPrimaryTouchPoint(UIElement relativeTo)**—Retrieves the `TouchPoint` representing the first finger that touched the screen. A `UIElement` can be specified to make the `TouchPoint` object's `Position` property relative to that element. If a `UIElement` is not specified (it is *null*), then the returned `TouchPoint` is relative to the top left of the page.

► **GetTouchPoints(UIElement relativeTo)**—Retrieves the collection of `TouchPoints` for the frame. The `UIElement` parameter works the same as the `GetPrimaryTouchPoint`. The parameter does not restrict the set of `TouchPoints` returned; all are returned and only the `Position` of each `TouchPoint` is affected.

► **SuspendMousePromotionUntilTouchUp()**—Prevents touch events from turning into mouse events. See the following section for a more detailed explanation.

Mouse Event Promotion

With the advent of Windows Phone, Silverlight has transitioned from being a browser and desktop only technology with a primarily mouse-driven UI, to a mobile device technology with a touch-driven UI.

To allow controls that were originally designed to work with mouse events to continue to function, the touch system was engineered so that touch events are automatically turned into (promoted to) mouse events. If a touch event is not suspended using the `SuspendMousePromotionUntilTouchUp` method, then mouse events are automatically raised.

> **NOTE**
>
> Promotion of a `TouchPoint` to a mouse event only occurs with the primary touch point.

To prevent a touch event from being promoted to a mouse event, call the `SuspendMousePromotionUntilTouchUp` within the `FrameReported` event handler, like so:

```
void HandleFrameReported(object sender, TouchFrameEventArgs e)
{
    TouchPoint primaryTouchPoint = e.GetPrimaryTouchPoint(null);
    if (primaryTouchPoint != null
        && primaryTouchPoint.Action == TouchAction.Down)
    {
        e.SuspendMousePromotionUntilTouchUp();
        /* custom code */
    }
}
```

> **NOTE**
>
> The `SuspendMousePromotionUntilTouchUp` method can be called only when the
> `TouchPoint.Action` property is equal to `TouchAction.Down`, or else an
> `InvalidOperationException` is raised.

In most cases, calling `SuspendMousePromotionUntilTouchUp` is something you should avoid, because doing so prevents the functioning of any controls that rely solely on mouse events and those that have not been built using the touch-specific API.

Handling the `Touch.FrameReported` Event

The following example shows how to change the color of a `Border` control by responding to the `Touch.FrameReported` event. Within the `TouchPointView` XAML file is a named `Border` control as shown:

```
<Grid x:Name="ContentPanel" Grid.Row="1" Margin="12,0,12,0">
    <Border x:Name="border"
        Height="100"
        Width="200"
        Background="{StaticResource PhoneAccentBrush}" />
</Grid>
```

The code-beside file, `TouchPointView.xaml.cs`, subscribes to the `Touch.FrameReported` event within the page constructor. The event handler retrieves the primary touch point, and if the `TouchPoint` is above the `Border`, then the `Border` object's `Background` is switched (see Listing 11.2).

LISTING 11.2   `TouchPointView` Class

```
public partial class TouchPointView : PhoneApplicationPage
{
    readonly SolidColorBrush directlyOverBrush
                = new SolidColorBrush(Colors.Orange);
    readonly Brush normalBrush;

    public TouchPointView()
    {
        InitializeComponent();

        normalBrush = border.Background;

        Touch.FrameReported += HandleFrameReported;
    }

    void HandleFrameReported(object sender, TouchFrameEventArgs e)
    {
        TouchPoint primaryTouchPoint = e.GetPrimaryTouchPoint(null);
```

LISTING 11.2   Continued

```
        if (primaryTouchPoint == null
            || primaryTouchPoint.TouchDevice.DirectlyOver != border)
        {
            return;
        }

        if (primaryTouchPoint.Action == TouchAction.Down)
        {             border.Background = directlyOverBrush;
        }
        else
        {
            border.Background = normalBrush;
        }
    }
}
```

Using the Touch and TouchPoint API provides you with the ability to respond to touch at a very low level. Subsequent sections of this chapter look at two higher level abstractions of the Touch and TouchPoint APIs, namely manipulation events and the Silverlight Toolkit for Windows Phone, beginning with manipulation events.

Manipulation Events

Manipulation events consolidate the touch activities of one or two fingers. Manipulation events combine individual touch point information, provided by the Touch.FrameReported event, and interpret them into a higher-level API with velocity, scaling, and translation information.

Moreover, unlike the Touch.FrameReported event, which provides touch notifications for your entire interface, a manipulation event is specific to the UIElement to which it is associated.

The manipulation events comprise three UIElement events, which are described in the following list:

▶ **ManipulationStarted**—Raised when the user touches the UIElement.

▶ **ManipulationDelta**—Raised when a second touch point is placed on the element, and when a touch input changes position. This event can occur multiple times during a manipulation. For example, if the user drags a finger across the screen, the ManipulationDelta event occurs multiple times during the finger's movement.

▶ **ManipulationCompleted**—Raised when the user's finger, or fingers, leaves the UIElement, and when any inertia applied to the element is complete.

These three events are routed events (they subclass the `RoutedEvent` class). In case you are not familiar with routed events, a `RoutedEvent` can be handled by an ancestor element in the visual tree. `RoutedEvents` *bubble* upwards through the visual tree, until they are either handled, indicated by the `Handled` property of the event arguments, or reach the root element of the visual tree. This means that you can subscribe to a manipulation event at, for example, the page level, and it gives you the opportunity to handle manipulation events for all elements in the page.

As you might expect, a manipulation begins with the `ManipulationStarted` event, followed by zero or more `ManipulationDelta` events, and then a single `ManipulationCompleted` event.

The event arguments for all three manipulation events have the following shared properties:

▶ **OriginalSource (provided by the RoutedEvent base class)**—This is the object that raised the manipulation event.

▶ **ManipulationContainer**—This is the topmost enabled `UIElement` being touched. Touch points on different `UIElement`s provide a separate succession of manipulation events and are distinguished by the `ManipulationContainer` property. The `OriginalSource` and `ManipulationContainer` properties are in most cases the same. Internally, `ManipulationContainer` is assigned to the `OriginalSource` property when a manipulation event is raised.

▶ **ManipulationOrigin**—This property, of type `Point`, indicates the location of the touch point relative to the top-left corner of the `ManipulationContainer` element. If two touch points exist on the element, then the `ManipulationOrigin` property indicates the middle position between the two points.

▶ **Handled**—A property of type `bool` that allows you to halt the bubbling of the routed event up the visual tree.

Handling Manipulation Events

When a manipulation begins, the `ManipulationStarted` event is raised. The event handler accepts a `ManipulationStartedEventArgs` parameter, as shown:

```
void HandleManipulationStarted(object sender, ManipulationStartedEventArgs e)
{
    /* method body */
}
```

Contrary to the low-level `TouchPoint` API, there is no need to store the id of the touch point to track its motion. In fact, the manipulation events do not offer individual touch point information. If you need that information, then the low-level `TouchPoint` API may be more suitable.

During manipulation, the `ManipulationDelta` event is raised when a touch point is added to the `ManipulationContainer` element, or when the position of a touch point on the element changes. The event handler accepts a `ManipulationDeltaEventArgs` parameter, as shown:

```
void HandleManipulationDelta(object sender, ManipulationDeltaEventArgs e)
{
    /* method body */
}
```

`ManipulationDeltaEventArgs` provides you with the most recent and the accumulated manipulation data. The following is a list of its properties, which have not yet been covered:

- **CumulativeManipulation**—Gets the accumulated changes of the current manipulation, as a `ManipulationDelta` instance. `ManipulationDelta` has the following two properties:
  - **Scale**—A `Point` indicating the horizontal and vertical scale amounts, relevant during multitouch manipulation.
  - **Translate**—A `Point` indicating the horizontal and vertical positional offset.
- **DeltaManipulation**—Gets the most recent changes of the current manipulation, as a `ManipulationDelta`.
- **IsInertial**—Gets whether the `ManipulationDelta` event was raised while a finger had contact with the element. In my experience the value of this property is always false during the `ManipulationDelta` event. This property is of more use during handling of the `ManipulationCompleted` event, as you soon see.
- **Velocities**—Gets the rates of the most recent changes to the manipulation. This property is of type `ManipulationVelocities`, which is a class with the following two properties:
  - **ExpansionVelocity**—Gets a `Point` representing the rate at which the manipulation was resized.
  - **LinearVelocity**—Gets a `Point` representing the speed of the linear motion.

Inertia is applied automatically to a manipulation and is based on the velocity of the manipulation. Both the `ManipulationCompletedEventArgs` and `ManipulationStartedEventArgs` classes contain a `Complete` method, which allows you to forcibly finish the manipulation event sequence, which raises the `ManipulationComplete` event and prevents the application of inertia.

The `ManipulationComplete` event handler accepts a `ManipulationCompletedEventArgs` parameter, as shown:

```
void HandleManipulationCompleted(
            object sender, ManipulationCompletedEventArgs e)
{
    /* method body */
}
```

`ManipulationCompletedEventArgs` provides you with the final velocities and overall manipulation data. The following is a list of its properties, which have not yet been covered:

- ▶ **FinalVelocities**—Gets the final expansion and linear velocities for the manipulation.

- ▶ **IsInertial**—Gets whether the `ManipulationDelta` event occurred while a finger has contact with the element.

- ▶ **IsInertial**—Gets whether the `ManipulationDelta` event was raised while a finger had contact with the element. If the manipulation consisted of a single touch point it is indicative of a flick gesture.

- ▶ **TotalManipulation**—Gets a `ManipulationDelta` object containing two `Points` representing the total scale and translation values for the manipulation.

Manipulation Events Example

The following example illustrates how to move and scale a `UIElement` using the various manipulation events.

Within the `ManipulationEventsView` XAML file, there is a `Border` control defined as shown:

```xml
<StackPanel x:Name="ContentPanel" Grid.Row="1" Margin="12,0,12,0">
    <Border
        Height="400"
        Width="400"
        Background="{StaticResource PhoneAccentBrush}"
        ManipulationStarted="HandleManipulationStarted"
        ManipulationDelta="HandleManipulationDelta"
        ManipulationCompleted="HandleManipulationCompleted">
        <TextBlock x:Name="TextBlock_Message" />
        <Border.RenderTransform>
            <CompositeTransform x:Name="compositeTransform"/>
        </Border.RenderTransform>
    </Border>
</StackPanel>
```

When the user touches the `Border`, the `ManipulationStarted` event is raised, calling the code-beside handler, which sets the background color of the `Border`. As the user moves her fingers, the `ManipulationDelta` event is raised repeatedly, each time the location and scale of the `Border` is adjusted using the `CompositeTransform` (see Listing 11.3).

LISTING 11.3   `ManipulationEventsView` Class

```csharp
public partial class ManipulationEventsView : PhoneApplicationPage
{
    readonly SolidColorBrush startManipulationBrush
```

LISTING 11.3   Continued

```
                                    = new SolidColorBrush(Colors.Orange);
    Brush normalBrush;

    public ManipulationEventsView()
    {
        InitializeComponent();
    }

    void HandleManipulationStarted(
            object sender, ManipulationStartedEventArgs e)
    {
        Border border = (Border)sender;
        normalBrush = border.Background;
        border.Background = startManipulationBrush;
    }

    void HandleManipulationDelta(object sender, ManipulationDeltaEventArgs e)
    {
        compositeTransform.TranslateX += e.DeltaManipulation.Translation.X;
        compositeTransform.TranslateY += e.DeltaManipulation.Translation.Y;

        if (e.DeltaManipulation.Scale.X > 0
            && e.DeltaManipulation.Scale.X > 0)
        {
            compositeTransform.ScaleX *= e.DeltaManipulation.Scale.X;
            compositeTransform.ScaleY *= e.DeltaManipulation.Scale.Y;
        }
    }

    void HandleManipulationCompleted(
            object sender, ManipulationCompletedEventArgs e)
    {
        Border border = (Border)sender;
        border.Background = normalBrush;
        TextBlock_Message.Text = string.Empty;
    }
}
```

Pinching or stretching the `Border` modifies the `CompositeTransform` scale values, which resizes the control. A tap and drag gesture modifies the `CompositeTransform` translation values, which repositions the control (see Figure 11.1).

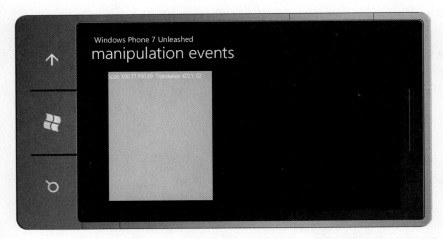

FIGURE 11.1   A Border is moved and resized in response to manipulation events.

UIElement Touch Gesture Events

Gestures are a high-level way of interpreting touch input data and include a set of common motions, such as tapping, flicking, and pinching. Controls, such as the WebBrowser, handle gestures such as the pinch gesture internally, allowing the user to pan and zoom in and out of content. By responding to gestures you can provide a natural and immersive experience for your users.

Support for basic single touch gestures has been incorporated into the Silverlight for Windows Phone SDK. Support for more complex gestures is provided by the Silverlight for Windows Phone Toolkit, discussed in the next section.

The sample code for this section is located in the UIElementTouchEventsView.xaml and UIElementTouchEventsView.xaml.cs files, in the Touch directory of the WindowsPhone7Unleashed.Examples project.

The UIElement class comes equipped to handle the following three touch gestures:

▶ Tap

▶ Double tap

▶ Hold

The UIElement includes three corresponding routed events: Tap, DoubleTap, and Hold.

The three tap events can be subscribed to in XAML, as the following excerpt demonstrates:

```
<Grid x:Name="ContentPanel" Grid.Row="1" Margin="12,0,12,0">
    <Border
        Tap="HandleTap"
        DoubleTap="HandleDoubleTap"
```

```
        Hold="HandleHold"
        Height="100"
        Width="200"
        Background="{StaticResource PhoneChromeBrush}">
        <TextBlock x:Name="textBlock"
                   HorizontalAlignment="Center" VerticalAlignment="Center"
                   Style="{StaticResource PhoneTextLargeStyle}"/>
    </Border>
</Grid>
```

Figure 11.2 shows the sample page responding to the double tap gesture.

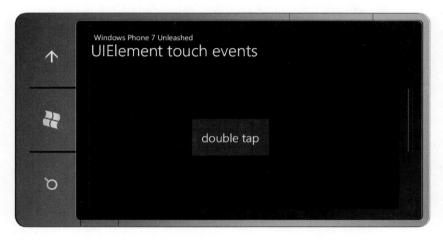

FIGURE 11.2   `UIElementTouchEventsView` page

Event handlers for all three events share the same signature and accept a `GestureEventArgs` object. `GestureEventArgs` contains a Boolean `Handled` property, which allows you to stop the event from continuing to bubble up the visual tree, and a `GetPosition` method that allows you to retrieve the location coordinates of where the touch occurred.

Each tap gesture supported by `UIElement` is examined in the following sections.

Tap Gesture

The simplest of all the gestures, a tap occurs when a finger touches the screen momentarily (see Figure 11.3).

This gesture is analogous to a single-click performed with a mouse. The tap gesture can be broken down into the following two parts:

► Finger down provides touch indication.

► Finger up executes the action.

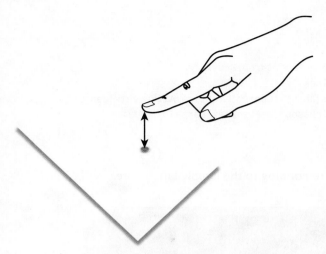

FIGURE 11.3   Tap gesture

The Tap event is raised when the user performs a tap gesture. If the user's finger remains in contact with the display for longer than one second, the tap event is not raised.

An event handler for the Tap event is shown in the following excerpt:

```
void HandleTap(object sender, GestureEventArgs e)
{
    textBlock.Text = "tap";
}
```

Double Tap Gesture

The double tap gesture occurs when a finger quickly touches the screen twice (see Figure 11.4). This gesture is analogous to a double-click performed with a mouse.

The double tap is primarily designed to be used to toggle between the *in* and *out* zoom states of a control.

An event handler for the DoubleTap event is shown in the following excerpt:

```
void HandleDoubleTap(object sender, GestureEventArgs e)
{
    textBlock.Text = "double tap";
}
```

Hold Gesture

The hold gesture is performed by touching the screen while continuing contact for a period of time (see Figure 11.5).

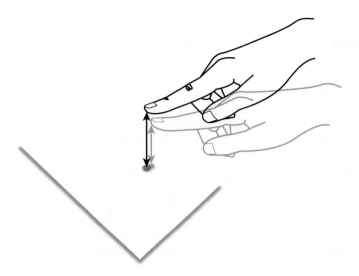

FIGURE 11.4   Double tap gesture

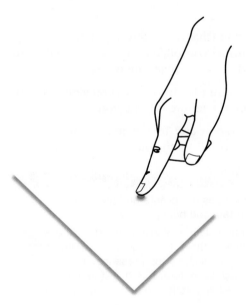

FIGURE 11.5   Hold gesture

The UIElement.Hold event is raised when the user touches the screen for one second.

An event handler for the Hold event is shown in the following excerpt:

```
void HandleHold(object sender, GestureEventArgs e)
{
    textBlock.Text = "hold";
}
```

As an aside, the UIElement Hold event is used by the Silverlight Toolkit's ContextMenu component. When used in this way, the hold gesture mimics the right-click of a mouse.

> **NOTE**
>
> UIElement and Silverlight Toolkit gesture events (discussed in the next section) are raised only if the UIElement is detected beneath the touch point. Make sure that the Background property of the UIElement is not null. If a background is not defined, touch events pass through the host control, and gestures are not detected. To achieve a see-through background, while still maintaining gesture support, set the background property of the UIElement to Transparent.

Silverlight Toolkit Gestures

Silverlight for Windows Phone Toolkit, introduced in Chapter 9, "Silverlight Toolkit Controls," abstracts low-level touch events and further consolidates touch event data into a set of events representing the various single and multitouch gesture types.

Toolkit gestures harness the Touch.FrameReported event (described in the previous section "Touch and TouchPoint Classes") to provide high-level gesture information.

Unless you require low-level touch point data, UIElement and Toolkit gestures are the recommended way to add single and multitouch capabilities to your apps.

> **NOTE**
>
> There is some overlap between the UIElement touch gesture events and the Toolkit gestures API; both allow you to handle tap, double tap, and hold gestures.
>
> The first release of the Windows Phone SDK did not include baked-in support for these three gestures, and they were subsequently added with the 7.1 release of the SDK. In the meantime, the Toolkit had already included gesture support, so the presence of these gestures in the Toolkit remains as somewhat of a legacy feature. It is therefore recommended that you use the UIElement touch gesture events, rather than the Toolkit gesture API, for the tap, double tap, and hold gestures.

Getting Started with Toolkit Gestures

Unlike the other techniques seen in this chapter, Toolkit gestures are provided as a separate assembly, as part of the Silverlight for Windows Phone Toolkit package.

You can obtain the Silverlight for Windows Phone Toolkit from the Toolkit website on CodePlex (http://silverlight.codeplex.com/). See Chapter 9 for more information.

The two main classes for working with Toolkit gestures are the `GestureService` and `GestureListener` classes. `GestureService` is used only to attach a `GestureListener` to a `UIElement`. Like manipulation events, Toolkit gestures are used in conjunction with a `UIElement`. Once attached, the `GestureListener` monitors the element for gestures that the element can support, such as tap, hold, pinch, and flick.

`GestureListener` allows you to specify handlers for each gesture type. The following example shows a `Border` control with subscriptions to these events via the attached `GestureListener`:

```xml
<Border Background="{StaticResource PhoneAccentBrush}">
    <toolkit:GestureService.GestureListener>
        <toolkit:GestureListener
            GestureBegin="HandleGestureBegin"
            GestureCompleted="HandleGestureCompleted"
            Tap="HandleTap"
            DoubleTap="HandleDoubleTap"
            Hold="HandleHold"
            DragStarted="HandleDragStarted"
            DragDelta="HandleDragDelta"
            DragCompleted="HandleDragCompleted"
            Flick="HandleFlick"
            PinchStarted="HandlePinchStarted"
            PinchDelta="HandlePinchDelta"
            PinchCompleted="HandlePinchCompleted">
        </toolkit:GestureListener>
    </toolkit:GestureService.GestureListener>
</Border>
```

The `GestureListener` class is designed for Silverlight's event-driven model. The class effectively wraps the low-level Silverlight touch mechanism to perform automatic conversion of the `Touch.FrameReported` events into unique Silverlight events for each gesture type.

GestureListener Events in Detail

This section looks at each gesture and the events that correspond to each.

Tap Gesture

When a tap gesture is detected, then the `GestureListener.Tap` event is raised. The event handler accepts a `GestureEventArgs` parameter, as shown:

```csharp
void HandleTap(object sender, GestureEventArgs e)
{
    /* method body. */
}
```

The GestureListener events are quasi routed events. That is, they behave like routed events, yet their event arguments do not inherit from the RoutedEvent class. Like the RoutedEventArgs class, the GestureEventArgs includes an OriginalSource property that allows you to retrieve a reference to the object that raised the event, which may differ from the sender argument provided to the event handler.

The routing mechanism for gesture events also allows you to handle any or all of the gesture events at a higher level in the visual tree. For example, to listen for a Tap event that may occur in a child element, you can subscribe to the Tap event at the page level, like so:

```
<phone:PhoneApplicationPage
    x:Class="DanielVaughan.WindowsPhone7Unleashed.Examples.GesturesView"
    ... >
    <toolkit:GestureService.GestureListener>
        <toolkit:GestureListener Tap="HandleTapAtPageLevel" />
    </toolkit:GestureService.GestureListener>
    ...
</phone:PhoneApplicationPage>
```

The routing mechanism gives you the power to control whether an event should continue to bubble up the visual tree. Set the GestureEventArgs.Handled property to true to prevent the event from being handled at a higher level (in this case by the page level handler), as shown in the following example:

```
void HandleTap(object sender, GestureEventArgs e)
{
    e.Handled = true;
}
```

By setting the Handled property to true, the HandleTapAtPageLevel method is not called.

The GestureEventArgs class is the base class for other gesture event arguments as shown later in this section.

Double Tap Gesture

When a double tap gesture is detected, the GestureListener.DoubleTap event is raised. The event handler accepts a GestureEventArgs parameter, as shown:

```
void HandleDoubleTap(object sender, GestureEventArgs e)
{
    /* method body. */
}
```

Hold Gesture

When a hold gesture is detected, then the GestureListener.Hold event is raised. The handler accepts a GestureEventArgs parameter, as shown:

```
void HandleHold(object sender, GestureEventArgs e)
{
    /* method body. */
}
```

Drag Gesture

The drag gesture is performed by touching the screen and moving the finger in any direction while still in contact with the screen (see Figure 11.6).

The drag gesture is normally used to reorder items in a list or to reposition an element by direct manipulation.

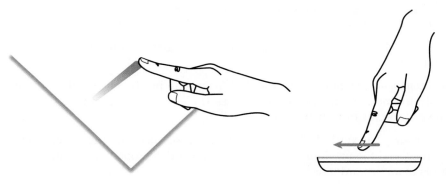

FIGURE 11.6   Drag gesture

The following three events are used to detect and coordinate activities during a drag gesture:

- **DragStarted**—Raised when the drag gesture begins, which is as soon as motion is detected following a touch event.

- **DragDelta**—Raised while a drag gesture is underway and the location of the touch point changes.

- **DragCompleted**—Raised on touch release after a drag, or when a second touch point is added.

When a drag gesture is detected, the GestureListener.DragStarted event is raised. The event handler accepts a DragStartedGestureEventArgs parameter, as shown:

```
void HandleDragStarted(object sender, DragStartedGestureEventArgs e)
{
    /* method body. */
}
```

DragStartedGestureEventArgs provides you with the initial direction of the drag gesture via its Direction property and can be either Horizontal or Vertical depending on the predominate direction.

As the user moves either finger during a drag gesture, the GestureListener.DragDelta event is raised. The event handler accepts a DragDeltaGestureEventArgs parameter, as shown:

```
void HandleDragDelta(object sender, DragDeltaGestureEventArgs e)
{
    /* method body. */
}
```

The DragDeltaGestureEventArgs parameter provides the difference between the current location of the touch point and its previous location. The DragDeltaGestureEventArgs has the following three properties:

- ▶ **Direction**—Provides the predominate direction of the drag gesture, either Horizontal or Vertical.

- ▶ **HorizontalChange**—The horizontal (x axis) difference in pixels between the current touch point location and the previous location. The value of this property is negative if the drag occurs from right to left.

- ▶ **VerticalChange**—The vertical (y axis) difference in pixels between the current touch point location and the previous location. The value of this property is negative if the drag occurs in an upward direction.

When the user completes the drag gesture by removing the touch points, the GestureListener.DragCompleted event is raised. This event provides the opportunity to conclude any activities that were being performed during the drag gesture. The handler accepts a DragCompletedGestureEventArgs parameter, as shown:

```
void HandleDragCompleted(object sender, DragCompletedGestureEventArgs e)
{
    /* method body. */
}
```

In addition to the data provided by the DragDeltaGestureEventArgs, the DragCompletedGestureEventArgs argument includes a VerticalVelocity property and a HorizontalVelocity property that measure the velocity of the drag. You may find that often both values are zero, when the user stops the dragging motion before removing the touch point.

The example presented later in this section explores the drag gesture in greater detail and shows how the drag gesture can be used to change the location of UIElements on a page.

Flick Gesture

A flick gesture is performed by dragging a finger across the screen and lifting the finger without stopping (see Figure 11.7). A flick gesture normally moves content from one area to another.

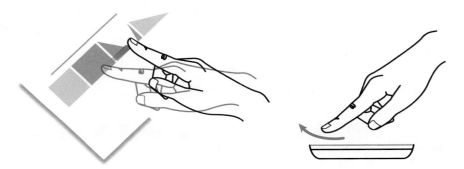

FIGURE 11.7   Flick gesture

When a flick gesture is detected, the GestureListener.Flick event is raised. The event handler accepts a FlickGestureEventArgs parameter, as shown:

```
void HandleFlick(object sender, FlickGestureEventArgs e)
{
    /* method body. */
}
```

FlickGestureEventsArgs provides you with the direction and velocity of the flick gesture via the following four properties:

- ▶ **Angle**—A double value, measured in degrees, indicating the angle of the flick. A downward flick results in an angle between 0 and 180 degrees; an upward flick in an angle between 180 and 360 degrees (see Figure 11.8). This value is calculated using the horizontal and vertical velocity of the flick.

- ▶ **Direction**—An Orientation value of either Horizontal or Vertical, indicating whether the flick was more horizontal than vertical, or vice versa.

- ▶ **HorizontalVelocity**—A double value indicating the horizontal (X) velocity of the flick.

- ▶ **VerticalVelocity**—A double value indicating the vertical (Y) velocity of the flick.

In the example code, presented later in this section, you see how to animate a UIElement in response to a flick gesture.

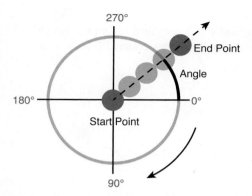

FIGURE 11.8   Origin of the `FlickGestureEventsArgs.Angle` property

Pinch Gesture

A pinch gesture is performed by pressing two fingers on the screen and moving either or both fingers together (see Figure 11.9). A stretch gesture is performed by moving the fingers apart. Both gestures are detected using the `GestureListener.Pinch` event.

The pinch gesture is the only multitouch gesture supported by the `GestureListener` and is typically used to zoom in or out of a page or element.

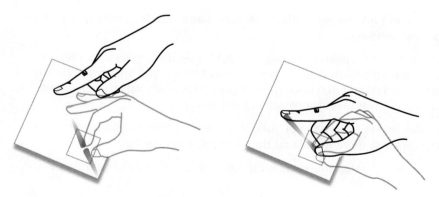

FIGURE 11.9   Pinch and stretch gestures

The following three events are used to detect and coordinate activities during a pinch gesture:

▶ **PinchStarted**—Raised when the pinch gesture begins, and occurring as soon as motion is detected when at least two fingers are touching the screen

▶ **PinchDelta**—Raised while a pinch gesture is underway and the location of either touch point changes

▶ **PinchCompleted**—Raised on touch release, of either touch points, after a pinch

When a pinch gesture is detected, the GestureListener.PinchStarted event is raised. The event handler accepts a PinchStartedGestureEventArgs parameter, as shown:

```
void HandlePinchStarted(object sender, PinchStartedGestureEventArgs e)
{
    /* method body. */
}
```

PinchStartedGestureEventArgs provides you with the direction and velocity of the pinch gesture via the following two properties:

▶ **Angle**—A double value, measured in degrees, indicating the angle from the first touch point, the first to make contact with the screen, to the second touch point (see Figure 11.10)

▶ **Distance**—A double value indicating the distance in pixels between the two touch points

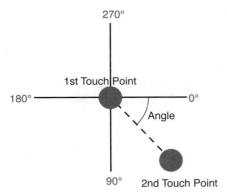

FIGURE 11.10   Determining the pinch angle

As the user moves either finger during a pinch gesture, the GestureListener.PinchDelta event is raised. The handler accepts a PinchGestureEventArgs parameter, as shown:

```
void HandlePinchDelta(object sender, PinchGestureEventArgs e)
{
    /* method body. */
}
```

The `PinchGestureEventArgs` argument provides the distance and angle of the touch points compared to the original touch points that were registered when the pinch gesture began. `PinchGestureEventArgs` has the following two properties:

▶ **DistanceRatio**—Provides the ratio of the current distance between touch points divided by the original distance between the touch points

▶ **TotalAngleDelta**—Provides the difference between the angles of the current touch positions and the original touch positions

The `PinchGestureEventArgs` derives from `MultiTouchGestureEventArgs`, which also provides a `GetPosition` method that allows you to determine the position of the first or second touch point relative to a specified `UIElement`. The method accepts a `UIElement` and an `int` value indicating the index of a touch point, either 0 or 1.

When the user completes the pinch gesture by removing either or both touch points, the `GestureListener.PinchCompleted` event is raised. This event provides the opportunity to conclude any activities that were being performed during the pinch gesture, such as finalizing the locations of elements. The handler accepts a `PinchStartedGestureEventArgs` parameter, as shown:

```
void HandlePinchDelta(object sender, PinchGestureEventArgs e)
{
    /* method body. */
}
```

The `PinchGestureEventArgs` argument provides the same information as described for the `GestureListener.PinchDelta` event.

GestureBegin and GestureCompleted Events

In addition to the gesture-specific events, two events are raised before and after every gesture event. These are the `GestureBegin` and `GestureCompleted` events. Handlers for these events resemble the following:

```
void HandleGestureBegin(object sender, GestureEventArgs e)
{
    /* method body. */
}


void HandleGestureCompleted(object sender, GestureEventArgs e)
{
    /* method body. */
}
```

Gesture Sample Code

This section looks at the `GesturesView` page in the downloadable sample code and demonstrates the various events of the `GestureListener` class. You see how to move, rotate, and resize a `UIElement` using gestures. You also see how to provide an animation that responds to a flick gesture to send a `UIElement` hurtling across a page.

The view contains a `Border`. Within the `Border` we attach the `GestureListener` and subscribe to its various events:

```xml
<Grid x:Name="ContentPanel" Grid.Row="1" Margin="12,0,12,0">
    <TextBlock x:Name="messageBlock"
            Style="{StaticResource PhoneTextNormalStyle}"
            VerticalAlignment="Top" />
    <Button Content="reset" Click="Button_Click"
            VerticalAlignment="Bottom"
            HorizontalAlignment="Left" />
    <Border x:Name="border"
            Width="300" Height="200"
            BorderBrush="{StaticResource PhoneBorderBrush}"
            BorderThickness="4,32,4,4"
            Background="{StaticResource PhoneAccentBrush}"
            RenderTransformOrigin="0.5,0.5"
            Opacity=".8"
            CacheMode="BitmapCache">
        <Border.RenderTransform>
            <CompositeTransform x:Name="compositeTransform"/>
        </Border.RenderTransform>
        <toolkit:GestureService.GestureListener>
            <toolkit:GestureListener
                Tap="HandleTap"
                DoubleTap="HandleDoubleTap"
                Hold="HandleHold"
                DragStarted="HandleDragStarted"
                DragDelta="HandleDragDelta"
                DragCompleted="HandleDragCompleted"
                Flick="HandleFlick"
                PinchStarted="HandlePinchStarted"
                PinchDelta="HandlePinchDelta"
                PinchCompleted="HandlePinchCompleted">
            </toolkit:GestureListener>
        </toolkit:GestureService.GestureListener>
    </Border>
</Grid>
```

A `CompositeTransform` is used to change the position, size, and rotation of the `Border`.

The following sections walk through each gesture event and show how the Border control is manipulated in response.

Handling the Tap, DoubleTap, and Hold Events

When the user performs a tap gesture, the HandleTap method in the code-beside is called. This method resets the CompositeTransform translate values to 0, which returns the Border to its original location.

```
void HandleTap(object sender, GestureEventArgs e)
{
    compositeTransform.TranslateX = compositeTransform.TranslateY = 0;
}
```

When the user performs a double tap gesture, the HandleDoubleTap method is called, which resets the amount of scaling applied to the Border, returning it to its original size.

```
void HandleDoubleTap(object sender, GestureEventArgs e)
{
    compositeTransform.ScaleX = compositeTransform.ScaleY = 1;
}
```

When a hold gesture is performed, the HandleHold method is called. This, in turn, calls the ResetPosition method, resetting the size and location of the Border.

```
void HandleHold(object sender, GestureEventArgs e)
{
    ResetPosition();
}
```

```
void ResetPosition()
{
    compositeTransform.TranslateX = compositeTransform.TranslateY = 0;
    compositeTransform.ScaleX = compositeTransform.ScaleY = 1;
    compositeTransform.Rotation = 0;
}
```

Dragging the Border Control

When a drag gesture is performed, the HandleDragStarted method is called. This method changes the background of the Border, like so:

```
void HandleDragStarted(object sender, DragStartedGestureEventArgs e)
{
    border.Background = dragBrush;
}
```

An event handler for the DragDelta event moves the element by the drag amount, via the translation properties of the CompositeTransform:

```
void HandleDragDelta(object sender, DragDeltaGestureEventArgs e)
{
    compositeTransform.TranslateX += e.HorizontalChange;
    compositeTransform.TranslateY += e.VerticalChange;
}
```

When the drag gesture completes the `DragCompleted` event handler resets the `Border` background:

```
void HandleDragCompleted(object sender, DragCompletedGestureEventArgs e)
{
    border.Background = normalBrush;
}
```

Rotating and Scaling in Response to a Pinch Gesture

When a pinch gesture is detected, the `Pinch` event handler records the amount of rotation applied to the element, along with the scale of the element:

```
double initialAngle;
double initialScale;

void HandlePinchStarted(object sender, PinchStartedGestureEventArgs e)
{
    border.Background = pinchBrush;

    initialAngle = compositeTransform.Rotation;
    initialScale = compositeTransform.ScaleX;
}
```

A change in the pinch gesture raises the `PinchDelta` event, at which point the level of rotation is applied to the `CompositeTransform`, and the element is scaled up or down using the `PinchGestureEventArgs.DistanceRatio` property:

```
void HandlePinchDelta(object sender, PinchGestureEventArgs e)
{
    compositeTransform.Rotation = initialAngle + e.TotalAngleDelta;
    compositeTransform.ScaleX
        = compositeTransform.ScaleY = initialScale * e.DistanceRatio;
}
```

The completion of a pinch gesture sees the border's background restored, as shown:

```
void HandlePinchCompleted(object sender, PinchGestureEventArgs e)
{
    border.Background = normalBrush;
}
```

Flick Gesture Animation

This section presents a technique for animating a UIElement in response to a flick gesture. When a flick occurs we install a StoryBoard with a timeline animation, which performs a translation on the UIElement.

The detection of a flick gesture causes the Flick event handler, named HandleFlick, to be called. This method calculates a destination point for the border control based on the velocity of the flick. It then creates an animation for the border using the custom AddTranslationAnimation. See the following excerpt:

```
const double brakeSpeed = 10;

void HandleFlick(object sender, FlickGestureEventArgs e)
{
    Point currentPoint = new Point(
        (double)compositeTransform.GetValue(
                    CompositeTransform.TranslateXProperty),
        (double)compositeTransform.GetValue(
                    CompositeTransform.TranslateYProperty));

    double toX = currentPoint.X + e.HorizontalVelocity / brakeSpeed;
    double toY = currentPoint.Y + e.VerticalVelocity / brakeSpeed;
    Point destinationPoint = new Point(toX, toY);

    var storyboard = new Storyboard { FillBehavior = FillBehavior.HoldEnd };

    AddTranslationAnimation(
        storyboard, border, currentPoint, destinationPoint,
        new Duration(TimeSpan.FromMilliseconds(500)),
        new CubicEase {EasingMode = EasingMode.EaseOut});

    storyboard.Begin();
}
```

The static method AddTranslationAnimation creates two DoubleAnimation objects: one for the horizontal axis, the other for the vertical axis. Each animation is assigned to the border's CompositeTransform, as shown:

```
static void AddTranslationAnimation(Storyboard storyboard,
    FrameworkElement targetElement,
    Point fromPoint,
    Point toPoint,
    Duration duration,
    IEasingFunction easingFunction)
```

```
{
    var xAnimation = new DoubleAnimation
                        {
                            From = fromPoint.X,
                            To = toPoint.X,
                            Duration = duration,
                            EasingFunction = easingFunction
                        };

    var yAnimation = new DoubleAnimation
                        {
                            From = fromPoint.Y,
                            To = toPoint.Y,
                            Duration = duration,
                            EasingFunction = easingFunction
                        };

    AddAnimation(
        storyboard,
        targetElement.RenderTransform,
        CompositeTransform.TranslateXProperty,
        xAnimation);

    AddAnimation(
        storyboard,
        targetElement.RenderTransform,
        CompositeTransform.TranslateYProperty,
        yAnimation);
}
```

The static method `AddAnimation` associates an animation `Timeline` with a `DependencyObject`, which in this case is the `Border` control:

```
static void AddAnimation(
    Storyboard storyboard,
    DependencyObject dependencyObject,
    DependencyProperty targetProperty,
    Timeline timeline)
{
    Storyboard.SetTarget(timeline, dependencyObject);
    Storyboard.SetTargetProperty(timeline, new PropertyPath(targetProperty));
    storyboard.Children.Add(timeline);
}
```

When launched, the `GestureView` page allows the user to flick the `Border` element across the page. A reset button exists to reset the position of the `Border` if it happens to leave the visible boundaries of the page (see Figure 11.11).

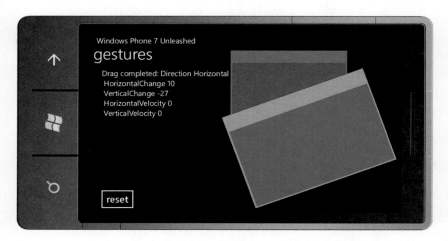

FIGURE 11.11   The `Border` can be moved, rotated, resized, and flicked in response to gesture events.

Toolkit gestures offer a high-level way of interpreting touch input data and make it easy to provide a natural and immersive experience for your users, without the bother of tracking low-level touch events.

Designing Touch Friendly User Interfaces

The design and layout of your user interface influences how easy your app is to use with touch input. When designing your UI, it is important to ensure that page elements are big enough and far enough apart to be conducive to touch input. It is also important to consider the nature of mobile devices, and that your app may be used in conditions where touch precision is compromised, such as standing aboard a moving train. Adhering to the advice presented in this section helps you to ensure that your apps are touch friendly.

Three Components of Touch

Touch UI can be broken down into the following three components:

▶ **Touch target**—The area defined to accept touch input, which is not visible to the user

▶ **Touch element**—The visual indicator of the touch target, which is visible to the user

▶ **Touch control**—A touch target that is combined with a touch element that the user touches

The touch target can be larger than the touch element, but should never be smaller than it. The touch element should never be smaller than 60% of the touch target.

Sizing and Spacing Constraints

Providing adequate spacing between touch targets helps to prevent users from selecting the wrong touch control. Touch targets should not be smaller than 34 pixels (9 mm) square and should provide at least 8 pixels (2 mm) between touchable controls (see Figure 11.12).

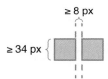

FIGURE 11.12   Touch target sizing and spacing constraints

In exceptional cases, controls can be smaller, but they should never be smaller than 26 pixels (7 mm) square.

It is recommend that some touch targets be made larger than 34 pixels (9 mm) when the touch target is a frequently touched control or the target resides close to the edge of the screen.

General Guidelines

The following is a list of some general guidelines when designing a touch-friendly interface:

▶ When designing your interface, you should allow all basic or common tasks to be completed using a single finger.

▶ Touch controls should respond to touch immediately. A touch control with even a slight lag, or one that seems slow when transitioning, has a negative impact on the user experience.

▶ Processing that would otherwise reduce the responsiveness of the UI should be performed on a background thread. If an operation takes a long time, consider providing incremental feedback.

▶ Try to use a gesture in the manner for which it was intended. For example, avoid using a gesture as a shortcut to a task.

Summary

This chapter began by looking at mouse events. Mouse events are an easy way to get basic touch support and allow you to detect simple, one-finger gestures such as tap and double tap.

The chapter examined the TouchPoint class and illustrated how it provides a low-level input system that you can use to respond to all touch activity in the UI.

The UIElement manipulation events also were discussed. Manipulation events are used to handle more complex gestures, such as multitouch gestures and gestures that use inertia and velocity data.

The chapter explored the gestures support in the Silverlight for Windows Phone SDK and the Silverlight for Windows Phone Toolkit, and you saw how they further consolidate the low-level touch API into a set of gesture-specific events and make it easy to handle complex single and multitouch gestures.

Finally, the chapter looked at the best practices for optimizing your user interfaces for touch input.

CHAPTER 12

Launchers and Choosers

Windows Phone apps execute within a sandbox and lack direct access to phone services like email and messaging. Launchers and choosers allow your app to reach outside the sandbox in a safe and system friendly way to give indirect access to a set of built-in system applications.

Launchers and choosers are fundamental to Windows Phone development. They enable users to perform common tasks in the same way across all apps, providing a consistent user experience.

This chapter begins by looking at the two types of tasks: launchers and choosers. It then explores the execution model of choosers, the internal workings of event subscriptions that span across application lifetimes. It then examines each launcher and chooser in detail.

Finally, the chapter examines how to programmatically retrieve contact and appointment information in a read-only manner.

Many launchers and choosers are presented in this chapter, so do not feel like you need to absorb them all at once. You may want to skim over them, just to get a feel for what is on offer, and then refer back to this chapter when you are implementing a particular launcher or chooser in your app.

API Overview

The launcher and chooser API is located in the Microsoft.Phone.Tasks namespace of the Microsoft.Phone.dll assembly.

Launchers and choosers share two characteristics. First, all contain a Show method, which initiates an associated system app. Second, all cause your app to be deactivated when the Show method is called. For more information on deactivation, see Chapter 3, "Application Execution Model."

Both launchers and choosers use an internal API, and there is little or no capability for custom launchers or choosers. In addition, nearly all are sealed classes, meaning that extending the existing implementations is not possible. The one exception is the MediaPlayerLauncher task, though subclassing it would serve little to no purpose since it has no virtual or protected members.

Launchers are a set of classes that do not return data to your application; they are fire and forget. Launchers, in general, do not share a common base class or interface.

Conversely, choosers derive from the ChooserBase<TTaskEventArgs> class, which contains a Completed event that is raised when the user either completes a task, such as selecting an image with the PhotoChooserTask, or when the user cancels the task, either explicitly within the system app or by using the hardware Back button.

The generic parameter TTaskEventArgs of the ChooserBase class specifies the type passed to the event handler for the Completed event.

> **NOTE**
>
> When your app is activated, after being deactivated by calling the Show method of a chooser, the chooser's Completed event is raised. This occurs even if the user takes a detour to another app or to the Start Experience (home screen), and then returns to your application via the hardware Back button.

The Windows Phone launchers and choosers available for your application are listed in Table 12.1.

TABLE 12.1   Launchers and Choosers

Launcher	Chooser
BingMapsDirectionsTask	AddressChooserTask
BingMapsTask	CameraCaptureTask
ConnectionSettingsTask	EmailAddressChooserTask
EmailComposeTask	GameInviteTask
MarketplaceDetailTask	PhoneNumberChooserTask
MarketplaceHubTask	PhotoChooserTask
MarketplaceReviewTask	SaveContactTask
MarketplaceSearchTask	SaveEmailAddressTask
MediaPlayerLauncher	SavePhoneNumberTask
PhoneCallTask	SaveRingtoneTask
SearchTask	
ShareLinkTask	
ShareStatusTask	
SmsComposeTask	
WebBrowserTask	

Choosers and the Application Execution Model

Recall from Chapter 3 that when tombstoned, your app is terminated, and therefore all regular CLR event subscriptions are discarded. Well, choosers use a subscription model that relies on CLR events, and using a chooser can lead to your app being tombstoned. To contend with this, the chooser infrastructure has some interesting plumbing that allows it to survive tombstoning and to reinstate subscriptions to the `ChooserBase.Completed` event when an app is reactivated.

Internal Workings of the `ChooserBase.Completed` Event

When subscription to the `ChooserBase.Completed` event occurs, the location of the subscription, in particular the class name and method name, is used as an identifier for the event subscription. This information is serialized to your app's transient state, allowing it to survive application termination. When the system application associated with the chooser completes, your app is restarted, and the OS signals that a chooser has completed by invoking a static method. When the event subscription occurs again in your class, the subscription identifier is re-created and compared with the list of subscription identifiers for that chooser. If there is a match, the event handler in your class is called.

> **NOTE**
>
> Subscribing to the `Completed` event causes the event to be raised.

To understand this further, consider the following code:

```
readonly SaveEmailAddressTask saveEmailAddressTask
    = new SaveEmailAddressTask();

public SomeViewModel()
{
    /* Step 2. */
    saveEmailAddressTask.Completed += saveEmailAddressTask_Completed;
    /* Step 4. */
    Debug.WriteLine("Constructor.");
}

public void ShowLauncher()
{
    /* Step 1. */
    saveEmailAddressTask.Show();
}

void saveEmailAddressTask_Completed(object sender, TaskEventArgs e)
{
    /* Step 3. */
    Debug.WriteLine("Task Completed.");
}
```

Subscription to the SaveEmailAddressTask.Completed event is performed in the view-model's constructor. When the Show method of the saveEmailAddressTask is called (step 1) the user app is deactivated. Presuming that the app is tombstoned, when the system app completes and the user app is restarted and activated, the viewmodel's constructor is called again (step 2). When the event subscription occurs this time, however, the Completed event is raised and the event handler is called (step 3). When the event handler returns, the code in the constructor resumes (step 4).

> **BEST PRACTICE**
>
> When subscribing to the Completed event of a chooser, declare the chooser at the class level and subscribe to the event within the class constructor.

Launchers and Choosers in Detail

The following sections cover each launcher and chooser class in detail. There is some repetition in the structure of several of the sections, but each is intended to be self-contained to allow you to look up a particular launcher or chooser when needed.

The examples presented in this chapter show tasks used directly from within viewmodel classes. Chapter 22, "Unit Testing," looks at techniques for removing the dependency on the Silverlight for Windows Phone SDK, which allows your code to be more portable across other platforms.

Retrieve Driving Directions Using the BingMapsDirectionsTask

The Bing Maps directions task launches the built-in Maps application and displays driving directions between two points. A start and an end point can be specified using the task's Start and End properties, which are of type LabeledMapLocation. If only one location is specified, the user's current location is used as the second location.

> **NOTE**
>
> At least one of the Start or End properties must be specified, or an InvalidOperationException is thrown when you call the BingMapsDirectionsTask.Show method.

Both Start and End properties allow you to specify a string label and geographic coordinates indicating the latitude and longitude of the location. If you omit the geographic coordinates, the Maps application searches for the label string.

The following example demonstrates how to launch the Maps application to search for two locations.

```
BingMapsDirectionsTask bingMapsDirectionsTask
                    = new BingMapsDirectionsTask();
...
```

```
bingMapsDirectionsTask.Start = new LabeledMapLocation("geneva", null);
bingMapsDirectionsTask.End = new LabeledMapLocation("london", null);
bingMapsDirectionsTask.Show();
```

To specify geographic coordinates, insert a using statement for System.Device.Location at the top of your class. A GeoCoordinate can then be passed to the task as shown:

```
GeoCoordinate geoCoordinate = new GeoCoordinate(46.25829, 6.20966);
bingMapsDirectionsTask.Start
                     = new LabeledMapLocation("Geneva", geoCoordinate);
bingMapsDirectionsTask.Show();
```

By specifying the geographic coordinates, the Maps application places a label at the location using the supplied text.

The sample for this section allows the user to enter the start and end search terms, and to launch the BingMapsDirectionsTask via an application bar button.

The sample can be found in the LaunchersAndChoosers/BingMaps directory of the WindowsPhone7Unleashed.Examples project.

The BingMapsDirectionsTaskViewModel class contains two string properties, which are used as search terms for a BingMapsDirectionsTask (see Listing 12.1).

An ICommand, named SearchCommand, initializes the BingMapsDirectionsTask and calls its Show method.

LISTING 12.1   BingMapsDirectionsTaskViewModel Class

```
public class BingMapsDirectionsTaskViewModel : ViewModelBase
{
    readonly BingMapsDirectionsTask bingMapsDirectionsTask
                                    = new BingMapsDirectionsTask();

    public BingMapsDirectionsTaskViewModel() : base("get directions")
    {
        searchCommand = new DelegateCommand(arg => ShowTask());
    }

    void ShowTask()
    {
        bingMapsDirectionsTask.Start
                            = new LabeledMapLocation(startLocation, null);
        bingMapsDirectionsTask.End
                            = new LabeledMapLocation(endLocation, null);
        bingMapsDirectionsTask.Show();
    }
```

LISTING 12.1   Continued

```csharp
readonly DelegateCommand searchCommand;

public ICommand SearchCommand
{
    get
    {
        return searchCommand;
    }
}

string startLocation;

public string StartLocation
{
    get
    {
        return startLocation;
    }
    set
    {
        Assign(() => StartLocation, ref startLocation, value);
    }
}

string endLocation;

public string EndLocation
{
    get
    {
        return endLocation;
    }
    set
    {
        Assign(() => EndLocation, ref endLocation, value);
    }
}
}
```

The `BingMapsDirectionsTaskView` page contains two `TextBox` controls that are bound to the viewmodel string properties, as shown:

```xml
<StackPanel x:Name="ContentPanel" Grid.Row="1">
    <TextBlock Text="start location"
```

```
                            Style="{StaticResource LabelTextStyle}" />
        <TextBox Text="{Binding StartLocation, Mode=TwoWay}" />

        <TextBlock Text="end location"
                            Style="{StaticResource LabelTextStyle}" />
        <TextBox Text="{Binding EndLocation, Mode=TwoWay}" />
    </StackPanel>
```

In addition, the view contains an `AppBarIconButton` that is used to execute the view-model's `SearchCommand`. See the following excerpt:

```
<u:AppBar>
    <u:AppBarIconButton
        Command="{Binding SearchCommand}"
        Text="Search"
        IconUri="/LaunchersAndChoosers/BingMaps/Images/AppBarSearch.png" />
</u:AppBar>
```

Figure 12.1 shows the view before launching the Bing Maps directions task.

FIGURE 12.1   `BingMapsDirectionsTaskView` page

Tapping the Search button launches the built-in Maps application (see Figure 12.2).

The Bing Maps directions task is a simple way to launch the built-in Maps application. Chapter 16, "Bing Maps," shows how to build similar capabilities directly into your app, allowing you to completely customize how direction information is presented.

FIGURE 12.2   Built-in Maps application

Displaying a Location on a Map Using the `BingMapsTask`

The Bing Maps task allows you to launch the built-in Maps application centered at the location specified by the `BingMapsTask.Center` property, which is of type `GeoCoordinate`. If not specified the map is centered at the user's current location. If provided, the `Center` property is ignored and the `BingMapsTask.SearchTerm` property is used to search for matching locations. The best match is then tagged on the map.

To use the `BingMapsTask` to search for a location, define it as a field in your class and set its `SearchTerm` property, as demonstrated:

```
BingMapsTask bingMapsTask = new BingMapsTask();
...
bingMapsTask.SearchTerm = "prague";
bingMapsTask.Show();
```

The following example demonstrates how to specify a geographic location:

```
bingMapsTask.Center = new GeoCoordinate(50.08021, 14.416983);
bingMapsTask.Show();
```

A sample for the `BingMapsTask` can be found in the LaunchersAndChoosers/BingMaps directory of the WindowsPhone7Unleashed.Examples project. The sample is almost identical to the previous `BingMapsDirectionsTask` sample.

Navigating to a Connection Setting Page Using the `ConnectionSettingsTask`

The connection settings task allows you to launch a settings page for a specified set of network connection related settings.

The `ConnectionSettingsType` property of the `ConnectionSettingsTask` class allows you to display the settings dialog using one of the following four `ConnectionSettingsType` values:

- AirplaneMode
- Bluetooth
- Cellular
- WiFi

To display the Wi-Fi settings dialog, for example, use the following:

```
ConnectionSettingsTask task = new ConnectionSettingsTask();
task.ConnectionSettingsType = ConnectionSettingsType.WiFi;
task.Show();
```

The four built-in settings pages available to the `ConnectionSettingsTask` are shown in Figure 12.3.

FIGURE 12.3   Connection settings pages

The sample for the `ConnectionSettingsTask` allows you to select one of the `ConnectionSettingsType` values from a Silverlight Toolkit `ListPicker` control (see Figure 12.4). Tapping the Settings button in the application bar executes an `ICommand` in the viewmodel, which initializes and calls the `Show` method of the `ConnectionSettingsTask`.

FIGURE 12.4   `ConnectionSettingsTaskView` page

Selecting an Email Address with the `EmailAddressChooserTask`

The email address chooser task launches the Windows Phone Contacts application and allows the user to select a contact. When the user completes the task, the `Completed` event is raised, and the event handler receives an `EmailResult` object that exposes a string containing the selected contact's email address.

> **NOTE**
>
> To query the user's contact list, without requiring the user to select a contact, use the `Contacts` class, which is described later in this chapter.

The `EmailAddressChooserTask` should be defined as a field in your class, like so:

```
readonly EmailAddressChooserTask emailAddressChooserTask
                                = new EmailAddressChooserTask();
```

Subscribe to the `EmailAddressChooserTask.Completed` event within your class constructor, as shown:

```
emailAddressChooserTask.Completed
   += new EventHandler<EmailResult>(HandleEmailAddressChooserTaskCompleted);
```

Use the `Show` method of the `EmailAddressChooserTask` to launch the built-in Contacts app. When the task completes the handler receives an `EmailResult` object, as shown:

```
void HandleEmailAddressChooserTaskCompleted(object sender, EmailResult e)
{
    if (e.TaskResult == TaskResult.OK)
    {
```

```
            ToAddress = e.Email;
        }
        else if (e.Error != null)
        {
            Message = "Unable to choose email address. " + e.ToString();
        }
        else if (e.TaskResult == TaskResult.Cancel)
        {
            Message = "Cancelled";
        }
    }
}
```

Sample Overview

Example code for the `EmailComposeTask` can be found in the `EmailViewModel` in the downloadable sample code. The `EmailView` allows the user to select the recipient and to launch a new `EmailComposeTask` via a button (see Figure 12.5).

FIGURE 12.5   The `EmailView` page

The viewmodel contains a public property of type `ICommand` called `ChooseRecipientCommand`. The view's Choose Email button is bound to the command.

When the `ChooseRecipientCommand` is executed, the `Show` method of the `emailAddressChooserTask` is called. This behavior is defined in the viewmodel constructor, as shown:

```
public EmailViewModel() : base("Email")
{
    emailAddressChooserTask.Completed
                            += HandleEmailAddressChooserTaskCompleted;
```

```
chooseRecipientCommand = new DelegateCommand(
    obj => emailAddressChooserTask.Show());
...
}
```

When the `EmailAddressChooserTask.Show` method is called, the built-in Contacts application is launched (see Figure 12.6).

FIGURE 12.6   The Windows Phone Contacts application

The result returned by the Contacts app is used by an `EmailComposeTask`, which is presented in the next section.

Preparing an Email with the `EmailComposeTask`

The `EmailComposeTask` launches the Windows Phone Email application, which displays a page allowing the user to create a new email.

NOTE

The email is not sent until it is initiated by the user.

You can optionally specify recipients, a message subject, and a message body, which are prepopulated in the new email, as shown in the following excerpt:

```
EmailComposeTask task = new EmailComposeTask
                {
                        To = "name1@example.com",
                        Cc = "name2@example.com",
```

```
                                 Subject = "Windows Phone",
                                 Body = "Hi from Windows Phone!"
                  };
task.Show();
```

Multiple recipients in the To and Cc properties can be specified by delimiting the address with a semicolon character.

Sample Overview

Example code for the EmailComposeTask can be found in the EmailViewModel in the downloadable sample code. The EmailView allows the user to select the recipient and to launch a new EmailComposeTask via a button (shown previously in Figure 12.5).

The view's Compose Email button is bound to a viewmodel command called ComposeCommand.

When executed, the ComposeCommand creates a new EmailComposeTask and sets its To property to the text supplied by the EmailAddressChooserTask. This behavior is defined in the EmailViewModel constructor, as shown:

```
public EmailViewModel() : base("Email")
{
...

    composeCommand = new DelegateCommand(
        delegate
           {
               EmailComposeTask emailComposeTask
                   = new EmailComposeTask
                       {
                           To = toAddress,
                           Subject = "Windows Phone 7 Unleashed",
                           Body = "Hi from Windows Phone 7!"
                       };
               emailComposeTask.Show();
           });
}
```

When the EmailComposeTask.Show method is called, the built-in Email application is launched. If the user has multiple email accounts defined on the device, the Email application prompts the user to select which account to use. The user is then presented with a new email message, prepopulated with the To, Cc, Subject, and Body properties of the EmailComposeTask.

Saving a Contact's Email Using the SaveEmailAddressTask

The SaveEmailAddressTask is a chooser that allows the user to save a specified email address using the built-in Contacts application. An email address can be saved to an existing contact, or to a new contact. SaveEmailAddressTask does not return data, but its Completed event can be handled to determine whether the task was completed correctly.

The SaveEmailAddressTask should be defined as a field in your class, like so:

```
readonly SaveEmailAddressTask saveEmailAddressTask
                                    = new SaveEmailAddressTask();
```

Subscribe to the SaveEmailAddressTask.Completed event within your class constructor, as shown:

```
saveEmailAddressTask.Completed += HandleSaveEmailAddressTaskCompleted;
```

Use the Show method of the SaveEmailAddressTask to launch the built-in Contacts app. When the task completes the handler receives a TaskEventArgs object, as shown:

```
void HandleSaveEmailAddressTaskCompleted(object sender, TaskEventArgs e)
{
    if (e.Error != null)
    {
        Message = "Unable to save the email address. " + e.Error;
        return;
    }

    if (e.TaskResult == TaskResult.OK)
    {
        Message = "Email address saved";
    }
    else if (e.TaskResult == TaskResult.Cancel)
    {
        Message = "Cancelled";
    }
}
```

Sample Overview

Example code for the SaveEmailAddressTask can be found in the SaveEmailAddressViewModel in the downloadable sample code.

The SaveEmailAddressView page allows the user to enter an email address and then to initiate the SaveEmailAddressTask using a button (see Figure 12.7).

The view's Email Address TextBlock has a two-way binding to the viewmodel's EmailAddress property, as shown:

```
<TextBox Text="{Binding EmailAddress, Mode=TwoWay}"
        InputScope="EmailSmtpAddress" />
```

FIGURE 12.7   `SaveEmailAddressView` page

The `InputScope` property of the `TextBox` causes the onscreen keyboard to be displayed with a set of keys suitable for typing an email address. For more information on `InputScopes`, see Chapter 6, "Text Elements."

To initiate the `SaveEmailAddressTask`, the viewmodel contains a public property called `SaveCommand`:

```
readonly DelegateCommand saveCommand;

public ICommand SaveCommand
{
    get
    {
        return saveCommand;
    }
}
```

When the `saveCommand` is executed, the `Show` method of the `saveEmailAddressTask` is called. This behavior is defined in the viewmodel's construct, as shown in the following excerpt:

```
public SaveEmailAddressViewModel() : base("Save Email Address")
{
    saveEmailAddressTask.Completed += saveEmailAddressTask_Completed;

    saveCommand = new DelegateCommand(
        delegate
            {
                Message = string.Empty;
                saveEmailAddressTask.Email = emailAddress;
```

```
            saveEmailAddressTask.Show();
        });
}
```

The view's Save button is bound to the `SaveCommand`, as shown:

```
<Button Command="{Binding SaveCommand}"
        Content="Save" />
```

When the `saveEmailAddressTask.Show` method is called, the built-in Contacts application is launched (see Figure 12.8).

FIGURE 12.8   The Contacts application allows the user to select an existing contact or create a new one.

When the user selects either an existing contact or the new contact option, the Edit Email page is displayed (see Figure 12.9).

If the user selects an existing contact, when the Save icon button is tapped, the Edit Phone Contact page is displayed (see Figure 12.10).

Alternatively, if the user opts to create a new contact, the New Contact page is displayed.

Once the contact information is saved using the disk icon, the sample application is activated, and the `HandleSaveEmailAddressTaskCompleted` handler is called.

Navigating to an App on the Marketplace with the `MarketplaceDetailTask`

The Marketplace detail task is used to launch the built-in Marketplace app, which shows the details page for a product specified by a unique identifier that you provide. If an identifier is not specified, the details page for the current application is shown.

FIGURE 12.9   Edit Email page

FIGURE 12.10   Edit Phone Contact page

The following code demonstrates how to launch the `MarketplaceDetailTask`:

```
MarketplaceDetailTask task
    = new MarketplaceDetailTask
        {
            ContentIdentifier = "<ID>",
            //ContentType = MarketplaceContentType.Applications
        };
task.Show();
```

The `MarketplaceDetailTask` has two properties: `ContentIdentifier` and `ContentType`. The `ContentIdentifier` is the unique product identifier for an app. When an application is published on the Windows Phone Marketplace it is assigned a unique identifier, which is located in a `ProductID` attribute of the WMAppManifest.xml file. This identifier can be used to launch the `MarketplaceDetailsTask` from other apps.

If the `ContentIdentifier` is specified, the value must be a valid product identifier. If the identifier has an invalid format, a `FormatException` is raised. The identifier format is 32 digits separated by hyphens and enclosed in braces, as shown in the following example:

```
{45dc3711-8af7-42bf-a749-6c491f2b427f}
```

As an aside, this format can be achieved using a `Guid`, by calling its `ToString` method with "B" as the format argument, as shown:

```
string productId = guid.ToString("B");
```

Retrieving Your Application's Product ID at Runtime

While the `ContentIdentifier` is not required to launch the `MarketplaceDetailTask` for the current app, it is required to launch the details page for a different app. This value can be read at runtime by retrieving the WMAppManifest.xml file using the `Application.GetResourceStream` method, and then by extracting the value using the System.Xml.Linq API, as shown in the following excerpt:

```
public string GetProductId()
{
    Uri uri = new Uri("WMAppManifest.xml", UriKind.Relative);
    StreamResourceInfo info
        = Application.GetResourceStream(uri);
    XElement manifestElement = XElement.Load(info.Stream);
    XElement appElement = manifestElement.Element("App");
    XAttribute idAttribute
        = appElement.Attribute("ProductID");
    return idAttribute.Value;
}
```

Sample Overview

Example code for the `MarketplaceDetailTask` can be found in the `MarketplaceViewModel` in the downloadable sample code. The `MarketplaceView` page includes a `ListBox` to select content type for the `MarketplaceHubTask` and the `MarketplaceSearchTask`, both of which are discussed later in this chapter, and buttons for exercising the various tasks (see Figure 12.11).

The viewmodel contains a `DetailCommand` defined as follows:

```
readonly DelegateCommand detailCommand;

public ICommand DetailCommand
{
    get
    {
```

```
        return detailCommand;
    }
}
```

FIGURE 12.11   `MarketplaceView` page

The `detailCommand` is instantiated in the `MarketplaceViewModel` constructor. When executed, the `detailCommand` creates a new `MarketplaceDetailTask` and calls its `Show` method. This behavior is defined in the viewmodel constructor, as shown:

```
public MarketplaceViewModel()
{
    detailCommand = new DelegateCommand(
            delegate
            {
                var task = new MarketplaceDetailTask();
                task.Show();
            });
// ...
}
```

The `MarketPlaceView` uses a button to execute the `DetailCommand` in the viewmodel:

```
<Button Command="{Binding DetailCommand}"
        Content="Marketplace Detail" />
```

Launching the Marketplace App with the `MarketplaceHubTask`

The Marketplace hub task is used to launch the built-in Marketplace app.

The marketplace category can be specified using the `ContentType` property of the `MarketplaceHubTask`. Set the `ContentType` property to a value from the `MarketplaceContentType` enumeration to launch the hub to a particular type of content, as shown in the following excerpt:

```
MarketplaceHubTask task
    = new MarketplaceHubTask
            {
                ContentType = MarketplaceContentType.Music
            };
task.Show();
```

`ContentType` allows you to specify one of two categories: Music or Applications.

> **NOTE**
>
> The only allowed value for the `ContentType` property is `MarketplaceContentType.Applications`, which is the default value if not supplied. If `MarketplaceContentType.Music` is used, an `ArgumentException` is raised.

Sample Overview

Example code for the `MarketplaceHubTask` can be found in the `MarketplaceViewModel` in the downloadable sample code.

The viewmodel contains an `ICommand` called `HubCommand`, which is instantiated in the `MarketplaceViewModel` constructor. A Silverlight Toolkit `ListPicker` allows the user to select the marketplace content type.

When executed, the `hubCommand` creates a new `MarketplaceHubTask`, sets its `ContentType` property, and calls its `Show` method, like so:

```
public MarketplaceViewModel()
{
    hubCommand = new DelegateCommand(
        delegate
            {
                MarketplaceHubTask task = new MarketplaceHubTask();
                if (contentType.HasValue)
                {
                    task.ContentType = contentType.Value;
                }
                task.Show();
            });
// ...
}
```

Allowing the User to Review Your App Using the `MarketplaceReviewTask`

The Marketplace review task is used to launch the built-in Marketplace application. A review page allows the user to enter a text review for the current app and give it a rating out of five. The user can also see the average rating of the application by other users.

The `MarketplaceReviewTask` has no settable properties and is launched like so:

```
MarketplaceReviewTask task = new MarketplaceReviewTask();
task.Show();
```

Sample Overview

Example code for the `MarketplaceReviewTask` can be found in the `MarketplaceViewModel` in the downloadable sample code. The `MarketPlaceView` uses a button to execute an `ICommand` called `ReviewCommand` in the viewmodel.

The `reviewCommand` is instantiated in the `MarketplaceViewModel` constructor. When executed, the `reviewCommand` creates a new `MarketplaceReviewTask` and calls its `Show` method, like so:

```
public MarketplaceViewModel()
{
    reviewCommand = new DelegateCommand(
        delegate
            {
                MarketplaceReviewTask task = new MarketplaceReviewTask();
                task.Show();
            });
// ...
}
```

Searching the Marketplace with the `MarketplaceSearchTask`

The Marketplace search task is used to launch the built-in Marketplace app, which displays the search results for a specified search string.

The `MarketplaceSearchTask` class has two properties: `SearchTerms` and `ContentType`. `SearchTerms` is a string that contains one or more search terms. `ContentType` can be set to either `MarketplaceContentType.Applications` or `MarketplaceContentType.Music`. If not specified, `ContentType` defaults to `MarketplaceContentType.Applications`. The following excerpt demonstrates how to create and launch a `MarketplaceSearchTask`:

```
MarketplaceSearchTask task
    = new MarketplaceSearchTask
        {
            ContentType = MarketplaceContentType.Applications,
            SearchTerms = "puzzle"
        };
task.Show();
```

The Marketplace app is not shown on the emulator's App List page. It does, however, exist on the emulator, and it is not necessary to have an unlocked emulator to use it. By calling the Show method on the MarketplaceSearchTask in an app running on the emulator, it allows you to launch the Marketplace app search page and to browse search results using real data.

Sample Overview

Example code for the MarketplaceSearchTask can be found in the MarketplaceViewModel in the downloadable sample code.

The MarketPlaceView has a button that executes an ICommand named SearchCommand in the viewmodel. The searchCommand is instantiated in the MarketplaceViewModel constructor. When executed it creates a new MarketplaceSearchTask, sets its SearchTerms property with the text supplied by a TextBox in the view, sets its ContentType property, and finally calls its Show method, like so:

```
public MarketplaceViewModel()
{
    searchCommand = new DelegateCommand(
        delegate
            {
                MarketplaceSearchTask task = new MarketplaceSearchTask
                    {
                        /* SearchTerms can't be null or empty,
                         * or else an ArgumentException is thrown. */
                        SearchTerms = string.IsNullOrEmpty(searchTerms)
                                        ? " " : searchTerms
                    };
                if (contentType.HasValue)
                {
                    task.ContentType = contentType.Value;
                }
                task.Show();
            });
// ...
}
```

If the MarketplaceSearchTask.SearchTerms property is null or empty, an ArgumentException is raised. To launch the MarketplaceSearchTask without providing search terms, set its SearchTerms property to a string consisting of a single space.

Playing a Media File Using the `MediaPlayerLauncher`

The media player launcher is used to launch the built-in Media Player app to play a speci-fied media file (see Figure 12.12).

FIGURE 12.12   Windows Phone Media Player application

Media files can be stored either locally on the device or externally using an absolute Uri. If stored locally, the `MediaPlayerLauncher.Media` property must be assigned a relative Uri to the file location. Relative Uri's are used for files located in either isolated storage or in the app's XAP file.

Files downloaded from the Internet are placed in isolated storage, whereas files accompa-nying the app are placed into the app's XAP file during the build process.

TIP

To include a media file in your XAP file be sure to set its Build Action to Content.

The `MediaPlayerLauncher.Location` property allows you to specify where the content is located, either in the XAP, isolated storage, or on a remote server.

The `MediaPlayerLauncher.Location` property must be set to `MediaLocationType.Install` for media files located within the app's XAP file. For content located in isolated storage, `MediaLocationType.Data` should be used. If not specified, `MediaPlayerLauncher.Location` defaults to `MediaLocationType.Data`. For content located on a remote server, `MediaLocationType.None` is used along with an absolute Uri. If `MediaLocationType.None` is used in conjunction with a relative Uri, a `FileNotFoundException` is raised when the `MediaPlayerLauncher.Show` method is called.

You can optionally specify that one or more playback controls should be shown by the Media Player, by setting the `MediaPlayerLauncher.Controls` property using bitwise *OR* combinations of the `MediaPlaybackControls` enum values.

The following is the list of possible `MediaPlaybackControls` enum values:

▶ **All**—All controls. The equivalent of using *OR* to combine all the other members of the enumeration.

▶ **FastForward**—The fast-forward control.

▶ **None**—No controls are shown.

▶ **Pause**—The pause control.

▶ **Rewind**—The rewind control.

▶ **Skip**—The skip control.

▶ **Stop**—The stop control.

If not specified, the `MediaPlayerLauncher.Controls` property defaults to `MediaPlaybackControls.All`, and the rewind, pause, and fast-forward buttons are displayed by the Media Player app.

> **NOTE**
>
> While it is possible to specify the Skip and Stop controls, the controls are not displayed, and it does not affect the Media Player app.

The following example shows how to use the `MediaPlayerLauncher` to play a local media file in the Media Player app, displaying a Pause and a Stop button:

```
MediaPlayerLauncher mediaPlayerLauncher
    = new MediaPlayerLauncher
        {
            Media = new Uri("LaunchersAndChoosers/Video.wmv",
                            UriKind.Relative),
            Location = MediaLocationType.Install,
            Controls = MediaPlaybackControls.Pause
                     | MediaPlaybackControls.Stop
        };
mediaPlayerLauncher.Show();
```

To specify a nonlocal media file, use an absolute `Uri`, as demonstrated in the following example:

```
MediaPlayerLauncher mediaPlayerLauncher
    = new MediaPlayerLauncher
        {
            Media = new Uri("http://www.example.com/Video.wmv",
                            UriKind.Absolute),
            Controls = MediaPlaybackControls.All
        };
mediaPlayerLauncher.Show();
```

Sample Overview

Example code for the `MediaPlayerLauncher` can be found in the
`MediaPlayerLauncherViewModel`, in the downloadable sample code.

The `MediaPlayerLauncherView` page has a button that executes an `ICommand` named
`SearchCommand` in the viewmodel.

When executed, the command instantiates a `MediaPlayerLauncher` and populates its
`Controls` property with the `playbackControls` field, using a lambda expression (see
Listing 12.2).

The lambda `Aggregate` extension method combines the values in the `IEnumerable` collection of `MediaPlaybackControls` enum flags by OR'ing each one with the previous result.

LISTING 12.2   `MediaPlayerLauncherViewModel` Class (excerpt)

```
public class MediaPlayerLauncherViewModel : ViewModelBase
{
    public MediaPlayerLauncherViewModel()
        : base("Media Player Launcher")
    {
        launchCommand = new DelegateCommand(
            delegate
            {
                MediaPlayerLauncher mediaPlayerLauncher
                    = new MediaPlayerLauncher
                    {
                        //Media = new Uri("http://example.com/Video.wmv",
                        //                        UriKind.Absolute),
                        Media = new Uri("LaunchersAndChoosers/Video.wmv",
                                            UriKind.Relative),
                        Location = MediaLocationType.Install,
                    };

                if (playbackControls.Count > 0)
                {
                    mediaPlayerLauncher.Controls
                        = playbackControls.Aggregate((a, b) => a | b);
                }

                mediaPlayerLauncher.Show();
            });
    }

    readonly List<MediaPlaybackControls> mediaPlaybackControls
        = new List<MediaPlaybackControls>
            {
                MediaPlaybackControls.FastForward,
```

LISTING 12.2   Continued

```
                MediaPlaybackControls.Pause,
                MediaPlaybackControls.Rewind,
                /* Not used by Media Player. */
                //MediaPlaybackControls.Skip,
                //MediaPlaybackControls.Stop
        };

    public IEnumerable<MediaPlaybackControls> AvailablePlaybackControls
    {
        get
        {
            return mediaPlaybackControls;
        }
    }

    readonly ObservableCollection<MediaPlaybackControls> playbackControls
        = new ObservableCollection<MediaPlaybackControls>();

    public ObservableCollection<MediaPlaybackControls> PlaybackControls
    {
        get
        {
            return playbackControls;
        }
    }
...
}
```

The view presents the list of available playback controls in a ListBox. A custom attached property is used to provide quasi binding support for the SelectedItems property of the ListBox. This attached property is discussed further in the next section. See the following excerpt:

```
<StackPanel x:Name="ContentPanel" Grid.Row="1">
    <TextBlock Text="Media Player Controls:"
        Style="{StaticResource PhoneTextTitle2Style}" />
    <ListBox ItemsSource="{Binding AvailablePlaybackControls}"
        SelectionMode="Multiple"
        unleashed:SelectedItems.Items="{Binding PlaybackControls}"
        Margin="15">
    </ListBox>
    <Button Command="{Binding LaunchCommand}"
        Content="Launch Media Player" />
```

```
<TextBlock Text="{Binding Message}"
      Style="{StaticResource PhoneTextMessageStyle}" />
</StackPanel>
```

Multiple items in the `ListBox` can be selected, and the Launch Media Player button initiates the `LaunchCommand` in the viewmodel (see Figure 12.13).

FIGURE 12.13   The media player launcher page

Binding to the `ListBox.SelectedItems` Property

Unfortunately, the `ListBox.SelectedItems` property is not a `DependencyProperty`, which means it cannot be the target of a databinding. A custom attached property is included in the downloadable sample code that allows you to bind the `SelectedItems` property to a collection (see Listing 12.3).

The `SelectedItems` class contains two `DependencyProperty`'s: an `ItemsProperty` and a `SelectedItemsBehaviorProperty`. `ItemsProperty` specifies the source property of the `DataContext` and is used to assign the selected items to the `ListBox`'s `DataContext`. When the `SelectionChanged` event of the `ListBox` is raised, the `DataContext`'s property is updated.

The `SelectedItemsBehavior` class contains the logic for updating the list of selected items, which also relies on the `DataContextChangedListener` class, which raises an event when the `DataContext` of the `ListBox` changes. For more information on the `DataContextChangedListener`, see Chapter 23, "Input Validation."

An instance of the `SelectedItemsBehavior` is associated with the `ListBox` using the `SelectedItemsBehaviorProperty`.

LISTING 12.3   SelectedItems Class

```
public static class SelectedItems
{
    public static readonly DependencyProperty ItemsProperty
```

LISTING 12.3   Continued

```
      = DependencyProperty.RegisterAttached(
          "Items",
          typeof(IList),
          typeof(SelectedItems),
          new PropertyMetadata(null, ItemsPropertyChanged));

  public static void SetItems(ListBox listBox, IList list)
  {
      listBox.SetValue(ItemsProperty, list);
  }


  public static IList GetItems(ListBox listBox)
  {
      return (IList)listBox.GetValue(ItemsProperty);
  }


  static readonly DependencyProperty SelectedItemsBehaviorProperty
      = DependencyProperty.RegisterAttached(
          "SelectedItemsBehavior",
          typeof(SelectedItemsBehavior),
          typeof(ListBox), null);


  static void ItemsPropertyChanged(
      DependencyObject d, DependencyPropertyChangedEventArgs e)
  {
      var target = d as ListBox;
      if (target != null)
      {
          GetOrCreateBehavior(target, (IList)e.NewValue);
      }
  }


  static SelectedItemsBehavior GetOrCreateBehavior(
      ListBox listBox, IList list)
  {
      var behavior = (SelectedItemsBehavior)listBox.GetValue(
                                      SelectedItemsBehaviorProperty);
      if (behavior == null)
      {
          behavior = new SelectedItemsBehavior(listBox, list);
          listBox.SetValue(SelectedItemsBehaviorProperty, behavior);
      }

      return behavior;
```

LISTING 12.3   Continued

```csharp
    }

    class SelectedItemsBehavior
    {
        readonly ListBox listBox;
        readonly IList sourceList;

        public SelectedItemsBehavior(ListBox listBox, IList sourceList)
        {
            this.listBox = ArgumentValidator.AssertNotNull(listBox, "listBox");
            this.sourceList = ArgumentValidator.AssertNotNull(
                                                sourceList, "sourceList");
            this.listBox.SelectionChanged += OnSelectionChanged;
            DataContextChangedListener.Subscribe(listBox, OnDataContextChanged);
        }

        void OnDataContextChanged(
            DependencyObject d, DependencyPropertyChangedEventArgs e)
        {
            UpdateList();
        }

        void OnSelectionChanged(object sender, SelectionChangedEventArgs e)
        {
            UpdateList();
        }

        void UpdateList()
        {
            sourceList.Clear();

            foreach (object item in listBox.SelectedItems)
            {
                sourceList.Add(item);
            }
        }
    }
}
```

Placing a Call with the PhoneCallTask

The phone call task is used to launch the built-in Phone app and displays the specified phone number and display name.

NOTE

The phone call is not placed until it is initiated by the user.

The following example demonstrates how to launch the phone call task:

```
PhoneCallTask phoneCallTask = new PhoneCallTask
                                {
                                        DisplayName = "Alan Turing",
                                        PhoneNumber = "882960"
                                };
phoneCallTask.Show();
```

If the `PhoneCallTask.PhoneNumber` is a null or empty string, calling the `PhoneCallTask.Show` method has no effect. If the `PhoneCallTask.PhoneNumber` has an invalid format, the Phone app prompts the user when the call is being made.

Sample Overview

Example code for the `PhoneCallTask` can be found in the `PhoneCallViewModel` in the downloadable sample code.

The `PhoneCallView` allows the user to enter a telephone number and place a call to that number when a button is tapped.

A Place Call button in the view is bound to the viewmodel's `CallCommand`.

The `callCommand` field is instantiated in the `PhoneCallViewModel` constructor. When executed, the `callCommand` creates a new `PhoneCallTask`, and sets its `PhoneNumber` property with the text supplied by a `TextBox` in the view, as shown:

```
public PhoneCallViewModel() : base("Phone Call Tasks")
{
    callCommand = new DelegateCommand(
        delegate
            {
                PhoneCallTask phoneCallTask = new PhoneCallTask
                                    {
                                            DisplayName = "someone",
                                            PhoneNumber = phoneNumber
                                    };
                phoneCallTask.Show();
            });
}
```

Figure 12.14 shows the `PhoneCallView` page.

When the `PhoneCallTask.Show` method is called, the Phone application is launched, which deactivates the sample application but leaves the sample app's UI visible in the background (see Figure 12.15).

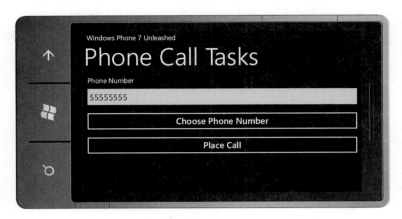

FIGURE 12.14   `PhoneCallView` page

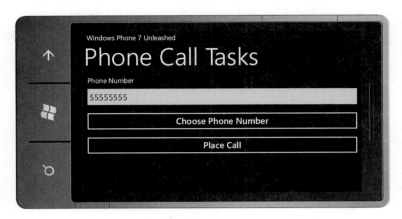

FIGURE 12.15   The built-in Phone app is superimposed on the sample application.

Selecting a Phone Number with the `PhoneNumberChooserTask`

The phone number chooser task is used to launch the built-in Contacts application and allows the user to select a contact. A phone number for the contact is then returned to your app.

> **NOTE**
>
> To query the user's contact list without requiring the user to select a contact, use the `Contacts` class, described later in this chapter.

The `PhoneNumberChooserTask` should be defined as a field in your class, like so:

```
readonly PhoneNumberChooserTask phoneNumberChooserTask
                            = new PhoneNumberChooserTask();
```

Subscribe to the `PhoneNumberChooserTask.Completed` event within your class constructor, as shown:

```
PhoneNumberChooserTask.Completed
    += new EventHandler<PhoneNumberResult>(
                            HandlePhoneNumberChooserTaskCompleted);
```

Use the `Show` method of the `PhoneNumberChooserTask` to launch the built-in Contacts app. When the task completes the handler receives a `PhoneNumberResult` object, as shown:

```
void HandlePhoneNumberChooserTaskCompleted(object sender,
                                        PhoneNumberResult e)
{
    if (e.TaskResult == TaskResult.OK)
    {
        PhoneNumber = e.PhoneNumber;
    }
    else if (e.Error != null)
    {
        Message = "Unable to choose number. " + e.ToString();
    }
    else if (e.TaskResult == TaskResult.Cancel)
    {
        Message = "Cancelled";
    }
}
```

Sample Overview

Example code for the `PhoneNumberChooserTask` can be found in the `PhoneCallViewModel` in the downloadable sample code. The `PhoneCallView` allows the user to populate the Phone Number `TextBox` by using a button that launches the `PhoneNumberChooserTask` (shown previously in Figure 12.14).

A button in the view is bound to a viewmodel `ICommand` property named `ChooseCommand`. The `chooseCommand` field is instantiated in the `PhoneCallViewModel` constructor. When executed, the command calls the `Show` method of the `PhoneNumberChooserTask`, as shown:

```
public PhoneCallViewModel() : base("Phone Call Tasks")
{
    phoneNumberChooserTask.Completed
                += HandlePhoneNumberChooserTaskCompleted;
```

```
chooseCommand = new DelegateCommand(
                        obj => phoneNumberChooserTask.Show());
...
}
```

When the Show method is called, the Contacts application is launched (see Figure 12.16).

CHOOSE A CONTACT

search

a

Andrew R. (Andy) ⊦

Arturo Lopez

FIGURE 12.16   Windows Phone Contacts application

When the user selects a contact from the Contacts app, the sample app is activated, and the Completed event handler is called, which updates the PhoneNumber property in the viewmodel.

Saving a Contact's Phone Number with the SavePhoneNumberTask

The save phone number task is used to launch the built-in Contacts app, allowing the user to save a specified phone number. This *chooser* does not return data, but you can handle the Completed event to determine whether the task was completed correctly.

SavePhoneNumberTask contains a single PhoneNumber property, which is passed to the Contacts application when the task's Show method is called.

The SavePhoneNumberTask should be defined as a field in your class, like so:

```
readonly SavePhoneNumberTask savePhoneNumberTask
                                = new SavePhoneNumberTask();
```

Subscribe to the SavePhoneNumberTask.Completed event within your class constructor, as shown:

```
savePhoneNumberTask.Completed
    += new EventHandler<TaskEventArgs>(HandleSavePhoneNumberTaskCompleted);
```

Use the Show method of the SavePhoneNumberTask to launch the built-in Contacts app. When the task completes the handler receives a TaskEventArgs object, as shown:

```
void HandleSavePhoneNumberTaskCompleted(object sender, TaskEventArgs e)
{
    if (e.Error != null)
    {
        Message = "Unable to save the phone number. " + e.Error;
        return;
    }

    if (e.TaskResult == TaskResult.OK)
    {
        Message = "Phone number saved";
    }
    else if (e.TaskResult == TaskResult.Cancel)
    {
        Message = "Cancelled";
    }
}
```

Sample Overview

Example code for the SavePhoneNumberTask can be found in the SavePhoneNumberViewModel in the downloadable sample code.

The SavePhoneNumberView page allows the user to enter a phone number into a TextBox and then to initiate the savePhoneNumberTask, using a button.

The button is bound to a viewmodel command named SaveCommand.

The TextBox is bound to the viewmodel's PhoneNumber property using a TwoWay data binding, as shown:

```
<TextBox Text="{Binding PhoneNumber, Mode=TwoWay}"
         InputScope="TelephoneNumber" />
```

The InputScope property of the TextBox causes the onscreen keyboard to be displayed with a set of keys suitable for typing a phone number. For more information on InputScopes, see Chapter 6.

When the SaveCommand is executed, the phoneNumber text is assigned to the task, and the task's Show method is called. See the following excerpt:

```
public SavePhoneNumberViewModel() : base("Save Phone Number")
{
    savePhoneNumberTask.Completed += savePhoneNumberTask_Completed;

    saveCommand = new DelegateCommand(
        delegate
```

```
        {
            Message = string.Empty;
            savePhoneNumberTask.PhoneNumber = phoneNumber;
            savePhoneNumberTask.Show();
        });
}
```

Figure 12.17 shows the custom `SavePhoneNumberView` page.

FIGURE 12.17   `SavePhoneNumberView` page

When the `savePhoneNumberTask.Show` method is called, the Contacts application is launched (shown previously in Figure 12.8).

When the user selects either an existing contact, or the new contact option, the Edit Phone Number page is displayed (see Figure 12.18).

When the save icon button is pressed, if the user selected an existing contact, the Edit Phone Contact page, shown previously in Figure 12.10, is displayed.

Alternatively, if the user opts to create a new contact, the New Contact page is displayed.

Once the contact information has been stored, the sample application is activated, and the `Completed` handler is called.

FIGURE 12.18   Edit Phone Number page

Searching the Web with the `SearchTask`

The Search task is used to launch the built-in Search application and performs a search for the specified search string. The Search application presents search results for the following three categories:

▶ **Web**—The search query is used to perform a web search.

▶ **Local**—Geographic location is used to provide search results that are relevant to the user's location. For example, searching for the term *restaurant* presents a map with the location of nearby restaurants.

▶ **News**—The search query is used to perform a search of various news-related websites and blogs.

The `SearchTask` class has a single string property called `SearchQuery`.

NOTE

If the `SearchQuery` property is null or empty, calling the `SearchTask.Show` method has no effect.

The following excerpt demonstrates how to initiate a `SearchTask`:

```
SearchTask searchTask = new SearchTask { SearchQuery = "restaurant" };
searchTask.Show();
```

Sample Overview

Example code for the `SearchTask` can be found in the `SearchViewModel` in the downloadable sample code.

The `SearchView` allows the user to populate a `TextBox` with a search query. The `TextBox` has a two-way data binding to the viewmodel's `SearchQuery` property.

A button is used to execute an `ICommand` named `SearchCommand`, which initiates the `SearchTask`.

The `searchCommand` field is instantiated in the `SearchViewModel` constructor. When executed, the `searchCommand` creates a new `SearchTask` and sets its `SearchQuery` property to the text supplied by a `TextBox` in the view, as shown in the following excerpt:

```
public SearchViewModel()
{
    searchCommand = new DelegateCommand(
        delegate
            {
                SearchTask searchTask = new SearchTask
                                            {
                                                SearchQuery = searchQuery
                                            };
                searchTask.Show();
            });
}
```

Figure 12.19 shows the custom `SearchView` page.

FIGURE 12.19   The sample search page allows the user to enter a search query.

When the `SearchTask.Show` method is called, the built-in Search app is launched (see Figure 12.20).

FIGURE 12.20   The built-in Search app

Sending Contacts a Link Using the `ShareLinkTask`

The share link task is used to enable the user to share a link on one or more social networks.

The `ShareLinkTask` allows you to specify a link URI, title, and message, as shown in the following excerpt:

```
ShareLinkTask task = new ShareLinkTask
    {
        LinkUri = new Uri("http://linkd.in/jnFoqE", UriKind.Absolute),
        Title = "Check out the Windows Phone Experts group.",
        Message = "Interested in Windows Phone development? "
                    + " Join the Windows Phone Experts group on Linked-In!"
    };

task.Show();
```

When the task's `Show` method is called, the built-in link sharing app is launched, allowing the user to select various social networks, such as Facebook, Twitter, and LinkedIn.

The sample for the `ShareLinkTask` is a page called `ShareLinkTaskView`, which allows the user to enter a URL, title, and message, and to launch the `ShareLinkTask` via an application bar button (see Figure 12.21).

Allowing the user to share a link with his contacts is a great way to connect your app with a wider audience.

FIGURE 12.21   ShareLinkTaskView page

Posting a Status Update to Social Networks Using the ShareStatusTask

The share status task is used to enable the user to post a status update to one or more social networks. The ShareStatusTask contains a single Status property of type string. When the Show method is called, the ShareStatusTask presents the built-in message sharing app. See the following excerpt:

```
ShareStatusTask task = new ShareStatusTask();
task.Status = "I'm loving the new features of the Windows Phone 7.5 API!";
task.Show();
```

The sample for the ShareStatusTask is a page called ShareStatusTaskView, which allows the user to enter some text and to launch the ShareLinkTask via an application bar button.

Preparing an SMS With the SmsComposeTask

The SMS compose task is used to launch the built-in Messaging app, allowing the user to create a new SMS message.

> **NOTE**
>
> The message is not sent until it is initiated by the user.

You can optionally specify recipients and a message body, which are prepopulated in the new message, as shown in the following excerpt:

```
SmsComposeTask smsComposeTask = new SmsComposeTask
                        {
                                To = "885729",
```

```
                                        Body = "Hi from Windows Phone!"
                        };
smsComposeTask.Show();
```

Sample Overview

Example code for the `SmsComposeTask` can be found in the `SmsView` page and `SmsViewModel`
classes in the downloadable sample code.

The `SmsView` allows the user to launch the built-in Messaging app when a button is tapped
(see Figure 12.22).

FIGURE 12.22   The built-in Messaging app

Navigating to a Web Page Using the `WebBrowserTask`

The web browser task is used to launch the built-in Web Browser app and optionally navigates the browser to a specified URL:

```
Uri uri = new Uri("http://msdn.microsoft.com", UriKind.RelativeOrAbsolute);
WebBrowserTask task = new WebBrowserTask { Uri = uri };
task.Show();
```

If the `Uri` results in a 404 HTTP standard response code (Not Found), no exception is
raised; instead the Windows Phone Search application is launched.

Sample Overview

Example code for the `WebBrowserTask` can be found in the `LaunchWebBrowserViewModel` in
the downloadable sample code.

The `LaunchWebBrowserView` page contains a `TextBox` in which the user can enter a URL and
a Launch Web Browser `Button` (see Figure 12.23).

FIGURE 12.23   Web Browser Launcher page

The view's `TextBox` has a `TwoWay` data binding to the viewmodel's `Url` property, as shown:

```
<TextBox Text="{Binding Url, Mode=TwoWay}" InputScope="Url" />
```

The `InputScope` property of the `TextBox` causes the onscreen keyboard to be displayed with a set of keys suitable for typing a URL. For more information on `InputScope`s, see Chapter 6.

A button is bound to an `ICommand` in the viewmodel named `LaunchCommand`. The command is instantiated in the viewmodel's constructor. When executed, `LaunchCommand` creates a new `WebBrowserTask` and sets its `Uri` property using the text supplied by a `TextBox` in the view. See the following excerpt:

```
public LaunchWebBrowserViewModel()
{
    launchCommand = new DelegateCommand(
        delegate
            {
                WebBrowserTask task = new WebBrowserTask { URL = url };
                task.Show();
            });
}
```

When the `WebBrowserTask.Show` method is called, the built-in Web Browser app is launched.

Selecting a Contact's Address Using the `AddressChooserTask`

The address chooser task is used to allow the user to provide your app with the street address of a contact. This task launches the built-in Contacts application so that the user can select a contact.

> **NOTE**
>
> To query the user's contact list without requiring the user to select a contact, use the `Contacts` class, described later in this chapter.

If the user completes the task, an event is raised and the task's `Completed` event handler receives an address in the result.

The sample for the `AddressChooserTask` consists of the `AddressChooserTaskView` page and `AddressChooserTaskViewModel` class.

The `AddressChooserTask` should be defined as a field in your class, like so:

```
readonly AddressChooserTask addressChooserTask = new AddressChooserTask();
```

Subscribe to the `AddressChooserTask.Completed` event within your class constructor, as shown:

```
addressChooserTask.Completed
                += new EventHandler<AddressResult>(HandleCompleted);
```

Use the `Show` method of the `AddressChooserTask` to launch the built-in Contacts application (see Figure 12.24).

FIGURE 12.24   Contacts application

When the task completes, the handler receives an `AddressResult` object that contains the display name and address of the contact. See the following excerpt from the `AddressChooserTaskViewModel` class:

```
void HandleTaskCompleted(object sender, AddressResult e)
{
    if (e.Error != null)
    {
        MessageService.ShowError("Unable to retrieve address");
    }

    if (e.TaskResult != TaskResult.OK)
    {
        return;
    }

    DisplayName = e.DisplayName;
    Address = e.Address;
}
```

Saving a Contact to the Phone's Contact List Using the SaveContactTask

The save contact task is used to enable a user to save a contact to the phone's contact list. The `SaveContactTask` class contains 26 string properties such as `FirstName`, `Company`, and `Website`, which allow you to pass detailed information to the built-in Contacts app.

When the user finishes saving the contact, cancels out of the task, or an error occurs, the task's `Completed` event is raised.

The sample for the `SaveContactTask` consists of the `SaveContactTaskView` page and the `SaveContactTaskViewModel` class.

The `SaveContactTask` should be defined as a field in your class, like so:

```
readonly SaveContactTask saveContactTask = new SaveContactTask();
```

Subscribe to the `SaveContactTask.Completed` event within your class constructor, as shown:

```
saveContactTask.Completed
                += new EventHandler<SaveContactResult>(HandleCompleted);
```

The sample page allows the population of just some of the `SaveContactTask` properties (see Figure 12.25).

When the application bar button is tapped, the `Show` method of the `SaveContactTask` launches the built-in Contacts application.

FIGURE 12.25   SaveContactTaskView page

When the task returns, the `Completed` event handler receives a `SaveContactResult` object that allows you to determine whether the task completed successfully. See the following excerpt:

```
void HandleTaskCompleted(object sender, SaveContactResult e)
{
    if (e.Error != null)
    {
        MessageService.ShowError("Unable to save contact.");
        return;
    }

    if (e.TaskResult == TaskResult.OK)
    {
        MessageService.ShowMessage("Contact saved.");
    }
}
```

Taking a Photo with the `CameraCaptureTask`

The camera capture task is a chooser that is used to launch the built-in Camera app. If the user completes the task by taking and confirming a photo, the `Completed` event is raised and the event handler receives a `PhotoResult` object, which exposes a stream containing the image data.

For information on working with photo image streams, see Chapter 18, "Extending the Windows Phone Picture Viewer."

The `CameraCaptureTask` should be defined as a field in your class, like so:

```
readonly CameraCaptureTask cameraCaptureTask
                                = new CameraCaptureTask();
```

Subscribe to the `CameraCaptureTask.Completed` event within your class constructor, as shown:

```
cameraCaptureTask.Completed
    += new EventHandler<PhotoResult>(HandleCameraCaptureTaskCompleted);
```

Use the `Show` method of the `CameraCaptureTask` to launch the built-in Camera app. When the task completes the handler receives a `PhotoResult` object, as shown:

```
void HandleCameraCaptureTaskCompleted(object sender, PhotoResult e)
{
    if (e.TaskResult == TaskResult.OK)
    {
        BitmapImage bitmapImage = new BitmapImage();
        bitmapImage.SetSource(e.ChosenPhoto);
        CapturedImage = bitmapImage;
    }
    else if (e.Error != null)
    {
        MessageService.ShowError("An error occurred. " + e.ToString());
    }
    else if (e.TaskResult == TaskResult.Cancel)
    {
        /* Cancelled. */
    }
}
```

Sample Overview

Example code for the `CameraCaptureTask` is located in the `CameraCaptureViewModel` in the downloadable sample code.

The view contains a button that is bound to a viewmodel `ICommand` property named `CaptureCommand`.

The `CameraCaptureView` allows the user to launch the `CameraCaptureTask` when she taps the button. When the `captureCommand` is executed, the `Show` method of the `cameraCaptureTask` is called, as shown in the following excerpt:

```
public CameraCaptureViewModel() : base("Camera Capture")
{
    cameraCaptureTask.Completed += cameraCaptureTask_Completed;
    captureCommand = new DelegateCommand(obj => cameraCaptureTask.Show());
}
```

Calling the task's Show method launches the built-in Camera application (see Figure 12.26).

FIGURE 12.26   The built-in Camera application

Once the photo has been taken and accepted by the user, the task's Completed event handler is called, and a new BitmapImage is created using the e.ChosenPhoto image Stream. It is then assigned to the CapturedImage property of the viewmodel, as shown:

```
BitmapImage bitmapImage = new BitmapImage();
bitmapImage.SetSource(e.ChosenPhoto);
CapturedImage = bitmapImage;
```

An Image control in the view is used to display the image, as shown:

```
<Image Source="{Binding CapturedImage}" />
```

When the CapturedImage property is updated, the image is displayed in the view (see Figure 12.27).

Inviting Game Players with the GameInviteTask

The game invite task is used to show a game invite screen that enables the user to invite players to a multiplayer game session that is in progress on a Windows Phone device. The invitation is sent asynchronously.

> **CAUTION**
>
> The game invite task works only when called from within a game that is approved for release on Xbox LIVE on Windows Phone.

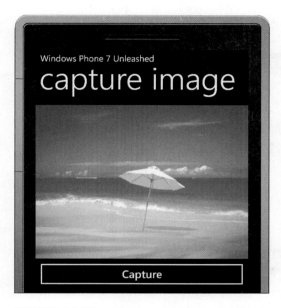

FIGURE 12.27   The captured image is displayed on the `CameraCaptureView` page.

When the user finishes sending the invite, cancels out of the task, or an error occurs, the task's `Completed` event is raised.

The `GameInviteTask` should be defined as a field in your class, like so:

```
readonly GameInviteTask gameInviteTask = new GameInviteTask();
```

Subscribe to the `GameInviteTask.Completed` event within your class constructor, as shown:

```
gameInviteTask.Completed
                += new EventHandler<TaskEventArgs>(HandleCompleted);
```

The `GameInviteTask` allows you to specify a unique session id. The only information that another player needs to join an active game session is the session id.

```
gameInviteTask.SessionId = "<session id>";
gameInviteTask.Show();
```

When the task's `Show` method is called, the built-in Game Invite app is launched, allowing the user to email recipients using either a gamer tag or an email address.

NOTE

Without a valid session id, the Game Invite app is not able to send invitations.

The built-in Game Invite app is shown in Figure 12.28.

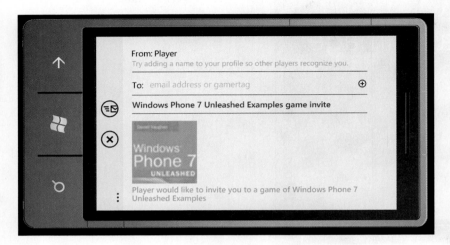

FIGURE 12.28   Built-in game invite page

Selecting a Photo from the Photo Hub Using the `PhotoChooserTask`

The photo chooser task is used to launch the built-in Photo Picker app, which allows a user to select an image from isolated storage or, optionally, to take a photo using the device's camera.

The following is a list of the `PhotoChooserTask` properties:

▶ **PixelHeight**—The maximum height, in pixels, of the resulting image.

▶ **PixelWidth**—The maximum width, in pixels, of the resulting image.

▶ **ShowCamera**—If set to `true`, the user is presented with the option to use the device's camera to take a photo. A button is displayed on the first page of the Photo Picker app. If not specified, this value defaults to `false`.

NOTE

When debugging with the Zune software running, the media database on the phone device is locked. To debug while using the `PhotoChooserTask` use the Windows Phone Connect tool discussed in Chapter 18.

The `PhotoChooserTask` should be defined as a field in your class, like so:

```
readonly PhotoChooserTask photoChooserTask = new PhotoChooserTask();
```

Subscribe to the `PhotoChooserTask.Completed` event within your class constructor, as shown:

```
PhotoChooserTask.Completed
    += new EventHandler<PhotoResult>(HandlePhotoChooserTaskCompleted);
```

Use the Show method of the PhotoChooserTask to launch the built-in Photo Picker app. When the task completes the handler receives a PhotoResult object, as shown:

```
void HandleTaskCompleted(object sender, PhotoResult e)
{
    if (e.TaskResult == TaskResult.OK)
    {
        BitmapImage bitmapImage = new BitmapImage();
        bitmapImage.SetSource(e.ChosenPhoto);
        CapturedImage = bitmapImage;
    }

    if (e.Error != null)
    {
        MessageService.ShowError("An error occurred. " + e.Error.ToString());
    }
}
```

When the task's Show method is called, the built-in Photo Picker app is launched, allowing the user to select or take a photo (see Figure 12.29).

FIGURE 12.29   The PhotoChooserTask.ShowCamera property determines whether the user is given the option to use the device's camera.

Once an image has been selected by the user, it can be cropped to the aspect ratio specified by the PhotoChooserTask's PixelHeight and PixelWidth properties.

> **NOTE**
>
> If neither the PixelHeight nor PixelWidth is specified, the Photo Picker application skips the step that allows the user to crop the image.

The PhotoChooserTask's Completed event is raised when an image has been selected or the user cancels out of the Photo Picker application. If the user completes the task of choosing an image, the Completed event is raised and the event handler receives a PhotoResult object that exposes a stream containing the image data. For information on working with image streams, see Chapter 18.

The properties of the PhotoResult class (a subclass of TaskEventArgs) are presented in the following list:

▶ **ChosenPhoto**—A System.IO.Stream for the selected image

▶ **OriginalFileName**—The path to the file in isolated storage

Sample Overview

The PhotoChooserViewModel class in the downloadable sample code demonstrates how to use the PhotoChooserTask (see Listing 12.4).

Subscription to the PhotoChooserTask.Completed event occurs in the class constructor. The chooseCommand's execute handler assigns the task's various properties and calls its Show method. When the Completed event of the task is raised, a BitmapImage is created using the chosen image Stream.

LISTING 12.4   PhotoChooserViewModel Class (excerpt)

```
public class PhotoChooserViewModel : ViewModelBase
{
    readonly PhotoChooserTask task = new PhotoChooserTask();

    public PhotoChooserViewModel()
    {
        task.Completed += HandleTaskCompleted;
        chooseCommand = new DelegateCommand(
            delegate
                {
                    task.PixelWidth = pixelWidth;
                    task.PixelHeight = pixelHeight;
                    task.ShowCamera = showCamera;
                    task.Show();
                });
    }
```

LISTING 12.4   Continued

```
    void HandleTaskCompleted(object sender, PhotoResult e)
    {
        if (e.TaskResult == TaskResult.OK)
        {
            BitmapImage bitmapImage = new BitmapImage();
            bitmapImage.SetSource(e.ChosenPhoto);
            CapturedImage = bitmapImage;
            PixelWidth = ImageWidth = bitmapImage.PixelWidth;
            PixelHeight = ImageHeight = bitmapImage.PixelHeight;
            OriginalFileName = e.OriginalFileName;
        }

        if (e.Error != null)
        {
            MessageService.ShowError("An error occurred. " + e.Error.ToString());
        }
    }
...
}
```

The `PhotoChooserView` is data-bound to the `PhotoChooserViewModel`, which allows the user to affect the properties of the `PhotoChooserTask` when the viewmodel's `ChooseCommand` is executed. The `ChooseCommand` is executed when the Capture button is pressed. The user can change the aspect ratio of the image by modifying the Width and Height Ratio `Sliders`.

A `PhotoChooserViewModel` instance is assigned to the view's `DataContext`, as shown in the following excerpt from the `PhotoChooserView` code-beside:

```
public PhotoChooserView()
{
    InitializeComponent();
    DataContext = new PhotoChooserViewModel();
}
```

The view uses data binding to populate its controls and to interact with the viewmodel. Once the user chooses an image via the `PhotoChooserTask`, the `Image` control is populated via its data binding to the `CapturedImage` property of the `PhotoChooserViewModel`. The Capture button causes the execution of the `ChooseCommand` (see Listing 12.5).

LISTING 12.5   PhotoChooserView.xaml (excerpt)

```xml
<StackPanel x:Name="ContentPanel" Grid.Row="1">
    <TextBlock Text="{Binding PixelWidth, StringFormat='Width Ratio\: \{0\}'}"
               Style="{StaticResource PhoneTextNormalStyle}" />
    <Slider Value="{Binding PixelWidth, Mode=TwoWay}"
```

LISTING 12.5   Continued

```
                Minimum="10" Maximum="200" LargeChange="50" SmallChange="10"/>
    <TextBlock Text="{Binding PixelHeight, StringFormat='Height Ratio\: \{0\}'}"
                Style="{StaticResource PhoneTextNormalStyle}" />
    <Slider Value="{Binding PixelHeight, Mode=TwoWay}"
                Minimum="10" Maximum="200" LargeChange="50" SmallChange="10"/>
    <CheckBox IsChecked="{Binding ShowCamera, Mode=TwoWay}"
                Content="Show Camera" />
    <Button Command="{Binding ChooseCommand}"
                Content="Choose" />
    <Image Source="{Binding CapturedImage}"
                Width="{Binding ImageWidth}" Height="{Binding ImageHeight}"
                HorizontalAlignment="Left" Margin="15,0,15,0" />
    <TextBlock Text="Path: "
                Style="{StaticResource PhoneTextSmallStyle}" />
    <TextBlock Text="{Binding OriginalFileName}"
                Style="{StaticResource PhoneTextSmallStyle}" TextWrapping="Wrap" />
</StackPanel>
```

The `PhotoChooserView` page is presented in Figure 12.30.

FIGURE 12.30   `PhotoChooserView` page

The `PixelWidth` and `PixelHeight` properties of the `PhotoChooserTask` determine the maximum dimensions of the resulting image. The Photo Picker crop page presents the image with a selection overlay conforming to the aspect ratio `PixelWidth/PixelHeight`, which spans either the entire width or height of the image. When the user confirms the selection, the image is reduced to the size specified by PixelWidth and PixelHeight (see Figure 12.31).

FIGURE 12.31   The Photo Picker crop page

When the user completes the PhotoChooserTask, the PhotoChooserTask.Completed event is handled by the PhotoChooserViewModel.HandleTaskCompleted method. A new BitmapImage is created using the resulting image stream, and it is assigned to the CapturedImage property of the viewmodel. The view is then automatically updated via the Image control's data binding (see Figure 12.32).

Creating a Ringtone with an Audio File Using the SaveRingtoneTask

The save ringtone task is used to launch the built-in Ringtones app, which enables the user to save an audio file to the system ringtones list and to optionally set it as the active ringtone on the device.

The ringtones list can be viewed by selecting the Ringtones + Sounds item on the phone's system settings page.

Once the audio file is added to the list, the user can set it as the ringtone for individual contacts in the Contacts application.

FIGURE 12.32   The chosen image is displayed in the view.

When the user finishes saving the contact, cancels out of the task, or an error occurs, the task's Completed event is raised.

The SaveRingtoneTask should be defined as a field in your class, like so:

```
readonly SaveRingtoneTask saveRingtoneTask = new SaveRingtoneTask();
```

Subscribe to the SaveRingtoneTask.Completed event within your class constructor, as shown:

```
saveRingtoneTask.Completed
                    += new EventHandler<TaskEventArgs>(HandleCompleted);
```

The SaveRingtoneTask allows you to specify a display name for the ringtone and the URI of the audio file. The audio file can be either located in isolated storage or within an assembly. Initialization and launching of the task is shown in the following excerpt:

```
saveRingtoneTask.DisplayName = displayName;
saveRingtoneTask.IsShareable = shareable;
saveRingtoneTask.Source = new Uri("appdata:/AudioFiles/Audio01.wma");
//saveRingtoneTask.Source = new Uri("isostore:/AudioFiles/Audio01.wma");
saveRingtoneTask.Show();
```

The appdata segment of the `Source Uri` value indicates that the file is located within the app's XAP file. In this case, the file is located in a project directory called AudioFiles.

> **NOTE**
>
> When using the appdata prefix, the file must have its Build Action set to Content; otherwise, it will be unresolvable.

Conversely, the isostore prefix indicates that the file is located in isolated storage. Files located in isolated storage must be placed there by your app.

Ringtone audio files must meet the following requirements.

▶ File must be of type MP3 or WMA.

▶ Files must be less than 1MB in size.

▶ Files must be less than 40 seconds in length.

▶ Files must not have digital rights management (DRM) protection.

When the task's `Show` method is called, the built-in Ringtone app is launched, allowing the user to edit the ringtone's display name and to optionally set the ringtone as the active ringtone.

The sample for the `SaveRingtoneTask` consists of the `SaveRingtoneTaskView` page and `SaveRingtoneTaskViewModel` class. The view allows the user to enter a display name for the ringtone and to launch the `SaveRingtoneTask` via an application bar button. The built-in Ringtone app is shown in Figure 12.33.

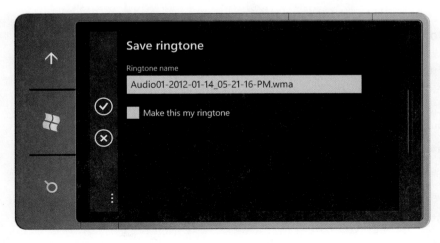

FIGURE 12.33   The built-in Ringtone app

When the task returns control to your app, the Completed event handler is called. The TaskEventArgs object allows you to determine whether the user successfully saved the ringtone, as shown in the following excerpt:

```
void HandleTaskCompleted(object sender, TaskEventArgs e)
{
    if (e.Error != null)
    {
        MessageService.ShowError("Unable to save ringtone.");
        return;
    }

    if (e.TaskResult == TaskResult.OK)
    {
        MessageService.ShowMessage("Ringtone saved.");
    }
}
```

The save ringtone task is a great way to extend an audio app. You could have your app procure audio from third-party websites or from your own website.

Contacts and Appointments

While the three choosers: AddressChooserTask, EmailAddressChooserTask, and PhoneNumberChooserTask enable the user to select a contact, your app may also query the user's contact list without user intervention. Read-only access to the user's contacts and appointments can be achieved using the Contacts and Appointment classes, located in the Microsoft.Phone.UserData namespace.

Retrieving Contacts

The Contacts class allows you to search the user's contacts for a string. The search can be restricted to a single field of the Contact class, or to contacts that have been pinned to the phone's Start Experience (home screen). Searches are performed using one of the following FilterKind enumeration values:

▶ None (default value)

▶ DisplayName

▶ EmailAddress

▶ PhoneNumber

▶ PinnedToStart

To query the user's contact list, define a `Contacts` instance as a field in a class, as shown:

```
Contacts contacts;
```

Instantiate the `Contacts` object, subscribe to its `SearchCompleted` event, and then call `SearchAsync`, as shown in the following excerpt:

```
void SearchContacts()
{
    contacts = new Contacts();

    contacts.SearchCompleted += HandleSearchCompleted;
    contacts.SearchAsync("andrew", FilterKind.DisplayName, null);
}
```

> **NOTE**
>
> To access the user's contact list the ID_CAP_CONTACTS capability must be present in the WMAppManifest.xml file.
>
> For more information on the phone's security capability model, see Chapter 2, "Fundamental Concepts in Silverlight Development for Windows Phone."

> **NOTE**
>
> The `Contacts.SearchAsync` method allows the use of an empty search string when `FilterKind` is set to DisplayName, PinnedToStart, or None. An exception is raised if you attempt to search for an empty string in conjunction with a `FilterKind` value equal to EmailAddress or PhoneNumber.

When the search completes, the specified event handler receives a list of matching `Contact` objects. See the following excerpt:

```
void HandleSearchCompleted(object sender, ContactsSearchEventArgs e)
{
    if (e.Results == null)
    {
        return;
    }
    Contacts = e.Results;
}
```

The list of retrieved `Contact` objects can be further refined using LINQ.

> **NOTE**
>
> Be mindful when using LINQ, however, that some users may have a lot of contacts, and it may be expensive to use LINQ to select a subset of the resulting `Contact` objects.
>
> Internally, the contact list has various indexes placed on fields corresponding to the `FilterKind` enumeration, which may offer superior performance during retrieval. Therefore, favor the use of filters rather than LINQ wherever possible.

Windows Phone aggregates contacts from various social networking accounts, including Windows Live, Facebook, Twitter, and LinkedIn (and potentially more to come). To determine the accounts from which contacts are available, use the `Contacts` class's `Accounts` property.

Sample Contacts Page

The example for this section allows the user to enter a search string, select a `FilterKind` enumeration value, and perform a search against the user's contact list.

Within the `ContactsViewModel` class a `SearchText` property and a `FilterKind` property restrict the results of the call to `contacts.SearchAsync` (see Listing 12.6).

The list of available filter values is exposed by the viewmodel's `FilterKinds` property.

A `DelegateCommand` named `SearchCommand` calls the `SearchContacts` method when it is executed. When the `SearchCompleted` handler is called, a `Contacts` property is populated with the result.

LISTING 12.6   ContactsViewModel Class

```
public class ContactsViewModel : ViewModelBase
{
    public ContactsViewModel() : base("search contacts")
    {
        searchCommand = new DelegateCommand(arg => SearchContacts());
    }

    Contacts contacts;

    void SearchContacts()
    {
        if (string.IsNullOrWhiteSpace(searchText)
                && (FilterKind == FilterKind.EmailAddress
                        || FilterKind == FilterKind.PhoneNumber))
        {
            MessageService.ShowMessage("Please enter the search text.");
            return;
        }
```

12

LISTING 12.6　Continued

```
    contacts = new Contacts();

    contacts.SearchCompleted += HandleSearchCompleted;
    contacts.SearchAsync(searchText, FilterKind, null);
}

void HandleSearchCompleted(object sender, ContactsSearchEventArgs e)
{
    if (e.Results == null)
    {
        return;
    }
    Contacts = e.Results;
}

IEnumerable<Contact> contactsList = new List<Contact>();

public IEnumerable<Contact> Contacts
{
    get
    {
        return contactsList;
    }
    private set
    {
        Assign(() => Contacts, ref contactsList, value);
    }
}

readonly DelegateCommand searchCommand;

public ICommand SearchCommand
{
    get
    {
        return searchCommand;
    }
}

string searchText;

public string SearchText
{
    get
```

LISTING 12.6   Continued

```csharp
    {
        return searchText;
    }
    set
    {
        Assign(() => SearchText, ref searchText, value);
    }
}

FilterKind filterKind = filterKinds.First();

public FilterKind FilterKind
{
    get
    {
        return filterKind;
    }
    set
    {
        Assign(() => FilterKind, ref filterKind, value);
    }
}

static readonly IEnumerable<FilterKind> filterKinds
    = EnumUtility.CreateEnumValueList<FilterKind>().OrderBy(x => x.ToString());

public IEnumerable<FilterKind> FilterKinds
{
    get
    {
        return filterKinds;
    }
}
}
```

The view contains a `TextBox` that is bound to the viewmodel's `SearchText` property, and a `ListPicker` whose `ItemsSource` property is bound to the `FilterKinds` viewmodel property (see Listing 12.7).

When the user selects an item in the `ListPicker`, the viewmodel's `FilterKind` property is updated.

Results are displayed using a `ListBox`, whose `ItemsSource` property is bound to the viewmodel's `Contacts` property. Each `Content` object is presented using a `TextBlock` to show its `DisplayName`, and a `ListBox` is used to display each of the contact's email addresses.

LISTING 12.7   `ContactsView.xaml` (excerpt)

```xml
<StackPanel x:Name="ContentPanel" Grid.Row="1">
    <TextBlock Text="search" Style="{StaticResource LabelTextStyle}" />
    <TextBox Text="{Binding SearchText, Mode=TwoWay}" />
    <toolkit:ListPicker
        ItemsSource="{Binding FilterKinds}"
        SelectedItem="{Binding FilterKind, Mode=TwoWay}"
        Header="filter" />
    <ListBox ItemsSource="{Binding Contacts}">
        <ListBox.ItemTemplate>
            <DataTemplate>
                <StackPanel Margin="0,0,0,20">
                    <TextBlock Text="{Binding DisplayName}"
                        Style="{StaticResource PhoneTextLargeStyle}" />
                    <ListBox ItemsSource="{Binding EmailAddresses}"
                        ScrollViewer.VerticalScrollBarVisibility="Disabled">
                        <ListBox.ItemTemplate>
                            <DataTemplate>
                                <StackPanel>
                                    <TextBlock Text="{Binding EmailAddress}"
                                        Style="{StaticResource
➥PhoneTextNormalStyle}" />
                                </StackPanel>
                            </DataTemplate>
                        </ListBox.ItemTemplate>
                    </ListBox>
                </StackPanel>
            </DataTemplate>
        </ListBox.ItemTemplate>
    </ListBox>
</StackPanel>
```

In addition, the view contains an `AppBarIconButton` that is bound to the viewmodel's `SearchCommand`, as shown:

```xml
<u:AppBar>
    <u:AppBarIconButton
                Command="{Binding SearchCommand}"
                Text="search"
                IconUri="/Images/ApplicationBarIcons/AppBarSearch.png" />
</u:AppBar>
```

When the user taps the application bar button, matching contacts are displayed at the bottom of the page (see Figure 12.34).

FIGURE 12.34   ContactsView page

Retrieving Appointments

The Appointments class allows you to retrieve appointments that fall between two specified dates.

> **NOTE**
>
> To access the user's appointments the ID_CAP_APPOINTMENTS capability must be present in the WMAppManifest.xml file.
>
> For more information on the phone's security capability model, see Chapter 2.

To query the user's appointments, define an Appointments instance as a field in a class, as shown:

```
Appointments appointments;
```

Instantiate the Appointments object, subscribe to its SearchCompleted event, and then call SearchAsync. The following excerpt demonstrates the retrieval of appointments that fall within the next six months:

```
void SearchAppointments()
{
    appointments = new Appointments();

    appointments.SearchCompleted += HandleSearchCompleted;
    appointments.SearchAsync(DateTime.Now, DateTime.Now.AddMonths(6), null);
}
```

When the search completes, the specified event handler receives a list of matching Appointment objects. See the following excerpt:

```csharp
void HandleSearchCompleted(object sender, AppointmentsSearchEventArgs e)
{
    if (e.Results == null)
    {
        return;
    }
    Appointments = e.Results;
}
```

To determine the accounts from which appointments are available, use the `Appointment` class's `Accounts` property.

Each appointment is represented by an `Appointment` object. The `Appointment` class provides various read-only properties, described in Table 12.2.

TABLE 12.2   Appointment Class Properties

Name	Description
Account	Gets the data source (e.g., Windows Live) associated with this appointment
Attendees	Gets the list of attendees associated with this appointment
Details	Gets a detailed description of the appointment
EndTime	Gets the date and time that the appointment ends
IsAllDayEvent	Gets a value that indicates whether the appointment is an all-day event
IsPrivate	Gets a bool value that indicates whether the appointment is private
Location	Gets the location of the appointment
Organizer	Gets the organizer of the appointment
StartTime	Gets the date and time that the appointment starts
Status	Gets information about how to treat the block of time of this appointment, such as busy or out of the office
Subject	Gets the subject of the appointment

The `Appointments.SearchAsync` method is overloaded to allow you to restrict the retrieval of appointments from specific accounts. For example, to retrieve only those appointments associated with the user's Windows Live account, use the following:

```csharp
Account account = appointments.Accounts.Where(
                    x => x.Name == "Windows Live").First();
appointments.SearchAsync(
    DateTime.Now, DateTime.Now.AddMonths(6), account, null);
```

Sample Appointments Page

The example for this section allows the user to retrieve the list of appointments for a specified period. The `AppointmentsViewModel` class, located in the downloadable sample code, contains a `StartTimeInclusive` property and an `EndTimeInclusive` property, which are used to specify the period (see Listing 12.8).

A `DelegateCommand` named `SearchCommand` calls the `SearchAppointments` method when it is executed. When the `SearchCompleted` handler is called, the `Appointments` property is populated with the result.

LISTING 12.8   AppointmentsViewModel Class

```
public class AppointmentsViewModel : ViewModelBase
{
    public AppointmentsViewModel() : base("appointments")
    {
        searchCommand = new DelegateCommand(arg => SearchAppointments());
    }

    Appointments appointments;

    void SearchAppointments()
    {
        appointments = new Appointments();
        appointments.SearchCompleted += HandleSearchCompleted;
        appointments.SearchAsync(startTimeInclusive, endTimeInclusive, null);
    }

    void HandleSearchCompleted(object sender, AppointmentsSearchEventArgs e)
    {
        if (e.Results == null)
        {
            return;
        }
        Appointments = e.Results;
    }

    IEnumerable<Appointment> appointmentList = new List<Appointment>();

    public IEnumerable<Appointment> Appointments
    {
        get
        {
            return appointmentList;
        }
        private set
        {
            Assign(() => Appointments, ref appointmentList, value);
        }
    }

    readonly DelegateCommand searchCommand;
```

LISTING 12.8   Continued

```
public ICommand SearchCommand
{
    get
    {
        return searchCommand;
    }
}


DateTime startTimeInclusive = DateTime.Now.AddYears(-1);

public DateTime StartTimeInclusive
{
    get
    {
        return startTimeInclusive;
    }
    set
    {
        Assign(() => StartTimeInclusive, ref startTimeInclusive, value);
    }
}


DateTime endTimeInclusive = DateTime.Now.AddYears(1);

public DateTime EndTimeInclusive
{
    get
    {
        return endTimeInclusive;
    }
    set
    {
        Assign(() => EndTimeInclusive, ref endTimeInclusive, value);
    }
}
}
```

The view contains two Silverlight Toolkit `ListPicker` controls that are bound to the view-model's `StartTimeInclusive` and `EndTimeInclusive` properties (see Listing 12.9).

Results are displayed using a `ListBox`, whose `ItemsSource` property is bound to the view-model's `Appointments` property. Each `Appointment` object is presented using a `TextBlock` to display its `StartTime`, `Subject`, and `Details` properties.

LISTING 12.9   AppointmentsView.xaml (excerpt)

```
<StackPanel x:Name="ContentPanel" Grid.Row="1">
    <toolkit:DatePicker Value="{Binding StartTimeInclusive, Mode=TwoWay}"
                        Header="start"/>
    <toolkit:DatePicker Value="{Binding EndTimeInclusive, Mode=TwoWay}"
                        Header="end"/>

    <ListBox ItemsSource="{Binding Appointments}">
        <ListBox.ItemTemplate>
            <DataTemplate>
                <StackPanel Margin="0,0,0,20">
                    <TextBlock Text="{Binding StartTime}"
                        Style="{StaticResource PhoneTextNormalStyle}" />
                    <TextBlock Text="{Binding Subject}"
                        Style="{StaticResource PhoneTextLargeStyle}" />
                    <TextBlock Text="{Binding Details}"
                        Style="{StaticResource PhoneTextNormalStyle}" />
                </StackPanel>
            </DataTemplate>
        </ListBox.ItemTemplate>
    </ListBox>
</StackPanel>
```

In addition, the view includes an AppBarIconButton that is bound to the viewmodel's SearchCommand, as shown:

```
<u:AppBar>
    <u:AppBarIconButton
            Command="{Binding SearchCommand}"
            Text="search"
            IconUri="/Images/ApplicationBarIcons/AppBarSearch.png" />
</u:AppBar>
```

When the user taps the application bar button, appointments that fall within the specified date range are displayed at the bottom of the page (see Figure 12.35).

By using the Appointments and Contacts classes you are able to further integrate your app with the social networking features of the phone.

FIGURE 12.35   AppointmentsView page

Summary

This chapter began by looking at the two types of tasks: launchers and choosers. Launchers have no common base class, yet choosers all derive from `ChooserBase<TTaskEventArgs>`, which has a `Completed` event.

The chapter then explored the execution model of choosers and the internal workings of `ChooserBase.Completed` event subscriptions that span across application lifetimes. Each launcher and chooser was discussed in detail.

Finally, the chapter examined how to programmatically retrieve contact and appointment information in a read-only manner.

CHAPTER 13

Push Notification

Push notification is a server to client, or cloud to phone, messaging system that allows notifications to be sent from the cloud to the phone and displayed to the phone user. Notifications are one-way messages that are normally associated with a particular application and may be delivered both while the application is running and not running. The main purpose of the push notification system is to reduce the power consumption of the phone device, thereby increasing battery life.

This chapter begins with an overview of push notification, starting with the three different types of push notifications: toast, tile, and raw notifications. The chapter examines the various types of channel errors that can occur during push notification and how the phone's battery level affects delivery of push notifications. Cloud service authentication using X.509 certificates is also discussed as well as how to update an application tile without tile notifications using shell tile schedules.

Finally, the chapter explores a custom stock ticker sample app that allows the user to enter a stock symbol into the phone, after which a cloud service periodically notifies the phone of stock price variations.

Push Notification Types

Windows Phone supports the following three types of push notifications:

▸ **Toast notification**—A systemwide notification that is shown for a few seconds at the top of the phone's display.

▸ **Tile notification**—Displays information using a tile on the Start Experience (home screen).

▶ **Raw notification**—Offers a completely flexible manner for delivering notifications to your running app. The OS does not display a raw notification, but rather the notification message is sent directly to your running app.

Benefits of Push Notification

The Microsoft Push Notification Service (MPNS) is designed to be resilient and to expose a persistent channel for sending notifications to Windows Phone devices.

Apart from some special cases, the Windows Phone platform does not allow multiple apps to be running at the same time.[1] The main reason is that, in most cases, it is not efficient to have background apps consuming device resources, such as maintaining an open connection and sending data over the wire. Network activity results in high power consumption and decreased battery life.

> **NOTE**
>
> By battery life I mean the amount of time a device runs before it requires a recharge. Conversely, battery lifespan means the total amount of time a battery lasts before it is discarded and replaced with a new battery.

Push notification reduces power consumption in several ways; most notably it uses a single shared network connection, eliminating the need for private persistent open connections. If an app needs to be running merely to receive updates from the cloud, a better approach is to use push notification. The push notification model has the following benefits:

▶ **Offline capability**—Windows Phone apps should be designed to be tolerant of interruptions as they may be deactivated or terminated at any time. Push notification allows the user to act on some information, even when your app is not running.

▶ **Notification aggregation**—Multiple notifications for different apps can be pushed at the same time.

▶ **Notification prioritization**—Notifications can be assigned a priority, which affects when the notification is delivered. This control allows a developer to assign lower priorities to those notifications that do not require immediate attention, thereby reducing the device's network activity.

▶ **Connection pooling**—It is more efficient to use a single shared network connection than to have each app owning its own connection.

▶ **Small message size**—Notifications are designed to carry a small payload. This forces you to think carefully about what information is really necessary to be conveyed.

---

1. *Background tasks allow an app to run in the background periodically for short periods. For more information, see Chapter 27, "Scheduled Actions."*

▶ **Deterministic behavior**—Tile and toast notifications use a well-defined format with a fixed set of data properties, which allows the OS to present them automatically.

▶ **Eliminates polling**—Apps that want to receive messages from a cloud service without the use of push notification must periodically poll the cloud service. Push notification eliminates the need for custom network communication code and for private persistent open connections.

Understanding Push Notification

Push notification relies on the MPNS to dispatch notifications to the phone. The process works like this:

1. A phone app requests subscription to the MPNS using a notification channel.

2. The MPNS returns a URI, where notifications can be sent.

3. The phone app forwards the URI to any third-party service (such as a web service created by you) that wants to send the phone app notifications (see Figure 13.1).

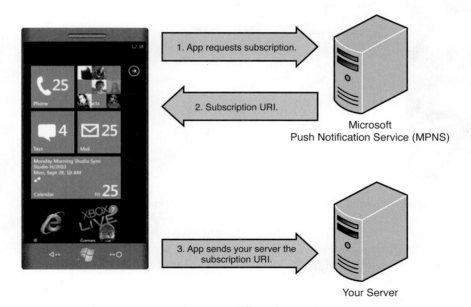

FIGURE 13.1   An app subscribes to the MPNS, which is then forwarded to a third-party server.

The Push Notification URI is the address of the MPNS plus an identifier for phone device. Having received the push notification URI, a third-party service is then able to send notifications to the phone, via the MPNS, as shown in Figure 13.2.

> **NOTE**
>
> The notification channel URI is not guaranteed to remain the same. Therefore, each time a phone app launches, it is expected to send its notification channel URI to its corresponding cloud service.

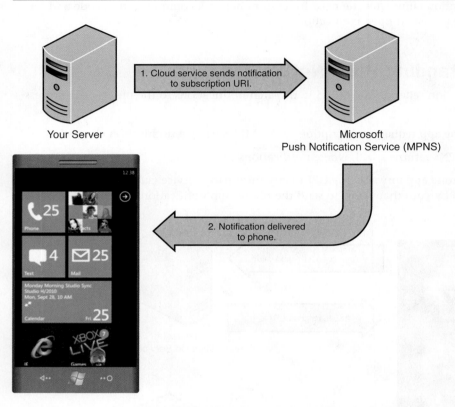

FIGURE 13.2   Your server sends a notification to the MPNS, which is then forwarded to the phone.

Notifications from the cloud service use a well-defined protocol for sending notifications to the MPNS. Subsequent sections of the chapter examine the protocol format for the various notification types.

> **NOTE**
>
> Microsoft does not offer a Service Level Agreement (SLA) for the delivery of push notifications.

Getting Started with Push Notification

The main CLR types used in push notification reside in the `Microsoft.Phone.Notification` namespace. To consume push notifications in an application, a reference to the `Microsoft.Phone` assembly is required (see Figure 13.3).

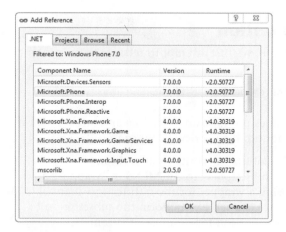

FIGURE 13.3   Add a reference to Microsoft.Phone.

To enable an application to use push notification, the ID_CAP_PUSH_NOTIFICATION capability must be present in the WMAppManifest.xml file. While not explicitly required for push notification, the ID_CAP_NETWORKING capability is also required if you want to notify a cloud service of the existence of an MNPS URI. Push notification is useless in most cases without the latter capability.

The following excerpt shows the capabilities needed for push notification in the WMAppManifest.xml file:

```
<Capabilities>
  <Capability Name="ID_CAP_NETWORKING" />
  <Capability Name="ID_CAP_PUSH_NOTIFICATION" />
</Capabilities>
```

For more information on application capabilities, see Chapter 2, "Fundamental Concepts in Silverlight Development for Windows Phone."

> **NOTE**
>
> To pass certification for the Windows Phone Marketplace, an app must provide the user with the ability to disable toast and tile notifications. The user must have the ability to perform this task from within the app.

Furthermore, before calling either the `HttpNotificationChannel.BindtoShellToast` or `HttpNotificationChannel.BindToShellTile` methods for the first time, an application must explicitly ask the user for permission.

These requirements give the user control over if and when push notification is used.

Subscribing to Push Notification

To subscribe to push notification within an app, we first attempt to retrieve an existing `HttpNotificationChannel` by name.

```
channel = HttpNotificationChannel.Find("<a channel name>");
```

The `HttpNotificationChannel.Find` method does not raise an `Exception` and returns `null` if the channel with the specified name is not found. If so, a new instance must be created.

The Push Notification sample in the downloadable code contains a class called `PushNotificationSubscriber`, which manages subscription to the MPNS by wrapping a notification channel. The main benefit of using a wrapper for the notification channel is that if the `PushNotificationSubscriber` instance is unable to perform the subscription to the MPNS, due to the absence of a network connection for example, it automatically retries.

If the channel cannot be found, a new channel is created as shown:

```
if (channel == null)
{
    channel = string.IsNullOrEmpty(serviceName)
        ? new HttpNotificationChannel(channelName)
        : new HttpNotificationChannel(channelName, serviceName);
}
```

The `HttpNotificationChannel` constructor has the following two overloads:

```
public HttpNotificationChannel(string channelName);
public HttpNotificationChannel(string channelName, string serviceName);
```

The `channelName` parameter is the name that the app uses to identify the notification channel instance. This allows an application to retrieve an existing channel by name using the static `HttpNotificationChannel.Find` method.

The `serviceName` parameter is the name of the cloud service to which the notification channel is associated. The `serviceName` parameter may be used to subscribe to an authenticated cloud service. For more information, see the section "Cloud Service Authentication" later in this chapter.

Once you have obtained a channel instance, it can be opened like so:

```
channel.Open();
```

Binding to the Shell

For the OS to display toast and tile notifications, the channel must call the `BindToShellToast` and `BindToShellTile` methods, as demonstrated in the following excerpt:

```
/* Toast Notifications. */
if (!channel.IsShellToastBound)
{
    channel.BindToShellToast();
}

/* Tile Notifications. */
if (!channel.IsShellTileBound)
{
    channel.BindToShellTile();
}
```

To stop receiving toast and tile notifications, the channel provides the `UnbindToShellToast` and `UnbindToShellTile` methods, respectively.

BEST PRACTICE

When creating an `HttpNotificationChannel`, avoid keeping it open if not subscribing to its events. It is not necessary for the channel to be kept open for the shell to receive either toast or tile notifications, and the channel itself consumes valuable resources.

`HttpNotificationChannel` implements `IDisposable` and can be safely disposed after binding it to the shell, as shown in the following excerpt:

```
using (HttpNotificationChannel channel
    = new  HttpNotificationChannel(channelName))
{
    channel.Open();
    channel.BindToShellTile();
    channel.BindToShellToast();
}
```

NOTE

Calling the `Open` method on a channel may immediately raise an `Exception`, most commonly an `InvalidOperationException`, if the channel fails to establish a connection with the MPNS.

After retrieving or creating a channel instance, you are able to subscribe to its various events.

CAUTION

Be mindful that each Windows Phone device is limited to a total of 15 apps registered for push notifications. If the user installs 15 apps that use push notifications and your app is the 16th one installed, an `InvalidOperationException` (channel quota exceeded) is raised if your app calls `BindToShellTile` or `BindToShellToast`.

`HttpNotificationChannel` Events

The following is a list of the `HttpNotificationChannel` events:

▶ **`ChannelUriUpdated`**—This event occurs when the push notification URI changes, which can be at any time. If and when the URI changes, the new URI must be forwarded to any cloud services that send push notifications to your app.

▶ **`HttpNotificationReceived`**—This event occurs when a raw notification is received.

▶ **`ShellToastNotificationReceived`**—This event occurs when a toast notification is received.

▶ **`ErrorOccurred`**—This event provides a handling mechanism for exceptions raised by the channel. The handler for this event receives a `NotificationChannelErrorEventArgs` object, which contains an `ErrorCode` property, an `ErrorType` property, and a `Message` property pertaining to the `Exception` that was raised.

Handling Channel Errors

When a channel error occurs, the `NotificationChannelErrorEventArgs.ErrorType` property can be used to determine the nature of the error, as the following excerpt demonstrates:

```
void HandleChannelErrorOccurred(
    object sender, NotificationChannelErrorEventArgs e)
{
    switch (e.ErrorType)
    {
        case ChannelErrorType.ChannelOpenFailed:
            // ...
            break;
        case ChannelErrorType.MessageBadContent:
            // ...
            break;
        case ChannelErrorType.NotificationRateTooHigh:
            // ...
            break;
        case ChannelErrorType.PayloadFormatError:
            // ...
            break;
```

```
        case ChannelErrorType.PowerLevelChanged:
            // ...
            break;
    }
}
```

The following list describes the `NotificationChannelErrorEventArgs.ErrorType` enumeration values:

▶ **ChannelOpenFailed**—Occurs when the push client is unable to establish a connection with the MPNS. Note that exceptions resulting from, for example, a channel already being open, are raised at the call to the `HttpNotificationChannel.Open` method.

▶ **MessageBadContent**—Occurs when using tile notifications and the `BackgroundImage` URI is pointing to a remote image, despite the `HttpNotificationChannel` not being bound to a list of URIs. Tile notifications are discussed in detail later in the chapter.

▶ **NotificationRateTooHigh**—Occurs when the push notification client is unable to receive messages because the cloud service is sending too many messages at too high a rate.

▶ **PayloadFormatError**—Occurs when the XML payload format, or the HTTP header of the push notification, is syntactically invalid. When this error occurs, the `HttpNotificationChannel` is closed and the channel must be reopened.

▶ **PowerLevelChanged**—Occurs when the device's battery level changes significantly enough to trigger a change in the push client's power policy. This topic is discussed in the next section "Power Management and Push Notification."

Additional error information can be obtained by examining the `NotificationChannelErrorEventArgs.ErrorCode` property, which identifies the `HRESULT` of the `Exception`. The `HRESULT` is a coded numerical value that is assigned to some specific exceptions.

Power Management and Push Notification

Even though push notification assists in reducing the power consumption of the phone, maintaining any kind of network connection unfortunately expends more power than most other device functions. Therefore, when the phone's battery level is low, to help reduce power consumption, the phone progressively prevents certain types of notifications from being received by the device (see Figure 13.4).

When an `HttpNotificationChannel` raises its `ErrorOccured` event with an `ErrorType` value of `PowerLevelChanged`, it indicates that there is a change to the types of notifications that are to be delivered to the device.

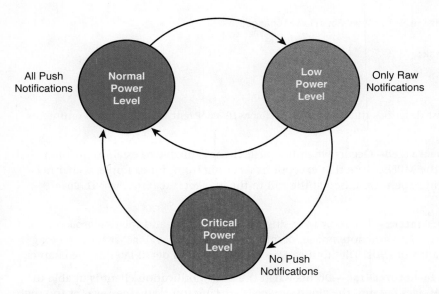

FIGURE 13.4   Device power states transition from a normal power level to low and to critically low.

The `NotificationChannelErrorEventArgs.ErrorAdditionalData` property can be used to obtain the `ChannelPowerLevel` enum value, as shown in the following excerpt:

```
void HandleChannelErrorOccurred(
        object sender, NotificationChannelErrorEventArgs e)
{
    switch (e.ErrorType)
    {
        case ChannelErrorType.PowerLevelChanged:
            if (e.ErrorAdditionalData == (int)ChannelPowerLevel.LowPowerLevel
                || e.ErrorAdditionalData
                        == (int)ChannelPowerLevel.CriticalLowPowerLevel)
            {
                /* Power level is too low. */
            }
            break;
    }
}
```

The following list describes each of the `ChannelPowerLevel` enum values:

▶ **NormalPowerLevel**—The battery level is not low. All push notification types are sent to the device.

▶ **LowPowerLevel**—The battery level is low. Only raw notifications are sent to the device.

▶ **CriticalLowPowerLevel**—The battery level is critically low. No push notifications of any type are sent to the device.

Sending Push Notifications

Sending a toast or tile push notification is done by creating an XML envelope containing the notification information, converting it to a byte array, and then sending it via an HttpWebRequest to the MPNS.

NOTE

When sending a push notification, only the HTTP POST method is allowed. Using any other method such as GET, PUT, CREATE, or DELETE results in a 405 MethodNotAllowed response. Moreover, a ProtocolViolationException results when writing to the request Stream.

For testing purposes, however, the HTTP GET method can be used, and results in a 200 OK response regardless.

An example of a push notification URL is http://sn1.notify.live.net/throttledthirdparty/01.00/AAGvdLTQzLGqRZ0FRZRVT1GBAgoOs1kPAQAAAAQOMDAwAAAAAAAAAAAAAAA.

The notification URL subscriber identifier, which is located after the final forward slash, does not need to resolve to an active subscription. This prevents a third party from fishing for an active subscription URL.

Raw notifications have more flexibility in their format; however, the process of sending a raw notification remains the same as that of tile and toast notifications. The following sections explore in detail how to send toast, tile, and raw notifications.

CAUTION

When sending a notification, the maximum size of a toast, tile, or raw notification body should not exceed 1KB. If this size is exceeded, a System.Net.WebException is raised, resulting from a 400 (Bad Request) response code returned from the MPNS.

For a complete list of MPNS response codes, see http://bit.ly/wd6SXy.

Toast Notifications

Toast notifications are systemwide action requests primarily designed for use with peer-to-peer communications. Toast notifications do not disrupt the user's workflow. They are, however, distracting and therefore should be used sparingly. Toast notifications are presented on the phone as a clickable overlay on the user's current screen even if the associated app is not running (see Figure 13.5). Toast notifications are, however, not displayed if the current app is the app that initiated the push notification subscription. If a user clicks on a toast notification, the associated app is launched.

13

BEST PRACTICE

Toast notifications should be time critical and personally relevant to the user.

Assume that toast notifications are not enabled for your app, as they require the user to explicitly opt-in to receive them.

FIGURE 13.5   Toast notifications are displayed as an overlay on the current application.

A toast notification consists of the application icon displayed at a reduced size and two text fields, one for a title, the other for the notification message.

Receiving a Toast Notification from Within an Application

The `HttpNotificationChannel.ShellToastNotificationReceived` event is used to receive toast notifications within your app, like so:

```
channel.ShellToastNotificationReceived +=
        channel_ShellToastNotificationReceived;
```

NOTE

Toast notifications are displayed only when your app is not running in the foreground. If your app is running in the foreground, the toast notification can still be received and handled in code.

When the `ShellToastNotificationReceived` event is raised, the handler receives a `NotificationEventArgs` object from which the relevant toast notification fields can be extracted, as shown:

```
void channel_ShellToastNotificationReceived(object sender,
                                    NotificationEventArgs e)
{
    string text1 = e.Collection["wp:Text1"];
    string text2 = e.Collection["wp:Text2"];
    //...
}
```

Sending a Toast Notification

Toast notifications require an XML envelope for the notification information. Listing 13.1 demonstrates how the creation of an XML envelope is constructed and sent to the MPNS. An `HttpWebRequest` is created using the push notification subscription URL. The notification XML is converted to a byte array, and then it is written to the outgoing request `Stream`. After sending the request, the response is examined to ensure that it was correctly received by the MPNS.

> **NOTE**
>
> For more information on the `X-NotificationClass` request header, and setting a notification's priority level, see the upcoming section "Notification Classes."

LISTING 13.1   PushNotifier Class (excerpt)

```
public PushNotificationSendResult SendToastNotification(
    string title, string message, string url, PushNotificationPriority priority)
{
    string priorityHeader;
    if (priority == PushNotificationPriority.RealTime)
    {
        priorityHeader = "2";
    }
    else if (priority == PushNotificationPriority.Priority)
    {
        priorityHeader = "12";
    }
    else
    {
        priorityHeader = "22";
    }
```

LISTING 13.1   Continued

```csharp
/* Create the http message that will be sent
 * to the Microsoft hosted server. */
HttpWebRequest request = (HttpWebRequest)WebRequest.Create(url);
request.Method = "POST";
request.ContentType = "text/xml";
request.Headers = new WebHeaderCollection
            {
                { "X-WindowsPhone-Target", "toast" },
                { "X-NotificationClass", priorityHeader }
            };

/* The XML envelope contains the notification text. */
string messageFormat = "<?xml version='1.0' encoding='utf-8'?>" +
                "<wp:Notification xmlns:wp='WPNotification'>" +
                    "<wp:Toast>" +
                        "<wp:Text1>{0}</wp:Text1>" +
                        "<wp:Text2>{1}</wp:Text2>" +
                    "</wp:Toast>" +
                "</wp:Notification>";

/* Insert the message string. */
string messageFormatted = string.Format(messageFormat, title, message);
/* The message will be sent as a byte array. */
byte[] messageBytes = Encoding.Default.GetBytes(messageFormatted);

request.ContentLength = messageBytes.Length;

using (Stream requestStream = request.GetRequestStream())
{
    requestStream.Write(messageBytes, 0, messageBytes.Length);
}

/* Get the response after the message is sent. */
HttpWebResponse response = (HttpWebResponse)request.GetResponse();
string notificationStatus = response.Headers["X-NotificationStatus"];
string deviceConnectionStatus
        = response.Headers["X-DeviceConnectionStatus"];
string subscriptionStatus = response.Headers["X-SubscriptionStatus"];

PushNotificationSendResult result = new PushNotificationSendResult(
    notificationStatus, deviceConnectionStatus, subscriptionStatus);

Debug.WriteLine(result);
return result;
}
```

An `HttpRequestHeader` named `WindowsPhone-Target` with the value toast is added to the request's `Headers` collection, indicating to the MPNS that it is a toast notification.

The XML format for a toast notification is shown in the following fragment:

```
<?xml version='1.0' encoding='utf-8'?>
<wp:Notification xmlns:wp='WPNotification'>
  <wp:Toast>
    <wp:Text1>WP7 Unleashed</wp:Text1>
    <wp:Text2>Toast example</wp:Text2> " +
  </wp:Toast>
</wp:Notification>
```

When the notification is displayed on the phone, the content of the `wp:Text1` element is placed in the title field of the notification overlay, while the content of the `wp:Text2` element is placed in the body field (see Figure 13.6).

FIGURE 13.6   Anatomy of a toast notification overlay

By default, the app icon is the ApplicationIcon.png file present in the root directory of the Windows Phone project. This can be customized from within the project's properties editor (see Figure 13.7).

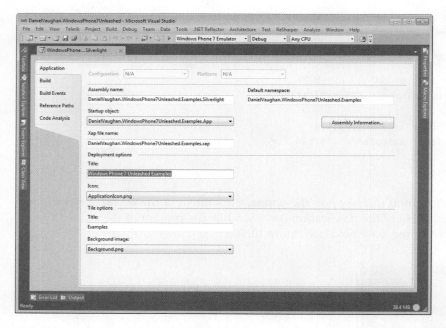

FIGURE 13.7   The application icon image can be set via the Application tab on the properties editor, within Visual Studio.

Alternatively, the path to the image for the application icon can be modified manually within the WMAppManifest.xml file at the Deployment/App/IconPath element.

```
<IconPath IsRelative="true"
          IsResource="false">ApplicationIcon.png</IconPath>
```

TIP

As you can see in Figure 13.6, it is wise to tailor the application icon so that it displays clearly at a small size when presented in a toast notification.

Tile Notifications

A tile is a dynamic visual representation of your app that resides on the phone's Start Experience. Each app on the phone can be associated with a single application tile and multiple secondary tiles. Tiles serve as a shortcut to an application.

Tile notifications allow the application tile to be modified periodically, using a data driven template model, with a fixed set of data properties. Each property corresponds to a UI element, with each UI element having a fixed position on the tile. A tile notification can be used to communicate information sent from the cloud, such as updates from an email service, a social networking service, or a weather service.

It is at the user's discretion to pin an application to the Start Experience, and having the app pinned to the Start Experience is essential for receiving tile notifications.

When an application is pinned to the Start Experience, tile notifications are displayed regardless of whether the app is running.

The template for a tile notification consists of three assignable data properties: a title property, a count property (also called a badge), and a background image property (see Figure 13.8). A cloud service may modify the content of an associated tile using tile notifications.

FIGURE 13.8   A tile notification consists of a count property, title property, and a background image property.

Tile Notification Anatomy

Tile notifications are comprised of three parts: a background, a title, and a count (or badge) field, as shown in Figure 13.9.

Background Image Property

The background image of a tile can be assigned a local resource URI or a remote URI to an image on the cloud. By using a remote image, you have the opportunity to dynamically generate it, giving you more control over information presented in the image but at the cost of bandwidth and power consumption.

The tile background image must be in either JPG or PNG format.

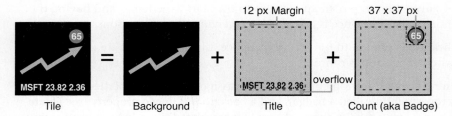

FIGURE 13.9   Tile notifications consist of three assignable fields: the background, a title field, and a count field.

Title Property

The title is a text field located at the bottom of the tile.

Count Property

The Count element must be a positive integer value between 0 and 99. This value is displayed on the count property, or badge, region of the tile. If the value is 0 then the badge is not displayed.

Sending a Tile Notification

Sending a tile notification is done in the same manner as sending a toast notification, the differences being in the request headers and the format of the XML message (see Listing 13.2). As with toast notifications, we create an HttpWebRequest, build the message, convert the message to a byte array, and then write it to the request Stream. Finally, we verify that the notification was correctly received by the MPNS.

An HttpRequestHeader named WindowsPhone-Target with the value tile is added to the request's Headers collection, indicating to the MPNS that it is a tile notification.

LISTING 13.2   Sending a Tile Notification

```
public PushNotificationSendResult SendTileNotification(string title, int count,
    string imagePath, string url, PushNotificationPriority priority)
{
    string priorityHeader;
    if (priority == PushNotificationPriority.RealTime)
```

LISTING 13.2   Continued

```
{
    priorityHeader = "1";
}
else if (priority == PushNotificationPriority.Priority)
{
    priorityHeader = "11";
}
else
{
    priorityHeader = "21";
}

/* Create the http message that will be sent
 * to the Microsoft hosted server. */
HttpWebRequest request = (HttpWebRequest)WebRequest.Create(url);
request.Method = "POST";
request.ContentType = "text/xml";
request.Headers = new WebHeaderCollection
            {
                { "X-WindowsPhone-Target", "token" },
                { "X-NotificationClass", priorityHeader }
            };

/* The XML envelope contains the notification text. */
string messageFormat = "<?xml version='1.0' encoding='utf-8'?>" +
                "<wp:Notification xmlns:wp='WPNotification'>" +
                    "<wp:Tile>" +
                        "<wp:BackgroundImage>{0}</wp:BackgroundImage>" +
                        "<wp:Count>{1}</wp:Count>" +
                        "<wp:Title>{2}</wp:Title>" +
                    "</wp:Tile>" +
                "</wp:Notification>";

/* Insert the message string. */
string messageFormatted = string.Format(
    messageFormat, imagePath, count, title);
/* The message is sent as a byte array. */
byte[] messageBytes = Encoding.Default.GetBytes(messageFormatted);

request.ContentLength = messageBytes.Length;

using (Stream requestStream = request.GetRequestStream())
{
    requestStream.Write(messageBytes, 0, messageBytes.Length);
}
```

LISTING 13.2   Continued

```
    /* Get the response after the message is sent. */
    HttpWebResponse response = (HttpWebResponse)request.GetResponse();
    string notificationStatus = response.Headers["X-NotificationStatus"];
    string subscriptionStatus = response.Headers["X-SubscriptionStatus"];
    string deviceConnectionStatus
            = response.Headers["X-DeviceConnectionStatus"];

    PushNotificationSendResult result = new PushNotificationSendResult(
        PushNotificationEnumConverter.ToNotificationStatus(notificationStatus),
        PushNotificationEnumConverter.ToDeviceConnectionStatus(
                                                deviceConnectionStatus),
        PushNotificationEnumConverter.ToSubscriptionStatus(subscriptionStatus)
        );
    Debug.WriteLine(result);
    return result;
}
```

The format for a tile notification is shown in the following fragment:

```
<?xml version='1.0' encoding='utf-8'?>
<wp:Notification xmlns:wp='WPNotification'>
  <wp:Tile>
    <wp:BackgroundImage>
            ProjectSubdirectory/ExampleImage.png
    </wp:BackgroundImage>
    <wp:Count>
            An integer n, with 0 <= n <= 99
    </wp:Count>
    <wp:Title>Example Title</wp:Title>
  </wp:Tile>
</wp:Notification>
```

When the notification is displayed on the phone, the content of the `wp:BackgroundImage` element specifies the URL of the tile's background image. This value can either be a local path within the project, or a remote URI such as http://www.example.com/ImageName.png.

> **CAUTION**
>
> A tile's background image size must not exceed 80KB. In addition, the download time for an image must not exceed 1 minute. If the image size is too large, or the download takes too long, then the default image for the tile is used.

The `wp:Title` element denotes the title text to be displayed at the bottom of the tile.

NOTE

For information on how to create shell tiles or modify tile properties directly from your app, see Chapter 27.

TIP

Presenting too much information can slow down comprehension of a tile. Therefore, keep the style simple to improve clarity. When designing a background image for a tile, it is important to make different states easily recognizable.

Do not presume that a background image will be placed on a particular screen color. Themes allow the phone's Start Experience color scheme to be modified. Therefore, when using PNG images as the tile image format, avoid using transparency if possible, as antialiasing may produce unintended discoloration around shape boundaries.

Updating an Application Tile Using a Shell Tile Schedule

You saw how to specify the background image of an application tile using push notification. There is, however, an alternative approach that lets you set the background image to a remote URI without using push notification, eliminating the need for a cloud service to issue tile notifications.

By using the ShellTileSchedule class the phone can be directed to periodically download an image from a remote server.

To create a schedule for a tile update, create a new instance of the ShellTileSchedule class and set the RemoteImageUri property, as shown in the following example:

```
string url = "http://www.example.com/ImageName.png";
ShellTileSchedule schedule = new ShellTileSchedule
{
    Interval = UpdateInterval.EveryHour,
    MaxUpdateCount = 10,
    Recurrence = UpdateRecurrence.Interval,
    RemoteImageUri = new Uri(url),
    StartTime = DateTime.Now
};
schedule.Start();
```

The following is a list of ShellTileSchedule properties that affect the download frequency:

▶ **Interval**—This property specifies the download frequency rate and is of type Microsoft.Phone.Shell.UpdateInterval. UpdateInterval is an enumeration with the following values:

 ▶ EveryHour   ▶ EveryWeek

 ▶ EveryDay   ▶ EveryMonth

If the shortest frequency, `EveryHour`, does not offer a short enough interval, push notification or a background agent should be considered instead.

▶ **MaxUpdateCount**—This property defines the number of times the schedule runs. If this value is not set or set to a number less than 1, then the schedule runs indefinitely. This value is ignored if `Recurrence` is set to `OneTime`.

▶ **Recurrence**—This property specifies whether the image is to be fetched periodically, or if retrieval of the image is to occur only once. The available values are `UpdateRecurrence.Interval` or `UpdateRecurrence.OneTime`.

▶ **RemoteImageUri**—This property is the fully qualified URI of the background image. It cannot point to a local image stored on the phone.

▶ **StartTime**—This property specifies the duration from the initial `ShellTileSchedule.Start` method call until the first time that the image is fetched. This property is used to delay the initial download of an image.

CAUTION

The same restrictions apply to images retrieved using a `ShellTileSchedule` as those in tile notifications. In particular, image size must not exceed 80KB, and the download time must not exceed 1 minute. If the image size is too large, or the download takes too long, not only is the default image used for the tile, but the tile schedule is also removed. The only way to reinstate a schedule is to re-run the schedule generation code.

Raw Notifications

Raw notifications are not displayed by the OS and are delivered directly to your running app, via an event. If your app is not running when a raw notification is received, then the notification is discarded.

Sending a Raw Notification

Sending a raw notification differs from sending tile and toast notifications in that there is greater flexibility over the contents of the body of the notification.

Listing 13.3 demonstrates sending an object as part of a raw notification, using a `DataContractJsonSerializer`. As with tile and toast notifications, we create an `HttpWebRequest`, convert the content to a byte array, and then write it to the request `Stream`. Finally, we verify that the notification was correctly received by the MPNS.

LISTING 13.3   `PushNotifier` Class (excerpt)—Sending a Raw Notification

```
public PushNotificationSendResult SendRawNotification(
    object content, string url, PushNotificationPriority priority)
{
    string priorityHeader;
```

LISTING 13.3   Continued

```
if (priority == PushNotificationPriority.RealTime)
{
    priorityHeader = "5";
}
else if (priority == PushNotificationPriority.Priority)
{
    priorityHeader = "16";
}
else
{
    priorityHeader = "26";
}

/* Create the http message that will be sent
 * to the Microsoft hosted server. */
HttpWebRequest request = (HttpWebRequest)WebRequest.Create(url);
/* HTTP POST is the only allowed method to send the notification. */
request.Method = "POST";
request.ContentType = "application/json; charset=utf-8";
request.Headers = new WebHeaderCollection {
{ "X-MessageID", Guid.NewGuid().ToString()},
{ "X-NotificationClass", priorityHeader } };

/* The message will be sent as a byte array. */
byte[] contentBytes;
var serializer = new DataContractJsonSerializer(content.GetType());

using (MemoryStream stream = new MemoryStream())
{
    serializer.WriteObject(stream, content);
    contentBytes = stream.ToArray();
}

request.ContentLength = contentBytes.Length;

using (Stream requestStream = request.GetRequestStream())
{
    requestStream.Write(contentBytes, 0, contentBytes.Length);
}

/* Get the response after the message is sent. */
HttpWebResponse response = (HttpWebResponse)request.GetResponse();
string notificationStatus = response.Headers["X-NotificationStatus"];
string subscriptionStatus = response.Headers["X-SubscriptionStatus"];
```

LISTING 13.3   Continued

```
string deviceConnectionStatus
        = response.Headers["X-DeviceConnectionStatus"];

PushNotificationSendResult result = CreateSendResult(
    notificationStatus, deviceConnectionStatus, subscriptionStatus);

return result;
}
```

The use of the DataContractJsonSerializer is convenient because it allows you to serialize an entire object on the server in a format that is compatible with Silverlight. With little effort the object can be rehydrated on the client. You could, however, use another payload format, such as a string, as shown in the tile and toast notification examples.

TIP

The DataContractJsonSerializer type, as shown in this example, was chosen over the more commonly used DataContractSerializer because JSON serialization is more space efficient than XML, producing a payload of much smaller size. This is important because the maximum body size for a toast, tile, or raw notification is 1KB.

The DataContractJsonSerializer approach relies on the content object's class being decorated with DataContract and DataMember attributes, as shown in the following example:

```
[DataContract]
public class StockQuote
{
    [DataMember]
    public string StockSymbol { get; set; }

    [DataMember]
    public double LastPrice { get; set; }

    [DataMember]
    public double ChangeInPrice { get; set; }
}
```

The DataContract and DataMember attributes provide the DataContractJsonSerializer with the information it needs to serialize the StockQuote object. Neglecting to decorate a property with a DataMember attribute causes that property to be ignored, and its value to be absent when the object is deserialized in the client application.

Receiving a Raw Notification

To receive a raw notification in an app, subscribe to the
`HttpNotificationChannel.HttpNotificationReceived` event, as shown:

```
channel.HttpNotificationReceived += channel_HttpNotificationReceived;
...
void channel_HttpNotificationReceived(object sender,
                                        HttpNotificationEventArgs e)
{
...
}
```

When the `HttpNotificationReceived` event is raised, the handler receives an
`HttpNotificationEventArgs` object that contains a `Notification` property of type
`HttpNotification`. `HttpNotification` contains the following properties:

▶ **Body**—The payload for the notification. This is the main property of interest. It is a
`Stream` containing the raw notification data.

▶ **Channel**—The channel to which the notification arrived.

▶ **Headers**—The request headers that were supplied during the creation of the
notification.

The following excerpt from the `PushNotificationViewModel` class in the downloadable
sample code demonstrates how raw notification is handled on the phone, and in particular how the content object (in this case, a `StockQuote`) is rehydrated:

```
void subscriber_HttpNotificationReceived(
    object sender, HttpNotificationEventArgs e)
{
    Message = "Raw notification received.";
    Stream bodyStream = e.Notification.Body;

    if (bodyStream != null)
    {
        DataContractJsonSerializer serializer
                = new DataContractJsonSerializer(typeof(StockQuote));

        StockQuote = (StockQuote)serializer.ReadObject(bodyStream);
    }
}
```

A `DataContractJsonSerializer` reverses the serialization process by transforming the
stream data back to a `StockQuote` object.

Identifying Notifications in an `HttpWebResponse`

Common to all push notification types is an optional custom header named `X-MessageID`, which can be added to the `HttpWebRequest.Headers` collection. Its purpose is to uniquely identify the notification message, and if present, the same value is able to be retrieved in the notification response. It must be a string that contains a universally unique identifier (UUID), as shown in the following excerpt:

```
request.Headers.Add("X-MessageID", "<UUID>");
```

At the time of writing, this header does not serve any purpose, because the resulting `HttpWebResponse` is retrieved using the original `HttpWebRequest`. It is, therefore, trivial to identify a notification based on an `HttpWebResponse`. In the future, however, this setting may be used in conjunction with an MPNS callback, to update the cloud service if a notification is impacted due to, for example, session expiry.

Notification Classes

Some kinds of notifications may be more time critical than others. For example, a notification indicating that tomorrow's weather forecast has changed may be less time critical than a notification about a traffic jam on your planned route home. The MPNS allows notifications to be assigned a batching interval, which works as a guide for the MPNS in determining when to deliver one or more notifications in a batch.

To inform the MPNS of the batching interval of a notification, a header named X-NotificationClass is added to the outgoing request. The batching interval is a string representation of an integer value. The set of valid priority values is determined by the kind of notification, be it a toast, tile, or raw notification.

When notifications are sent to the MPNS, they are placed in queues (see Figure 13.10). Each queue is serviced at different intervals according to its notification class. Accordingly, a queue for a lower notification class may be serviced more frequently than one with a higher notification class. For example, a raw notification with an *X*-NotificationClass of 3 means that the message is delivered by the MPNS immediately, a value of 13 means that the message is delivered within 450 seconds, and a value of 23 means the message is delivered within 900 seconds.

When sending a push notification, the X-NotificationClass may be omitted, in which case a default regular priority is used. Table 13.1 lists the push notification classes for each notification type.

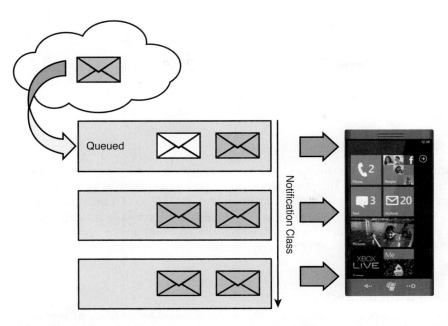

FIGURE 13.10   Notifications are queued and the notifications from each queue are periodically sent to the phone.

TABLE 13.1   Push Notification Classes

Level	Description	Notification Class		
		Toast	**Title**	**Raw**
Real Time	Indicates that the toast notification is to be delivered as soon as possible.	2	1	3-10
Priority	Indicates that the toast notification is to be delivered at the next priority batch send. The interval is predefined. In most cases it is delivered within 450 seconds.	12	11	13-20
Regular	Indicates that the toast notification is to be delivered at the next regular batch interval. The interval is predefined, and it is longer than the priority interval. In most cases it is delivered within 900 seconds.	22	21	23-31

In the downloadable sample code, the notification class is represented as an enum called `PushNotificationPriority` and provides for strongly typed notification class values.

```
public enum PushNotificationPriority
{
    Regular,
    Priority,
    RealTime
}
```

Cloud Service Authentication

The Push Notification protocol enables a cloud service to send a notification to a phone application using a RESTful API. The cloud service can choose to operate as authenticated or unauthenticated by registering an X.509 certificate with the MPNS. An unauthenticated cloud service is limited to sending 500 notification requests a day for each subscription. While in most cases this will suffice, having an authenticated cloud service removes this limitation, and an unlimited number of push notifications can be sent for the life of a subscription.

Authenticating a Cloud Service

To authenticate a cloud service, obtain an X.509 certificate issued by a Microsoft trusted root certificate authority. The certificate can then be registered on the Windows Phone Marketplace. The certificate is used to establish a Secure Sockets Layer (SSL) connection between the cloud service and the MPNS.

Creating a Notification Channel for an Authenticated Cloud Service

As mentioned earlier in this chapter, the `HttpNotificationChannel` has a constructor that accepts the fully qualified domain name (FQDN) of the cloud service certificate. The FQDN must match the registered certificate's subject name, which is the CN attribute. An example of an FQDN is www.example.com. Creating a channel using an FQDN is demonstrated in the following excerpt:

```
using (HttpNotificationChannel channel
        = new HttpNotificationChannel(channelName, "www.example.com"))
{
    channel.Open();
    channel.BindToShellEntryPoint();
    channel.BindToShellNotification();
}
```

Building a Stock Ticker Application

The main sample for this app demonstrates the three kinds of push notifications: tile, toast, and raw notifications. It is a stock ticker application that allows the user to enter a stock symbol into the phone, after which a cloud service periodically notifies the phone of stock price variations.

> **NOTE**
>
> When debugging using a phone device (not the emulator) a local WCF service is unreachable from the app. To allow a device to communicate with a local WCF service, configure Visual Studio to use IIS and use a machine name or external IP address in your WCF client configuration.

The server side component of the sample application consists of a WCF service that allows the phone app to register itself to receive stock price update notifications. The server side implementation retrieves stock price information periodically from Yahoo! Finance (see Figure 13.11).

FIGURE 13.11   The sample Stock Quoter application monitors stock prices according to stock symbol.

Input controls for the application include a text box, which allows the user to enter a stock symbol to be monitored, a Register button, and an Unregister button. Clicking on the Register button causes the viewmodel's `RegisterForPushNotification` method to be called. This causes a `PushNotificationSubscriber` to be initialized and its events subscribed to, as shown in the following excerpt.

```
void Subscribe()
{
    if (subscriber == null)
    {
```

```
        InitializeSubscriber();
    }
    subscriber.Subscribe();
}

void InitializeSubscriber()
{
    subscriber = new PushNotificationSubscriber(
                    channelName, null, RegisterWithCloudService);
    subscriber.HttpNotificationReceived
                            += subscriber_HttpNotificationReceived;
    subscriber.ChannelUriUpdated += subscriber_ChannelUriUpdated;
    subscriber.ErrorOccurred += subscriber_ErrorOccurred;
}
```

A delegate is passed to the subscriber, which is used to notify the cloud service of the push notification URI once it is received from the MPNS.

As mentioned earlier in the chapter, the PushNotificationSubscriber handles the creation and opening of the HttpNotificationChannel (see Listing 13.4). When the Subscribe method is called, a channel is retrieved if it already exists; otherwise, a new channel is created. Subscription occurs to the channel's various events and the channel is opened. The channel then nominates itself to receive tile and toast notifications.

LISTING 13.4   PushNotificationSubscriber.Subscribe Method

```
public void Subscribe()
{
    try
    {
        channel = HttpNotificationChannel.Find(channelName);
        if (channel == null)
        {
            channel = string.IsNullOrEmpty(serviceName)
                ? new HttpNotificationChannel(channelName)
                : new HttpNotificationChannel(channelName, serviceName);
        }
        else
        {
            channel.UnbindToShellTile();
            channel.UnbindToShellToast();
            channel.Close();
            Subscribe();
            return;
        }
```

LISTING 13.4   Continued

```
        UnsubscribeFromChannelEvents();
        SubscribeToChannelEvents();

        try
        {
            channel.Open();
        }
        catch (Exception ex)
        {
            channel.UnbindToShellTile();
            channel.UnbindToShellToast();
            channel.Close();
            WaitAndRetryChannelConnect();
            return;
        }

        /* Toast Notifications. */
        if (!channel.IsShellToastBound)
        {
            channel.BindToShellToast();
        }

        /* Tile Notifications. */
        if (!channel.IsShellTileBound)
        {
            channel.BindToShellTile();
        }

        if (channel.ChannelUri != null)
        {
            RegisterChannel(channel.ChannelUri);
        }
    }
    catch (Exception ex)
    {
        Debug.WriteLine("Unable to subscribe. " + ex.ToString());
        WaitAndRetryChannelConnect();
    }
}
```

If something goes wrong during the subscription phase, the subscriber waits 30 seconds and then tries again, as the following excerpt shows:

```
void WaitAndRetryChannelConnect()
{
    if (retryTimer == null)
    {
        /* Create a timer and have it fire once. */
        retryTimer = new Timer(o => Subscribe(), null, retryDueTimeMs,
            Timeout.Infinite);
    }
    else
    {
        /* The timer is changed to fire once after the period expires. */
        retryTimer.Change(retryDueTimeMs, Timeout.Infinite);
    }
}
```

PushNotificationSubscriber contains a field of type Action<string> named
registerWithServer, whose task is to send the URI of the MPNS subscription to the
StockQuoteService cloud service, along with the stock symbol for the stock that the user
wants to monitor. By plugging in this behavior you can test the app without relying on
the cloud service being present.

> **NOTE**
>
> The StockQuoteService implementation is for demonstration purposes only and lacks the
> capability to support multiple concurrent users. In supporting multiple users, it would be
> advisable to use a database to record each user's stock symbols, and to use a worker
> process to periodically query the database and to send notifications only when a price
> change occurs.

When the StockQuoteService.RegisterForStockQuoteNotifications method is called on
the server, a Timer causes tile, toast, and raw notifications to be periodically sent to the
subscriber (Listing 13.5).

The StockQuote result is provided by the StockQuoter class, discussed next.

LISTING 13.5   StockQuoteService Class

```
[AspNetCompatibilityRequirements(
    RequirementsMode = AspNetCompatibilityRequirementsMode.Allowed)]
[ServiceBehavior(InstanceContextMode = InstanceContextMode.Single)]
public class StockQuoteService : IStockQuoteService
{
    Timer timer;
    bool notify = true;
    int tilePushCount;
    string subscriptionUrl;
    string stockSymbol;
```

LISTING 13.5   Continued

```csharp
StockQuote stockQuote;
bool sendingNotifications;
const int notificationPeriodMs = 30000;

public void RegisterForStockQuoteNotifications(
    PushNotificationSubscriberId pushNotificationSubscriberId,
    string stockSymbol)
{
    subscriptionUrl = pushNotificationSubscriberId.PushNotificationUrl;
    this.stockSymbol = stockSymbol;
    notify = true;

    if (timer == null)
    {
        timer = new Timer(delegate
                        {
                            /* An exception must not be raised. */
                            try
                            {
                                NotifyWithStockQuote();
                            }
                            catch (Exception ex)
                            {
                                Debug.WriteLine("Unable to notify.", ex);
                            }
                        }, null,
            2000 /* 2000 MS = 5 seconds. */, notificationPeriodMs);
    }
}

void NotifyWithStockQuote()
{
    if (!notify || sendingNotifications)
    {
        return;
    }

    if (tilePushCount > 98)
    {
        tilePushCount = 0;
    }

    try
    {
        sendingNotifications = true;
```

LISTING 13.5   Continued

```
try
{
    StockQuoter stockQuoter = new StockQuoter();
    stockQuote = stockQuoter.GetStockQuote(this.stockSymbol);
}
catch (Exception ex)
{
    Debug.WriteLine("Unable to retrieve stock quote." + ex);
    return;
}

DateTime now = DateTime.Now;
Debug.WriteLine(
    "Sending notifications at " + now.ToLongTimeString());
PushNotifier notifier = new PushNotifier();

string background;
if (stockQuote.ChangeInPrice > 0)
{
    background = "PushNotification/Images/StockUp.png";
}
else if (stockQuote.ChangeInPrice < 0)
{
    background = "PushNotification/Images/StockDown.png";
}
else
{
    background = "PushNotification/Images/StockNone.png";
}

try
{
    notifier.SendTileNotification(
        stockQuote.ToString(),
        ++tilePushCount,
        background,
        subscriptionUrl,
        PushNotificationPriority.RealTime);
}
catch (Exception ex)
{
    Debug.WriteLine("Unable to send tile notifications:" + ex);
}
```

LISTING 13.5   Continued

```csharp
            try
            {
                notifier.SendToastNotification("Stock Quote",
                                    stockQuote.ToString(),
                                        subscriptionUrl,
                            PushNotificationPriority.RealTime);
            }
            catch (Exception ex)
            {
                Debug.WriteLine("Unable to send toast notification:" + ex);
            }

            try
            {
                notifier.SendRawNotification(stockQuote,
                    subscriptionUrl, PushNotificationPriority.RealTime);
            }
            catch (Exception ex)
            {
                Debug.WriteLine("Unable to send raw notification: " + ex);
            }
        }
        finally
        {
            sendingNotifications = false;
        }
    }

    public void UnregisterForStockQuoteNotifications(
        PushNotificationSubscriberId pushNotificationSubscriberId)
    {
        notify = false;
        tilePushCount = 0;
    }
}
```

The GetStockQuote method creates an HttpWebRequest that is sent to the Yahoo! Finance
stock quote URL. This request produces a CSV (comma-separated values) file containing
the stock information of interest, including the price of the stock and the change in price
for the day. The following excerpt shows the GetStockQuote method:

```csharp
public StockQuote GetStockQuote(string stockSymbol)
{
string queryString = string.Format(
    "s={0}&f=sl1p2d1t1c1hgvba", stockSymbol);
```

```
string url = "http://download.finance.yahoo.com/d/quotes.csv?"
                    + queryString;
HttpWebRequest request = (HttpWebRequest)WebRequest.Create(url);

string responseString;
using (HttpWebResponse response
                    = (HttpWebResponse)request.GetResponse())
{
    using (var reader = new StreamReader(
        response.GetResponseStream(), Encoding.ASCII))
    {
        responseString = reader.ReadLine();
    }
}

Debug.WriteLine("Stock Quote: " + responseString);

var cells = responseString.Split(',');
if (cells.Length < 3)
{
    throw new Exception("Invalid response.");
}
if (cells[1].ToLower() == @"\na\")
{
    throw new UnknownStockSymbolException(stockSymbol);
}

StockQuote stockQuote = new StockQuote();
string changeInPrice = cells[2].Replace("\"", "").Replace("%", "");
stockQuote.ChangeInPrice = double.Parse(changeInPrice,
    NumberStyles.AllowLeadingSign | NumberStyles.AllowDecimalPoint);
stockQuote.LastPrice = double.Parse(cells[1].Replace("\"", ""));
stockQuote.StockSymbol = cells[0].Replace("\"", "");
return stockQuote;
}
```

The information that is sent back from Yahoo! Finance depends on the contents of the query string in the request URL. The format is like so:

```
http://finance.yahoo.com/d/quotes.csv?s=
                    <stock symbols separated by +>&f=<field identifiers>
```

For more information regarding the Yahoo! stock data format, see http://bit.ly/C5MPu.

The StockQuote class is a container for the information retrieved from Yahoo! Finance. It is decorated with DataContract and DataMember attributes so that it can be serialized for raw notifications, as shown in the following excerpt:

```
[Serializable
[DataContract]
public class StockQuote
{
    [DataMember]
    public string StockSymbol { get; set; }

    [DataMember]
    public double LastPrice { get; set; }

    [DataMember]
    public double ChangeInPrice { get; set; }

    public override string ToString()
    {
        return string.Format("{0} {1} {2}",
                        StockSymbol, LastPrice, ChangeInPrice);
    }
}
```

Sample App Notifications

The Stock Quoter app uses all three types of push notifications, which are described in the following sections.

Tile Notifications

Tile notifications are sent periodically from the StockQuoteService and are displayed as shown in Figure 13.8. The tile notification contains a Text1 data property equal to Stock Quote and a Text2 data property that is the result of calling the ToString method of the StockQuote object, which produces a combination of the stock symbol, the stock's last price, and its change in price.

Toast Notifications

Toast notifications are sent periodically from the StockQuoteService and are displayed as shown in Figure 13.5. The sample uses the title property of the tile notification to display the stock symbol, its price, and its change in price for the day. The count property is populated with an incrementing value, which is just for demonstration purposes.

Sample Background Images

For tile and raw notifications, the sample makes use of three images: StockUp.png, StockNone.png, and StockDown.png, located in the PushNotification/Images directory of the WindowsPhone7Unleashed.Examples project.

The logic for determining the background image for a tile notification is located server-side, as this excerpt from the `StockQuoteService` shows:

```
string background;
if (stockQuote.ChangeInPrice > 0)
{
    background = "PushNotification/Images/StockUp.png";
}
else if (stockQuote.ChangeInPrice < 0)
{
    background = "PushNotification/Images/StockDown.png";
}
else
{
    background = "PushNotification/Images/StockNone.png";
}
```

Image paths are relative to the application project.

Raw Notifications

Raw notifications make use of the serialized `StockQuote` instance as the following excerpt from the `StockQuoteService` class shows:

```
notifier.SendRawNotification(
    stockQuote, subscriptionUrl, PushNotificationPriority.RealTime);
```

The `StockQuote` instance is serialized to a `byte` array, which is then used as the content for the raw notification. For more information on the serialization process see the previous section "Receiving a Raw Notification."

When a raw notification is received by the phone app and the `StockQuote` object is rehydrated in the `PushNotificationViewModel` class, the object is assigned to the viewmodel's `StockQuote` property.

The view displays the stock information via the viewmodel's `StockQuote` property, as shown in the following excerpt from the `PushNotificationView.xaml` file (style attributes have been removed for clarity):

```
<TextBlock Text="Price:" />
<TextBlock Text="{Binding StockQuote.LastPrice}" />
<TextBlock Text="Change:" />
<TextBlock Text="{Binding StockQuote.ChangeInPrice}" />
```

The stock direction image is presented using the viewmodel's `StockPriceDirection` property. When the `StockQuote` changes in the viewmodel, the `StockPriceDirection` property is reevaluated and a different image displayed in the view. The following excerpt shows the `StockQuote` property in the viewmodel:

```
StockQuote stockQuote;

public StockQuote StockQuote
{
    get
    {
        return stockQuote;
    }
    set
    {
        Assign("StockQuote", ref stockQuote, value);
        /* Set the direction so that the view
         * doesn't need to do any evaluation. */
        if (stockQuote == null || stockQuote.ChangeInPrice == 0)
        {
            StockPriceDirection = StockPriceDirection.None;
        }
        else if (stockQuote.ChangeInPrice > 0)
        {
            StockPriceDirection = StockPriceDirection.Up;
        }
        else
        {
            StockPriceDirection = StockPriceDirection.Down;
        }
    }
}
```

The view itself subscribes to the viewmodel's `PropertyChanged` event. When the `StockPriceDirection` property changes, it determines what image should be displayed depending on its value.

```
void viewModel_PropertyChanged(object sender, PropertyChangedEventArgs e)
{
    if (e.PropertyName == "StockPriceDirection")
    {
        string url;
        switch (ViewModel.StockPriceDirection)
        {
            case StockPriceDirection.Down:
                url = "Images/StockDown.png";
                break;
            case StockPriceDirection.Up:
                url = "Images/StockUp.png";
                break;
            default:
```

```
            url = "Images/StockNone.png";
            break;
    }
    Image_StockQuote.Source = new BitmapImage(
        new Uri(url, UriKind.Relative));
    }
}
```

NOTE

Updating the UI based on a viewmodel property could be better orchestrated using the page's `VisualStateManager`. In Chapter 16, "Bing Maps," we discuss a custom `VisualStateUtility` class that allows you to bind the visual state of a UI element to a viewmodel property.

Opting Out of Stock Price Updates

The Stock Quoter application allows a user to unregister from receiving stock updates. By clicking the Unregister button, the viewmodel's `UnregisterPushNotification` method is called, which calls the `PushNotificationSubscriber` object's `Unsubscribe` method, as shown:

```
public void UnregisterForPushNotification()
{
    try
    {
        Message = "Unregistering for notifications.";
        if (subscriber != null)
        {
            subscriber.Unsubscribe();
            subscriber.Dispose();
            subscriber = null;
        }
        Message = "Unregistered for notifications.";
    }
    catch (Exception ex)
    {
        Message = "Problem unregistering: " + ex.ToString();
    }

    if (channelUri != null)
    {
        try
        {
            UnregisterWithServer(channelUri.ToString());
        }
```

```
        catch (Exception ex)
        {
            Message = "Problem unregistering with server: " + ex.ToString();
        }
    }
}
```

When the `PushNotificationSubscriber` is disposed, its `Timer` and `HttpNotificationChannel` are also disposed. The cloud service is then notified that push notifications should no longer be sent.

Summary

This chapter looked at the advantages of push notification, and how it can be used to extend the battery life of the device.

The chapter began with an overview of push notification, starting with the three different types of push notifications: toast, tile, and raw notifications. The various types of channel errors that can occur during push notification were examined, and you saw how the phone's battery level affects delivery of push notifications. The chapter also looked at cloud service authentication using X.509 certificates, and at how to update an application tile without tile notifications using shell tile schedules.

Finally, the chapter explored a stock ticker sample app that allows the user to enter a stock symbol into the phone, after which a cloud service periodically notifies the phone of stock price variations.

Chapter 11, "Touch," looked at touch input and gestures, which is ordinarily the first choice for user input in most Windows Phone apps. Yet the hardware of Windows Phone devices provides additional sensors that can be used for input, including an accelerometer, compass, and gyroscope, along with a combined virtual sensor called the motion sensor.

This chapter examines each sensor in detail, beginning with the accelerometer. You see how to process accelerometer readings, and how to simulate acceleration within the Windows Phone emulator. You learn how to apply data smoothing to accelerometer readings to decrease jittering of UI elements without sacrificing responsiveness. You also see how to calibrate the accelerometer, and how to perform shake detection using the accelerometer.

The chapter then looks at the compass sensor and how to use the compass's magnetic heading to build a custom compass app that displays the heading using an arrow. How compass calibration is performed is also discussed.

The chapter then moves to the gyroscope sensor, and you see how to build a UI to display the angular rotation of the phone.

Finally, the chapter discusses the motion sensor, which is a virtual sensor that harnesses the other hardware sensors to improve accuracy and provide extended orientation and motion information.

Sensors Overview

All sensor classes derive from the class `SensorBase<TSensorReading>`, allowing you to work with what will become a familiar programming model. `SensorBase` ensures that sensors and readings are treated in the same way, a consistency that you will come to appreciate the more you work with sensors. The only variation occurs in the type of data that each sensor provides as a reading.

`SensorBase<TSensorReading>` has the following three properties:

- ▶ `CurrentValue`
- ▶ `IsDataValid`
- ▶ `TimeBetweenUpdates`

Windows Phone sensors use an event-based model for monitoring changes to sensor readings. When new data arrives from the sensor, the `SensorBase<TSensorReading>.` `CurrentValueChanged` event is raised, providing the ability to periodically process sensor readings. The type of reading depends on the type of sensor you are using. For example, the accelerometer uses an `AccelerometerReading`.

> **NOTE**
>
> The `CurrentValueChanged` event is not raised on the UI thread. It is therefore important to invoke any updates to the UI using a `Dispatcher`. This, however, poses no challenge if you choose to use the property change notification infrastructure present in the downloadable sample code.

The interval between sensor readings can be set using the `TimeBetweenUpdates` property, which is of type `TimeSpan`. By default, this value is 17, 20, or 25 milliseconds, depending on the type of sensor. Setting the `TimeBetweenUpdates` to a value not supported by the sensor silently fails.

> **NOTE**
>
> If you require a specific value for the `TimeBetweenUpdates` interval, be sure to test the value of the property after it is set to ensure that the value was actually assigned.

The `CurrentValue` property holds the value of the most recent sensor reading taken. A good habit to get into is to make sure you check the `IsDataValid` property, which indicates whether the sensor's `CurrentValue` property contains valid data before retrieving the value from the `CurrentValue` property.

Two methods, `Start` and `Stop`, are used to start and stop acquisition of data from the sensor. Sensors consume native resources on the device and may unduly impact battery consumption if they are kept alive for longer than they are needed. It is therefore important to call `Start` only when sensor readings are needed, and to call `Stop` as soon as the new sensor readings are no longer needed.

`SensorBase<TSensorReading>` implements `IDisposable`. Calling `Dispose` on a sensor releases the managed and unmanaged resources used by the sensor. Obviously it is wise to dispose of sensors once they are not needed, such as when your app is deactivated; however, `SensorBase<T>` automatically subscribes to the `PhoneApplicationService.Closing` event, and when the event is raised, calls its own `Dispose` method. This means that, no matter what happens, resources related to the native sensor are correctly released when your app exits.

> **NOTE**
>
> The accelerometer, compass, motion, and gyroscope are limited to 10 instances of each type. If this number is exceeded, a `SensorFailedException` is raised when the sensor class's `Start` method is called. If this occurs, you can notify the user, providing this reason as a potential cause, and instruct him to uninstall another app that uses the same sensor type.

The sensor classes available in the Windows Phone 7.1 SDK reside in the Microsoft. Devices.Sensors namespace, and include the `Accelerometer`, `Compass`, `Gyroscope`, and `Motion` classes. To use any of the sensors add a reference to the Microsoft.Devices.Sensors assembly.

The following sections look at each sensor, beginning with the accelerometer.

Measuring Force with the Accelerometer

The accelerometer sensor measures the force applied to the device. The sensor detects the force of gravity along with any forces resulting from the movement of the phone. When the device is stationary, this force is equal to that of earth's gravity. Thus, when stationary, the accelerometer provides the position of the phone relative to the earth. When in the hands of a user, the accelerometer can be used to determine in which direction the user is moving the device, and when the phone is moved suddenly, while playing a game for example, the force may exceed that of gravity.

The accelerometer is normally used for determining whether the phone is tilted. But it can also be used to allow the device to become the controller, such as steering a car in a game.

The accelerometer measures force in gravitational units (g's), where 1 g equals (by definition) 9.80665 m/s^2 (32.1740 ft/s^2).

Ideally, when stationary, accelerator readings range from -1 to 1. Slight variations introduced by differences in the earth's gravity around the world may take the value outside this range.[1]

Theoretically, if you dropped your phone, in free fall the phone's accelerometer should read 0.

---

1. Gravity ranges at it is lowest in Mexico City (9.779 m/s^2) and highest in Oslo (Norway) and Helsinki (Finland) (9.819 m/s^2). Source: http://en.wikipedia.org/wiki/Gravity_of_Earth

The accelerometer measures force in three directions. The acceleration value is represented as a three-dimensional vector, representing the dimension components X, Y, and Z axes (see Figure 14.1). The three-dimensional vector represents the direction from the point (0, 0, 0). For example, when the device is placed on a level surface with its screen facing upward, the Z-axis registers a value of -1 g. You can get a feel for the acceleration effects of tilting and flipping the phone using the sample page for this chapter, discussed in a moment.

FIGURE 14.1   Effects on axis values when facing upward

Using the `Accelerometer` Class

`Accelerometer`, like the other sensor types, uses an event-based model for monitoring changes to sensor readings.

NOTE

Accelerometer contains a `ReadingChanged` event, which should not be used as it is a remnant of the first release of the Windows Phone OS and has been deprecated in the 7.1 release of the SDK.

The event to use is the base class `SensorBase` event: `CurrentValueChanged`. Subscribing to the event can be done as follows:

```
var accelerometer = new Accelerometer();
accelerometer.CurrentValueChanged += HandleSensorValueChanged;
accelerometer.Start();
```

When the `CurrentValueChanged` event is raised, the event handler receives a `SensorReadingEventArgs<AccelerometerReading>` object, as shown:

```
void HandleSensorValueChanged(
    object sender, SensorReadingEventArgs<AccelerometerReading> e)
{
    ProcessReading(e.SensorReading);
}
```

`SensorReadingEventArgs` provides a reference to the `Accelerometer` via its single `Sensor` property. `AccelerometerReading` contains an `Acceleration` property, which is a `Microsoft.Xna.Framework.Vector3`. Silverlight does not have a type representing a three-dimensional vector baked into the SDK, thus there is some crossover here, and `Vector3` is used throughout the phone sensor API.

Rather than relying on the XNA `Vector3` type in the sample code, a custom `ThreeDimensionalVector` class is used that has a markedly simpler implementation and uses properties rather than fields to access vector dimension values, which improves its compatibility with the Silverlight data binding infrastructure.

Simulating Acceleration with the Emulator

At times it may be difficult to test an app directly on a real device, such as when you are developing an app for a new version of the Windows Phone SDK that has not yet been rolled out to phone devices. Fortunately, the emulator has a tool for simulating the accelerometer, which can be accessed by clicking on the Additional Tools button of the emulator menu (see Figure 14.2).

FIGURE 14.2   Click the bottom arrow on the emulator menu to launch the Additional Tools window.

The Accelerometer tab of the Additional Tools window allows you to manipulate the position of the virtual device; moving the small red circle affects the reading taken by the `Accelerometer` class (see Figure 14.3).

> **NOTE**
>
> Within the emulator, the accelerometer is not subject to environmental effects, and readings taken within the emulator are perfectly stable.
>
> While the emulator provides the means to test code that relies on the accelerometer, it is important to test your code on an actual device, to see how it behaves in real-world conditions.

FIGURE 14.3   The emulator's accelerometer simulator

Smoothing Accelerometer Readings

The `Accelerometer`'s `CurrentValueChanged` event is raised, by default, 50 times a second and reflects the raw hardware sensor readings. Updating UI elements based on the raw values from the accelerometer can make elements appear jittery, much like the effects of Brownian motion under a microscope. You can allow your app to appear more stable by smoothing the readings received by the accelerometer through ignoring small changes in acceleration.

Some apps may benefit from some degree of smoothing, yet may need to react quickly to sudden fluctuations in reading values, such as games, which usually need input to be as direct as possible. This section looks at applying various data smoothing techniques to reduce jitter while also minimizing latency.

Much of the code and theory in this section is based on an article on the Windows Team Blog by Dave Edson http://bit.ly/cXJ2EC. It is recommended that you take a look at the article to better understand the theory behind the smoothing algorithms employed in the sample code. The advantage of the sample code provided here is that you also have a number of other features included that you can take and use immediately in your own apps.

The example code for this section is located in the Devices/Sensors directory of the WindowsPhone7Unleashed project in the downloadable sample code.

In the example, a custom class called EnhancedAccelerometer is used in place of the built-in Accelerometer. The EnhancedAccelerometer class uses an Accelerometer, allowing the application of smoothing algorithms based on previous readings. EnhancedAccelerometer has a number of features that the Accelerometer does not, such as calibration support, shake detection, and of course data smoothing.

Like the Accelerometer, the EnhancedAccelerometer is IDisposable. When the EnhancedAccelerometer is disposed, it in turn disposes the built-in Accelerometer. So too, EnhancedAccelerometer is started by calling its Start method, which instantiates an Accelerometer, subscribes to its CurrentValueChanged event, and starts the Accelerometer as shown:

```
public void Start()
{
    if (accelerometer == null)
    {
        lock (accelerometerLock)
        {
            if (accelerometer == null)
            {
                accelerometer = new Accelerometer();
                accelerometer.CurrentValueChanged
                                      += HandleSensorValueChanged;
                accelerometer.Start();
            }
        }
    }
}
```

EnhancedAccelerometer has a Reading property of type EnhancedAccelerometerReading, which not only supplies the raw value supplied by the Accelerometer, but also the following three smoothed reading values:

▶ AverageAcceleration

▶ LowPassFilteredAcceleration

▶ OptimallyFilteredAcceleration

Each value is the result of the application of a particular smoothing algorithm. The first, AverageAcceleration, has the highest latency (lag) of the three, while the other two attempt to combat the latency by responding to large reading variations immediately so that you get smoothing as well as responsiveness. These properties are examined in greater detail in the following sections.

AverageAcceleration

The AverageAcceleration property provides an average value of the last 25 readings. As stated, this approach has the highest latency; a large change in acceleration is less evident as the previous readings average it out. This approach may suit an app that requires input to be very steady—a spirit level app for example—but would not be suitable for a game that needs to respond quickly to user input.

LowPassFilteredAcceleration

The LowPassFilteredAcceleration property is calculated using the current reading and the previously calculated output. This approach has less latency than averaging, yet still does not respond to large changes in acceleration immediately.

The EnhancedAccelerometer.LowPassFilterCoefficient property allows you to adjust the level of smoothing applied to the output value. Each reading dimension value is calculated like so:

```
double newOutputValue = priorOutputValue
    + LowPassFilterCoefficient * (newInputValue - priorOutputValue);
```

By decreasing the LowPassFilterCoefficient, more smoothing is applied.

OptimallyFilteredAcceleration

The OptimallyFilteredAcceleration property uses a low pass filter in conjunction with a threshold value, which causes the output value to be set to the raw reading immediately if the reading exceeds the threshold value. This approach eliminates the latency of the pure low pass approach for sharp changes in acceleration.

If the difference between a new reading and the previous output is greater than the noise threshold, then the raw value is used, as shown in the following excerpt:

```
double ApplyLowPassFilterWithNoiseThreshold(
            double newInput, double previousOutput)
{
    double newOutputValue = newInput;
    if (Math.Abs(newInput - previousOutput) <= NoiseThreshold)
    {
        /* A simple low-pass filter. */
        newOutputValue = previousOutput
            + LowPassFilterCoefficient * (newInput - previousOutput);
    }
    return newOutputValue;
}
```

The noise threshold of the filter can be adjusted using the `EnhancedAccelerometer.` `NoiseThreshold` property. Its default value is 0.05, and by increasing the value you increase the level of acceleration needed to produce an immediate response.

Calibrating the Accelerometer

The built-in `Accelerometer` does not provide calibration support out of the box. Moreover, there is no systemwide calibration setting that your app can update. It is up to your app to have the user place the phone in a level position, calculate an offset value, and save the offset value in isolated storage.

The custom `EnhancedAccelerometer` provides support for calibrating a device placed on a level surface. It includes the following two calibration related methods:

▶ `bool CanCalibrate()`

▶ `bool Calibrate()`

`CanCalibrate` determines whether the device is stable enough for calibration to take place and is determined by measuring the variation of the last several readings and whether the current X, Y, and Z axes do not stray too far from the ideal level position. The level of allowed variation can be specified using the `MaximumStabilityTiltDeltaAngle` property, which is set to half a degree (0.5 * Math.PI / 180.0) by default.

The ideal level vector is (0,0,-1). The allowed variation from the ideal vector can be specified using the `EnhancedAccelerometer`'s `MaximumCalibrationTiltAngle` property, which is set to 20 degrees (20.0 * Math.PI / 180.0) by default.

Sample Accelerometer View

The sample for this section is located in the Sensors/Accelerometer directory of the WindowsPhone7Unleashed.Examples project in the downloadable sample code. It uses the `EnhancedAccelerometer` via a custom `IAccelerometer` interface. This enables a mock accelerometer to be supplanted for testing purposes.

The `AccelerometerView` page presents four sliders for viewing the various readings from the `EnhancedAccelerometer`. Its viewmodel, the `AccelerometerViewModel` class, contains the following three commands:

▶ `StartCommand`

▶ `StopCommand`

▶ `CalibrateCommand`

`StartCommand` subscribes to the `IAccelerometer.ReadingChanged` event and calls the `IAccelerometer`'s `Start` method, while `StopCommand` unsubscribes from the event and calls `IAccelerometer`'s `Stop` method (see Listing 14.1).

`CalibrateCommand` uses the `IAccelerometer.CanCalibrate` method to determine whether the command can execute, which in turn sets the enabled state of the view's `AppBar` button.

14

LISTING 14.1   AccelerometerViewModel Constructor

```csharp
public AccelerometerViewModel(IAccelerometer accelerometer) : base("accelerometer")
{
    startCommand = new DelegateCommand(
        obj =>
            {
                accelerometer.ReadingChanged -= HandleReadingChanged;
                accelerometer.ReadingChanged += HandleReadingChanged;
                accelerometer.Start();
            });

    stopCommand = new DelegateCommand(
        obj =>
            {

                accelerometer.ReadingChanged -= HandleReadingChanged;
                accelerometer.Stop();
            });

    calibrateCommand = new DelegateCommand(
        obj => MessageService.ShowMessage(accelerometer.Calibrate()
                                ? "Successfully calibrated."
                                : "Unable to calibrate."),
        obj => accelerometer.CanCalibrate());
}
```

When a new reading is received, the viewmodel's HandleReadingChanged handler sets the viewmodel's Reading property to the IAccelerometer's EnhancedAccelerometerReading, as shown:

```csharp
void HandleReadingChanged(object sender, EventArgs e)
{
    IAccelerometer accelerometer = (IAccelerometer)sender;
    Reading = accelerometer.Reading;
    UpdateCommands();
}
```

The UpdateCommands method calls calibrateCommand.RaiseCanExecuteChanged(), which updates the enabled state of an AppBar button.

The view executes the viewmodel's Start command within the OnNavigatedTo method and the Stop command in the OnNavigatedFrom method, thus ensuring that the native Accelerometer is disposed when another page is shown or the app is deactivated (see Listing 14.2).

LISTING 14.2 AccelerometerView Class

```
public partial class AccelerometerView : PhoneApplicationPage
{
    public AccelerometerView()
    {
        InitializeComponent();

        DataContext = new AccelerometerViewModel(
            new EnhancedAccelerometer(new IsolatedStorageUtility()));
    }

    AccelerometerViewModel ViewModel
    {
        get
        {
            return (AccelerometerViewModel)DataContext;
        }
    }

    protected override void OnNavigatedTo(NavigationEventArgs e)
    {
        base.OnNavigatedTo(e);
        ViewModel.StartCommand.Execute(null);
    }

    protected override void OnNavigatedFrom(NavigationEventArgs e)
    {
        base.OnNavigatedFrom(e);
        ViewModel.StopCommand.Execute(null);
    }
}
```

The view's XAML contains a custom AppBar with an AppBarIconButton that is bound to the viewmodel's CalibrateCommand, as shown:

```
<u:AppBar>
    <u:AppBarIconButton
            Command="{Binding CalibrateCommand}"
            Text="Calibrate"
            IconUri="/Sensors/Accelerometer/Icons/AppbarCalibrate.png" />
</u:AppBar>
```

The view's main content panel contains several grids, each displaying a value from the EnhancedAccelerometerReading:

```
<Grid>
    <TextBlock Text="raw"
               Style="{StaticResource PhoneTextGroupHeaderStyle}" />
    <Slider Value="{Binding Reading.RawAcceleration.X,
            Converter={StaticResource SquashConverter}}"
            Style="{StaticResource SliderStyle}" Margin="0" />
    <Slider Value="{Binding Reading.RawAcceleration.Y,
            Converter={StaticResource SquashConverter}}"
            Style="{StaticResource SliderStyle}" Margin="0,30,0,0" />
    <Slider Value="{Binding Reading.RawAcceleration.Z,
            Converter={StaticResource SquashConverter}}"
            Style="{StaticResource SliderStyle}" Margin="0,60,0,0" />
    <TextBlock Text="{Binding Reading.RawAcceleration}"
               Margin="16,90,0,0" />
</Grid>
```

The SquashConverter is a custom IValueConverter that ensures the Slider always has a positive value that is within the range of 0 and 2, thus preventing binding failures.

The AccelerometerView page allows you to get a feel for the behavior of the accelerometer and to experiment with the various smoothing functions provided by the custom EnhancedAccelerometer (see Figure 14.4).

By placing your phone device face up on a flat surface, the calibrate button becomes enabled.

FIGURE 14.4   AccelerometerView page

Shake Detection

The phone SDK does not come with any built-in support for detecting when the device is being shaken. This section extends the custom EnhancedAccelerometer to provide shake detection.

The EnhancedAccelerometer.IsShake method returns true if the difference between the current and previous acceleration readings exceeds a threshold value for two or more dimensional components, in which case, the movement is deemed a shake. Thanks to Mark Monster, http://bit.ly/9GMDJX, on which this code is based. See the following excerpt:

```
static bool IsShake(Vector3 currentAcceleration,
                Vector3 previousAcceleration, double threshold)
{
    double deltaX = Math.Abs(previousAcceleration.X - currentAcceleration.X);
    double deltaY = Math.Abs(previousAcceleration.Y - currentAcceleration.Y);
    double deltaZ = Math.Abs(previousAcceleration.Z - currentAcceleration.Z);

    return deltaX > threshold && deltaY > threshold
            || deltaX > threshold && deltaZ > threshold
            || deltaY > threshold && deltaZ > threshold;
}
```

A Shake event has been added to the IAccelerometer interface. When a new reading is received from the Accelerometer within the EnhancedAccelerometer, the DetectShake method is called (see Listing 14.3). If a shake is detected, then the Shake event is raised.

Two threshold properties control sensitivity during shake detection. Both threshold properties are of type double, representing the threshold in radians. The first, ShakeThreshold, is used to determine when a shake has begun; the second, ShakeEndThreshold, defines the maximum value of the acceleration delta, used for detecting when the device is no longer being shaken.

LISTING 14.3   EnhancedAccelerometer.DetectShake Method

```
void DetectShake(Vector3 acceleration)
{
    EventHandler tempEvent = Shake;

    if (tempEvent == null || !previousAcceleration.HasValue)
    {
        return;
    }

    Vector3 previousValue = previousAcceleration.Value;
    bool shakeDetected = IsShake(acceleration, previousValue, shakeThreshold);
```

LISTING 14.3   Continued

```
    if (shakeDetected && !shaking && shakeCount > 0)
    {
        shaking = true;
        shakeCount = 0;
        OnShake(EventArgs.Empty);
    }
    else if (shakeDetected)
    {
        shakeCount++;
    }
    else if (!IsShake(acceleration, previousValue, shakeEndThreshold))
    {
        shakeCount = 0;
        shaking = false;
    }
}
```

The `AccelerometerViewModel` subscribes to the `IAccelerometer.Shake` event. When the event is raised, the viewmodel's `ShakeCount` property is incremented. `ShakeCount` is displayed using a `TextBlock`, as shown:

```
<TextBlock Text="{Binding ShakeCount, StringFormat='\{0\} shakes'}"
                Style="{StaticResource LabelTextStyle}"
                Foreground="{StaticResource PhoneAccentBrush}"
                HorizontalAlignment="Right" />
```

All Windows Phone devices are required to have an accelerometer, and the accelerometer API has been present since the first release of the phone SDK. It is, therefore, a staple piece of Windows Phone tech that offers a reliable way of enriching your app with movement sensing.

Measuring Direction with the Compass

The compass, also known as the magnetometer, is a Windows Phone required sensor that allows your app to determine which direction the phone is pointing, in particular, the offset from magnetic or geographic north.

The compass is useful in applications that use geographic location; for example, you may want to provide a compass arrow as a supplement for a mapping app. The compass also allows you to monitor raw magnetometer readings and to detect changes to magnetic forces around the device.

The sample code for this section creates a page that displays a compass arrow and the various compass readings, and you see how to allow the user to calibrate the compass.

The sample code for this section resides in the /Sensors/Compass/ directory of the WindowsPhone7Unleashed.Examples project in the downloadable sample code.

NOTE

The compass sensor is rather subject to interference. Bringing the device into close proximity of large metallic objects or other electronic devices, for example, a laptop, throws off the reading.

Using the Compass Sensor

The compass sensor is a required component of Windows Phone devices. In the first release of the Windows Phone OS (7.0), however, no API was provided for the compass, and some devices lacked the native drivers necessary to use the compass even when running the Windows Phone 7.5 OS (mango). If you are maintaining an app for a pre-mango device it is therefore important to verify that the compass is supported before attempting to use it. For this, the static `Compass.IsSupported` property is used, as demonstrated in the `CompassViewModel` class (see Listing 14.4). The `Start` method of the `CompassViewModel` oversees the creation of the `Compass` instance.

The default value of the compass `TimeBetweenUpdates` property is 25 milliseconds, which on my test device was the minimum allowed value.

As with all sensor types, the `CurrentValueChanged` event is used to receive periodic updates from the sensor.

The `Calibrate` event allows your app to respond to when the phone is calibrating the sensor. Calibration is discussed further later in this section.

NOTE

Calibration is an activity triggered by the OS; there is no `PerformCalibration` method that you can call to cause the device to begin calibration.

LISTING 14.4   `CompassViewModel.Start` Method (excerpt 1)

```
public void Start()
{
    if (!Compass.IsSupported)
    {
        MessageService.ShowMessage("Compass is not supported on this device.");
        return;
    }

    compass = new Compass();
    compass.TimeBetweenUpdates = TimeSpan.FromMilliseconds(updateIntervalMs);
    UpdateIntervalMs = (int)compass.TimeBetweenUpdates.TotalMilliseconds;
```

14

LISTING 14.4   Continued

```
    compass.CurrentValueChanged += HandleCompassCurrentValueChanged;
    compass.Calibrate += HandleCompassCalibrate;
    compass.Start();
...
}
```

When the CurrentValueChanged event is raised, the event handler receives a
SensorReadingEventArgs<CompassReading> object. CompassReading contains the five
properties listed in Table 14.1.

TABLE 14.1   CompassReading Properties

Property Name	Description
HeadingAccuracy	A double value that indicates the level of accuracy of the reading in degrees.
MagneticHeading	A double value between 0 and 359 that is the difference between the earth's magnetic north and the direction of the phone device. This value is in degrees, and measured clockwise from the earth's magnetic north.
MagnetometerReading	The raw sensor readings provided as an XNA Vector3 struct.
Timestamp	A DateTimeOffset indicating the time when the sensor reading was taken.
TrueHeading	Similar to MagneticHeading, this property is a double value between 0 and 359 that indicates in degrees the direction of the devices, measured clockwise from the earth's geographic north.

The handler for the Compass object's CurrentValueChanged event in the CompassViewModel
extracts the values from the event arguments and assigns them to various viewmodel
properties of the same name. XNA's Vector3 data type is not amenable to data binding
because it exposes its X, Y, and Z dimensions as public fields. Rather than use Vector3, a
custom ThreeDimensionalVector object is created using the Vector3 values, as shown in the
following excerpt:

```
void HandleCompassCurrentValueChanged(
        object sender, SensorReadingEventArgs<CompassReading> e)
{
    MagneticHeading = e.SensorReading.MagneticHeading;
    TrueHeading = e.SensorReading.TrueHeading;
    HeadingAccuracy = e.SensorReading.HeadingAccuracy;
    Vector3 reading = e.SensorReading.MagnetometerReading;
    MagnetometerReading = new ThreeDimensionalVector(reading.X,
                                                     reading.Y,
                                                     reading.Z);
```

```
SmoothedReading
    = readingSmoother.ProcessReading(e.SensorReading.MagneticHeading);
}
```

The raw sensor readings for `MagneticHeading` and `TrueHeading` are subject to slight variations in magnetic forces and, like the accelerometer, can make elements look unsteady when bound directly to the UI. A custom class, called `ReadingSmoother`, is used to dampen the stream of sensor reading values. I have abstracted the data smoothing code of the `EnhancedAccelerometer`, which was presented in the "Smoothing Accelerometer Readings" section of this chapter, into a new class called `ReadingSmoother`. The `ReadingSmoother` class uses the strategy pattern to allow you to change its filtering behavior via an `IFilterStrategy` interface provided to its constructor, as shown:

```
public ReadingSmoother(
            IFilterStrategy filterStrategy = null, int samplesCount = 25)
{
...
}
```

Listing 14.5 shows the `ReadingSmoother.ProcessReading` method. `ReadingSmoother` tracks the previous 25 values provided to it and uses the `IFilterStrategy` to smooth the data.

LISTING 14.5   ReadingSmoother.ProcessReading Method

```
public double ProcessReading(double rawValue)
{
    double result = rawValue;

    if (!initialized)
    {
        lock (initilizedLock)
        {
            if (!initialized)
            {
                /* Initialize buffer with first value. */
                sampleSum = rawValue * samplesCount;
                averageValue = rawValue;

                for (int i = 0; i < samplesCount; i++)
                {
                    sampleBuffer[i] = averageValue;
                }

                initialized = true;
            }
        }
    }
```

LISTING 14.5   Continued

```
double latestValue;
if (filterStrategy != null)
{
    latestValue = result = filterStrategy.ApplyFilter(rawValue, result);
}
else
{
    latestValue = rawValue;
}

/* Increment circular buffer insertion index. */
if (++sampleIndex >= samplesCount)
{
    /* If at max length then wrap samples back
        * to the beginning position in the list. */
    sampleIndex = 0;
}

/* Add new and remove old at sampleIndex. */
sampleSum += latestValue;
sampleSum -= sampleBuffer[sampleIndex];
sampleBuffer[sampleIndex] = latestValue;

averageValue = sampleSum / samplesCount;

/* Stability check */
double deltaAcceleration = averageValue - latestValue;

if (Math.Abs(deltaAcceleration) > StabilityDelta)
{
    /* Unstable */
    deviceStableCount = 0;
}
else
{
    if (deviceStableCount < samplesCount)
    {
        ++deviceStableCount;
    }
}

if (filterStrategy == null)
{
```

LISTING 14.5   Continued

```
        result = averageValue;
    }

    return result;
}
```

The ReadingSmoother instance is defined as a field of the viewmodel, like so:

```
readonly ReadingSmoother readingSmoother
            = new ReadingSmoother(new LowPassFilterStrategy());
```

LowPassFilterStrategy removes noise from the raw sensor values, while allowing fast changes of sufficient amplitude to be detected. See the LowPassFilterStrategy source in the downloadable sample code for more detail.

The content panel of the CompassView page displays the various viewmodel properties, including the current magnetic heading and the accuracy of the compass. In addition, the viewmodel's SmoothedReading is displayed using an arrow. The arrow is defined as a Silverlight Path. An enclosing Canvas uses a RotateTransform, which is bound to the SmoothedReading property, to rotate to the compass heading value. See the following excerpt:

```
<Canvas Width="280" Height="100">
    <Path Width="275" Height="95"
            Canvas.Left="0" Canvas.Top="0" Stretch="Fill"
            Fill="{StaticResource PhoneAccentBrush}"
            Data="** Arrow points omitted **">
        <Path.RenderTransform>
            <RotateTransform Angle="-90"
                             CenterX="140" CenterY="48" />
        </Path.RenderTransform>
    </Path>
    <Canvas.RenderTransform>
        <RotateTransform Angle="{Binding SmoothedReading,
                         Converter={StaticResource NegateConverter}}"
                         CenterX="140" CenterY="48" />
    </Canvas.RenderTransform>
</Canvas>
```

A custom IValueConverter, called NegateConverter, is used to negate the value so that the arrow's heading corresponds to north, rather than the offset value. The NegateConverter. Convert method is shown in the following excerpt:

```
public object Convert(
    object value, Type targetType, object parameter, CultureInfo culture)
{
```

14

```
    double degrees = (double)value;
    return -degrees;
}
```

Figure 14.5 shows the `CompassView` page with the heading arrow pointing to magnetic north. As the phone is rotated, the arrow maintains its heading.

FIGURE 14.5   `CompassView` page with arrow pointing to magnetic north

The *compass orientation* value, shown in Figure 14.5, is determined by the accelerometer. This value is discussed in the following section.

Compass Orientation

The compass API uses a single axis to calculate the heading, depending on the orientation of the device. The device may be flat with its screen facing up, or it may be in an upright portrait position.

The `Compass` class does not provide the means to determine which orientation it is using; rather, you use an `Accelerometer` to tell you.

The viewmodel's `Start` method also includes the initialization of an `Accelerometer` (see Listing 14.6).

LISTING 14.6   `CompassViewModel.Start` Method (excerpt 2)

```
public void Start()
{
    ...
    accelerometer = new Accelerometer();
    accelerometer.CurrentValueChanged += HandleAccelerometerCurrentValueChanged;
    accelerometer.Start();
}
```

The orientation of the compass is represented using a custom enum called `CompassOrientation`. It has two values: Flat and Portrait. Listing 14.7 shows how the `Accelerometer`'s `CurrentValueChanged` event handler calculates the orientation of the device using the Y and Z dimensional components of the reading vector.

LISTING 14.7   `HandleAccelerometerCurrentValueChanged` Method

```
void HandleAccelerometerCurrentValueChanged(
        object sender, SensorReadingEventArgs<AccelerometerReading> e)
{
    Vector3 accelerationVector = e.SensorReading.Acceleration;

    bool usingNegativeZAxis = false;

    /* Determine the orientation of the device. */
    if (Math.Abs(accelerationVector.Z) < Math.Cos(Math.PI / 4)
        && accelerationVector.Y < Math.Sin(7 * Math.PI / 4))
    {
        usingNegativeZAxis = true;
    }

    CompassOrientation = usingNegativeZAxis
                            ? CompassOrientation.Portrait
                            : CompassOrientation.Flat;
}
```

Calibrating the Compass

Over time, the compass sensor can become inaccurate, and this is exacerbated if it is exposed to magnetic fields. Calibration of the device is performed by the user, by moving the phone repeatedly in a figure eight pattern (see Figure 14.6). The `Compass.Calibrate` event is raised whenever the OS detects that the heading accuracy is worse than 20 degrees, at which point it is your app's responsibility to display a dialog to the user with instructions on how to perform the calibration motion.

The `CompassView` page includes a `StackPanel` with the calibration UI, consisting of an image with instructions for performing the figure eight motion (see Listing 14.8).

As the user performs the calibration motion, the accuracy level is displayed in a `TextBlock` that is bound to the viewmodel's `HeadingAccuracy` property. Once the user is satisfied that she has improved the accuracy of the sensor sufficiently, she taps a done button. The button is bound to the viewmodel's `ToggleCalibrationCommand`.

LISTING 14.8   Calibration UI XAML (excerpt from `CompassView.xaml`)

```
<StackPanel x:Name="stackPanel_Calibration" Visibility="Collapsed"
            Background="{StaticResource PhoneBackgroundBrush}">
    <Image Source="/Sensors/Compass/Images/CalibrateCompass.png"
           HorizontalAlignment="Center"/>
    <TextBlock TextWrapping="Wrap" TextAlignment="Center">
        The compass on your device needs to be calibrated.
        Hold the device in front of you and sweep it through
        a figure eight pattern as shown, until the calibration is complete.
    </TextBlock>
    <StackPanel Orientation="Horizontal" Margin="0,10"
                HorizontalAlignment="Center">
        <TextBlock Text="accuracy is "
                   Style="{StaticResource LabelTextStyle}" />
        <TextBlock Text="{Binding HeadingAccuracy, StringFormat=\{0\}°}"
                   Style="{StaticResource PhoneTextAccentStyle}"
                   FontSize="{StaticResource PhoneFontSizeLarge}"/>
    </StackPanel>
    <Button Content="done"
            Command="{Binding ToggleCalibrationCommand}"
            HorizontalAlignment="Center" />
</StackPanel>
```

The `Calibrate` handler in the `CompassViewModel` sets its `VisualState` property to a custom enum value Calibrating, as shown:

```
void HandleCompassCalibrate(object sender, CalibrationEventArgs e)
{
    VisualState = VisualStateValue.Calibrating;
}
```

The visual state of the page is controlled using a custom `VisualStateUtility.VisualState` attached property, presented earlier in this chapter. The attached property is bound to the `VisualState` property of viewmodel, as shown:

```
<phone:PhoneApplicationPage
    ...
    u:VisualStateUtility.VisualState="{Binding VisualState}">
    ...
</phone:PhoneApplicationPage>
```

The Calibrating visual state affects the `Visibility` property of the calibration `StackPanel`, as shown:

```xml
<VisualState x:Name="Calibrating">
    <Storyboard>
        <ObjectAnimationUsingKeyFrames Duration="0"
                    Storyboard.TargetProperty="Visibility"
                    Storyboard.TargetName="stackPanel_Calibration">
            <DiscreteObjectKeyFrame KeyTime="0">
                <DiscreteObjectKeyFrame.Value>
                    <Visibility>Visible</Visibility>
                </DiscreteObjectKeyFrame.Value>
            </DiscreteObjectKeyFrame>
        </ObjectAnimationUsingKeyFrames>
    </Storyboard>
</VisualState>
```

The `ToggleCalibrationCommand` is initialized in the viewmodel constructor. When executed it changes the `VisualState` from Calibrating to NotCalibrating, and vice versa. This hides the calibration UI when the user taps the done button.

```csharp
public CompassViewModel() : base("compass")
{
    toggleCalibrationCommand
                    = new DelegateCommand(obj => ToggleCalibration());
}

void ToggleCalibration()
{
    VisualState = VisualState == VisualStateValue.Calibrating
                    ? VisualStateValue.NotCalibrating
                    : VisualStateValue.Calibrating;
}
```

Figure 14.6 shows the calibration UI after having performed the calibration, bringing the accuracy to five degrees.

The compass sensor enables you to easily add heading information to your app, and to build specialized apps that can detect changes in magnetic forces around the device.

FIGURE 14.6   `CompassView` page showing calibration instructions

Sensing Rotation with the Gyroscope

The gyroscope is an optional hardware sensor that can sense rotation. While the accelerometer is able to gauge the orientation of the phone when it is stationary, it is not able to sense rotation. If the device is in free fall, the accelerometer reading is theoretically zero. In contrast, the gyroscope measures the rate of rotation around a particular axis, so that while the device continues to be in rotation the reading is non-zero. The disadvantage, however, is that because the gyroscope measures rotational velocity, and not position, it is subject to drift.

The sample code for this section creates a page that displays raw readings from the gyroscope, as well as providing a visual representation of the angular rotation of the device.

The sample code for this section is located in the /Sensors/Gyroscope/ directory of the WindowsPhone7Unleashed.Examples project in the downloadable sample code.

Using the Gyroscope Sensor

The gyroscope sensor is not a required component of Windows Phone devices. It is therefore important to verify that it is supported before attempting to use it. For this, the static `Gyroscope.IsSupported` property is used, as demonstrated in the `GyroscopeViewModel` class (see Listing 14.9). The `Start` method of the `GyroscopeViewModel` oversees the creation of the `Gyroscope` instance.

The default value of the `Gyroscope`'s `TimeBetweenUpdates` property is 20 milliseconds, which on my test device was the minimum allowed value.

As with all sensor types, the `CurrentValueChanged` event is used to receive periodic updates from the sensor.

LISTING 14.9   `GyroscopeViewModel.Start` Method

```
public void Start()
{
    if (!Gyroscope.IsSupported)
    {
        MessageService.ShowMessage(
            "Gyroscope is not supported on this device.");
        return;
    }

    gyroscope = new Gyroscope();
    gyroscope.TimeBetweenUpdates = TimeSpan.FromMilliseconds(20);
    gyroscope.CurrentValueChanged += HandleGyroscopeCurrentValueChanged;
    gyroscope.Start();
}
```

When the `CurrentValueChanged` event is raised, the event handler receives a `SensorReadingEventArgs<GyroscopeReading>` object. `GyroscopeReading` contains two properties: a `Timestamp` property of type `DateTimeOffset`, which indicates when the sensor reading was taken, and a `RotationRate` property of type `Vector3`, which retrieves the rotational velocity around each axis of the device (X, Y, and Z) in radians per second.

The handler for the compass's `CurrentValueChanged` event in the `GyroscopeViewModel` converts the `RotationRate` property of the event arguments, which is of type `Vector3`, to a custom `ThreeDimensionalVector` instance and assigns it to the viewmodel's `RotationRate` property (see Listing 14.10).

The viewmodel tracks the angular rotation of the device by accumulating the value of each reading into a `ThreeDimensionalVector` called `cumulativeRotationRadians`. The amount of rotation since the last `CurrentValueChanged` event is calculated by multiplying the rotation rate by the time since the last event was raised. Put simply: (radians/second) * secondsSinceLastReading = radiansSinceLastReading.

LISTING 14.10   `HandleGyroscopeCurrentValueChanged` Method

```
void HandleGyroscopeCurrentValueChanged(
    object sender, SensorReadingEventArgs<GyroscopeReading> e)
{
    GyroscopeReading reading = e.SensorReading;
    Vector3 rate = reading.RotationRate;
    RotationRate = new ThreeDimensionalVector(rate.X, rate.Y, rate.Z);
```

LISTING 14.10   Continued

```
    if (lastUpdateTime.Equals(DateTimeOffset.MinValue))
    {
        lastUpdateTime = e.SensorReading.Timestamp;
        cumulativeRotationRadians = rotationRate;
        return;
    }

    TimeSpan timeSinceLastUpdate = e.SensorReading.Timestamp - lastUpdateTime;

    cumulativeRotationRadians
                    += rotationRate * (timeSinceLastUpdate.TotalSeconds);
    CumulativeRotation = new RotationAngles(
        MathHelper.ToDegrees((float)cumulativeRotationRadians.X),
        MathHelper.ToDegrees((float)cumulativeRotationRadians.Y),
        MathHelper.ToDegrees((float)cumulativeRotationRadians.Z));

    lastUpdateTime = e.SensorReading.Timestamp;
}
```

The viewmodel's `CumulativeRotation` property is of type `RotationAngle`, a simple custom class with three readonly properties: X, Y, and Z, all of which are of type `double`.

As with most of the examples in this chapter, the page calls the viewmodel's `Start` method within its `OnNavigatedTo` method and calls the `Stop` method within its `OnNavigatedFrom` method.

The `Stop` method of the viewmodel disposes the `Gyroscope` instance, as shown:

```
public void Stop()
{
    if (gyroscope == null)
    {
        return;
    }

    gyroscope.Stop();
    gyroscope.CurrentValueChanged -= HandleGyroscopeCurrentValueChanged;
    gyroscope.Dispose();
    gyroscope = null;
}
```

The `GyroscopeView` page contains `TextBlock` elements that display both the raw reading values in radians/second and the accumulated angular rotation values in degrees.

The cumulative rotation values serve to rotate colored rectangles. As the device is rotated, a `RotateTransform` is applied to each rectangle, as shown:

```
<Canvas Width="400" Height="400" Margin="0,50,0,0">
    <Ellipse Width="400" Height="400" StrokeThickness="2"
                Stroke="{StaticResource PhoneSubtleBrush}" />
    <Rectangle Canvas.Left="195" Canvas.Top="0"
                Width="10" Height="200" Fill="Honeydew">
        <Rectangle.RenderTransform>
            <RotateTransform Angle="{Binding CumulativeRotation.X}"
                        CenterX="5" CenterY="200" />
        </Rectangle.RenderTransform>
    </Rectangle>
    <Rectangle Canvas.Left="195" Canvas.Top="0"
                Width="10" Height="200" Fill="Red">
        <Rectangle.RenderTransform>
            <RotateTransform Angle="{Binding CumulativeRotation.Y}"
                        CenterX="5" CenterY="200" />
        </Rectangle.RenderTransform>
    </Rectangle>
    <Rectangle Canvas.Left="195" Canvas.Top="0"
                Width="10" Height="200" Fill="Orange">
        <Rectangle.RenderTransform>
            <RotateTransform Angle="{Binding CumulativeRotation.Z}"
                        CenterX="5" CenterY="200" />
        </Rectangle.RenderTransform>
    </Rectangle>
</Canvas>
```

Figure 14.7 shows the `GyroscopeView` page with the rotation of the device across three dimensions indicated by the three colored lines.

You may notice, while running the sample, that the cumulative rotation drifts over time. This drift is indicative of the main disadvantage of the gyroscope; the gyroscope measures changes in angular rotation, and not the absolute angular rotation of the device. This is where the `Accelerometer` has an advantage, as it can provide the same rotational information without drift. In the case of the accelerometer, however, the magnitude of the signal is biased by gravity. This is not the case with the gyroscope.

The next section explores the `Motion` class, which promises to overcome the disadvantages of the individual sensors by unifying them into a single software virtual sensor.

14

FIGURE 14.7   GyroscopeView page

Improving Sensor Accuracy with the Motion Sensor

The Motion class provides access to a virtual sensor. There is no dedicated motion sensor per se, rather the motion API combines the readings of the accelerometer, compass, and gyroscope to provide an enhanced API that overcomes the shortcomings of the individual sensors. The motion sensor provides the greatest accuracy of all the sensors, eliminating possible sensor inaccuracy issues that occur when relying on a single hardware sensor. For this reason, it is recommended that the motion sensor is used when available.

As mentioned in the previous section, the gyroscope is subject to drift. The motion API alleviates the drifting of the gyroscope by combing its readings with the compass and accelerometer readings.

Accelerometer readings include the force of gravity applied to the device as well as the force resulting from the motion of the device. The motion API separates the gravity vector from the device acceleration and provides you with the device's attitude, consisting of yaw, pitch, and roll.

The Motion API can use two different sensor modes: normal and enhanced. Normal mode uses the compass and the accelerometer sensor and is less accurate than enhanced mode, which uses the compass, the accelerometer, and the gyroscope (see Table 14.2).

TABLE 14.2   Motion Sensor Availability

Motion	Compass	Gyroscope	Accelerometer
✓ (enhanced mode)	✓	✓	✓
✓ (normal mode)	✓	X	✓
X	X	✓	✓
X	X	X	✓

If your app requires the accuracy of enhanced mode, you should verify that the device supports the gyroscope sensor. If the gyroscope is supported then enhanced mode is used automatically.

> **NOTE**
>
> Determining whether a device supports all the sensors required by your app happens before the app is deployed to the device. When a user views an app on Windows Phone Marketplace, a warning is issued if the user's device does not support a sensor that is used by the app.
>
> The Marketplace uses the compass sensor to determine whether the motion API is supported on a device. If a user views an app that uses the motion API and her device lacks a compass, a warning is displayed stating that the application requires a compass sensor.

Using the Motion Sensor

The sample code for this section follows the same pattern as the code for the gyroscope. The viewmodel's Start method first tests whether the motion sensor is supported, and then creates a new Motion instance, subscribes to its CurrentValueChangedEvent, and calls its Start method. See the following excerpt:

```
public void Start()
{
    if (!Motion.IsSupported)
    {
        MessageService.ShowMessage(
            "Motion is not supported on this device.");
        return;
    }

    motion = new Motion();
    double interval = motion.TimeBetweenUpdates.TotalMilliseconds;
    motion.CurrentValueChanged += HandleMotionCurrentValueChanged;
    motion.Start();
}
```

The Motion sensor's TimeBetweenUpdates property is, by default, set to 17 milliseconds.

14

When the `CurrentValueChanged` event is raised, a `SensorReadingEventArgs<MotionReading>` object is passed to your event handler. `MotionReading` reading contains the following properties:

- ▶ **Attitude (of type `AttitudeReading`)**—Gets the attitude (yaw, pitch, and roll) of the device, in radians

- ▶ **DeviceAcceleration (of type `Vector3`)**—Gets the linear acceleration of the device, in gravitational units

- ▶ **DeviceRotationRate (of type `Vector3`)**—Gets the rotational velocity of the device, in radians per second

- ▶ **Gravity (of type `Vector3`)**—Gets the gravity vector associated with the `Microsoft.Devices.Sensors.MotionReading`

- ▶ **Timestamp (of type `DateTimeOffset`)**—Gets the time at which the reading was calculated

The `Attitude` reading is useful in allowing you to determine the position of the device, which is broken down into pitch, roll, and yaw. Table 14.3 describes each of the `AttitudeReading` properties.

TABLE 14.3   `AttitudeReading` Struct Properties

Property Name	Description
Pitch	A float value indicating the vertical relationship in radians between the Y axis of the device and the horizon. See Figure 14.8 for a depiction of the X, Y, and Z dimensional components.
Roll	A float value indicating the vertical relationship in radians between the X axis of the device and the horizon.
Yaw	A float value indicating the direction of the device in radians.
Quaternion	An alternative representation of the attitude reading. The `Quaternion` data type is an XNA struct that defines a four-dimensional vector (x, y, z, w), which is used to represent the rotation of an object about the (x, y, z) vector by the angle theta, where w = cos(theta/2).
RotationMatrix	An alternative representation of the attitude reading using an XNA Matrix struct.
Timestamp	A `DateTimeOffset` value indicating when the reading was calculated.

The `CurrentValueChanged` handler, within the viewmodel, assigns the reading to various properties within the viewmodel. The reading's `DeviceAcceleration` and `DeviceRotationRate` `Vector3` properties are converted to a `ThreeDimensionalVector` using an extension method. See the following excerpt:

```
void HandleMotionCurrentValueChanged(
    object sender, SensorReadingEventArgs<MotionReading> e)
{
    MotionReading reading = e.SensorReading;
```

```
AttitudeReading = reading.Attitude;
DeviceAcceleration
            = reading.DeviceAcceleration.ToThreeDimensionalVector();
DeviceRotationRate
            = reading.DeviceRotationRate.ToThreeDimensionalVector();
Gravity = reading.Gravity.ToThreeDimensionalVector();
AttitudeReading attitude = reading.Attitude;
Attitude = new ThreeDimensionalVector(
                attitude.Pitch, attitude.Roll, attitude.Yaw);
}
```

Within the view the reading vector values are represented in the same manner as for the gyroscope; lines are rotated using a `RotateTransform` that is bound to the reading value. In this case, however, values are supplied in radians and must be converted to degrees. For this, a custom `IValueConverter` called `RadiansToDegreesConverter` is used (see Listing 14.11).

LISTING 14.11   RadiansToDegreesConverter Class

```
public class RadiansToDegreesConverter : IValueConverter
{
    public object Convert(
        object value, Type targetType, object parameter, CultureInfo culture)
    {
        float f = System.Convert.ToSingle(value);
        float result = MathHelper.ToDegrees(f);
        return result;
    }

    public object ConvertBack(
        object value, Type targetType, object parameter, CultureInfo culture)
    {
        float f = (float)value;
        float result = MathHelper.ToRadians(f);
        return result;
    }
}
```

A `ControlTemplate` is used to display the four `ThreeDimensionalVector` objects on the page. A `Rectangle` represents each vector component, and the `RadiansToDegreesConverter`, defined as page level resource, converts the source value to degrees for the `RotateTransform`. See the following excerpt:

```
<Rectangle Canvas.Left="195" Canvas.Top="0"
        Width="10" Height="200" Fill="Honeydew">
    <Rectangle.RenderTransform>
        <RotateTransform Angle="{Binding X,
```

```
            Converter={StaticResource RadiansToDegressConverter}}"
            CenterX="5" CenterY="200" />
    </Rectangle.RenderTransform>
</Rectangle>
```

Figure 14.8 shows the various readings displayed on the `MotionView` page. The attitude meter shows the pitch, roll, and yaw as the vector components X, Y, and Z, respectively. The other three reading types—acceleration, rotation rate, and gravity—are also displayed.

FIGURE 14.8   MotionView page

The `Motion` class also includes a `Calibrate` event that indicates when the compass needs calibrating. This event provides your app with the opportunity to display the calibration dialog, as discussed previously in the "Measuring Direction with the Compass" section of this chapter.

Summary

This chapter examined each Windows Phone sensor in detail, beginning with the accelerometer. You saw how to process accelerometer readings, and how to simulate acceleration within the Windows Phone emulator. The chapter explored how to apply data smoothing to accelerometer readings to decrease jittering of UI elements without sacrificing responsiveness. You also learned how to calibrate the accelerometer, and how to perform shake detection using the accelerometer.

The chapter then looked at the compass sensor and explained how to use the compass's magnetic heading to build a custom compass app that displays the heading using an arrow. The chapter also discussed compass calibration.

The chapter then moved to the gyroscope sensor, and you saw how to build a UI to display the angular rotation of the phone.

Finally, the chapter examined the motion sensor, which is a virtual sensor that harnesses the hardware sensors to improve accuracy and provide extended orientation and motion information.

CHAPTER 15

Geographic Location

Geographic location has become one of the principal uses of smartphones, and for good reason. Smartphones are portable, they go with us nearly everywhere, and offer the kind of processing power required to make displaying and interacting with complex maps possible.

The Windows Phone SDK provides an API that makes working with geographic location straightforward. The geographic location APIs on the phone abstract the location-sensing technologies and unburden the developer from having to know anything about the specific hardware in the device. Your app can specify a desired accuracy, either low or high, and the phone does the rest; it decides what location sensing components to use.

The .NET location API is consistent across platforms and can be used in much the same way in a phone app as it can in a desktop CLR application.

This chapter begins with an overview of the location sensing technologies available on Windows Phone and then dives into the location API. The chapter looks at monitoring location changes and at simulating location changes using both the emulator's location simulator and a custom class compatible with unit testing and testing on a physical device.

Finally, the chapter delves into the Reactive Extensions (Rx) and looks at sampling events to make rapidly firing position changes manageable.

Location Sensing Technologies

Windows Phone uses the following strategies to determine its geographic location:

- ▶ A-GPS
- ▶ Wi-Fi triangulation
- ▶ Cell tower triangulation

Each strategy has advantages and disadvantages, depending on environmental factors and power efficiency requirements (see Figure 15.1). The following sections discuss the pros and cons of each technology.

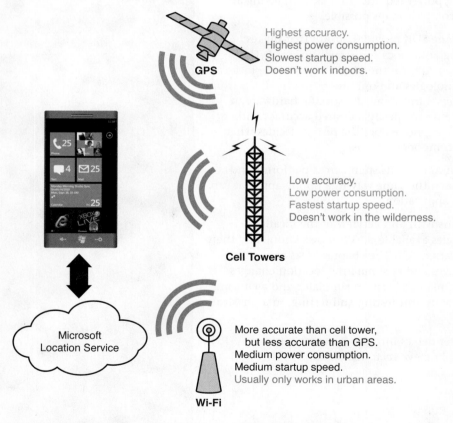

GPS

Highest accuracy.
Highest power consumption.
Slowest startup speed.
Doesn't work indoors.

Cell Towers

Low accuracy.
Low power consumption.
Fastest startup speed.
Doesn't work in the wilderness.

Microsoft
Location Service

Wi-Fi

More accurate than cell tower,
    but less accurate than GPS.
Medium power consumption.
Medium startup speed.
Usually only works in urban areas.

FIGURE 15.1   Sensor technologies available to Windows Phone

NOTE

The term *accuracy*, used frequently in this chapter, describes how close a location reading is to the true physical location.

A-GPS

A-GPS (Assisted Global Positioning System) is a satellite-based positioning system, which is generally the most accurate of the geo location methods available on the phone. The accuracy afforded by A-GPS, however, comes with a power penalty. It uses significantly more power than the other two sensing technologies. Because of this, it should only be used when an application needs a high level of accuracy.

GPS uses radio signals from satellites and does not perform as well in dense urban areas. In poor signal conditions, signals may suffer multipath errors; signals bounce off buildings, or are weakened by passing through tree cover. Later in the chapter, you see how to reduce the effect of multipath errors by applying a movement threshold to signal readings.

A-GPS is an extension to GPS. It improves GPS's startup performance by using an assistance server to supply satellite orbital information to the device over the network. This is faster than acquiring the information from the satellite itself, which can also prove difficult in low signal conditions.

Cell Tower Triangulation

Cell tower location uses triangulation against multiple cell towers to pinpoint the phone's location based on the ping time from each tower. The distance from a single cell tower can be roughly determined by the time it takes for a phone to respond to a ping. The location of the cell towers, combined with their ping times, allows the phone's location to be pinpointed (see Figure 15.2).

Accuracy increases as more towers are included in the calculation.

While cell tower triangulation uses less power than A-GPS, it is less accurate. Cell tower triangulation works best where there are more cell towers. Thus, areas such as city fringes or countryside may not provide an adequate level of accuracy. Unlike A-GPS, however, cell tower triangulation works indoors.

Wi-Fi Triangulation

Wi-Fi triangulation provides a middle ground between A-GPS and cell tower triangulation. Wi-Fi triangulation uses less power than GPS and can provide better accuracy than cell tower triangulation in some environments.

Wi-Fi location relies on a global location database of Wi-Fi networks and the ability of a phone device to detect Wi-Fi networks within its vicinity.

Wi-Fi triangulation works by detecting networks that are in range, measuring the signal strength of each network, and then triangulating the result using the Wi-Fi network location database.

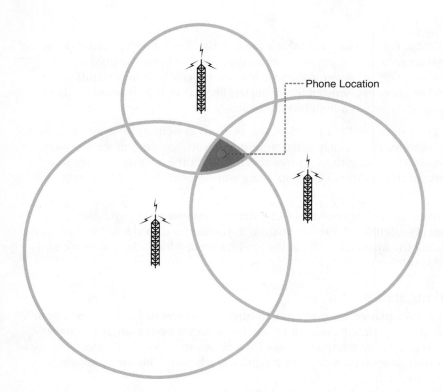

Phone Location

FIGURE 15.2   A phone's location can be pinpointed using cell tower triangulation.

Geographic Location Architecture

The Windows Phone location architecture consists of three layers: a hardware layer, a native code layer, and a managed layer (see Figure 15.3).

The hardware layer comprises the location related hardware components in the phone device, which includes a GPS receiver, a Wi-Fi interface, and a cellular radio. Each serves as a provider of location information with varying degrees of accuracy and power consumption.

The second layer, a native code layer, communicates directly with the hardware devices to determine the location of the device. The choice of hardware component, or combination of components, depends on the accuracy level requested by the app and the availability of data; there may not be any Wi-Fi networks in the vicinity for example.

The native code layer also uses a Microsoft web service to provide location related information from a database.

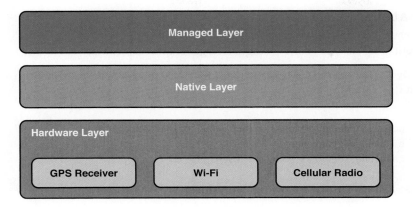

FIGURE 15.3   Location architecture layers

Code cannot be written to directly interact with the native layer, nor the hardware layer. For this, a managed code layer exists, which provides a hardware agnostic API. Recall from Chapter 2, "Fundamental Concepts in Silverlight Development for Windows Phone," that P/Invoke is not allowed at all on the phone. All interoperation with location components on the phone must therefore be done via the managed layer.

Getting Started with Location

The CLR types pertaining to geographic location reside in the `System.Device` assembly. To use geographic location in your Windows Phone project, add a reference to the `System.Device` assembly (see Figure 15.4).

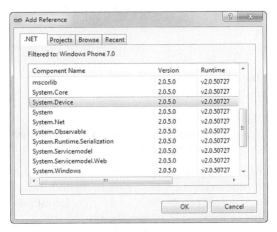

FIGURE 15.4   Adding a reference to the `System.Device` assembly

The geographic location types are located in the namespace System.Device.Location. Of these types, the GeoCoordinateWatcher class is discussed in detail in the next section.

GeoCoordinateWatcher Class

The GeoCoordinateWatcher class can be used by your app to monitor the location of the phone. It contains events for hardware state changes and geographic coordinate changes.

When instantiating a GeoCoordinateWatcher, you request a desired accuracy level, which can be either the default accuracy level, which lets the OS decide the accuracy level, or a high accuracy level, which causes the OS to prefer A-GPS. See the following example:

```
GeoCoordinateWatcher defaultAccuracyWatcher = new GeoCoordinateWatcher();
GeoCoordinateWatcher highAccuracyWatcher
    = new GeoCoordinateWatcher(GeoPositionAccuracy.High);
```

The GeoPositionAccuracy enum has the following two values:

▶ **Default**—Results in a power optimized (or low power) configuration at the probable cost of decreased accuracy. Moreover, the phone device favors the use of cell towers triangulation and Wi-Fi triangulation above GPS.

▶ **High**—Favors GPS when available at the cost of greater power usage and, thus, reduced battery life.

DesiredAccuracy Property

This property retrieves the desired accuracy level specified when the GeoCoordinateWatcher was instantiated. It has no setter.

BEST PRACTICE

Use the default (power optimized) accuracy setting unless a higher level of accuracy is required. Using lower accuracy minimizes power consumption, thereby increasing battery life.

MovementThreshold Property

In some environments, signal noise can cause a GPS device to register movement when there is no movement. This can be caused by surface reflection, which occurs when signals bounce off walls or other structures, or by other environmental factors. It is also exacerbated by the absence of a GPS antenna on Windows Phone devices.

The MovementThreshold property of the GeoCoordinateWatcher allows you to specify the minimum amount of movement required to register a change in position. When a change is registered the GeoCoordinateWatcher's PositionChanged event is raised.

MovementThreshold is a double value, which indicates the distance in meters, relative to the last coordinate received. The MovementThreshold property allows position change notifications to be smoothed. If the value is set too low, the PositionChanged event may be raised too frequently, or when there is no actual change in location. Conversely, setting the value too high reduces the ability of the device to provide up-to-date location coordinates.

A road navigation app, for example, with a `MovementThreshold` value set too high, may cause a user to miss a turn. Set too low, the application may provide continuous directions when the phone is, in fact, stationary.

Monitoring Position Changes

The `GeoCoordinateWatcher` class exposes the following three events:

▶ **PositionChanged**—This event is raised when a change in location is detected.

▶ **StatusChanged**—This event is raised when the underlying location service changes state; for example, when the location component is receiving data or when it has been disabled.

▶ **PropertyChanged**—This event is raised when a property changes and satisfies the `INotifyPropertyChanged` implementation.

PositionChanged *Event*

The `PositionChanged` event is raised whenever a significant change is detected in the phone's location. How large the change needs to be is determined by the `GeoCoordinateWatcher` object's `MovementThreshold` property.

The following code fragment demonstrates how to subscribe to the `PositionChanged` event:

```
geoPositionWatcher.PositionChanged += HandleGeoPositionWatchPositionChanged;
```

When the `PositionChanged` event is raised, the handler receives a `GeoPositionChangedEventArgs<GeoCoordinate>` object that contains a `GeoPosition<GeoCoordinate>` property, as shown:

```
void HandleGeoPositionWatchPositionChanged(
    object sender, GeoPositionChangedEventArgs<GeoCoordinate> e)
{
    GeoPosition<GeoCoordinate> position = e.Position;
    GeoCoordinate location = position.Location;
    DateTimeOffset timestamp = position.Timestamp;
}
```

In the context of the Geo Location API, a *position* can be thought of as a location at a point in time. The `Position` property of the `GeoPositionChangedEventArgs<GeoCoordinate>` is a `GeoPosition` instance containing the following two properties:

- ▶ Location (of type `GeoCoordinate`)
- ▶ Timestamp (of type `DateTimeOffset`)

StatusChanged *Event*

The status of the underlying geographic location provided is indicated by the `GeoCoordinateWatcher` object's `Status` property, which is of type `GeoPositionStatus`. `GeoPositionStatus` is an enum that contains the following four values:

- ▶ **Disabled**—The location provider is disabled. No position updates occur.
- ▶ **Initializing**—The location provider is initializing. This status occurs, for example, when the A-GPS component is obtaining a fix.
- ▶ **NoData**—No location data is available from any location provider.
- ▶ **Ready**—A location provider is ready to supply new data. Once in this state, the `GeoCoordinateWatcher` is able to raise its `PositionChanged` event.

The location provider transitions between these states as depicted in Figure 15.5.

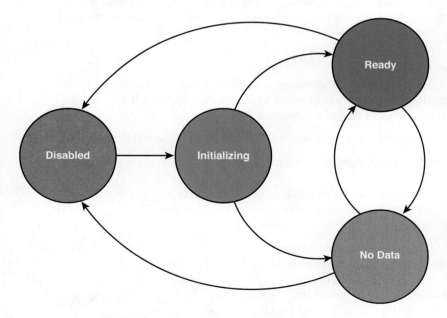

FIGURE 15.5   `GeoCoordinateWatcher.Status` property transitions between `GeoPositionStatus` values.

The following example demonstrates how to subscribe to the StatusChanged event:

```
geoPositionWatcher.StatusChanged += HandleGeoPositionWatcherStatusChanged;
```

When the StatusChanged event is raised, the handler receives a
GeoPositionStatusChangedEventArgs object, as shown in the following excerpt:

```
void HandleGeoPositionWatcherStatusChanged(
    object o, GeoPositionStatusChangedEventArgs args)
{
    GeoPositionStatus status = args.Status;
    switch (status)
    {
        case GeoPositionStatus.Disabled:
        // ...
        break;
        case GeoPositionStatus.Initializing:
        // ...
        break;
        case GeoPositionStatus.NoData:
        // ...
        break;
        case GeoPositionStatus.Ready:
        // ...
        break;
    }
}
```

Starting the GeoCoordinateWatcher

When you instantiate the GeoCoordinateWatcher it does not start monitoring the location
provider until its Start method is called, as shown in the following excerpt:

```
geoPositionWatcher.Start();
```

BEST PRACTICE

GeoCoordinateWatcher leverages phone hardware that consumes power. Only start a
GeoCoordinateWatcher when it is needed by your app, and stop it as soon as it is no
longer needed. This reduces power consumption and increases the battery life of the
phone.

The Start method has an overload that accepts a Boolean parameter named
suppressPermissionPrompt. This parameter, however, is designed to be used by Silverlight
for the Browser and is unused in the Windows Phone implementation.

Similarly, the Windows Phone implementation of the GeoCoordinateWatcher.TryStart
method does not use either the suppressPermissionPrompt parameter or the timeout

parameter. Its method name is misleading in its current implementation since it returns true if the `GeoCoordinateWatcher` is already started and false otherwise, even if it is successfully started during the method call. For this reason, it is recommended that you do not use the method.

Testing Apps That Use the `GeoCoordinateWatcher`

The Windows Phone emulator includes a tool for simulating location tracking, which can be accessed by clicking the Additional Tools button on the emulator menu (this was shown in Figure 14.2), and then selecting the Location tab on the Additional Tools window.

The location simulator works in two modes: a live mode that allows you to interact with the map to send location data to the emulator as soon as you click on the map and a playback mode that causes the location simulator to step through a sequence of map points, which you enter by clicking on the map (see Figure 15.6).

Map points can be saved to a file and loaded again at a later time.

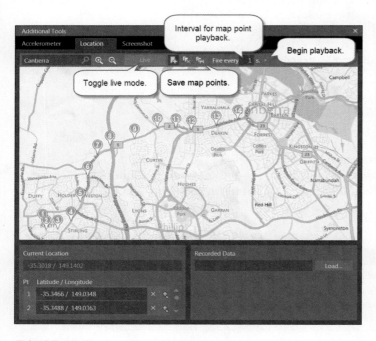

FIGURE 15.6   Location simulator

> **NOTE**
>
> The Play button is enabled only when the Live button is toggled off.

When using the location simulator, any GeoCoordinateWatcher instances in your app respond as though they are receiving actual location data, giving you the opportunity to test your app's geo location features.

Code Driven Location Simulation

The Windows Phone emulator's location simulator is useful for testing your app while it is executing within the emulator. To test the geo location features of your app on a physical device or within a unit test requires a different, code driven approach.

For this you must supplant the GeoCoordinateWatcher object with your own implementation of the IGeoPositionWatcher<GeoCoordinate> interface.

Included in the downloadable sample code is a class called MockGeoCoordinateWatcher, which does just that. It works like the GeoCoordinateWatcher but allows you to supply a list of GeoCoordinate values, which are analogous to the location simulator's map points (see Listing 15.1).

MockGeoCoordinateWatcher implements INotifyPropertyChanged, just like the built-in GeoCoordinateWatcher class.

In addition to the properties of the IGeoCoordinateWatcher class, MockGeoCoordinateWatcher has the following three properties that allow you to tailor when the PositionChanged event is raised:

▶ **InitializationMs**—The time, in milliseconds, before the watcher's Status transitions to the NoData state

▶ **FixDelayMs**—The time before the watcher's Status transitions from the NoData state to the Ready state

▶ **PositionChangedDelayMs**—The time interval between PositionChanged events

MockGeoCoordinateWatcher allows you to add waypoints to a list of GeoCoordinate values using its WayPoints property.

The MockGeoCoordinateWatcher.WalkPath method runs on a background thread and processes the waypoints sequentially (see Listing 15.1).

If there are no waypoints specified, then the MockGeoCoordinateWatcher uses a default list of coordinates.

The first time WalkPath is called, the watcher simulates initialization by pausing for the duration specified by the InitializationMs value. It then updates its Status to Ready and iterates over the WayPoints collection, raising the PositionChanged event for each one.

15

LISTING 15.1   `MockGeoCoordinateWatcher.WalkPath` Method

```
void WalkPath()
{
    if (wayPoints.Count < 1)
    {
        List<GeoCoordinate> defaultWayPoints = GetDefaultCoordinates();
        wayPoints.AddRange(defaultWayPoints);
    }

    if (firstRun)
    {
        Status = GeoPositionStatus.Initializing;
        Wait(InitializationMs);
    }

    Status = GeoPositionStatus.NoData;
    Wait(FixDelayMs);

    GeoCoordinate coordinate = wayPoints.First();

    if (firstRun)
    {
        Position = new GeoPosition<GeoCoordinate>(
                            DateTimeOffset.Now, coordinate);
        firstRun = false;
    }
    Status = GeoPositionStatus.Ready;
    Wait(PositionChangeDelayMs);
    int index = 1;

    while (started)
    {
        if (wayPoints != null && wayPoints.Count > index)
        {
            coordinate = wayPoints[index++];
        }
        SetPosition(coordinate);
        Wait(PositionChangeDelayMs);
    }
}
```

The `Wait` method uses the `Monitor` to block the background thread for the specified number of milliseconds (see Listing 15.2).

Using the `Monitor` to block the thread is preferable to calling `Thread.Sleep` because, unlike `Monitor.Wait`, `Thread.Sleep` cannot be unblocked.

LISTING 15.2   Wait Method

```
static readonly object waitLock = new object();

static void Wait(int delayMs)
{
    if (delayMs > 0)
    {
        lock (waitLock)
        {
            Monitor.Wait(waitLock, delayMs);
        }
    }
}
```

Both `MockGeoCoordinateWatcher` and the built-in `GeoCoordinateWatcher` implement `IGeoPositionWatcher<GeoCoordinate>`. This allows us to use either type without referring to a concrete implementation. This is demonstrated in the next section.

A Walkthrough of the Position Viewer Sample

The sample for this chapter includes a set of classes for monitoring location using either a `GeoCoordinateWatcher` or a `MockGeoCoordinateWatcher`. The UI includes three input controls: a start and a stop `Button` to toggle monitoring location changes on and off and a `Slider`.

The sample code for this section is located in the GeographicLocation directory of the WindowsPhone7Unleashed.Examples project.

GeoPositionViewModel Class

The `GeoPositionViewModel.Start` method instantiates either a mock or a built-in `IGeoPositionWatcher<GeoCoordinate>` object (see Listing 15.3).

Rather than requiring the viewmodel to determine which `IGeoPositionWatcher<GeoCoordinate>` implementation it should use, Inversion of Control (IoC) could also be employed to resolve the object. IoC is discussed in Chapter 22, "Unit Testing."

15

The Start method subscribes to the PositionChanged and StatusChanged events of the watcher, and then calls the watcher's Start method to begin receiving location notifications.

When the PositionChanged event is raised, the viewmodel's GeoCoordinate property is set to the current location.

LISTING 15.3   GeoPositionViewModel.Start Method (excerpt)

```
void Start()
{
    if (running)
    {
        return;
    }

    Running = true;
    CanStart = false;

    geoPositionWatcher = EnvironmentValues.UsingEmulator
        ? new MockGeoCoordinateWatcher()
        : (IGeoPositionWatcher<GeoCoordinate>)new GeoCoordinateWatcher
                                              {MovementThreshold = 20};

    geoPositionWatcher.PositionChanged
        += (o, args) =>
            {
                GeoCoordinate = args.Position.Location;
                ResolveAddress(args.Position.Location);
            };

    geoPositionWatcher.StatusChanged
        += (o, args) => GeoPositionStatus = args.Status;

    geoPositionWatcher.Start();
}
```

Determining whether the application is running within the emulator is done using the custom static EnvironmentValues.UsingEmulator property, shown in the following excerpt:

```
static bool? usingEmulator;

public static bool UsingEmulator
{
    get
    {
        if (!usingEmulator.HasValue)
```

```
        {
            usingEmulator = Environment.DeviceType == DeviceType.Emulator;
        }
        return usingEmulator.Value;
    }
}
```

The viewmodel contains two `DelegateCommands` that are used to start and stop position monitoring. The commands are initialized in the viewmodel constructor, as shown:

```
public GeoPositionViewModel()
{
    startCommand = new DelegateCommand(obj => Start(), arg => CanStart);
    stopCommand = new DelegateCommand(obj => Stop(), arg => Running);
    PropertyChanged += delegate { RefreshCommands(); };
}
```

Tapping the Stop button causes the viewmodel's `StopCommand` to execute, which calls the `Stop` method of the `geoPositionWatcher`. This prevents the `PositionChanged` event from being raised. The `Stop` method is shown in the following excerpt:

```
void Stop()
{
    if (!running || geoPositionWatcher == null)
    {
        return;
    }

    if (sampler != null)
    {
        sampler.Dispose();
    }

    geoPositionWatcher.Stop();
    Running = false;
    CanStart = true;
}
```

Displaying Location Using the `GeoPositionView` Page

The view has two buttons, which are bound to the viewmodel's `StartCommand` and `StopCommand` (see Listing 15.4).

The `GeoPositionView` contains several `TextBlock` elements that are bound to viewmodel properties.

A `Slider` is bound to the viewmodel's `SampleIntervalMs` property, allowing the user to control the sample frequency. The sampling feature is explored later in the chapter.

LISTING 15.4   `GeoPositionView` Page (excerpt showing main content panel)

```
<StackPanel Grid.Row="1" Margin="21,30,21,0">
    <Grid>
        <Grid.RowDefinitions>
            <RowDefinition Height="80" />
            <RowDefinition Height="80" />
            <RowDefinition Height="*" />
        </Grid.RowDefinitions>
        <Grid.ColumnDefinitions>
            <ColumnDefinition />
            <ColumnDefinition />
        </Grid.ColumnDefinitions>

        <TextBlock Text="Latitude"
                   Style="{StaticResource LatLongTitleStyle}" Margin="20"/>
        <TextBlock Text="{Binding GeoCoordinate.Latitude}"
                   Style="{StaticResource LatLongStyle}" Grid.Row="1"/>
        <TextBlock Text="Longitude"
                   Style="{StaticResource LatLongTitleStyle}"
                   Grid.Column="1" Margin="20" />
        <TextBlock Text="{Binding GeoCoordinate.Longitude}"
                   Style="{StaticResource LatLongStyle}"
                   Grid.Row="1" Grid.Column="1" />
    </Grid>
    <TextBlock Text="Status: "
               Style="{StaticResource PhoneTextTitle3Style}" />
    <TextBlock Text="{Binding GeoPositionStatus}"
               Style="{StaticResource PhoneTextNormalStyle}"
               Foreground="{StaticResource PhoneAccentBrush}"
               Height="50" />
    <TextBlock>Sample interval in milliseconds (0 for realtime):</TextBlock>
    <Slider Minimum="0"
            Maximum="10000"
            Value="{Binding SampleIntervalMs, Mode=TwoWay}"
            IsEnabled="{Binding CanStart}"
            LargeChange="1000" SmallChange="1000"/>
    <TextBlock Text="{Binding SampleIntervalMs}"
               Width="100" Height="50" HorizontalAlignment="Left"
               Style="{StaticResource PhoneTextNormalStyle}" />
    <TextBlock Text="Message"
               Style="{StaticResource PhoneTextTitle3Style}" />
    <TextBlock Text="{Binding Message}" Height="50"
```

LISTING 15.4   Continued

```xml
                Style="{StaticResource PhoneTextNormalStyle}" />
    <StackPanel Orientation="Horizontal">
        <Button Content="Start"
                Command="{Binding StartCommand}"
                Margin="0,20,0,0" Width="150" HorizontalAlignment="Left" />
        <Button Content="Stop"
                Command="{Binding StopCommand}"
                Margin="0,20,0,0" Width="150" HorizontalAlignment="Left" />
    </StackPanel>
</StackPanel>
```

Tapping the Start button causes the current location to be displayed whenever the
`IGeoCoordinateWatcher` object's `PositionChanged` event is raised (see Figure 15.7).

FIGURE 15.7   `GeoPositionView` page

Civic Address Resolution

`CivicAddressResolver` is supposed to be able to resolve a street address from a geographic
coordinate. It has not, however, been fully implemented yet and is unable to resolve an
address.

> **NOTE**
>
> In the 7.5 release of the Windows Phone OS the `CivicAddressResolver` class has not been fully implemented.

In Chapter 16, "Bing Maps," you see how to use the Bing Maps Geocode Service to resolve an address from a geo coordinate, and vice versa.

The `GeoPositionViewModel` class demonstrates how to use the `CivicAddressResolver`, but the `CivicAddressResolver.ResolveAddressCompleted` handler always receives an unknown address value.

Sampling the `PositionChanged` Event with Rx

If the `GeoCoordinateWatcher` class is assigned too low a `MovementThreshold` value, the event handler for the `GeoCoordinateWatcher.PositionChanged` event may be raised more frequently than needed, which can potentially degrade the performance of your app. The Reactive Extensions (Rx) can eliminate this issue by modulating, or sampling, the event, restricting calls to the `PositionChanged` event handler to a certain number each second.

Rx is a managed library that has been included as part of the Windows Phone Framework Class Library (FCL). At its essence, Rx allows events to be treated as a data stream. Rx allows you to subscribe to this data stream, and to manipulate and filter the data stream before it is handled by your app.

Rx can be thought of as LINQ to Events, and includes all the standard LINQ query operators. Rx provides a convenient mechanism for passing around event streams, which makes working with events easier. It uses the Dispose pattern and the `IDisposable` interface in conjunction with event subscriptions, and automatically unsubscribes from events, eliminating potential memory leaks.

If you are new to Rx, it is recommended that you learn more about it because it is an invaluable tool when working with an asynchronous programming model. Rx is being used evermore frequently by developers for asynchronous programming. The Silverlight Toolkit team, for example, used Rx to write reliable, event-based asynchronous tests for many of the Toolkit components.

Getting Started with Rx for Windows Phone

To use Rx in your app add a reference to the System.Observable and the Microsoft.Phone.Reactive assemblies (see Figure 15.8).

Rx types reside in the Microsoft.Phone.Reactive namespace.

The key to using Rx is to understand the two principal interfaces: `IObserver` and `IObservable`. Rx's `IObservable` and `IObserver` are analogous to `IEnumerable` and `IEnumerator`, except for one key difference: They do not block.

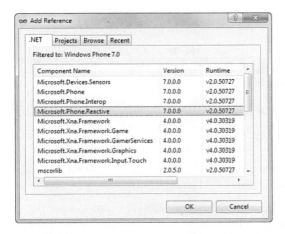

FIGURE 15.8   Add a reference to the System.Observable and Microsoft.Phone.Reactive assemblies.

Rx allows you to create an IObservable object from an event. In the following excerpt, an IObservable is created using the GeoPositionWatcher<GeoCoordinate> instance's PositionChanged event:

```
IObservable<IEvent<GeoPositionChangedEventArgs<T>>> observable
    = Observable.FromEvent<GeoPositionChangedEventArgs<T>>(
        ev => watcher.PositionChanged += ev,
        ev => watcher.PositionChanged -= ev);
```

By supplying both an add handler and a remove handler, the PositionChanged event is automatically unsubscribed once the observable instance is disposed.

Once an IObservable has been acquired, you can limit the frequency of event notifications by using the Sample extension method for the IObservable<T> type, as shown in the following excerpt:

```
IObservable<IEvent<GeoPositionChangedEventArgs<T>>> sampled
    = observable.Sample(TimeSpan.FromMilliseconds(sampleIntervalMs));
```

The final step is to subscribe to the data stream. This is done by calling the Subscribe extension method, passing it a delegate. The following excerpt calls the Subscribe method and passes a lambda expression for the PositionChanged event handler:

```
sampled.Subscribe(
    args =>
        {
            GeoPosition<T> position = args.EventArgs.Position;
            Location = position.Location;
            TimeStamp = position.Timestamp;
        });
```

If the `sampleIntervalMs` value is equal to 1000, the `PostionChanged` event handler is called, at most, once each second.

CAUTION

Using the `Subscribe` method results in an object that implements `IDisposable`. It is critical that the `Dispose` method be called on the object when it is no longer needed, as not doing so can lead to a memory leak. The event source (in this case the `GeoPositionWatcher`) may keep the target (`GeoPositionSampler`) alive.

The downloadable sample code contains a class called `GeoPositionSampler` that encapsulates this sampling functionality into a reusable class (see Listing 15.5).

`GeoPositionSampler` wraps a `GeoCoordinateWatcher` instance and allows you to sample the `IGeoPositionWatcher<T>.PositionChanged` event. It implements `INotifyPropertyChanged` so that a UI element can bind to its `Location` property if needed.

`GeoPositionSampler` implements `IDisposable` so that when it is disposed, it disposes its Rx subscription object and unsubscribes from the watcher's `StatusChanged` event.

LISTING 15.5   `GeoPositionSampler<T>` Class (excerpt)

```
public class GeoPositionSampler<T> : NotifyPropertyChangeBase, IDisposable
{
    readonly IDisposable subscription;
    readonly IGeoPositionWatcher<T> watcher;

    public GeoPositionSampler(
        IGeoPositionWatcher<T> watcher, int sampleIntervalMs)
    {
        this.watcher = ArgumentValidator.AssertNotNull(watcher, "watcher");

        IObservable<IEvent<GeoPositionChangedEventArgs<T>>> observable
            = Observable.FromEvent<GeoPositionChangedEventArgs<T>>(
                ev => watcher.PositionChanged += ev,
                ev => watcher.PositionChanged -= ev);

        IObservable<IEvent<GeoPositionChangedEventArgs<T>>> sampled
            = observable.Sample(
                TimeSpan.FromMilliseconds(sampleIntervalMs));

        subscription = sampled.Subscribe(
            args =>
                {
                    GeoPosition<T> position = args.EventArgs.Position;
                    Location = position.Location;
                    TimeStamp = position.Timestamp;
                });
```

LISTING 15.5   Continued

```
        watcher.StatusChanged += WatcherOnStatusChanged;
}

void WatcherOnStatusChanged(
    object o, GeoPositionStatusChangedEventArgs args)
{
    Status = args.Status;
}

T location;

public T Location
{
    get
    {
        return location;
    }
    private set
    {
        Assign("Location", ref location, value);
    }
}

DateTimeOffset timeStamp;

public DateTimeOffset TimeStamp
{
    get
    {
        return timeStamp;
    }
    private set
    {
        Assign("TimeStamp", ref timeStamp, value);
    }
}

GeoPositionStatus status;

public GeoPositionStatus Status
{
    get
    {
        return status;
```

LISTING 15.5   Continued

```
        }
        set
        {
            Assign("Status", ref status, value);
        }
    }
...
}
```

The GeoPositionSampler initialization has been incorporated into the
GeoPositionViewModel.Start method, as shown:

```
if (sampleIntervalMs > 0)
{
    sampler = new GeoPositionSampler<GeoCoordinate>(
                        geoPositionWatcher, sampleIntervalMs);

    sampler.PropertyChanged += (o, args) =>
                                {
                                    ResolveAddress(sampler.Location);
                                    GeoCoordinate = sampler.Location;
                                    GeoPositionStatus = sampler.Status;
                                };
}
```

The GeoPositionSampler constructor accepts an IGeoPositionWatcher<T>, which is normally
a GeoCoordinateWatcher, and a sample interval in milliseconds.

The GeoPositionView page uses a Slider control to set the sample interval of the
GeoPositionSampler (see Figure 15.9).

Increasing the sample interval causes the latitude and longitude display values to be
updated less frequently.

Sampling the PositionChanged event allows your app to respond periodically to location
changes and can improve the behavior of your app when the GeoCoordinateWatcher
object's movement threshold is set too low for the current conditions.

FIGURE 15.9   A Slider control is used to set the sample interval.

Summary

This chapter looked at the various location sensing technologies, and how they compare in terms of power usage and accuracy. The chapter also explored how to monitor position changes using the GeoCoordinateWatcher class, and how to simulate position changes using both the emulator's location simulator and a custom class that is compatible with unit testing and testing on a physical device.

Finally, the chapter demonstrated how Rx can be used to modulate, or restrict, the frequency of PositionChanged event handler calls.

CHAPTER 16

Bing Maps

Mapping capabilities are now an expected part of just about every smartphone, and, as you might expect, Windows Phone has a rich built-in Maps application that leverages Bing Maps as its principal mapping service. Yet not only is Bing Maps integrated into the built-in apps on the phone, the Windows Phone SDK includes a Bing Maps control, enabling you to incorporate mapping features into your own apps.

This chapter begins with an overview of the Bing Maps control and walks through the creation of a Bing Maps API key. You look at customizing the Bing Maps control by hiding the Bing logo and the copyright text and see how to programmatically manipulate the map view, in particular how to pan and zoom, as well as how to create a customized zoom bar.

The chapter then continues on from the previous chapter. You see how to track the phone's location on a map using the `IGeoPositionWatcher.PositionChanged` event. The `Pushpin` control is examined, and you see how it is used to identify locations of interest on the map. You look at generating pushpins from POCO (plain old CLR object) collections and at customizing the appearance of pushpins using a custom style and control template.

The chapter then examines Bing SOAP services and how they can be leveraged to locate a route between two user-provided addresses. The chapter illustrates how Rx (Reactive Extensions) is used to coordinate asynchronous SOAP service calls and to decrease search time. You also look at hiding and revealing page elements using a viewmodel `VisualState` property in conjunction with an attached property and a custom `VisualStateUtility` class.

Finally, the chapter demonstrates how to present a list of itinerary items on the Bing Maps control and as an expandable list.

Getting Started with Bing Maps

An API key is required to use the Bing Maps control in production. While you can use the control during development without having an API key, the Bing Maps control displays a warning message if a valid key is not used. This message is displayed as an overlay across the map at runtime (see Figure 16.1). The warning message does not prevent interacting with the map, but you are required to use a valid key if you want to publish an application to the Windows Phone marketplace.

FIGURE 16.1   The Bing Maps control without a valid API key

Registering for a Bing Maps API Key

Registering for an API key is a short and simple process, which usually takes a couple of minutes. Having an API key also gives you access to other services such as the Bing Route service, which can be used to request directions between two locations, and the Bing Geocode service, which can be used to convert a street address to a geographic coordinate. Each of these services is discussed later in the chapter.

To obtain a Bing Maps API key, create a Bing Maps account at http://www.bingmapsportal.com (see Figure 16.2).

Select the Create button, and proceed to enter your details. Once your account is created, you are able to create an API key using the Create or View Keys hyperlink in the Map APIs menu section (see Figure 16.3).

NOTE

There is a limit of five Bing Maps keys per account.

FIGURE 16.2   Creating a Bing Maps account

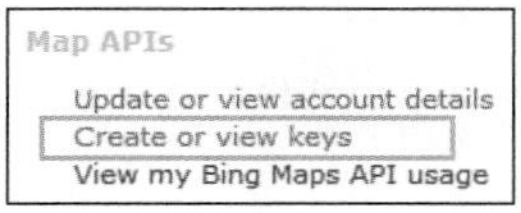

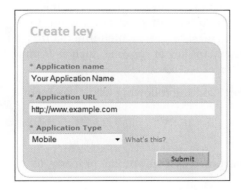

FIGURE 16.3   Select the Create or View Keys link in the Map APIs section.

Enter your application's details (see Figure 16.4). This information can be changed at a later time via the same Create or View Keys link.

FIGURE 16.4   Creating a new key

On creation, the key is displayed on the My Keys page. The actual API key, represented by a series of *x*'s in Figure 16.5, is a string of 64 alphanumeric characters that is copied and pasted into your code. In the next section, you see how this value is used.

Application name	Key / URL	Update Key
Your Application	XXXXXXXXXXXXXXXXXXXXXXXXXXXXXXXXXXXXXXXXXXXXXXXXXXXXXXXXXXXXXXXXXX http://www.example.com Mobile	Update

FIGURE 16.5   The API key is a string of 64 alphanumeric characters.

Adding a Map Control to a Page

The Bing Maps control downloads map information as you manipulate the control. For the Bing Maps control to function at runtime, you need an active Internet connection.

Adding a Bing Map control to a page requires a reference to the assembly Microsoft.Phone.Controls.Maps, which is included in the Windows Phone SDK. A namespace definition is placed at the top of your page, like so:

```
xmlns:m="clr namespace:Microsoft.Phone.Controls.Maps;assembly=
    Microsoft.Phone.Controls.Maps"
```

An m:Map element can then be placed on your host page. The API key is provided to the control via its CredentialsProvider property, as shown:

```
<m:Map CredentialsProvider="Your Bing Maps Key" />
```

The API key can be provided in XAML, and also by using a data binding, like so:

```
<m:Map CredentialsProvider="{Binding CredentialsProvider}" />
```

The Map.CredentialsProvider property is of type CredentialsProvider class, an abstract class that contains an abstract method called GetCredentials. A single class is present in the Windows Phone SDK named ApplicationIdCredentialsProvider, which inherits from Credentials provider. If you need to retrieve the Bing Maps key at runtime, such as from a web service, you can do so by creating a custom CredentialsProvider.

To provide the key to a Map control via a data binding, add the following using statement to your viewmodel:

```
using Microsoft.Phone.Controls.Maps;
```

An ApplicationIdCredentialsProvider can then be exposed as a viewmodel property, as shown in the following example:

```
readonly CredentialsProvider credentialsProvider
    = new ApplicationIdCredentialsProvider("Your Bing Maps Key");

public CredentialsProvider CredentialsProvider
{
    get
    {
```

```
        return credentialsProvider;
    }
}
```

Before delving deeper into the Bing Maps control, briefly familiarize yourself with the sample for this chapter.

Sample Code Overview

The sample code for this chapter resides in the BingMaps directory of the WindowsPhone7Unleashed.Examples project within the downloadable sample code.

The sample code demonstrates various uses of the Bing Maps control, in particular it demonstrates:

▶ Tracking a user's geographic location

▶ Identifying locations of interest using pushpins

▶ Searching and displaying routes using Bing services

The `BingMapsView.xaml` contains four application bar icon buttons and a single menu item (see Figure 16.6).

FIGURE 16.6   Sample Bing Maps view

The application bar items perform the tasks described in Table 16.1.

TABLE 16.1   BingMapsView Application Bar Items

Text	Description
Track	A button that causes the viewmodel to begin tracking the device's geographic location using an IGeoPositionWatcher implementation.
Add Pin	A button that allows the user to enter a title for a new pushpin, which is placed on the map.
Route	A button that presents the user with a search dialog, to locate a path from one street address to another.
Itinerary	A button that expands the itinerary view, which contains the route information present after a route search has completed.
Road View/Aerial View	A menu item that toggles the Map control's map mode. Map modes are presented in the next section.

Map Modes

Out of the box, the Bing Maps control can be viewed using a road or aerial (satellite) view. The choice of view is controlled by the Map object's Mode property.

A map mode represents a 2D projection of the Earth. The Bing Maps control relies on two map modes on which all other map modes are based: FlatMapMode and MercatorMode (see Figure 16.7). The two standard map modes available with the Bing Maps control are derived from MercatorMode and include RoadMode and AerialMode.

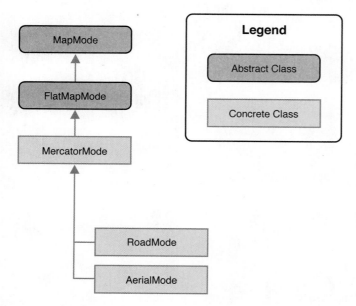

FIGURE 16.7   MapMode class hierarchy

The FlatMapMode is a flattened representation of the Earth. MercatorMode is derived from FlatMapMode and represents a cylindrical projection of the Earth onto a 2D surface with perpendicular straight lines representing latitude and longitude.

The Map object's Mode property can be set to one of the built-in map modes, or to an instance of your own custom MapMode class. Deriving from one of these classes provides you with a base tile layer, useful when defining the behavior of a new map mode. Creating a custom MapMode is, however, beyond the scope of this chapter.

NOTE

AerialMode displays satellite imagery and allows for street and place names to be switched off. RoadMode does not allow you to switch off street names.

The Mode property can be set programmatically in code-beside, or defined in XAML as shown in the following example:

```
<m:Map Name="map">
    <m:Map.Mode>
        <m:AerialMode ShouldDisplayLabels="True" />
    </m:Map.Mode>
</m:Map>
```

Unfortunately, the Mode property does not allow you to bind to it directly in XAML. The Map control is quirky in that it traverses the visual tree when it is instantiated and raises a NullReferenceException if you try to define a binding to its Mode property before the page has loaded. As a workaround, binding the Mode property can be accomplished by creating the binding in a Loaded event handler, as shown:

```
public BingMapsView()
{
…
    Loaded += HandleLoaded;
}

void HandleLoaded(object sender, RoutedEventArgs e)
{
    Binding binding = new Binding("MapMode") {Source = ViewModel};
    BindingOperations.SetBinding(map, MapBase.ModeProperty, binding);
}
```

The BingMapsViewModel signals which MapMode the Map control should use, via a property. See the following excerpt:

```
MapMode mapMode = new AerialMode(true);

public MapMode MapMode
```

16

```
{
    get
    {
        return mapMode;
    }
    set
    {
        Assign(() => MapMode, ref mapMode, value);
        OnPropertyChanged(() => MapModeCommandText);
    }
}
```

A custom `AppBarMenuItem` is data-bound to the `MapModeCommandText`, as shown:

```xml
<u:AppBar>
    ...
    <u:AppBar.MenuItems>
        <u:AppBarMenuItem Command="{Binding ToggleMapModeCommand}"
                          Text="{Binding MapModeCommandText}" />
    </u:AppBar.MenuItems>
</u:AppBar>
```

For more information on the `AppBarMenuItem` see Chapter 8, "Taming the Application Bar."

Tapping the menu item causes the `ToggleMapModeCommand` to be executed. The command is initialized in the viewmodel's constructor, like so:

```
toggleMapModeCommand = new DelegateCommand(obj => ToggleMapMode());
```

The command calls the `ToggleMapMode` method, which changes between modes as shown:

```
void ToggleMapMode()
{
    MapMode = mapMode is AerialMode
        ? (MapMode)new RoadMode() : new AerialMode(true);
}
```

Hiding the Bing Logo and Copyright Text

By default the Bing Maps control overlays the Bing logo and a copyright text (see Figure 16.8).

To remove the logo and/or the copyright text, set the maps `LogoVisibility` and `CopyrightVisibility` properties to Collapsed like so:

```xml
<m:Map Name="map"
       LogoVisibility="Collapsed"
       CopyrightVisibility="Collapsed" />
```

FIGURE 16.8   The Bing logo and copyright text

Panning and Zooming

The bindable `Map.Center` property is a `GeoCoordinate` that is used to set the center location of the map view. The following example shows how to set the `Center` property of a `Map` control by providing the latitude and longitude (in that order):

```
<m:Map Center="45.8, 6.15" />
```

Conversely, the `Center` property can be data-bound, as shown in the following example:

```
<m:Map Center="{Binding Center, Mode=TwoWay}" />
```

By using a `TwoWay` data binding, it allows you to track the current viewable center point of the map from your viewmodel.

An alternative way of setting the viewable area of the map is to use the `Map.SetView` method. The `SetView` method accepts a `LocationRect` object, which specifies a rectangular region of the map.

The `BingMapsViewModel` contains a `LocationRect` property that is applied to the map within the viewmodel's `PropertyChanged` event handler, as shown in the following excerpt:

```
public BingMapsView()
{
...
    viewModel.PropertyChanged
```

```
        += (o, args) =>
            {
                switch (args.PropertyName)
                {
                    case "LocationRect":
                        map.SetView(ViewModel.LocationRect);
                        break;
                }
            };
}
```

Later in this chapter you see how the `Map.SetView` method is used to pan and zoom to an area of the map to display the shortest path between two points.

When the lifespan of the viewmodel exceeds that of the view, subscribing to a viewmodel's `PropertyChanged` event from the view can cause a memory leak. This happens because the target of an event subscription (in this case the view) is kept alive by the garbage collector while the event source (the viewmodel) exists in memory. To prevent this from occurring, you may choose to forgo the use of the `PropertyChanged` event in favor of an alternative approach, such as weak events, or a messaging system to communicate with the view, both of which are to be found in various Model-View-ViewModel (MVVM) frameworks including the Calcium SDK project.

The `Map.ZoomLevel` property allows you to control the altitude of the viewpoint. This property ranges between 0 and 21, with 0 being completely zoomed out so that the entire map is visible, and 21 being zoomed in as close as possible. 21 is not a hard limit, in that you can attempt to assign the zoom level to a higher value. Doing so, however, has no effect on the level of detail displayed.

To demonstrate the `ZoomLevel` property of the `Map` control, the sample view uses a data binding to the viewmodel's `ZoomLevel` property, as shown:

```
<m:Map Name="map"
       ZoomLevel="{Binding ZoomLevel, Mode=TwoWay}">
...
</m:Map>
```

A `Slider` is used to indicate and control the map's zoom level via a data binding to the `BingMapsViewModel`, as shown:

```
<Slider Value="{Binding ZoomLevel, Mode=TwoWay}"
        Minimum="1"
```

```
Maximum="{Binding ZoomLevelMaximum}"
Orientation="Vertical"
Grid.Row="1"
Margin="0,0,20,0" />
```

The `ZoomLevelMaximum` property is defined within the viewmodel and restricts the `ZoomLevel` from being set to a value greater than 21.

Zoom Buttons

The Bing Maps control has buttons for zooming in and out (see Figure 16.9). These buttons are hidden by default, and they can be shown by setting the `Map` object's `ZoomBarVisibility` property to Visible.

FIGURE 16.9   Setting the `ZoomBarVisibility` property to Visible causes the zoom buttons to be shown.

Zooming in and out can be accomplished using a pinch gesture, making the zoom bar unnecessary in most cases.

The style and location of the zoom bar is not customizable. This, however, does not prevent you from defining your own zoom buttons, which accomplishes the same task as the built-in zoom bar. For example, buttons can be added as content on the map like so:

```
<my:Map Name="Map">
    <StackPanel>
        <Button x:Name="Button_ZoomIn" Tap="Handle_ZoomIn_Tap" />
```

```
        <Button x:Name="Button_ZoomOut" Tap="Handle_ZoomOut_Tap" />
    </StackPanel>
</my:Map>
```

The button `Tap` event handlers should increment or decrement the `ZoomLevel` property of the `Map` control.

```
void Handle_ZoomIn_Tap(object sender, RoutedEventArgs e)
{
    if (map.ZoomLevel < 21)
    {
        map.ZoomLevel += 1;
    }
}
```

Here we see that the zoom level is limited to values less than 21, the maximum zoom level available using the Bing Maps control.

> **TIP**
>
> Rather than using a `Tap` event handler to control the map's zoom level, I suggest binding the buttons to a viewmodel command instead. That way you can keep your UI logic within the viewmodel.

Location Tracking

In Chapter 15, "Geographic Location," you saw how a `GeoCoordinateWatcher` provides geographic location updates. In this section you see how the custom `IGeoPositionWatcher` (presented in that chapter) can be used to track the location of the device using a Bing Maps control.

The `BingMapsViewModel` class constructor instantiates either a `GeoCoordinateWatcher` or a `MockGeoCoordinateWatcher`, depending on whether the class is executing within the emulator. See the following excerpt:

```
public BingMapsViewModel(IRouteCalculator routeCalculator)
{
...
    geoPositionWatcher = EnvironmentValues.UsingEmulator
            ? new MockGeoCoordinateWatcher(2000)
            : (IGeoPositionWatcher<GeoCoordinate>)new GeoCoordinateWatcher();

    geoPositionWatcher.PositionChanged
      += delegate(object o, GeoPositionChangedEventArgs<GeoCoordinate> args)
        {
```

```
        GeoCoordinate geoCoordinate = args.Position.Location;
        Center = geoCoordinate;

        Message = string.Format("{0} Lat, {1} Long",
            geoCoordinate.Latitude, geoCoordinate.Longitude);
    };

geoPositionWatcher.StatusChanged
    += delegate(object o, GeoPositionStatusChangedEventArgs args)
    {
        GeoPositionStatus = args.Status;
    };

trackCommand = new DelegateCommand(obj => Start());
...
}
```

The `IGeoPositionWatcher` instance is used to monitor the position of the phone. When the watcher's `PositionChanged` event is raised, the visible center point of the Bing Maps control is set to the `Center` property of the viewmodel via a data binding.

The viewmodel's `TrackCommand` property is data-bound to an `AppBarIconButton` in the view, and when executed, calls the `Start` method of the viewmodel. The `Start` method uses a Boolean `tracking` field to prevent tracking if it is already underway.

> **NOTE**
>
> To pass the Windows Phone Marketplace Certification your app must ask the user whether it is okay to use location services. Additionally, you must provide an option in the settings page of your app to allow the user to disable location services.

Before tracking can take place, prompt the user to confirm the use of location services. This is done by using the `ViewModelBase` class's `IMessageService`. If the `AskYesNoQuestion` method returns true, the `geoPositionWatcher` is started. See the following excerpt:

```
void Start()
{
    if (tracking)
    {
        return;
    }

    lock (startLock)
    {
```

```
        if (tracking)
        {
            return;
        }

        /* Before using geo location, it is a certification requirement
         * that you seek permission from the user first. */
        bool canTrack = MessageService.AskYesNoQuestion(
            "Is it OK to use the geographic location system on your phone?");

        if (!canTrack)
        {
            return;
        }

        tracking = true;
        OnPropertyChanged(() => Tracking);
        geoPositionWatcher.Start();
    }
}
```

For more information regarding the IMessageService see Chapter 2, "Fundamental Concepts in Silverlight Development for Windows Phone."

When the PositionChanged event is raised, the viewmodel's Center property is set to the event argument's Position.Location property. This raises the viewmodel's PropertyChanged event and moves the map view to that location.

The BingMapsView.xaml contains a custom AppBar control, shown in the following excerpt, with various AppBarIconButtons, including one that executes the TrackCommand:

```
<u:AppBar BarOpacity="0.7">
    <u:AppBarIconButton
        Command="{Binding TrackCommand}"
        Text="Track"
        IconUri="/BingMaps/Images/ApplicationBarIcons/Route.png" />
...
</u:AppBar>
```

Tapping the Track button causes the watcher to begin raising events. The map center is moved to the location as reported by the GeoPositionChangedEventArgs (see Figure 16.10).

FIGURE 16.10   Use the track button to emulate location changes that are displayed on the map.

Pushpins

Pushpins are markers placed on the Bing Maps control's surface that indicate a specific location on the map. They can be used to identify particular places of interest, and with the use of custom styles, they can be customized to use shapes, images, or indeed any `UIElement`. Pushpins are generally placed within a map layer, on a `Map` control.

The `Pushpin` class provides a `Location` property, which can be used to position the `Pushpin`; this is useful when a collection is being used to generate a series of `Pushpin` objects. While the position of any `UIElement` can be positioned using the `MapLayer` API, doing so can be cumbersome, and the `Pushpin.Location` property is far more amenable to data templates and data binding.

Map Layers

While any `UIElement` can be added directly to the `Map` control, it is best to place content within a map layer as it provides greater control over location and the z-index of content. You can add shapes, controls, and media such as images and even video to the map using map layers.

The following excerpt demonstrates how to create and add a new `MapLayer` to a `Map` control, and then how to add a `Pushpin` to the `MapLayer`:

```
MapLayer mapLayer = new MapLayer();
map.Children.Add(mapLayer);
Pushpin pushpin = new Pushpin { Content = "Pushpin Example" };
mapLayer.AddChild(pushpin, map.Center, PositionOrigin.Center);
```

The result is depicted in Figure 16.11. The appearance of the Pushpin can be customized using a control template, as you see later in this section.

FIGURE 16.11   The default appearance of a Pushpin

An alternative approach to populating the map directly is to bind a collection of objects to a MapItemsControl. MapItemsControl uses a MapLayer to lay out items. A control template can be used to generate each Pushpin object. This allows you to populate the map with Pushpin objects from your viewmodel without direct reliance on the Pushpin class.

Populating a MapItemsControl with Pushpins Via a Data-Bound Collection

In this section you see how a collection of POCO classes can be represented as Pushpin controls within a Map control. You also see how to prompt the user for pushpin text from within a viewmodel method, using the custom IMessageService.

The BingMapsViewModel class contains an ObservableCollection of PushpinViewModels named pushpins. The custom PushpinViewModel class (see Listing 16.1) provides the relevant information for displaying an actual Pushpin control in the view.

LISTING 16.1   PushpinViewModel Class

```
public class PushpinViewModel
{
    public object Text { get; private set; }
    public GeoCoordinate Location { get; private set; }
    public PushpinIcon Icon { get; private set; }

    public PushpinViewModel(
                object text, GeoCoordinate location, PushpinIcon icon)
    {
        Text = ArgumentValidator.AssertNotNull(text, "text");
        Location = location;
        Icon = icon;
    }
}
```

The PushpinViewModel properties, shown in the following list, determine how a Pushpin is represented on the map:

▶ **Text**—A string that is displayed as a pushpin label

▶ **Icon**—An enum value that indicates the icon shown on the map

▶ **Location**—The geographic coordinate, which indicates where the Pushpin is to be placed on the map

The BingMapsViewModel class adds new items to the pushpins collection within its CreateNewPushPin method. This method leverages the IMessageService to present the user with a dialog requesting the name for the new pushpin. If a valid response is received, a new PushpinViewModel is created and assigned a random icon enum value. The new PushpinViewModel is then added to the pushpins collection. See the following excerpt:

```
void CreateNewPushPin()
{
    var question = new TextResponseQuestion(
                        "Please provide a name for the new pushpin.");

    var messageService = Dependency.Resolve<IMessageService>();
    messageService.AskQuestion(question,
        questionResult =>
        {
            if (!questionResult.HasValidResponse)
            {
                return;
            }
```

```
            Random random = new Random();
            PushpinIcon randomIcon = (PushpinIcon)random.Next(0, 8);
            PushpinViewModel pushpin = new PushpinViewModel(
                questionResult.Response.Text, Center, randomIcon);

            pushpins.Add(pushpin);
        });
}
```

A control template is used to display a PushpinViewModel as a Pushpin control. The Bing Maps control in the view contains a MapItemsControl whose ItemsSource property is bound to the Pushpins property of the viewmodel, as shown in the following excerpt:

```xml
<m:Map Name="map">
    <m:MapItemsControl ItemsSource="{Binding Pushpins}">
        <m:MapItemsControl.ItemTemplate>
            <DataTemplate>
                <m:Pushpin Location="{Binding Location}"
                    Style="{StaticResource PushpinStyle}" >
                    <Image Source="{Binding Icon,
                    Converter={StaticResource PushpinIconConverter}}" />
                </m:Pushpin>
            </DataTemplate>
        </m:MapItemsControl.ItemTemplate>
    </m:MapItemsControl>
</m:Map>
```

Pushpin controls are presented using the PushpinStyle XAML style as shown (you see what this style looks like in Figure 16.14, at the end of this section):

```xml
<Style x:Key="PushpinStyle" TargetType="m:Pushpin">
    <Setter Property="BorderBrush" Value="#FFF4F4F5" />
    <Setter Property="Template">
        <Setter.Value>
            <ControlTemplate>
                <Canvas Height="0"
                Width="0"
                RenderTransformOrigin="0.5,0.5">
                    <Canvas RenderTransformOrigin="0.5,0.5"
                        Height="1" Width="1">
                        <Path>
                        ...
                        </Path>
                        <Path>
                        ...
                        </Path>
                    </Canvas>
```

```xml
            <ContentPresenter Width="35"
                Height="35"
                RenderTransformOrigin="0.5,0.5"
                Canvas.Top="-3.5">
                <ContentPresenter.RenderTransform>
                    <CompositeTransform
                        TranslateX="-18"
                        TranslateY="-54"/>
                </ContentPresenter.RenderTransform>
            </ContentPresenter>
            <StackPanel Width="200" Margin="-100, 0, 0, 0">
                <TextBlock Text="{Binding Text}"
                    Style="{StaticResource PhoneTextNormalStyle}"
                    HorizontalAlignment="Center" />
            </StackPanel>
        </Canvas>
    </ControlTemplate>
  </Setter.Value>
 </Setter>
</Style>
```

The `PushpinViewModel` class contains an `Icon` property, which is a `PushpinIcon` enum value (see Listing 16.2). Each value of the `PushpinIcon` enum corresponds to an image file.

LISTING 16.2   PushpinIcon Enum

```csharp
public enum PushpinIcon
{
    Bar,
    Bicylce,
    Car,
    Fuel,
    House,
    Location,
    Restaurant,
    Shop
}
```

A custom `IValueConverter`, called `PushpinIconConverter`, is used to turn the `PushpinIcon` enum value into an image path (see Listing 16.3). The advantage of using an enum value (or even a string without an extension) to represent an icon is that it does not depend on the structure of the project, making it easier to port the project to another technology, such as Silverlight for the browser, which may have different resolution requirements for the image.

LISTING 16.3   PushpinIconConverter Class

```
public class PushpinIconConverter : IValueConverter
{
    public object Convert(
        object value, Type targetType, object parameter, CultureInfo culture)
    {
        PushpinIcon icon = (PushpinIcon)value;
        return new Uri(string.Format(
            "/BingMaps/Images/PushpinIcons/{0}.png", icon), UriKind.Relative);
    }

    public object ConvertBack(
        object value, Type targetType, object parameter, CultureInfo culture)
    {
        throw new NotImplementedException();
    }
}
```

The PushpinIconConverter uses the PushpinIcon value to construct a path to the PNG files located in the project's PushpinIcons directory, shown in Figure 16.12.

FIGURE 16.12   Pushpin icon images

The viewmodel's addPushpinCommand is used to call the CreateNewPushPin method. The command is initialized within the viewmodel's constructor, as shown:

```
addPushpinCommand = new DelegateCommand(obj => CreateNewPushPin());
```

The custom AppBar control in the view contains an AppBarIconButton that is data-bound to the AddPushpinCommand:

```
<u:AppBarIconButton
        Command="{Binding AddPushpinCommand}"
        Text="Add Pin"
        IconUri="/BingMaps/Images/ApplicationBarIcons/Pushpin.png" />
```

When the user taps the Add Pin application bar button, the `AddPushpinCommand` executes, which presents the user with the dialog shown in Figure 16.13.

FIGURE 16.13   The user is prompted to name the new pushpin.

Each time the Add Pin button is used, a new pushpin is added to the current center location of the map. Figure 16.14 shows the map after several uses of the Add Pin button.

`Pushpins` provide a way to highlight map locations of interest and, as you have seen, allow you to easily position elements via the `Pushpin`'s `Location` property.

Route Calculation Using Bing Maps SOAP Services

Bing Maps services include a set of SOAP services that enable things like determining the geographic coordinates of a street address or finding the shortest route to get from one location to another.

This section looks at harnessing these services to allow the user to enter a start and an end location. The app then locates the shortest path between the two points by road and displays the itinerary.

FIGURE 16.14   Various pushpins placed on the map

Bing SOAP Services

The following list provides a description of each of the core Bing SOAP services:

▶ **Geocode service**—This service is used to convert street addresses to geographic coordinates, and vice-versa. Service URL: http://dev.virtualearth.net/webservices/v1/geocodeservice/geocodeservice.svc

▶ **Route service**—This service is used to find a path between two or more locations. It can also be used to generate routes based on more obscure requirements, such as party maps. Party maps show directions from main roads. For example, when you host a party or a large gathering, it is often a requirement to include a map showing driving directions to the party. This can be a difficult task because often attendees are coming from different areas. The Route service can be used to calculate a route to the location from all major roads. Service URL: http://dev.virtualearth.net/webservices/v1/routeservice/routeservice.svc

▶ **Imagery service**—Allows you to retrieve information about imagery data as well as retrieving URIs for maps, which can then be downloaded. The Imagery service is outside the scope of this chapter. Service URL: http://dev.virtualearth.net/webservices/v1/imageryservice/imageryservice.svc

▶ **Search service**—This service is used to query the Bing search engine. The Search service is outside the scope of this chapter. Service URL: http://dev.virtualearth.net/webservices/v1/searchservice/searchservice.svc

This chapter looks at the Geocode and Route services.

Bing SOAP services can be consumed in your project by adding a service reference for each (see Figure 16.15). To open the Add Service Reference, right-click on the project node in the Solution Explorer within Visual Studio and select Add Service Reference.

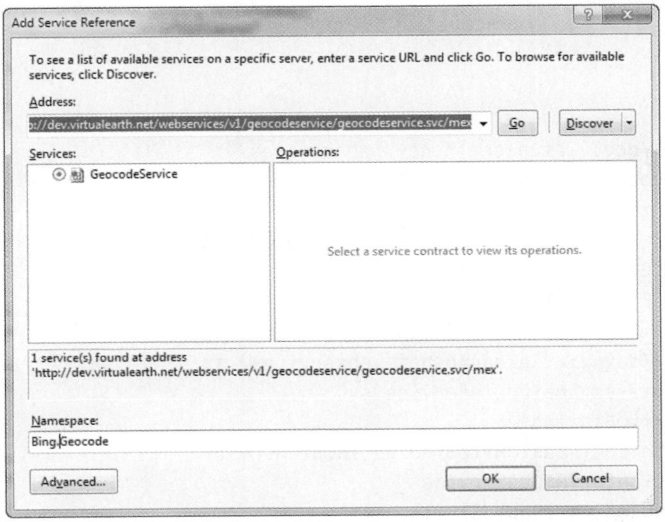

FIGURE 16.15 Adding a service reference to the Bing Geocode service

The Namespace field of the Add Service Reference allows you to group the Bing services under a common root namespace. In the sample, Bing was chosen arbitrarily as the root namespace, but you can choose whatever namespace you want.

Once a service reference has been added, the ServiceReferences.ClientConfig configuration file, in the root directory of the project, is automatically generated by Visual Studio. Within this file, CustomBindings for the Bing services can be removed and replaced with basic HttpBinding elements.

Listing 16.4 shows the ServiceReferences.ClientConfig after it has been edited.

LISTING 16.4 ServiceReferences.ClientConfig (excerpt)

```
<configuration>
    <system.serviceModel>
        <bindings>
            <basicHttpBinding>
                <binding name="BasicHttpBinding_IGeocodeService"
                maxBufferSize="2147483647"
                maxReceivedMessageSize="2147483647">
                    <security mode="None" />
                </binding>
```

LISTING 16.4   Continued

```xml
                <binding name="BasicHttpBinding_IRouteService"
            maxBufferSize="2147483647"
            maxReceivedMessageSize="2147483647">
                    <security mode="None" />
                </binding>
            </basicHttpBinding>
        </bindings>
        <client>
            <endpoint
                address="http://dev.virtualearth.net/webservices/v1
                            /geocodeservice/GeocodeService.svc"
                binding="basicHttpBinding"
                bindingConfiguration="BasicHttpBinding_IGeocodeService"
                contract="Bing.Geocode.IGeocodeService"
                name="BasicHttpBinding_IGeocodeService" />
            <endpoint
                address="http://dev.virtualearth.net/webservices/v1/
                            routeservice/routeservice.svc"
                binding="basicHttpBinding"
                bindingConfiguration="BasicHttpBinding_IRouteService"
                contract="Bing.Route.IRouteService"
                name="BasicHttpBinding_IRouteService" />
        </client>
    </system.serviceModel>
</configuration>
```

Calculating a Route Using Bing Services

Recall that the Bing Geocode service is used to convert a street address to a geographic coordinate, while the Bing Route service is used to calculate the shortest path from one coordinate to another.

To decouple our viewmodel code from the generated Bing services code, a custom interface called IRouteCalculator, located in the downloadable sample code, is used to consume the services. IRouteCalculator contains a single method called CalculateAsync (see Listing 16.5).

LISTING 16.5   IRouteCalculator

```csharp
public interface IRouteCalculator
{
    void CalculateAsync(
        string fromAddress,
        string toAddress,
        Action<RouteCalculationResult> completeAction);
}
```

CalculateAsync accepts a `fromAddress` and a `toAddress` argument. We use the Bing Geocode service to search for these two locations to resolve a geographic coordinate for each.

The return type of the `CalculateAsync` method is void. When the `CalculateAsync` method has completed, it invokes the specified `completeAction` argument, passing the `Action` a `RouteCalculationResult` containing the result of the calculation. The `RouteCalculationResult` object either contains the route found using the Bing Route service, or an error (see Listing 16.6).

LISTING 16.6   `RouteCalculationResult` Class

```
public class RouteCalculationResult
{
    public RouteResult RouteResult { get; private set; }
    public RouteCalculationError Error { get; private set; }

    public RouteCalculationResult(
        RouteResult routeResult, RouteCalculationError error = null)
    {
        RouteResult = routeResult;
        Error = error;
        if (routeResult == null && error == null)
        {
            throw new ArgumentException("Both arguments cannot be null.");
        }
    }
}
```

The custom `RouteCalculator` class implements `IRouteCalculator` and is used to call the Bing Geocode and Route services. The `RouteCalculator` relies on a `CredentialsProvider`, provided to it when it is created. See the following excerpt:

```
public class RouteCalculator : IRouteCalculator
{
    readonly CredentialsProvider credentialsProvider;
    readonly GeocodeServiceClient geocodeClient
                                    = new GeocodeServiceClient();
    readonly RouteServiceClient routeClient = new RouteServiceClient();

    public RouteCalculator(CredentialsProvider credentialsProvider)
    {
        this.credentialsProvider = ArgumentValidator.AssertNotNull(
                                    credentialsProvider,
                                    "credentialsProvider");
    }

    // Further content is presented later in this section.
}
```

16

The `CredentialsProvider` class also uses an asynchronous pattern to fetch credentials; its `GetCredentials` method has a void return type and accepts an `Action<Credentials>` parameter, which is invoked when the credentials have been retrieved.

> **NOTE**
>
> While the `CredentialsProvider.GetCredentials` method uses an asynchronous pattern, its default implementation, the `ApplicationIdCredentialsProvider` class, uses a blocking call to construct the `Credentials` and invoke the supplied `Action`.

The `RouteCalculator.CalculateAsync` method uses its `CalculateAsyncCore` method in combination with the `GetCredentials` method, as shown:

```
public void CalculateAsync(
    string fromAddress,
    string toAddress,
    Action<RouteCalculationResult> completeAction)
{
    ArgumentValidator.AssertNotNullOrEmpty(toAddress, "toAddress");
    ArgumentValidator.AssertNotNullOrEmpty(fromAddress, "fromAddress");
    ArgumentValidator.AssertNotNull(completeAction, "completeAction");

    credentialsProvider.GetCredentials(
        credentials => CalculateAsyncCore(
            credentials, fromAddress, toAddress, completeAction));
}
```

Figure 16.16 depicts what happens when the `CalculateAsync` method is called. The following list describes the process of retrieving a route:

1. The `RouteCalculator` resolves the credentials using the `CredentialsProvider` and dispatches two asynchronous calls to the Bing Geocode service client proxy.

2. The `RouteCalculator` waits for both geographic coordinates representing the origin (to) and the destination (from) addresses to be returned from the SOAP service. The `RouteCalculator` then uses the Bing Route service client proxy to retrieve attempts to find a route between the two coordinates.

3. When the Bing Route service client proxy responds, the route is placed in a new `RouteCalculationResult` and returned to the viewmodel.

Retrieving the route from the Bing Route service requires that you know the geographic coordinates for both the *to* and the *from* addresses. You could perform this task synchronously; you could retrieve the toAddress coordinate, wait until you have a result, then retrieve the fromAddress coordinate, and so on. A more efficient approach, however, is to dispatch both calls in parallel and then wait until you have both results, at which point you can request the route.

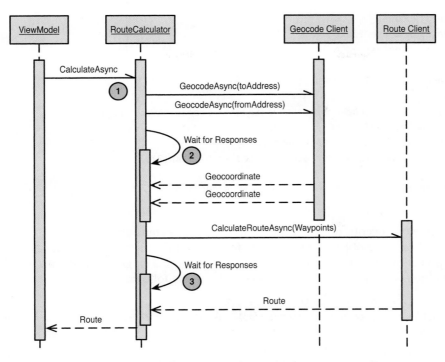

FIGURE 16.16   Retrieving a `Route` using the `RouteCalculator.CalculateAsync` method

Using Rx to Coordinate SOAP Service Calls

Rather than building a complicated state machine to accomplish the retrieval of the to and the from addresses, this section shows how Rx (Reactive Extensions) can be used to coordinate the SOAP service calls.

For more information on Rx, see Chapter 15.

> **NOTE**
>
> If you are new to Rx, you may find this section challenging. Feel free to skip over it and return to it when you face a similar scenario in one of your apps.

The first step is to coordinate the retrieval of the two geographic locations using the Bing Geocode service.

The following excerpt shows how an `IObservable` is created for the `GeocodeCompleted` event using the static `FromEvent` method of the `Observable` class. The `Take` extension method is used to specify that you want to automatically remove the subscription to the event after the event is raised twice.

```
void CalculateAsyncCore(
        Credentials credentials,
        string fromAddress,
        string toAddress,
        Action<RouteCalculationResult> completeAction)
{
    IObservable<IEvent<GeocodeCompletedEventArgs>> geocodingCompleted
        = Observable.FromEvent<GeocodeCompletedEventArgs>
            (h => geocodeClient.GeocodeCompleted += h,
            h => geocodeClient.GeocodeCompleted -= h).Take(2);


    // Further content is presented later in this section.
}
```

To coordinate these two events, append a call to the TakeLast extension method; this creates another IObservable object, which is used to retrieve the last two events. The Zip extension method allows you to merge sequences of events into a single event stream so that you are notified when both events have occurred. See the following excerpt:

```
var geocodeEvents = geocodingCompleted.TakeLast(2)
    .Let(observable => observable.Zip(observable.Skip(1),
        (previous, current) => new
                        {
                            Args1 = previous.EventArgs,
                            Args2 = current.EventArgs
                        }));
```

The Skip extension method is used to supply the Zip method with the second event occurrence. Zip combines the event arguments of the two event occurrences into a new anonymous type.

By using the Subscribe method on the IObservable object, a handler is called when the GeocodeCompleted event occurs twice, at which point you are able to dispatch the call to the Bing Route service, as shown in the following excerpt:

```
geocodeEvents.Subscribe(
    x =>
    {
        RouteCalculationError error
            = RouteCalculationError.CreateErrorIfInvalid(x.Args1)
                ?? RouteCalculationError.CreateErrorIfInvalid(x.Args2);

        if (error != null)
        {
            OnRouteCalculated(
                new RouteCalculationResult(null, error), completeAction);
            return;
        }
```

```
        RouteRequest request = new RouteRequest
            {
                Culture = CultureInfo.CurrentUICulture.Name,
                Waypoints = new ObservableCollection<Waypoint>(),
                /* Suppress exceptions. */
                ExecutionOptions = new ExecutionOptions
                {
                    SuppressFaults = true
                },
                Options = new RouteOptions
                {
                    RoutePathType = RoutePathType.Points
                }
            };

        request.Waypoints.Add(ToWaypoint(x.Args1.Result.Results.First()));
        request.Waypoints.Add(ToWaypoint(x.Args2.Result.Results.First()));
        request.Credentials = credentials;
        routeClient.CalculateRouteAsync(request);
    });
```

Each geographic coordinate resulting from the Bing Geocode service call in the previous step is converted to a `Waypoint` and then placed in the `Waypoints` collection of the `RouteRequest`.

You subscribe to the Bing Route client proxy's `CalculateRouteCompleted` in the same manner as the `GeocodeCompleted` event. This time, however, instead of waiting for the event to occur twice, you unsubscribe after its first occurrence. See the following excerpt:

```
var routeEvent = Observable.FromEvent<CalculateRouteCompletedEventArgs>
            (h => routeClient.CalculateRouteCompleted += h,
             h => routeClient.CalculateRouteCompleted -= h)
                            .Take(1).ObserveOnDispatcher();


routeEvent.Subscribe(x => HandleRouteCalculated(
    new RouteCalculationResult(x.EventArgs.Result.Result,
        RouteCalculationError.CreateErrorIfInvalid(x.EventArgs)),
        completeAction));
```

When the `routeClient.CalculateRouteCompleted` event is raised, the `RouteCalculator.HandleRouteCalculated` method is called. Before examining the `HandleRouteCalculated` method, let us look at the last two lines of the `CalculateAsyncCore` method.

Once subscription to the various event streams has been performed, you are able to dispatch the calls to the `geocodeClient` proxy, both of which occur asynchronously.

```
geocodeClient.GeocodeAsync(CreateGeocodeRequest(toAddress, credentials));
geocodeClient.GeocodeAsync(CreateGeocodeRequest(fromAddress, credentials));
```

The `RouteCalculator.HandleRouteCalculated` method is called as the final step in the route calculation process. This method invokes the `completeAction` that was passed to the `CalculateAsync` method.

```
protected virtual void HandleRouteCalculated(
    RouteCalculationResult calculationResult,
    Action<RouteCalculationResult> completeAction)
{
    ArgumentValidator.AssertNotNull(calculationResult, "calculationResult");
    Deployment.Current.Dispatcher.InvokeIfRequired(
                          () => completeAction(calculationResult));
}
```

By using a custom `Dispatcher` extension method called `InvokeIfRequired`, you are able to ensure that the callback is always invoked on the UI thread. This is useful when interacting with `DependencyObjects`, which have UI thread affinity.

Using the `IRouteCalculator`

When the to and from addresses have been provided by the user the `BingMapsViewModel` class leverages the `IRouteCalculator`. The viewmodel contains two string properties: `FromAddress` and `ToAddress`, which are populated using two `TextBox` controls in the view.

When the viewmodel's `RouteSearchCommand` is executed, the command first ensures that the address fields have been populated. It then uses the `IRouteCalculator` to calculate the route, as shown in the following excerpt:

```
public BingMapsViewModel(IRouteCalculator routeCalculator)
{
    ...
    routeSearchCommand = new DelegateCommand(
        obj =>
        {
            if (!string.IsNullOrEmpty(fromAddress)
                    && !string.IsNullOrEmpty(toAddress))
            {
                Message = "searching...";
                routeCalculator.CalculateAsync(
                    fromAddress, toAddress, HandleCalculationResult);
            }
            SetItineraryVisibility(false);
            SetRouteSearchVisibility(false);
        });
    ...
}
```

When the IRouteCalculator completes its search for a route, the HandleCalculationResult method is called. The following list describes the three main tasks of the HandleCalculationResult method:

▶ Populate the list of itinerary items for the route

▶ Create a Route object containing the geographic coordinates within the RouteCalculationResult

▶ Set the LocationRect property of the viewmodel to the routes coordinates, so that the view pans and zooms to display the entire route

The following excerpt shows the HandleCalculationResult method in full:

```
void HandleCalculationResult(RouteCalculationResult routeCalculationResult)
{
    Message = string.Empty;
    if (routeCalculationResult.Error != null)
    {
        return;
    }

    ObservableCollection<MapItineraryItem> items
            = new ObservableCollection<MapItineraryItem>();

    RouteLeg routeLeg = routeCalculationResult.RouteResult.Legs[0];
    foreach (ItineraryItem itineraryItem in routeLeg.Itinerary)
    {
        items.Add(new MapItineraryItem(itineraryItem));
    }
    ItineraryItems = items;

    Routes.Clear();
    ObservableCollection<Location> routePoints
            = routeCalculationResult.RouteResult.RoutePath.Points;
    Route route = new Route(routePoints);
    Routes = new ObservableCollection<Route> { route };
    LocationRect = LocationRect.CreateLocationRect(route.GeoCoordinates);
}
```

The Route class is a custom class that contains a read-only Microsoft.Phone.Controls.Maps.LocationCollection, representing the waypoints of the route (see Listing 16.7). By using the Route class, you could potentially create multiple routes and have them displayed within the view.

LISTING 16.7 Route Class

```
public class Route
{
    readonly LocationCollection geoCoordinates = new LocationCollection();

    public IEnumerable<GeoCoordinate> GeoCoordinates
    {
        get
        {
            return geoCoordinates;
        }
    }

    public Route(IEnumerable<Location> locations)
    {
        ArgumentValidator.AssertNotNull(locations, "locations");

        foreach (var location in locations)
        {
            geoCoordinates.Add(location);
        }
    }
}
```

Searching for a Route Using the View

The BingMapsView contains a Border control named RouteSearchView. This control is used to prompt the user for the origin (from) and destination (to) addresses (see Figure 16.17).

A visual state is used to hide and show the Border. When the Border is shown it provides the user with the means to enter two addresses. When the user taps the Search button, the viewmodel's SearchCommand executes.

The following excerpt shows the RouteSearchView Border:

```
<Border x:Name="RouteSearchView"
        Height="160" Margin="0" Padding="8"
        RenderTransformOrigin="0.5,0.5" Width="480"
        Background="{StaticResource PhoneBackgroundBrush}"
        Grid.ColumnSpan="2">
    <Border.RenderTransform>
        <CompositeTransform TranslateY="-160"/>
    </Border.RenderTransform>
    <Grid>
        <Grid.RowDefinitions>
            <RowDefinition />
```

```
        <RowDefinition />
    </Grid.RowDefinitions>
    <Grid.ColumnDefinitions>
        <ColumnDefinition Width="50" />
        <ColumnDefinition Width="0.8*" />
        <ColumnDefinition Width="0.4*"/>
    </Grid.ColumnDefinitions>
    <TextBlock Text="from" VerticalAlignment="Center" />
    <TextBox Text="{Binding FromAddress, Mode=TwoWay}"
        Grid.Column="1" Grid.ColumnSpan="2" />
    <TextBlock Text="to"
        Grid.Row="1" VerticalAlignment="Center" />
    <TextBox Text="{Binding ToAddress, Mode=TwoWay}"
        Grid.Row="1" Grid.Column="1" />
    <Button Command="{Binding RouteSearchCommand}"
        Content="search" Grid.Column="2" Grid.Row="1" />
    </Grid>
</Border>
```

FIGURE 16.17   The RouteSearchView Border control allows the user to search for a route.

When the Search button is tapped, the RouteSearchView Border is hidden via the VisualState property in the viewmodel.

Visual States

The visibility of the search panel and itinerary list is controlled using visual states. The visual state of either control is set via an associated string property in the viewmodel. Using a visual state, rather than a Boolean property for visibility, affords greater flexibility because you can create any number of visual state values, whereas a Boolean value allows you just two. See the following viewmodel excerpt:

```
public const string ShowRouteSearchState = "ShowRouteSearch";
public const string HideRouteSearchState = "HideRouteSearch";
string routeSearchVisualState = HideRouteSearchState;
public const string ShowItineraryState = "ShowItinerary";
public const string HideItineraryState = "HideItinerary";
string itineraryVisualState = HideItineraryState;

string visualState;

public string VisualState
{
    get
    {
        return visualState;
    }
    private set
    {
        Assign(() => VisualState, ref visualState, value);
    }
}
```

The routeSearchToggleCommand and the itineraryToggleCommand are used to switch the visual state properties. The commands are initialized in the viewmodel constructor as shown:

```
public BingMapsViewModel(IRouteCalculator routeCalculator)
{
...

    routeSearchToggleCommand = new DelegateCommand(
        obj => ToggleRouteSearchVisibility());

    itineraryToggleCommand = new DelegateCommand(
        obj => ToggleItineraryVisibility());
}
```

The RouteSearchToggleCommand and the ItineraryToggleCommand methods both set their corresponding visual state property to its alternate state via the ToggleItineraryVisibility and ToggleRouteSearchVisibility methods, as shown:

```
void ToggleRouteSearchVisibility()
{
    if (routeSearchVisualState == ShowRouteSearchState)
    {
        VisualState = routeSearchVisualState = HideRouteSearchState;
    }
    else
    {
        VisualState = routeSearchVisualState = ShowRouteSearchState;
    }
}

void ToggleItineraryVisibility()
{
    if (itineraryVisualState == ShowItineraryState)
    {
        VisualState = itineraryVisualState = HideItineraryState;
    }
    else
    {
        VisualState = itineraryVisualState = ShowItineraryState;
    }
}
```

16

The BingMapsView page contains various visual states that coincide with the viewmodel's VisualState properties (see Listing 16.8).

The task of the Storyboad elements within the visual states is to either contract or expand their associated target control.

LISTING 16.8   BingMapsView Page Visual State Groups (excerpt)

```
<Grid x:Name="LayoutRoot" Background="Transparent">
...
    <VisualStateManager.VisualStateGroups>
        <VisualStateGroup x:Name="RouteStates">
            <VisualStateGroup.Transitions>
                <VisualTransition To="ShowRouteSearch" />
                <VisualTransition To="HideRouteSearch" />
            </VisualStateGroup.Transitions>
            <VisualState x:Name="ShowRouteSearch">
                <Storyboard>
                    <DoubleAnimation Duration="0:0:0.3" To="0"
                        Storyboard.TargetProperty=
                            "(UIElement.RenderTransform)
                                    .(CompositeTransform.TranslateY)"
                        Storyboard.TargetName="RouteSearchView"
```

LISTING 16.8   Continued

```xml
                        d:IsOptimized="True">
                        <DoubleAnimation.EasingFunction>
                            <CircleEase EasingMode="EaseIn" />
                        </DoubleAnimation.EasingFunction>
                    </DoubleAnimation>
                </Storyboard>
            </VisualState>
            <VisualState x:Name="HideRouteSearch">
                <Storyboard>
                    ...
                </Storyboard>
            </VisualState>
        </VisualStateGroup>
        <VisualStateGroup x:Name="ItineraryStates">
            <VisualStateGroup.Transitions>
                <VisualTransition To="ShowItinerary" />
                <VisualTransition To="HideItinerary" />
            </VisualStateGroup.Transitions>
            <VisualState x:Name="ShowItinerary">
                <Storyboard>
                    ...
                </Storyboard>
            </VisualState>
            <VisualState x:Name="HideItinerary">
                <Storyboard>
                    ...
                </Storyboard>
            </VisualState>
        </VisualStateGroup>
    </VisualStateManager.VisualStateGroups>
</Grid>
```

When the VisualState of the viewmodel changes to ShowRouteSearch, for example, the VisualStateManager is directed to that state and the RouteSearchView Border control is brought into view. This is all orchestrated using a custom VisualStateUtility class and an attached property (see Listing 16.9).

The VisualState attached property can be placed on a Control element and automatically transitions the visual state of the control using the VisualStateManager according to the value of the attached property.

LISTING 16.9   VisualStateUtility Class

```
public static class VisualStateUtility
{
    public static readonly DependencyProperty VisualStateProperty
        = DependencyProperty.RegisterAttached(
            "VisualState",
            typeof(string),
            typeof(VisualStateUtility),
            new PropertyMetadata(HandleVisualStateChanged));

    public static string GetVisualState(DependencyObject obj)
    {
        return (string)obj.GetValue(VisualStateProperty);
    }

    public static void SetVisualState(DependencyObject obj, string value)
    {
        obj.SetValue(VisualStateProperty, value);
    }

    static void HandleVisualStateChanged(
        object sender, DependencyPropertyChangedEventArgs args)
    {
        var control = sender as Control;
        if (control != null)
        {
            string stateName = args.NewValue != null
                                ? args.NewValue.ToString() : null;
            if (stateName != null)
            {
                /* Call is invoked as to avoid missing
                 * the initial state before the control has loaded. */
                Deployment.Current.Dispatcher.BeginInvoke(
                    delegate
                        {
                            VisualStateManager.GoToState(
                                        control, stateName, true);
                        });
            }
        }
        else
        {
            throw new ArgumentException(
                "VisualState is only supported for Controls.");
        }
    }
}
```

The attached property is set on the `phone:PhoneApplicationPage` element of the view as shown:

```
u:VisualStateUtility.VisualState="{Binding VisualState}"
```

When the viewmodel `VisualState` property changes, the `HandleVisualStateChanged` method of the `VisualStateUtility` class is called, which calls the built-in `VisualStateManager.GoToState` method.

The advantage of this approach is that it becomes unnecessary to subscribe to viewmodel property changed events from the page code-beside.

Displaying the Route and Itinerary

When a search completes successfully, the resulting route is displayed as a bending line on the map, connecting itinerary waypoints. A separate expandable view displays the detailed itinerary.

Constructing the collection of itinerary items to be displayed on the map and itinerary view involves converting the Bing Route service `ItineraryItems` into objects that are more easily consumable by a `MapLayer` or a `ListBoxItem` data template.

Recall that the viewmodel's `HandleCalculationResult` populates the list of `ItineraryItems` using the `RouteCalculationResult`, as shown in the following excerpt:

```
RouteLeg routeLeg = routeCalculationResult.RouteResult.Legs[0];
foreach (ItineraryItem itineraryItem in routeLeg.Itinerary)
{
    items.Add(new MapItineraryItem(itineraryItem));
}
ItineraryItems = items;
```

The custom `MapItineraryItem` class is used to extract the relevant information from the Bing `ItineraryItem`. The following excerpt shows the `MapItineraryItem` constructor:

```
public MapItineraryItem(ItineraryItem item)
{
    ArgumentValidator.AssertNotNull(item, "item");
    Text = Extract(item.Text);
    Location = item.Location;
    Distance = item.Summary.Distance;
}
```

The `MapItineraryItem.Extract` method converts the text segment of the Bing response (which is in a quasi XML format) into a string that can be displayed as an itinerary item in the UI. The text response from the Bing Route service cannot be parsed as is because it contains an undefined XML namespace and no root node. The following excerpt shows how we construct the root element, inserting the service response text, which has been cleaned of any errant ampersand symbols:

```csharp
static string Extract(string value)
{
    ArgumentValidator.AssertNotNull(value, "value");

    var stringBuilder = new StringBuilder();

    string cleanedXml = value.Replace("&", "&amp;");
    string validXmlText = string.Format(
     "<Root xmlns:VirtualEarth=\"http://BingMaps\">{0}</Root>", cleanedXml);

    XDocument document = XDocument.Parse(validXmlText);

    XElement childElement = document.FirstNode as XElement;
    if (childElement != null)
    {
        foreach (XNode node in childElement.Nodes())
        {
            XElement element = node as XElement;
            stringBuilder.Append(
                element != null ? element.Value : node.ToString());
            stringBuilder.Append(' ');
        }
    }

    return stringBuilder.Replace("  ", " ").ToString();
}
```

The `BingMapsView` presents the itinerary items, both as pushpins on the `Map` control and in an expandable `ListBox`.

Itinerary items are displayed on the map using a `MapItemsControl` in the same manner as the earlier pushpin example in this chapter. The following excerpt shows the itinerary `MapItemsControl` from the `BingMapsView` XAML:

```xml
<m:Map Name="map">
...
    <m:MapItemsControl ItemsSource="{Binding ItineraryItems}">
        <m:MapItemsControl.ItemTemplate>
            <DataTemplate>
                <m:Pushpin Location="{Binding Location}"
                        Style="{StaticResource ItineraryPushpinStyle}" />
            </DataTemplate>
        </m:MapItemsControl.ItemTemplate>
    </m:MapItemsControl>

</m:Map>
```

When a route is located, the map view is panned and zoomed to display the path and waypoints (see Figure 16.18).

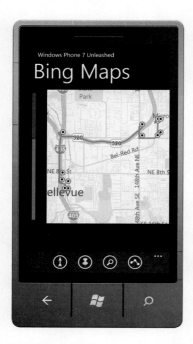

FIGURE 16.18   The BingMapsView after a route search completes

The style of each itinerary item pushpin is defined by the ItineraryPushpinStyle, located in the BingMapsView Resources element.

An ellipse is used to highlight the waypoint using the static resource PhoneAccentBrush as its Stroke. The use of the PhoneAccentBrush means that the Ellipse changes color according to the active theme on the phone. The following excerpt shows the ItineraryPushpinStyle:

```
<Style x:Key="ItineraryPushpinStyle" TargetType="m:Pushpin">
    <Setter Property="Template">
        <Setter.Value>
            <ControlTemplate TargetType="m:Pushpin">
                <Grid Height="20" Width="20">
                    <Ellipse x:Name="ellipse" Width="20" Height="20"
                            RenderTransformOrigin="0.5,0.5" Fill="White"
                            Stroke="{StaticResource PhoneAccentBrush}"
                            StrokeThickness="3" >
                        <Ellipse.RenderTransform>
                            <CompositeTransform/>
                        </Ellipse.RenderTransform>
```

```
            </Ellipse>
            <Ellipse x:Name="ellipse_Center" Width="8" Height="8"
                    RenderTransformOrigin="0.5,0.5" Fill="Black"
                    Stroke="{x:Null}" StrokeThickness="2" >
                <Ellipse.RenderTransform>
                    <CompositeTransform/>
                </Ellipse.RenderTransform>
            </Ellipse>
        </Grid>
    </ControlTemplate>
    </Setter.Value>
  </Setter>
</Style>
```

The `ListBox`'s `ItemsSource` property is bound to the `ItineraryItems` property in the view-model. Each custom `MapItineraryItem` has its `Text` and `DistanceString` property displayed within a `DataTemplate`, as shown in the following excerpt:

```
<Border x:Name="ItineraryView"
    VerticalAlignment="Bottom" Width="480" Height="260"
    RenderTransformOrigin="0.5,0.5" Grid.Row="2" Grid.ColumnSpan="2">

    <ListBox ItemsSource="{Binding ItineraryItems}" Margin="0,10">
        <ListBox.ItemTemplate>
            <DataTemplate>
                <StackPanel Orientation="Horizontal" Margin="5,2.5">
                    <TextBlock Text="{Binding Text}"
                            TextWrapping="Wrap"
                            Width="380" FontWeight="Light" />
                    <TextBlock Text="{Binding DistanceString}"
                            Margin="4,0,4,0" FontWeight="Light"
                            Foreground="{StaticResource PhoneAccentBrush}" />
                </StackPanel>
            </DataTemplate>
        </ListBox.ItemTemplate>
    </ListBox>

</Border>
```

The parent `Border` control is used to hide or display the `ListBox` via a visual state defined by the `ItineraryVisualState` string property of the viewmodel. The itinerary button in the application bar executes the `ItineraryToggleCommand` in the viewmodel, which toggles the `VisualState` from ShowItinerary to HideItinerary and vice-versa. The ShowItinerary state sets the height of the `ItineraryView Border` control so that it comes into view, while the HideItinerary state reduces the `Border`'s height to zero. When the `VisualState` is set to ShowItinerary, the list of itinerary items is presented (see Figure 16.19).

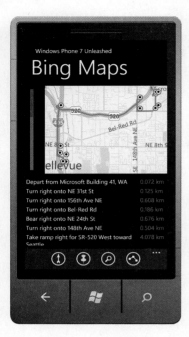

FIGURE 16.19   The itinerary button expands the itinerary view.

Summary

This chapter began with an overview of the Bing Maps control and walked through the creation of a Bing Maps API key. You saw how to customize the Bing Maps control by hiding the Bing logo and copyright text, how to programmatically zoom and pan the map, and how to create a customized zoom bar.

The chapter then continued on from the previous chapter to look at tracking the `IGeoPositionWatcher.PositionChanged` event within the Bing Maps control.

Next the chapter examined the `Pushpin` control and illustrated how it is used to identify locations of interest on the map. The `Pushpin` control contains a `Location` property, allowing it to be automatically positioned on a map layer. You saw how to generate pushpins from POCO collections and how to customize the appearance of pushpins using a custom style and control template.

The chapter then examined Bing SOAP services and how they can be leveraged to locate a route between two user-provided addresses. You saw how Rx can be used to coordinate asynchronous SOAP service calls to decrease overall search time. Hiding and revealing page elements using a viewmodel `VisualState` property in conjunction with an attached property and a custom `VisualStateUtility` class was also discussed.

Finally, you saw how a list of itinerary items can be presented both on the Bing Maps control and as a detailed expandable list.

CHAPTER 17

Internationalization

Internationalization is the process of building an application so that it can be adapted for different languages and regions. The Windows Phone Marketplace provides the opportunity to market an app to people from all over the world. Reaching such a broad audience of users requires that your software can be translated and otherwise adapted at runtime to be linguistically and culturally relevant to whomever is using it. This is the realm of internationalization and this chapter looks at the techniques to make your app world-ready.

It is crucial to devise efficient strategies for internationalization from the beginning of an app's development. As development progresses, it becomes increasingly difficult to retrofit support for multiple cultures.

This chapter begins by describing the terminology around internationalization, and then walks you through techniques and examples showing how to provide for dynamic localizability and image localizability in your Silverlight for Windows Phone apps.

Finally, the chapter touches on right to left support in Windows Phone.

Terminology

The term *internationalization* is an umbrella term for the process of presenting an application in multiple languages. The terms *internationalization*, *globalization*, and *localization* are sometimes used interchangeably, yet they have different meanings.

Globalization describes engineering an application so that it does not have cultural preconceptions. For example, in the United States dates are presented using the convention month/day/year, whereas in the United Kingdom and other countries, they are shown using the convention day/month/year. Fortunately, for developers working with .NET Microsoft provides considerable infrastructure for provisioning for globalization.

Localizability describes the capacity of an application to have its resources replaced at runtime with culturally specific resources. Localization is the process of providing the sets of culturally specific resources. Such resources may include strings, icons, images, and sound files.

This chapter focuses on localizability.

The primary means for implementing localizability in Silverlight for Windows Phone apps is through the use of resx files. While the main ingredients exist in Silverlight for localizability, there are techniques, demonstrated in this chapter, that improve compatibility with resx files and, in particular, enable them to be used with the Silverlight data binding infrastructure. This allows the UI to respond to culture settings changes at runtime, something that Silverlight does not provide out of the box.

Localizability Using Resx Files

Windows Phone apps follow the same hub and spoke model for localization that .NET desktop CLR applications do. Satellite assemblies provide culture specific resources, while a main assembly contains a default set of resources that are used to fall back on. This process of producing the main assembly and satellite assemblies is done automatically at build time.

At runtime the CLR selects the appropriate composite set of resources to use. The culture settings of a Windows Phone app and the language displayed are dependent on the culture settings of the phone itself.

Resx files have been employed to localize .NET applications since .NET 2.0 and Windows Forms. Resx files support the production of what is known as localized satellite assemblies. These are assemblies that are discovered at runtime and contain culture-specific resources.

In Silverlight browser applications, and desktop CLR projects, a major benefit of satellite assemblies is that they can be used to reduce the overall package size of an application. By storing culturally specific resources separately from the main assembly, culturally specific resources can be downloaded on demand. For example, if an application supports 10 languages, and each set of localized strings and images is 1MB, then one can reduce the overall download size by 9MB (10MB – 1MB = 9MB). In some scenarios this can prove to be critical, such as in Silverlight browser applications, where the proper use of bandwidth can play a large factor in an application's success. It is, however, largely irrelevant for Windows Phone apps, since the manner in which satellite assemblies are deployed to the phone, in particular the bundling of all assemblies into a single XAP file, including satellite assemblies, means that without the use of multiple resource projects, all satellite assemblies are deployed to the phone anyway, and therefore it does not reduce the overall footprint of an app. Moreover, the Windows Phone Marketplace requires each app to come complete with localized resources for all languages supported by the app. The topic of separate deployment of satellite assemblies, therefore, is not covered in this book.

Getting Started with Resx Files

The first step in enabling a project to support localizable resx files involves editing the project file manually. Curiously, while you can change the *neutral language* for a project via the Assembly Information dialog, via the Visual Studio project properties tab, there is no facility to change the supported cultures for a project within Visual Studio 2010.

To allow a project to support multiple languages, follow these steps:

1. Right-click on the project node in the Solution Explorer within Visual Studio and select Unload Project.

2. Right-click again on the project node and select Edit YourProjectName.csproj.

3. Locate the `SupportedCultures` element, which, by default, is located in the first `PropertyGroup` element.

4. Add the culture codes that are supported. For example, if intending to support both US English and French, the `SupportedCultures` element may look like this:
   `<SupportedCultures>fr;en-US</SupportedCultures>`
   The culture name format is discussed in the next section.

5. Save the project file, close it, and then right-click on the project node and select Reload Project.

After the previous steps are completed, compiling the project with culturally specific resx files produces independent satellite assemblies located together within the resulting XAP file.

Working with Resx Files

To create a resx file, right-click on a project node in the Solution Explorer and select Add and then New Item, or alternatively press Ctrl+Shift+A (see Figure 17.1).

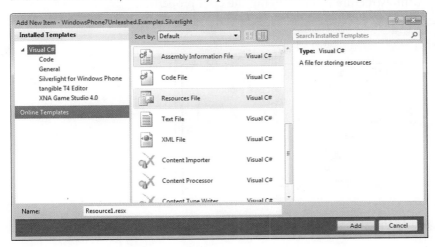

FIGURE 17.1   Creating a new resx file

17

Once the first default resource file has been created, enabling support for alternate languages is achieved by adding a new resource file for each additional language (see Figure 17.2), and by employing the following naming convention:

```
<Name of the default language resource file>.<Culture Name>.resx
```

Names differ only by culture name, where the culture name has the following format:

```
<Lowercase two letter language code>-<Uppercase two letter region code>
```

If not specifying a region, then use the following format:

```
<Lowercase two letter language code>
```

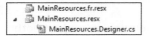

FIGURE 17.2   By using different culture codes when naming resx files, Visual Studio generates satellite assemblies for specific cultures.

NOTE

The culture code present in the name of a resx file must match a `SupportedCultures` string within the project file. Otherwise, no satellite assembly is generated. This also applies when the region is defined with a wider scope without a locale in the `SupportedCultures` project element.

When editing a resx file, the resx editor allows the access modifier of the generated class to be set to internal or public (see Figure 17.3). As the resource file is going to be used within XAML bindings, it must be set to public because the use of internal prevents the Silverlight binding infrastructure from resolving the class properties.

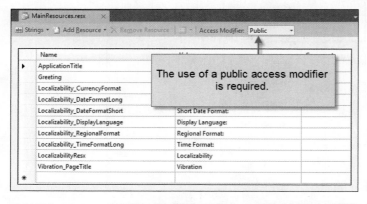

FIGURE 17.3   Setting the access modifier to public enables properties to be used in XAML binding expressions.

While setting the access modifier to Public produces public properties, it unfortunately does not produce a public constructor. The resx file's generated designer class is left with an internal constructor, which prevents it from being used directly as a resource in a XAML file. Furthermore, modifying the generated designer class is not a practical solution, because any changes to it are lost if the resx file is modified, causing the resx custom tool to run.

> **CAUTION**
>
> Unfortunately the generated output of the `PublicResXFileCodeGenerator` (the tool that converts the resx file XML to a class) does not generate an extensibility point that is compatible with the XAML resource infrastructure. That is, it is not possible to include the generated output directly as an application resource via XAML. The generated class that it produces is not partial, and subclassing it breaks the ability to data bind to the static resource properties in the base class.

One possible approach is to use an intermediary class, whose task is to create an instance of the generated class and expose it as a public static property, thereby making it compatible with the Silverlight data binding infrastructure. This class, called `BindableResources`, is shown in Listing 17.1 and is available in the downloadable sample code.

LISTING 17.1   BindableResources Class

```
public class BindableResources
{
    static readonly BindableChangeNotifier<MainResources> resources
        = new BindableChangeNotifier<MainResources>(new MainResources());

    public static BindableChangeNotifier<MainResources> Resources
    {
        get
        {
            return resources;
        }
    }

    public static void RaiseNotifyPropertyChanged()
    {
        resources.RaisePropertyChanged();
    }
}
```

As new resx files are added to a project, they should also be added to the `BindableResources` class and exposed as static properties. For convenience, the default resources class, MainResources, is named `Resources`.

While the approach presented here may at first appear complicated, it provides for change notification, allowing the Silverlight data binding infrastructure to be coerced into rereading the static properties of the localizable resources when the application culture changes.

The BindableResources class uses the BindableChangeNotifier to expose the localizable resources. When the culture is changed, the BindableResources class signals to each BindableChangeNotifier instance that the PropertyChanged event should be raised. Once the event is raised, all data bindings associated with the resources are refreshed.

The BindableResources class can be defined as a resource in an application-wide resource file or directly in your app's App.xaml file, as shown in the following excerpt:

```
<Application ...>
    <Application.Resources>
        <local:BindableResources x:Key="BindableResources" />
    </Application.Resources>
</Application>
```

This allows an instance of the BindableResources proxy to be resolved in binding expressions, like so:

```
<TextBlock Text="{Binding Resources.Instance.ApplicationTitle,
        Source={StaticResource BindableResources}}" />
```

Here the Source property of the Text property's binding expression points to the BindableResources instance. The path accesses the ApplicationTitle resource string via the Instance property of the BindableChangeNotifier, which happens to be an instance of the resx generated designer class.

> **NOTE**
>
> Validation of Silverlight binding expressions is performed at runtime. Unlike WPF, Silverlight does not support the x:Static markup extension, which would otherwise provide the means to validate the binding expression at compile time.

Dynamic Localizability—Updating the UI When the Culture Changes

Silverlight's data binding infrastructure relies on change notification to signal that a property in a data binding expression should be reevaluated. Generated resource designer classes do not provide change notification. Simply exposing the generated resource class for data binding does not allow the UI to be updated when there is a culture change at runtime. Therefore, some other means is required to update the UI when the app's culture changes. This is the purpose of the custom BindableChangeNotifier class, shown in Listing 17.2. By using the BindableChangeNotifier class to wrap the resource's designer class, change notification can be surreptitiously added for all properties.

> **NOTE**
>
> If the desired `CurrentCulture` of the thread is set to the appropriate value before the UI is shown, then refreshing the data bindings is not required. If, however, the user is provided with the ability to change the language, after the UI is loaded, then the `BindableChangeNotifier` or some other mechanism is necessary to refresh the data bindings within the active view.

The `ResourceBase` class implements `System.ComponentModel.INotifyPropertyChanged` to signal to the data binding infrastructure that properties should be reread (see Listing 17.2).

LISTING 17.2   BindableChangeNotifier Class

```
public sealed class BindableChangeNotifier<T> : INotifyPropertyChanged
{
    public event PropertyChangedEventHandler PropertyChanged;

    static T instance;

    public T Instance
    {
        get
        {
            return instance;
        }
    }

    public BindableChangeNotifier(T observableObject)
    {
        instance = observableObject;
    }

    public void RaisePropertyChanged()
    {
        var temp = PropertyChanged;
        if (temp != null)
        {
            temp(this, new PropertyChangedEventArgs(string.Empty));
        }
    }
}
```

The `BindableChangeNotifier` class contains a public method called `RaisePropertyChanged`. By using `string.Empty` as the property name, it signals to the data binding infrastructure that all source properties within the resources object should be reread. Thus, it is not necessary to raise the `PropertyChanged` event for each resource property.

Localizing Images Using Resx Files

The resx designer in Visual Studio 2010 behaves in a manner typical of the .NET 2.0 days, when the main client side presentation technology was Windows Forms. This is made evident by its preference to use various Windows Forms types for certain kinds of resources, such as images, which are represented by the type `System.Drawing.Bitmap`. This type does not exist in the Windows Phone FCL (Framework Class Library), which makes localizing images in Silverlight somewhat more difficult. Because of the absence of this class, using a resx file to localize images, such as those that are in the JPG or PNG formats, fails to generate a compilable resource designer class. This is a limitation of the Visual Studio custom tool.

As a workaround, the image can be stored in another format within the resx file. This approach involves tricking Visual Studio into storing the image as an `UnmanagedMemoryStream` by temporarily renaming the image. To store an image in a Silverlight resx file follow these steps:

1. Change the file extension of the image to .wav.

2. Select Add Resource and then Add Existing File from the resx designer toolbar.

3. Browse to the renamed image file and select Open.

4. Save and close the resx designer.

5. Rename the image file in the Solution Explorer. Visual Studio places resources into a directory called Resources.

6. Open the resx file using the XML editor. This is done by right-clicking on the resx file, selecting Open With, and then selecting XML Editor.

7. Edit the data element for the newly added resource to reflect the correct file extension. Here, AnImage.wav becomes AnImage.jpg:

```xml
<data name="AnImage"
      type="System.Resources.ResXFileRef, System.Windows.Forms">
  <value>
    Resources\AnImage.jpg;System.IO.MemoryStream, mscorlib,
    Version=2.0. 5.0, Culture=neutral, PublicKeyToken=7cec85d7bea7798e
  </value>
</data>
```

> **NOTE**
>
> Steps 5 to 7, while not entirely necessary, do help to avoid confusion by eliminating the .wav extensions for application images.

An `Image` control can now be bound to a localized image as shown in the following excerpt:

```
<Image Source="{Binding Resources.Instance.ImageResourceName,
        Source={StaticResource BindableResources},
        Converter={StaticResource BitmapImageConverter}}" />
```

As in the previous string resources example, the data binding's `Source` property uses the
`ResourceBindingWrapper` `BindableResources` instance defined in the app's resources. The
data binding's `Path` property is set to `Resources.Instance.ImageResourceName`, which is the
`UnmanagedMemoryStream` property for the image.

Notice the use of the `BitmapImageConverter` in the previous excerpt. This `IValueConverter`
is responsible for taking the image data in the form of an `UnmanagedMemoryStream` and
converting it into an image (see Listing 17.3).

LISTING 17.3   `BitmapImageConverter` Class

```
public class BitmapImageConverter : IValueConverter
{
    public object Convert(object value, Type targetType,
        object parameter, System.Globalization.CultureInfo culture)
    {
        UnmanagedMemoryStream memoryStream = (UnmanagedMemoryStream)value;
        BitmapImage bitmapImage = new BitmapImage();
        bitmapImage.SetSource(memoryStream);
        return bitmapImage;
    }

    public object ConvertBack(object value, Type targetType,
        object parameter, System.Globalization.CultureInfo culture)
    {
        throw new NotImplementedException();
    }
}
```

The Resx Localizability Sample

The sample for this chapter demonstrates how to leverage resource files to support multiple UI languages. The interface allows the user to set the application thread's culture value via a `ListBox` (see Figure 17.4). The interface includes fields to demonstrate the various culture-dependent data formats, such as currency, as well as demonstrating the use of a localizable image.

Selecting a language endonym (name) changes the app's culture, and results in the image being replaced and the data format fields being updated to reflect the new selection.

NOTE

An *endonym* refers to the name of a language that is used by speakers of the language in the language itself.

FIGURE 17.4   The Localizability sample demonstrates how to change the UI language at runtime.

BEST PRACTICE

Allow users to switch languages using endonyms. It makes little sense to display a pick list of languages and/or cultures, where the names are displayed in the current interface language. Odds are that if you are seeking to change the interface language, it is because you are having difficulty understanding it. If the interface language happens to be in Japanese, for example, and you are unable to read Japanese, then being shown a list of languages to pick from in Japanese is not helpful. This is an all too common UI faux-pas.

The source code for this sample is located in Localizability directory of the WindowsPhone7Unleashed.Example project, in the downloadable sample code.

CultureName Class

Available cultures are represented using the custom CultureName class, which contains a CultureCode property and an Endonym property (see Listing 17.4).

LISTING 17.4   CultureName Class

```
public sealed class CultureName
{
    public string CultureCode { get; private set; }
    public string Endonym { get; private set; }

    public CultureName(string cultureCode, string endonym)
    {
        CultureCode = cultureCode;
        Endonym = endonym;
    }
}
```

Controlling the UI Culture from the `LocalizabilityViewModel`

The viewmodel exposes a list of `CultureName` objects via its `SupportedCultures` property. The list of supported cultures is initialized as shown:

```
readonly List<CultureName> supportedCultures = new List<CultureName>
                    {
                        new CultureName("en-US", "English US"),
                        new CultureName("fr-FR", "Français"),
                        /* Not supported. */
                        new CultureName("ar-AE", "???????")
                    };
```

A method called `SetCulture` is used to change the `CurrentCulture` and `CurrentUICulture` of the UI thread, as shown in the following excerpt:

```
void SetCulture(string cultureName)
{
    CultureInfo cultureInfo = new CultureInfo(cultureName);

    Thread.CurrentThread.CurrentCulture = cultureInfo;
    Thread.CurrentThread.CurrentUICulture = cultureInfo;

    BindableResources.RaiseNotifyPropertyChanged();
    Message = string.Empty;

    SetCurrentCultureValues();
}
```

`CurrentCulture` affects the formatting of currency values, dates, and so forth, while `CurrentUICulture` determines the language and consequently the primary resource dictionary that is used by your app.

17

Not all culture names are supported in Windows Phone. Attempting to instantiate a
`CultureInfo` class using an unsupported culture name raises a
`PlatformNotSupportedException` (see Figure 17.5).

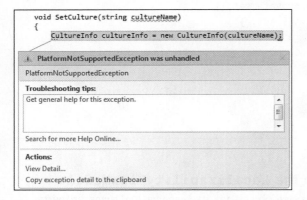

```
void SetCulture(string cultureName)
{
    CultureInfo cultureInfo = new CultureInfo(cultureName);
```

FIGURE 17.5   A `PlatformNotSupportedException` is raised if a specific culture name is not
supported.

The viewmodel contains a `CultureName` property that controls the current culture of the
app. The `CultureName` set accessor calls the `SetCulture` method if assignment succeeds. If a
`PlatformNotSupportedException` is raised, the value falls back to the previous value. See
the following excerpt:

```
CultureName cultureName;

public CultureName CultureName
{
    get
    {
        return cultureName;
    }
    set
    {
        CultureName temp = cultureName;
        AssignmentResult result
            = Assign(() => CultureName, ref cultureName, value);

        if (result == AssignmentResult.Success && value != null)
        {
            try
            {
                SetCulture(value.CultureCode);
            }
            catch (PlatformNotSupportedException)
            {
```

```
            CultureName = temp;
            Message = "Platform not supported";
            return;
        }
    }
}
}
```

The viewmodel contains various properties that indicate the culture specific date, time, and currency formatting. These properties are initialized in the SetCurrentCultureValues method, which is shown in the following excerpt:

```
void SetCurrentCultureValues()
{
    CultureInfo culture = Thread.CurrentThread.CurrentCulture;
    CultureInfo uiCulture = Thread.CurrentThread.CurrentUICulture;
    DisplayLanguage = uiCulture.DisplayName;
    RegionalFormat = culture.NativeName;
    DateTime date = DateTime.Now;
    try
    {
        DateFormatLong = culture.DateTimeFormat.LongDatePattern
                                + " " + date.ToString("D");
        DateFormatShort = culture.DateTimeFormat.ShortDatePattern
                                + " " + date.ToString("d");
        TimeFormat = culture.DateTimeFormat.LongTimePattern + " "
                                + date.ToString("T");
    }
    catch (IndexOutOfRangeException)
    {
        Message = "DateTimeFormat is not defined for culture.";
    }
    const int monetaryAmount = 123456789;
    CurrencyFormat = monetaryAmount.ToString("C");
}
```

Displaying Localized Text and Images within the LocalizabilityView Page

The view's XAML file is entirely absent of literal strings. The BindableResources instance is used to retrieve all localized resource strings (see Listing 17.5).

A ListBox is bound to the viewmodel's SupportedCultures property. Selecting a value causes the current thread's CurrentCulture and CurrentUICulture to be set to a new CultureInfo instance. The BindableResources.RaisePropertyChanged method is then called to trigger an update of the UI.

The flag image is also bound to the `BindableResources`. The binding uses an `IValueConverter` called `BitmapImageConverter`, to transform the localized image bytes into a `BitmapImage`. The `BitmapImageConverter` class was presented earlier in Listing 17.3.

LISTING 17.5 `LocalizabilityResxView.xaml` (excerpt)

```xml
<Grid x:Name="LayoutRoot" Background="{StaticResource PhoneBackgroundBrush}">
    <Grid.RowDefinitions>
        <RowDefinition Height="140"/>
        <RowDefinition Height="*"/>
    </Grid.RowDefinitions>

    <Grid>
        <TextBlock x:Name="ApplicationName"
                   Text="{Binding Resources.Instance.ApplicationTitle,
                          Source={StaticResource BindableResources}}"
                   Style="{StaticResource PhoneTextNormalStyle}"/>
        <TextBlock x:Name="ListName"
                   Text="{Binding Resources.Instance.LocalizabilityResx,
                          Source={StaticResource BindableResources}}"
                   Style="{StaticResource PhoneTextTitle1Style}"
                   Margin="0,5,0,0"/>
    </Grid>

    <StackPanel Grid.Row="1" Margin="20">
        <ListBox ItemsSource="{Binding SupportedCultures}"
                 SelectedItem="{Binding CultureName, Mode=TwoWay}">
            <ListBox.ItemTemplate>
                <DataTemplate>
                    <TextBlock Text="{Binding Path=Endonym}" />
                </DataTemplate>
            </ListBox.ItemTemplate>
        </ListBox>

        <!-- Flag and greeting. -->
        <StackPanel Orientation="Horizontal">
            <Image Width="100" Height="100"
                   Source="{Binding Resources.Instance.Flag,
                        Source={StaticResource BindableResources},
                        Converter={StaticResource BitmapImageConverter}}"
                   Margin="5,5,20,5"/>
            <TextBlock Text="{Binding Resources.Instance.Greeting,
                            Source={StaticResource BindableResources}}"
                       Style="{StaticResource PhoneTextLargeStyle}"
                       VerticalAlignment="Center" Width="122" />
        </StackPanel>
```

LISTING 17.5   Continued

```xml
<!-- Culture details. -->
<StackPanel>
    <TextBlock
     Text="{Binding Resources.Instance.Localizability_DisplayLanguage,
                    Source={StaticResource BindableResources}}"
            Style="{StaticResource PhoneTextTitle3Style}" />
    <TextBlock Text="{Binding DisplayLanguage}"
            Style="{StaticResource PaddedTextStyle}" />
    <TextBlock
        Text="{Binding Source={StaticResource BindableResources},
                Path=Resources.Instance.Localizability_RegionalFormat}"
        Style="{StaticResource PhoneTextTitle3Style}" />
    <TextBlock Text="{Binding RegionalFormat}"
            Style="{StaticResource PaddedTextStyle}" />
    <TextBlock
        Text="{Binding Source={StaticResource BindableResources},

            Path=Resources.Instance.Localizability_DateFormatLong}"
        Style="{StaticResource PhoneTextTitle3Style}" />
    <TextBlock Text="{Binding DateFormatLong}"
             Style="{StaticResource PaddedTextStyle}" />
    <TextBlock
        Text="{Binding Source={StaticResource BindableResources},
                Path=Resources.Instance.Localizability_DateFormatShort}"
        Style="{StaticResource PhoneTextTitle3Style}" />
    <TextBlock Text="{Binding DateFormatShort}"
             Style="{StaticResource PaddedTextStyle}" />
    <TextBlock
        Text="{Binding Source={StaticResource BindableResources},
          Path=Resources.Instance.Localizability_TimeFormatLong}"
             Style="{StaticResource PhoneTextTitle3Style}" />
    <TextBlock Text="{Binding TimeFormat}"
            Style="{StaticResource PaddedTextStyle}" Grid.Row="4" />
    <TextBlock
        Text="{Binding Source={StaticResource BindableResources},
              Path=Resources.Instance.Localizability_CurrencyFormat}"
             Style="{StaticResource PhoneTextTitle3Style}" />
    <TextBlock Text="{Binding CurrencyFormat}"
             Style="{StaticResource PaddedTextStyle}" />
</StackPanel>

<TextBlock Text="{Binding Message}"
        Foreground=" {StaticResource PhoneAccentBrush}"
```

LISTING 17.5   Continued

```
                    Style="{StaticResource PhoneTextSubtleStyle}" />
    </StackPanel>
</Grid>
```

When a new culture is selected by the user, the flag and various string fields are updated, as shown in Figure 17.6.

FIGURE 17.6   Changing the UI language at runtime

TIP

Consider in advance that translated strings may end up being longer or shorter in length than your intended design allows. Be generous when allocating space for text, and allow for as much as a 50% increase in length, when the text is localized.

Data binding expressions for localizable properties may be edited manually within Visual Studio's XAML editor or in the design view by selecting the property in the Properties pane (see Figure 17.7).

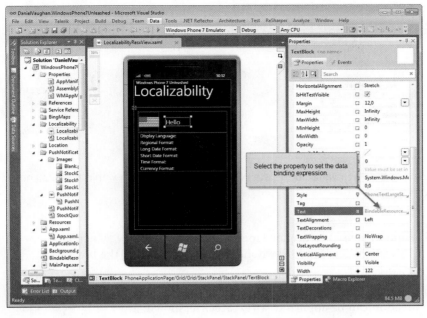

FIGURE 17.7   Selecting a resource property within Visual Studio

Selecting the property in the property pane allows the data binding expression's Source property to be set using the floating window. In Figure 17.8 you see that the binding's Source property is set to the resource with name BindableResources, which is defined at the application resources level within the App.xaml file.

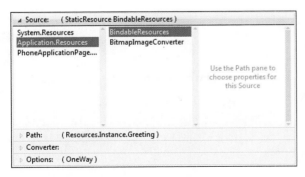

FIGURE 17.8   Setting the Source value for a data binding expression from within the designer

Similarly, the data binding's Path property can be set by expanding the Path tab in the floating window. Figure 17.9 shows that the Text property is bound to the Greeting string property.

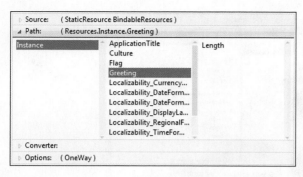

FIGURE 17.9   Setting the `Path` value for a data binding expression, from within the designer

RTL Support

Right to left (RTL) support is used to display languages, such as Hebrew, which are right-aligned by default. Silverlight for Windows Phone supports RTL out of the box.

By setting the `FlowDirection` property on any `FrameworkElement` object, you can control whether text is presented from left to right (the default) or right to left. For example, a right to left flow direction can be applied to a `TextBlock` as shown:

```
<TextBlock FlowDirection="RightToLeft" />
```

Alternatively, a right to left flow direction can be applied to all elements on a page, like so:

```
<phone:PhoneApplicationPage
...
    FlowDirection="RightToLeft">
...
</phone:PhoneApplicationPage>
```

Figure 17.10 demonstrates the effect of a right to left flow direction on the sample page.

FIGURE 17.10   `LocalizabilityResxView` with right to left flow direction

Summary

This chapter looked at how to use resx files to provide localizability for a Silverlight for Windows Phone app. The chapter explored techniques that allow resource designer classes to be readily consumed by the Silverlight data binding infrastructure. You also saw how to provision for runtime language changes, without requiring an application restart or the closing of a view.

Finally, the chapter touched on using the `FrameworkElement.FlowDirection` property to display text from right to left.

17

FIGURE 1.17 Localizer. (Courtesy of Baxter Mfg. Company)

SUMMARY

Extending the Windows Phone Picture Viewer

The Windows Phone photo experience is a key aspect of the phone OS. These days, just about everyone who uses a smartphone wants to be able to alter and share photos with friends and family via social networks.

The Windows Phone picture viewer app displays local or online photos in a consistent way. You can reach the picture viewer on a Windows Phone by navigating to the Windows Phone Pictures Hub and then selecting any image. The picture viewer's menu is activated by tapping the three dots at the bottom of the page.

While most of the built-in Windows Phone apps do not offer points of extensibility, the built-in picture viewer app is one exception.

With the picture viewer, it is possible to give users the ability to launch your app directly from the picture viewer itself, to provide extended image processing capabilities, or to send an image to a third-party cloud service.

The picture viewer provides two extensibility points: photo extras applications and photo share applications.

Photo extras application extensibility allows you to integrate your photo altering app with the OS, giving users the ability to launch your app from the picture viewer, alter a photo, and save it back to the phone's picture library.

Photo share application extensibility allows you to integrate your photo upload app into the picture viewer application, giving users the ability to upload an image to a third-party service via your app.

This chapter begins by looking at photo Extras applications. You see how to add an app to the picture viewer's Extras menu, and how to create an Extras application that traces the edges within an image and allows the user to save the image back to the phone's picture library.

The chapter then looks at photo Share applications. You learn how to add an app to the picture viewer's Share menu, and how to create a photo Share application that uploads images to a custom WCF service.

Finally, this chapter looks at the Windows Phone Connect Tool and how it is used to unlock the phone's media library during debugging.

For developing Windows Phone apps, we are fortunate to have two technologies at our disposal: Silverlight and XNA. In Chapter 7, "Media and Web Elements," you saw how an XNA API was used to play sound effects efficiently. In this chapter, you see how some of the picture and media capabilities are, once again, provided by XNA APIs.

NOTE

Windows Phone supports either 16 or 32 bpp (bits per pixel). By default Windows Phone apps use 16 bpp, which can cause some images to appear to be of low quality. Gradients in particular are most subject to the apparent effects of low pixel density, and when using 16 bpp banding may be detected in some images.

To use 32 bpp in your app, modify its WMAppManifest.xml file by adding a BitsPerPixel attribute to the App element, as shown in the following excerpt:

```
<App …
  BitsPerPixel="32">
</App>
```

Be aware that using 32 bpp may impact the performance of your app, especially if you are rendering a lot of images in a list, for example. Where possible apply dithering as preprocessing to image assets instead.

Debugging Apps That Rely on the Pictures Hub

The Windows Phone 7.5 emulator does not include access to the Pictures Hub on the device. Therefore, if you do not have a device, you may find working through certain parts of this chapter difficult.

While it is possible to unlock the Windows Phone emulator to allow access to various hubs, including the Pictures Hub, using it for phone development is not recommended as it takes substantially longer to boot, and it is not supported by Microsoft.

Debugging an app that relies on the Windows Phone Pictures Hub is awkward and in most cases does not work. A workaround for this, which uses an image resource during development, is presented later in the chapter.

If you have a device on hand and you want to test an app that uses the Pictures Hub, follow these steps.

1. Tether your phone to your computer and wait for it to be recognized by the Zune software.

2. Make sure that the solution is set to deploy to the Windows Phone Device.

3. Select Debug from the menu, and select Start Debugging.

4. When the application is visible, go back to the Debug menu and select Stop Debugging.

5. Disconnect the device from your computer, navigate to the Windows Phone application list, and locate your application.

Creating a Photos Extras Application

The Extras menu of the built-in picture viewer app allows you to add a link to your app so that the user can quickly launch your app from within the picture viewer. This effectively allows you to extend the picture viewer with your own app.

An Extras application may be used to enhance an image's color, crop an image, convert an image to monochrome, or even read a photo's Exchangeable image file format (EXIF) information to display where the photo was taken on a map.

For an example of an app that reads EXIF data, see the Photo Location app on the Windows Phone Marketplace. (Full disclosure: The app is written by my wife.)

When a user taps the three dots on the application bar in the picture viewer, he is presented with a menu containing a link to the Extras menu (see Figure 18.1).

18

FIGURE 18.1   Users can activate a photo Extras application or a photo Share application.

Selecting the Extras menu item presents the list of apps that are registered as Extras applications (see Figure 18.2).

FIGURE 18.2   The sample Extras application displayed in the Extras menu

When a user selects your app from the Extras menu, your app is launched, and it receives an identifier (a token) that is used to retrieve the image from the phone's image library.

Adding Your App to the Extras Menu

To indicate to the Windows Phone picture viewer that your app should be included in the Extras menu, the inclusion of an XML file called Extras.xml is required in the root of your XAP file.

To add the Extras.xml file to your project, follow these steps:

1. Right-click the name of your project in the Solution Explorer, and select Add, New Item.

2. On the Add New Item page select XML File, and name the file Extras.xml.

3. Select Add.

> **NOTE**
>
> Make sure that the Extras.xml file is set to Content. Contrary to the official documentation on MSDN, the Copy to Output Directory option should be set to Do Not Copy. You can do this via the Visual Studio Properties window after selecting the file in the Solution Explorer.

Edit the Extras.xml file so that it matches Listing 18.1.

LISTING 18.1   Extras.xml

```xml
<?xml version="1.0" encoding="utf-8" ?>
<Extras>
    <PhotosExtrasApplication>
        <Enabled>true</Enabled>
    </PhotosExtrasApplication>
</Extras>
```

When an app is installed on the phone, the OS scans the XAP file. When it discovers the Extras.xml file, it adds your app to the picture viewer's Extras menu.

An Edge Tracing Extras Application

This section looks at building an Extras application that converts an image to a line drawing by tracing its edges, and then allows the user to save the image to the Saved Pictures folder in the Pictures Hub. The example app for this section is located in the WindowsPhone7Unleashed.ExtrasExample project in the downloadable sample code.

When your app is selected from the Extras menu, your app is launched and the main page of your app has its query string populated with a string identifier named token. The token value is then used to retrieve the image from the phone's image library, as shown later in this section.

18

To hasten the pace of development and to enable testing of your app without deploying to a Windows Phone device, it is useful to feed your app with a dummy image so that it does not have to rely on the Pictures Hub.

In the following excerpt from MainPage.xaml.cs, you see how to detect whether the app is executing on the emulator using the `Microsoft.Devices.Environment.DeviceType` property. If so, substitute the image, which would otherwise be supplied by the picture viewer, with a sample image stored as an embedded resource.

Conversely, if not executing within the emulator, attempt to extract the token from the page's query string, as shown:

```
protected override void OnNavigatedTo(NavigationEventArgs e)
{
    base.OnNavigatedTo(e);

    /* Equivalent to: Environment.DeviceType == DeviceType.Emulator */
    if (EnvironmentValues.UsingEmulator)
    {
        ProcessTestImage();
    }
    else
    {
        string token;
        if (NavigationContext.QueryString.TryGetValue("token", out token))
        {
            ProcessImageUsingToken(token);
        }
        else
        {
            if (image.Source == null)
            {
                photoChooserTask.Show();
            }
        }
    }
}
```

When the query string does not contain a token, it indicates that the app has been launched from either the Start Experience (if the app has been pinned there), or from the Application List.

> **NOTE**
>
> It is a Windows Phone Marketplace certification requirement that if your Extras application is launched from the application list (not from the Extras menu) it must invoke the PhotoChooser task to allow the user to select an image or take a photo. Conversely, it is also a requirement that if your app is launched from the Extras menu, it should not require further image selection steps.

To retrieve an image from the phone's image library, we leverage the XNA framework, in particular the `Microsoft.Xna.Framework.Media.MediaLibrary` class located in the Microsoft.Xna.Framework assembly. This assembly should be added as a reference to your project (see Figure 18.3).

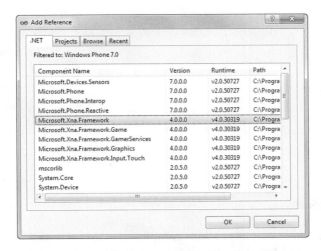

FIGURE 18.3   Add a reference to the `Microsoft.Xna.Framework` assembly.

The XNA `MediaLibrary` class is used to retrieve the image with the specified token. The `MediaLibrary` class implements `IDisposable`, and hence it is wrapped in a using statement, as shown in the following excerpt:

```
void ProcessImageUsingToken(string token)
{
    imageName = token;

    Picture picture;
    using (MediaLibrary mediaLibrary = new MediaLibrary())
    {
        picture = mediaLibrary.GetPictureFromToken(token);
    }
    Stream imageStream = picture.GetImage();
    ProcessImage(imageStream);
}
```

When the image `Stream` has been retrieved, the `ProcessImage` method is called, which creates a `BitmapImage` object. The `BitmapImage` is assigned to an `Image` control on the page (see Figure 18.4).

FIGURE 18.4   The sample Extras application

The image is displayed until processing has completed. Once complete the `Image` control's `Source` property is assigned to the processed image in the `HandleEdgesFound` method.

The `ProcessImage` method creates a new `BitmapImage` object and passes it to the `BitmapUtility.FindEdgesUsingSobel` method (see Listing 18.2).

NOTE

The `CreateOptions` property of the `BitmapImage` class allows you to specify when the image is to be created. By default the value is `BitmapCreationOptions.BackgroundCreation`, which causes the image to be created on a background thread and frees the UI thread from processing the image.

Because we require the `BitmapImage` immediately, the `CreateOptions` property is explicitly set to `BitmapCreateOptions.None`.

The `saveCommand` is disabled by setting the `canSave` flag to false.

LISTING 18.2   `MainPage.ProcessImage` Method

```
void ProcessImage(Stream imageStream)
{
    BitmapImage sourceImage = new BitmapImage();
    sourceImage.CreateOptions = BitmapCreateOptions.None;
    sourceImage.SetSource(imageStream);
    image.Source = sourceImage;

    canSave = false;
    saveCommand.RaiseCanExecuteChanged();

    progressBar.Visibility = Visibility.Visible;
    BitmapUtility.FindEdgesUsingSobel(sourceImage, HandleEdgesFound);
}
```

The custom `BitmapUtility` class contains a `FindEdgesUsingSobel` method, which attempts to reduce an image to a line drawing by locating the distinct edges within the image. Unlike Silverlight for the browser, Silverlight for Windows Phone does not support `UIElement` pixel shader effects. You therefore must resort to processing the image in code, which is unfortunately much slower than using a custom pixel shader.

To allow the app to remain responsive during processing, the image is processed asynchronously using a thread from the thread pool. When processing completes, the `resultAction` is invoked on the UI thread using the default `Dispatcher`, as shown:

```
public static void FindEdgesUsingSobel(BitmapSource bitmapSource,
    Action<ResultEventArgs<WriteableBitmap>> resultAction)
{
    ArgumentValidator.AssertNotNull(bitmapSource, "bitmapSource");
    ArgumentValidator.AssertNotNull(resultAction, "resultAction");

    WriteableBitmap sourceBitmap = new WriteableBitmap(bitmapSource);
    int[] sourcePixels = sourceBitmap.Pixels;
    int imageWidth = bitmapSource.PixelWidth;
    int imageHeight = bitmapSource.PixelHeight;

    ThreadPool.QueueUserWorkItem(
        delegate
        {
            try
            {
                int[] resultPixels = FindEdgesUsingSobelCore(
                                        sourcePixels,
                                        imageWidth,
                                        imageHeight);
                Deployment.Current.Dispatcher.BeginInvoke(
```

18

```
            delegate
            {
                WriteableBitmap resultBitmap
                    = new WriteableBitmap(bitmapSource);

                for (int i = 0; i < resultPixels.Length; i++)
                {
                    resultBitmap.Pixels[i] = resultPixels[i];
                }

                resultAction(new ResultEventArgs<WriteableBitmap>(
                                    resultBitmap));
            });

        }
        catch (Exception ex)
        {
            resultAction(new ResultEventArgs<WriteableBitmap>(null, ex));
        }
    });
}
```

The FindEdgesUsingSobelCore method is where the main processing takes place. FindEdgesUsingSobelCore produces an int array representing the image pixels of the traced image. On completion, these pixels are copied to a new WriteableBitmap and returned to the caller via the resultAction.

A Sobel filter is implemented within the FindEdgesUsingSobelCore method. The method produces either white or black pixels, depending on a pixel's intensity and that of its neighbors. See the following excerpt:

```
static int[] FindEdgesUsingSobelCore(
    int[] sourcePixels, int imageWidth, int imageHeight)
{
    /* Sobel Matrices */
    int[,] gx = new[,] { { -1, 0, 1 }, { -2, 0, 2 }, { -1, 0, 1 } };
    int[,] gy = new[,] { { 1, 2, 1 }, { 0, 0, 0 }, { -1, -2, -1 } };

    int[] resultPixels = new int[sourcePixels.Length];

    for (int i = 1; i < imageHeight - 1; i++)
    {
        for (int j = 1; j < imageWidth - 1; j++)
        {
            float newX = 0;
            float newY = 0;
            float c;
```

```
            for (int hw = -1; hw < 2; hw++)
            {
                for (int wi = -1; wi < 2; wi++)
                {
                    int row = j + wi;
                    int column = i + hw;
                    int position = column * imageWidth + row;
                    int pixel = sourcePixels[position];
                    var bytes = BitConverter.GetBytes(pixel);
                    c = (bytes[0] + bytes[1] + bytes[2]) / 3;
                    int index0 = hw + 1;
                    int index1 = wi + 1;
                    newX += gx[index0, index1] * c;
                    newY += gy[index0, index1] * c;
                }
            }

            int resultPosition = i * imageWidth + j;
            int colorIntValue;

            if (newX * newX + newY * newY > 16384 /* 128 * 128 */)
            {
                colorIntValue = ToInt(Color.White);
            }
            else
            {
                colorIntValue = ToInt(Color.Black);
            }
            resultPixels[resultPosition] = colorIntValue;
        }
    }

    return resultPixels;
}
```

To produce either a black or white pixel, convert a `Microsoft.Xna.Framework.Color` value to an integer value by combining the A,R,G, and B byte color components, as shown:

```
static int ToInt(Color color)
{
    return (color.A << 24) | (color.R << 16)
            | (color.G << 8) | (color.B << 0);
}
```

When the asynchronous portion of the FindEdgesUsingSobel method completes, the resulting WriteableBitmap is passed back to the caller within an instance of the ResultEventArgs. The ResultEventArgs contains a generic Result property, which, in this case, holds the resulting WriteableBitmap and an Error property if something goes awry:

```
public class ResultEventArgs<T> : EventArgs
{
    public T Result { get; private set; }
    public Exception Error { get; private set; }

    public ResultEventArgs(T result, Exception error = null)
    {
        Result = result;
        Error = error;
    }
}
```

The HandleEdgesFound method within the MainPage class handles the result of the FindEdgesUsingSobel method. If no errors occurred during processing, the WriteableBitmap is assigned to the Source property of the Image control:

```
void HandleEdgesFound(ResultEventArgs<WriteableBitmap> obj)
{
    progressBar.Visibility = Visibility.Collapsed;

    if (obj.Error != null)
    {
        MessageBox.Show("Unable to find edges.");
        return;
    }
    image.Source = obj.Result;

    canSave = true;
    saveCommand.RaiseCanExecuteChanged();
}
```

Once processing completes the image is displayed (see Figure 18.5).

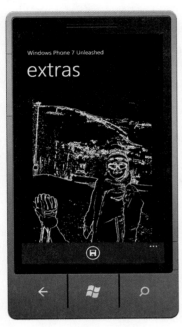

FIGURE 18.5   The sample Extras application after processing of the image is complete

As mentioned earlier in this section, when debugging using the emulator, a dummy image is used. The location of this image is defined as a constant within the `ProcessTestImage` method, as shown:

```
void ProcessTestImage()
{
    const string testImageUrl = @"/DanielVaughan.WindowsPhone7Unleashed"
        + ".ExtrasExample;component/Images/TestImage.jpg";

    var imageUri = new Uri(testImageUrl, UriKind.Relative);

    using (Stream stream = Application.GetResourceStream(imageUri).Stream)
    {
        BitmapSource bitmapSource = new BitmapImage();
        bitmapSource.SetSource(stream);
        image.Source = bitmapSource;

        progressBar.Visibility = Visibility.Visible;
        BitmapUtility.FindEdgesUsingSobel(bitmapSource, HandleEdgesFound);
    }
}
```

When the app is launched from the Application List, rather than from the Extras menu, the app must use the `PhotoChooserTask` to allow the user to select an image. Accordingly, a `PhotoChooserTask` is defined as a field, and its `Completed` event is subscribed to in the page constructor, as shown:

```
readonly PhotoChooserTask photoChooserTask = new PhotoChooserTask();

public MainPage()
{
    InitializeComponent();
    ...
    photoChooserTask.Completed += HandlePhotoChooserTaskCompleted;
}
```

For more information on the `PhotoChooserTask` see Chapter 12, "Launchers and Choosers."

The `HandlePhotoChooserTaskCompleted` method takes the resulting image `Stream` and, like the `ProcessImageUsingToken` method shown earlier, calls the `ProcessImage` method, as shown:

```
void HandlePhotoChooserTaskCompleted(object sender, PhotoResult e)
{
    if (e.TaskResult != TaskResult.OK)
    {
        return;
    }
    imageName = e.OriginalFileName;

    if (!string.IsNullOrWhiteSpace(imageName))
    {
        int index = imageName.LastIndexOf(@"\");
        if (index >= 0)
        {
            imageName = "Unleashed_" + imageName.Substring(index + 1);
        }
    }
    else
    {
        imageName = string.Format(
            "Unleashed_{0:yyyy-MM-dd-HH-mm-ss}.jpg", DateTime.Now);
    }
    Stream imageStream = e.ChosenPhoto;
    ProcessImage(imageStream);
}
```

The `imageName` field is constructed using the original filename of the image.

Saving the Image

Once processing is complete, the user is provided with the means to save the image via an application bar icon button. The page contains an `ICommand` called `SaveCommand`, as shown:

```
readonly ICommand saveCommand;

public ICommand SaveCommand
{
    get
    {
        return saveCommand;
    }
}
```

The command is instantiated in the constructor and when executed calls the page's `SaveImage` method, which is shown in the following excerpt:

```
public MainPage()
{
    InitializeComponent();

    saveCommand = new DelegateCommand(obj => SaveImage());

    DataContext = this;

    photoChooserTask.Completed += HandlePhotoChooserTaskCompleted;
}
```

The `SaveImage` method retrieves the `WriteableBitmap` from the `Image` control and then uses the `WriteableBitmap` extension method `SaveJpeg` to write the image bytes to a `MemoryStream`. The `MemoryStream` is then passed to the `MediaLibrary.SavePicture` method, as shown:

```
void SaveImage()
{
    var writeableBitmap = (WriteableBitmap)image.Source;
    if (writeableBitmap == null)
    {
        return;
    }

    const int jpegQuality = 90;

    using (MemoryStream memoryStream = new MemoryStream())
    {
        writeableBitmap.SaveJpeg(
            memoryStream,
            writeableBitmap.PixelWidth, // target width
```

18

```
            writeableBitmap.PixelHeight, // target height
            0, // orientation.
            jpegQuality);

    memoryStream.Seek(0, SeekOrigin.Begin);
    using (MediaLibrary mediaLibrary = new MediaLibrary())
    {
        Picture savedPicture
            = mediaLibrary.SavePicture(imageName, memoryStream);
    }
    }

    MessageBox.Show("Image saved to Saved Pictures.");
}
```

The `MediaLibrary.SavePicture` method requires that the specified image name is not null or an empty string. The `SavePicture` method has two overloads; one accepts a `Stream` of image bytes, the other a byte array representing the image. Both save the image to the Saved Pictures album in the Pictures Hub.

The XAML for the `MainPage` class contains an `AppBarIconButton` with a binding to the `SaveCommand` (see Listing 18.3). For more information on the custom `AppBarIconButton` see Chapter 8, "Taming the Application Bar."

LISTING 18.3   Extras Example `MainPage` XAML (excerpt)

```
<Grid x:Name="LayoutRoot" Background="Transparent">
  <Grid.RowDefinitions>
    <RowDefinition Height="Auto"/>
    <RowDefinition Height="*"/>
  </Grid.RowDefinitions>

  <u:AppBar>
    <u:AppBarIconButton
                x:Name="button_Save"
                Command="{Binding SaveCommand}"
                Text="Save"
                IconUri="/Images/appbar.save.rest.png" />
  </u:AppBar>
```

LISTING 18.3   Continued

```
<StackPanel x:Name="TitlePanel" Grid.Row="0" Margin="12,17,0,28">
  <TextBlock Text="Windows Phone 7 Unleashed"
             Style="{StaticResource PhoneTextNormalStyle}"/>
  <TextBlock Text="extras" Margin="9,-7,0,0"
             Style="{StaticResource PhoneTextTitle1Style}"/>
</StackPanel>

<Grid x:Name="ContentPanel" Grid.Row="1" Margin="12,0,12,0">
  <Image x:Name="image" />
  <ProgressBar x:Name="progressBar" IsIndeterminate="True" />
</Grid>
</Grid>
```

When the `SaveImage` method completes, a message is displayed informing the user that the image was successfully saved (see Figure 18.6).

FIGURE 18.6   The message box confirms that the image has been saved.

Share Menu Extensibility

The Share menu of the pictures viewer functions in much the same way as the Extras menu. The Share menu enables users to select a particular app to transfer an image somewhere, such as via email or to a third-party service like Twitter. When selected from the picture viewer, a list of registered Share applications is presented (see Figure 18.7).

18

FIGURE 18.7   The picture viewer Share menu

The title displayed in the Share menu is taken from your app's WMAppManifest.xml file. The screen displays the text *upload to*, followed by the App element's Title attribute. The length of the displayed title is limited to two lines and is truncated if it exceeds that number.

While some services are available by default, you can extend the share picker with additional apps in a similar manner as the Extras menu.

Adding Your App to the Share Menu

To extend the share menu to include your photo share application, create a new file called E0F0E49A-3EB1-4970-B780-45DA41EC7C28.xml in the root directory of your main project. Rather than typing the name by hand, you may prefer to copy the XML file to your project from the downloadable sample code.

> **NOTE**
>
> Using the Visual Studio Properties window, make sure that the XML file Build Action is set to Content. Set the Copy to Output Directory option to Do Not Copy.

The existence of this file in the root of your XAP file indicates to the phone OS that your app participates as a Share application.

The awkwardly named XML file uses a GUID in its name. This appears to be an attempt to avoid collisions with other filenames. It is an unfortunate choice because it is unconventional and not in line with the Extras.xml filename.

A Simple Photo Upload Share Application

This section looks at building a photo Share application that takes an image and uploads it as a byte array to a WCF service. The example app is located in the WindowsPhone7Unleashed.ShareExample project in the downloadable sample code. The WCF service that the app communicates with is located in the WindowsPhone7Unleashed.Web project.

When your app is selected from the Share menu in the built-in picture viewer, your app is launched and the main page of your app has its query string populated with a string identifier named FileId. Extras applications use Token as their identifier; Share applications use FileId.

The FileId value is used to retrieve the image from the Pictures Hub in the same manner as an Extras application retrieves the image.

In the following excerpt from MainPage.xaml.cs, the code to detect whether the app is executing within the emulator has been abstracted to a custom class called EnvironmentValues, which provides for greater flexibility during testing and potentially increases the portability of your code.

If the code is executing within the emulator, we rely on a dummy image, or else the image is retrieved using the file ID provided in the page query string. If no file ID is present, the PhotoChooserTask is used to allow the user to select an image from the Pictures Hub:

```
protected override void OnNavigatedTo(NavigationEventArgs e)
{
    base.OnNavigatedTo(e);

    /* Equivalent to: Environment.DeviceType == DeviceType.Emulator */
    if (EnvironmentValues.UsingEmulator)
    {
        ProcessShareTestImage();
    }
    else
    {
        string fileId;
        if (NavigationContext.QueryString.TryGetValue("FileId", out fileId))
        {
            imageName = fileId;
            ProcessShareImage(fileId);
        }
        else
        {
            photoChooserTask.Show();
```

18

```
            }
        }
    }
```

NOTE

It is a Windows Phone Marketplace certification requirement that if your Share application is launched from the application list (not from the Share menu) that it must invoke the PhotoChooser task to allow the user to select an image or take a photo. Conversely, it is also a requirement that if your app is launched from the Share menu, no further image selection steps should be required.

To determine whether your app has been launched from the Share menu in the Picture Viewer, you can either test for the presence of the FileId query string parameter, as demonstrated in the previous example, or test whether the query string contains an *Action* parameter set to ShareContent, as shown in the following example:

```
string action;
NavigationContext.QueryString.TryGetValue("action", out action);
if (action == "ShareContent")
{
    /* Launched from Share menu. */
}
```

As with the Extras application in the previous section, Share applications rely on the XNA `MediaLibrary` class for retrieving the selected image. Your project needs to reference the Microsoft.Xna.Framework assembly, and the following using statements should be included at the top of your page:

```
using System.IO;
using System.Windows.Media.Imaging;
using Microsoft.Phone.Tasks;
using Microsoft.Xna.Framework.Media;
```

The custom `ProcessShareImage` method uses the token provided in the query string to retrieve the image from the phone's media library, as shown:

```
void ProcessShareImage(string token)
{
    MediaLibrary mediaLibrary = new MediaLibrary();
    Picture picture = mediaLibrary.GetPictureFromToken(token);
    SetImageStream(picture.GetImage());
}
```

The `SetImageStream` method takes the `Stream` returned from the `Picture.GetImage` method and creates a new `BitmapImage`, which is then assigned to an `Image` control on the page:

```
void SetImageStream(Stream imageStream)
{
```

```
    BitmapSource bitmapSource = new BitmapImage();
    bitmapSource.SetSource(imageStream);
    image.Source = bitmapSource;
}
```

When executing within the emulator, the `ProcessShareTestImage` takes a different approach and uses an image stored as a resource within the project. As stated previously, this facilitates development by removing the reliance on the Pictures Hub and is useful for testing purposes. See the following excerpt:

```
string testImageUrl = @"/DanielVaughan.WindowsPhone7Unleashed" +
                        ".ShareExample;component/Images/TestImage.jpg";
string imageName = "WindowsPhone7UnleashedTestImage";

void ProcessShareTestImage()
{
    var imageUri = new Uri(testImageUrl, UriKind.Relative);

    using (Stream stream = Application.GetResourceStream(imageUri).Stream)
    {
        SetImageStream(stream);
    }
}
```

So far you have seen how the image is retrieved from the image library and displayed using an `Image` control. However, the real value of a photo Share application lies in its ability to send the image somewhere. In the sample the image is sent to a web service located in the WindowsPhone7Unleashed.Web project.

An `ICommand` named UploadCommand is used to begin the upload and is defined as shown:

```
readonly DelegateCommand uploadCommand;

public ICommand UploadCommand
{
    get
    {
        return uploadCommand;
    }
}
```

`UploadCommand` is initialized within the class constructor like so:

```
public MainPage()
{
    InitializeComponent();
```

```
    uploadCommand = new DelegateCommand(obj => UploadImage());

    DataContext = this;

    client.UploadImageCompleted += HandleUploadImageCompleted;
    photoChooserTask.Completed += HandlePhotoChooserTaskCompleted;
}
```

The uploadCommand field is a DelegateCommand that calls the UploadImage method when the command is executed.

The DataContext of the page is set to the page itself. This enables you to easily bind to any commands within the page and acts as a quasi viewmodel.

Once the command is executed and you have the image, you need to upload it somewhere. This chapter uses a simple web service called ImageUploadService that accepts a byte array representing an image and the name of the image.

To create a Silverlight compatible web service, right-click on your project node and select Add, New Item. This presents the Add New Item dialog. From there, select the Silverlight-enabled WCF Service from the list of Silverlight templates (see Figure 18.8).

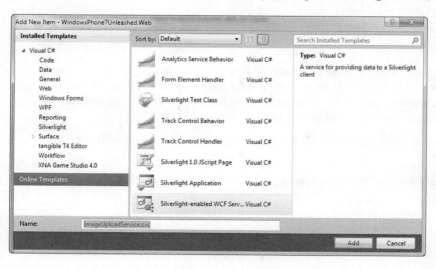

FIGURE 18.8   Creating a Silverlight enabled WCF service using the Visual Studio Add New Item dialog

The Silverlight-enabled WCF Service option produces a skeleton WCF service. The WCF configuration is located in the project's web.config file.

The `ImageUploadService` with its single `UploadImage` method is shown in Listing 18.4.

LISTING 18.4   `ImageUploadService` Class

```
[ServiceContract(Namespace = "WindowsPhone7Unleashed")]
[AspNetCompatibilityRequirements(RequirementsMode
                                = AspNetCompatibilityRequirementsMode.Allowed)]
public class ImageUploadService
{
    [OperationContract]
    public void UploadImage(byte[] imageBytes, string name)
    {
        Debug.WriteLine(string.Format("Saving image {0}.", name));
        /* TODO: Save the image to a database or directory. */

    }
}
```

Ordinarily, the generated XML configuration for the WCF service would be adequate to send most objects over the wire. However, sending an image as a large byte array to the WCF service fails if the configuration is not modified. Specifically, the maxArrayLength and maxReceivedMessageSize need to be explicitly defined, as shown in the following excerpt:

```
<binding name="ImageUploadService.customBinding0">
  <binaryMessageEncoding>
    <readerQuotas
        maxArrayLength="2147483647" />
  </binaryMessageEncoding>
  <httpTransport
      maxReceivedMessageSize="2147483647" />
</binding>
```

To consume the WCF service from the Windows Phone app, a service reference is created by right-clicking on the project node and selecting Add Service Reference (see Figure 18.9).

18

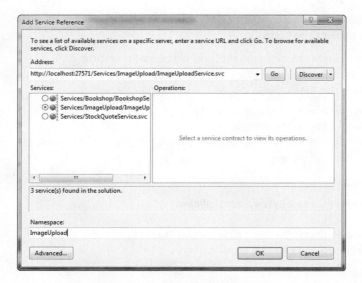

FIGURE 18.9   Adding a service reference for the custom ImageUploadService

We then consume the service using the generated service client, which, in this case, is called `ImageUploadServiceClient`. It is defined as a field in the main page.

`UploadCommand` calls `UploadImage` when it is executed. The `UploadImage` method retrieves the `BitmapImage` from the `Source` property of the `Image` control, and then uses it to create a `WriteableBitmap`. A `WriteableBitmap` is used because it provides access to the image's pixels, whereas a `BitmapImage` does not.

Once the image has been converted to a byte array using a custom extension method, the bytes are sent to the WCF service, as shown:

```
void UploadImage()
{
    BitmapImage bitmapImage = (BitmapImage)image.Source;
    if (bitmapImage == null)
    {
        return;
    }

    WriteableBitmap writeableBitmap = new WriteableBitmap(bitmapImage);
    byte[] imageBytes = writeableBitmap.ToByteArray();

    try
    {
        SetProgressBarVisibility(true);
        client.UploadImageAsync(imageBytes, imageName);
    }
```

```
    catch (Exception)
    {
        SetProgressBarVisibility(false);
        throw;
    }
}
```

To convert the `WriteableBitmap` to a `byte` array, we use a custom `BitmapExtensions` class that contains the `ToByteArray` method, shown in the next excerpt. The `WriteableBitmap` represents each pixel using an integer value. An integer contains four bytes, representing the red, green, blue, and alpha components of a pixel. The `ToByteArray` method splits the integer values into its consecutive bytes using the static `Buffer.BlockCopy` method, as shown:

```
public static byte[] ToByteArray(this WriteableBitmap writeableBitmap)
{
    ArgumentValidator.AssertNotNull(writeableBitmap, "writeableBitmap");
    int[] pixels = writeableBitmap.Pixels;
    int arrayLength = pixels.Length * 4;
    byte[] result = new byte[arrayLength];
    Buffer.BlockCopy(pixels, 0, result, 0, arrayLength);
    return result;
}
```

The `MainPage` XAML file contains an `AppBarIconButton`, which, when tapped by the user, executes the `UploadCommand` in the code-beside. The image is displayed in an `Image` control. During the upload process, a Silverlight Toolkit `PerformanceProgressBar` is made visible to indicate to the user that the image is being uploaded (see Listing 18.5).

LISTING 18.5   MainPage.xaml (excerpt)

```
<Grid x:Name="LayoutRoot" Background="Transparent">
    <Grid.RowDefinitions>
        <RowDefinition Height="Auto"/>
        <RowDefinition Height="*"/>
    </Grid.RowDefinitions>

    <u:AppBar>
      <u:AppBarIconButton
                x:Name="button_Upload"
                Command="{Binding UploadCommand}"
                Text="Upload"
                IconUri="/Images/appbar.upload.rest.png" />
    </u:AppBar>

    <StackPanel x:Name="TitlePanel" Grid.Row="0" Margin="12,17,0,28">
        <TextBlock Text="Windows Phone 7 Unleashed"
```

18

LISTING 18.5   Continued

```
                    Style="{StaticResource PhoneTextNormalStyle}"/>
        <TextBlock Text="share" Margin="9,-7,0,0"
                    Style="{StaticResource PhoneTextTitle1Style}"/>
    </StackPanel>

    <Grid x:Name="ContentPanel" Grid.Row="1" Margin="12,0,12,0">
        <Image x:Name="image" />
        <toolkit:PerformanceProgressBar x:Name="progressBar"
                    IsIndeterminate="True"
                    Visibility="Collapsed" />
    </Grid>
</Grid>
```

As soon as an image is selected by the user, it is displayed in the Image control. The user can then use the application bar icon button to upload the image to the WCF service (see Figure 18.10).

FIGURE 18.10   The sample photo share application

When the WCF service client completes the image upload, the completed handler is called, as shown:

```
void HandleUploadImageCompleted(object sender, AsyncCompletedEventArgs e)
{
```

```
    SetProgressBarVisibility(false);
    if (e.Error != null)
    {
        MessageBox.Show("Error uploading image.");
        return;
    }
    MessageBox.Show("Image uploaded");
}
```

If the image bytes are successfully uploaded, a confirmation message is displayed (see Figure 18.11).

FIGURE 18.11   A message box confirms that the image was successfully uploaded.

Using the Windows Phone Connect Tool

When debugging with the Zune software running, the media database on the phone device is locked. The *Windows Phone Connect Tool*, also known as *WPConnect*, allows you to establish serial or USB connectivity to the device without running the Zune software. This permits access to media during debugging and allows you to debug your app during various media related activities while the device is tethered.

Examples of media related activities include the following:

▶ Media launchers or choosers

▶ XNA framework playback of song objects

▶ Silverlight playback of video or audio content using the MediaElement control

To use the WPConnect tool perform the following steps:

1. Connect your phone to the computer.

2. The Zune software starts automatically. If the Zune software does not start, then start it manually.

3. Wait a few seconds while your phone is connected, and then close the Zune software.

4. Open a command prompt and navigate to the directory containing the Windows Phone Connect Tool (WPConnect.exe). It can be found in one of the following locations:

   ▶ %ProgramFiles%\Microsoft SDKs\Windows Phone\v7.1\Tools\WPConnect

   ▶ %ProgramFiles (x86)%\Microsoft SDKs\Windows Phone\v7.1\Tools\ WPConnect

5. At a command prompt, enter the command WPConnect.exe.

6. You receive confirmation that your device is connected. You can now test your app without the Zune software running.

You do not need to disconnect from the WPConnect tool. You can reestablish connectivity with the Zune software at any time by launching the Zune software. After reestablishing connectivity with the Zune software however, you must repeat the preceding steps if you want to debug an app with media activities.

When you run WPConnect.exe, the connection is made and then the process exits. You will not, therefore, find the WPConnect process in the Windows task manager after it has completed.

> **NOTE**
>
> There is no advantage to using the WPConnect tool over the Zune software apart from unlocking the local media database on the device; neither is faster than the other, and both use the same infrastructure to connect to the phone.

To expedite the process of closing the Zune software and launching WPConnect, I have written a small batch file, which can be placed on your file system and executed either as a custom tool within Visual Studio, or via a shortcut in your Start menu. The batch file is included in the Resources directory in the downloadable sample code for this book.

The batch file attempts to close the Zune software, allowing it a few seconds to exit. It then launches the WPConnect tool from a location specific to your Windows architecture type—either 32 or 64 bit (see Listing 18.6).

LISTING 18.6   Launch WPConnect.bat

```
@ECHO OFF
ECHO WM Connect Script. For updates see http://danielvaughan.org

SET %errorlevel% = 0
taskkill /IM zune.exe
ECHO Waiting for Zune to close...

REM Wait for 15 seconds.
@choice /T 15 /C y /CS /D y | REM

IF PROCESSOR_ARCHITECTURE == x86 (
    "%ProgramFiles(x86)%\Microsoft SDKs\Windows Phone\v7.1\Tools
      \WPConnect\x86\WPConnect.exe"
) ELSE "%ProgramFiles(x86)%\Microsoft SDKs\Windows Phone\v7.1\Tools
        \WPConnect\x64\WPConnect.exe"

REM Wait for 5 seconds.
@choice /T 5 /C y /CS /D y | REM
```

Summary

This chapter began by looking at photo Extras applications. You saw how to add an application to the picture viewer's Extras menu, and how to create an Extras application that traces the edges within an image and allows the user to save the image back to the phone's picture library.

The chapter then looked at photo Share applications. You learned how to add an app to the picture viewer's Share menu, and how to create a photo Share application that uploads an image to a custom WCF service.

Finally, this chapter looked at the Windows Phone Connect Tool and how it is used to unlock the phone's media library during debugging.

18

CHAPTER 19

Camera

The camera has become an essential component of all mobile phones. Indeed, the manufacturing requirements for Windows Phone devices require them to have a camera with at least a 5 megapixel capability and an LED flash.

Most of the first generation Windows Phone devices, however, did not have great cameras. New phones that have arrived after Windows Phone 7.5 (mango) have seen their cameras much improved; mango brings with it programmatic access to both front and rear facing cameras, enabling scenarios such as video chat, image recognition, and augmented reality.

You saw in Chapter 12, "Launchers and Choosers," how the CameraCaptureTask chooser can be used to launch the Windows Phone Camera app, allowing the user to take a photo and have it returned to your app. While convenient in some scenarios, the CameraCaptureTask limits the capabilities of the capture process to that of the built-in camera app, which supports only photos and not video capture. By using the direct access camera APIs on the phone, you can control the camera directly from your app to capture both photos and video. The APIs allow you to control many aspects of the camera, including the flash, the hardware shutter button, and the autofocus mechanism.

The Windows Phone SDK includes two distinct APIs for the camera. The first is Windows Phone specific and centers on the Microsoft.Devices.PhotoCamera class. The second is the Silverlight 4 webcam API.

The main difference between the webcam API and the PhotoCamera class is that the PhotoCamera allows you to make the camera perform autofocus, and to set the camera's flash mode, which the webcam API cannot.

Conversely, the webcam API allows you to capture video with audio and save it to isolated storage. The webcam API is platform agnostic, and code that uses the webcam API can also be used in Silverlight desktop and browser applications.

When deciding whether to use the PhotoCamera or the webcam API, you can make your decision based on the following criteria:

▶ If your app needs to take stills only, use PhotoCamera.

▶ If your app needs to capture audio and video, use the webcam API.

▶ If your app needs to be cross-platform and must support Silverlight for the browser, use the webcam API.

This chapter explores both approaches, beginning with PhotoCamera. You see how to capture still images and display live video using PhotoCamera, and you also look at leveraging the hardware shutter button and adding a live video effect.

The second part of this chapter looks at the Silverlight 4 webcam API and how to use it to capture audio and video and to save it as an MP4 in isolated storage.

> **NOTE**
>
> For the camera application to function, the Windows Phone application manifest, WMAppManifest.xml, must include a capability named ID_CAP_ISV_CAMERA. Without it, the application will not function correctly.
>
> The following capabilities element must be present in the WMAppManifest.xml file:
>
> `<Capability Name="ID_CAP_ISV_CAMERA" />`
>
> To use a device's front facing camera, if it exists, you must add the ID_HW_FFCCAMERA capability, as shown:
>
> `<Capability Name=" ID_HW_FFCCAMERA" />`
>
> ID_HW_FFCCAMERA is not added automatically during the Windows Phone Marketplace capabilities detection process.
>
> If a particular camera capability is not present, then an InvalidOperationException is raised when an attempt is made by your app to use the camera. Moreover, it may not be immediately apparent that the exception is due to the missing capability definition.

PhotoCamera

The advantage of the PhotoCamera class is that it gives control over the flash and autofocus when capturing images.

PhotoCamera is usually defined as a field in a page or viewmodel and then instantiated when needed. The device camera needs time to ready itself for use and cannot be used until it is initialized, indicated by an `Initialized` event. Initialization commences when the `PhotoCamera` is assigned to the source of a `VideoBrush`, using its `SetSource` method.

NOTE

Failure to call `VideoBrush.SetSource` with the `PhotoCamera` instance prevents the `Initialized` event from being raised.

The following example shows how to create and initialize a `PhotoCamera` using a `VideoBrush` within a `PhoneApplicationPage`:

```
PhotoCamera photoCamera;

protected override void OnNavigatedTo(NavigationEventArgs e)
{
    photoCamera = new PhotoCamera();
    photoCamera.Initialized += HandlePhotoCameraInitialized;

    videoBrush_Preview.SetSource(photoCamera);

    base.OnNavigatedTo(e);
}
```

The `Initialized` event allows the configuration of the camera. This may include setting the image resolution for captured images, setting the flash mode of the camera, and allows subscription to the various `PhotoCamera` events, as demonstrated in the following excerpt:

```
void HandlePhotoCameraInitialized(
        object sender, CameraOperationCompletedEventArgs e)
{
    PhotoCamera camera = (PhotoCamera)sender;
    camera.Resolution = camera.AvailableResolutions.ElementAt(0);

    camera.AutoFocusCompleted += HandleAutoFocusCompleted;
    camera.CaptureCompleted += HandleCaptureCompleted;
    camera.CaptureThumbnailAvailable += HandleCaptureThumbnailAvailable;
    camera.CaptureImageAvailable += HandleCaptureImageAvailable;

    if (camera.IsFlashModeSupported(FlashMode.Auto))
    {
        FlashMode = FlashMode.Auto;
    }
}
```

Each of the events and the `PhotoCamera` properties are discussed in greater detail in the following section.

Building a PhotoCamera App

This section looks at using the PhotoCamera to create a custom camera app that allows the user to view live video from the camera and to take still image captures that are saved to the phone's media library. You look at performing post-processing of the PhotoCamera's preview buffer to create a live video effect. In addition, this section looks at extending the app to provide a page that includes a list of photo thumbnails that link to images saved in the media library images.

The sample code for this section resides in the /Sensors/Camera directory of the WindowsPhone7Unleashed.Examples project in the downloadable sample code.

The section begins with the custom PhotoCameraViewModel class, which contains a Start and a Stop method that allows the PhotoCamera instance to be created on demand and disposed as soon as it is no longer required (see Listing 19.1).

Some phone devices support a front facing camera. The Camera.IsCameraTypeSupported method is used to determine whether a particular camera type is available on the device. Devices are required to have at least one camera, and by using the parameterless constructor of the PhotoCamera class, the primary (non-front facing) camera is used.

LISTING 19.1   PhotoCameraViewModel Class (excerpt)

```
public class PhotoCameraViewModel: ViewModelBase
{
    public PhotoCameraViewModel() : base("PhotoCamera")
    {
        /* Intentionally left blank. */
    }

    PhotoCamera photoCamera;

    public Camera Camera
    {
        get
        {
            return photoCamera;
        }
    }

    public void Start()
    {
        if (photoCamera != null)
        {
            return;
        }

        if (Camera.IsCameraTypeSupported(CameraType.FrontFacing))
        {
```

LISTING 19.1   Continued

```
        photoCamera = new PhotoCamera(CameraType.FrontFacing);
    }
    else //if (PhotoCamera.IsCameraTypeSupported(CameraType.Primary))
    {
        photoCamera = new PhotoCamera(); /* Defaults to CameraType.Primary */
    }

    photoCamera.Initialized += HandlePhotoCameraInitialized;
}
...
}
```

When the `PhotoCamera`'s `Initialized` event is raised, the `PhotoCamera` is ready for configuration, and the resolution and flash mode of the camera are set (see Listing 19.2). The first element of the camera's `AvailableResolutions` property indicates the lowest resolution that the camera supports. On my device, the available resolutions are 320x240, 640x480, 800x600, 1280x960, 1600x1200, 2048x1536, and 2592x1944.

When in operation, the `AutoFocusCompleted` event is raised indeterminately by the device itself whenever it decides to focus. The event is also raised following a call to the `PhotoCamera.Focus` method.

The `CaptureImageAvailable` and `CaptureThumbnailAvailable` events are raised after your code calls the camera's `CaptureImage` method, providing the opportunity to process the captured image and to, for example, save it to isolated storage. In the sample, two things are performed when an image is captured: We handle the `CaptureImageAvailable` event to save the image to the phone's media library, and we handle the `CaptureThumbnailAvailable` event to save a thumbnail of the image to isolated storage.

The `CaptureCompleted` event is raised after the `CaptureImageAvailable` event, providing the opportunity to update the UI in response. In the sample app, we overlay the video stream with a custom focus indicator image when the user presses the hardware shutter button and hide the image when the `CaptureCompleted` event is raised.

LISTING 19.2   `PhotoCameraViewModel.HandlePhotoCameraInitialized` Method

```
void HandlePhotoCameraInitialized(
        object sender, CameraOperationCompletedEventArgs e)
{
    cameraInitialized = true;

    PhotoCamera camera = (PhotoCamera)sender;
    camera.Resolution = camera.AvailableResolutions.ElementAt(0);

    camera.AutoFocusCompleted += HandleAutoFocusCompleted;
    camera.CaptureImageAvailable += HandleCaptureImageAvailable;
```

LISTING 19.2   Continued

```
    camera.CaptureThumbnailAvailable += HandleCaptureThumbnailAvailable;
    camera.CaptureCompleted += HandleCaptureCompleted;

    FlashModes = flashModes.Where(
                    mode => photoCamera.IsFlashModeSupported(mode)).ToList();

    if (camera.IsFlashModeSupported(FlashMode.Auto))
    {
        FlashMode = FlashMode.Auto;
    }

    CameraButtons.ShutterKeyPressed += HandleShutterKeyPressed;
    CameraButtons.ShutterKeyHalfPressed += HandleShutterKeyHalfPressed;
    CameraButtons.ShutterKeyReleased += HandleShutterKeyReleased;
}
```

The viewmodel contains a `FlashModes` property that is populated with a list of `FlashMode` enumeration values that the camera supports. The potential `FlashMode` values are as follows:

▶ Auto

▶ Off

▶ On

▶ RedEyeReduction

`FlashMode.Auto` lets the device decide whether the flash is warranted. You can force the camera to use, or not use, the flash using the Off and On values. `FlashMode.RedEyeReduction` is the most commonly unsupported flash mode. With red eye reduction enabled, the camera performs a brief flash cycle before taking the photo, causing the subjects' pupils to close and thereby eliminating the red eye effect.

`PhotoCamera.IsFlashModeSupported` allows you to determine whether a particular flash mode is supported and should be used before setting the camera's `FlashMode`.

NOTE

Attempting to set the camera's `FlashMode` to an unsupported value does not raise an exception but rather silently defaults the `FlashMode` to Off, effectively disabling the flash.

The `CameraButtons` class is used to monitor the device's hardware camera button. The three events: `ShutterKeyPressed`, `ShutterKeyHalfPressed`, and `ShutterKeyReleased`, allow you to emulate the behavior of the phone's built-in camera app. `CameraButtons` is independent of the PhotoCamera and can also be used in conjunction with the Silverlight webcam API if you so choose.

CameraButtons does nothing apart from allowing you to monitor the pressed state of the phone's camera shutter button. It is up to you to subscribe to the CameraButtons events and to control camera behavior accordingly.

The PhotoCameraViewModel contains a VisualState property that determines the set of controls available in the view. The following excerpt shows that when the CameraButtons.ShutterKeyHalfPressed event is raised, the PhotoCamera.Focus method is called, which causes the device camera to attempt to automatically focus on the scene:

```
void HandleShutterKeyHalfPressed(object sender, EventArgs e)
{
    VisualState = VisualStateValue.Focusing;
    photoCamera.Focus();
}
```

When the user fully presses the hardware button, the CameraButtons.ShutterKeyPressed event is raised. The viewmodel's event handler calls the camera's CaptureImage method, which causes the camera to acquire the current frame as a still image and to raise the PhotoCamera.CaptureImageAvailable event.

Prior to calling CaptureImage, we take the opportunity to generate a filename (based on the current time), which is used for two image files: one stored in the phone's media library, the other a thumbnail representation stored in isolated storage. Generating the filename at this point is necessary because the order in which the two PhotoCamera events, CaptureImageAvailable and CaptureThumbnailAvailable, are raised is indeterminable. See the following excerpt:

```
volatile string fileName;

void HandleShutterKeyPressed(object sender, EventArgs e)
{
    fileName = string.Format(
                "Unleashed_{0:yyyy-MM-dd-HH-mm-ss}.jpg", DateTime.Now);
    photoCamera.CaptureImage();
}
```

The use of the volatile keyword prevents the CLR from caching the fileName value, so that all threads use the field's most recent value.

When the user releases the hardware camera button, the camera's CancelFocus method is called to halt any auto focusing that is underway, and the visual state is returned to NotFocusing, which hides the focus indicator image in the view. See the following excerpt:

```
void HandleShutterKeyReleased(object sender, EventArgs e)
{
```

```
    photoCamera.CancelFocus();

    VisualState = VisualStateValue.NotFocusing;
}
```

The `PhotoCamera.CaptureImage` method causes the `PhotoCamera` events `CaptureImageAvailable` and `CaptureThumbnailAvailable` to be raised on a non-UI thread. This means that event handler code must invoke any changes to UI elements on the UI thread. In the following excerpt the viewmodel's `SaveImage` method is invoked using the current `Dispatcher` instance:

```
void HandleCaptureImageAvailable(object sender, ContentReadyEventArgs e)
{
    Deployment.Current.Dispatcher.BeginInvoke(
        () => SaveImage(e.ImageStream,
                        (int)photoCamera.Resolution.Width,
                        (int)photoCamera.Resolution.Height));
}
```

> **NOTE**
>
> Once the `PhotoCamera.CaptureImage` method is called, subsequent calls must occur after the `CaptureCompleted` event has been raised; otherwise an `InvalidOperationException` is thrown.

The viewmodel's `SaveImage` method uses the `Microsoft.Xna.Framework.Media.MediaLibrary` class to save the picture to the media library, making it available from the phone's Pictures Hub. The built-in `WriteableBitmap.LoadJpeg` extension method is used to place the captured image into an `ObservableCollection`, which is bound to a `ListBox` in the view. See the following excerpt:

```
void SaveImage(Stream imageStream, int width, int height)
{
    ArgumentValidator.AssertNotNull(imageStream, "imageStream");

    var mediaLibrary = new MediaLibrary();
    mediaLibrary.SavePicture(fileName, imageStream);
    imageStream.Position = 0;

    var bitmap = new WriteableBitmap(width, height);
    bitmap.LoadJpeg(imageStream);

    CapturedImages.Add(bitmap);
}
```

The `HandleCaptureThumbnailAvailable` method saves the thumbnail of the image to isolated storage, allowing you to use the name to retrieve the image from the media library at a later time (see Listing 19.3). Building a page to view the thumbnails is discussed later in this chapter.

LISTING 19.3   `PhotoCameraViewModel.HandleCaptureThumbnailAvailable` Method

```
void HandleCaptureThumbnailAvailable(object sender, ContentReadyEventArgs e)
{
    using (e.ImageStream)
    {
        /* Save thumbnail as JPEG to isolated storage. */
        using (IsolatedStorageFile storageFile
                = IsolatedStorageFile.GetUserStoreForApplication())
        {
            if (!storageFile.DirectoryExists(imageDirectory))
            {
                storageFile.CreateDirectory(imageDirectory);
            }

            using (IsolatedStorageFileStream targetStream
                    = storageFile.OpenFile(
                        imageDirectory + "/" + fileName,
                        FileMode.Create, FileAccess.Write))
            {
                /* Initialize the buffer for 4KB disk pages. */
                byte[] readBuffer = new byte[4096];
                int bytesRead;

                /* Copy the thumbnail to isolated storage. */
                while ((bytesRead = e.ImageStream.Read(
                                    readBuffer, 0, readBuffer.Length)) > 0)
                {
                    targetStream.Write(readBuffer, 0, bytesRead);
                }
            }
        }
    }
}
```

The viewmodel's `Stop` method unsubscribes from the various `PhotoCamera` events and calls `Dispose` on the `PhotoCamera` instance to free all managed and unmanaged resources, as shown:

```
public void Stop()
{
```

```
    cameraInitialized = false;

    if (photoCamera == null)
    {
        return;
    }

    photoCamera.Initialized -= HandlePhotoCameraInitialized;
    photoCamera.AutoFocusCompleted -= HandleAutoFocusCompleted;
    photoCamera.CaptureCompleted -= HandleCaptureCompleted;
    photoCamera.CaptureThumbnailAvailable -= HandleCaptureThumbnailAvailable;
    photoCamera.CaptureImageAvailable -= HandleCaptureImageAvailable;

    CameraButtons.ShutterKeyPressed -= HandleShutterKeyPressed;
    CameraButtons.ShutterKeyHalfPressed -= HandleShutterKeyHalfPressed;
    CameraButtons.ShutterKeyReleased -= HandleShutterKeyReleased;

    photoCamera.Dispose();
    photoCamera = null;
}
```

The viewmodel is instantiated in the `PhotoCameraView` page (see Listing 19.4). The page's `OnNavigatedTo` method is used to call the `Start` method of the viewmodel, and the page's `OnNavigatedFrom` method calls the viewmodel's `Stop` method, thus ensuring that the `PhotoCamera` is disposed as soon as the user leaves the page.

> **NOTE**
>
> While the approach taken in this section explicitly calls the `Start` and `Stop` methods of the viewmodel, it is feasible that this approach could be further abstracted by placing the infrastructure for handling navigation events in the `ViewModelBase` class. This is, however, outside the scope of this book. The Calcium SDK project (http://calciumsdk.com) has this infrastructure in place.

Once the `PhotoCamera` has been instantiated by the viewmodel, it can be attached to a `VideoBrush`, which causes the initialization of the `PhotoCamera`.

LISTING 19.4   PhotoCameraView Class

```
public partial class PhotoCameraView : PhoneApplicationPage
{
    readonly PhotoCameraViewModel viewModel = new PhotoCameraViewModel();

    public PhotoCameraView()
    {
        InitializeComponent();
```

LISTING 19.4   Continued

```
        DataContext = viewModel;
    }

    PhotoCameraViewModel ViewModel
    {
        get
        {
            return (PhotoCameraViewModel)DataContext;
        }
    }

    protected override void OnNavigatedTo(NavigationEventArgs e)
    {
        ViewModel.Start();
        videoBrush_Preview.SetSource(ViewModel.Camera);

        base.OnNavigatedTo(e);
    }

    protected override void OnNavigatedFrom(NavigationEventArgs e)
    {
        ViewModel.Stop();
        base.OnNavigatedFrom(e);
    }
}
```

The view contains a Rectangle whose Fill property is set to the VideoBrush connected to the viewmodel's PhotoCamera (see Listing 19.5).

The viewmodel contains an EffectImage property of type ImageSource. As you see in a moment, this image is used to display the video in grayscale.

An Image control is bound to the EffectImage property in the view, and a Silverlight Toolkit ToggleSwitch is used to switch the effect on and off.

When the PhotoCamera is performing an automatic focus, the Image named image_Focus is made visible.

A ListBox is bound to the CapturedImages property of the viewmodel and displays each captured image as a thumbnail on the left side of the page.

A ListPicker control is bound to the list of FlashModes in the viewmodel. Selecting a flash mode causes the viewmodel's FlashMode property to be updated, and in turn, the PhotoCamera.FlashMode.

19

LISTING 19.5   PhotoCameraView Page (excerpt)

```xml
<Grid x:Name="LayoutRoot" Background="Transparent">

    <Rectangle Width="800" Height="480">
        <Rectangle.Fill>
            <VideoBrush x:Name="videoBrush_Preview" />
        </Rectangle.Fill>
    </Rectangle>

    <Image x:Name="image_Effect"
            Source="{Binding EffectImage}"
            Visibility="Collapsed" Stretch="Fill" Width="800" Height="480" />

    <Image x:Name="image_Focus" Source="/Sensors/Camera/Images/Focus.png"
            Margin="314, 197.5" Visibility="Collapsed"/>

    <ListBox ItemsSource="{Binding CapturedImages}">
        <ListBox.ItemTemplate>
            <DataTemplate>
                <Border BorderThickness="2,2,2,8" BorderBrush="White">
                    <Image Stretch="Uniform" Width="80" Source="{Binding}"/>
                </Border>
            </DataTemplate>
        </ListBox.ItemTemplate>
    </ListBox>

    <StackPanel Style="{StaticResource PageTitlePanelStyle}">
        <TextBlock Text="Windows Phone 7 Unleashed"
                    Style="{StaticResource PhoneTextAppTitleStyle}" />
        <TextBlock Text="{Binding Title}"
                    Style="{StaticResource PhoneTextPageTitleStyle}"/>
    </StackPanel>

    <StackPanel Width="200"
                HorizontalAlignment="Right" VerticalAlignment="Bottom">
        <TextBlock Text="effect"
                    FontSize="{StaticResource PhoneFontSizeMediumLarge}"/>
        <toolkit:ToggleSwitch IsChecked="{Binding EffectEnabled, Mode=TwoWay}"
                        FontSize="{StaticResource PhoneFontSizeExtraLarge}" />

        <TextBlock Text="flash mode"
                    FontSize="{StaticResource PhoneFontSizeMediumLarge}"/>
        <toolkit:ListPicker ItemsSource="{Binding FlashModes}"
                        SelectedItem="{Binding FlashMode, Mode=TwoWay}" />
    </StackPanel>
```

LISTING 19.5   Continued

```xml
<VisualStateManager.VisualStateGroups>
    <VisualStateGroup x:Name="FocusStates">
        <VisualState x:Name="Focusing">
            <Storyboard>
                <ObjectAnimationUsingKeyFrames Duration="0"
                        Storyboard.TargetProperty="Visibility"
                        Storyboard.TargetName="image_Focus">
                    <DiscreteObjectKeyFrame KeyTime="0">
                        <DiscreteObjectKeyFrame.Value>
                            <Visibility>Visible</Visibility>
                        </DiscreteObjectKeyFrame.Value>
                    </DiscreteObjectKeyFrame>
                </ObjectAnimationUsingKeyFrames>
            </Storyboard>
        </VisualState>
        ...
    </VisualStateGroup>
    <VisualStateGroup x:Name="EffectStates">
        ...
    </VisualStateGroup>
</VisualStateManager.VisualStateGroups>
</Grid>
```

All, apart from one of the VisualStateGroup elements, have been omitted from the excerpt to reduce its length.

The VisualStateGroup is set according to the VisualState property of the viewmodel. When the VisualState of the viewmodel changes to Focusing, for example, the VisualStateManager is directed to that state. This is all orchestrated using the custom VisualStateUtility class and an attached property named VisualState. For more information on the VisualStateUtility class see Chapter 16, "Bing Maps."

The attached property is set on the phone:PhoneApplicationPage element of the view as shown:

```
u:VisualStateUtility.VisualState="{Binding VisualState}"
```

When the viewmodel's VisualState property changes, the HandleVisualStateChanged method of the VisualStateUtility class is called, which calls the built-in VisualStateManager.GoToState method.

Figure 19.1 shows the PhotoCameraView page with a number of still captures displayed on the left and the flash mode selected as Auto.

FIGURE 19.1   `PhotoCameraView` page

The next section looks at enabling a grayscale effect for the video stream.

Adding a Video Effect

The viewmodel contains an `EffectEnabled` property to toggle the video effect on and off, shown in the following excerpt:

```
volatile bool effectEnabled;

public bool EffectEnabled
{
    get
    {
        return effectEnabled;
    }
    set
    {
        if (Assign(() => EffectEnabled, ref effectEnabled, value)
                                    == AssignmentResult.Success)
        {
            SetEffectState(value);
        }
    }
}
```

When the `EffectEnabled` property is set, the `SetEffectState` method is called, which assigns the `EffectImage` property to a new `WriteableBitmap` and begins updating the `WriteableBitmap` as new frames are received on another thread. See the following excerpt:

```
void SetEffectState(bool enabled)
{
```

```
if (enabled)
{
    EffectImage = new WriteableBitmap(
        (int)photoCamera.PreviewResolution.Width,
        (int)photoCamera.PreviewResolution.Height);

    effectThread = new Thread(ProcessEffectFrames);
    effectThread.Start();
}

VisualState = enabled ? VisualStateValue.EffectOn
                      : VisualStateValue.EffectOff;
}
```

Unlike Silverlight for the browser, Silverlight for Windows Phone does not support custom pixel shaders. Consequently, image post-processing must be performed in custom code. This, unfortunately, does not provide for great performance, as you see when switching on the effect on your own phone device.

The viewmodel's `ProcessEffectFrames` method, as you saw, is called from a non-UI thread. Its task is to retrieve an array of pixels from the `PhotoCamera`. It then converts each pixel (represented as an `int` value) to grayscale and uses the UI thread, via the apps `Dispatcher`, to write the pixels to the `effectImage` (see Listing 19.6). An `AutoResetEvent` is used to prevent a new frame from being processed until the current frame has been written to the effect image.

The `GetPreviewBufferArgb32` of the `PhotoCamera` class copies the current frame into a buffer array so that it can be further manipulated. We use this to retrieve the frame pixels.

LISTING 19.6   ProcessEffectFrames Method

```
readonly AutoResetEvent frameResetEvent = new AutoResetEvent(true);

void ProcessEffectFrames()
{
    try
    {
        while (effectEnabled)
        {
            frameResetEvent.WaitOne();

            int width = (int)photoCamera.PreviewResolution.Width;
            int height = (int)photoCamera.PreviewResolution.Height;
            int[] pixelArray = new int[width * height];

            photoCamera.GetPreviewBufferArgb32(pixelArray);
```

19

LISTING 19.6   Continued

```csharp
                int[] effectPixels = new int[pixelArray.Length];

                for (int i = 0; i < pixelArray.Length; i++)
                {
                    effectPixels[i] = ConvertColorToGrayScale(pixelArray[i]);
                }

                Deployment.Current.Dispatcher.BeginInvoke(
                    delegate
                        {
                            /* Copy pixels to the WriteableBitmap. */
                            effectPixels.CopyTo(effectImage.Pixels, 0);

                            effectImage.Invalidate();
                            frameResetEvent.Set();
                        });
            }
        }
        catch (Exception ex)
        {
            Debug.WriteLine("Unable to process effect frames." + ex);
            EffectEnabled = false;
            frameResetEvent.Set();
        }
    }
}
```

There are two other preview related PhotoCamera methods that are not shown in the example: GetPreviewBufferYCbCr and GetPreviewBufferY. Both also copy the current frame from the camera, yet do so without transforming the pixels to 32-bit ARGB values. GetPreviewBufferYCbCr provides the frame expressed using the YCbCr color space, while GetPreviewBufferY copies only the luminance data.

By avoiding the conversion to ARGB, retrieving the preview can be done much faster. According to René Schulte (http://kodierer.blogspot.com/2011/05/why-is-y-in-windows-phone-mango-camera.html), GetPreviewBufferYCbCr not only excludes the alpha channel in the YCrCb buffer, but in addition the Cr and Cb color components are stored with reduced resolution, keeping the buffer size substantially smaller and making the method approximately four times faster than GetPreviewBufferArgb32. Extracting the color components and brightness when using the YCbCr methods requires some more effort, however, and is outside the scope of this book.

Converting a pixel to grayscale involves first extracting the ARGB color components, as performed by the viewmodel's ConvertColorToArgb method, shown in the following excerpt:

```
void ConvertColorToArgb(
        int color, out int alpha, out int red, out int green, out int blue)
{
    alpha = color >> 24;
    red = (color & 0x00ff0000) >> 16;
    green = (color & 0x0000ff00) >> 8;
    blue = (color & 0x000000ff);
}
```

The red, green, and blue components are averaged to provide the grayscale value, as shown:

```
int ConvertColorToGrayScale(int color)
{
    int alpha, red, green, blue;
    ConvertColorToArgb(color, out alpha, out red, out green, out blue);

    int average = (red + green + blue) / 3;
    red = green = blue = average;

    int result = ConvertArgbToColor(alpha, red, green, blue);
    return result;
}
```

Finally, the color components are converted back to a color value using the viewmodel's ConvertArgbToColor method, as shown:

```
int ConvertArgbToColor(int alpha, int red, int green, int blue)
{
    int result = ((alpha & 0xFF) << 24)
                    | ((red & 0xFF) << 16)
                    | ((green & 0xFF) << 8)
                    | (blue & 0xFF);
    return result;
}
```

Figure 19.2 shows the result of the video effect, with the video displayed in grayscale.

19

FIGURE 19.2   `PhotoCameraView` page showing grayscale video effect

Using the `PhotoCamera`'s preview buffer is a way to produce live video effects. It does, however, suffer from suboptimal performance when each frame is redrawn. For improved performance, we must wait until Silverlight for Windows Phone supports custom pixel shaders.

Viewing Thumbnails

Earlier in the chapter you saw that the `PhotoCamera.CaptureThumbnailAvailable` event can be used to save a thumbnail image to isolated storage. This section looks at materializing those thumbnails on a page so that the user can tap a thumbnail and retrieve its associated full-size image from the phone's media library, all from within your app.

Recall that within the `PhotoCameraViewModel` when the user releases the hardware shutter button, the `PhotoCamera.CaptureImage` method is called, which raises the `PhotoCamera`'s `CaptureThumbnailAvailable` and `CaptureImageAvailable` events.

The `CaptureImageAvailable` handler saves the image to the media library, while the `CaptureThumbnailAvailable` handler saves the thumbnail version of the image to isolated storage. Both images share the same name, however, which allows the retrieval of corresponding media library image using the name of the thumbnail image.

The `PhotoCameraViewModel` saves all full-size images to a default PhotoCameraImages directory in isolated storage. The task of the `ThumbnailsViewModel` is to provide the names of these image files to the `ThumbnailsView` page, via an `ObservableCollection` of custom `ImageInfo` objects.

The `ImageInfo` class has two properties, which identify the location of the thumbnail in isolated storage and the name of the media library image (see Listing 19.7).

LISTING 19.7   ImageInfo Class

```csharp
public class ImageInfo
{
    public string MediaLibraryUrl { get; private set; }
    public Uri ThumbnailUri { get; private set; }

    public ImageInfo(Uri thumbnailUri, string mediaLibraryUrl)
    {
        ThumbnailUri = ArgumentValidator.AssertNotNull(
                            thumbnailUri, "thumbnailUri");
        MediaLibraryUrl = ArgumentValidator.AssertNotNullOrEmpty(
                            mediaLibraryUrl, "mediaLibraryUrl");
    }
}
```

The ThumbnailsViewModel.Populate method creates an ImageInfo object for each JPG image it finds in the isolated storage directory (see Listing 19.8).

The viewmodel's Populate method is called in the OnNavigatedTo method of the ThumbnailsView page. This causes new images present in the directory to be detected immediately after returning from the PhotoCameraView page.

LISTING 19.8   ThumbnailsViewModel.Populate Method

```csharp
public void Populate()
{
    string imageDirectory = PhotoCameraViewModel.ImageDirectory;

    ObservableCollection<ImageInfo> tempImages
                = new ObservableCollection<ImageInfo>();

    using (IsolatedStorageFile storageFile
                = IsolatedStorageFile.GetUserStoreForApplication())
    {
        string[] fileNames = storageFile.GetFileNames(
                            imageDirectory + @"\*.jpg");
        foreach (string fileName in fileNames)
        {
            ImageInfo info = new ImageInfo(
                new Uri(imageDirectory + "/" + fileName, UriKind.Relative),
                fileName);
            tempImages.Add(info);
        }
    }

    Images = tempImages;
}
```

The ThumbnailsViewModel contains a ViewImageCommand, whose task is to navigate to the MediaLibraryImageView page. The name of the image is provided as a querystring parameter, allowing the MediaLibraryImageView to retrieve the image from the phone's media library. See the following excerpt:

```
public ThumbnailsViewModel() : base("photos")
{
    viewImageCommand = new DelegateCommand<string>(ViewImage);
}

void ViewImage(string name)
{
    Navigate("/Sensors/Camera/MediaLibraryImageView.xaml?image=" + name);
}
```

Thumbnails are presented by binding to the viewmodel's Images property, as shown:

```
ObservableCollection<ImageInfo> images
                = new ObservableCollection<ImageInfo>();

public ObservableCollection<ImageInfo> Images
{
    get
    {
        return images;
    }
    private set
    {
        Assign(() => Images, ref images, value);
    }
}
```

To convert a path to an image stored in isolated storage, a custom IValueConverter is used (see Listing 19.9).

NOTE

It would be useful if the URI prefix isostore, which is used when working with local databases, worked with the Image.Source property. This would make the custom IValueConverter unnecessary. Unfortunately, though, the isostore prefix does not work with images.

LISTING 19.9   StringToImageConverter Class

```
public class StringToImageConverter : IValueConverter
{
    public object Convert(
```

LISTING 19.9   Continued

```
        object value, Type targetType, object parameter, CultureInfo culture)
    {
        if (value == null)
        {
            return null;
        }

        using (IsolatedStorageFile storageFile
                    = IsolatedStorageFile.GetUserStoreForApplication())
        {
            using (IsolatedStorageFileStream stream
                    = storageFile.OpenFile(value.ToString(), FileMode.Open))
            {
                BitmapImage image = new BitmapImage();
                image.SetSource(stream);
                return image;
            }
        }
    }

    public object ConvertBack(
        object value, Type targetType, object parameter, CultureInfo culture)
    {
        throw new NotImplementedException();
    }
}
```

Within the ThumbnailsView page, thumbnail images are presented using a ListBox in combination with a Silverlight Toolkit WrapPanel, as shown in the following excerpt:

```
<Grid x:Name="ContentPanel" Grid.Row="1" Margin="12,0,12,0">
    <ListBox ItemsSource="{Binding Images}">
        <ListBox.ItemsPanel>
            <ItemsPanelTemplate>
                <toolkit:WrapPanel ItemHeight="150" ItemWidth="150" />
            </ItemsPanelTemplate>
        </ListBox.ItemsPanel>
        <ListBox.ItemTemplate>
            <DataTemplate>
                <Image Source="{Binding ThumbnailUri,
                    Converter={StaticResource StringToImageConverter}}"
                    c:Commanding.Command="{Binding Content.ViewImageCommand,
                    Source={StaticResource bridge}}"
                    c:Commanding.CommandParameter="{Binding MediaLibraryUrl}"
```

```
                    Width="120" Height="120" Margin="10" />
            </DataTemplate>
        </ListBox.ItemTemplate>
    </ListBox>
</Grid>
```

The data context of each `Image` control is an `ImageInfo` object.

To reach out of the `DataTemplate` and execute the viewmodel's `ViewImageCommand`, a `ContentControl` whose content is set to the page is defined as resource and serves as a bridge between items in the `DataTemplate` and the viewmodel. See the following excerpt:

```
<phone:PhoneApplicationPage.Resources>
    <ValueConverters:StringToImageConverter
                x:Name="StringToImageConverter" />
    <ContentControl x:Name="bridge"
                Content="{Binding Path=DataContext, ElementName=page}" />
</phone:PhoneApplicationPage.Resources>
```

The custom `Command` attached property (introduced in Chapter 2, "Fundamental Concepts in Silverlight Development for Windows Phone") is used to execute the `ViewImageCommand` when the user taps a thumbnail image. The path to the image in the media library is passed as the command parameter.

`ThumbnailsView` also contains an `AppBar` with a single `AppBarHyperlinkButton` that, when tapped, navigates to the `PhotoCameraView` page:

```
<u:AppBar>
    <u:AppBarHyperlinkButton
                NavigateUri="/Sensors/Camera/PhotoCameraView.xaml"
                Text="PhotoCameraView"
                IconUri="/Sensors/Camera/Icons/TakePhoto.png" />
</u:AppBar>
```

Figure 19.3 shows the `ThumbnailsView` page, populated with several images.

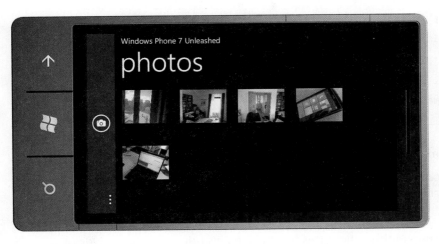

FIGURE 19.3   ThumbnailsView page

When the user taps a thumbnail image, the app is directed to the `MediaLibraryImageView`
page. The name of the image to display is supplied as a querystring parameter. The
`MediaLibraryImageViewModel` retrieves the specified image from the phone's media
library and exposes it via its `Image` property. The viewmodel's `LoadImageCommand` calls its
`LoadImage` method, in which the `Picture` object is retrieved from the media library (see
Listing 19.10).

`Picture.GetImage` is used to retrieve a `Stream` object, which then becomes the source of a
`BitmapImage`.

In addition, the `Title` property of the viewmodel is set to the name of the `Picture`, which
is subsequently displayed in the view.

LISTING 19.10   `MediaLibraryImageViewModel.LoadImage` Method

```
void LoadImage(string name)
{
    MediaLibrary mediaLibrary = new MediaLibrary();
    Picture picture = mediaLibrary.SavedPictures.Where(
                                x => x.Name == name).FirstOrDefault();

    if (picture == null)
    {
        MessageService.ShowError(
            string.Format("The picture {0} was not found.", name));
        return;
    }

    BitmapImage bitmapImage;
    using (Stream stream = picture.GetImage())
    {
        bitmapImage = new BitmapImage();
```

LISTING 19.10   Continued

```
        bitmapImage.SetSource(stream);
    }

    Image = bitmapImage;
    Title = name;
}
```

The view contains an `Image` that is bound to the viewmodel's `Image` property, as shown:

```
<Grid x:Name="ContentPanel" Grid.Row="1" Margin="12,0,12,0">
    <Image Source="{Binding Image}"  />
</Grid>
```

As with most examples throughout this book, the page's title container includes a `TextBlock` that is bound to the `Title` property of the `ViewModelBase` class. By following this pattern, it provides the viewmodel the ability to change the title of the page. As you saw in the `LoadImage` method, the `Title` property is set to the name of the image. See the following excerpt:

```
<StackPanel Grid.Row="0" Style="{StaticResource PageTitlePanelStyle}">
    <TextBlock Text="Windows Phone 7 Unleashed"
                Style="{StaticResource PhoneTextAppTitleStyle}" />
    <TextBlock Text="{Binding Title}"
                Style="{StaticResource PhoneTextPageTitleStyle}"
                FontSize="{StaticResource PhoneFontSizeMediumLarge}" />
</StackPanel>
```

Figure 19.4 shows the `MediaLibraryImageView` page displaying an image from the media library.

FIGURE 19.4   `MediaLibraryImageView` page

By using the `PhotoCamera` class combined with the Media Library API, you can create a full-featured camera app. The `PhotoCamera` class is, however, not suitable for apps that need to capture audio and video. The next section explores the Silverlight webcam API and how it is used to save audio and video to isolated storage.

Using the Silverlight Webcam API

The Silverlight webcam API comes to the phone with Silverlight 4. If you already have code for processing audio and video using the `System.Windows.Media.CaptureSource` class, you will feel right at home. `CaptureSource` allows you to capture both audio and video, and when used in conjunction with a `FileSink` class, allows you to save video to isolated storage.

This section creates a simplified version of the Photo Camera page presented in the previous section. A page is created that allows the user to capture still images as well as video, and in both cases, you see how captured data is written to isolated storage.

The sample for this section includes a page named `CaptureSourceView` and its viewmodel `CaptureSourceViewModel`, both located in the /Sensors/Camera directory of the WindowsPhone7Unleashed.Examples project in the downloadable sample code.

To begin, the viewmodel contains a property named `CaptureSource`, which is of type `CaptureSource`. The `CaptureSource` class is analogous to the `PhotoCamera` class.

The `CaptureSource` backing field is initialized in the viewmodel's `Start` method (see Listing 19.11).

NOTE

In Silverlight for Windows Phone, `CaptureDeviceConfiguration.AllowedDeviceAccess` is always true, even if the app does not have the ID_CAP_ISV_CAMERA capability specified in its WMAppManifest.xml file.

In Listing 19.11, both the test for `AllowedDeviceAccess` and the subsequent call to `RequestDeviceAccess` exist to retain compatibility with Silverlight for the browser, which does not use a capabilities model, but instead requires that the user authorize the request to use the camera via a confirmation dialog.

A `CaptureSource` instance is initialized using static methods of the `System.Windows.Media.CaptureDeviceConfiguration` class, which connects the `CaptureSource` to the video and audio capture device classes.

NOTE

If your app does not have the ID_CAP_ISV_CAMERA capability, an exception is raised after the call to `CaptureSource.Start`.

Wrapping the `Start` call in a try/catch block does not allow the ensuing `COMException` to be caught because the exception is raised at an indeterminate point after the `Start` call returns.

LISTING 19.11   `CaptureSourceViewModel.Start Method`

```
public void Start()
{
    Stop();

    if (CaptureDeviceConfiguration.AllowedDeviceAccess
            || CaptureDeviceConfiguration.RequestDeviceAccess())
    {
        captureSource = new CaptureSource
            {
                VideoCaptureDevice
                    = CaptureDeviceConfiguration.GetDefaultVideoCaptureDevice(),
                AudioCaptureDevice
                    = CaptureDeviceConfiguration.GetDefaultAudioCaptureDevice()
            };

        captureSource.CaptureImageCompleted += HandleCaptureImageCompleted;
        captureSource.CaptureFailed += HandleCaptureFailed;

        captureSource.Start();
        started = true;
        UpdateCommands();
    }
}
```

Specifying the image format, including the resolution of captured images, is done by setting the `CaptureSource` object's `VideoCaptureDevice.DesiredFormat` property. To determine which formats are supported the `VideoCaptureDevice.SupportedFormats` property is used. On my device there are two supported formats, both with a resolution of 640 by 480, but one offering 32-bit color while the other offers 8-bit grayscale. The desired format can be indicated using one of the supported formats, as shown:

```
captureSource.VideoCaptureDevice.DesiredFormat
    = captureSource.VideoCaptureDevice.SupportedFormats[1];
```

> **NOTE**
>
> Setting the `DesiredFormat` affects still image captures, and not captured video.

In addition, the audio format can be specified by setting the `DesiredFormat` property of the `AudioCaptureDevice` to one of the supported formats, like so:

```
foreach (AudioFormat supportedFormat
                in captureSource.AudioCaptureDevice.SupportedFormats)
{
```

```
    if (supportedFormat.BitsPerSample > 16)
    {
        captureSource.AudioCaptureDevice.DesiredFormat = supportedFormat;
        break;
    }
}
```

CaptureSourceViewModel

The viewmodel contains the following three commands:

▶ TakePhotoCommand

▶ ToggleVideoCaptureCommand

▶ PlayVideoCommand

TakePhotoCommand uses the CaptureSource to save a still image to isolated storage. ToggleVideoCaptureCommand starts and stops the recording of video and initially causes the CaptureSource to be attached to a FileSink object so that a video file is written to isolated storage.

The commands are instantiated in the viewmodel constructor like so:

```
public CaptureSourceViewModel() : base("CaptureSource")
{
    takePhotoCommand
        = new DelegateCommand(obj => TakePhoto(), obj => started);

    toggleVideoCaptureCommand
        = new DelegateCommand(obj => ToggleCapturingVideo());

    playVideoCommand
        = new DelegateCommand(obj => PlayVideo(),
                              obj => !capturingVideo && IsVideoCaptured());
}
```

Whenever something takes place that may alter the executable state of a command, the viewmodel's UpdateCommands method is called, which is shown in the following excerpt:

```
void UpdateCommands()
{
    takePhotoCommand.RaiseCanExecuteChanged();
    playVideoCommand.RaiseCanExecuteChanged();
}
```

The viewmodel's TakePhoto method calls the CaptureImageAsync method of the CaptureSource object, as shown:

19

```
void TakePhoto()
{
    if (captureSource != null && captureSource.State == CaptureState.Started)
    {
        captureSource.CaptureImageAsync();
    }
}
```

CaptureImageAsync attempts to use the device camera to capture an image.

> **NOTE**
>
> If CaptureImageAsync is called without first calling the CaptureSource.Start method, then an InvalidOperationException is raised.

The CaptureSource.CaptureImageCompleted event is raised if the call completes asynchronously, which does not necessarily mean that an image has been successfully acquired. If an error occurs during image capture, the CaptureSource.CaptureFailed event is raised.

> **NOTE**
>
> Although the resulting CaptureImageCompletedEventArgs has an Error property (inherited from its AsyncCompletedEventArgs), this property is never set, and therefore cannot be used for error detection.

The resulting image is saved to the phone's photo hub using the MediaLibrary class (see Listing 19.12). The dimensions of the image are supplied by the event arguments. Just as the PhotoCamera example maintained a collection of captured images, so too does the CaptureSourceViewModel.

LISTING 19.12   CaptureSourceViewModel.HandleCaptureImageCompleted Method

```
void HandleCaptureImageCompleted(object sender, CaptureImageCompletedEventArgs e)
{
    if (e.Result != null)
    {
        Deployment.Current.Dispatcher.BeginInvoke(() =>
        {
            MediaLibrary mediaLibrary = new MediaLibrary();
            string imageName = string.Format(
                    "Unleashed_{0:yyyy-MM-dd-HH-mm-ss}.jpg", DateTime.Now);
            using (MemoryStream stream = new MemoryStream())
            {
                e.Result.SaveJpeg(
                    stream, e.Result.PixelWidth, e.Result.PixelHeight,
                    0, 100);
```

LISTING 19.12   Continued

```
                stream.Position = 0;
                mediaLibrary.SavePicture(imageName, stream);
            }
            CapturedImages.Add(e.Result);
        });
    }
}
```

The `CaptureSource.State` property, which is an enum value of type `CaptureState`, indicates the state of the `CaptureSource` object and can be either Failed, Started, or Stopped.

Recording the audio and video of a `CaptureSource` instance requires the attachment of a `FileSink` (see Listing 19.13). The `FileSink` object is assigned the location of a file in isolated storage, to which it writes the video file in MP4 format.

> **NOTE**
>
> The `CaptureSource` object must be in a stopped state to attach or detach a `FileSink`. Attempting to set the `FileSink.CaptureSource` property while the `CaptureSource` object is in a Started state raises an `InvalidOperationException`.

Stopping the capture of video involves detaching the `FileSink` from the `CaptureSource` object. Again, the `FileSink` can only be removed if the `CaptureSource` is not started; `CaptureSource.State` must not equal `CaptureState.Started`.

LISTING 19.13   `CaptureSourceViewModel.ToggleCapturingVideo` Method

```
FileSink fileSink;

void ToggleCapturingVideo()
{
    if (!capturingVideo)
    {
        fileSink = new FileSink {IsolatedStorageFileName = videoFileName};

        captureSource.Stop();
        fileSink.CaptureSource = captureSource;
        captureSource.Start();
    }
    else
    {
        captureSource.Stop();
        fileSink.CaptureSource = null;
        captureSource.Start();
```

LISTING 19.13   Continued

```
    }

    CapturingVideo = !capturingVideo;
    UpdateCommands();
}
```

Once a video has been recorded to isolated storage it can be played back using either a `MediaPlayer` control within the app or via the `MediaPlayerLauncher`, as shown in the following excerpt:

```
void PlayVideo()
{
    MediaPlayerLauncher mediaPlayerLauncher = new MediaPlayerLauncher
            {
                Media = new Uri(videoFileName, UriKind.Relative),
                Location = MediaLocationType.Data,
            };

    mediaPlayerLauncher.Show();
}
```

> **NOTE**
>
> Although `AppBar` buttons were used to demonstrate the `CaptureSource` class, there is no reason that the `Microsoft.Devices.CameraButtons` class (presented earlier in this chapter) cannot be used instead. `CameraButtons` can be used in conjunction with the `CaptureSource` class to allow the hardware shutter button to start and stop video capture.

Displaying Video in the `CaptureSourceView`

As with the `PhotoCamera` example earlier in this chapter, the view displays video using a `VideoBrush`, which is defined as shown:

```
<Rectangle Width="780" Height="460" Margin="10">
    <Rectangle.Fill>
        <VideoBrush x:Name="videoBrush_Preview" />
    </Rectangle.Fill>
</Rectangle>
```

The `CaptureSourceViewModel.Start` method is called in the `OnNavigatedTo` method of the page. Once started, the `VideoBrush` has its source set to the viewmodel's `CaptureSource` property. See the following excerpt:

```
protected override void OnNavigatedTo(NavigationEventArgs e)
{
```

```
    base.OnNavigatedTo(e);
    Dispatcher.BeginInvoke(
        delegate
            {
                ViewModel.Start();
                videoBrush_Preview.SetSource(ViewModel.CaptureSource);
            });
}
```

The Dispatcher is used to push the `ViewModel.Start` call onto the work stack of the UI thread. This workaround, for what appears to be an issue with the `CaptureSource` class, prevents the `CaptureSource` from raising a `COMException` when the app is activated.

Unlike the `PhotoCamera`, no `Initialized` event is raised when the `CaptureSource` is attached to a `VideoBrush`.

Captured images overlay the video preview and are displayed using a `ListBox`, as shown:

```xml
<ListBox ItemsSource="{Binding CapturedImages}" Margin="12">
    <ListBox.ItemTemplate>
        <DataTemplate>
            <Border BorderThickness="2,2,2,8" BorderBrush="White" Margin="3">
                <Image Source="{Binding}" Stretch="Uniform" Width="80" />
            </Border>
        </DataTemplate>
    </ListBox.ItemTemplate>
</ListBox>
```

An `AppBar` contains buttons that are bound to the three viewmodel commands: `PlayVideoCommand`, `ToggleVideoCaptureCommand`, and `TakePhoneCommand`.

An `AppBarToggleButton` changes its icon depending on the value of the viewmodel's `CapturingVideo` property. See the following excerpt:

```xml
<u:AppBar>
    <u:AppBarIconButton
                Command="{Binding PlayVideoCommand}"
                Text="play video"
                IconUri="/Sensors/Camera/Icons/Play.png" />
    <u:AppBarToggleButton
                Command1="{Binding ToggleVideoCaptureCommand}"
                Text1="record video"
                Icon1Uri="/Sensors/Camera/Icons/Record.png"
                Text2="stop"
                Icon2Uri="/Sensors/Camera/Icons/Stop.png"
                Toggled="{Binding CapturingVideo}" />
    <u:AppBarIconButton
                Command="{Binding TakePhotoCommand}"
```

```
                    Text="take photo"
                    IconUri="/Sensors/Camera/Icons/TakePhoto.png" />
</u:AppBar>
```

Figure 19.5 shows the `CaptureSourceView` page with the three application bar buttons, allowing the user to take a still capture and to record and play back video.

FIGURE 19.5   `CaptureSourceView` page

`CaptureSource` is the recommended way for recording video to isolated storage, and offers exciting possibilities for creating rich multimedia apps.

Summary

This chapter explored two approaches for capturing still images and video. Beginning with `PhotoCamera`, you saw how to capture still images and display live video using the `PhotoCamera`'s preview buffer. You also looked at leveraging the phone's hardware shutter button and how to create a live video effect.

The second part of this chapter covered the Silverlight 4 webcam API, specifically how to use the webcam API to capture audio and video and to save it as an MP4 in isolated storage.

CHAPTER 20

Incorporating XNA Graphics in Silverlight

Silverlight and XNA are fundamentally different technologies; each is suited to particular scenarios: Silverlight for line of business apps and XNA for games. Yet, both have limitations that are otherwise solved by the other.

Previously, allowing Silverlight and XNA to coexist within a single app was not possible. The initial release of Windows Phone 7 saw Silverlight and XNA graphics inhabiting two different application types. It was a case of never the twain shall meet. In fact, attempting to employ XNA graphics in a Silverlight app, or vice versa, would see your app fail marketplace certification.

With the Mango release of the Windows Phone SDK, all this has changed, and you can now incorporate the performance and 2D and 3D graphics engine of XNA into your Silverlight apps, or build XNA games that are able to harness the richness of Silverlight's controls and navigation system.

Combining the two technologies, into what is referred to as a hybrid app, gives you the best of both worlds. For example, Silverlight has a richer set of controls that makes creating a user interface for your XNA game, such as a high score table or menu, easier.

Building a hybrid app does, however, come at the cost of portability. Silverlight for the browser does not support XNA, and XBox360 does not provide support for Silverlight (although this may change in the near future). Thus, the downside to mixing Silverlight and XNA is, at present, that it limits your app to the phone. This is something to be mindful of, especially if you are looking to monetize your app on the XBox360.

This chapter begins with a brief overview of the key components that make hybrid apps possible. You then look at the Visual Studio project templates for creating hybrid apps and explore the shared graphics device manager that is used to allow immediate mode rendering within a Silverlight app. You also see how to use the GameTimer class to subscribe to XNA game loop events. The chapter then takes a closer look at the plumbing that allows hybrid apps to function and puts it all together by demonstrating how to display an XNA model with superimposed Silverlight content. Finally, processing XNA gesture input from within a PhoneApplicationPage is discussed.

The focus of this book is Silverlight and not XNA, and for that reason, this chapter's emphasis is placed firmly on hybrid apps and not XNA.

Supporting Components

The infrastructure supporting hybrid apps allows Silverlight and XNA to coexist on the same PhoneApplicationPage within what is a Silverlight app. The two technologies, however, differ significantly in their respective UI programming models, and integrating them relies on the following three components:

▶ **SharedGraphicsDeviceManager**—This class is used to provide side-by-side rendering of Silverlight and XNA.

▶ **GameTimer**—This class provides notifications of XNA game loop events.

▶ **UIElementRenderer**—This class allows you to display Silverlight UIElements within XNA.

Much of this chapter is devoted to exploring these components in detail. The chapter begins, however, by looking at the Visual Studio project templates used to create hybrid apps.

Project Templates for Creating Hybrid Apps

With the Windows Phone SDK installed, Visual Studio provides two project templates for creating a Silverlight app with XNA integration. The first template is named XNA Windows Phone Rich Graphics Application and is located in the XNA Game Studio 4.0 section of the Add New Project dialog. The second template is named Windows Phone 3D Graphics Application within the Silverlight for Window Phone section (see Figure 20.1). These templates are henceforth referred to as the *hybrid project templates*.

NOTE

Even though the XNA Windows Phone Rich Graphics Application resides in the XNA Game Studio 4.0 section of the Add New Project dialog, it is actually a Silverlight app; an App class is generated, along with PhoneApplicationPage files.

Both templates are almost identical. Both generate three projects: a principal Silverlight project, an XNA Game Library project, and an XNA Content project. Both templates create the plumbing required for displaying XNA graphics alongside Silverlight.

The difference between the two templates is that the Silverlight project starts you off with a basic animation. While the XNA template starts you with a stock standard CornflowerBlue background.

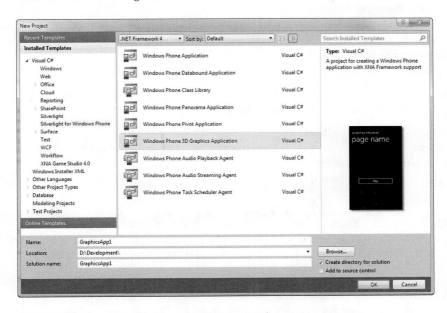

FIGURE 20.1   Windows Phone 3D Graphics Application project

XNA games ordinarily subclass `Microsoft.Xna.Framework.Game` to provide the bootstrapping that is otherwise performed by the subclassed `App` class in a pure Silverlight app. When a hybrid app is created, using either of the hybrid project templates, the generated app uses the Silverlight model and an `App` subclass is used (not a `Game` subclass).

The key ingredient that makes rendering Silverlight and XNA possible is a class called `SharedGraphicsDeviceManager`.

Rendering Modes and the `SharedGraphicsDeviceManager` Class

Silverlight and XNA differ in the way graphic objects are rendered. The `SharedGraphicsDeviceManager` class allows your app to use both XNA's immediate mode rendering and Silverlight's retained mode rendering. In retained mode, the rendering system has a complete model of the objects to be rendered. Conversely, in immediate mode, there is no model and graphics are rendered directly on the display. In XNA, your code is responsible for periodically drawing all content within each pass of the game loop; if you do not explicitly draw something, it will not show up on the screen. Conversely, in Silverlight, elements are drawn automatically, which is more convenient yet may suffer

20

poorer performance due to the overhead of managing the visualization of the entire visual tree.

SharedGraphicsDeviceManager is used instead of the GraphicsDeviceManager class in the hybrid programming model to allow immediate mode XNA rendering in the Silverlight app.

SharedGraphicsDeviceManager Initialization

A single instance of the SharedGraphicsDeviceManager must be created within your app before it can be used to render XNA content. Ordinarily, this is done when your App is instantiated. When using either of the hybrid project templates, the SharedGraphicsDeviceManager is initialized in the App.xaml file.

SharedGraphicsDeviceManager implements IApplicationService and is placed in the ApplicationLifetimeObjects collection as shown in the following excerpt:

```
<Application.ApplicationLifetimeObjects>
    <!--Required object that handles lifetime events for the application-->
    <xna:SharedGraphicsDeviceManager />
</Application.ApplicationLifetimeObjects>
```

> **NOTE**
>
> SharedGraphicsDeviceManager is intended to be used as a singleton. If more than one SharedGraphicsDeviceManager is instantiated, an InvalidOperationException is raised.

To display XNA content from a PhoneApplicationPage, the sharing mode of the SharedGraphicsDeviceManager graphics device must be enabled. The recommended location for setting the sharing mode is in the page's OnNavigatedTo handler, as shown:

```
protected override void OnNavigatedTo(NavigationEventArgs e)
{
    SharedGraphicsDeviceManager.Current.GraphicsDevice.SetSharingMode(true);

    base.OnNavigatedTo(e);
}
```

> **NOTE**
>
> If an app is in Silverlight's retained rendering mode, an exception is raised if you attempt to load graphical content via XNA's ContentManager. All nongraphical content, however, can be loaded at any time.

When the user navigates away from a page, shared mode should be disabled. Doing so reverts to retained mode rendering and allows subsequent Silverlight content to be displayed. The OnNavigatedFrom page event handler can be used to disable the sharing mode, as shown:

```
protected override void OnNavigatedFrom(NavigationEventArgs e)
{
    SharedGraphicsDeviceManager.Current.GraphicsDevice.SetSharingMode(false);

    base.OnNavigatedFrom(e);
}
```

> **NOTE**
>
> Neglecting to disable sharing mode before navigating away from the page prevents
> Silverlight from rendering the next page.

Harnessing the XNA Game Loop Via the GameTimer Class

In XNA, responding to user input, updating your app's state, and drawing content all
happen periodically within the *game loop*. The game loop is the heart of every XNA game,
and understanding it is fundamental to XNA development.

Unlike pure XNA games, which use the Game class for the game loop, hybrid apps rely on
the Microsoft.Xna.Framework.GameTimer, which is unique to the phone.

In a pure XNA game, a Game class is used instead of an Application class. XNA games rely
on overloading Game class methods that are specific to the game loop, such as Update and
Draw, while hybrid apps use the GameTimer class for the same purpose, and instead
subscribe to game loop related events. To make things easier, GameTimer events correspond
to methods of the same name in ordinary XNA games.

GameTimer has three events: Draw, FrameAction, and Update. When raised, the Draw and
Update events deliver a GameTimerEventArgs object, which contains the same timing information as the GameTime object provided to the Game.Update and Game.Draw methods.

The GameTimer class extends the functionality around the game loop, going beyond the
Game class by allowing you to create multiple GameTimer instances, each dedicated to
drawing particular objects or sets of objects in your UI. The order in which the Draw event
is raised for different GameTimer instances can be controlled using the GameTimer.DrawOrder
property. DrawOrder indicates the order in which Draw events are called when more than
one timer has the event raised at the same time. GameTimer objects with lower DrawOrder
values have their event handlers called before those of GameTimer objects with higher
values.

For example, the following excerpt shows three GameTimers. Each has a subscription to its
Draw event, and each specifies a different DrawOrder value:

```
timer1.Draw += delegate { Debug.WriteLine("Timer 1"); };
timer1.DrawOrder = 10;

timer2.Draw += delegate { Debug.WriteLine("Timer 2"); };
timer2.DrawOrder = 100;
```

```
timer3.Draw += delegate { Debug.WriteLine("Timer 3"); };
timer3.DrawOrder = 1;
```

By specifying a lower `DrawOrder` value, the event handler of `timer3` is called first, while `timer2`, having the highest `DrawOrder`, is called last. See the following output:

```
Timer 3
Timer 1
Timer 2
Timer 3
Timer 1
Timer 2
...
```

The other two `GameTimer` properties, `GameTimer.UpdateOrder` and `FrameActionOrder`, are analogous to the `DrawOrder` property, yet pertain to the `Update` and `FrameAction` events, respectively.

Controlling the Interval Between Updates

The `GameTimer.UpdateInterval` property allows you to explicitly set the time between updates. By default, this value is 333333 ticks or ~33 ms. A tick is the smallest unit of time, equal to 100 nanoseconds. This equates to 30 frames a second.

> **NOTE**
>
> Be careful when explicitly setting `UpdateInterval`. If set too short and the event handler consistently runs longer than the time interval set by `UpdateInterval`, game performance is adversely affected.

XNA Environment Initialization

When a hybrid project template is used to create a hybrid app, a region is generated within the `App` class for the purpose of initializing the XNA content manager and starting a `GameTimer` object. By default, a `ContentManager` is exposed as a public property within your `App` class, allowing it to be consumed across your application. You can, however, create new instances of the `ContentManager` class if you want.

When instantiating a `ContentManager`, it must be passed an `IServiceProvider` that can later be used to retrieve an `IGraphicsDeviceService`. The `App` class implements `IServiceProvider`, and the `IServiceProvider.GetService` method implementation returns objects that reside in the `ApplicationLifetimeObjects` collection.

Because the `App` class implements the `IServiceProvider` interface, it is able to pass itself to the `ContentManager` constructor, providing the `ContentManager` access to an `IGraphicsDeviceService`, which, in this case, is a `SharedGraphicsDeviceManager`. See the following excerpt:

```
#region XNA application initialization

// Performs initialization of the XNA types required for the application.
void InitializeXnaApplication()
{
    // Create the ContentManager
    // so the application can load precompiled assets.
    ContentManager = new ContentManager(this, "Content");

    // Create a GameTimer to pump the XNA FrameworkDispatcher.
    GameTimer frameworkDispatcherTimer = new GameTimer();
    frameworkDispatcherTimer.FrameAction += FrameworkDispatcherFrameAction;
    frameworkDispatcherTimer.Start();
}

// An event handler that pumps the FrameworkDispatcher each frame.
// FrameworkDispatcher is required for a lot of the XNA events and
// for certain functionality such as SoundEffect playback.
void FrameworkDispatcherFrameAction(object sender, EventArgs e)
{
    FrameworkDispatcher.Update();
}

#endregion
```

The `FrameworkDispatcher.Update` method triggers event processing in the XNA framework. In a pure XNA app, it is automatically called whenever `Game.Update` is called. In Silverlight, however, the absence of a `Game` class means that you rely on a `GameTimer` instance to raise a manual call to `FrameworkDispatcher.Update`.

Displaying a 3D XNA Model in a Hybrid App

The example for this chapter is located in the `SilverlightXnaHybrid` solution in the downloadable sample code. In the sample, we use a `PhoneApplicationPage` to display an XNA model and integrate Silverlight elements with the XNA content.

The viewmodel for this example is called `GamePageViewModel`. It contains a custom `ModelMetadata` property, which provides the view with the information it needs to display a particular 3D model using XNA.

The `ModelMetadata` field is initialized in the viewmodel constructor. An XNA asset, called Spaceship, is specified, and various other properties that are used when drawing the 3D model are defined as shown:

```
public GamePageViewModel()
{
    modelMetadata = new ModelMetadata
```

20

```
    {
        Asset = "Spaceship",
        Name = "Spaceship",
        Description = "Alien spaceship model",
        World = Matrix.Identity,
        ViewMatrix = Matrix.CreateLookAt(
            new Vector3(3500, 400, 0) + new Vector3(0, 250, 0),
            new Vector3(0, 250, 0),
            Vector3.Up),
        FieldOfViewDivisor = 1f,
        AspectRatio = 1.66666663f,
        NearPlaneDistance = 10f,
        FarPlaneDistance = 20000f,
    };

    displayMessageCommand = new DelegateCommand(
                            obj => Message = "Silverlight Message");
}
```

The example uses an alien spacecraft model, which can be found in the App Hub game development resources at http://create.msdn.com/en-US/education/gamedevelopment.

Rendering Silverlight Elements in XNA

While it may seem that Silverlight is able to coexist with XNA in the same UI, it is somewhat of an illusion. Within any app, only a single renderer can paint to the screen at any given time. This means that when displaying XNA content, you cannot display Silverlight content without using a special proxy called `UIElementRenderer`, which takes the Silverlight content and renders it as a 2D XNA texture. XNA is responsible for triggering Silverlight touch events for the elements represented by the texture. The Silverlight content still exists behind the scenes, but it remains invisible because it is not able to be rendered by the XNA renderer.

This section demonstrates how to use the `UIElementRenderer` class to enable Silverlight content to be rendered above XNA content.

To begin, within the view XAML a `Button` is bound to the `DisplayMessageCommand` property of the viewmodel. The command updates the viewmodel's `Message` property, which is then displayed using a `TextBlock`. See the following excerpt:

```
<Grid x:Name="LayoutRoot" Margin="12">
    <StackPanel Orientation="Horizontal">
        <Button Content="tap me" Command="{Binding DisplayMessageCommand}"
            HorizontalAlignment="Left" VerticalAlignment="Top" />
        <TextBlock Text="{Binding Message}" />
    </StackPanel>
</Grid>
```

The view code-beside (GamePage.xaml.cs) contains a single `GameTimer` field. In the view's constructor we subscribe to the `GameTimer` object's `Update` and `Draw` events. The `DataContext` is assigned a `GamePageViewModel` instance, as shown in the following excerpt:

```
public GamePage()
{
    InitializeComponent();
    DataContext = viewModel = new GamePageViewModel();

    gameTimer.Update += HandleGameTimerUpdate;
    gameTimer.Draw += HandleGameTimerDraw;

    LayoutUpdated += HandleLayoutUpdated;

    /* Enable gestures - Pinch for zoom and horizontal drag for rotate. */
    TouchPanel.EnabledGestures
        = GestureType.FreeDrag
            | GestureType.Pinch
            | GestureType.PinchComplete;
}
```

The view contains a `UIElementRenderer` field. When a change occurs within the visual tree, the `UIElementRenderer` must be replaced. When the page's `LayoutUpdated` event is raised, indicating that the visual tree has changed, the `HandleLayoutUpdated` method reassigns the `uiElementRenderer`, as shown:

```
void HandleLayoutUpdated(object sender, EventArgs e)
{
    if (uiElementRenderer == null
        || LayoutRoot.ActualWidth > 0 && LayoutRoot.ActualHeight > 0)
    {
        uiElementRenderer = new UIElementRenderer(
            LayoutRoot,
            (int)LayoutRoot.ActualWidth,
            (int)LayoutRoot.ActualHeight);
    }
}
```

The `UIElementRenderer` constructor accepts a `UIElement`, which is the top level control to be rendered (along with its children). The width and height of the area to render is also specified using the constructor. If either the width or height is less than that of the `UIElement`, then the `UIElement` is clipped.

The `GameTimer.Update` event provides an opportunity to process user input and to update the model's position and rotation based on that input. This is discussed in a moment, but first we turn our attention to the `OnNavigatedTo` method (see Listing 20.1).

20

When navigating to the page, the shared mode of the graphics device is set. This allows you to create a SpriteBatch object that is used to draw various objects in XNA. The ContentManager, provided by the App class, is used to retrieve the background texture. It is also used to retrieve the XNA model with the asset name specified by the ModelMetadata. Finally, the GameTimer is started, which begins listening for game loop events.

LISTING 20.1   OnNavigatedTo Method

```
protected override void OnNavigatedTo(NavigationEventArgs e)
{
    GraphicsDevice graphicsDevice
        = SharedGraphicsDeviceManager.Current.GraphicsDevice;
    /* Set the sharing mode of the graphics device
     * to turn on XNA rendering. */
    graphicsDevice.SetSharingMode(true);

    spriteBatch = new SpriteBatch(graphicsDevice);

    App app = (App)Application.Current;
    ContentManager contentManager = app.ContentManager;

    background = contentManager.Load<Texture2D>("Background");

    string modelName = GetModelMetadata().Asset;
    Model xnaModel = contentManager.Load<Model>(modelName);
    modelWrapper.Load(xnaModel);

    gameTimer.Start();

    base.OnNavigatedTo(e);
}
```

When the GameTimer.Update event is raised, we process any gesture input that has occurred since the last update using the ProcessInput method (discussed later in the chapter). The custom ModelMetadata contains various properties relating to the XNA Model instance (see Listing 20.2).

LISTING 20.2   HandleGameTimerUpdate Method

```
void HandleGameTimerUpdate(object sender, GameTimerEventArgs e)
{
    ProcessInput();

    float yaw = MathHelper.Pi + MathHelper.PiOver2 + rotationX / 100;
    float pitch = rotationY / 100;
    ModelMetadata metadata = GetModelMetadata();
```

LISTING 20.2   Continued

```
modelWrapper.Rotation
    = metadata.World * Matrix.CreateFromYawPitchRoll(yaw, pitch, 0);
modelWrapper.View = metadata.ViewMatrix;
modelWrapper.IsTextureEnabled = true;
modelWrapper.IsPerPixelLightingEnabled = true;
modelWrapper.Projection = Matrix.CreatePerspectiveFieldOfView(
    MathHelper.ToRadians(cameraFieldOfView) / metadata.FieldOfViewDivisor,
    metadata.AspectRatio,
    metadata.NearPlaneDistance,
    metadata.FarPlaneDistance);
}
```

Drawing to the screen does not take place until the GameTimer.Draw event is raised. The event handler, HandleGameTimerDraw (see Listing 20.3), draws the background, XNA model, and Silverlight controls in that order. The background is painted using the traditional CornFlowerBlue. The background image is then drawn, followed by the spaceship model. Finally, the Silverlight root Grid and all children are rendered into an XNA framework Texture2D object and then drawn.

LISTING 20.3   HandleGameTimerDraw Method

```
void HandleGameTimerDraw(object sender, GameTimerEventArgs e)
{
    GraphicsDevice graphicsDevice
        = SharedGraphicsDeviceManager.Current.GraphicsDevice;

    graphicsDevice.Clear(Color.CornflowerBlue);

    /* Draw the background. */
    spriteBatch.Begin();
    spriteBatch.Draw(background, Vector2.Zero, Color.White);
    spriteBatch.End();

    graphicsDevice.DepthStencilState = DepthStencilState.Default;
    graphicsDevice.BlendState = BlendState.Opaque;
    graphicsDevice.RasterizerState = RasterizerState.CullCounterClockwise;
    graphicsDevice.SamplerStates[0] = SamplerState.LinearWrap;

    /* Draw the XNA model. */
    modelWrapper.Draw();

    /* Render the Silverlight UI. */
    uiElementRenderer.Render();
```

LISTING 20.3   Continued

```
/* Draw the Silverlight elements. */
spriteBatch.Begin();
spriteBatch.Draw(uiElementRenderer.Texture, Vector2.Zero, Color.White);
spriteBatch.End();
}
```

Figure 20.2 shows the resulting page with the XNA model drawn alongside the Silverlight content. When the button is tapped, a message is displayed in a Silverlight TextBlock.

FIGURE 20.2   Silverlight elements are rendered alongside an XNA model.

> **NOTE**
>
> Pop-up controls are not supported in hybrid interfaces. This means that controls like the Silverlight Toolkit's AutoComplete and ListPicker do not work when in shared mode.

Processing Gesture Input

Handling touch manipulation in a hybrid app can be done by either relying solely on the XNA gesture support for both XNA and Silverlight elements or by using XNA gestures in combination with the techniques for handling touch in Silverlight, presented in Chapter 11, "Touch."

Processing XNA input in a hybrid app is normally done during the game loop and can be achieved by first setting the TouchPanel.EnabledGestures property to the gestures you want to support.

In the sample, the enabled gestures are specified in the `GamePage` constructor as shown:

```
TouchPanel.EnabledGestures
    = GestureType.FreeDrag
        | GestureType.Pinch
        | GestureType.PinchComplete;
```

Unlike the Silverlight's event driven touch model, XNA gestures are normally processed during an update pass. In the sample, the `GamePage.HandleGameTimerUpdate` method calls the `ProcessInput` method when the `GameTimer.Update` event is raised (see Listing 20.4).

If a `FreeDrag` gesture occurs, then the rotation fields are modified. This causes the model to be drawn in a rotated position. In addition, a pinch gesture causes the model's field of view to simulate a zoom-in or zoom-out effect.

LISTING 20.4   `ProcessInput` Method

```
void ProcessInput()
{
    while (TouchPanel.IsGestureAvailable)
    {
        GestureSample gestureSample = TouchPanel.ReadGesture();
        switch (gestureSample.GestureType)
        {
            case GestureType.FreeDrag:
                rotationX += gestureSample.Delta.X;
                rotationY -= gestureSample.Delta.Y;
                break;

            case GestureType.Pinch:
                const float fieldOfViewMin = 80;
                const float fieldOfViewMax = 20;
                const float gestureLengthToZoomScale = 10;

                Vector2 gestureDiff
                        = gestureSample.Position - gestureSample.Position2;
                float gestureValue
                        = gestureDiff.Length() / gestureLengthToZoomScale;
                /* Skip the first pinch event.*/
                if (previousGestureValue != null)                {
                    cameraFieldOfView
                        -= gestureValue - previousGestureValue.Value;
                }

                cameraFieldOfView = MathHelper.Clamp(
                    cameraFieldOfView, fieldOfViewMax, fieldOfViewMin);

                previousGestureValue = gestureValue;
                break;
```

20

LISTING 20.4   Continued

```
        case GestureType.PinchComplete:
            previousGestureValue = null;
            break;

        default:
            break;
    }
  }
}
```

Be mindful that Silverlight touch events do not prevent XNA gestures from being registered. Having more than one way of processing touch in a hybrid app means that you are
able to pick and choose how you handle touch for the Silverlight portion of your UI. It
also means, however, that your app may exhibit unexpected behavior when touch
intended for Silverlight elements is misinterpreted by your app as an XNA gesture and
vice versa.

Summary

This chapter began with a brief overview of the key components that make hybrid apps
possible. You then looked at the Visual Studio project templates for creating hybrid apps.
The chapter explored the shared graphics device manager that is used to allow immediate
mode rendering within a Silverlight app and how to use the GameTimer class to subscribe
to XNA game loop events. You then took a closer look at the plumbing that allows hybrid
apps to function and put it all together by demonstrating how to display an XNA model
with superimposed Silverlight content. Finally, you looked at processing XNA gesture
input from within a PhoneApplicationPage.

CHAPTER 21

Microphone and FM Radio

Every Windows Phone device is required to have an FM radio tuner, and likewise, without a microphone, the phone would be no more than a smart camera.

This chapter begins by looking at using the XNA microphone API to record audio. You have some fun with the microphone and create a helium voice app that allows the user to record audio and to modulate the pitch of the recorded audio during playback.

The chapter then looks at the FM radio. You see how to create a custom radio app that uses a Silverlight Toolkit LoopingSelector to change the radio's frequency.

Recording Audio with the Microphone

The XNA Microphone class allows you to capture audio data from the phone's microphone. Microphone resides in the Microsoft.Xna.Framework.Audio namespace.

To use the Microphone class you need to perform the following two steps:

1. Add a reference to the Microsoft.Xna.Framework assembly.

2. Create a GameTimer to pump the XNA FrameworkDispatcher, discussed next.

XNA components usually rely on initialization of the XNA environment before they can be used, and the Microphone class is no exception. Creating a GameTimer to pump the XNA FrameworkDispatcher usually involves adding some code to your `App` class that creates a `GameTimer` and subscribes to its `FrameAction` event. When creating a Silverlight/XNA hybrid application, this plumbing is automatically put in place when using the "Windows Phone Rich Graphics Application" Visual Studio new project template.

For more information on initializing the XNA environment, see Chapter 20, "Incorporating XNA Graphics in Silverlight."

`Microphone` does not have a public constructor; an instance is retrieved using the static `Microphone.Default` property, as shown:

```
Microphone microphone = Microphone.Default;
```

`Microphone` uses an event driven approach to periodically deliver audio data while it is recording. The `Microphone.BufferReady` event is raised as soon as the `Microphone` instance's buffer is full. The size of the buffer is specified using the `Microphone.BufferDuration` property, like so:

```
microphone.BufferDuration = TimeSpan.FromSeconds(1);
```

The `Microphone.GetSampleSizeInBytes` can be used to determine the space requirements for reading the sample data when the `BufferReady` event is raised.

```
int sampleSizeInBytes
        = microphone.GetSampleSizeInBytes(microphone.BufferDuration);
```

This provides the opportunity to create a byte array for storing the sample bytes when the buffer has been filled:

```
byte[] buffer = new byte[sampleSizeInBytes];
```

The buffer can later be copied to a stream and saved in isolated storage, as shown:

```
void HandleBufferReady(object sender, EventArgs e)
{
    microphone.GetData(buffer);
    stream.Write(buffer, 0, buffer.Length);
}
```

The next section looks at putting this together to create a page that allows the user to record and play back audio.

Creating a Helium Voice App

They are a dime a dozen, and you may be surprised by just how simple it is to create a helium voice app, which can modulate the pitch of the user's voice. This section creates a page that allows the user to record audio, which is saved to isolated storage, and to play back the sample with the option to change the pitch of the playback using a slider.

The code for this section is located in the Sensors/Microphone directory of the WindowsPhone7Unleashed.Examples project in the downloadable sample code.

The MicrophoneViewModel class includes the following two commands:

▶ **ToggleRecordCommand**—Starts the microphone recording if not recording; otherwise, recording is stopped and the sample saved to isolated storage.

▶ **PlayCommand**—Plays the previously saved sample, if it exists, from isolated storage.

MicrophoneViewModel initializes the default Microphone instance to a BufferDuration of 1 second. A byte array field is initialized using the microphone's sample size (see Listing 21.1).

LISTING 21.1   MicrophoneViewModel Class (excerpt)

```
public class MicrophoneViewModel : ViewModelBase
{
    readonly Microphone microphone = Microphone.Default;
    readonly byte[] buffer;
    const string fileName = "MicrophoneSample.bytes";
    MemoryStream stream = new MemoryStream();
    readonly object fileLock = new object();

    public MicrophoneViewModel() : base("microphone")
    {
        microphone.BufferDuration = TimeSpan.FromSeconds(1);
        microphone.BufferReady += HandleBufferReady;

        int sampleSizeInBytes = microphone.GetSampleSizeInBytes(
                                        microphone.BufferDuration);
        buffer = new byte[sampleSizeInBytes];

        toggleRecordCommand = new DelegateCommand(obj => ToggleRecording());
        playCommand = new DelegateCommand(obj => Play(), obj => !recording);
    }
...
}
```

Recording Audio

The viewmodel's ToggleRecording method either calls the StopRecording or StartRecording method, depending on the current recording state, as shown:

```
void ToggleRecording()
{
    if (recording)
    {
```

```
        StopRecording();
    }
    else
    {
        StartRecording();
    }
}
```

The viewmodel's `StartRecording` method instantiates a new `MemoryStream`, which is used to copy the sample data each time the `Microphone.BufferReady` event is raised. When the `Microphone` object is started, the `BufferReady` event is raised after 1 second of recording time. See the following excerpt:

```
void StartRecording()
{
    stream = new MemoryStream();
    microphone.Start();
    Recording = true;
    UpdateCommands();
}
```

The `UpdateCommands` method disables the play command if playback is in progress, as shown:

```
void UpdateCommands()
{
    playCommand.RaiseCanExecuteChanged();
}
```

The viewmodel's `StopRecording` method tests the state of the microphone. The `Microphone.Stop` method is not in the `StopRecording` method because doing so would prevent the last `BufferReady` event from being raised, which can cause the audio to be cut off. See the following excerpt:

```
void StopRecording()
{
    if (microphone.State != MicrophoneState.Stopped)
    {
        Recording = false;
        UpdateCommands();
    }
}
```

The stop request is, instead, dealt with in the viewmodel's `HandleBufferReady` method, in which the sample data is read into the buffer byte array and then written to a `MemoryStream`. If a stop recording request has been made at this point, the stream is flushed, the microphone stopped, and the `MemoryStream` is written to isolated storage, as shown:

```
void HandleBufferReady(object sender, EventArgs e)
{
    microphone.GetData(buffer);
    stream.Write(buffer, 0, buffer.Length);

    if (!recording)
    {
        stream.Flush();
        microphone.Stop();
        WriteFile(stream);
    }
}
```

Writing the sample to isolated storage involves retrieving an IsolatedStorageFileStream and writing the MemoryStream to it, as shown:

```
void WriteFile(MemoryStream memoryStream)
{
    lock (fileLock)
    {
        using (var isolatedStorageFile
                    = IsolatedStorageFile.GetUserStoreForApplication())
        {
            using (IsolatedStorageFileStream fileStream
                = isolatedStorageFile.OpenFile(fileName, FileMode.Create))
            {
                memoryStream.WriteTo(fileStream);
            }
        }
    }
}
```

Playback of the audio begins with the retrieval of the sample bytes from isolated storage, as shown:

```
void Play()
{
    byte[] bytes = null;

    lock (fileLock)
    {
        using (var userStore
                    = IsolatedStorageFile.GetUserStoreForApplication())
        {
            if (userStore.FileExists(fileName))
            {
                using (IsolatedStorageFileStream fileStream
```

```
                                    = userStore.OpenFile(fileName,
                                                FileMode.Open,
                                                FileAccess.Read))
                {
                    bytes = new byte[fileStream.Length];
                    fileStream.Read(bytes, 0, bytes.Length);
                }
            }
        }
    }

    if (bytes != null)
    {
        PlayAudio(bytes);
    }
}
```

Playback

An XNA `SoundEffect` instance is used to play the sample bytes. The microphone's sample rate is used to match the sample rate of the `SoundEffect`. A `SoundEffectInstance` field is used to vary the pitch of the audio during playback. See the following excerpt:

```
SoundEffectInstance effectInstance;

void PlayAudio(byte[] audioBytes)
{
    if (audioBytes == null || audioBytes.Length == 0
        || effectInstance != null
        && effectInstance.State == SoundState.Playing)
    {
        return;
    }

    var soundEffect = new SoundEffect(audioBytes,
                                microphone.SampleRate,
                                AudioChannels.Mono);
    if (effectInstance != null)
    {
        effectInstance.Dispose();
    }
    effectInstance = soundEffect.CreateInstance();
    effectInstance.Pitch = (float)pitch;
    effectInstance.Play();
}
```

The `Pitch` property adjusts the playback of the `SoundEffectInstance` during playback, as shown:

```
double pitch;

public double Pitch
{
    get
    {
        return pitch;
    }
    set
    {
        Assign(() => Pitch, ref pitch, value);
        if (effectInstance != null)
        {
            effectInstance.Pitch = (float)value;
        }
    }
}
```

MicrophoneView

The `MicrophoneView` page includes a custom `AppBar` definition with buttons bound to the commands in the view. The first button is an `AppBarToggleButton`, which changes its icon according to the value of the viewmodel's `Recording` property. See the following excerpt:

```
<u:AppBar>
    <u:AppBarToggleButton
                Command1="{Binding ToggleRecordCommand}"
                Toggled="{Binding Recording}"
                Text1="Record"
                Text2="Stop"
                Icon1Uri="/Sensors/Microphone/Icons/Record.png"
                Icon2Uri="/Sensors/Microphone/Icons/StopRecording.png" />
    <u:AppBarIconButton
                Command="{Binding PlayCommand}"
                Text="Play"
                IconUri="/Sensors/Microphone/Icons/Play.png" />
</u:AppBar>
```

The main content panel includes a `Slider` that is bound to the viewmodel's `Pitch` property, as shown:

```
<StackPanel x:Name="ContentPanel" Grid.Row="1" Margin="12,0,12,0">
    <TextBlock Text="pitch"
                Style="{StaticResource LabelTextIndentedStyle}" />
    <Slider Value="{Binding Pitch, Mode=TwoWay}" Minimum="-1" Maximum="1" />
</StackPanel>
```

By moving the slider to the left the pitch decreases during playback; by moving it to the right the helium voice effect is achieved (see Figure 21.1).

FIGURE 21.1   MicrophoneView page with a Slider to control pitch

The Microphone class provides an easy way to capture audio and provides interesting opportunities for adding voice enabled services such as voice recognition and streaming communications.

Controlling the Phone's FM Radio

The FMRadio class allows you to control the Windows Phone hardware FM radio component. It is a singleton, providing access to a single FMRadio object via its static Instance property.

The FMRadio class has the following four nonstatic properties:

▶ PowerMode

▶ Frequency

▶ CurrentRegion

▶ SignalStrength

PowerMode allows you to turn the FM radio device on or off. PowerMode is of type RadioPowerMode, an enum with two values: Off and On.

Frequency is a double property that allows you to control the stations that the radio is tuned to. The set of radio frequency bands available for tuning is determined by the CurrentRegion property, which is of type RadioRegion, an enum with the following three values:

▶ Europe

▶ Japan

▶ UnitedStates

The differences in frequency ranges for each of these regions are as follows

Europe*	88 to 108 MHz
Japan	76 to 90 MHz
United States	88.1 to 107.9 MHz

There are variations to the frequency range depending on country. See Wikipedia's article for FM broadcasting at http://en.wikipedia.org/wiki/FM_broadcasting.

NOTE

The `CurrentRegion` property is used to determine whether a `Frequency` value is valid. When setting the `Frequency` property, the value must fall within the range as described by the `CurrentRegion` property. For example, if the `CurrentRegion` property is set to Japan and you attempt to set the `Frequency` above 90MHz, an `ArgumentException` is raised.

`FMRadio.SignalStrength` indicates the reception quality. The FM radio on Windows Phone devices is designed to work with the user's headphones plugged in, which act as an aerial for the device. It is good practice to inform the user of this fact when a low signal strength is detected. This is demonstrated in the following section.

```
FMRadio fmRadio = FMRadio.Instance;

fmRadio.PowerMode = RadioPowerMode.On;
fmRadio.CurrentRegion = RadioRegion.UnitedStates;
fmRadio.Frequency = 99.5;

if (fmRadio.SignalStrength < 0.01)
{
    MessageBox.Show("This phone uses your headphones "
                    + "as an FM radio antenna. "
                    + "To listen to radio, connect your headphones.",
                    "No antenna", MessageBoxButton.OK);
}
```

To switch off the radio, set the `PowerMode` to Off, as shown:

```
FMRadio.Instance.PowerMode = RadioPowerMode.Off;
```

Building a Custom FM Radio App

This section looks at using the `FMRadio` class to create a custom FM radio app that allows the user to switch the radio on and off, to set the region and frequency of the FM radio, and to view the radio's signal strength. You also look at the Silverlight Toolkit's `LoopSelector` control and how it is used to provide an infinitely scrolling list that allows the user to set the FM radio's frequency.

The sample code for this section resides in the /Sensors/FMRadio directory of the WindowsPhone7Unleashed.Examples directory in the downloadable sample code.

To begin, the viewmodel's `PoweredOn` property controls the `FMRadio`'s `PowerMode` property (see Listing 21.2).

Setting the `FMRadio`'s `Frequency` property causes the `SignalStrength` property to be updated immediately. If the `Frequency` property is not set, you need to wait momentarily for the `SignalStrength` property to be updated. We therefore use another thread to wait a moment before determining whether the user needs to be informed that she should plug in headphones.

LISTING 21.2   `FMRadioViewModel.PoweredOn` Property

```
public bool PoweredOn
{
    get
    {
        return FMRadio.Instance.PowerMode == RadioPowerMode.On;
    }
    set
    {
        bool state = FMRadio.Instance.PowerMode == RadioPowerMode.On;
        if (state != value)
        {
            FMRadio.Instance.PowerMode = value
                ? RadioPowerMode.On : RadioPowerMode.Off;

            if (value)
            {
                ThreadPool.QueueUserWorkItem(
                    delegate
                        {
                            Wait(2000);
                            if (SignalStrength < 0.01)
                            {
                                MessageService.ShowMessage(
                                  "This phone uses your headphones "
                                + "as an FM radio antenna. "
                                + "To listen to radio, connect your headphones.",
                                  "No antenna");
```

LISTING 21.2   Continued

```
                        }
                    });
            }

            OnPropertyChanged(() => PoweredOn);

            if (FMRadio.Instance.PowerMode == RadioPowerMode.On)
            {
                OnPropertyChanged(() => Frequency);
            }
        }
    }
}
```

The custom `Wait` method blocks the thread without resorting to a `Thread.Sleep` call. For more information see Listing 15.2, "Wait Method."

The view contains a `ToggleSwitch` that is bound to the viewmodel's `PoweredOn` property, as shown:

```
<toolkit:ToggleSwitch IsChecked="{Binding PoweredOn, Mode=TwoWay}"
                      Header="Power" />
```

The binding is two way, so that when the user taps the switch, the viewmodel property is updated.

The viewmodel's `Frequency` property sets the frequency of the `FMRadio`. The minimum allowed frequency is determined using the frequency range for the current region. See the following excerpt:

```
public double Frequency
{
    get
    {
        return FMRadio.Instance.Frequency < 1
            ? frequencyMin : FMRadio.Instance.Frequency;
    }
    set
    {
        if (Math.Abs(FMRadio.Instance.Frequency - value) >= .1)
        {
            FMRadio.Instance.Frequency = value;
            OnPropertyChanged(() => Frequency);
        }
    }
}
```

The viewmodel exposes the RadioRegion enum values as a property, which is bound to a Silverlight Toolkit ListPicker in the view, as shown:

```
<toolkit:ListPicker ItemsSource="{Binding Regions}"
                    SelectedItem="{Binding Region, Mode=TwoWay}" />
```

Rather than hard-coding each enum value in the viewmodel, a custom class called EnumUtility is used to create an IEnumerable<RadioRegion> (see Listing 21.3).

LISTING 21.3   EnumUtility Class

```
public static class EnumUtility
{
    public static IEnumerable<TEnum> CreateEnumValueList<TEnum>()
    {
        Type enumType = typeof(TEnum);
        IEnumerable<FieldInfo> fieldInfos
            = enumType.GetFields().Where(x => enumType.Equals(x.FieldType));
        return fieldInfos.Select(
            fieldInfo => (TEnum)Enum.Parse(enumType,
                                           fieldInfo.Name, true)).ToList();
    }
}
```

The viewmodel's Regions property and its backing field are defined as shown:

```
readonly IEnumerable<RadioRegion> radioRegions
                = EnumUtility.CreateEnumValueList<RadioRegion>();

public IEnumerable<RadioRegion> Regions
{
    get
    {
        return radioRegions;
    }
}
```

The complement of the Regions property is the viewmodel's nonplural Region property, which exposes the FMRadio's CurrentRegion property, as shown:

```
public RadioRegion Region
{
    get
    {
        return FMRadio.Instance.CurrentRegion;
    }
    set
```

```
    {
        FMRadio fmRadio = FMRadio.Instance;
        if (fmRadio.CurrentRegion != value)
        {
            fmRadio.CurrentRegion = value;
            UpdateFrequencyRanges();

            OnPropertyChanged(() => Region);
        }
    }
}
```

When the `Region` property is changed, the list of valid frequency ranges is updated using the viewmodel's `UpdateFrequencyRangesMethod`.

The `Frequency` double value is split into two parts so that its fractional and nonfractional components can be binding sources for two controls in the view; two Silverlight Toolkit `LoopingSelector` controls allow the user to select the desired frequency (see Figure 21.2).

FIGURE 21.2   Frequency is modified using `LoopingSelector` controls.

For information on the `LoopingSelector`, see Chapter 9, "Silverlight Toolkit Controls."

The radio frequency is split into two using two custom `NumericDataSource` objects. The nonfractional segment is defined by the viewmodel field `frequenciesNonFractional`, while the fractional component is defined by the field `frequenciesFractional`, as shown:

```
readonly NumericDataSource frequenciesFractional
                    = new NumericDataSource { Minimum = 0, Maximum = 9 };
```

The `SelectedItem` of the `frequenciesFractional` field is set to the fractional component of the current frequency in the viewmodel constructor, like so:

```
frequenciesFractional.SelectedItem = (int)(Frequency % 1 * 10);
```

The viewmodel subscribes to each `NumericDataSource` object's `SelectChanged` event. When the nonfractional part of the frequency is changed, the handler determines the new frequency by adding the existing fractional part (frequency modulo 1) to the selected value, as shown:

```
void HandleFrequencyLargeChanged(object sender, SelectionChangedEventArgs e)
{
    NumericDataSource dataSource = (NumericDataSource)sender;
    var newFrequency = Frequency % 1 + dataSource.SelectedNumber;
    if (newFrequency > frequencyMax || newFrequency < frequencyMin)
    {
        return;
    }
    Frequency = newFrequency;
}
```

When the fractional part of the frequency is changed, the handler determines the new frequency by removing the fractional component of the existing frequency and adding it to the selected item, as shown:

```
void HandleFrequencyFractionPartChanged(
        object sender, SelectionChangedEventArgs e)
{
    NumericDataSource dataSource = (NumericDataSource)sender;
    double f = Frequency;
    double newFrequency = f - f % 1 + dataSource.SelectedNumber / 10.0;
    if (newFrequency > frequencyMax || newFrequency < frequencyMin)
    {
        return;
    }
    Frequency = newFrequency;
}
```

When the viewmodel is instantiated, or when the Region property changes, the UpdateFrequencyRanges method is called, which creates a new NumericDataSource object for the nonfractional frequency component and sets its Minimum and Maximum properties according to the region's frequency range (see Listing 21.4).

LISTING 21.4   UpdateFrequencyRanges Method

```
void UpdateFrequencyRanges()
{
    if (frequenciesNonFractional != null)
    {
        frequenciesNonFractional.SelectionChanged -= HandleFrequencyLargeChanged;
    }

    NumericDataSource dataSource = new NumericDataSource();

    switch (Region)
    {
```

LISTING 21.4   Continued

```
        case RadioRegion.Europe:
            FrequencyMin = 88;
            FrequencyMax = 108;
            dataSource.Minimum = 88;
            dataSource.Maximum = 108;
            break;
        case RadioRegion.Japan:
            FrequencyMin = 76;
            FrequencyMax = 90;
            dataSource.Minimum = 76;
            dataSource.Maximum = 90;
            break;
        case RadioRegion.UnitedStates:
            FrequencyMin = 88.1;
            FrequencyMax = 107.9;
            dataSource.Minimum = 88;
            dataSource.Maximum = 107;
            break;
    }

    double tempFrequency = Frequency;
    dataSource.SelectedNumber = (int)(tempFrequency - tempFrequency % 1);
    FrequenciesNonFractional = dataSource;
    dataSource.SelectionChanged += HandleFrequencyLargeChanged;
}
```

The viewmodel also indicates the current signal strength of the radio and contains a SignalStrength property that gets its value directly from the FMRadio instance, as shown:

```
public double SignalStrength
{
    get
    {
        return FMRadio.Instance.SignalStrength;
    }
}
```

The device FM radio can also be controlled by the user using the hardware volume buttons, which, when pressed (while the FM radio is powered on) causes an onscreen menu to be displayed. The onscreen menu allows the user to skip forward and backward between stations. The FMRadio class provides no events for monitoring changes to frequency or signal strength, nor any other property. To monitor changes to the FMRadio instance, a Timer is used, which periodically polls the FMRadio for changes.

> **TIP**
>
> It is generally best to avoid the use of timers within your app, as it can unduly degrade battery life. Use a `Timer` only if your app absolutely requires the functionality and it is not obtainable by other means.

The `Timer` is instantiated in the viewmodel constructor, like so:

```
timer = new Timer(HandleTimerTick, null, timerIntervalMs, timerIntervalMs);
```

When the interval elapses, the `Timer` instance calls the `HandleTimerTick` method. If the previous frequency value is markedly different from the current frequency value, a property changed event for the `Frequency` property is raised and the UI updated, as shown:

```
double previousFrequency;

void HandleTimerTick(object state)
{
    OnPropertyChanged(() => SignalStrength);
    double frequency = FMRadio.Instance.Frequency;
    if (Math.Abs(previousFrequency - frequency) >= 0.1)
    {
        double fraction = frequency % 1;
        Deployment.Current.Dispatcher.BeginInvoke(delegate
        {
            frequenciesFractional.SelectedNumber = (int)(fraction * 10);
            frequenciesNonFractional.SelectedNumber
                                    = (int)(frequency - fraction);
            OnPropertyChanged(() => Frequency);
        });
    }
    previousFrequency = frequency;
}
```

The `FMRadioView` page displays the raw frequency value using a `TextBlock`. A `TextBlock` and a `ProgressBar` are used to display the `SignalStrength` property (see Listing 21.5).

> **NOTE**
>
> It is critical to set a number of properties of the `LoopingSelector` for it to be displayed correctly, in particular, its `ItemSize`, `Width`, and `Height`.

LISTING 21.5   `FMRadioView.xaml` (excerpt)

```xml
<Grid x:Name="ContentPanel" Grid.Row="1" Margin="12,0,12,0">
    <StackPanel>
        <toolkit:ToggleSwitch IsChecked="{Binding PoweredOn, Mode=TwoWay}"
                              Header="Power" />

        <TextBlock Text="frequency" Style="{StaticResource LabelTextStyle}" />
        <TextBlock Text="{Binding Frequency}"
                   Style="{StaticResource ValueTextStyle}" />

        <StackPanel Orientation="Horizontal" HorizontalAlignment="Center">
            <toolkitPrimitives:LoopingSelector
                DataSource="{Binding FrequenciesNonFractional}"
                Margin="12" Width="128" Height="128" ItemSize="128,128"
                ItemTemplate="{StaticResource LoopNumberTemplate}"
                IsEnabled="{Binding PoweredOn}" />
            <TextBlock Text="." FontSize="54" VerticalAlignment="Bottom"
                       FontFamily="{StaticResource PhoneFontFamilySemiBold}" />
            <toolkitPrimitives:LoopingSelector
                DataSource="{Binding FrequenciesFractional}"
                Margin="12" Width="128" Height="128" ItemSize="128,128"
                ItemTemplate="{StaticResource LoopNumberTemplate}"
                IsEnabled="{Binding PoweredOn}" />
        </StackPanel>

        <TextBlock Text="region" Style="{StaticResource LabelTextStyle}" />
        <toolkit:ListPicker ItemsSource="{Binding Regions}"
                            SelectedItem="{Binding Region, Mode=TwoWay}" />

        <TextBlock Text="signal strength"
                   Style="{StaticResource LabelTextStyle}" />
        <TextBlock Text="{Binding SignalStrength}"
                   Style="{StaticResource ValueTextStyle}" />
        <ProgressBar Value="{Binding SignalStrength}" Maximum="5" />
    </StackPanel>
</Grid>
```

A `DataTemplate` called `LoopNumberTemplate` is used for presenting the numbers within the `LoopingSelectors`. It is defined as a page resource as shown:

```xml
<phone:PhoneApplicationPage.Resources>
    <DataTemplate x:Key="LoopNumberTemplate">
        <Grid>
            <TextBlock Text="{Binding}" FontSize="54"
                       FontFamily="{StaticResource PhoneFontFamilySemiBold}"
```

```
                        HorizontalAlignment="Center"
                        VerticalAlignment="Center" />
        </Grid>
    </DataTemplate>
</phone:PhoneApplicationPage.Resources>
```

Figure 21.3 shows the `FMRadioView` page with the radio powered on and the region list expanded. The signal strength field is periodically updated.

FIGURE 21.3   `FMRadioView` page

The FM radio is a core piece of phone hardware that allows users to listen to audio without having a data connection. The built-in radio app provides the bare essentials for listening, and having programmatic access to the FM radio allows you to create an advanced radio app or to enhance your audio app by including radio capabilities.

Summary

This chapter began by looking at using the XNA microphone API to record audio. You had some fun with the microphone and created a helium voice app that allows the user to record audio and to modulate the pitch of the recorded audio during playback.

The chapter then looked at the FM radio and how to create a custom radio app that uses a Silverlight Toolkit `LoopingSelector` to change the FM radio's frequency.

CHAPTER 22

Unit Testing

Unit testing saves time and helps to find defects early in the development cycle. Unit tests become assets that provide assurance that further development or refactoring has not broken something. The more tests you create, the more confidence you have when adding features and fixing bugs. This is especially true if you are working with a team of developers.

Manual ad hoc testing becomes less effective as an app increases in size and complexity. Having a solid suite of unit tests can actually decrease the time it takes to get your app to the marketplace. This is because often an exorbitant amount of time is spent on ad hoc testing in the last stages of development before a release.

Another benefit of unit tests is that they can act as a tacit form of documentation. There is a distinct lack of code documentation in many software houses today; unfortunately it is all too common. Unit tests can assist a developer in understanding how an app works, and unit tests are less susceptible than traditional system documentation to implementation drift, where design changes and feature creep can see the documentation of an app become outdated. Unit tests tend to fare better because they are verifiable. Relying solely on unit tests to document a system is, however, not wise. Unit tests should be considered production code, requiring their own adequate documentation.

For all its benefits, unit testing does have a cost. It takes time and skill to write effective unit tests. In your career, you may have experienced the reluctance of management to support unit testing because it is invariably seen as time stolen from writing product code. It is that old story: Developers craft a product and then scramble in the last moments to iron out defects, producing fixes that frequently introduce new bugs. Unit testing can help to alleviate that last minute scramble.

Some may also see unit tests as a liability because when there are substantial changes to an app, unit tests have to be rewritten. This cost is, however, usually overstated and can sometimes reflect unsound development practices.

Testing and patterns of testing vary, and divided opinion on the topic has spurred many a heated debate. This chapter is not about affirming one approach over another. The techniques and tools presented in this chapter should, however, make a worthy addition to your development toolbox.

Throughout this book you have seen the use of Model-View-ViewModel (MVVM). MVVM comes into its own when combined with unit testing. In fact, it is one of the key motivations for using the pattern. MVVM allows you to separate UI technology specific code so that it can be tested without the user interface.

This chapter delves into the Silverlight UTF (Unit Testing Framework) for Windows Phone. The chapter begins with a walk-through of the creation of a unit test project from scratch. You see how to create test classes and test methods, and get to know the tag expressions editor, which provides a useful mechanism for selecting which tests are to be run.

The UTF is then explored more deeply by creating a simple chat client app, in which you see how to verify a viewmodel before creating its UI. Following the creation of the view, the test suite is extended to include code driven UI tests, where we manipulate the user interface, simulating button clicks and other user actions from a unit test. The chapter illustrates how to perform asynchronous testing and touches on the Microsoft Automation framework.

Some advanced topics such as Inversion of Control (IoC) and mocking are also discussed, and you learn how to use a custom IoC container.

Finally, we put it all together to see how to perform testing of trial applications and how to hide or reveal content based on a mock licensing service. You then look at a custom API for mocking launchers and choosers.

There is a lot to cover in this chapter, and the tools and techniques presented here can help spot unintended side effects, increase the robustness of code, assist in focusing the development effort, and perhaps save you some time.

Automated Testing

By finding and guarding against defects, an automated test can save you many times the cost of creating it over the lifetime of a project. This chapter looks at three kinds of automated testing: unit testing, integration testing, and coded UI testing.

Unit Testing

A unit test verifies that a single unit of work, usually a class method, works correctly. Unit tests should generally avoid accessing the file system, database, or network resources.

Types requiring this kind of access ideally rely on an abstracted API and have the types used in production substituted with stubs or mock types during testing. Unit tests should execute rapidly and cause no side effects that affect other unit tests.

Integration Testing

Integration tests verify that multiple classes function correctly together. Integration occurs after unit testing. It involves testing groups of classes that have been unit tested.

Coded UI Testing

Coded UI tests simulate a user interacting with the application. These tests rely on an automation API to allow programmatic access to UI elements. For example, an automation object can be used to raise a button's `Click` event.

There are other types of tests as well, including acceptance testing, performance testing, and stress testing. You often use different tools or extensions to your testing framework for these types of tests. Despite some tests not being formally unit tests, it's fine to use the existing unit testing framework and tools to perform other kinds of testing. The unit testing tools presented in this chapter are a good starting point for many other types of tests.

It is important to partition your tests by test type. For example, unit tests should execute quickly. By grouping integration tests with unit tests, you risk slowing the execution of the group, which may make running the tests tedious, resulting in avoidance of unit testing altogether by you or another developer. Other test types, such as system tests, which test the entirety of your app, may rely on resources that are unavailable during a unit testing session. By including a system test with your unit tests, you may inadvertently prevent the test suite from passing.

Introduction to the Windows Phone Unit Test Framework

The API of the Silverlight UTF for Windows Phone is the same as the Silverlight UTF for the browser. In fact, it is almost a superset of the Microsoft desktop CLR UTF. This cross-screen compatibility means that you can run all your existing unit tests just as they are.

Unfortunately tooling support for the Silverlight UTF for Windows Phone is nonexistent. Unlike the Microsoft desktop UTF, there is no Visual Studio integration whatsoever. This means you cannot run individual unit tests from Visual Studio as you might with a desktop application. Windows Phone test projects are Silverlight for Windows Phone applications. Therefore, do not bother trying to create a new unit test from the Test menu in Visual Studio, as it is unsupported for Windows Phone.

While the tooling support is absent, all of the metadata and assertions, discussed later in this chapter, are identical for both the desktop CLR and Silverlight for Windows Phone, and creating a unit test project is easy, as you see in the following section.

Creating a Test Project

Download the Silverlight UTF for Windows Phone from Microsoft's Jeff Wilcox's blog at http://bit.ly/krk41Q. These assemblies are also present in the downloadable sample code, but to be sure you have the latest, download them from Jeff's blog.

The download contains two assemblies: Microsoft.Silverlight.Testing.dll and Microsoft.VisualStudio.QualityTools.UnitTesting.Silverlight.dll.

As stated previously, a unit test project is a bona fide Windows Phone application. To create a test project, create a new Windows Phone Application project by using the Add New Project dialog (see Figure 22.1).

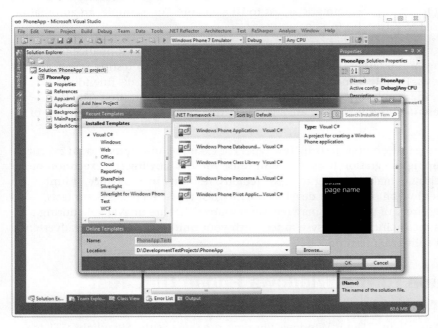

FIGURE 22.1   Creating a new Windows Phone Application for testing

Once the test project has been created, add a reference to the two assemblies.

> **TIP**
>
> If you are working in a team and using a source control system, I recommend checking-in all non-FCL assemblies, regardless of whether an installer exists to place the assemblies in a known location. This allows you to propagate updated assemblies easily and helps prevent issues around incorrect installer versions.

Some changes need to be made in the new project's MainPage.xaml.cs. The `OnNavigatedTo` method override should disable the system tray so that it does not intrude on the UTF test harness. A test page can then be created using the Microsoft.Silverlight.Testing.UnitTestSystem.CreateTestPage method (see Listing 22.1).

The app's root visual is assigned to the test page instance. Windows Phone does not allow the assignment of the `RootVisual` in App.xaml.cs. This is why the code to create the test page is placed in the `MainPage` class and not in the `App` class.

The `BackKeyPress` method is overridden so that pressing the hardware button causes the `IMobileTestPage` object's `NavigateBack` method to be called. If the `NavigateBack` method returns false, such as when the first test page is displayed, then the navigation is cancelled, preventing navigation.

LISTING 22.1   Test Project MainPage.xaml.cs

```
public partial class MainPage
{
    public MainPage()
    {
        InitializeComponent();
    }

    IMobileTestPage mobileTestPage;

    protected override void OnNavigatedTo(NavigationEventArgs e)
    {
        base.OnNavigatedTo(e);

        SystemTray.IsVisible = false;

        UnitTestSettings settings = UnitTestSystem.CreateDefaultSettings();
        /* To set the TagExpression use the following: */
        // UnitTestSettings settings = UnitTestSystem.CreateDefaultSettings();
        // settings.TagExpression = "UnitTest";

        /* Add test assemblies as shown: */
        // settings.TestAssemblies.Add(typeof(Class1).Assembly);
        // settings.TestAssemblies.Add(typeof(TestClass2).Assembly);

        UIElement testPage = UnitTestSystem.CreateTestPage();

        Application.Current.RootVisual = testPage;
        Application.Current.Host.Settings.EnableFrameRateCounter = false;
```

LISTING 22.1   Continued

```
        mobileTestPage = testPage as IMobileTestPage;
    }

    protected override void OnBackKeyPress(CancelEventArgs e)
    {
        if (mobileTestPage != null)
        {
            e.Cancel = mobileTestPage.NavigateBack();
        }

        base.OnBackKeyPress(e);
    }
}
```

Creating a Test Class

To create a test class, add a new class to your test project. Then add the following two using statements to the top of the class:

```
using Microsoft.Silverlight.Testing;
using Microsoft.VisualStudio.TestTools.UnitTesting;
```

Test related attributes and assertion types can be found within the namespace Microsoft.VisualStudio.TestTools.UnitTesting. Even if you have not used the Visual Studio UTF before, it is easy to pick up since the attributes are self-descriptive.

Tests consist of test classes and test methods. The unit test framework relies on metadata in the form of attributes for identifying unit test classes and methods at runtime. To indicate that a class is a unit test class, decorate it with the TestClassAttribute, as shown in the following example:

```
[TestClass]
public class FirstTest : SilverlightTest
{
    [TestMethod]
    [Description("A first unit test.")]
    public void ShouldAlwaysPass()
    {
        Assert.IsTrue(true);
    }
}
```

To run the test, set the test project as the startup project by right-clicking on the project node in the Visual Studio Solution Explorer and selecting Set as Startup Project. Then debug the solution by selecting Start Debugging from the Debug menu or by pressing F5. When the app starts, the tag expressions editor is presented (see Figure 22.2).

FIGURE 22.2   The tag expressions editor

The tag expressions editor allows you to run all or a subset of the tests. It has a count-down timer that automatically commences testing after 5 seconds.

When the test completes, a review page is presented in the test harness (see Figure 22.3).

The test harness allows you to drill down to see the details of each test method (see Figure 22.4). The content of the test method's Description attribute is presented beneath the test method's name.

FIGURE 22.3   The test harness displays that the unit test passed.

FIGURE 22.4   Viewing a detailed test result

Tests run on a single thread and are executed within the Silverlight sandbox.

Tag Expressions

When you have a large number of tests, you need some way to execute just one, or a subset, of the tests. The UTF includes a tagging language, which allows you to create tag expressions that specify which tests should be run during a unit testing session.

Every test class and test method has an implicit set of tags, shown in the following list:

- ▶ Type or method name, for example, TestClass1, TestMethod1.

- ▶ Full type or method name, for example, TestClass1.TestMethod1.

- ▶ The priority specified by a `Priority` attribute if present. For further information on tag expressions and the `Priority` attribute, see the section "Priority Attribute" later in the chapter.

You can also explicitly assign a test class or test method with a tag using the `Tag` attribute. The `Tag` attribute accepts a single string parameter, which is used to associate a test with a group of tests.

The following is an example of a test method decorated with a `Tag` attribute:

```
[TestMethod]
[Tag("UITest")]
public void AlwaysPass()
{
    Assert.IsTrue(true, "Test method intended to always pass.");
}
```

Multiple `Tag` attributes can be applied to any test class or method in your test suite. Tags can also be useful in selecting different kinds of tests to run.

When the testing session begins, you have the opportunity to enter a tag expression. To run the test method from the previous excerpt, or any other test methods with a matching attribute, you could enter `UITest` as the tag expression.

The tag expression syntax provides a set of operators to control test selection. The `!` (not) operator, for example, allows you to prevent those tests with a particular tag from being executed. A tag expression of `!UITest` causes all tests that do not have the tag `UITest` to be executed. A tag of `All-(UITest+IntegrationTest)` causes all tests that do not have the `UITest` or `IntegrationTest` tag to execute.

The tag expression syntax uses Extended Backus-Naur Form (EBNF). You can use the symbols presented in Table 22.1 in tag expressions.

TABLE 22.1   Tag Expression Symbols

Symbol	Description
All	Represents all test methods.
!	Compliment of two tag subexpressions.
-	Difference of two tag subexpressions.
*	Intersection of two tag subexpressions.
+	Union of two tag subexpressions.
( )	Parentheses allow you to group tag subexpressions.

Setting the Tag Expression Programmatically

To set the tag expression without using the UTF tag expressions editor, use the
TagExpression property of the UnitTestSettings class, as shown in the following example:

```
void OnLoaded(object sender, RoutedEventArgs e)
{
    SystemTray.IsVisible = false;

    UnitTestSettings settings = UnitTestSystem.CreateDefaultSettings();

    /* To set the TagExpression use the following: */
    UnitTestSettings settings = UnitTestSystem.CreateDefaultSettings();
    settings.TagExpression = "UnitTest";
    UIElement testPage = UnitTestSystem.CreateTestPage(settings);

    Application.Current.RootVisual = testPage;
    Application.Current.Host.Settings.EnableFrameRateCounter = false;

    mobileTestPage = testPage as IMobileTestPage;
}
```

Metadata and Assertions

As you have seen, attributes are used to identify test classes and methods. Attributes can
also be used to provide other metadata information to the UTF. This section examines
each of the UTF attributes in greater detail and provides descriptions of their usage,
purpose, and effect on test execution.

TestClass Attribute

The TestClass attribute indicates that a class contains test methods.

TestMethod Attribute

The `TestMethod` attribute indicates that a method should be included in the suite of tests. The `Ignore` attribute can be used to temporarily exclude a test method from the suite of tests. Methods decorated with the `TestMethod` attribute should be public and have a void return type.

Metadata for Test Initialization and Cleanup

The UTF provides attributes that allow you to specify methods that should be run before and after test execution. You can provide methods that are executed once for each test assembly, once for each test class, and once for each test method. The order in which methods decorated with each particular attribute are run is presented in Figure 22.5.

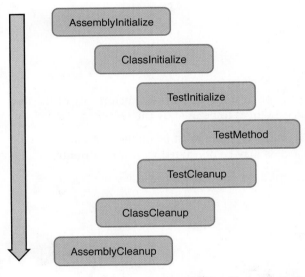

FIGURE 22.5   Test execution order is affected by initialization and cleanup metadata.

AssemblyInitialize Attribute

The `AssemblyInitialize` attribute identifies a method that contains code to be used before all tests in an assembly are run and to allocate resources obtained by the assembly. A method decorated with the `AssemblyInitialize` attribute must be public and static, and have a void return type. The following demonstrates the use of the `AssemblyInitialize` attribute:

```
[AssemblyInitialize]
public static void AssemblyInitialize()
{
    /* Assembly initialization logic goes here. */
}
```

> **NOTE**
>
> The test framework runs a method that is marked with the `AssemblyInitialize` attribute only if that method is a member of a class that is marked with the `TestClass` attribute.

AssemblyCleanup Attribute

The `AssemblyCleanup` attribute is analogous to the `AssemblyInitialize` attribute but occurs at the end of the test run. As with the `AssemblyInitialize` attribute, a method decorated with this attribute should be located in a test class. The following shows an example of a method decorated with the `AssemblyCleanup` attribute:

```
[AssemblyCleanup]
public static void AssemblyCleanup()
{
    /* Assembly cleanup logic goes here. */
}
```

ClassInitialize Attribute

The `ClassInitialize` attribute provides the opportunity to run code before any of the tests in the test class have run and to allocate resources to be used by the test class.

A method decorated with the `ClassInitialize` attribute must be public and static with a void return type. Only one method in a class may be decorated with this attribute.

The following shows an example of a method decorated with the `ClassInitialize` attribute:

```
[ClassInitialize]
public static void ClassInitialize()
{
    /* Class initialization logic goes here. */
}
```

ClassCleanup Attribute

The `ClassCleanup` attribute is analogous to the `ClassInitialize` attribute but occurs after all test methods have completed within the test class. The following shows an example of a method decorated with the `ClassCleanup` attribute:

```
[ClassCleanup]
public static void ClassCleanup()
{
    /* Class cleanup logic goes here. */
}
```

`TestInitialize` Attribute

The `TestInitialize` attribute is used to indicate that a method decorated with this attribute should be called before every test method within a test class. A method decorated with the `TestInitialize` attribute must be public and have a void return type. The following shows an example of a method decorated with the `TestInitialize` attribute:

```
[TestInitialize]
public void TestInitialize()
{
    /* Test initialization logic goes here. */
}
```

TIP

If more than one method is decorated with the `TestInitialize` attribute in a test class, it prevents the execution of all test methods. Furthermore, it does so silently. If you find that the debugger is failing to hit a break point in a test method, look for a duplication of the `TestInitialize` attribute.

`TestCleanup` Attribute

The `TestCleanup` attribute is useful for resetting the state of shared resources in between test methods, such as an object that is used by all tests within a test class.

```
[TestCleanup]
public void TestCleanup()
{
    /* Test cleanup logic goes here. */
}
```

Miscellaneous Metadata

The following attributes allow you to control various other aspects of test execution.

`TestProperty` Attribute

The `TestProperty` attribute allows arbitrary metadata to be associated with a test method. For example, you could use it to store the name of a test pass that this test covers by decorating the test method with `[TestProperty("TestPass", "Accessibility")]`. Unlike the Silverlight UTF for the browser and the Visual Studio desktop CLR unit testing tools, the Windows Phone UTF does not display `TestProperty` information within the test harness.

`Ignore` Attribute

The `Ignore` attribute can be used to temporarily exclude a specific test from execution. This can be useful for excluding a test that is blocking other tests from running. It allows you to retain compilation of the test, rather than merely commenting out the code.

> **NOTE**
>
> The number of tests listed in the unit test harness is unaffected by the `Ignore` attribute.

Description Attribute

The `Description` attribute is used on test methods and allows you to provide a string describing the purpose and/or behavior of the test method. The description is then presented beneath the title of the test result details screen on the phone (refer to Figure 22.4). The following example demonstrates the use of the `Description` attribute:

```
[TestMethod]
[Description("An example test demonstrating the Description attribute.")]
public void ShouldAlwaysPass()
{
    Assert.IsTrue(true);
}
```

Timeout Attribute

The `Timeout` attribute allows you to specify an amount in milliseconds in which a test method must complete or the test method fails.

The following is an example of using the `Timeout` attribute to prevent an asynchronous test method from taking longer than 100 milliseconds to execute:

```
[TestMethod]
[Asynchronous]
[Timeout(100)]
public void ShouldFailDueToAsyncTestTimeout()
{
    EnqueueDelay(1000);
    EnqueueTestComplete();
}
```

This test method fails because the call to `EnqueueDelay` delays the completion of the test by 1000 ms (1 second), and the `Timeout` attribute specifies that the test should take no longer than 100 ms. The `EnqueueDelay` attribute and the other asynchronous related attributes are discussed later in this chapter.

Owner Attribute

The `Owner` attribute is used to specify the person responsible for maintaining, running, and/or debugging the test. This attribute accepts a single string parameter, indicating the name of the owner, as shown in the following example:

```
[TestMethod]
[Owner("Daniel Vaughan")]
public void ShouldAlwaysPass()
{
```

```
    Assert.IsTrue(true);
}
```

The value of the attribute is not displayed within the test harness of the current Windows Phone UTF.

ExpectedException Attribute

Verifying that your code produces a correct response to a known set of values is one thing; verifying that it responds appropriately when given bad input is another. This is called negative testing, and it allows you to verify that code behaves correctly even when exceptional conditions arise.

Ordinarily, if a test method raises an exception, the exception causes that test to fail. In a negative test, however, raising an exception may be the expected behavior. In that case, the ExpectedException attribute can be used to indicate that if an exception of a particular type, with a particular message, is not thrown, then the test should fail. The following example demonstrates the use of the ExpectedException attribute:

```
[TestMethod]
[ExpectedException(typeof(ArgumentException))]
public void ShouldFailDueToArgumentException()
{
    throw new ArgumentException("Invalid argument supplied.");
}
```

> **NOTE**
>
> The TagAttribute, AsynchronousAttribute, and BugAttribute are not available in the Microsoft desktop CLR test framework. Using any of them, therefore, means that your unit tests will not be compatible with the desktop CLR.

Asynchronous Attribute

The Asynchronous attribute informs the UTF that a test method should be considered to be in a running state until the SilverlightTest.EnqueueTestComplete method is called.

> **TIP**
>
> Use the Asynchronous attribute in combination with the Timeout attribute to prevent the test method from taking forever if it fails to call EnqueueTestComplete.

For more information on the Asynchronous attribute, see the section "Asynchronous Testing."

Bug Attribute

The Bug attribute allows you to associate a known bug with a unit test. Its key characteristic is that it reverses the result of a test, so you can first use it to demonstrate the existence of a bug, and once the bug is resolved, the `Fixed` property indicates that the test should pass. For example, if a method is able to reproduce a bug in the software, it may first look like this:

```
[Bug("TFS 123")]
[TestMethod]
public void ExerciseBuggyCode()
{
    Assert.IsTrue(false); /* Simulates some broken code. */
}
```

Consider the preceding test method. It passes because the `Bug` attribute's `Fixed` property is false by default.

When the issue is resolved, you can add the `Fixed` property to the `Bug` attribute, which removes the inversion behavior of the `Bug` attribute.

```
[Bug("TFS 123", Fixed = true)]
[TestMethod]
public void ExerciseBuggyCode()
{
    Assert.IsTrue(true); /* Simulates issue resolved. */
}
```

Priority Attribute

Contrary to first assumptions, the `Priority` attribute is not used by the test system. Its purpose can be defined by you. It is, however, added to the set of implicit expression tags. The attribute requires an integer constructor argument, which specifies the priority value. For example:

```
[TestMethod]
[Priority(1)]
public void AlwaysPass()
{
    Assert.IsTrue(true, "Test method intended to always pass.");
}
```

We can then use the tag expression `Priority1` to execute this test method.

SilverlightTest: The Base TestClass Type

UTF test classes normally inherit from the `SilverlightTest` class. While inheriting from this class is not strictly required, it does provide for some advanced features such as asynchronous testing.

Asynchronous unit test methods are a key feature of the UTF for Silverlight, and one that is notably absent from the Microsoft UTF for the desktop CLR.

> **NOTE**
>
> By inheriting from `SilverlightTest`, you lose compatibility with the Desktop CLR Visual Studio unit test framework. Therefore, do not inherit from this class if you want to retain cross-screen compatibility and do not require advanced UI testing facilities, such as asynchronous tests.

Verifying Conditions with Assertions

Assertions are the cornerstone of UTF. The `Assert` class has a multitude of test related method overloads that allow you to ensure the validity of your app's state and behavior. The following is the core set of assertions used by most test classes:

▶ **AreEqual and AreNotEqual**—These methods rely on the `Object.Equals` method to determine object equality. There are various overloads for primitives, as well as reference types.

▶ **AreSame and AreNotSame**—Tests for whether two variables refer to the same object instance. These methods rely on the `Object.ReferenceEquals` method. There are various overloads for primitives, as well as reference types.

▶ **Fail**—Allows you to explicitly fail a test based on logic within the test method.

▶ **Inconclusive**—Allows you to explicitly set the outcome of a test to inconclusive.

▶ **IsTrue and IsFalse**—Verifies that a Boolean value is either `true` or `false`.

▶ **IsInstanceOfType and IsNotInstanceOfType**—Verifies that an object instance does or does not inherit from a specified type.

▶ **IsNull and IsNotNull**—Verifies that an object is, or is not, `null`.

If an `Assert` method fails, it raises a `UnitTestAssertException`, which is handled by the UTF infrastructure and reported back to you as a test failure.

To complement the set methods provided by the `Assert` classes, there exists a `CollectionAssert` class with methods particular to collections, and a `StringAssert` class, which provides assertions based on regular expressions.

Verifying Collection Conditions with `CollectionAssert`

The following is the list of collection assertions that enable you to verify the contents of collections:

▶ **AllItemsAreInstancesOfType**—Verifies that all items in a collection are, or inherit from, a specified type.

▶ **AllItemsAreNotNull**—Verifies that no item in the collection is null.

▶ **AllItemsAreUnique**—Verifies that a collection is a set; each item occurs only once.

▶ **AreEqual and AreNotEqual**—Verifies that two collections have the same number of items, and that each item in the first collection is equal to the item at the same index in the second collection.

▶ **AreEquivalent and AreNotEquivalent**—Verifies that two collections have the same number of items and that each item in the first collection has an item that is equal to it in the second collection. This differs from AreEqual and AreNotEqual in that order does not matter.

▶ **Contains and DoesNotContain**—Verifies that a collection contains a specified item.

▶ **IsSubsetOf and IsNotSubsetOf**—Verifies that all items in one collection exist in another specified collection.

Verifying String Conditions with `StringAssert`

The StringAssert class provides various methods for verifying the contents of strings:

▶ **Contains**—Verifies that a string contains a specified substring.

▶ **Matches and DoesNotMatch**—Uses a regular expression to verify that the specified string matches, or does not match, a specified pattern.

▶ **StartsWith and EndsWith**—Verifies that a string starts or ends with a specified string.

Hiding the Expressions Editor

Sometimes you may like to execute your tests without having to interact with the UTF interface. It can be annoying to have to tap the Use Tag button to kick of the unit tests before the countdown timer reaches zero.

> **NOTE**
>
> Unfortunately, the test harness does not allow you to hide the tag expressions editor in the current version of the Windows Phone UTF. Nonetheless, it is shown here in anticipation of a future release of the UTF.

To hide the tag expressions editor (in a future release) and to run the tests as soon as the test harness launches, you need to modify two properties in the UnitTestSettings class; set the StartRunImmediately property to true, and set the ShowTagExpressionEditor to false. This is demonstrated in this excerpt from the MainPage.xaml.cs file in the downloadable sample code:

```
void OnLoaded(object sender, RoutedEventArgs e)
{
    SystemTray.IsVisible = false;
```

```
UnitTestSettings settings = UnitTestSystem.CreateDefaultSettings();
settings.StartRunImmediately = true;
settings.ShowTagExpressionEditor = false;

UIElement testPage = UnitTestSystem.CreateTestPage(settings);
Application.Current.RootVisual = testPage;
Application.Current.Host.Settings.EnableFrameRateCounter = false;

mobileTestPage = testPage as IMobileTestPage;
}
```

Testing Multiple Assemblies

The current implementation of the UTF for Windows Phone does not support inclusion of tests from assemblies outside the test project; all tests must reside in the Windows Phone test project.

When this shortcoming is rectified, if you want to have a single project for testing and include other test assemblies, add assemblies to the `TestAssemblies` collection of the `UnitTestSettings` class, as shown:

```
UnitTestSettings settings = UnitTestSystem.CreateDefaultSettings();
settings.TestAssemblies.Add(typeof(TestClass1).Assembly);
settings.TestAssemblies.Add(typeof(TestClass2).Assembly);
UIElement testPage = UnitTestSystem.CreateTestPage(settings);
```

Testing Non-Public Members

Sometimes, you need to test classes and members that are not public but are internal to a project, such as during system testing, where you need to interact with UI elements directly. To have access to internal members, you must allow the test project access to the internal members of the main project. You do this by placing an `InternalsVisibleTo` attribute into the `AssemblyInfo` class of the main project, as shown:

```
[assembly: InternalsVisibleTo("WindowsPhone7Unleashed.Tests.Silverlight")]
```

The `InternalsVisibleTo` attribute accepts a single parameter, which is the name of the assembly. If the test project has a strong name, then the full name of the assembly must be used, including its public key token.

Examples of the `InternalsVisibleTo` attribute are in the downloadable sample code.

A Testable Chat Client

This section explores a simple chat client app. First, a custom chat service that is used to send and receive messages is discussed. Next, you examine how to substitute types using mocking and look at mocking the chat service. You see how to test the functionality of a viewmodel without needing to create a view for it. Finally, you learn how to create coded UI tests using the UTF TestPanel in combination with the Microsoft Automation framework.

The code for this section is located in the ChatClientView and ChatClientViewModel classes in the downloadable sample code.

The chat client app relies on a chat service, represented by an IChatService interface. The IChatService specifies a method to send a message, presumably to a cloud service, and an event to indicate when the service receives a message. The interface is shown in the following excerpt:

```
public interface IChatService
{
    void SendMessage(string message);
    event EventHandler<ChatMessageEventArgs> MessageReceived;
}
```

A mock chat service is used during unit testing. Mock objects mimic the behavior of real objects in controlled ways. In this case, MockChatService acts as loopback; when the SendMessage method is called, the MessageReceived event is raised, as shown:

```
public class MockChatService : IChatService
{
    public bool MessageSent { get; private set; }
    public string LastMessage { get; private set; }

    public void SendMessage(string message)
    {
        MessageSent = true;
        LastMessage = message;
        OnMessageReceived(new ChatMessageEventArgs(message));
    }

    public event EventHandler<ChatMessageEventArgs> MessageReceived;

    public void OnMessageReceived(ChatMessageEventArgs e)
    {
        MessageReceived.Raise(this, e);
    }
}
```

The viewmodel for the chat client uses the chat service to send messages using a SendCommand (see Listing 22.2). When the SendCommand executes, the IChatService.SendMessage method receives the message.

The viewmodel subscribes to the `IChatService.MessageReceived` event. When a message is received, it is placed into an `ObservableCollection` of messages, which are then presented in the view.

LISTING 22.2   `ChatClientViewModel` Class (excerpt)

```
public class ChatClientViewModel : ViewModelBase
{
    readonly IChatService chatService;

    public ChatClientViewModel(IChatService chatService)
    {
        this.chatService = ArgumentValidator.AssertNotNull(
                                    chatService, "chatService");

        sendCommand = new DelegateCommand(
            delegate
            {
                if (string.IsNullOrEmpty(message))
                {
                    return;
                }
                chatService.SendMessage(message);
                Message = string.Empty;
            },
            delegate { return !string.IsNullOrEmpty(message); });

        chatService.MessageReceived
            += (sender, args) => messages.Add(args.Message);

        PropertyChanged += delegate { sendCommand.RaiseCanExecuteChanged(); };

        /* The rest of the constructor is shown later in the chapter. */
    }

    readonly ObservableCollection<string> messages
                = new ObservableCollection<string>();

    public ObservableCollection<string> Messages
    {
        get
        {
            return messages;
        }
    }
```

LISTING 22.2   Continued

```
    string message;

    public string Message
    {
        get
        {
            return message;
        }
        set
        {
            Assign(() => Message, ref message, value);
        }
    }

    readonly DelegateCommand sendCommand;

    public ICommand SendCommand
    {
        get
        {
            return sendCommand;
        }
    }

    /* The rest of the class is shown later in the chapter. */
}
```

With the infrastructure in place, you can create some unit tests for the viewmodel.

NOTE

An alternative approach, known as Test Driven Development (TDD), sees the creation of the unit tests first. If you are willing to take an interface first approach or have a tool such as Resharper that allows you to quickly generate class members, you may choose to create the unit tests before you implement the class that is the subject of the unit tests.

Listing 22.3 shows various test methods for verifying that the viewmodel is able to send a message correctly and that it is able to respond correctly when it receives a message from the chat service.

LISTING 22.3   Chat Client ViewModel Tests

```
[TestClass]
public class ChatClientTests : SilverlightTest
{
    [TestMethod]
    public void ShouldSendMessage()
    {
        string testMessage = "Hello from unit test.";
        MockChatService chatService = new MockChatService();
        ChatClientViewModel viewModel = new ChatClientViewModel(chatService);
        viewModel.Message = testMessage;
        viewModel.SendCommand.Execute(null);
        Assert.AreEqual(chatService.LastMessage, testMessage);
    }


    [TestMethod]
    public void ShouldNotSendMessageIfEmpty()
    {
        MockChatService chatService = new MockChatService();
        ChatClientViewModel viewModel = new ChatClientViewModel(chatService);
        viewModel.Message = string.Empty;
        viewModel.SendCommand.Execute(null);
        Assert.IsFalse(chatService.MessageSent);
    }


    [TestMethod]
    public void CommandShouldBeDisabledIfMessageIfEmpty()
    {
        MockChatService chatService = new MockChatService();
        ChatClientViewModel viewModel = new ChatClientViewModel(chatService);
        viewModel.Message = string.Empty;
        Assert.IsFalse(viewModel.SendCommand.CanExecute(null));
    }


    [TestMethod]
    [Description(@"When the chat service receives a message,
        the client displays it.")]
    public void CommandShouldBeEnabledIfMessageNotEmpty()
    {
        MockChatService chatService = new MockChatService();
        ChatClientViewModel viewModel = new ChatClientViewModel(chatService);
        viewModel.Message = "Test";
        Assert.IsTrue(viewModel.SendCommand.CanExecute(null));
    }


    [TestMethod]
```

LISTING 22.3   Continued

```
public void ShouldReceiveMessage()
{
    string testMessage = "Hello from unit test.";
    MockChatService chatService = new MockChatService();
    ChatClientViewModel viewModel = new ChatClientViewModel(chatService);
    chatService.OnMessageReceived(new ChatMessageEventArgs(testMessage));
    CollectionAssert.Contains(viewModel.Messages, testMessage);
}
}
```

The result of running the unit tests is shown in Figure 22.6.

FIGURE 22.6   Chat client test results

Building the View

The view allows the user to send and receive messages via the viewmodel. The view consists of the following elements:

▶ A TextBox to allow the user to enter a message to send.

▶ An AppBar that includes an AppBarIconButton to execute the viewmodel's SendCommand. For more information on the AppBar, see Chapter 8, "Taming the Application Bar."

▶ A ListBox to display all incoming messages.

The following excerpt shows the main content from the `ChatClientView.xaml` page:

```xml
<StackPanel Grid.Row="1"
        Style="{StaticResource PageContentPanelStyle}">
    <u:AppBar>
        <u:AppBarIconButton
        Command="{Binding SendCommand}"
        Text="Send"
        IconUri="/ChatClient/Images/AppBarMessageSend.png"
        x:Name="button_Send"
        AutomationProperties.AutomationId="button_Send" />
    </u:AppBar>

    <TextBox x:Name="textBlock_Message"
        Text="{Binding Message, Mode=TwoWay,
        UpdateSourceTrigger=Explicit}"
        TextWrapping="Wrap" AcceptsReturn="True"
        u2:UpdateSourceTriggerExtender.UpdateSourceOnTextChanged="True"/>
    <TextBlock Text="Messages" Style="{StaticResource LabelTextStyle}"/>
    <ListBox x:Name="listBox" ItemsSource="{Binding Messages}" Height="400">
        <ListBox.ItemTemplate>
            <DataTemplate>
                <TextBlock Text="{Binding}"
                    Style="{StaticResource NormalTextStyle}" />
            </DataTemplate>
        </ListBox.ItemTemplate>
    </ListBox>
</StackPanel>
```

The various input controls have been named. You see later in this chapter how the naming of elements allows you to directly manipulate them from a coded UI unit test.

TIP

If you are not creating coded UI tests, it is better to refrain from naming elements unless you need to refer to them in the code-beside. This helps identify those elements that are referred to in the code-beside, and decreases the verbosity of the XAML.

The view's code-beside (`ChatClientView.xaml.cs`) instantiates the viewmodel and supplies the viewmodel with an instance of the `MockChatService`, as shown in the following excerpt:

```csharp
public ChatClientView()
{
    InitializeComponent();
    DataContext = new ChatClientViewModel(new MockChatService());
}
```

Later in the chapter you see how to replace the MockChatService for a *real* chat service implementation using Inversion of Control (IoC).

The final result of the chat page is shown in Figure 22.7.

FIGURE 22.7   ChatClientView page

Code Driven UI Testing

A key benefit of the MVVM pattern is that it allows you to unit test an app without needing to display its UI. Sometimes, however, you may want to verify the behavior of the UI by emulating user interaction. This can be achieved using coded UI tests.

The advantage of coded UI tests is that they provide your app with a test environment that is closer to the real world; they allow you to simulate the tapping of buttons or entering of text while the app is running.

The downside of coded UI tests is that they are tightly coupled to the user interface, which is often the most likely thing to change over time. If the UI is modified, it can mean having to rewrite your coded UI tests.

Coded UI tests can be performed with the UTF by populating the `SilverlightTest` object's `TestPanel` with the page or control that you want to test, as demonstrated in the following excerpt:

```
[TestClass]
public class ChatClientUITests : SilverlightTest
{
    ChatClientView view;

    [TestInitialize]
    public void PreparePage()
    {
        view = new ChatClientView();
        TestPanel.Children.Add(view);
    }
...
}
```

Recall that the `TestInitialize` attribute causes the method to be called before each test method in the parent class. You see that when the `PreparePage` method is called, it creates a new instance of the `ChatClientView` and places it into a container control within the test harness.

This section looks at the three test methods in the `ChatClientUITests` class.

The first test method simply verifies that the `PhoneApplicationPage` is presented in the `TestPanel`, as shown:

```
[TestMethod]
public void ShouldDisplayDefaultSize()
{
    Assert.IsTrue(view.ActualWidth > 0);
}
```

The `ShouldDisplayDefaultSize` method demonstrates that you are able to interact with the UI elements from code. In fact, while the tests are running their actions are viewable within the test harness (see Figure 22.8).

FIGURE 22.8   A UI test in execution

To interact with controls on the page, give the test project access to the internal members of the main project. This is done by placing an InternalsVisibleTo attribute in the AssemblyInfo class of the main project, shown in the previous section "Testing Non-Public Members."

When the InternalsVisibleTo is placed in the target project, IntelliSense is enabled for controls on the page.

To test that the Send button is enabled when the message TextBox is populated, set the text and then perform an assert using the button, as shown in the following excerpt:

```
[TestMethod]
public void ButtonShouldBeEnabled()
{
    view.textBlock_Message.Text = "Test";
    Assert.IsTrue(view.button_Send.IsEnabled);
}
```

Asynchronous Testing

The UTF is designed to run tests on a single thread. The Silverlight UI thread uses a message pump and often calls to update properties or reactions to property changed events are driven forward using Dispatcher calls. The result is that a UIElement may not be in the state that you think it should be when you are performing an assertion. Fortunately, the Silverlight UTF compensates with some built-in asynchronous features.

The `Asynchronous` attribute tells the UTF to keep running the test until the test class's base method, `SilverlightTest.EnqueueTestComplete` is called or until an unhandled exception occurs. This allows you to spin off work to other threads or queue work to happen on the UI thread, while keeping the test alive.

The `SilverlightTest.EnqueueCallback` method allows actions to be queued on the UI thread. This may include actions such as verifying the value of a `UIElement`'s property after a `PropertyChanged` event has been given the opportunity to propagate.

The following excerpt demonstrates how to use the `Asynchronous` attribute in combination with the `EnqueueCallback` method to set the text of a sample view's message box. It simulates a tap to the Send Message button and then verifies that the `ListBox` has been correctly populated:

```
[TestMethod]
[Asynchronous]
public void ButtonShouldSendMessage()
{
    view.textBlock_Message.Text = "Test";
    EnqueueCallback(() => ((IAppBarItem)view.button_Send).PerformClick());
    EnqueueCallback(() => Assert.IsTrue(view.listBox.Items.Count > 0));
    EnqueueTestComplete();
}
```

When the `textBlock_Message.Text` property is set, the Send button is not enabled until the viewmodel's `SendCommand` responds to the `Message` property's `PropertyChanged` event. Once it has had a chance to respond, the command enables itself.

The `EnqueueCallback` method queues the `PerformClick` method, so that by the time it is called, the button is enabled. Similarly, verification that the `ListBox` has been populated must occur after the UI has responded to the new item in the `Messages` collection in the viewmodel.

The UTF is notified that all nonblocking activity has been completed by calling the base class's `SilverlightTest.EnqueueTestComplete` method.

Using Automation Peers to Manipulate UI Elements at Runtime

When performing code driven UI testing, often you need to manipulate elements in ways that are not possible using the API of the elements themselves. The `Button` class, for example, does not have a `PerformTap` method to raise the `Tap` event. The built-in Silverlight controls are generally well encapsulated and are not designed to simulate interaction via code. For this, we turn to the Microsoft UI Automation framework, which consists of a secondary API for manipulating UI elements from code. The Automation framework is designed for accessibility software, allowing third-party software to manipulate the UI on behalf of a user with a disability.

The Automation API is able to manipulate elements, such as a `Button`, using internal methods of the various built-in `FrameworkElement` types, which are ordinarily off-limits.

In this example, a button is placed on the ChatClientView page. When tapped, it sets the view's custom ButtonClicked property to true. The XAML for the button is as follows:

```
<Button x:Name="button_AutomationTest"
        Content="AutomationTestButton"
        Click="button_AutomationTest_Click" />
```

The code-beside for the view contains the event handler for the Click event of the button:

```
public bool ButtonClicked { get; private set; }

void button_AutomationTest_Click(object sender, RoutedEventArgs e)
{
    ButtonClicked = true;
}
```

An AutomationPeer, located in the System.Windows.Automation.Peers namespace, is used to verify that the button was indeed clicked. The AutomationPeer object is then used to retrieve an IInvokeProvider specific to the Button class, which allows you to invoke the button's Click event, shown in the following excerpt:

```
[TestMethod]
[Asynchronous]
public void DemonstrateButtonClick()
{
    AutomationPeer peer
            = FrameworkElementAutomationPeer.CreatePeerForElement(
                                        view.button_AutomationTest);
    IInvokeProvider provider
            = (IInvokeProvider)peer.GetPattern(PatternInterface.Invoke);
    provider.Invoke();

    EnqueueCallback(() => Assert.IsTrue(view.ButtonClicked));
    EnqueueTestComplete();
}
```

Behind the scenes, the AutomationPeer is simply calling an internal method of the ButtonBase named AutomationButtonBaseClick, which raises the button's Click event.

NOTE

The ButtonAutomationPeer raises the button's Click event and not its Tap event. Unfortunately, the Tap event is not supported by the Automation API in the current 7.5 release of the Windows Phone SDK.

Inversion of Control (IoC)

Windows Phone presents some interesting challenges for testing apps in various deployment scenarios. For example, a common requirement for phone apps is the need to behave differently depending on whether the app has been purchased or whether it is in trial mode. Furthermore, the launcher and chooser API does not play well with unit tests because launchers and choosers cause the app to be deactivated. Hence, there is a need for some mechanism to alter the behavior of an app, depending on its deployment scenario, and to decouple and replace various phone-specific types so that code can be more easily tested. One way to achieve these things is by using Inversion of Control.

IoC encompasses two key concepts presented in this chapter: service location and dependency injection.

Service location allows you to associate a type, often an interface, with a concrete implementation of that type so that when another component requests the first type, they are automatically delivered an instance of the associated type. This allows your code to be decoupled from any particular concrete implementation, which increases flexibility, and allows the behavior of your app to be modified, without having to change all references to a particular concrete implementation.

Dependency Injection (DI) assists in the creation of objects by automatically supplying known types to the objects constructor during instantiation.

Employing IoC in Windows Phone apps helps overcome the challenges brought on by the rigid infrastructure and numerous sealed classes that account for many of the key types in the SDK and that hinder both unit testing and ad hoc testing.

Numerous IoC frameworks have been designed for Silverlight for the browser and the desktop CLR. Silverlight for Windows Phone, however, is based on the Microsoft .NET Compact Framework (.NET CF) and lacks the ability to generate Microsoft Intermediate Language (MSIL) and, in particular, `Reflection.Emit`, a key ingredient in generating types at runtime. This limitation means that none of the well-known IoC projects, such as the Microsoft Patterns and Practices Unity framework, exist for the phone. I have, however, created an IoC container and DI framework, based on work by Ian Randall (http://microioc.codeplex.com/), for use with Windows Phone.

Like much of the code presented in this book, these classes are present in the downloadable sample code. I recommend, however, that you procure the latest code from http://calciumsdk.com, where you are sure to have the most up-to-date version.

A Custom IoC Container and DI Framework

The custom `Dependency` class is a static class used to associate types or resolve instances of types at runtime. The `Dependency` class serves as a proxy to an instance of IoC container, allowing you to change the underlying IoC container implementation. It does this by leveraging the Microsoft.Practices.ServiceLocation API, which provides a container agnostic type resolution mechanism. The `Dependency` class also uses a custom `IDependencyRegistrar` to create type associations, something notably absent from the Microsoft.Practices.ServiceLocation API.

To use the Dependency class, an IoC container implementation must be specified.

Initialization of the IoC infrastructure should be performed as soon as possible before the app displays its UI. This helps prevent type resolution failures.

In the sample, located in the WindowsPhone7Unleashed.Examples project, the container initialization code is placed in the App class, as shown in the following excerpt:

```
void InitializeContainer()
{
    SimpleContainer container = new SimpleContainer();
    container.InitializeServiceLocator();

#if DEBUG
    Dependency.Register<ILicensingService>(new MockLicensingService
    {
        IsTrial = true
    });
    Dependency.Register<IMarketplaceDetailTaskAdapter>(
        new MockMarketplaceDetailTaskAdapter(
            () => Debug.WriteLine("Launching Marketplace Detail...")));
#else
    Dependency.Register<ILicensingService, LicensingService>();
    Dependency.Register<IMarketplaceDetailTaskAdapter,
                        MarketplaceDetailTaskAdapter>();
#endif
}
```

Once the container is initialized, the Dependency class is used to register type associations. Creating a different set of type associations, depending on the build configuration, can be achieved using preprocessor directives. When using a DEBUG build configuration, mock implementations of the ILicensingService interface and the IMarketplaceDetailTaskAdapter interface are used. These types wrap and substitute the functionality provided by the built-in MarketDetailTask and LicenseInformation classes.

> **TIP**
>
> Rather than duplicating your type mappings across test and core projects, you may choose instead to create a dedicated class that includes type associations for each scenario you are covering: test, release, trial, and so on.

If you are familiar with unit testing in Silverlight for the browser, you may wonder why there is no coverage of dynamic mocking in this chapter. The reason is that dynamic mocking does not exist in Windows Phone due to, as previously mentioned, the absence of Reflection.Emit.

Testing Trial Conditions

Providing a trial version of your app may help to improve its monetization. If someone has the opportunity to try out your app, they may be more likely to purchase it (assuming that it is any good). A usual requirement for an app employing a trial version is to provide the user with a link to buy the app within the app itself. In the following demonstration you see how to display an application bar button when an app is in trial mode.

The `Microsoft.Phone.MarketPlace.LicenseInformation` class contains a single method called `IsTrial()`, which indicates whether your app has been purchased. When a user downloads the trial version of your app from the marketplace, this method returns true. On all other occasions, such as when debugging, this method returns false.

To ensure that an app functions correctly in both scenarios, you abstract the `LicenseInformation` class.

Abstracting the `LicenseInformation` Class

The downloadable sample code includes a custom `ILicenseService` interface, which contains a single property called `Trial`, indicating the trial state of the app. There are two implementations of this interface: one for testing and one for production.

The production implementation named `LicensingService` wraps a `LicenseInformation` instance, as shown in the following excerpt:

```
public class LicensingService : ILicensingService
{
    public bool Trial
    {
        get
        {
            LicenseInformation licenseInformation
                            = new LicenseInformation();
            return licenseInformation.IsTrial();
        }
    }
}
```

During development and testing, the `LicensingService` class is replaced by a `MockLicensingService` class, which allows you to change the value of its `Trial` property. See the following excerpt:

```
public class MockLicensingService : ILicensingService
{
    bool trial = true;

    public bool Trial
    {
        get
```

```
    {
        return trial;
    }
    set
    {
        trial = value;
    }
  }
}
```

The particular implementation that is used depends on the type association within the IoC container. When the project is built using a release configuration, then LicensingService is used; otherwise the MockLicensingService is used.

Within the ChatClientView page, there is a button whose visibility depends on a view-model property called BuyOptionVisible. See the following excerpt:

```
bool buyOptionVisible;

public bool BuyOptionVisible
{
    get
    {
        return buyOptionVisible;
    }
    private set
    {
        Assign(() => BuyOptionVisible, ref buyOptionVisible, value);
    }
}
```

In the viewmodel constructor the value of the buyOptionVisible field is determined using the ILicensingService, which is resolved via the static Dependency method called Resolve:

```
var licensingService = Dependency.Resolve<ILicensingService>();
buyOptionVisible = licensingService.IsTrial;
```

An AppBarMenuItem is bound to the BuyOptionVisible property, as shown:

```
<u:AppBar.MenuItems>
    <u:AppBarMenuItem Text="Buy"
        Command="{Binding BuyCommand}"
        Visibility="{Binding BuyOptionVisible,
        Converter={StaticResource BooleanToVisibilityConverter}}" />
</u:AppBar.MenuItems>
```

A value converter is used to convert the Boolean value to a `Visibility` enum value.

When the user taps the button, the `BuyCommand` is executed. In the next section you see how the `BuyCommand` uses an abstracted `MarketPlaceDetailTask` to launch the built-in marketplace application on the phone.

Testing with Launchers and Choosers

Unit testing code that uses a launcher or chooser directly is a challenge because both types of tasks cause your app to be deactivated. No means to abstract launchers or choosers exists out of the box, therefore I have included in the downloadable sample code a set of classes that do just that.

Just as we abstracted the built-in `LicenseInformation` class in the previous section, here we do the same with the `MarketDetailTask`. The `MarketDetailTask` is a launcher which, when shown, takes the user to the built-in marketplace application. When showing the `MarketplaceDetailTask` during a debugging session, the native marketplace application displays an error because it expects an app with an id that has been officially published to the marketplace.

The main issue, however, is that when the `MarketplaceDetailTask` is shown, it deactivates the app. Thus, it makes sense to abstract the task as in the `LicenseInformation` class in the previous section.

The abstracted custom interface for the `MarketplaceDetailTask` is named `IMarketDetailTask` and contains a single method named `Show`. There are two implementations of this interface. The first, named `MarketplaceDetailTaskAdapter`, calls the `Show` method of a built-in `MarketplaceDetailTask` instance when its own `Show` method is called, as shown in the following excerpt:

```
public class MarketplaceDetailTaskAdapter : IMarketplaceDetailTask
{
    public void Show()
    {
        var marketplaceDetailTask = new MarketplaceDetailTask();
        marketplaceDetailTask.Show();
    }
}
```

The unit test compatible implementation of the `IMarketplaceDetailTask` is called `MockMarketplaceDetailTask` and allows a specified `Action` to be invoked when the `Show` method is called:

```
public class MockMarketplaceDetailTask : IMarketplaceDetailTask
{
    readonly Action action;

    public MockMarketplaceDetailTask(Action action)
    {
```

```
        this.action = action;
    }

    public void Show()
    {
        if (action != null)
        {
            action();
        }
    }
}
```

The `ChatClientViewModel` class contains an `ICommand` named `BuyCommand`, which, when executed, retrieves the `IMarketplaceDetailTask` from the IoC container and calls its `Show` method. `BuyCommand` is initialized in the viewmodel's constructor, as shown:

```
buyCommand = new DelegateCommand(
    obj =>
    {
      var marketplaceDetailTask
              = Dependency.Resolve<IMarketplaceDetailTask>();
      marketplaceDetailTask.Show();
    });
```

When the `BuyCommand` is executed, it causes the `IMarketDetailTask` instance to be resolved using the static `Dependency.Resolve` method. Recall that a particular implementation of the `IMarketDetailTask` is registered according to the selected build configuration, as described in the earlier section, "A Custom IoC Container and DI Framework." If the build is using a Release configuration, then an instance of the `MarketplaceDetailTaskAdapter` is resolved, which, in turn, causes an instance of the built-in `MarketplaceDetailTask` to be shown. Conversely, if the build is using a Debug configuration, then the `MockMarketplaceDetailTask` is used, which does not disrupt unit testing or any manual ad hoc testing.

Summary

This chapter explored the Silverlight Unit Testing Framework (UTF) for Windows Phone. The chapter began with a walk-through of the creation of a unit test project. You saw how to create test classes and test methods and looked at the tag expressions editor, which provides a useful mechanism for selecting which tests are to be run during a test session.

The chapter then examined the UTF in greater detail by creating a simple chat client app. You saw how to test a viewmodel's behavior before creating a UI and explored code driven UI testing. You also learned how to perform asynchronous testing and touched on the Microsoft Automation framework.

The chapter then examined some advanced topics such as Inversion of Control, mocking, and how to use a custom IoC container.

Finally, you saw how to perform testing of trial applications. You learned how to hide or reveal content based on a mock licensing service and examined a custom API for mocking launchers and choosers.

22

Input Validation

Input validation is the process of validating input to an application before it is used. Most line-of-business applications rely on input validation to ensure that user input is correctly formatted, meaningful, safe to use, and that it properly conveys the intent of the user.

Input validation in a Windows Phone app may be purely client-side, or it can involve sending input to a web service for validation, which normally entails asynchronous processing.

Silverlight for Windows Phone comes equipped to support input validation. There are, however, some crucial validation related control styles missing from the SDK, which need to be put in place before visual indicators are displayed for validation errors.

This chapter begins by looking at the two types of input validation: syntactic and semantic, and then at the Silverlight data binding system as it relates to input validation, its features, and limitations.

The chapter then provides a walk-through for adding custom control styles for enabling visualization of data validation errors and shows how to create a custom error validation summary control.

Finally, the chapter explores an alternative approach to validation, one that leverages the validation system that is new to Silverlight 4 and allows for asynchronous and composite validation.

Defining Input Validation

Alexander Jung does a great job on his blog (http://ajdotnet.wordpress.com/2010/02/28/understanding-validation-in-silverlight/) of defining input validation. He states that input validation involves ensuring that user input passes two types of validation: syntactic and semantic.

Syntactic Validation

Syntactic validation ensures that data entered by a user can be converted to the type required by the application. For example, when a user enters a date string into a `TextBox`, the input fails syntactic validation if it cannot be converted to a date.

In most cases, the Silverlight data binding system attends to syntactic validation, coercing values to and from source property types.

> **NOTE**
>
> The Silverlight data binding system performs syntactic validation before assigning a value to a property.

Semantic Validation

Unlike syntactic validation, semantic validation can occur after a value has been assigned. Semantic validation deals with more complex validation and usually encompasses the evaluation of business rules.

The following examples require semantic validation:

▶ Required fields.

▶ String length restrictions, for example, the length of a string input must not exceed 140 characters.

▶ Numeric range restrictions, for example, value must be greater than 0 but less than 100.

▶ Date range restrictions, for example, a date must occur in the future.

▶ Mutually dependent fields, for example, value A is required if value B has been provided.

▶ Distinguishing between absent and invalid fields. The application must be able to distinguish between when a user has chosen not to enter a field, from when a field has been provided by the user, but it is an empty string for example.

Input Validation Using Property Setters

The first validation system discussed in this chapter is the property setter validation system. This system has been with the phone since the first 7.0 release of the Windows Phone SDK and is part of Silverlight 3.

The Silverlight data binding system provides validation support when assigning a value to the source of a data binding expression. For example, when a `FrameworkElement` (the binding target) has a binding to a property in a viewmodel (the binding source) and the value in the `FrameworkElement` changes, validation occurs as the value is being assigned to the property in the viewmodel.

To enable property setter validation for an input control, set the binding's `NotifyOnValidationError` and `ValidatesOnExceptions` to true, as shown in the following example:

```
<TextBox Text="{Binding PropertyName, Mode=TwoWay,
        NotifyOnValidationError=True, ValidatesOnExceptions=True}" />
```

`ValidatesOnExceptions` enables property validation for the binding, and `NotifyOnValidationError` causes an event to be raised when a validation error occurs.

The Silverlight data binding system performs the following three actions during assignment of a source object property:

▶ Conversion of the target `DependencyProperty` value using an `IValueConverter`. This occurs if the target's binding has its `ValueConverter` set.

▶ Type conversion of the result of step 1 to the source property type.

▶ Assignment of the result of step 2 to the source property, and detection and handling of exceptions raised in the source's property set accessor.

The validation and assignment of a source property is explored in greater detail in Figure 23.1, which is based on Alexander Jung's diagram at http://ajdotnet.wordpress.com/2010/02/28/understanding-validation-in-silverlight/.

The following list refers to numbered items in Figure 23.1, and describes each step performed by the data binding system:

1. The change event is raised for the target's `DependencyProperty`. This event is subscribed to by the target's `BindingExpression` for the `DependencyProperty`. When the `FrameworkElement`'s property is changed, the `BindingExpression`'s `TargetPropertyChanged` method is called. The `BindingExpression` then calls its own `UpdateValue` method.

2. If there is a `ValueConverter` defined for the binding, then its `ConvertBack` method is called. If an exception is raised in the `ConvertBack` method, it is not handled and must be handled by the `Application.UnhandledException` event handler, or the app exits.

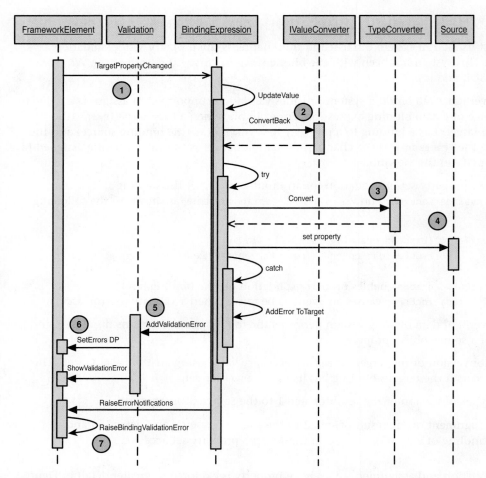

FIGURE 23.1   A change in a target property causes validation and assignment of its source property.

3. An internal `IValueConverter`, called `DynamicValueConverter`, uses a `TypeConverter` to convert the target value to the source type. The `DynamicValueConverter` comes into play when, for example, a `TextBox.Text` string value needs to be converted to an `int` value. During conversion, noncritical `Exceptions` are treated as validation errors. Critical `Exceptions` are described in a later section.

4. The property setter is called using the result from the `TypeConverter`. Once again, if a noncritical exception is raised, it is treated as a validation error. Be mindful that if the property setter raises the `PropertyChanged` event and an event handler throws an `Exception`, it results in a validation error.

5. The `BindingExpression` class uses the static `Validation` class to assign validation errors for the `FrameworkElement`.

6. The Validation class records validation information about a FrameworkElement using the DependencyProperty's Validation.ErrorsProperty and Validation.HasErrorProperty. Once the error has been set, the FrameworkElement is prompted to display the error. This is normally done by transitioning the VisualState of the control to an invalid state. We look at displaying validation errors, using VisualState and the VisualStateManager, later in this chapter.

7. If the binding has been set to notify of validation errors, discussed further in the following section, the BindingValidationError event is raised.

NOTE

IValueConverters are unable to participate in input validation because if an IValueConverter throws an exception, it is re-thrown by the BindingExpression.

Validation Class

The static Validation class is used to determine whether a control has validation errors and to retrieve the errors if they exist. The Validation class has the methods: GetHasError and GetErrors, and provides two dependency properties for storing the validation information: ErrorsProperty and HasErrorsProperty.

Critical Exceptions

Most exceptions that occur during the assignment of a value to a source property are handled by the BindingExpression class. Several exception types, however, are deemed critical exceptions and are re-thrown by the BindingExpression. The following is the list of critical exceptions:

▶ OutOfMemoryException

▶ StackOverflowException

▶ AccessViolationException

▶ ThreadAbortException

Binding Errors

Binding errors occur when a noncritical exception is raised after the ConvertBack method of the ValueConverter is called. The following is a list of the three types of binding errors that can occur when modifying the value of a target property:

▶ The user enters a value that fails to be converted to the source binding type (syntactic validation).

▶ An exception is raised within the property set accessor.

▶ The property does not have a set accessor and is, therefore, read-only.

> **NOTE**
>
> When a binding error occurs, the target, a `TextBox` for example, retains the entered value, but the source property is not updated.

By default, the Silverlight data binding infrastructure fails silently when a binding error occurs. The `NotifyOnValidationError` and the `ValidatesOnExceptions` binding properties allow you to provide the user with feedback when a value is incorrectly set.

NotifyOnValidationError Binding Property

With the `Binding.NotifyOnValidationError` property set to true, Silverlight's data binding system raises a `BindingValidationError` event when a binding error occurs. The following example demonstrates enabling validation on a `TextBox` element:

```
<TextBox Text="{Binding ValidatedString2, Mode=TwoWay,
        NotifyOnValidationError=True, ValidatesOnExceptions=True}"
        Style="{StaticResource ValidatingTextBoxStyle}" />
```

The `BindingValidationError` is a `RoutedEvent`, allowing it to be handled by an ancestor element in the visual tree. `RoutedEvents` bubble upwards through the visual tree until they are either handled, indicated by the `Handled` property of the event arguments, or they reach the root element of the visual tree. Subscription to the `BindingValidationError` event at the page level, therefore, provides the opportunity to handle validation errors for all elements in the page. We leverage this fact later in the chapter to create a validation summary control.

ValidatesOnExceptions Property

The `Binding` class's `NotifyOnValidationError` property works in unison with its `ValidatesOnExceptions` property. If the `ValidatesOnExceptions` property is not explicitly set to true and a binding error results from a noncritical exception being raised from a property accessor, the error is silently ignored. Furthermore, the `VisualState` of the `FrameworkElement` is not changed, and the `BindingValidationError` event is not raised.

Defining Validation Visual States in Silverlight for Windows Phone

When a binding error occurs, the data binding system transitions the `VisualState` of the `FrameworkElement` to an invalid state. In Silverlight for the browser, various controls come ready to display validation errors. Unfortunately, those styles have not been incorporated into Silverlight for Windows Phone because the styles are not immediately transferable to the phone because of the reduced size of the phone display. Consequently, if you want to harness the existing validation infrastructure, you must replace the template for each control for which you intend to display validation errors.

Replacing a control's template can be done using Expression Blend. A copy can be made of the template, and error related `VisualStates` can then be modified.

23

NOTE

If you do not have Microsoft Expression Blend already installed, it can be downloaded from http://www.microsoft.com/expression/windowsphone/.

To make a copy of a control's template, right-click on a control within Expression Blend, select Edit Template, and then select Edit a Copy (see Figure 23.2).

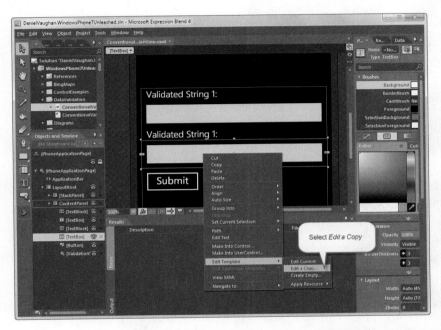

FIGURE 23.2   Editing a copy of a control's template from within Expression Blend

To allow the template to be reused across the entire app from any page, define the style at the application level (see Figure 23.3). This causes a style containing the template to be placed in the project's app.xaml file.

Once the style has been created, a new Style element is placed in the App.xaml file. See the following excerpt:

```
<Style x:Key="ValidatingTextBoxStyle" TargetType="TextBox">
    ...
</Style>
```

The States tab in Expression Blend allows you to define different ways of displaying the control depending on its visual state. The control is placed into a named state by the VisualStateManager. To customize the way the control is displayed when a validation error occurs, select the InvalidUnfocused state (see Figure 23.4).

FIGURE 23.3 Defining the location of a new style in Expression Blend

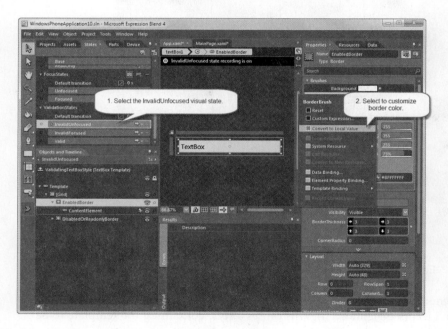

FIGURE 23.4 Converting the BorderBrush to a local value

To modify the TextBox border so that it is displayed in a different manner when in the InvalidUnfocused state, select the yellow button next to the BorderBrush item in the Properties tab and choose Convert to Local Value.

Converting the BorderBrush to a local value allows the brush to be customized for the particular VisualState, and for its color to be set to one that better represents the state of the control when a validation error occurs.

Just as the TextBox style was made globally available by placing it in the app's resources, converting the new color to a resource enables its use in other styles (see Figure 23.5).

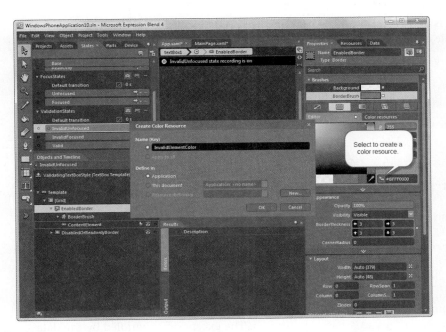

FIGURE 23.5 Creating a new color resource for the BorderBrush color

When the color resource has been created, the template in the style resource contains a definition for the InvalidUnfocused state, with a reference to the InvalidElementColor resource, as shown in the following excerpt:

```
<VisualState x:Name="InvalidUnfocused">
    <Storyboard>
        <ColorAnimation Duration="0"
            To="{StaticResource InvalidElementColor}"
            Storyboard.TargetProperty
                ="(Border.BorderBrush).(SolidColorBrush.Color)"
            Storyboard.TargetName="EnabledBorder"
            d:IsOptimized="True"/>
    </Storyboard>
</VisualState>
```

Subsequently, whenever you want to display validation errors for a TextBox, the Style property of the TextBox is set to ValidatingTextBoxStyle, like so:

```
<TextBox Text="{Binding ValidatedString1, Mode=TwoWay,
        NotifyOnValidationError=True}"
        Style="{StaticResource ValidatingTextBoxStyle}" />
```

If a binding error occurs, the VisualState of the TextBox automatically transitions to the InvalidUnfocused state.

The following is an excerpt from the ConventionalValidationViewModel class in the down-loadable sample code, which contains validation logic for the ValidatedString1 property:

```
public string ValidatedString1
{
    get
    {
        return validatedString1;
    }
    set
    {
        if (string.IsNullOrEmpty(value))
        {
            throw new ArgumentException("Validated String 1 is required.");
        }
        validatedString1 = value;
    }
}
```

When a user removes all the text from the TextBox that is bound to this property, the property set accessor raises an ArgumentException. The exception is handled by the data binding system, and the TextBox is placed into the InvalidUnfocused state, which now provides visual indication that the value is invalid (see Figure 23.6).

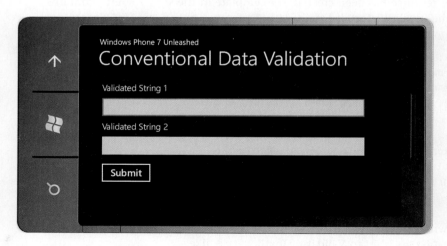

FIGURE 23.6   ConventionalValidationView page. A TextBox with a validation error is displayed with the custom BorderBrush.

This approach can be used to validate a variety of semantic rules. For example, data can be made to conform to a valid range. If the data falls outside a specified range, an exception can be thrown.

Custom validation logic can be applied to other control types as well. In some cases, however, it is necessary to provide a style for the InvalidFocused state as well as the InvalidUnfocused state. The InvalidUnfocused state is used in this example because, by default, the TextBox.Text property is set only when the TextBox loses focus.

Validating a TextBox as the User Types

The BindingExpression class's UpdateSource method forces the target property value to be assigned to its source property. This allows you to perform input validation while the user is entering text into a TextBox, rather than after the TextBox loses focus.

I have created a class called UpdateSourceTriggerExtender, which contains an attached property that is used to trigger an update of the binding source whenever the TextBox's text changes.

When the attached property is placed on a TextBox, the UpdateSourceTriggerExtender class's HandleUpdatePropertyChanged method is called, which subscribes to the TextBox.TextChanged event (see Listing 23.1). When the text is changed the BindingExpression for the TextProperty is retrieved, and its UpdateSource method is called, which effectively pushes the Text string value to the source property.

The attached property can also be placed on a PasswordBox, in which case its PasswordChanged event is used to monitor for user input.

> **NOTE**
>
> The TextBox.LostFocus event is used to explicitly set the visual state of the TextBox. This is required because the Silverlight data binding system does not place the TextBox into the correct visual state when it loses focus if the Text property has not changed, which is the case when you call UpdateSource on the TextChanged event.

LISTING 23.1   UpdateSourceTriggerExtender Class

```
public class UpdateSourceTriggerExtender
{
    public static readonly DependencyProperty UpdateSourceOnTextChanged
        = DependencyProperty.RegisterAttached(
            "UpdateSourceOnTextChanged", typeof(bool),
            typeof(UpdateSourceTriggerExtender),
            new PropertyMetadata(HandleUpdatePropertyChanged));

    public static bool GetUpdateSourceOnTextChanged(DependencyObject d)
    {
        return (bool)d.GetValue(UpdateSourceOnTextChanged);
    }

    public static void SetUpdateSourceOnTextChanged(
        DependencyObject d, bool value)
```

LISTING 23.1   Continued

```csharp
{
    d.SetValue(UpdateSourceOnTextChanged, value);
}

static void HandleUpdatePropertyChanged(
    DependencyObject d, DependencyPropertyChangedEventArgs e)
{
    TextBox textBox = d as TextBox;
    if (textBox != null)
    {
        if ((bool)e.OldValue)
        {
            textBox.TextChanged -= HandleTextBoxTextChanged;
            textBox.LostFocus -= HandleBoxLostFocus;
        }

        if ((bool)e.NewValue)
        {
            textBox.TextChanged += HandleTextBoxTextChanged;
            textBox.LostFocus += HandleBoxLostFocus;
        }
        return;
    }

    PasswordBox passwordBox = d as PasswordBox;
    if (passwordBox == null)
    {
        throw new Exception("UpdateSourceTrigger can only be used "
                            + "on a TextBox or PasswordBox.");
    }

    /* Wire up for password box. */
    if ((bool)e.OldValue)
    {
        passwordBox.PasswordChanged -= HandlePasswordBoxTextChanged;
        passwordBox.LostFocus -= HandleBoxLostFocus;
    }

    if ((bool)e.NewValue)
    {
        passwordBox.PasswordChanged += HandlePasswordBoxTextChanged;
        passwordBox.LostFocus += HandleBoxLostFocus;
    }
}
```

LISTING 23.1   Continued

```csharp
static void HandlePasswordBoxTextChanged(object sender, RoutedEventArgs e)
{
    UpdateSource((PasswordBox)sender, PasswordBox.PasswordProperty);
}

static void HandleTextBoxTextChanged(object sender, TextChangedEventArgs e)
{
    UpdateSource((TextBox)sender, TextBox.TextProperty);
}

static void UpdateSource(
    FrameworkElement element, DependencyProperty property)
{
    if (element == null)
    {
        return;
    }

    BindingExpression bindingExpression
            = element.GetBindingExpression(property);
    if (bindingExpression != null)
    {
        bindingExpression.UpdateSource();
    }
}

static void HandleBoxLostFocus(object sender, RoutedEventArgs e)
{
    /* This method prevents the control from being placed
     * into the valid state when it loses focus. */
    var control = sender as Control;
    if (control == null)
    {
        return;
    }
    bool hasError = Validation.GetHasError(control);
    if (hasError)
    {
        VisualStateManager.GoToState(control, "InvalidFocused", false);
    }
}
```

The following example demonstrates how the UpdateSourceTriggerExtender can be applied to a TextBox:

```xml
<TextBox Text="{Binding ValidatedString1, Mode=TwoWay,
                        UpdateSourceTrigger=Explicit,
                        NotifyOnValidationError=True,
                        ValidatesOnExceptions=True}"
         Style="{StaticResource ValidatingTextBoxStyle}"
         u:UpdateSourceTriggerExtender.UpdateSourceOnTextChanged="True" />
```

The UpdateSourceTrigger binding property determines when the source property is updated. It can be set to either Default or Explicit. Default causes the source property to be updated when the TextBox loses focus, and Explicit prevents the source being updated until the binding's UpdateSource method is explicitly called.

As soon as the text changes, the source property named ValidatedString1 is updated, which causes the input to be validated.

Performing Group Validation

Validating a series of input fields usually entails validating each field as the user leaves the field and then checking for completeness and validity of all fields when the Submit button is tapped (see Figure 23.7).

The UpdateSource method of the BindingExpression class can be used to validate all controls on a form. As you saw in the preceding section, the UpdateSource method causes the target value to be reassigned to its source property. In other words, the value in the control is pushed to its data context, allowing the discovery of any input validation errors.

The following excerpt from ConventionalValidationView.xaml.cs in the downloadable sample code demonstrates how to validate all TextBox fields on a form:

```csharp
void Button_Click(object sender, System.Windows.RoutedEventArgs e)
{
    IEnumerable<TextBox> children = ContentPanel.GetDescendents<TextBox>();
    foreach (TextBox textBox in children)
    {
        BindingExpression bindingExpression
            = textBox.GetBindingExpression(TextBox.TextProperty);
        if (bindingExpression != null)
        {
            bindingExpression.UpdateSource();
        }
    }
}
```

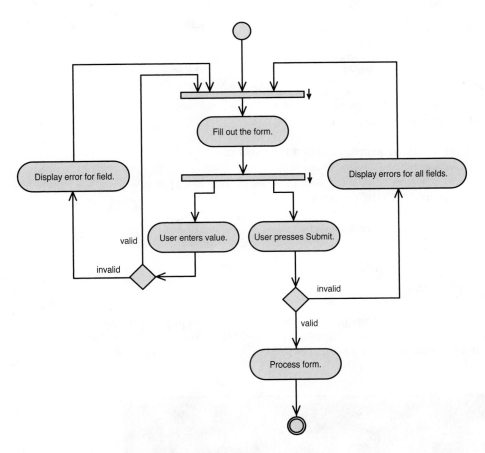

FIGURE 23.7   Form validation activity diagram

The custom `GetDescendents` extension method recursively retrieves all children, children's children, and so on, of a particular type for the specified `FrameworkElement`. The method is located in the `VisualTree` class in the downloadable sample code and is shown in the following excerpt:

```
public static IEnumerable<TChild> GetDescendents<TChild>(
    this FrameworkElement parent) where TChild : class
{
    ArgumentValidator.AssertNotNull(parent, "parent");

    int childCount = VisualTreeHelper.GetChildrenCount(parent);
    for (int i = 0; i < childCount; i++)
    {
        DependencyObject child = VisualTreeHelper.GetChild(parent, i);
        TChild candidate = child as TChild;
```

```
if (candidate != null)
{
    yield return candidate;
}

FrameworkElement element = child as FrameworkElement;
if (element != null)
{
    /* Could be improved with tail recursion. */
    IEnumerable<TChild> descendents
                = element.GetDescendents<TChild>();
    foreach (TChild descendent in descendents)
    {
        yield return descendent;
    }
}
        }
    }
}
```

When the Submit button of the ConventionalValidationView page is tapped, all TextBoxes are retrieved and the UpdateSource method is called for each control's Text property binding. If any input validation errors are present, they are displayed in the UI (see Figure 23.8).

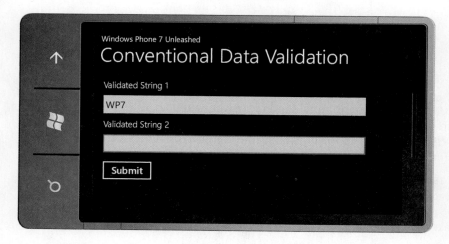

FIGURE 23.8   ConventionalValidationView page. Tapping the Submit button causes all fields to be validated.

Displaying Error Details

Highlighting an invalid field indicates that the field needs attention, but it does not tell the user why. Feedback should be provided describing the nature of the error and how it

can be corrected. In Silverlight for the browser, this is achieved using the
`ValidationSummary` control. Unfortunately, no such control exists in the Windows
Phone FCL. But that does not stop us from making our own!

A Custom `ValidationSummary` Control

Included in the downloadable sample code is a simple control for displaying all errors that
occur on a page. It is named the same as its browser counterpart: `ValidationSummary`.
When placed on a page, it retrieves the page and subscribes the page's `BindingValidation`
`Error` event during its `Loaded` event. When an unhandled validation error occurs for any
control on the page, the error is placed in an `ObservableCollection` and displayed in the
view (see Listing 23.2).

LISTING 23.2   `ValidationSummary` Class (excerpt)

```
public partial class ValidationSummary : UserControl
{
    readonly ObservableCollection<object> errors
                    = new ObservableCollection<object>();

    readonly Dictionary<string, List<object>> errorLookup
                        = new Dictionary<string, List<object>>();
    const int lineHeight = 30;

    public IEnumerable<object> Errors
    {
        get
        {
            return errors;
        }
    }

    public ValidationSummary()
    {
        InitializeComponent();
        Loaded += HandleLoaded;
    }

    bool loaded;

    void HandleLoaded(object sender, System.Windows.RoutedEventArgs e)
    {
        if (loaded)
        {
            return;
        }
        loaded = true;
```

LISTING 23.2   Continued

```csharp
        Page page = this.GetVisualAncestors<Page>().FirstOrDefault();

        if (page == null)
        {
            throw new InvalidOperationException(
                        "Unable to locate parent page.");
        }
        page.BindingValidationError += HandleBindingValidationError;
        ...
    }

    /// <summary>
    /// Performs property setter validation.
    /// </summary>
    void HandleBindingValidationError(
            object sender, ValidationErrorEventArgs e)
    {
        string content = e.Error.ErrorContent.ToString();

        if (e.Action == ValidationErrorEventAction.Added)
        {
            AddError(content);
        }
        else
        {
            RemoveError(content);
        }
    }

    void AddError(object error)
    {
        string content = error.ToString();

        if (!errors.Contains(content))
        {
            errors.Add(content);
        }
        MinHeight += lineHeight;
    }

    void RemoveError(object error)
    {
        string content = error.ToString();
```

LISTING 23.2   Continued

```
        errors.Remove(content);
        MinHeight -= lineHeight;
    }
...
}
```

The `ValidationSummary` control's XAML file contains a `ListBox`, whose `ItemsSource` has a data binding to the `Errors` property (see Listing 23.3).

LISTING 23.3   ValidationSummary Control XAML

```xml
<UserControl x:Class="DanielVaughan.WindowsPhone7Unleashed.ValidationSummary"
             x:Name="control"
...
>
    <StackPanel x:Name="LayoutRoot"
            Background="{StaticResource PhoneBackgroundBrush}">
        <ListBox ItemsSource
                ="{Binding ElementName=control, Path=Errors}">
            <ListBox.ItemTemplate>
                <DataTemplate>
                    <TextBlock Text="{Binding}"
                        Style="{StaticResource PhoneTextSmallStyle}"
                        Height="30" />
                </DataTemplate>
            </ListBox.ItemTemplate>
        </ListBox>
    </StackPanel>
</UserControl>
```

As soon as the `BindingValidationError` event is raised in the host page, the `ObservableCollection` of errors is updated, and the user is provided with detailed feedback for each validation error (see Figure 23.9).

Property Setter Validation Limitations

While the Silverlight 3 property setter validation system is simple and easy to use, it has two significant limitations: mutually dependent property validation is cumbersome, and there is no support for asynchronous validation.

The Silverlight 3 property setter validation system allows you to validate one property at a time. Some properties, however, may be mutually dependent, with the value of one property altering the validity of another property.

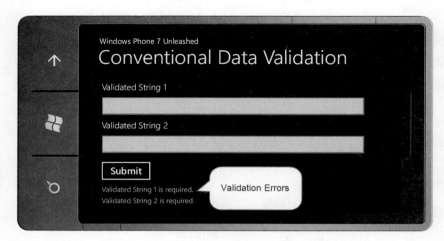

FIGURE 23.9   The `ValidationSummary` control displays validation errors as they occur.

One approach to solving this problem, while still using the property setter validation system, is to use a set of shadow properties, which perform composite semantic validation. This approach, however, falls short because it adds undue complexity and often leads to substantial code duplication.

The asynchronous validation features of Silverlight 4 decouple input validation from properties and provide a better solution where composite validation is required.

Furthermore, asynchronous validation is needed in situations such as validating input on a remote server, where asynchronous WCF service calls are performed.

Asynchronous and Composite Validation

New to Windows Phone 7.1 SDK is the `INotifyDataErrorInfo` interface, which is present in Silverlight 4. Silverlight 4 eliminates the need to rely on exceptions to indicate invalid property values. In addition, implementing `INotifyDataErrorInfo` makes it possible to evaluate the validity of a property on a secondary thread.

The `INotifyDataErrorInfo` interface contains three members (see Figure 23.10). The `HasErrors` property is used to determine whether the control contains validation errors. The `GetErrors` method returns all errors that are detected, while the `ErrorsChanged` event notifies listeners when an error has been added or removed from the set of known errors.

To enable validation using the `INotifyDataErrorInfo` interface, the binding expression's `NotifyOnValidationError` property is set to true as shown:

```
<TextBox Text="{Binding ValidatedString1, Mode=TwoWay,
                NotifyOnValidationError=True}" />
```

The next section looks at implementing `INotifyDataErrorInfo` so that it can be reused across your entire app.

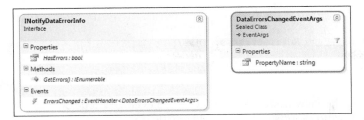

FIGURE 23.10   INotifyDataErrorInfo interface is used to monitor input validation errors.

A Reusable Implementation of the `NotifyDataErrorInfo` Interface

The `DataErrorNotifier` class in the downloadable sample code is a reusable implementation of the `INotifyDataErrorInfo` interface.

`DataErrorNotifier` makes implementing asynchronous validation easy. With the addition of a single validation method to your viewmodel, `DataErrorNotifier` manages the list of errors and takes care of raising data error events. Furthermore, validation can be restricted by registering only those properties that you want to be validated.

`DataErrorNotifier` is designed to validate classes that implement a custom `IValidateData` interface, such as the `ViewModelBase` class. The validation logic has been decoupled from the `ViewModelBase` class to be reusable for other types as well.

The `DataErrorNotifier` requires an instance of `IValidateData`. The `IValidateData` interface defines an asynchronous validation mechanism with a nonblocking `BeginValidate` method and an event to signal when validation is complete (see Figure 23.11).

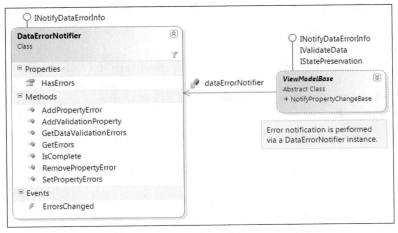

FIGURE 23.11   `DataErrorNotifier` provides validation for the `ViewModelBase` class.

The `ViewModelBase` class implements `IValidateData`. `ViewModelBase` creates an instance of the `DataErrorNotifier` class and passes itself to the `DataErrorNotifier`'s constructor, as shown:

```
protected ViewModelBase()
{
    dataErrorNotifier = new DataErrorNotifier(this, this);
...
}
```

DataErrorNotifier subscribes to the viewmodel's PropertyChanged event. When the PropertyChanged event is raised, validation is performed automatically.

The DataErrorNotifier takes responsibility for the INotifyDataErrorInfo implementation. Ordinarily, a viewmodel calls only the ViewModelBase's AddValidationProperty and IsComplete methods. Both the ViewModelBase class and the DataErrorNotifier implement INotifyDataErrorInfo. The ViewModelBase class, however, merely calls through to its DataErrorNotifier instance.

Leveraging the DataErrorNotifier Class

To register a property for validation in a viewmodel, the AddValidationProperty is called in the constructor of the viewmodel, as demonstrated in the following excerpt:

```
AddValidationProperty(() => ARequiredStringProperty);
```

AddValidationProperty causes the DataErrorNotifier to automatically attempt to validate the property when the property changes or when the viewmodel is being validated in its entirety.

The lambda expression provides the ViewModelBase class with the means to resolve both the property and the name of the property. The ViewModelBase.AddValidationProperty method retrieves the name of the property and passes it and a Func to the DataErrorNotifier, as shown:

```
protected void AddValidationProperty(Expression<Func<object>> expression)
{
    PropertyInfo propertyInfo = PropertyUtility.GetPropertyInfo(expression);
    string name = propertyInfo.Name;
    Func<object> getter = (Func<object>)Delegate.CreateDelegate(
                            typeof(Func<object>),
                            this,
                            propertyInfo.GetGetMethod());

    dataErrorNotifier.AddValidationProperty(name, getter);
}
```

`DataErrorNotifier` stores the association between the property name and the `Func`, which allows the property to be retrieved by name during validation.

The `AddValidationProperty` method of the `DataErrorNotifier` is shown in the following excerpt:

```
public void AddValidationProperty(string name, Func<object> property)
{
    lock (propertyDictionaryLock)
    {
        propertyDictionary[name] = property;
    }
}
```

Provisioning for Asynchronous or Synchronous Validation

The validation infrastructure contained in the `ViewModelBase` and the `DataErrorNotifier` classes caters for both asynchronous and synchronous validation models. When using this system, validation code should reside in one of two overridable methods: `BeginValidation` or `GetPropertyErrors`.

`BeginValidation` uses an asynchronous event driven validation model, while `GetPropertyErrors` provides for a simpler synchronous model for when asynchronous processing is not required.

DataValidationError Class

When using either the synchronous or asynchronous validation models, validation errors are represented using a custom class named `DataValidationError`. `DataValidationError` has an `ErrorMessage` property of type string and an `Id` property of type int. The purpose of the `Id` property is that it allows you to use the same error message for multiple fields.

Provisioning for Synchronous Validation

The `ViewModelBase.GetPropertyErrors` method allows your viewmodel to perform input validation using a simple synchronous approach. The `GetPropertyErrors` method is overridden to validate specific properties in your viewmodel. The method returns all errors for the specified property as an `IEnumerable<DataValidationError>`.

In the following example, the `GetPropertyErrors` method has been overridden in a viewmodel containing two properties, neither of which is allowed to be null or to consist of entirely whitespace:

```
protected override IEnumerable<DataValidationError> GetPropertyErrors(
    string propertyName, object value)
{
    if (!string.IsNullOrWhiteSpace((string)value))
    {
        yield break;
    }
```

```
    switch (propertyName)
    {
        case "ValidatedString1":
            yield return new DataValidationError(1,
                "ValidatedString1 is required.");
            break;
        case "ValidatedString2":
            yield return new DataValidationError(2,
                "ValidatedString2 is required.");
            break;
    }
    yield break;
}
```

If an exception is raised during the execution of this method, it is handled by the
ViewModelBase class. Exception handling is discussed further in the next section.

Provisioning for Asynchronous Validation

The BeginValidation method of the ViewModelBase class is the main extensibility point for
providing asynchronous validation. This method should be overridden in subclasses to
perform composite validation or validation of property values using, for example, WCF
services.

The ViewModelBase class implementation of the BeginValidation method calls the virtual
GetPropertyErrors method, which, as you saw in the preceding section, retrieves the list
of errors for a specified property. See the following excerpt:

```
public virtual void BeginValidation(string memberName, object value)
{
    IEnumerable<DataValidationError> errors;
    try
    {
        errors = GetPropertyErrors(memberName, value);
    }
    catch (Exception ex)
    {
        OnValidationComplete(
            new ValidationCompleteEventArgs(memberName, ex));
        return;
    }
    OnValidationComplete(
            new ValidationCompleteEventArgs(memberName, errors));
}
```

The base implementation of the BeginValidation method executes synchronously, retrieving the list of errors and raising the ValidationComplete event.

> **NOTE**
>
> Once the `BeginValidation` method has finished validating, it is imperative that the `ValidationComplete` event is raised; otherwise, the `DataErrorNotifier` will not raise the `INotifyDataErrorInfo.ErrorsChanged` event, which prevents the UI from signalling that a validation error exists.

The following excerpt provides an example implementation of the `BeginValidation` method:

```csharp
public override void BeginValidation(string memberName, object value)
{
    try
    {
        if (string.IsNullOrEmpty((string)value))
        {
            List<DataValidationError> errors
                = new List<DataValidationError>();
            DataValidationError error = null;

            switch (memberName)
            {
                case "ValidatedString1":
                    error = new DataValidationError(1,
                        "ValidatedString1 is required.");
                    break;
                case "ValidatedString2":
                    error = new DataValidationError(2,
                        "ValidatedString2 is required.");
                    break;
            }

            if (error != null)
            {
                errors.Add(error);
            }
            OnValidationComplete(
                new ValidationCompleteEventArgs(memberName, errors));
        }
        else
        {
            OnValidationComplete(
                new ValidationCompleteEventArgs(memberName));
        }
    }
    catch (Exception ex)
```

```
    {
        OnValidationComplete(
            new ValidationCompleteEventArgs(memberName, ex));
    }
}
```

The `ViewModelBase` class contains a string keyed `Dictionary` of errors for each property, which is of type `Dictionary<string, List<DataValidationError>>`.

Decoupling Validation

The `DataErrorNotifier` instance relies on an `IValidateData` object to perform the actual semantic validation of viewmodel property values. Thus, the strategy for validating the viewmodel can be decoupled from the viewmodel itself. In most cases, however, the viewmodel implements `IValidateData`.

Validating Properties as They Change

The `DataErrorNotifier` class subscribes to the viewmodel's `PropertyChanged` event so that when a property is changed, it is also validated. See the following excerpt:

```
public DataErrorNotifier(
    INotifyPropertyChanged owner, IValidateData validator)
{
    this.validator
            = ArgumentValidator.AssertNotNull(validator, "validator");
    ArgumentValidator.AssertNotNull(owner, "owner");

    validator.ValidationComplete += validator_ValidationComplete;
    owner.PropertyChanged += HandleOwnerPropertyChanged;
}

void HandleOwnerPropertyChanged(object sender, PropertyChangedEventArgs e)
{
    if (e == null || e.PropertyName == null)
    {
        return;
    }
    BeginGetPropertyErrorsFromValidator(e.PropertyName);
}
```

When a viewmodel property changes, a potentially asynchronous validation operation is commenced from the `BeginGetPropertyErrorsFromValidator` method, shown in the following excerpt:

```
void BeginGetPropertyErrorsFromValidator(string propertyName)
{
    Func<object> propertyFunc;
    lock (propertyDictionaryLock)
```

```
    {
        if (!propertyDictionary.TryGetValue(propertyName, out propertyFunc))
        {
            /* No property registered with that name. */
            return;
        }
    }
    validator.BeginValidation(propertyName, propertyFunc());
}
```

The `BeginGetPropertyErrorsFromValidator` method performs the following tasks:

▶ The property `Func` is retrieved from the property `Dictionary`.

▶ The property value is retrieved by invoking the property `Func`.

▶ The `BeginValidation` method of the viewmodel (implementing `IValidateData`) is called using the property name and the property value.

When the `IValidateData` finishes validating a property value, it raises the `IValidateData.ValidationComplete` event. This event is handled by the `HandleValidationComplete` method.

The first thing that the `HandleValidationComplete` method does is update the list of validation errors for the specified property. It does this by calling the `SetPropertyErrors` method, which attempts to retrieve the list of errors for that property. If the specified list of errors is different from the existing list of known errors for that property, the list of known errors is updated (or removed if empty) and the `ErrorsChanged` event is raised:

```
public void SetPropertyErrors(
    string propertyName, IEnumerable<DataValidationError> dataErrors)
{
    ArgumentValidator.AssertNotNullOrEmpty(propertyName, "propertyName");

    List<DataValidationError> list;
    bool raiseEvent = false;
    lock (errorsLock)
    {
        bool created = false;

        int paramErrorCount = dataErrors == null ? 0 : dataErrors.Count();
        if ((errorsField == null || errorsField.Count < 1)
            && paramErrorCount < 1)
        {
            return;
        }
```

```csharp
        if (errorsField == null)
        {
            errorsField
                = new Dictionary<string, List<DataValidationError>>();
            created = true;
        }

        bool listFound = false;
        if (created ||
            !(listFound = errorsField.TryGetValue(propertyName, out list)))
        {
            list = new List<DataValidationError>();
        }

        if (paramErrorCount < 1)
        {
            if (listFound)
            {
                errorsField.Remove(propertyName);
                raiseEvent = true;
            }
        }
        else
        {
            var tempList = new List<DataValidationError>();
            foreach (var dataError in dataErrors)
            {
                if (created || list.SingleOrDefault(
                    e => e.Id == dataError.Id) == null)
                {
                    tempList.Add(dataError);
                    raiseEvent = true;
                }
            }
            list.AddRange(tempList);
            errorsField[propertyName] = list;
        }
    }

    if (raiseEvent)
    {
        OnErrorsChanged(propertyName);
    }
}
```

The `OnErrorsChanged` method raises the `ErrorsChanged` event on the UI thread using the app's `Dispatcher`. An extension method is used to ensure that the method is invoked only if the thread is not the UI thread; otherwise, the delegate is called from the current thread.

```
protected virtual void OnErrorsChanged(string property)
{
    Dispatcher dispatcher = Deployment.Current.Dispatcher;
    dispatcher.InvokeIfRequired(
        delegate
        {
            ErrorsChanged.Raise(this,
                new DataErrorsChangedEventArgs(property));
        });
}
```

Asynchronous Validation of All Properties

As the user completes a form, individual properties are validated. To validate an entire form at once, the same approach is used; however, each property is validated, one by one, until all are validated, or until one is deemed invalid.

The `IsComplete` method of the `DataErrorValidator` attempts to validate each known property and accepts handlers that are invoked when one of the following three conditions is met:

▸ **completeAction**—The viewmodel is complete; that is, no properties have associated data validation errors.

▸ **incompleteAction**—The viewmodel is incomplete; that is, one or more properties has an associated data validation error.

▸ **unknownAction**—Determination of the viewmodel's completeness failed because an exception was raised.

To validate each property, the `DataErrorValidator` creates a list of all known property names, and as each property is validated, the property name is removed from the list, as shown in the following excerpt:

```
public void IsComplete(Action completeAction,
                       Action incompleteAction,
                       Action<Exception> unknownAction)
{
    this.completeAction = completeAction;
    this.incompleteAction = incompleteAction;
    this.unknownAction = unknownAction;

    try
    {
```

```
        if (!LockedOperations.TrySetTrue(
            ref isEvaluating, isEvaluatingLock))
        {
            return;
        }

        if (propertyDictionary == null)
        {
            if (completeAction != null)
            {
                completeAction();
            }
            return;
        }

        lock (waitingForPropertiesLock)
        {
            waitingForProperties.Clear();
            foreach (KeyValuePair<string, Func<object>> pair
                                            in propertyDictionary)
            {
                waitingForProperties.Add(pair.Key);
            }
        }
        foreach (KeyValuePair<string, Func<object>> pair
            in propertyDictionary)
        {
            validator.BeginValidation(pair.Key, pair.Value());
        }
    }
    catch (Exception ex)
    {
        isEvaluating = false;
        if (unknownAction != null)
        {
            unknownAction(ex);
        }
    }
}
```

The LockedOperations.TrySetTrue method provides for thread safety when reading and setting the isEvaluating flag. If isEvaluating is already true, the call to the IsComplete method is ignored, as shown:

```
public static bool TrySetTrue(ref bool value, object valueLock)
{
    ArgumentValidator.AssertNotNull(valueLock, "valueLock");
    if (!value)
    {
        lock (valueLock)
        {
            if (!value)
            {
                value = true;
                return true;
            }
        }
    }
    return false;
}
```

The TrySetTrue method reduces the amount of locking related code in the IsComplete method.

When the list of property names in the IsComplete method is empty or an exception is raised, the evaluation of the IsComplete method is deemed to be complete.

At completion, one of the three IsComplete action arguments is invoked. If the ValidationCompleteEventArgs contains an Exception, the unknownAction is invoked. If there are any data validation errors for the property, the incompleteAction is invoked. If there are no properties left to validate, the completeAction is invoked. See the following excerpt:

```
void HandleValidationComplete(object sender, ValidationCompleteEventArgs e)
{
    try
    {
        if (e.Exception == null)
        {
            SetPropertyErrors(e.PropertyName, e.Errors);
        }
    }
    catch (Exception ex)
    {
        Debug.WriteLine("Unable to set property error." + ex);
    }

    if (!isEvaluating)
    {
        return;
    }
```

```
lock (isEvaluatingLock)
{
    if (!isEvaluating)
    {
        return;
    }

    try
    {
        bool finishedEvaluating;
        lock (waitingForPropertiesLock)
        {
            waitingForProperties.Remove(e.PropertyName);
            finishedEvaluating = waitingForProperties.Count < 1;
        }

        if (e.Exception != null)
        {
            isEvaluating = false;
            if (unknownAction != null)
            {
                unknownAction(e.Exception);
            }
        }

        if (e.Errors != null && e.Errors.Count() > 0)
        {
            isEvaluating = false;
            if (incompleteAction != null)
            {
                incompleteAction();
            }
        }

        if (finishedEvaluating)
        {
            bool success = isEvaluating;
            isEvaluating = false;
            if (success && completeAction != null)
            {
                completeAction();
            }
        }
    }
    catch (Exception ex)
    {
        Debug.WriteLine("Unable to validate property." + ex);
```

```
            isEvaluating = false;
        }
    }
}
```

An Example of Asynchronous Input Validation

The downloadable sample code contains a number of examples of asynchronous input validation. The simplest of which is located in the `AsyncValidationViewModel` class.

The `AsyncValidationView` contains two string properties that are required to be non-null or whitespace strings (see Figure 23.12).

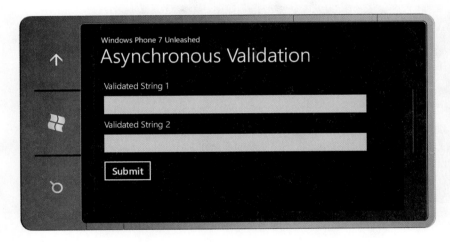

FIGURE 23.12   `AsyncValidationView` page

When either of the two properties is set to an empty or whitespace string, a data validation error is created for that property. This validation occurs when the user modifies the text or when the Submit button is tapped (see Figure 23.13).

The two `TextBox` controls are each bound to a property in the viewmodel, as shown in the following excerpt:

```xml
<StackPanel x:Name="ContentPanel" Grid.Row="1" Margin="12,60,12,0">
    <TextBlock Text="Validated String 1"
                Style="{StaticResource PhoneTextTitle3Style}" />
    <TextBox Text="{Binding ValidatedString1, Mode=TwoWay,
                            NotifyOnValidationError=True}"
                Style="{StaticResource ValidatingTextBoxStyle}" />
    <TextBlock Text="Validated String 2"
                Style="{StaticResource PhoneTextTitle3Style}" />
    <TextBox Text="{Binding ValidatedString2, Mode=TwoWay,
                            NotifyOnValidationError=True}"
```

```
                     Style="{StaticResource ValidatingTextBoxStyle}" />
        <StackPanel Orientation="Horizontal">
            <Button Content="Submit"
                Command="{Binding SubmitCommand}"
                Width="144" Height="75" HorizontalAlignment="Left" />
            <controls:ValidationSummary />
        </StackPanel>
        <TextBlock Text="{Binding Message}"
                     Style="{StaticResource PhoneTextNormalStyle}" />
    </StackPanel>
```

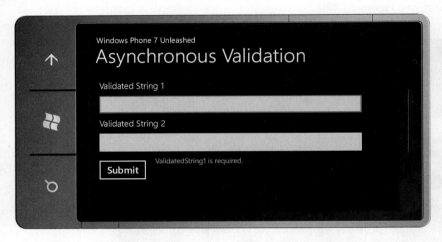

FIGURE 23.13   The Validated String 1 form field is deemed invalid.

The submit Button is bound to the viewmodel's SubmitCommand. The SubmitCommand is instantiated in the constructor of the AsyncValidationViewModel class, as shown in the following excerpt:

```
public AsyncValidationViewModel()
{
    AddValidationProperty(() => ValidatedString1);
    AddValidationProperty(() => ValidatedString2);

    submitCommand = new DelegateCommand(
        delegate
        {
            IsComplete(
                () => Message = "Data Submitted!",
                () => Message = string.Empty,
                obj => Message = "An error occured: " + obj.Message);
        });
}
```

When the button is pressed, the SubmitCommand calls the IsComplete method of the ViewModelBase class, which calls the DataErrorNotifier.IsComplete method with the same signature. Recall that the IsComplete method has the following three parameters:

▶ An Action to perform if there are no validation errors.

▶ An Action to perform if there are validation errors.

▶ A Func to perform if an exception is raised and the validation process fails.

The IsComplete method causes the overridden BeginValidation method of the AsyncValidationViewModel class to be called. Asynchronous behavior is simulated by calling a private Validate method using a thread from the ThreadPool. In a less trivial application, we could imagine that this call could be to a web service for example.

```
public override void BeginValidation(string memberName, object value)
{
    try
    {
        /* Perform validation asynchronously. */
        ThreadPool.QueueUserWorkItem(state => Validate(memberName, value));
    }
    catch (Exception ex)
    {
        OnValidationComplete(
            new ValidationCompleteEventArgs(memberName, ex));
    }
}
```

As previously stated, it is imperative that the ValidationComplete event is raised no matter what the outcome of the validation activity. Therefore, the validation logic is wrapped in a try-catch block, so that if an exception occurs, the ValidationComplete event is still raised, as shown in the following excerpt:

```
void Validate(string propertyName, object value)
{
    try
    {
        IEnumerable<DataValidationError> errors
            = GetPropertyErrors(propertyName, value);
        if (errors != null && errors.Count() > 0)
        {
            OnValidationComplete(
                new ValidationCompleteEventArgs(propertyName, errors));
        }
        else
        {
            OnValidationComplete(
```

23

```
                new ValidationCompleteEventArgs(propertyName));
        }
    }
    catch (Exception ex)
    {
        OnValidationComplete(
            new ValidationCompleteEventArgs(propertyName, ex));
    }
}
```

If either of the viewmodel's string properties fails validation, a `DataValidationError` for the property is added to the list of validation errors for that property.

Detecting a Change of Data Context

The `FrameworkElement.DataContext` property is a fundamental part of the Silverlight data binding system and allows an object to be associated with a top level element in the visual tree and then inherited by descendants of that element.

Unfortunately, Silverlight 4 for Windows Phone does not include a public event for detecting when the `DataContext` of a `FrameworkElement` is changed. As a workaround, I have included in the downloadable sample code a class named `DataContextChangedListener` that uses attached properties to emulate a `DataContextChanged` event, which allows you to receive notification when a `FrameworkElement`'s data context is changed (see Listing 23.4).

The `Subscribe` method of the `DataContextChangedListener` associates a `PropertyChangedCallback` delegate with a specified `FrameworkElement`. The delegate is invoked when a change to the `DataContextProperty` is detected.

The `HandleDataContextChanged` handler is called when the `FrameworkElement` object's `DataContext` is changed because changing the `DataContext` of the `FrameworkElement` causes all bindings for the `FrameworkElement` to be reevaluated.

The fact that the `DataContextProperty` is named DataContextProperty is arbitrary and has no effect on the association between the attached property and the `FrameworkElement.DataContext` property.

LISTING 23.4 `DataContextChangedListener` Class

```
public class DataContextChangedListener
{
    static readonly DependencyProperty DataContextProperty
        = DependencyProperty.RegisterAttached(
            "DataContextProperty",
            typeof(object),
            typeof(FrameworkElement),
            new PropertyMetadata(HandleDataContextChanged));
```

LISTING 23.4   Continued

```
static readonly DependencyProperty HandlersProperty
    = DependencyProperty.RegisterAttached(
        "HandlersProperty",
        typeof(PropertyChangedCallback),
        typeof(FrameworkElement),
        new PropertyMetadata(
            (object)((PropertyChangedCallback)(delegate { }))));

public static void Subscribe(
    FrameworkElement element, PropertyChangedCallback handler)
{
    ArgumentValidator.AssertNotNull(element, "element");
    ArgumentValidator.AssertNotNull(handler, "handler");

    PropertyChangedCallback handlers
        = (PropertyChangedCallback)element.GetValue(HandlersProperty);

    handlers += handler;

    element.SetValue(HandlersProperty, handlers);

    if (element.GetBindingExpression(DataContextProperty) == null)
    {
        element.SetBinding(DataContextProperty, new Binding());
    }
}

public static void Unsubscribe(
    FrameworkElement element, PropertyChangedCallback handler)
{
    ArgumentValidator.AssertNotNull(element, "element");
    ArgumentValidator.AssertNotNull(handler, "handler");

    PropertyChangedCallback handlers
        = (PropertyChangedCallback)element.GetValue(HandlersProperty);

    handlers -= handler;
    element.SetValue(HandlersProperty, handlers);
}

static void HandleDataContextChanged(
    DependencyObject d, DependencyPropertyChangedEventArgs e)
{
    FrameworkElement element = (FrameworkElement)d;
```

LISTING 23.4   Continued

```
        PropertyChangedCallback handlers
            = (PropertyChangedCallback)element.GetValue(HandlersProperty);

        PropertyChangedCallback tempEvent = handlers;
        if (tempEvent != null)
        {
            tempEvent(d, e);
        }
    }
}
```

The `ValidationSummary` control uses the `DataContextChangedListener` to subscribe to the `INotifyDataErrorInfo.ErrorsChanged` event of the viewmodel.

When the control is loaded, the control uses the static `DataContextChangedListener.Subscribe` method to add its `HandleDataContextChanged` method to the list of handlers.

If and when the handler is called, the control unsubscribes from the previous `INotifyDataErrorInfo` and subscribes to the new object's event. See the following excerpt:

```
void HandleLoaded(object sender, System.Windows.RoutedEventArgs e)
{
...
    DataContextChangedListener.Subscribe(this, HandleDataContextChanged);
}


void HandleDataContextChanged(
    DependencyObject d, DependencyPropertyChangedEventArgs e)
{
    /* Unsubscribe to previous notifier. */
    INotifyDataErrorInfo oldNotifier = e.OldValue as INotifyDataErrorInfo;
    if (oldNotifier != null)
    {
        oldNotifier.ErrorsChanged -= HandleErrorsChanged;
    }

    /* When the DataContext is an INotifyDataErrorInfo,
     * monitor it for errors. */
    INotifyDataErrorInfo notifier = DataContext as INotifyDataErrorInfo;
    if (notifier != null)
    {
        notifier.ErrorsChanged += HandleErrorsChanged;
    }
}
```

We can expect to see the `FrameworkElement.DataContextChanged` event made public in the next major release of the Windows Phone OS; in the meantime, however, the custom `DataContextChangedListener` is a simple solution that can be used wherever we need to respond to a change of an element's data context.

Adding `INotifyDataErrorInfo` Support to the `ValidationSummary` Control

Now that you have looked at the `INotifyDataErrorInfo` interface and at the inner workings of the custom validation system, let us examine how the `ValidationSummary` control has been extended to support the `INotifyDataErrorInfo` interface.

As you saw in the previous section, the `ValidationSummary` control monitors its data context for validation errors if the data context implements `INotifyDataErrorInfo`. When the `INotifyDataErrorInfo.ErrorsChanged` event is raised by the data context, the control's `HandleErrorsChanged` handler is called (see Listing 23.5).

`ValidationSummary` maintains a dictionary of validation errors, which are keyed by the associated property name. The `HandleErrorsChanged` method retrieves the list of validation errors from the `INotifyDataErrorInfo` and combines the list with the list in its own dictionary. If no list exists for the particular property name, then a new list is added to the dictionary.

LISTING 23.5   `ValidationSummary.HandleErrorsChanged` Method

```
void HandleErrorsChanged(object sender, DataErrorsChangedEventArgs args)
{
    INotifyDataErrorInfo notifier = sender as INotifyDataErrorInfo;
    if (notifier == null)
    {
        return;
    }

    string propertyName = args.PropertyName;
    if (string.IsNullOrEmpty(propertyName))
    {
        return;
    }

    IEnumerable notifierErrors = notifier.GetErrors(args.PropertyName);

    List<object> errorList;
    if (!errorLookup.TryGetValue(propertyName, out errorList))
    {
        errorList = new List<object>();
    }
```

LISTING 23.5   Continued

```
    foreach (var error in errorList)
    {
        RemoveError(error);
    }

    errorList.Clear();

    foreach (var error in notifierErrors)
    {
        AddError(error);
    }
    errorLookup[propertyName] = errorList;

    foreach (var error in errorList)
    {
        AddError(error);
    }
}
```

The ValidationSummary control now has support for both the property setter validation approach and for the Silverlight 4 INotifyDataErrorInfo validation approach.

Incorporating Group Validation

In the previous example, you saw how the ViewModelBase.IsComplete method is used to trigger validation of a viewmodel. This section looks at extending the validation to set control-enabled states based on the presence of validation errors and at hiding validation errors until the user has had a chance to fill out the form.

Before proceeding, you may want to briefly review the section "Performing Group Validation" earlier in the chapter and in particular Figure 23.7.

The SendEmailViewModel in the downloadable sample code is a more complex example of asynchronous input validation. In it, the sendEmailCommand is prevented from executing if it is already in execution or if the form is invalid.

When SendEmailView is first displayed, the Send button is enabled and no validation errors are displayed (see Figure 23.14).

When the Send button is tapped, the viewmodel is validated. If invalid, the Send button is disabled (see Figure 23.15).

FIGURE 23.14   SendEmailView page. The Send button is enabled and no validation errors are shown, even though the form is not complete.

FIGURE 23.15   SendEmailView page. The Send button is disabled once the form is deemed incomplete.

The Send button is bound to the viewmodel's `ICommand` named `SendEmailCommand`, as shown:

```
<Button Content="Send"
        Command="{Binding SendEmailCommand}" />
```

Evaluation of whether the command can execute depends on the following criteria:

- ▶ If the command is in execution, it cannot be executed.
- ▶ If an attempt to execute the command has not occurred before, it can be executed.
- ▶ If the viewmodel has validation errors, it cannot be executed.

`SendEmailCommand` is instantiated in the viewmodel constructor, as shown:

```
sendEmailCommand = new DelegateCommand(arg => SendEmail(),
                        arg => !sending && (!sendAttempted || !HasErrors));
```

The `SendEmail` method passes three Lambda expressions to the `ViewModelBase` class's `IsComplete` method (see Listing 23.6). The first action is performed if the form is deemed complete, in which case an `EmailComposeTask` is used to dispatch the email. The second action is performed if the form is not complete, and the third displays a warning message if an error is raised.

LISTING 23.6   `SendEmailViewModel.Send` Method

```
void SendEmail()
{
    if (sending)
    {
        return;
    }

    try
    {
        sending = sendAttempted = true;
        Message = string.Empty;
        RefreshCommands();
        IsComplete(() =>
                    {
                        sending = false;
                        EmailComposeTaskAdapter task = getEmailTaskAdapter();
                        task.Body = body;
                        task.Cc = cc;
                        task.Subject = subject;
                        task.To = to;
                        task.Show();
```

LISTING 23.6   Continued

```
            },
            () =>
            {
                sending = false;
                RefreshCommands();
            },
            obj =>
            {
                sending = false;
                RefreshCommands();
                string errorMessage = obj != null
                            ? obj.Message : string.Empty;
                Message = "Unable to send email: "
                            + errorMessage;
            });
    }
    catch (Exception ex)
    {
        sending = false;
        Message = "Unable to send email: " + ex.Message;
    }
}
```

A call to `RefreshCommands` raises the `CanExecuteChanged` event of the command, which in turn sets the `IsEnabled` property of the Button:

```
void RefreshCommands()
{
    sendEmailCommand.RaiseCanExecuteChanged();
}
```

Summary

This chapter began by defining the two types of input validation: syntactic and semantic. Syntactic validation ensures that user input has the correct format and can be converted to the correct type, while semantic validation may entail more complex validation such as the evaluation of business rules.

This chapter then looked at the Silverlight 3 property setter validation system. You saw how this system relies on the raising of exceptions to indicate validation errors. Noncritical exceptions raised in property setters produce binding errors, which signal validation errors.

You saw how Silverlight for Windows Phone requires custom templates for enabling visualization of input validation errors, and you looked at using Expression Blend to copy and customize the way error related visual states are displayed.

Finally, the chapter examined the Silverlight 4 validation system, which enables asynchronous and composite input validation. You looked at setting control enabled states based on the presence of validation errors and at hiding validation errors until the user has had a chance to fill out the form.

CHAPTER 24

Network Services

Network services have the potential to broaden your app's capabilities by connecting it to a vast collection of online resources. Many services such as Twitter and Facebook offer web APIs that allow your app to interact or even extend the services.

Windows Phone devices have low power mobile processors, which limit their processing power. By leveraging network services, your app can provide capabilities more akin to a desktop application.

This chapter begins by looking at the types of network services available on the phone. It then looks at monitoring network connectivity and at determining the type of network connection that the phone is using—Wi-Fi or cellular—enabling you to tailor the amount of data traffic your app uses accordingly.

Finally, the chapter focuses on the Open Data Protocol (OData) and how to create an app that consumes the eBay OData service. The chapter examines a useful custom component that allows your app to fetch data from a service as soon as the user scrolls to the end of a ListBox.

Network Service Technologies

Windows Phone provides various ways of consuming network services, including the following:

▶ **SOAP services**—SOAP stands for Simple Object Access Protocol. SOAP uses an XML format. In Windows Phone, SOAP services are usually consumed using Windows Communication Foundation (WCF).

▶ **REST services**—REST stands for Representational State Transfer. REST relies on HTTP and uses unique URLs to identify resource entities. CRUD (Create Read

Update Delete) operations are performed using HTTP GET, POST, PUT, and DELETE. Various open-source projects are available for consuming REST services.

▶ **OData**—OData stands for Open Data Protocol. It is a web protocol for querying and updating data. OData is the main topic of this chapter.

▶ **Plain HTTP services**—Some services are provided using nonstandardized protocols, where HTTP GET requests are used to consume an API. For example, Google search can be queried using a URL, and the results returned in JSON.

Silverlight for Windows Phone clients can access these services directly, or in the case of WCF or OData, may use a proxy that is generated from the service's published metadata.

Visual Studio generates proxy classes for SOAP and OData services by selecting the Add Service Reference from the Project menu.

A network service can be hosted on your own server or on the cloud. It may be a service that you have written in-house, or it could also be a third-party service where you can query the service but may not have access to its source code.

Monitoring Network Connectivity

While most phones have a data plan from a cellular network provider, a network connection will most likely not be available at all times. In fact, in some areas it can be difficult staying connected to a network. Therefore, it is imperative that your app is engineered to be resilient to network disruptions.

Furthermore, awareness of the type of network connection that the device is using allows you to tailor the volume of data traffic that it uses. When connected to a local area network via Wi-Fi or a USB cable, it may be acceptable for an app to download large data files. Conversely, depleting a user's cellular broadband connection by transferring a lot of data is probably not acceptable.

Connection Priorities

The Windows Phone OS automatically chooses a connection type based on the following ordered priorities:

▶ Network connection to a PC via the Zune software or the Windows Phone Connect Tool.

▶ Wi-Fi

▶ Mobile broadband

For more information on the Windows Phone Connect Tool, see Chapter 18, "Extending the Windows Phone Picture Viewer."

A network connection via a PC is favored above all other connection types. The phone periodically checks whether a higher priority connection is available and switches connections accordingly.

The API for determining the connection status of the device is located in the Microsoft.Phone.Net.NetworkInformation and System.Net.NetworkInformation namespaces. Within this API is an event for notification when a connection change occurs.

The System.Net.NetworkInformation.NetworkInterface class and the System.Net.NetworkInformation.NetworkChange class represent the non-phone specific portion of the API, while the Microsoft.Phone.Net.NetworkInformation.NetworkInterface inherits from System.Net.NetworkInformation.NetworkInterface and is specific to the phone (see Figure 24.1).

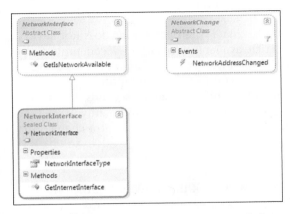

FIGURE 24.1   Network connection related classes

The NetworkInterface.GetIsNetworkAvailable method allows you to determine whether any network connection is available; however, there is one caveat (see the following note).

> **NOTE**
>
> GetIsNetworkAvailable is not always a *true* indicator of whether a useable network is available. A network connection is considered to be available if any network interface is marked "up" and is not a loopback or tunnel interface. There are cases where the phone may not be connected to a network, yet a network is still considered available, and GetIsNetworkAvailable returns true.

An alternative and albeit more reliable method for determining network availability is the NetworkInterface.NetworkInterfaceType property. While the NetworkInterfaceType enum includes many values, the phone implementation supports only the following five values:

▶ **None**—Indicates that no network connection is established.

▶ **MobileBroadbandCdma**—Indicates a connection to a CDMA cellular network.

▶ **MobileBroadbandGsm**—Indicates a connection to a GSM cellular network.

▶ **Ethernet**—Indicates a network connection is established via a PC. Ordinarily, this is done with a USB cable.

▶ **Wireless80211**—Indicates a Wi-Fi connection is established to a LAN.

To determine whether the phone is connected to a network, the NetworkInterfaceType property can be compared to the NetworkInterfaceType.None enum value, as shown:

```
bool connected = NetworkInterface.NetworkInterfaceType
                            != NetworkInterfaceType.None;
```

The NetworkInterfaceType.None value represents a state where the phone does not have Internet access. As Dolhai points out in an article available at http://www.codeproject.com/KB/windows-phone-7/ZuneDetectAndNetworking.aspx, under some circumstances, such as disconnecting the phone from an Ethernet connection, reading the NetworkInterfaceType property can block the calling thread for many seconds. It is advisable, therefore, to read the property from a background thread. In a moment you see how to do that using a custom class, but first let us briefly look at how to monitor changes to the network connection state.

Monitoring Connection Events

The NetworkChange.NetworkAddressChanged event is raised if the IP address of the phone changes and typically occurs when any of the following events occur:

▶ The device connects to, or disconnects from, a Wi-Fi or mobile network.

▶ The phone is linked to the PC via the Zune software or the Windows Phone Connect Tool.

▶ The phone is unlinked from the PC when either the Zune software or the Windows Phone Connect Tool is closed or when the USB cable is disconnected.

NOTE

When linked to a PC with no Internet connection present (via the Zune software or Windows Phone Connect Tool), the phone device does not automatically switch to an available Wi-Fi connection.

When the phone switches connections, the NetworkAddressChanged event may be raised several times. This can be troublesome if your event handler performs some expensive task. To remedy this, the custom NetworkConnectionMonitor class, provided in the downloadable sample code, uses Rx (Reactive Extensions) to sample the event so that, at most, only one NetworkAddressChanged event is raised each second (see Listing 24.1).

When the event is handled, the `NetworkConnectionMonitor.Update` method is called, which sets the network connection type and raises the `NetworkConnectionMonitor.NetworkConnectionChanged` event on the UI thread.

For more information on Rx, see Chapter 15, "Geographic Location."

LISTING 24.1   `NetworkConnectionMonitor` Class

```
public class NetworkConnectionMonitor : INetworkConnectionMonitor
{
    const int sampleRateMs = 1000;
    IDisposable subscription;

    public event EventHandler<EventArgs> NetworkConnectionChanged;
    public NetworkConnectionType NetworkConnectionType  { get; private set; }

    public bool Connected
    {
        get
        {
            return NetworkConnectionType != NetworkConnectionType.None;
        }
    }

    public NetworkConnectionMonitor()
    {
        Update();

        var observable
            = Observable.FromEvent<NetworkAddressChangedEventHandler, EventArgs>(
                handler => new NetworkAddressChangedEventHandler(handler),
                handler => NetworkChange.NetworkAddressChanged += handler,
                handler => NetworkChange.NetworkAddressChanged -= handler);

        IObservable<IEvent<EventArgs>> sampler
            = observable.Sample(TimeSpan.FromMilliseconds(sampleRateMs));

        subscription = sampler.ObserveOn(Scheduler.ThreadPool).Subscribe(
                                                    args => Update());
    }

    void Update()
    {
        switch (NetworkInterface.NetworkInterfaceType)
        {
            case NetworkInterfaceType.None:
                NetworkConnectionType = NetworkConnectionType.None;
```

LISTING 24.1   Continued

```
            break;
        case NetworkInterfaceType.MobileBroadbandCdma:
        case NetworkInterfaceType.MobileBroadbandGsm:
            NetworkConnectionType = NetworkConnectionType.MobileBroadband;
            break;
        /* These values do not apply to Windows Phone. */
        case NetworkInterfaceType.AsymmetricDsl:
        case NetworkInterfaceType.Atm:
        /* Content omitted. */
        /* Phone values */
        case NetworkInterfaceType.Ethernet:
        case NetworkInterfaceType.Wireless80211:
        default:
            NetworkConnectionType = NetworkConnectionType.Lan;
            break;
    }

    Deployment.Current.Dispatcher.BeginInvoke(new Action(
        () => NetworkConnectionChanged.Raise(this, EventArgs.Empty)));
    }
}
```

The custom NetworkConnectionMonitor class does not expose a NetworkInterfaceType property since only three values apply to the phone. Instead, it uses a custom enum type called NetworkConnectionType, which provides a simplified view on the type of connection with the following three values:

▶ **None**—Indicates that no network connection is established

▶ **Lan**—Indicates that a connection to a local area network is established, and that the app can probably be more indulgent with the amount of data it transfers

▶ **MobileBroadband**—Indicates that the phone is using a cellular network and that data usage should be used more sparingly, if at all

To use the NetworkConnectionMonitor, define it as a field in your class and subscribe to the NetworkConnectionChanged event, as shown:

```
readonly INetworkConnectionMonitor networkConnectionMonitor;

public YourViewModel()
{
    networkConnectionMonitor = new NetworkConnectionMonitor();
    networkConnectionMonitor.NetworkConnectionChanged
        += delegate
```

```
        {
            WebServiceAvailable = networkConnectionMonitor.Connected;
            CanPerformDownloadLargeFile
                = networkConnectionMonitor.NetworkConnectionType
                                == NetworkConnectionType.Lan;
        };
}
```

Alternatively, an implementation of the INetworkConnectionMonitor can be passed to the viewmodel, allowing it to be replaced with a mock for unit testing. This is demonstrated later in this chapter.

Introduction to OData

The example app for this section consumes live eBay data, which is exposed using the Open Data Protocol (OData). OData is a web protocol for querying and updating data. It defines operations on resources using HTTP verbs (PUT, POST, UPDATE, and DELETE), and it identifies those resources using a standard URI syntax. Data is transferred over HTTP using the AtomPub or JSON standards. For AtomPub, the OData protocol defines some conventions on the standard to support the exchange of query and schema information.

For in-depth information on the OData standard, visit http://odata.org.

A key advantage of the OData protocol is its accessibility by a broad range of clients. Client libraries are available for Windows Phone, iPhone, Silverlight 4, PHP, AJAX/Javascript, Ruby, and Java.

An OData service can be implemented on any server that supports HTTP. The .NET implementation is supported through WCF Data Services, which is a .NET Framework component that used to be known as ADO.Net Data Services (codename Astoria). WCF Data Services provides a framework for creating OData web services and includes a set of client libraries (one for the desktop CLR, and one for the Silverlight CLR) for building clients that consume OData feeds.

Services that expose their data using the OData protocol are referred to as OData producers, and clients that consume data exposed using the OData protocol are referred to as consumers. OData producers allow CRUD operations to be performed using query string parameters. The odata.org website provides a list of current producers and consumers. Among the producers, there are applications such as SharePoint 2010, Windows Azure Storage, and IBM WebSphere, as well as several live OData services such as the eBay data service, which is used in the sample app.

Consuming OData

The OData tools that accompany the Windows Phone SDK have been much improved since the first release of Windows Phone. In the first release, an external tool had to be downloaded and used to generate the OData service proxies. In addition, the LINQ interpreter on the phone did not support closures on local variables, which meant that using a variable inside a LINQ expression caused a runtime failure. That made LINQ to OData on the phone mostly unusable. This has since been rectified, and service proxies can now be generated using the Add Service Reference dialog.

Before you see how to create an OData consumer using LINQ, you should become familiar with the OData URI syntax.

OData URI Structure

A URI used by an OData consumer has up to three significant parts, as follows:

- ▶ A service root URI
- ▶ A resource path
- ▶ Query string options

An example of an OData URI is
http://ebayodata.cloudapp.net/Items?search=mobile&$top=5&$skip=5.

The components of this URI are then broken down as follows:

- ▶ http://ebayodata.cloudapp.net is the service root.
- ▶ /Items is the resource path.
- ▶ search=phone&$top=3&$skip=5 are the query string options.

If you use IE to navigate to this URI, you should see something like Figure 24.2. The page shows real eBay items for sale. The query retrieves three items—the sixth, seventh, and eighth items from a search result set—that match the phrase *phone*. This was done using the query string parameters *search*, *$top*, and *$skip*.

IE has a built-in feed reader that is enabled by default. A quick way to view the XML result is to right-click on the page and select View Source. This is a nuisance when developing, however, and you may prefer to disable the feed reader instead.

To disable the feed reader within IE, complete the following steps:

1. Select the Tools menu.
2. Select the Internet Options submenu.
3. Select the Content tab.
4. Click on the Settings button of Feed and Web Slices section to present the Feed Settings dialog.
5. Uncheck the Turn on Feed Reading View option.
6. Click OK, closing all dialog boxes.

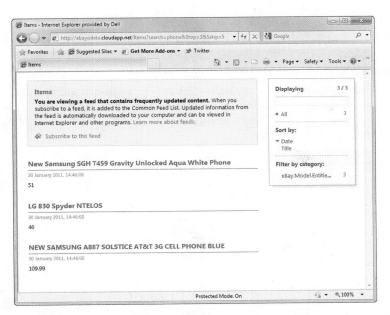

FIGURE 24.2   By default, IE presents the query result using its built-in feed reader.

Once the feed reader has been switched off, the entire XML query result can be viewed with syntax highlighting, as shown in Figure 24.3.

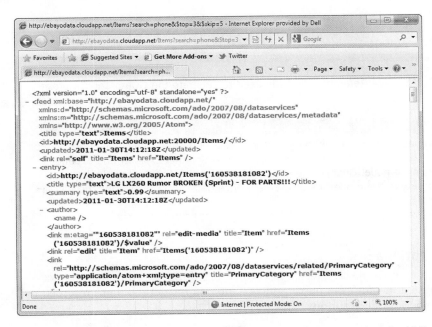

FIGURE 24.3   Disabling the built-in feed reader allows you to view the XML.

In this case, the format of the XML is an Atom feed. Some services are capable of supporting other formats, which can be specified using the $format query option.

Generating an OData Proxy

To generate the proxies for the eBay OData service, right-click on the project node in the Visual Studio Solution Explorer and select Add Service Reference. The Add Service Reference is displayed, allowing you to enter the OData service URL (see Figure 24.4).

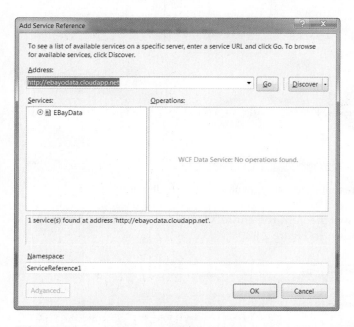

FIGURE 24.4   Add Service Reference dialog is used to generate the OData service proxies.

> **TIP**
>
> Changing the namespace of the generated service proxy and entity classes can be achieved by selecting Show All Files in the Visual Studio Solution Explorer and expanding the Service Reference node. Change the namespace by setting the Custom Tool Namespace property in the properties of the Reference.datasvcmap file using the Visual Studio properties pane.

OData Query Options

To retrieve data from an OData service, a URI is constructed that specifies the resources that you are interested in—for example, Products—and you restrict the items returned by the service using various query options.

The following are the three types of OData query string options:

▶ **System query options**—System query options are used to control the amount and order of the data that an OData service returns for the resource identified by the URI. The names of all System Query Options are prefixed with a "$" character. Not all system query options need to be supported by a producer. If not supported, the server should return an HTTP status code 405 (Method Not Allowed). The following is a summary list of OData system query options defined by the standard:

  ▶ **$orderby**—This option allows you to order the results of a query by an entity property. For example, to retrieve the list of eBay product categories ordered by Name, the following query could be used: http://ebayodata.cloudapp.net/ Categories?$orderby=Name.

  ▶ **$top**—This option allows you to select the first N items from a result set— where N is positive integer specified in the query. For example, the following query selects the first five items from the complete list of eBay items: http://ebayodata.cloudapp.net/Items?$top=5.

  ▶ **$skip**—This option allows you to select items that occur after a particular index in the result set and is useful when performing paging. By default, an OData service usually limits the number of items returned at any one time. In the case of the eBay OData service, this limit is 500 items. The $skip option, in conjunction with the $top option, can be used to page through results.

  ▶ **$filter**—This option allows you to restrict the results to those matching the specified criteria. The $filter option supports various logical, arithmetic, and grouping operators, as well as a set of functions such as substringof. See the OData website http://www.odata.org/developers/protocols/uri-conventions# QueryStringOptions for more information on the $filter option.

  ▶ **$expand**—This option allows you to retrieve a graph of entities. For example, rather than retrieving the first three product categories and then the products within those three categories in another query, by using the $expand option you are able to retrieve them all at once. This is done as shown in the following example: http://services.odata.org/OData/OData.svc/Categories?$top= 3&$expand=Products.

  The syntax of an $expand query option is a comma-separated list of navigation properties. Additionally, each navigation property can be followed by a forward slash and another navigation property to enable identifying a multilevel relationship.

  ▶ **$format**—This option allows you to specify the format of the response. Valid $format values include Atom, XML, and JSON. The $format value may also be set to a custom value specific to a particular OData service.

  ▶ **$select**—This option allows you to retrieve only the data that you are interested in and can be important for performance when working with OData on the phone. The value of a $select option is a comma-separated list of selection

24

clauses. Each selection clause may be a property name, navigation property name, or the "*" character. To select only the names of the top five search results for the phrase *phone*, the following query could be used: http://ebayodata.cloudapp.net/Items?search=phone&$top=5&$select=Title.

▶ **$inlinecount**—This option allows you to retrieve a count of the number of items in a result set, along with the entity elements. When combined with a $top option of 0 (specified by &$top=0), you can retrieve the number of items in a set without having to go to the trouble of downloading unnecessary bytes.

▶ **Custom query options**—Custom query options are specific to the OData service that uses them. They differ in that they are not prefixed by a $ symbol. The following is an example of a custom query option, where *xname* is the parameter name, and *xvalue* is its value: http://services.odata.org/OData/OData.svc/Products?*xname=xvalue*.

▶ **Service operation parameters**—A service operation is a function specific to the particular OData service. Service operation parameters work much like custom query options, where key/value pairs are provided to a custom function as arguments. For example, a service operation exists on the OData sample website that retrieves all products with a particular rating. The rating is specified using the *rating* service operation parameter, as shown: http://services.odata.org/OData/OData.svc/GetProductsByRating?rating=5.

Using an OData Proxy

To query an OData producer, such as the eBay OData service, first create an instance of the generated OData model class, using the service root URI, like so:

```
EBayData ebayData = new EBayData(new Uri("http://ebayodata.cloudapp.net/"));
```

We then create a DataServiceCollection, which is used to query the OData service asynchronously and to populate itself with the objects representing items in the response feed. The DataServiceCollection type inherits from ObservableCollection, which means it supports INotifyCollectionChanged out of the box, and it can be used directly within the user interface.

To instantiate a DataServiceCollection, an OData model instance is passed to its constructor, like so:

```
searchResult = new DataServiceCollection<Item>(ebayData);
```

Because the DataServiceCollection queries the OData producer asynchronously, we subscribe to its LoadCompleted handler to be notified when the query has completed, as shown in the following example:

```
searchResult.LoadCompleted
    += (sender, args) =>
    {
        if (args.Error != null)
        {
            /* Handle search error. */
        }
    };
```

Subscribing to the LoadCompleted event is, however, optional. Regardless of whether it is handled, if an error does not occur, then the collection is populated automatically once the call completes.

A second URI is used to specify the resources and query options:

```
var itemsUri = new Uri("/Items?search=phone&$top=5&$select=Title",
    UriKind.Relative);
```

This second URI is then used to fetch the results, using the LoadAsync method of the DataServiceCollection:

```
searchResult.LoadAsync(itemsUri);
```

Alternatively, a DataServiceQuery can be created, which eliminates the manual creation of the request URI, as shown:

```
IQueryable<Item> serviceQuery
= ebayData.Items.AddQueryOption("search", "phone")
                .AddQueryOption("$top", 5);
```

With an IQueryable<T> the search results can be further restricted using LINQ to OData, as demonstrated in the following example:

```
serviceQuery = from item in serviceQuery
               where item.CurrentPrice > 100.0
               select item;


searchResult.LoadAsync(serviceQuery);
```

When the query completes, the searchResult DataServiceCollection is automatically populated with strongly typed objects representing the resource; in this case it produces eBay Item objects.

Although OData is a standard, OData services differ in their coverage of query options; all query options are not provided by all services. Be sure to read any relevant documentation for the OData service that you intend to consume in your app.

The full API documentation for the eBay OData service can be found at http://ebayodata.cloudapp.net/docs.

Building an eBay OData Consumer Application

This section creates an eBay search app that uses the eBay OData service to search for items and to present search results on a page. The section also looks at how to retrieve data on demand when the user scrolls to the bottom of the ListBox.

Creating an OData Wrapper

The previous section looked at querying an OData service using the OData model class. While accessing the OData service model classes directly from a viewmodel is possible, it can make unit testing difficult because it relies on the actual OData producer.

In the sample for this chapter, an intermediary class called EbayClient performs all OData queries. EbayClient implements the custom IEbayClient interface, shown in the following excerpt:

```
public interface IEbayClient
{
    void SearchItemsAsync(string query,
                          int beginIndex = 0, int maxItems = 0);
    event EventHandler<SearchItemsCompleteEventArgs> SearchItemsComplete;
}
```

By using the IEbayClient interface and not a concrete implementation, we are able to substitute the EbayClient implementation for a mock type to enable testing of the user interface without needing to send data over the wire.

The IEbayClient interface is designed to be used asynchronously; the SearchItemsAsync method has a void return type, and an event is used to signal that the call has completed. When the search completes, the SearchItemsComplete method is raised using a custom extension method (see Listing 24.2).

The static HttpUtility.UrlEncode method transforms any special characters entered by the user into URL compatible characters. This prevents the user from injecting OData query options or inadvertently causing the request to fail.

LISTING 24.2   EbayClient Class

```
public class EbayClient : IEbayClient
{
    DataServiceCollection<Item> searchResult;

    public void SearchItemsAsync(string query,
                                 int beginIndex = 0, int maxItems = 0)
    {
        EBayData ebayData
                = new EBayData(new Uri("http://ebayodata.cloudapp.net/"));

        searchResult = new DataServiceCollection<Item>(ebayData);
```

LISTING 24.2   Continued

```
        searchResult.LoadCompleted
            += (sender, args) =>
                {
                    if (args.Error != null)
                    {
                        SearchItemsComplete.Raise(this,
                            new SearchItemsCompleteEventArgs(
                                null, query, args.Error));
                        return;
                    }
                    SearchItemsComplete.Raise(this,
                        new SearchItemsCompleteEventArgs(searchResult, query));
                };

        string parameter = HttpUtility.UrlEncode(query);

        IQueryable<Item> serviceQuery
            = ebayData.Items.AddQueryOption("search", parameter)
                        .AddQueryOption("$skip", beginIndex)
                        .AddQueryOption("$top", maxItems);

        //serviceQuery = from item in serviceQuery
        //                where item.CurrentPrice > 100.0
        //                select item;

        searchResult.LoadAsync(serviceQuery);
    }

    public event EventHandler<SearchItemsCompleteEventArgs> SearchItemsComplete;
}
```

The SearchItemsCompleteEventArgs class extends the custom ResultEventArgs, which contains the result produced by the OData proxy, the type of which is defined by a generic parameter. An optional parameter allows it to supply an Exception instance if the call fails (see Listing 24.3).

LISTING 24.3   ResultEventArgs Class

```
public class ResultEventArgs<T> : EventArgs
{
    public T Result { get; private set; }
    public Exception Error { get; private set; }

    public ResultEventArgs(T result, Exception error = null)
```

LISTING 24.3 Continued

```
    {
        Result = result;
        Error = error;
    }
}
```

The `SearchItemsCompleteEventArgs` adds a string `Query` property, which identifies the original query (see Listing 24.4).

LISTING 24.4 SearchItemsCompleteEventArgs Class

```
public class SearchItemsCompleteEventArgs
    : ResultEventArgs<ObservableCollection<Item>>
{
    public string Query { get; private set; }

    public SearchItemsCompleteEventArgs(
        ObservableCollection<Item> result, string query, Exception error = null)
        : base(result, error)
    {
        Query = query;
    }
}
```

The sample also comprises a view named `EbaySearchView` and its viewmodel: `EbaySearchViewModel`.

EbaySearchViewModel Class

The viewmodel uses the `IEbayClient` instance to query the eBay OData service. The viewmodel exposes two commands:

▶ **SearchCommand**—Triggered by entering text into a `TextBox` in the view, this command calls the `Search` method, which calls the `IEbayClient`'s `SearchItemsAsync` method.

▶ **FetchMoreDataCommand**—This command allows the search results to be paged.

The commands are initialized in the `EbaySearchViewModel` constructor, which is shown in the following excerpt:

```
public EbaySearchViewModel(
    Func<IEbayClient> getEbayClientFunc,
    INetworkConnectionMonitor networkConnectionMonitor)
{
    this.networkConnectionMonitor = ArgumentValidator.AssertNotNull(
                networkConnectionMonitor, "networkConnectionMonitor");
```

```
this.getEbayClientFunc = ArgumentValidator.AssertNotNull(
                    getEbayClientFunc, "getEbayClientFunc");

networkConnectionMonitor.NetworkConnectionChanged
    += (sender, args) => UpdateCommands();

SearchText = "star wars action figure";

searchCommand = new DelegateCommand<string>(
    query =>
    {
        if (!string.IsNullOrEmpty(query))
        {
            Search(query);
        }
    }, obj => networkConnectionMonitor.Connected);

fetchMoreDataCommand = new DelegateCommand(
    obj =>
    {
        if (!string.IsNullOrEmpty(lastQuery))
        {
            Search(lastQuery, true);
        }
    }, obj => networkConnectionMonitor.Connected);
}
```

The enabled state of each command depends on the `Connected` property of the `INetworkConnectionMonitor`. When the `NetworkConnectionChanged` event is raised, the viewmodel's `UpdateCommands` method is called, which calls the `RaiseCanExecuteChanged` method on each command, causing their `Enabled` state to be reevaluated:

```
void UpdateCommands()
{
    searchCommand.RaiseCanExecuteChanged();
    fetchMoreDataCommand.RaiseCanExecuteChanged();
}
```

The viewmodel's `Search` method uses a `Func` named `getEbayClientFunc` to retrieve an `IEbayClient` (see Listing 24.5). The `Search` method sets the viewmodel's `Busy` property to true, causing a `PerformanceProgressBar` in the view to be made visible.

To reduce the amount of data retrieved from the OData service, the number of records retrieved by the `IEbayClient` is restricted to 10.

LISTING 24.5   `EbaySearchViewModel.Search` Method and Related Members

```
const int chunkSize = 10;
string lastQuery;
bool appendResult;

void Search(string query, bool append = false)
{
    if (lastQuery == query && Busy)
    {
        return;
    }

    lastQuery = query;
    appendResult = append;

    IEbayClient ebayClient = getEbayClientFunc();
    ebayClient.SearchItemsComplete -= HandleEbayClientSearchItemsComplete;
    ebayClient.SearchItemsComplete += HandleEbayClientSearchItemsComplete;
    int beginIndex = appendResult ? Items.Count : 0;

    try
    {
        Busy = true;
        ebayClient.SearchItemsAsync(query, beginIndex, chunkSize);
    }
    catch (Exception ex)
    {
        Busy = false;
        Console.WriteLine("Unable to perform search." + ex);
        MessageService.ShowError("Unable to perform search.");
    }
}
```

If the call to `SearchItemsAsync` fails immediately, then the `ViewModelBase` class's `MessageService` is used to present a dialog to the user.

For more information on the `MessageService`, see Chapter 2, "Fundamental Concepts in Silverlight Development for Windows Phone."

When the search completes, the `HandleEbayClientSearchItemsComplete` handler is called. Old requests are ignored. The method returns immediately if the search query does not match the last query (see Listing 24.6).

If the search was not a new search but a request to fetch the next page of the current search results, the results are added to the end of the `Items` collection.

LISTING 24.6   EbaySearchViewModel.HandleEbayClientSearchItemsComplete Method

```
void HandleEbayClientSearchItemsComplete(
    object sender, SearchItemsCompleteEventArgs args)
{
    /* Ignore old query results. */
    if (args.Query != lastQuery)
    {
        return;
    }

    Busy = false;
    if (args.Error == null)
    {
        if (args.Result.Count > 0)
        {
            if (appendResult)
            {
                foreach (var item in args.Result)
                {
                    Items.Add(item);
                }
            }
            else
            {
                Items = new ObservableCollection<Item>(args.Result);
            }
        }
        else
        {
            MessageService.ShowMessage("No match found.");
        }
    }
    else
    {
        MessageService.ShowError(
            "An error occured while attempting to search.");
    }
}
```

EbaySearchView Page

When the viewmodel is created within the view, it receives a Func that allows it to resolve the EbayClient (see Listing 24.7).

The view contains a TextBox to allow the user to enter a search query.

The view subscribes to the KeyUp event of the TextBox, which allows the app to detect when the user taps the Enter key on the Software Input Panel (SIP) and to execute the viewmodel object's SearchCommand.

LISTING 24.7   EbaySearchView Class

```
public partial class EbaySearchView : PhoneApplicationPage
{
    public EbaySearchView()
    {
        InitializeComponent();
        DataContext = new EbaySearchViewModel(
            () => new EbayClient(), new NetworkConnectionMonitor());
    }

    EbaySearchViewModel ViewModel
    {
        get
        {
            return (EbaySearchViewModel)DataContext;
        }
    }

    void TextBox_KeyUp(object sender, KeyEventArgs e)
    {
        if (e.Key == Key.Enter)
        {
            e.Handled = true;
            TextBox textBox = (TextBox)sender;
            this.Focus();
            ViewModel.SearchCommand.Execute(textBox.Text);
        }
    }
}
```

The view contains a ListBox for displaying search results (see Listing 24.8). The ListBox contains a custom attached property ScrollViewerMonitor.AtEndCommand, which automatically causes the ListBox to be populated with more records when the user scrolls to end of the list. The ScrollViewerMonitor class is discussed in detail in the next section.

LISTING 24.8   EbaySearchView.xaml (excerpt)

```
<Grid x:Name="ContentPanel" Grid.Row="1">
    <Grid.RowDefinitions>
        <RowDefinition Height="Auto" />
        <RowDefinition Height="*" />
        <RowDefinition Height="Auto" />
```

LISTING 24.8   Continued

```xml
    </Grid.RowDefinitions>
    <TextBox Text="{Binding SearchText}"
            KeyUp="TextBox_KeyUp" />
    <ListBox Grid.Row="1"
        ItemsSource="{Binding Items}"
        u:ScrollViewerMonitor.AtEndCommand="{Binding FetchMoreDataCommand}">
        <ListBox.ItemTemplate>
            <DataTemplate>
                <Grid Margin="14,5,4,10">

                    <!-- Content omitted. -->
                    <Image Source="{Binding GalleryUrl}"
                        MaxWidth="100" MaxHeight="100"
                        Margin="0, 0, 10, 0"
                        Grid.RowSpan="4" />

                    <TextBlock Text="{Binding Title}"
                            Grid.Column="1" Grid.ColumnSpan="3"
                            Style="{StaticResource PhoneTextSmallStyle}" />

                    <TextBlock Text="current price:"
                            Grid.Row="1" Grid.Column="1"
                            HorizontalAlignment="Right" />
                    <TextBlock Text="{Binding CurrentPrice,
                            Converter={StaticResource StringFormatConverter},
                            ConverterParameter=\{0:C\}}"
                            Grid.Row="1" Grid.Column="2"
                            Margin="10,0,0,0" />

                    <TextBlock Text="time left:"
                            Grid.Row="2" Grid.Column="1"
                            HorizontalAlignment="Right" />
                    <TextBlock Text="{Binding TimeLeftCustom}"
                            Grid.Row="2" Grid.Column="2"
                            Margin="10,0,0,0" />

                    <HyperlinkButton NavigateUri="{Binding ViewItemUrl}"
                                Content="view"
                                TargetName="_blank"
                                Margin="0, 0, 10, 0"
                                Grid.Row="2" Grid.Column="3"
                                HorizontalAlignment="Left" />
                </Grid>
            </DataTemplate>
```

LISTING 24.8   Continued

```
        </ListBox.ItemTemplate>
    </ListBox>
    <Grid Grid.Row="2"
        Visibility="{Binding Busy,
        Converter={StaticResource BooleanToVisibilityConverter}}">
        <Grid.RowDefinitions>
            <RowDefinition />
            <RowDefinition />
        </Grid.RowDefinitions>
        <TextBlock Text="Loading..."
                Style="{StaticResource LoadingStyle}"/>
        <PerformanceProgressBar IsIndeterminate="True"
                VerticalAlignment="Bottom"
                Grid.Row="1" />
    </Grid>
</Grid>
```

In the grid row beneath the ListBox there is another Grid containing a TextBlock and a ProgressBar. This grid becomes visible when the viewmodel's Busy property is true.

When text is entered into the search query TextBox and the SIP's Enter button is tapped, the viewmodel's SearchCommand is executed (see Figure 24.5).

FIGURE 24.5   The eBay search page

The eBay logo is displayed using a `TextBlock` located in the title panel with a `Run` for each letter of the eBay logo, as shown in the following excerpt:

```
<StackPanel Grid.Row="0" Style="{StaticResource PageTitlePanelStyle}">
    <TextBlock Text="Windows Phone 7 Unleashed"
            Style="{StaticResource PhoneTextAppTitleStyle}" />
    <TextBlock Style="{StaticResource PhoneTextPageTitleStyle}"
            FontFamily="{StaticResource LogoFontFamily}">
    <Run Foreground="#ff0000">e</Run><Run Foreground="#000099">b</Run>
    <Run Foreground="#ffcc00">a</Run><Run Foreground="#99cc00">y</Run>
    <Run FontFamily="{StaticResource PhoneFontFamilyNormal}">search</Run>
    </TextBlock>
</StackPanel>
```

For more information on the `TextBlock` and `Run` classes, see Chapter 6, "Text Elements."

The next section demonstrates how the viewmodel's `FetchMoreDataCommand` is executed when the user scrolls to the end of the list.

Fetching Data When the User Scrolls to the End of a List

Most phone users are concerned about network usage. Network traffic comes at a premium, and a user's perception of the quality of your app depends a lot on its responsiveness. When it comes to fetching data from a network service, it should be done in the most efficient way possible. Making the user wait while your app downloads a lot of data is a bad idea. Instead, data should be retrieved in bite-sized chunks.

I have created a `ScrollViewerMonitor` class that uses an attached property to monitor a `ListBox` and fetch data as the user needs it. You use it by adding an attached property to a control that contains a `ScrollViewer`, such as a `ListBox`, as shown in the following example:

```
<ListBox ItemsSource="{Binding Items}"
    u:ScrollViewerMonitor.AtEndCommand="{Binding FetchMoreDataCommand}" />
```

The `AtEndCommand` property specifies a command that is executed when the user scrolls to the end of the list.

The `ScrollViewerMonitor` works by retrieving the first child `ScrollViewer` control from its target (usually a `ListBox`). It then listens to its `VerticalOffset` property for changes. When a change occurs and the `ScrollableHeight` of the `scrollViewer` is the same as the `VerticalOffset`, the `AtEndCommand` is executed (see Listing 24.9).

The `VerticalOffset` property is a dependency property, and to monitor it for changes I borrowed some of Pete Blois's code (http://blois.us/), which allows you to detect changes to any dependency property. This class is called `BindingListener` and is located in the downloadable sample code.

LISTING 24.9   ScrollViewerMonitor Class

```
public class ScrollViewerMonitor
{
    public static DependencyProperty AtEndCommandProperty
        = DependencyProperty.RegisterAttached(
            "AtEndCommand", typeof(ICommand),
            typeof(ScrollViewerMonitor),
            new PropertyMetadata(OnAtEndCommandChanged));

    public static ICommand GetAtEndCommand(DependencyObject obj)
    {
        return (ICommand)obj.GetValue(AtEndCommandProperty);
    }

    public static void SetAtEndCommand(DependencyObject obj, ICommand value)
    {
        obj.SetValue(AtEndCommandProperty, value);
    }

    public static void OnAtEndCommandChanged(
        DependencyObject d, DependencyPropertyChangedEventArgs e)
    {
        FrameworkElement element = (FrameworkElement)d;
        if (element != null)
        {
            element.Loaded -= element_Loaded;
            element.Loaded += element_Loaded;
        }
    }

    static void element_Loaded(object sender, RoutedEventArgs e)
    {
        FrameworkElement element = (FrameworkElement)sender;
        element.Loaded -= element_Loaded;
        ScrollViewer scrollViewer = FindChildOfType<ScrollViewer>(element);
        if (scrollViewer == null)
        {
            throw new InvalidOperationException("ScrollViewer not found.");
        }

        var listener = new DependencyPropertyListener();
        listener.Changed
            += delegate
                {
```

LISTING 24.9   Continued

```
                    bool atBottom = scrollViewer.ScrollableHeight > 0
                                 && scrollViewer.VerticalOffset
                                        >= scrollViewer.ScrollableHeight;

                    if (atBottom)
                    {
                        var atEnd = GetAtEndCommand(element);
                        if (atEnd != null)
                        {
                            atEnd.Execute(null);
                        }
                    }
                };
            Binding binding = new Binding("VerticalOffset") {
                                        Source = scrollViewer };
            listener.Attach(scrollViewer, binding);
        }

        static T FindChildOfType<T>(DependencyObject root) where T : class
        {
            var queue = new Queue<DependencyObject>();
            queue.Enqueue(root);

            while (queue.Count > 0)
            {
                DependencyObject current = queue.Dequeue();
                int start = VisualTreeHelper.GetChildrenCount(current) - 1;

                for (int i = start; 0 <= i; i--)
                {
                    var child = VisualTreeHelper.GetChild(current, i);
                    var typedChild = child as T;
                    if (typedChild != null)
                    {
                        return typedChild;
                    }
                    queue.Enqueue(child);
                }
            }
            return null;
        }
}
```

The `EbaySearchViewModel` contains a `FetchMoreDataCommand`. When the user scrolls to the bottom of the list, the command is executed, which then sets a `Busy` flag and calls the network service asynchronously.

Extending OData Entity Classes

When adding a service reference to an OData service, the generated entities classes are made *partial* classes. This provides a useful extensibility point for extending the model and for providing custom logic within entities themselves.

The `EbayModel.Item` class, for example, contains a `TimeLeft` property. This property is provided as a string. If it was of type `TimeSpan`, however, it would be easier to work with.

This section creates a new partial `Item` class and, within it, a `TimeSpan` property that converts the string value provided by the OData service into a `TimeSpan` value.

The following is an example of the format used by the `TimeLeft` string:

```
P0DT0H13M8S
```

The string contains tokens that indicate value positions for days, hours, minutes, and seconds. Unfortunately, this format is not compatible with the `TimeSpan.Parse` method. We, therefore, need to break up the string into its constituents parts. This can be done using a regular expression.

When constructing regular expressions, they can quickly become complex. Having a decent work bench for constructing them can make life easier. I really like the free regular expression tool called Expresso (http://www.ultrapico.com). Expresso allows you to specify sample text to see whether your regular expression produces the appropriate result (see Figure 24.6). It also includes other interfaces that assist in the construction of regular expressions.

The regular expression to deconstruct the `TimeLeft` value can be plugged in to a new partial `Item` class (see Listing 24.10).

LISTING 24.10   Custom `Item` Class

```
public partial class Item
{
    public TimeSpan? TimeLeftCustom
    {
        get
        {
            return ConvertToTimeSpan(TimeLeft);
        }
    }

    TimeSpan? ConvertToTimeSpan(string timeLeft)
    {
        Regex regex  = new Regex(
```

LISTING 24.10   Continued

```
        @"P(?<Days>\d+)DT(?<Hours>\d+)H(?<Minutes>\d+)M(?<Seconds>\d+)S");
    Match match = regex.Match(timeLeft);
    if (match.Success)
    {
        string timeSpanString = string.Format("{0}.{1}:{2}:{3}",
            match.Groups["Days"].Value,
            match.Groups["Hours"].Value,
            match.Groups["Minutes"].Value,
            match.Groups["Seconds"].Value);
        TimeSpan result;
        if (TimeSpan.TryParse(timeSpanString, out result))
        {
            return result;
        }
    }
    return null;
    }
}
```

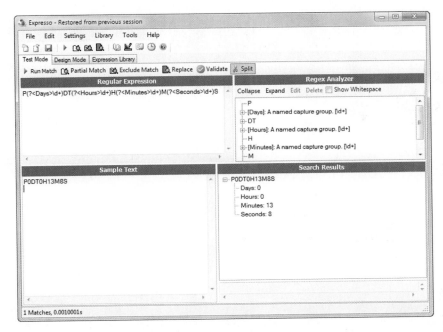

FIGURE 24.6   Expresso, regular expression editor

The TimeLeftCustom property is now able to be used in the view, like any of the other Item class's properties.

Summary

This chapter began by looking at the types of network services available on the phone. It then looked at monitoring network connectivity. You saw how to determine the type of network connection that the phone is using: Wi-Fi or cellular, enabling you to tailor the amount of data traffic accordingly. You saw how `GetIsNetworkAvailable` is not a reliable means of determining the network connection state.

Finally, the chapter focused on the OData protocol and how to create an app that consumes an OData service.

CHAPTER 25

Isolated Storage and State Preservation

P reserving the app's state is one of the key challenges facing Windows Phone developers.

To capture and restore state that is maintained across application launches, Silverlight provides a segregated storage area called isolated storage. Isolated storage is a managed storage area where your app can read and write data, and is inaccessible to other apps.

This chapter begins with a conceptual overview of isolated storage and looks at managing files and directories within the isolated storage data store. You see how to read and write files to isolated storage and explore the `IsolatedStorageSettings` class and how it is used to automatically persist application settings.

The chapter then examines a custom state preservation system, which uses an attribute based mechanism for preserving viewmodel property values automatically. You see that by decorating your viewmodel's properties with an attribute, the property's value can be preserved using binary serialization, either transiently using an OS managed `State` dictionary or persistently in isolated storage.

Finally, you learn how the custom state preservation API is used to preserve fields and to inject logic during state operations.

Understanding Isolated Storage

In Silverlight, applications do not have direct access to the underlying file system and must instead use the managed storage API of isolated storage. This helps to prevent unauthorized access to files by applications other than your own.

Isolated storage for Windows Phone works in much the same way as Silverlight for the browser. There is, however, no quota imposed on how much data can be stored on the phone; you are limited only by the storage capacity of the device. There is also no user-specific isolated storage as there is for the browser; each app has only one isolated storage area assigned to it when it is installed.

While the relaxation of the storage quota may appear convenient, it comes with the added responsibility of respecting the needs of your users and not consuming space unnecessarily. Phone users generally like to install new apps, download media from the Internet, and sync media to the phone from a PC. This means that storage on the device can be filled up quickly.

When a Windows Phone has only 10% of storage space remaining, the user receives a notification. The user then has the option to delete pictures, music, and apps to recover the necessary storage space. Reaching this point is not favorable from the user's perspective.

To minimize the amount of isolated storage space that your app uses, adhere to the following points:

▶ If your application creates temporary files, delete them when they are no longer needed.

▶ Allow the user to delete data that she has created.

▶ Consider using the cloud to store data when the phone is connected to a LAN.

▶ Trim application data periodically. For example, if your app caches a list of products, periodically remove items that have been in the list the longest.

> **NOTE**
>
> If an app is uninstalled, the isolated storage area for that app is deleted.
>
> In addition, when an application is updated in the Marketplace, its isolated storage folder is left untouched. It is your responsibility to ensure that any data saved in isolated storage is transformed to be compatible with the new version of your application.

Besides being able to read and write files in isolated storage, isolated storage also provides a managed dictionary for saving app settings (see Figure 25.1).

This managed dictionary is the IsolatedStorageSettings class, discussed later in the chapter.

Isolated Storage for Files and Directories

Isolated storage uses the same stream-based model that is present in .NET for the desktop. The isolated storage API is located in the System.IO.IsolatedStorage namespace.

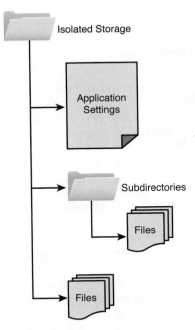

FIGURE 25.1   Logical representation of an application's isolated storage area

The IsolatedStorageFile class allows access to the virtual file system for reading and writing files, creating and deleting directories, and listing directory contents. The IsolatedStorageFile for an application can be retrieved using the static GetUserStoreForApplication method, as shown in the following example:

```
using (IsolatedStorageFile storageFile
        = IsolatedStorageFile.GetUserStoreForApplication())
{
...
}
```

IsolatedStorageFile implements IDisposable and should therefore be disposed of when it is no longer needed. Placing it within a using block is a convenient way of disposing of the object.

The class IsolatedStorageFile has a misleading name because rather than representing a single file in isolated storage, it represents the virtual file system. The public members of the IsolatedStorageFile class are presented in Table 25.1.

TABLE 25.1   `IsolatedStorageFile` Methods for File Management

Name	Description
CreateDirectory	Creates a new folder in the virtual file system.
DeleteDirectory	Deletes a folder in the virtual file system.
DirectoryExists	Determines whether the specified path refers to an existing directory in the virtual file system.
GetDirectoryNames	Returns an array of strings, which are the directories in the root of an isolated store. This method includes an overload that allows you to locate directories and subdirectories using a search pattern. Within the search pattern, single-character ? and multicharacter * wildcards are supported.
CreateFile	Creates a file in the virtual file system and returns an `IsolatedStorageFileStream`, which is used to write data to the file.
DeleteFile	Deletes a file in the virtual file system.
FileExists	Determines whether the specified path refers to an existing file in the isolated store.
GetFileNames	Enumerates files in isolated storage scope that match a given pattern. This method includes an overload that allows you to locate files using a search pattern. Within the search pattern, single-character ? and multicharacter * wildcards are supported.
OpenFile	Opens a named file and returns an `IsolatedStorageFileStream`, which is used to access the file. By providing various `FileMode`, `FileAccess`, and `FileShare` arguments, you can specify the kind of access you need to the file, such as reading or writing to the file, and appending or overwriting the file.

Measuring the Amount of Available Free Space

The `AvailableFreeSpace` property of the `IsolatedStorageFile` allows you to determine the amount of space remaining on the device. This property returns a long value indicating the number of bytes remaining.

The `Quota` property, of the `IsolatedStorageFile` class, serves no real purpose because no storage limit is imposed on Windows Phone apps.

Reading and Writing Data to Isolated Storage

Chapter 7, "Media and Web Elements," discussed storing web content to isolated storage. The following (slimmed down) example taken from that chapter tests for the existence of a directory called WebContent. If it does not exist, it is created. We then create a file named Webpage.html. If the file already exists, it is overwritten. We then write some HTML to the file, as shown:

```
using (IsolatedStorageFile isolatedStorageFile
            = IsolatedStorageFile.GetUserStoreForApplication())
{
```

```
if (!isolatedStorageFile.DirectoryExists("WebContent"))
{
    isolatedStorageFile.CreateDirectory("WebContent");
}

using (IsolatedStorageFileStream isolatedStorageFileStream
    = isolatedStorageFile.OpenFile(
        @"WebContent\Webpage.html", FileMode.Create))
{
    using (StreamWriter streamWriter
        = new StreamWriter(isolatedStorageFileStream))
    {
        streamWriter.Write(@"<html><head></head><body>
            <h2>Stored in Isolated Storage</h2></body></html>");
    }
}
}
```

Using `FileMode.Create` in an `OpenFile` call is equivalent to requesting that if the file does not exist, then `FileMode.CreateNew` should be used; otherwise, `FileMode.Truncate` should be used.

25

NOTE

The file system used by Windows Phone is TexFat and supports file names that are no longer than 247 characters. Files placed into isolated storage sit in the apps install directory, which has a path resembling the following:

\APPLICATIONS\INSTALL\45DC3711-8AF7-42BF-A749-6C491F2B427F\INSTALL

The length of this path, minus the native path to this directory leaves approximately 161 characters. If you attempt to write a file whose path is longer, an `IsolatedStorageException` is raised.

After the file is written to isolated storage, it can be retrieved, as shown in the following example:

```
string html;

using (IsolatedStorageFile isolatedStorageFile
        = IsolatedStorageFile.GetUserStoreForApplication())
{
    using (IsolatedStorageFileStream isolatedStorageFileStream
            = isolatedStorageFile.OpenFile(
                @"WebContent\Webpage.html", FileMode.Open))
    {
        using (StreamReader streamReader
                = new StreamReader(isolatedStorageFileStream))
```

```
    {
        html = streamReader.ReadToEnd();
    }
  }
}
```

NOTE

Attempting to open a file using a `FileMode.Open` argument raises an exception if the file does not exist. While `FileMode.OpenOrCreate` specifies that the operating system should open a file if it exists; otherwise, a new file should be created.

Serialization Performance Implications

When your app is transitioning from a nonrunning state to a running state and vice versa, it is important that it completes all activities as quickly as possible. Being slow at startup or shutdown can make your app appear sluggish and poorly engineered. Furthermore, there is a limit of 10 seconds before an app's process is terminated when it is being closed or deactivated.

To improve performance, consider favoring binary serialization over other types of serialization, such as XML or JSON serialization.

Unlike interacting with the user interface, there is no requirement to perform isolated storage activities on the main thread. When loading state at startup or while performing arbitrary CRUD operations, the use of a background thread can improve the responsiveness of your app during long-running storage operations.

TIP

To prevent locking the UI unnecessarily, if a storage operation takes more than 100 milliseconds to complete, move the operation to a background thread.

Application Settings

Saving objects in persistent state is such a common task that the isolated storage API includes an `IDictionary<string, object>` class named `IsolateStorageSettings` that is automatically persisted to isolated storage when your app is closed or tombstoned. `IsolateStorageSettings` is a convenient way to store global application state (see Figure 25.2).

`IsolateStorageSettings` is a singleton, accessible via the `IsolatedStorageSettings.ApplicationSettings` property. The `ApplicationSettings` property can be used just as you would any other `IDictionary`.

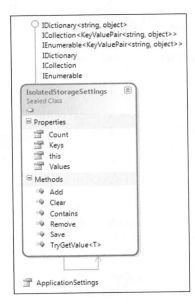

FIGURE 25.2   An app's `IsolatedStorageSettings` instance is retrieved using the `IsolatedStorageSettings.ApplicationSettings` property.

To place an object in persistent state, add a key value pair to the collection, like so:

```
IsolatedStorageSettings.ApplicationSettings["Foo"] = "Bah";
```

To retrieve the item from persistent state, the following can be used:

```
string value = (string)IsolatedStorageSettings.ApplicationSettings["Foo"];
```

If it is uncertain whether an item exists in `ApplicationSettings`, use the `TryGetValue` method as shown:

```
string value;
if (!IsolatedStorageSettings.ApplicationSettings.TryGetValue("Foo",
                                                    out value))
{
    value = "Unknown";
}
```

The `Contains` method can also be used to test whether an item exists in the dictionary.

Serialization Requirements

Objects placed in `ApplicationSettings` have the same serialization requirements as a transient application state (see Chapter 3, "Application Execution Model"); data placed in `ApplicationSetting` must be a primitive type, a known serializable type (for example, `Decimal`), or be capable of being serialized using a `DataContractSerializer`. If an object is unable to be serialized, an exception is raised.

CAUTION

If even a single object in the `ApplicationSettings` raises an exception when the `IsolatedStorageSettings.Save` method is called, all settings are prevented from being saved.

When the user exits your app, Windows Phone automatically calls `Save` to preserve the `IsolatedStorageSettings` object so that it can be automatically reinstated when your application starts again.

Abstracting `IsolatedStorageSettings`

This section briefly touches on the topic of abstracting the `IsolatedStorageSettings` class. By providing a custom API for application settings, it decouples your code from the Silverlight-specific `IsolatedStorageSettings` and allows you to change the way settings are stored, thereby increasing the portability of your code.

The `IsolatedStorageSettings` class uses a `DataContractSerializer` that serializes objects using XML, which is significantly slower than, for example, a binary serializer.

In the Calcium project there exists an `ISettingsService` that includes methods to retrieve items from persistent storage. The Calcium settings API allows you to retrieve a value from isolated storage, while supplying a default value, which is returned if no value exists, as shown in the following example:

```
var settingsService = Dependency.Resolve<ISettingsService>();
int exampleSetting = settingsService.GetSetting("Example Setting Key", 5);
```

The `GetSetting` method uses generics to return an object of the correct type, matching the default value's type.

To set a value, the `SetSetting` method is called like so:

```
settingsService.SetSetting("Example Setting Key", 2);
```

We do not delve deeper into the code in this chapter, but if you are interested in this topic, the source code is open source and freely available at http://calciumsdk.com.

Building an Automatic State Preservation System

App tombstoning presents a new challenge for developers moving to the Windows Phone platform. As the complexity of your app increases so too does the task of preserving your app's transient and persistent state.

For this chapter I have created an automatic state preservation system, which you are free to use. I intend to continue to refine and integrate it into the open source Calcium project.

The system presented in this section allows you to register properties for state preservation using a custom attribute. In addition, there is an API that uses lambda expressions for registering properties with nonpublic accessors and fields.

Using the system involves registering a property so that it is automatically saved and restored after tombstoning. This is done by decorating the property with the custom Stateful attribute, as shown in the following example:

```
[Stateful(ApplicationStateType.Persistent)]
public int SomeProperty { get; set; }
```

The Stateful attribute receives an ApplicationStateType value, which indicates the type of state persistency that the property requires. ApplicationStateType enum has the following two values:

- ▶ **Persistent**—State is saved to isolated storage.

- ▶ **Transient**—State is saved to the PhoneApplicationService.Current.State.

The attribute based approach is the simplest way for preserving the state of a property. Yet, to register fields or inject custom logic, the ViewModelBase class also provides the methods shown in Table 25.2.

TABLE 25.2   ViewModelBase State Related Methods

Method Name	Description
RegisterStatefulProperty	Allows you to specify a property using a lambda expression and a type of application state that should be applied, either transient or persistent. Calling this method causes the property to be automatically saved and restored.
DeregisterStatefulProperty	Removes a property from the list of registered state properties.
RegisterState	Allows you to supply a Func for reading a value and an Action for writing a value. This method offers more flexibility than the RegisterStatefulProperty method and is suitable, for example, when a property does not have a public setter.
DeregisterState	Removes the set of delegates from the list of registered state delegates, identified by a string key.

The eBay Search example from the Chapter 24, "Network Services," has been augmented to demonstrate the use of the state preservation system.

A SearchCount property has been added to the new EbaySearchStateViewModel (replacing the EbaySearchViewModel) to demonstrate the State attribute. This property is incremented each time a search takes place. It is preserved in isolated storage by using the Stateful attribute, as shown in the following excerpt:

```
[Stateful(ApplicationStateType.Persistent)]
public int SearchCount { get; set; }
```

When the viewmodel is instantiated, the ViewModelBase class identifies all properties that have been decorated with the attribute and registers them with a custom ViewState class.

Additionally, within the viewmodel's constructor there now exists various state registration statements. The first, shown in the following excerpt, registers the SearchText property for transient state preservation:

```
RegisterStatefulProperty(ApplicationStateType.Transient, () => SearchText);
```

A lambda expression is used to identify the property. As part of this call, the expression is deconstructed to determine the name of the property and to create the property accessor (get and set) delegates, which are used to retrieve and set the SearchText property during state preservation operations. If the app is deactivated, the SearchText property (and any other registered transient state properties) are placed in the PhoneApplicationService's State dictionary and reinstated if and when the app is reactivated.

In the following example, the Items collection is registered for transient state preservation:

```
RegisterStatefulProperty(
    ApplicationStateType.Transient, () => Items, x => Items = x);
```

Persisting an object to isolated storage works in the same way; however, we specify that the value is to be placed in persistent storage using the Persistent enum value, as shown:

```
RegisterStatefulProperty(
    ApplicationStateType.Persistent, () => SearchCount);
```

Customizing ViewModel State Preservation

A viewmodel has the opportunity to customize how its state is persisted by overriding the SaveState method from the ViewModelBase class, as shown:

```
public override void SaveState(
    IDictionary<string, object> persistentDictionary,
    IDictionary<string, object> transientDictionary)
{
    base.LoadState(persistentDictionary, transientDictionary);
    byte[] state = Serialize(items);
    transientDictionary[itemsStateKey] = state;
    transientDictionary[queryStateKey] = lastQuery;
}
```

The Serialize and Deserialize methods of the ViewModelBase class are able to convert an object to and from a byte array. The serialization mechanism is discussed in more detail in the next section.

Conversely, a viewmodel may restore its own state by overriding the `LoadState` method, as shown in the following example:

```
public override void LoadState(
    IDictionary<string, object> persistentDictionary,
    IDictionary<string, object> transientDictionary)
{
    base.SaveState(persistentDictionary, transientDictionary);
    object state;
    if (transientDictionary.TryGetValue(itemsStateKey, out state))
    {
        byte[] bytes = state as byte[];
        Items = Deserialize<ObservableCollection<Item>>(bytes);
    }

    if (transientDictionary.TryGetValue(queryStateKey, out state))
    {
        lastQuery = (string)state;
        SearchText = lastQuery;
    }
}
```

Automatic State Preservation Inner Workings

This section looks at how the state preservation system works behind the scenes. You see how properties decorated with the `Stateful` attribute are identified and how delegates for property accessors are created to store and retrieve property value. You also see how a custom `ViewState` class is used to load and save state via the `ViewModelBase` class.

The following sections are advanced in nature. Feel free to skip ahead. If you choose to use the custom state preservation system, you may return to this chapter at a later time.

Identifying Stateful ViewModels

The custom `IStatePreservation` interface is implemented by viewmodels that want to save and restore state. If a viewmodel implements `IStatePreservation` it has its `LoadState` or `SaveState` method called during page navigation.

`LoadState` and `SaveState` accept two parameters: a persistent state dictionary, which is normally the `IsolatedStorageSettings.ApplicationSettings` dictionary, and a transient state dictionary, which is normally the `PhoneApplicationService` state dictionary.

To coordinate this activity, the custom `StateManager` class is used. When the application starts, the `StateManager` class subscribes to the relevant navigation events of the `PhoneApplicationFrame`, as shown:

```
public static void Initialize()
{
    PhoneApplicationService.Current.Deactivated += OnDeactivated;
```

```
    var frame = (PhoneApplicationFrame)Application.Current.RootVisual;
    frame.Navigating += OnNavigating;
    frame.Navigated += OnNavigated;
}
```

When navigating away from a page, the StateManager requests that the associated view-model save its state, if it implements IStatePreservation:

```
static void OnNavigating(object sender, NavigatingCancelEventArgs e)
{
    var frame = (PhoneApplicationFrame)Application.Current.RootVisual;
    var element = frame.Content as FrameworkElement;
    if (element != null)
    {
        IStatePreservation preserver
            = element.DataContext as IStatePreservation;
        if (preserver != null)
        {
            preserver.SaveState(
                IsolatedStorageSettings.ApplicationSettings,
                PhoneApplicationService.Current.State);
        }
    }
}
```

When navigating to a page, the StateManager requests that the viewmodel load its state:

```
static void OnNavigated(object sender, NavigationEventArgs e)
{
    var element = e.Content as FrameworkElement;
    if (element != null)
    {
        IStatePreservation statePreservation
            = element.DataContext as IStatePreservation;
        if (statePreservation != null)
        {
            statePreservation.LoadState(
                IsolatedStorageSettings.ApplicationSettings,
                PhoneApplicationService.Current.State);
        }
    }
}
```

It is not necessary to implement IStatePreservation on each viewmodel because the ViewModelBase class implements it. When the ViewModelBase class is instantiated, it locates all attributes decorated with the StateFul attribute and registers those properties with the custom `ViewState` class. The `ProperyInfo` class is used to create a delegate for both the get and set property accessors, as shown in the following excerpt:

```
void ReadStateAttributes()
{
    var properties = GetType().GetProperties();

    foreach (PropertyInfo propertyInfo in properties)
    {
        object[] attributes = propertyInfo.GetCustomAttributes(
                                typeof(StatefulAttribute), true);

        if (attributes.Length <= 0)
        {
            continue;
        }

        StatefulAttribute attribute
            = (StatefulAttribute)attributes[0];
        var persistenceType = attribute.StateType;

        if (!propertyInfo.CanRead || !propertyInfo.CanWrite)
        {
            throw new InvalidOperationException(string.Format(
                "Property {0} must have a getter and a setter.",
                propertyInfo.Name));
        }

        /* Prevents access to internal closure warning. */
        PropertyInfo info = propertyInfo;

        viewState.RegisterState(
            propertyInfo.Name,
            () => info.GetValue(this, null),
            obj => info.SetValue(this, obj, null),
            persistenceType);
    }
}
```

The `ViewState` class provides thread state access to two dictionaries: one for persistent state, the other for transient state. The `RegisterState` method places the `Func` and `Action` associated with the state into its respective dictionary, as shown:

```
public void RegisterState<T>(
    string stateKey,
    Func<T> getterFunc,
    Action<T> setterAction,
```

```
        ApplicationStateType stateType)
{
    ArgumentValidator.AssertNotNull(stateKey, "propertyName");
    ArgumentValidator.AssertNotNull(getterFunc, "propertyGetterFunc");
    ArgumentValidator.AssertNotNull(setterAction, "propertySetterAction");

    if (stateType == ApplicationStateType.Persistent)
    {
        lock (persistentStateLock)
        {
            persistentState[stateKey]
                = new Accessor<T>(getterFunc, setterAction);
        }
    }
    else
    {
        lock (transientStateLock)
        {
            transientState[stateKey]
                = new Accessor<T>(getterFunc, setterAction);
        }
    }
}
```

The nested Accessor class is a container for a Func and an Action, and is usually populated with lambda expressions for the getter and setter of a viewmodel property. The following excerpt shows the nested Accessor class:

```
class Accessor<T> : IStateAccessor
{
    readonly Func<T> getter;
    readonly Action<T> setter;

    public Accessor(Func<T> getter, Action<T> setter)
    {
        this.getter = getter;
        this.setter = setter;
    }

    public object Value
    {
        get
        {
            return getter();
        }
        set
```

```
    {
        setter((T)value);
    }
  }
}
```

When the `StateManager` calls the `IStatePreservation.SaveState` method of the `ViewModelBase` instance, the `ViewModelBase` class calls the `ViewState` object's `SavePersistentState` and `SaveTransientState` methods, which are shown in the following excerpt:

```
public void SavePersistentState(IDictionary<string, object> stateDictionary)
{
    SaveState(stateDictionary, persistentState, persistentStateLock);
}

public void SaveTransientState(IDictionary<string, object> stateDictionary)
{
    SaveState(stateDictionary, transientState, transientStateLock);
}
```

The `ViewState.SaveState` method enumerates the `Accessor` objects in the specified accessors dictionary and resolves the value to be serialized using the `Accessor.Value` property. The value is then serialized to a byte array, which is then stored in the specified state dictionary, as shown in the following excerpt:

```
void SaveState(
        IDictionary<string, object> stateDictionary,
        Dictionary<string, IStateAccessor> accessors,
        object propertiesLock)
{
    lock (propertiesLock)
    {
        foreach (KeyValuePair<string, IStateAccessor> pair in accessors)
        {
            string stateKey = pair.Key;
            IStateAccessor accessor = pair.Value;

            object accessorValue = accessor.Value;

            if (accessorValue == null)
            {
                stateDictionary.Remove(stateKey);
                continue;
            }
```

```
        byte[] bytes;
        try
        {
            bytes = Serialize(accessorValue);
        }
        catch (Exception ex)
        {
            stateDictionary[pair.Key] = null;
            Debug.Assert(false,
                        "Unable to serialize state value. " + ex);
            continue;
        }

        stateDictionary[stateKey] = bytes;
    }
  }
}
```

Using the Silverlight Serializer for Binary Serialization

Mike Talbot's Silverlight Serializer is used in the sample code to serialize objects. The Silverlight Serializer has better performance and is easier to use than the built-in `DataContractSerializer`.

See http://whydoidoit.com/silverlight-serialize for more information on the Silverlight Serializer.

When using the Silverlight Serializer, an object can be converted to and from a byte array without the need to decorate it with a myriad of `DataMember` attributes, as is necessary with the `DataContractSerializer`.

The `SilverlightSerializer` class is used in the custom `ViewState` class to serialize and deserialize viewmodel data, as shown in the following excerpt:

```
protected byte[] Serialize(object value)
{
    byte[] state = SilverlightSerializer.Serialize(value);
    return state;
}

protected T Deserialize<T>(byte[] data) where T : class
{
    T result = SilverlightSerializer.Deserialize<T>(data);
    return result;
}
```

Within the `ViewState` class, state restoration works in much the same way as state persistence, but in reverse. We enumerate over the `Accessor` objects and attempt to retrieve a corresponding state value from the state dictionary. This value is then converted from a byte array to an object using the `Deserialize` method, as shown in the following excerpt:

```
void LoadState(
        IDictionary<string, object> stateDictionary,
        Dictionary<string, IStateAccessor> accessors,
        object propertiesLock)
{
    lock (propertiesLock)
    {
        foreach (KeyValuePair<string, IStateAccessor> pair in accessors)
        {
            object stateValue;
            string stateKey = pair.Key;
            IStateAccessor accessor = pair.Value;

            if (!stateDictionary.TryGetValue(stateKey, out stateValue))
            {
                continue;
            }

            byte[] bytes = stateValue as byte[];

            if (bytes == null)
            {
                Debug.Assert(false, "state value is not a byte[]");
                continue;
            }

            object deserializedValue;
            try
            {
                deserializedValue = Deserialize(bytes);
            }
            catch (Exception ex)
            {
                string message = "Unable to deserialize bytes. " + ex;
                Debug.Assert(false, message);
                continue;
            }

            if (deserializedValue == null)
            {
                const string message
                        = "Deserialized object should not be null.";
                Debug.Assert(false, message);
```

```
        continue;
    }

    try
    {
        accessor.Value = deserializedValue;
    }
    catch (Exception ex)
    {
        Console.WriteLine("Unable to set state value. " + ex);
        continue;
    }
    }
  }
}
```

The `ViewModelBase` class includes various state registration methods that can be used instead of the `State` attribute to specify stateful properties. The `RegisterStatefulProperty` method, for example, allows you to specify a stateful property using a lambda expression, as shown in the following example:

```
RegisterStatefulProperty(ApplicationStateType.Transient, () => SearchText);
```

The `RegisterStatefulProperty` method has an optional `setAction` parameter, which allows you to provide an alternative handler for setting the value; this is useful for properties that lack a public set accessor. The `RegisterStatefulProperty` calls the overloaded private method by the same name, as shown:

```
protected void RegisterStatefulProperty<TProperty>(
    ApplicationStateType applicationStateType,
    Expression<Func<TProperty>> expression,
    Action<TProperty> setAction = null)
{
    RegisterStatefulProperty((name, getter, setter)
        => viewState.RegisterState(
                name, getter, setter, applicationStateType),
                expression, setAction);
}
```

The private `RegisterStatefulProperty` method retrieves the `PropertyInfo` instance for the expression (described in the next section) and uses it to create delegates for the property accessors. It then invokes the specified `registerAction`, which, in this case, is a call to `viewState.RegisterState`. The `RegisterStatefulProperty` method is shown in the following excerpt:

```
void RegisterStatefulProperty<T>(
    Action<string, Func<T>, Action<T>> registerAction,
    Expression<Func<T>> expression, Action<T> setAction = null)
{
    ArgumentValidator.AssertNotNull(registerAction, "registerAction");
    ArgumentValidator.AssertNotNull(expression, "expression");

    PropertyInfo propertyInfo = PropertyUtility.GetPropertyInfo(expression);
    string name = propertyInfo.Name;
    var propertyGetterFunc = propertyInfo.CreateGetter<T>(this);

    if (setAction == null)
    {
        try
        {
            setAction = propertyInfo.CreateSetter<T>(this);
        }
        catch (Exception ex)
        {
            string message = string.Format(
                "Unable to get setter for property '{0}' {1} ", name, ex);
            Console.WriteLine(message);
            Debug.Assert(false, message);
            return;
        }
    }
    registerAction(name, propertyGetterFunc, setAction);
}
```

Unwinding a Property Lambda Expression

Resolving a property's name and creating delegates for its get and set property accessors involves unwinding of the Lambda expression and retrieving the PropertyInfo instance. In the sample code, this is done using the custom PropertyUtility.GetPropertyInfo method, which retrieves the PropertyInfo instance from the expression's Member property, as shown:

```
public static PropertyInfo GetPropertyInfo<T>(Expression<Func<T>> expression)
{
    var memberExpression = expression.Body as MemberExpression;
    if (memberExpression == null)
    {
        throw new ArgumentException(
            "MemberExpression expected.", "expression");
    }
```

```
    if (memberExpression.Member == null)
    {
        throw new ArgumentException("Member should not be null.");
    }

    if (memberExpression.Member.MemberType != MemberTypes.Property)
    {
        throw new ArgumentException("Property expected.", "expression");
    }

    PropertyInfo propertyInfo = (PropertyInfo)memberExpression.Member;
    return propertyInfo;
}
```

Creating Property Accessor Delegates

When the `PropertyInfo` instance has been obtained, it is used to create a delegate for the get and set accessors. For this, the `Delegate.CreateDelegate` method is used via a custom `PropertyInfo` extension method called `CreateGetter`, in the `PropertyUtility` class. Within the `CreateGetter` method, the type argument required by the `Delegate.CreateDelegate` method is generated using the `Expression.GetFuncType` method. If the property is of type string, for example, a type representing a `Func<string>` is produced. See the following excerpt:

```
public static Func<TProperty> CreateGetter<TProperty>(
    this PropertyInfo propertyInfo, object owner)
{
    ArgumentValidator.AssertNotNull(propertyInfo, "propertyInfo");
    ArgumentValidator.AssertNotNull(owner, "owner");

    Type getterType = Expression.GetFuncType(
                    new[] { propertyInfo.PropertyType });

    object getter = Delegate.CreateDelegate(
                    getterType, owner, propertyInfo.GetGetMethod());

    return (Func<TProperty>)getter;
}
```

The `Expression.GetFuncType` method is also equivalent to the `Type` method `MakeGenericType`, which could have been used instead, like so:

```
Type getterType = typeof(Func<>).MakeGenericType(propertyInfo.PropertyType);
```

Creating a delegate for the set accessor means resolving the generic `Action` type in the same manner:

```
public static Action<TProperty> CreateSetter<TProperty>(
    this PropertyInfo propertyInfo, object owner)
{
    ArgumentValidator.AssertNotNull(propertyInfo, "propertyInfo");
    ArgumentValidator.AssertNotNull(owner, "owner");

    var propertyType = propertyInfo.PropertyType;
    var setterType = Expression.GetActionType(new[] { propertyType });

    Delegate setter = Delegate.CreateDelegate(
                setterType, owner, propertyInfo.GetSetMethod());

    return (Action<TProperty>)setter;
}
```

These two methods provide the delegates that are retained by the ViewState class.

Summary

This chapter began with a conceptual overview of isolated storage and then looked at managing files and directories and reading and writing files within the isolated storage data store. The chapter then explored the IsolatedStorageSettings class, and you saw how it is used to automatically persist application settings.

The chapter then examined a custom state preservation system, which uses an attribute-based mechanism for preserving viewmodel property values automatically. You saw that by decorating your viewmodel's properties with an attribute, the property's value can be preserved either transiently using the PhoneApplicationService object's State dictionary or persistently in isolated storage using binary serialization.

Finally, you saw how the custom state preservation API is used to preserve fields and to inject logic during state operations.

Local Databases

For some apps, having to rely on a cloud service for storing application data is not practical. Some scenarios cry out for local storage of structured data on the phone.

With the Mango release of Windows Phone (7.5), Microsoft introduced a relational database system to the phone, allowing you to place a local database in either isolated storage or in your app's XAP file.

Windows Phone apps use LINQ to SQL for all database operations; LINQ to SQL is used to define the database schema, and to select, insert, update, and delete data from the database. LINQ to SQL provides an object-oriented approach to working with relational data and is comprised of an object model and a runtime. With LINQ to SQL, classes represent database tables, and foreign key relationships between tables are represented by aggregated collections.

This chapter begins with an overview of how local databases are deployed to the phone and discusses the main elements of LINQ to SQL.

The chapter then explores the code-first approach to data model creation and walks through a sample Twitter timeline viewer that caches data in a local database, during which you explore several facets of LINQ to SQL including entity creation, change tracking, and entity multiplicity (one-to-many relationships).

The database-first approach to data model creation is then discussed. You see how to retrieve a local database file from isolated storage and how to use the SqlMetal tool to generate a data model from a database.

The chapter then takes a short deviation and examines a custom navigation service that allows navigation from a viewmodel without being coupled to the built-in navigation of the phone, which can increase the testability of your viewmodel classes.

The chapter then gets back on topic to examine a technique for observing LINQ to SQL queries using a custom log. You see how to upgrade a schema without losing data and how to use version numbering to provide incremental updates to your database schema.

Finally, you look at mapping inheritance hierarchies using LINQ to SQL, and at concurrency and conflict detection when performing updates.

SQL Server Compact

The database used on the phone is based on SQL Server Compact Edition (SQL CE). SQL CE shares a common API with the other Microsoft SQL Server editions. Each SQL CE database resides in a single .sdf file, which can be up to 4GB in size. The .sdf file can be encrypted, using a password, with 128-bit encryption for data security.

NOTE

On Windows Phone, the database filename is required to use the .sdf file extension. A `NotSupportedException` is raised if you attempt to create a database with a name not ending in .sdf.

Deployment of Local Databases

Understanding how local databases can be deployed to the phone is important when determining the best approach for your app. This section looks behind the scenes at what happens when an app is installed on the phone and at the two locations for local database deployment.

It so happens that a XAP file, which is produced when you build your project, is also a Zip file. When an app is installed on the phone, the *package manager* extracts the app's XAP file into an install directory (see Figure 26.1).

For more information on XAP files see the section "Understanding the Role of XAP Files" in Chapter 2, "Fundamental Concepts in Silverlight Development for Windows Phone."

The install directory is read-only. An app is not able to add or remove items from its install directory, nor is it able to make any changes to any items in the directory.

During installation, the app is also assigned a data directory. The contents of this directory and all subdirectories are readable and writable by the app.

NOTE

An app's root directory, and all contents therein, are off-limits to any other app.

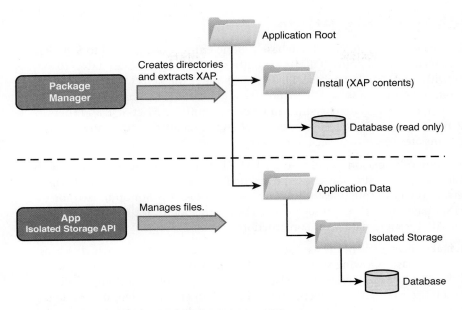

FIGURE 26.1   Install and Application Data directories

A local database can be placed either in isolated storage or in the app's install directory by including it within the XAP. You see why the choice of where to place a local database is important in a moment.

An app's data directory is persistent, while its install directory is not. When publishing an update for your app on the Windows Phone Marketplace, the install directory of your app is replaced, but the data directory for your app remains intact.

Moreover, when placed in the install directory, a database is read-only. This suits certain scenarios, such as when you want to include structured reference data with your app, data that may change with each application update, but that is not modifiable by the app itself. An example of this kind of data is a dictionary of word definitions.

The most common place for a database, however, is in isolated storage. When in isolated storage the database is readable and writable, and is retained during an app update.

There are two common scenarios for deploying a database to isolated storage. The first is where your app has a complex domain model and you want to persist its state. Perhaps your app is a shopping cart or a todo list. The second scenario is where you fetch a subset of reference data from the cloud, cache it locally, and combine it with user-specific data.

This chapter demonstrates each deployment option and focuses on using a local database as a cache by creating a Twitter app that downloads timeline information and caches it in a database so that it is available when the phone is offline.

26

LINQ to SQL on the Phone

Retrieval and storage of data in a local database is done entirely using LINQ to SQL, which provides object-relational mapping (ORM) capabilities, allowing you to use LINQ to communicate with a relational database. LINQ to SQL maps the object model, which you define by decorating entity classes with attributes, to a relational database. When your app runs, LINQ to SQL translates language-integrated queries into Transact-SQL and then sends the queries to the database for execution. When the database returns the results, LINQ to SQL translates the results back to objects.

When first learning of Microsoft's choice to go with LINQ to SQL in Windows Phone, I was somewhat dismayed that it was chosen over the Entity Framework. Yet, while the Entity Framework offers a more powerful API and set of tools, it is not optimized for mobile devices. I have since come to see LINQ to SQL as a good fit for the phone, as it offers a simple API for rapid data layer construction.

LINQ to SQL makes heavy use of the `System.Data.Linq.DataContext` class, which serves as a proxy to your database, allowing you to query the database via `Table` objects representing tables in the database (see Figure 26.2). Each `Table` member of a `DataContext` allows the storage and retrieval of entity objects; an instance of an entity represents a table row. Persisting changes to the local database is done using the `DataContext.SubmitChanges` method.

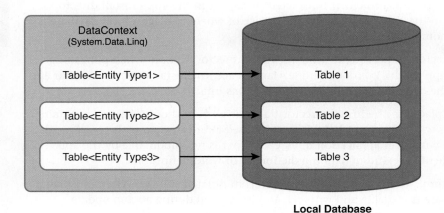

Local Database

FIGURE 26.2   `DataContext Table` members are associated with database tables.

By default, `DataContext` also tracks changes to your entity objects so that you can easily push changes back to your database.

An entity is a POCO (Plain Old CLR Object), representing a domain object, and is decorated with a `System.Data.Linq.Mapping.Table` attribute. Other data related attributes, placed on and within each entity class, define the mapping between the object model and the schema of the database and determine the structure of the database.

LINQ to SQL Platform Differences

Windows Phone supports most of the features of LINQ to SQL, apart from several notable absences present on other platforms, and some additional features not seen in LINQ to SQL on other platforms. The following is a list of some of the most notable differences:

▶ LINQ to SQL on Windows Phone does not directly support the execution of Transact-SQL, which includes Data Definition Language (DDL) and Data Modeling Language (DML) statements.

▶ Local databases run in your app's process and not in a background process, as is the case with most desktop based databases.

▶ A local database cannot be accessed by other apps; it lives in the sandboxed execution environment of your app.

▶ Transactions are not directly supported.

For more detailed information on the various API differences see http://bit.ly/xQMxmm.

New features have also been added to LINQ to SQL, specifically for Windows Phone apps. These include support for multiple table indexes and the ability to programmatically alter the database schema (described later in this chapter).

Getting Started with Local Databases

Using LINQ to SQL in your phone app requires referencing the assembly `System.Data.Linq`, which is included in the Windows Phone Framework Class Library (FCL).

There are two commonly used approaches to the creation of an application's data model: code-first and database-first. Code-first entails writing your classes first and then using those classes to generate the database. Conversely, database-first entails creating your database schema and then using a tool to generate an object model for interacting with the database. The database-first approach is discussed later in the chapter. For now, though, we concentrate on the code-first approach.

Code-First Data Model Creation

Code-first is the recommended approach for creating your data model in Windows Phone. It involves writing your classes and then generating your database using metadata contained in those classes.

Until now, I have never been a fan of code-first when building desktop and client-server applications because I saw how it can lead to a lack of attention being paid to the database schema—to its structure, constraints, and indexes. Yet, applied wisely, code-first offers some key advantages. One such advantage is that you do not break the application by forgetting to propagate a schema change to other developers on your team, since all changes to the schema are done via code metadata.

The following list outlines the steps for creating a data model and generating a database using the code-first approach and LINQ to SQL:

1. Manually create POCO classes representing your domain entities.

2. Create a class deriving from `DataContext`, with properties within the class representing tables within the database.

3. When instantiating your `DataContext`, provide a connection string with the location of your database file in isolated storage. The `DataContext` creates a database with the relationships defined in your data model.

Once the database is in place, you are able to interact with the `DataContext` and the entity objects using LINQ to SQL.

The following section looks at each of these steps in detail during the creation of a sample Twitter timeline viewer.

Sample Twitter Timeline Viewer

The principle example for this chapter is a Twitter timeline viewer that downloads the tweets of a specified Twitter user, caches them in a local database, and displays them on a page. The code for this example is located in the DataDrivenApps/TwitterExample directory of the WindowsPhone7Unleashed.Examples project.

The Twitter timeline viewer has a simple data model consisting of two entities representing a Twitter user and a tweet or `TimelineItem` (see Figure 26.3), and demonstrates using a local database to cache cloud data.

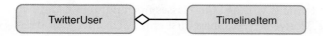

FIGURE 26.3   A `TwitterUser` has many `TimelineItem`s.

`TimelineItem` represents a status update (tweet) that contains information including the tweet text, the time the tweet occurred, and the user's id (see Listing 26.1). The `TwitterUser` class holds a collection, specifically an `EntitySet` of `TimelineItem` objects.

LISTING 26.1   `TimelineItem` Class (excerpt)

```
[Table]
public class TimelineItem : NotifyPropertyChangeBase
{
    string id;

    [Column(IsPrimaryKey = true)]
    public string Id
    {
```

LISTING 26.1   Continued

```
        get
        {
            return id;
        }
        set
        {
            Assign("Id", ref id, value);
        }
    }

    string text;

    [Column(DbType = "NVarChar(140)")]
    public string Text
    {
        get
        {
            return text;
        }
        set
        {
            Assign("Text", ref text, value);
        }
    }

    DateTime? receivedTime;

    [Column]
    public DateTime? ReceivedTime
    {
        get
        {
            return receivedTime;
        }
        set
        {
            Assign("ReceivedTime", ref receivedTime, value);
        }
    }

    string twitterUserId;

    [Column(CanBeNull = false)]
    public string TwitterUserId
```

LISTING 26.1   Continued

```
{
    get
    {
        return twitterUserId;
    }
    set
    {
        Assign("TwitterUserId", ref twitterUserId, value);
    }
}

EntityRef<TwitterUser> user;

[Association(Storage = "user",
            ThisKey = "TwitterUserId",
            IsForeignKey = true)]
public TwitterUser TwitterUser
{
    get
    {
        return user.Entity;
    }
    set
    {
        user.Entity = value;
    }
}
}
```

To declare the TimelineItem class as representing a table in the database, it is decorated with a Table attribute. The TableAttribute class includes a Name property, which allows you to explicitly define the name of the database table. If it is not provided, the name of the class is used as the table name. For example, to override the TimelineItem table name to something else, the following could be used:

```
[Table(Name = "SomethingElse")]
public class TimelineItem : NotifyPropertyChangeBase
{ ... }
```

Using the Column Attribute

Each property of the TimelineItem is decorated with a Column attribute, which tells the DataContext that the property is stored in a column by the same name. As with

`TableAttribute`, you can use its `Name` property to specify a different name for the column in the database.

`ColumnAttribute` includes various other properties described in the following sections.

IsPrimaryKey

`IsPrimaryKey` is used to designate the member or members of the entity class that comprise the primary key of the table. Composite keys are also supported by supplying more than one property decorated with a `Column` attribute with `IsPrimaryKey` set to true.

At least one member of an entity class must be designated as the primary key or else the entity is deemed to be read-only. If an attempt is made to create, update, or delete a read-only entity, an `InvalidOperationException` is raised.

AutoSync

`AutoSync` is used to specify whether the column is automatically synchronized from the value generated by the database on insert or update commands.

The following is a list of valid values for this property:

- `Default`
- `Always`
- `Never`
- `OnInsert`
- `OnUpdate`

If the column in your database provides a default value, set this property to `OnInsert`, `OnUpdate`, or `Always`.

CanBeNull

`CanBeNull` indicates whether a column can contain null values. This property is relevant when inserting data into the database but not during the creation of the table.

> **NOTE**
>
> The `DataContext.CreateDatabase` method uses only the `ColumnAttribute.DbType` property and not the `ColumnAttribute.CanBeNull` property when determining whether a column should allow null values. For this reason, you must specify whether a column can contain null values in the `DbType` property as well as setting `CanBeNull` to true.

If not specified, `CanBeNull` defaults to *true* if the member is a reference type; if the member is a value type, such as an `int`, then `CanBeNull` defaults to false.

DbType

`DbType` specifies the text that defines the column in a Transact-SQL create table statement. Using this property allows you to tailor a column data type to better match the data being stored in the column. If used correctly, it can help to decrease the size of your database and may improve the speed of some queries.

For example, by not specifying the `DbType` of a string property, LINQ to SQL generates DDL for a column containing up to 4000 Unicode characters (*NVARCHAR(4000)*). If you, however, know that a field will always contain values of relatively the same length (within two characters difference), then NCHAR can be faster and more space efficient for data, and it may pay dividends to specify it using `DbType`.

> **NOTE**
>
> SQL CE is a Unicode-only database so you must use Unicode data types when assigning the `DbType` property. In particular, use NVARCHAR instead of VARCHAR, and NCHAR instead of CHAR.

Expression

`Expression` allows you to automatically populate a field using a SQL expression. Use this property to define a column as containing computed values when you use `DataContext.CreateDatabase` to generate your database.

For example, if you want to create a column defined in SQL as *InventoryValue AS UnitPrice * UnitsInStock*, use the following `Expression` string:

`UnitPrice * UnitsInStock`

> **NOTE**
>
> LINQ to SQL does not support computed columns as primary keys.

IsDbGenerated

Entity members with `IsDbGenerated` are synchronized immediately after the row of data representing the entity is inserted into the database. The entity member's value is set when `DataContext.SubmitChanges` completes.

IsDescriminator

`IsDescriminator` is used in conjunction with the `InheritanceMapping` attribute to provide an inheritance hierarchy in your data model. For more information, see the section "Mapping an Inheritance Hierarchy," later in this chapter.

IsVersion

`IsVersion` allows you to designate an entity class member to be used for optimistic concurrency control (OCC). This property is discussed in the later section "Concurrency."

UpdateCheck

`UpdateCheck` tells the data context when to detect change conflicts. This property is discussed in the later section "Concurrency."

DataContext Change Tracking

The dirty state of an entity is monitored by the data context. This is usually accomplished with change notifications, provided through the INotifyPropertyChanging.PropertyChanging and INotifyPropertyChanged.PropertyChanged events, raised in the property setters of the entity.

Combining the PropertyChanged and PropertyChanging events raising into every property setter can add up to a lot of plumbing code. Fortunately, the Assign method in the custom ViewModelBase class used throughout this book raises the events required for change tracking.

For more information on the property change notification, in relation to the ViewModelBase class, see Chapter 2.

For entities that do not implement INotifyPropertyChanging, LINQ to SQL maintains a copy of their values. When DataContext.SubmitChanges is called, the current and original values are compared to determine whether the object has changed.

> **TIP**
>
> To decrease the amount of memory used by your app, ensure that entity classes implement INotifyPropertyChanged and INotifyPropertyChanging.

TwitterUser Class

The TwitterUser class contains various properties, such as the screen name of the Twitter user. It also includes a collection of TimelineItem objects that are maintained using an EntitySet. An EntitySet provides for deferred loading and manages the relationship of the collection side of one-to-many relationships between entities.

The TwitterUser constructor initializes the EntitySet, specifying two handlers: one that is called when a TimelineItem is added to its collection; the other, when a TimelineItem is removed (see Listing 26.2).

The TwitterUser class also uses the Index attribute, which tells the DataContext to create a database index for the secondary column ScreenName.

Indexes improve the speed of data retrieval operations by allowing the database engine to quickly locate a record. Without an index, potentially all rows in a table need to be scanned, an expensive O(n) operation.[1]

---

1. O(n) describes algorithm complexity. For more information on Big O notation see http://en.wikipedia.org/wiki/Big_O_notation.

LISTING 26.2   TwitterUser Class (excerpt)

```
[Table]
[Index(Columns = "ScreenName")]
public class TwitterUser : NotifyPropertyChangeBase
{
    public TwitterUser()
    {
        timelineItems = new EntitySet<TimelineItem>(
                            AttachTimelineItem, DetachTimelineItems);
    }

    string id;

    [Column(IsPrimaryKey = true)]
    public string Id
    {
        get
        {
            return id;
        }
        set
        {
            Assign("Id", ref id, value);
        }
    }

    string screenName;

    [Column]
    public string ScreenName
    {
        get
        {
            return screenName;
        }
        set
        {
            Assign("ScreenName", ref screenName, value);
        }
    }

... (ImageUrl and Description properties omitted)

    readonly EntitySet<TimelineItem> timelineItems;

    [Association(
```

LISTING 26.2   Continued

```
        Storage = "timelineItems",
        OtherKey = "TwitterUserId")]
    public EntitySet<TimelineItem> TimelineItems
    {
        get
        {
            return timelineItems;
        }
        set
        {
            timelineItems.Assign(value);
        }
    }

    void AttachTimelineItem(TimelineItem entity)
    {
        OnPropertyChanging("TimelineItems", timelineItems, timelineItems);
        entity.TwitterUser = this;
        OnPropertyChanged("TimelineItems");
    }

    void DetachTimelineItems(TimelineItem entity)
    {
        OnPropertyChanging("TimelineItems", timelineItems, null);
        entity.TwitterUser = null;
        OnPropertyChanged("TimelineItems");
    }
}
```

The PropertyChanging event is raised manually before the assignment of the TimelineItem.TwitterUser property, and the PropertyChanged event is raised after it has been assigned. These calls indicate to the change tracking infrastructure that the TwitterUser object is dirty and differs from the stored value in the database.

Multiplicity and the Association Attribute

One-to-many entity relationships can be defined by decorating entity properties with Association attributes. Two entities participating in a one-to-many relationship with each other each use properties of the Association attribute to indicate on which side each resides.

One-to-many entity relationships are represented as foreign key relationships in the database.

The one-to-many relationship between TwitterUser and TimelineItem is defined with an Association attribute placed on the TwitterUser property of the TimelineItem class. The attribute declares that the `TwitterUserId` column of the `TimelineItem` table is a foreign key of the `TwitterUser` table. It also declares that the user field holds a reference (an `EntityRef`) to a `TwitterUser` object.

Conversely, on the many side of the relationship, the `TwitterUser` property of the `TimelineItem` declares that the `TwitterUserId` property holds the foreign key of the `TwitterUser`.

An `EntityRef` represents the one side of a one-to-many relationship, while an `EntitySet` is the reciprocal and represents the many side.

Twitter DataContext

The `TwitterDataContext` class is the proxy to the Twitter local database and includes two public `Table<TSource>` properties: `TwitterUsers` and `TimelineItems` (see Listing 26.3).

The assignment of the `DataContext.Log` property allows you to monitor the activities of the `DataContext` at runtime, and in particular, to observe the generated SQL as it is being sent to the database. This customized logging is examined later in the chapter.

The `GetTable` property of the `DataContext` class retrieves a `Table<TEntity>` object representing a table in the underlying database. `Table` objects can be queried using LINQ to SQL.

LISTING 26.3   `TwitterDataContext` Class

```
public class TwitterDataContext : DataContext
{
    public TwitterDataContext(string connection) : base(connection)
    {
        Log = new DebugStreamWriter();
    }

    public Table<TwitterUser> TwitterUsers
    {
        get
        {
            return GetTable<TwitterUser>();
        }
    }

    public Table<TimelineItem> TimelineItems
    {
        get
        {
            return GetTable<TimelineItem>();
        }
    }
}
```

The `Table<TEntity>` class allows you to perform CRUD (create, read, update, delete) operations on a table. For example, you can insert a row (representing an entity) into the underlying table using the `Table.InsertOnSubmit(TEntity entity)` method.

The `Table<TEntity>` class also allows you to attach a disconnected (or detached) entity to a new `DataContext`.

As an aside, the `DataContext` base class automatically initializes its public fields of type `Table<TEntity>`. By placing a public field in a `DataContext` derived class, such as the following, the field is automatically assigned when the `DataContext` is instantiated:

```
public Table<TwitterUser>;
```

While this offers a way of exposing `Table` objects from your `DataContext` using less code, the use of public fields is not recommended because it breaks the convention that fields should have private visibility; nonprivate fields violate the encapsulation of the class and make the class less amenable to change.

Database Utilities

While `DataContext` enables you to create and delete a database file, a custom class, called `DatabaseUtility`, is used to directly create and delete the database in isolated storage and to build the connection string for the database.

`TwitterDatabaseUtility` extends the `DatabaseUtility` class, providing the default database filename. `TwitterDatabaseUtility` is used in various locations to create a `DataContext` for the Twitter database.

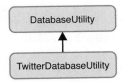

`DatabaseUtility` includes an `InitializeDatabase` method that creates the isolated storage file for the database. When it is called, if the `wipe` parameter is true and the database already exists, then it is deleted before being re-created. See the following excerpt:

```
public void InitializeDatabase(DataContext dataContext, bool wipe = false)
{
    ArgumentValidator.AssertNotNull(dataContext, "dataContext");

    if (localDatabaseMode != LocalDatabaseMode.ReadWrite
        && localDatabaseMode != LocalDatabaseMode.Exclusive)
    {
        return;
    }
```

```
    if (wipe && dataContext.DatabaseExists())
    {
        dataContext.DeleteDatabase();
    }

    if (!dataContext.DatabaseExists())
    {
        dataContext.CreateDatabase();
    }
}
```

Initialization of the local database occurs when the `Launching` event of the `PhoneApplicationService` is raised. For testing purposes, if a debugger is attached, the database is deleted so as to begin with a clean slate. The following excerpt shows the `Launching` event handler:

```
void Application_Launching(object sender, LaunchingEventArgs e)
{
    Debug.WriteLine("Application Launching");

    StateManager.Initialize();

    /* For the Twitter demo. */
    var twitterDatabaseUtility = new TwitterDatabaseUtility();
    bool wipeDatabase = Debugger.IsAttached;
    twitterDatabaseUtility.InitializeDatabase(wipeDatabase);
}
```

When the app is launched, the handler ensures that the database file is created in isolated storage.

Connection Strings

When instantiating a `DataContext`, a connection string must be supplied, indicating the location of the database file and an optional password. See the following example:

```
string connectionString
 = "Data Source='isostore:/DirectoryName/FileName.sdf';Password='password'";
DataContext dataContext = new DataContext(connectionString);
```

The Data Source parameter defines the location of the database file in isolated storage, while the Password parameter is used to access (or create) an encrypted database.

The *isostore* prefix of the Data Source value specifies that the file is located in isolated storage. By omitting the *isostore* prefix, it indicates that the file is located in the XAP file relative to its root directory. You see an example of using a database located in the XAP file later in the chapter.

Table 26.1 describes the database connection string parameters in more detail.

TABLE 26.1   Local Database Connection String Parameters for Windows Phone

Parameter	Description
data source alias: datasource	The name of the database file. This is a required parameter.
Password aliases: Pwd, database password, ssce:database password	A password that is used to encrypt a database or to access an already encrypted database. The string can be up to 40 characters in length. When creating a database, if you specify a password, encryption is automatically enabled on the database. If you specify a blank password, the database is not encrypted.
max buffer size alias: ssce:max buffer size	The largest amount of memory, in kilobytes, that a local database can use before it starts flushing changes to disk. If not specified, the default value is 384. The maximum value is 5120.
max database size alias: ssce:max database size	The maximum size of a local database, in megabytes. If not specified, the default value is 32. The maximum value is 512.
Mode aliases: file mode ssce:mode	The locking mode to use when opening the database file. The following values are valid: *Read Write*: Allows multiple contexts to open and modify the database. This is the default setting if the mode property is not specified. *Read Only*: Allows you to open a read-only copy of the database. This value must be used when using a database located in your app's XAP file. *Exclusive*: Prevents other contexts from opening or modifying the database. *Shared Read*: Allows other contexts to read, but not modify, the database while you have it open. Typically either *Read Write* or *Read* is used. Sometimes it can be beneficial for performance to use two distinct data contexts in an app—one that opens the database in *Read* only mode, and another, used less frequently for updates, which opens it in *Read Write* mode.
Culture Identifier	The culture code to use with the database. For example, en-US for United States English. For the full list of culture codes supported by Windows Phone, see http://bit.ly/yAsBuU. This property is ignored if used when connecting to an existing database.

26

TABLE 26.1   Continued

Parameter	Description
Case Sensitive alias: CaseSensitive	A Boolean value that determines whether the database collation is case-sensitive. This must be set to true to enable case-sensitive collation or false for case-insensitive collation. If not specified, the default value is false. This property is ignored if used when connecting to an existing database.

> **NOTE**
>
> A database must be encrypted when it is created; a password cannot be used to encrypt the database after it has been created.

The ConnectionString property of the custom DatabaseUtility class constructs a connection string using its DatabasePassword property, its DataSource property, and the localDatabaseMode field represented as a custom enum value. See the following excerpt:

```
public string ConnectionString
{
    get
    {
        if (string.IsNullOrWhiteSpace(DatabasePassword))
        {
            return string.Format("Data Source='{0}';Mode={1}",
                DataSource, localDatabaseMode.ToConnectionStringValue());
        }
        return string.Format("Data Source='{0}';Password='{1}';Mode={2}",
                DataSource,
                DatabasePassword,
                localDatabaseMode.ToConnectionStringValue());
    }
}
```

The following excerpt shows the LocalDatabaseMode enum, which represents the four connection string Mode values that were listed in Table 26.1:

```
public enum LocalDatabaseMode
{
    ReadWrite,
    ReadOnly,
    Exclusive,
    SharedRead
}
```

An extension method is used to convert an enum value to a valid Mode value. Using an enum, combined with an extension method for conversion, is an elegant alternative to loosely typed strings. The following excerpt shows the ToConnectionStringValue method:

```
public static class LocalDatabaseModeExtensions
{
    public static string ToConnectionStringValue(
        this LocalDatabaseMode mode)
    {
        switch (mode)
        {
            case LocalDatabaseMode.ReadWrite:
                return "Read Write";
            case LocalDatabaseMode.ReadOnly:
                return "Read Only";
            case LocalDatabaseMode.Exclusive:
                return "Exclusive";
            case LocalDatabaseMode.SharedRead:
                return "Shared Read";
            default:
                throw new ArgumentException(
                    "Unknown mode: " + mode);
        }
    }
}
```

Connection Strings for XAP File Databases

To target a database file in your app's XAP file, do not include the isostore prefix in the Data Source segment of its connection string. The following example shows a connection string for an .sdf file located in a XAP file:

```
string connectionString
    = "Data Source='/ProjectDirectoryName/FileName.sdf';Mode=Read Only";
DataContext dataContext = new DataContext(connectionString);
```

> **NOTE**
>
> The connection string for a database located in your XAP file must use the Mode of Read Only; otherwise a System.Data.SqlServerCe.SqlCeException is raised when attempting to access the database, regardless of whether your query is only attempting to read, such as with a select operation.

The custom DatabaseUtility class takes care of building the connection string. A preprocessor directive in the TwitterDatabaseUtility class allows you to change the location of the Twitter database to the XAP file. If enabled, the Read Only mode is

26

automatically introduced into the connection string. Being in read-only mode, however, breaks the app, because the `TwitterService` needs to write to the database.

Leveraging a Custom Twitter Service

A custom Twitter service is used for all communication with the Twitter web API. The service also provides the ability to cache the results of calls to Twitter using a local database.

The viewmodel, which presents the Twitter timeline information, consumes the Twitter service using an `ITwitterService` interface.

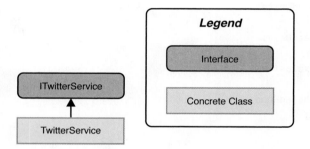

The `ITwitterService` contains two methods designed to execute asynchronously. They are as follows:

▶ `GetTimeline(string screenName,`
                `Action<ResultEventArgs<TwitterUser>> completeAction)`

▶ `GetCachedTimeline(`
                `string screenName,`
                `Action<ResultEventArgs<TwitterUser>> completeAction)`

A caller of either method provides an `Action` argument, which, on completion of the method, is invoked, notifying the caller of the result.

The `ResultEventArgs` class either contains the result produced by the operation, or an `Exception` object. `ResultEventArgs` is presented in Chapter 24, "Network Services."

`GetTimeline` uses the Twitter web API to retrieve a Twitter user's details and her list of status updates. Once a response is received from the Web, the result is converted into entity objects representing the Twitter user and the status updates (`TimelineItem` objects).

`GetCachedTimeline` is used to retrieve a `TwitterUser` from the database. This method does not produce a result until `GetTimeline` has successfully completed at least once because until then no data has been placed in the database.

The default implementation of the `ITwitterService` is the `TwitterService` class. `TwitterService` relies on the `TwitterDatabaseUtility`. A `TwitterDataContext` is created when the `TwitterService` is instantiated, as shown:

```
public class TwitterService : ITwitterService
{
    readonly TwitterDatabaseUtility twitterDatabaseUtility
                                = new TwitterDatabaseUtility();
    readonly TwitterDataContext dataContext;

    public TwitterService()
    {
        dataContext = twitterDatabaseUtility.CreateContext();
    }
...
}
```

The public GetTimeline method queues the Twitter call on a ThreadPool thread. To demonstrate population using the local database, the ThreadPool thread is made to wait for 3 seconds before calling the main GetTimelineCore method. If an exception is raised, the complete action is called, as shown:

```
public void GetTimeline(
    string screenName, Action<ResultEventArgs<TwitterUser>> completeAction)
{
    ArgumentValidator.AssertNotNullOrWhiteSpace(screenName, "userName");
    ArgumentValidator.AssertNotNull(completeAction, "completeAction");

    ThreadPool.QueueUserWorkItem(
        delegate
        {
            try
            {
                /*Wait for a moment to demonstrate the database retrieval.*/
                Wait(3000); /* Equivalent to Thread.Sleep(3000); */
                GetTimelineCore(screenName, completeAction);
            }
            catch (Exception ex)
            {
                Console.WriteLine(ex);
                completeAction(new ResultEventArgs<TwitterUser>(null, ex));
            }
        });
}
```

GetTimelineCore uses the Twitter web API (see Listing 26.4). A WebClient is used to dispatch an HTTP request to the site. When the call returns it is handled within a lambda expression. The result of the call is an XML fragment, which we convert to an XElement using the XElement.Parse method.

The user information is then extracted from the root element before building a list of
TimelineItems. Finally, the data context is used to store the TwitterUser and its associated
TimelineItems in the database.

LISTING 26.4   GetTimelineCore Method

```
void GetTimelineCore(
        string screenName, Action<ResultEventArgs<TwitterUser>> completeAction)
{
    WebClient twitterClient = new WebClient();
    twitterClient.DownloadStringCompleted
        += (o, args) =>
        {
            if (args.Error != null)
            {
                completeAction(
                        new ResultEventArgs<TwitterUser>(null, args.Error));
                return;
            }

            try
            {
                XElement rootElement = XElement.Parse(args.Result);

                XElement element = rootElement.Descendants("status").First();
                XElement userElement = element.Descendants("user").First();
                var twitterUser = new TwitterUser
                {
                    Id = userElement.Element("id").Value,
                    ScreenName = userElement.Element("screen_name").Value,
                    Description = userElement.Element("description").Value,
                    ImageUrl = userElement.Element("profile_image_url").Value,
                };

                IEnumerable<TimelineItem> items = from statusElement
                            in rootElement.Descendants("status")
                        select new TimelineItem
                        {
                            Id = statusElement.Element("id").Value,
                            ReceivedTime = ConvertToDateTime(
                                statusElement.Element("created_at").Value),
                            Text = statusElement.Element("text").Value
                        };

                TwitterUser storedUser = dataContext.TwitterUsers.Where(
                    user => user.ScreenName == screenName).FirstOrDefault();
```

LISTING 26.4   Continued

```
                if (storedUser != null)
                {
                    dataContext.TimelineItems.DeleteAllOnSubmit(
                        dataContext.TimelineItems.Where(
                            item => item.TwitterUserId == storedUser.Id));
                    dataContext.TwitterUsers.DeleteOnSubmit(storedUser);
                    dataContext.SubmitChanges();
                }

                twitterUser.TimelineItems.AddRange(items);
                dataContext.TwitterUsers.InsertOnSubmit(twitterUser);

                dataContext.SubmitChanges();

                completeAction(new ResultEventArgs<TwitterUser>(twitterUser));
            }
            catch (Exception ex)
            {
                Debug.WriteLine("Unable to get timeline. " + ex);
                completeAction(new ResultEventArgs<TwitterUser>(null, ex));
                return;
            }
        };

    twitterClient.DownloadStringAsync(new Uri(
        "http://api.twitter.com/1/statuses/user_timeline.xml?screen_name="
        + screenName));
}
```

Once the Twitter web API has been queried and the result stored in the database, the cached data can be retrieved from the database. This allows the Twitter timeline information to remain viewable when no network connection is available.

> **NOTE**
>
> Changes to the entity model are not persisted to the database until
> DataContext.SubmitChanges is called. New entity objects that have been
> added to the data context are not inserted into the database until SubmitChanges
> is called, and entities that have been removed from the data context are not
> deleted from the database until SubmitChanges is called.

Retrieving the cached data from the local database is the task of the TwitterService object's GetCachedTimeline method.

You see the same pattern applied as earlier; the principle `GetCachedTimelineCore` method is called from a `ThreadPool` thread as shown:

```
public void GetCachedTimeline(
    string screenName, Action<ResultEventArgs<TwitterUser>> completeAction)
{
    ArgumentValidator.AssertNotNullOrWhiteSpace(screenName, "userName");
    ArgumentValidator.AssertNotNull(completeAction, "completeAction");

    ThreadPool.QueueUserWorkItem(
        delegate
        {
            try
            {
                GetCachedTimelineCore(screenName, completeAction);
            }
            catch (Exception ex)
            {
                Console.WriteLine(ex);
                completeAction(new ResultEventArgs<TwitterUser>(null, ex));
            }
        });
}
```

The `GetCachedTimelineCore` method uses the data context to retrieve the Twitter user with the specified screen name, shown in the following excerpt:

```
void GetCachedTimelineCore(
        string userName, Action<ResultEventArgs<TwitterUser>> completeAction)
{
    TwitterUser storedUser = dataContext.TwitterUsers.Where(
            user => user.ScreenName == userName).FirstOrDefault();

    completeAction(new ResultEventArgs<TwitterUser>(storedUser));
}
```

You saw how the `TwitterService` is able to retrieve live data from the Twitter web API and then cache it using a local database. Subsequent sections look at presenting this data to the user.

Gathering the User's Credentials with the Sign-In View

The `TwitterSignInView` and associated viewmodel provide the UI for gathering the user's Twitter credentials. The sample, however, does not actually require the user to sign in to Twitter because we are merely retrieving the timeline for the user, and this does not require authentication.

A sign-in screen is included to provide the infrastructure to extend the app in the direction of being a fully blown Twitter app. It also provides a nice segue to demonstrate the custom INavigationService, which is discussed later in the chapter.

The TwitterSignInViewModel class contains properties for the user's Twitter credentials and a property that causes the password to be retained by the app (see Listing 26.5).

The viewmodel relies on the ViewModelBase class for state persistency. The Username, Password, and RememberPassword properties are each decorated with the custom State attribute so that they are persisted to isolated storage. For details on the custom state preservation system, see Chapter 25, "Isolated Storage and State Preservation."

When executed, the viewmodel's SignInCommand is responsible for navigating to the TwitterTimeline page and for deregistering state preservation for the Password property if the user has indicated that the app should not remember the password.

The Navigate method and the custom navigation functionality are discussed later in this chapter.

LISTING 26.5   TwitterSignInViewModel Class

```
public class TwitterSignInViewModel : ViewModelBase
{
    public TwitterSignInViewModel()
    {
        signInCommand = new DelegateCommand(
            obj =>
            {
                if (!rememberPassword)
                {
                    DeregisterStatefulProperty(
                            ApplicationStateType.Persistent, () => Password);
                }
                Navigate("/TwitterTimeline/" + username);
            });
    }

    string username;

    [Stateful(ApplicationStateType.Persistent)]
    public string Username
    {
        get
        {
            return username;
        }
        set
        {
```

26

LISTING 26.5   Continued

```csharp
            Assign(() => Username, ref username, value);
    }
}

string password;

[Stateful(ApplicationStateType.Persistent)]
public string Password
{
    get
    {
        return password;
    }
    set
    {
        Assign(() => Password, ref password, value);
    }
}


readonly DelegateCommand signInCommand;

public ICommand SignInCommand
{
    get
    {
        return signInCommand;
    }
}


bool rememberPassword = true;

[Stateful(ApplicationStateType.Persistent)]
public bool RememberPassword
{
    get
    {
        return rememberPassword;
    }
    set
    {
        Assign(() => RememberPassword, ref rememberPassword, value);
    }
}
}
```

Within the view's XAML, an `AppBarIconButton` is bound to the `SignInCommand`.

A `ToggleSwitch` from the Silverlight Toolkit is used to set the `RememberPassword` property of the viewmodel. See the following excerpt:

```xaml
<Grid x:Name="LayoutRoot" Background="Transparent">
    <Grid.RowDefinitions>
        <RowDefinition Height="Auto"/>
        <RowDefinition Height="*"/>
    </Grid.RowDefinitions>

    <u:AppBar>
        <u:AppBarIconButton
            Command="{Binding SignInCommand}"
            Text="Sign In"
         IconUri="/Images/ApplicationBarIcons/ApplicationBar.Check.png" />
    </u:AppBar>

    <StackPanel Grid.Row="0" Style="{StaticResource PageTitlePanelStyle}">
        <TextBlock Text="Windows Phone 7 Unleashed"
            Style="{StaticResource PhoneTextAppTitleStyle}" />
        <TextBlock Text="Twitter sign in"
            Style="{StaticResource PhoneTextPageTitleStyle}" />
    </StackPanel>

    <StackPanel x:Name="ContentPanel" Grid.Row="1"
            Margin="{StaticResource PhoneHorizontalMargin}">
        <TextBlock Text="username"
            Style="{StaticResource LabelTextIndentedStyle}" />
        <TextBox Text="{Binding Username, Mode=TwoWay}" />
        <TextBlock Text="password"
            Style="{StaticResource LabelTextIndentedStyle}" />
        <!--<PasswordBox Password="{Binding Password, Mode=TwoWay}" />-->
        <TextBox Text="not required in this example." IsReadOnly="True" />
        <toolkit:ToggleSwitch
            IsChecked="{Binding RememberPassword, Mode=TwoWay}"
                    Header="Remember Password" />
    </StackPanel>

</Grid>
```

Tapping the application bar button executes the `SignInCommand`, which causes the app to navigate to the timeline view page (see Figure 26.4).

FIGURE 26.4   Twitter sign-in page

If the app happens to be tombstoned or exited, the state of the various controls is retained in persistent storage.

Tapping the `ApplicationBarIconButton` navigates the app to the timeline view page.

Viewing Tweets with the Timeline View

The timeline view presents a Twitter user's list of recent tweets (status updates). The `TwitterTimelineViewModel` class relies on the `ITwitterService` to retrieve the list of tweets.

`TwitterTimelineViewModel` contains several properties, which are described in the following list:

▶ **TimelineItems**—An `IEnumerable` of `TimelineItem` objects, which is populated using the `ITwitterService`. This list is bound to a `ListBox` control in the view.

▶ **ScreenName**—The Twitter screen name that was supplied by the user on the sign-in view.

▶ **ImageUrl**—The URL to the Twitter user's avatar. This is retrieved from the Twitter web API.

▶ **Message**—An arbitrary string used to supply feedback to the user during retrieval.

▶ **Busy**—A `bool` value indicating whether an asynchronous operation is under way.

The viewmodel also includes a command of type `DelegateCommand<string>` named `loadUserTimelineCommand`, which coordinates the retrieval of the list of status updates. `LoadUserTimelineCommand` receives a Twitter screen name, which is passed to the `ITwitterService`. See the following excerpt:

```
public class TwitterTimelineViewModel : ViewModelBase
{
    readonly ITwitterService twitterService;

    public TwitterTimelineViewModel(ITwitterService twitterService)
    {
        this.twitterService = ArgumentValidator.AssertNotNull(
                                twitterService, "twitterService");

        loadUserTimelineCommand = new DelegateCommand<string>(LoadTimeline);
    }
...
}
```

When the `LoadUserTimelineCommand` executes, the `LoadTimeline` method is called. This method first ensures that a Twitter screen name has been supplied; if not, it navigates back to the sign-in page.

The `ITwitterService.GetCachedTimeline` method executes asynchronously and attempts to retrieve the cached timeline from the local database. When it returns, the viewmodel is populated using the `HandleGetTimelineResult`. After attempting to restore the cached timeline, the `ITwitterService.GetTimeline` method is used to retrieve the latest data from the Twitter web API. See the following excerpt:

```
void LoadTimeline(string twitterScreenName)
{
    if (string.IsNullOrWhiteSpace(twitterScreenName))
    {
        var messageService = Dependency.Resolve<IMessageService>();
        messageService.ShowError("Please provide a twitter screen name.");

        var navigationService = Dependency.Resolve<INavigationService>();
        navigationService.GoBack();

        return;
    }

    if (twitterScreenName == screenName)
    {
        return;
    }

    Busy = true;

    try
    {
```

```
                Message = "Retrieving cached timeline from database.";

                twitterService.GetCachedTimeline(twitterScreenName,
                    args =>
                        {
                            HandleGetTimelineResult(args);
                            Message = "Retrieving real data from Twitter.";
                            Busy = true;
                            twitterService.GetTimeline(
                                twitterScreenName, HandleGetTimelineResult);
                        });
            }
            catch (Exception ex)
            {
                Busy = false;
                Message = string.Format("Error retrieving items.");
                Console.WriteLine(ex);
            }
        }
```

The `HandleGetTimelineResult` method is called twice, once for the cached items and then for the live Twitter data. The `Error` property of the `ResultEventArgs` is used to determine whether the call completed successfully, and if so, the viewmodel's properties are populated accordingly:

```
void HandleGetTimelineResult(ResultEventArgs<TwitterUser> e)
{
    Busy = false;

    if (e.Error != null)
    {
        Message = "Unable to retrieve timeline.";
        return;
    }

    if (e.Result == null)
    {
        Message = "No result";
        return;
    }

    Message = "Received result.";
    TimelineItems = e.Result.TimelineItems.ToList();
    ScreenName = e.Result.ScreenName;
    ImageUrl = e.Result.ImageUrl;
}
```

When the viewmodel is instantiated, in the view's code-beside class, it is passed a `TwitterService` object, as shown:

```
public TwitterTimelineView()
{
    InitializeComponent();
    DataContext = new TwitterTimelineViewModel(new TwitterService());
}
```

The view executes the `LoadUserTimelineCommand` in its `OnNavigatedTo` handler, as shown:

```
protected override void OnNavigatedTo(NavigationEventArgs e)
{
    base.OnNavigatedTo(e);

    string twitterName;
    if (NavigationContext.QueryString.TryGetValue("name", out twitterName))
    {
        ViewModel.LoadUserTimelineCommand.Execute(twitterName);
    }
}
```

The view XAML contains controls to display the Twitter timeline information, as well as the Twitter user information. A `ListBox` presents each `TimelineItem` using a `DataTemplate`, as shown in the following excerpt:

```
<Grid x:Name="ContentPanel" Grid.Row="1">
    <Grid.RowDefinitions>
        <RowDefinition Height="Auto" />
        <RowDefinition Height="*" />
        <RowDefinition Height="Auto" />
    </Grid.RowDefinitions>

    <Grid Margin="{StaticResource PhoneMargin}">
        <Grid.ColumnDefinitions>
            <ColumnDefinition Width="Auto" />
            <ColumnDefinition Width="*" />
        </Grid.ColumnDefinitions>

        <Image Source="{Binding ImageUrl}"
                MaxWidth="60" MaxHeight="60" />
        <TextBlock Grid.Column="1" Text="{Binding ScreenName}"
            Style="{StaticResource PhoneTextExtraLargeStyle}" />
    </Grid>

    <ListBox Grid.Row="1"
        ItemsSource="{Binding TimelineItems}"
```

```
                    Margin="{StaticResource PhoneHorizontalMargin}">
            <ListBox.ItemTemplate>
                <DataTemplate>
                    <Border CornerRadius="10"
                    BorderBrush="{StaticResource PhoneBorderBrush}"
                    BorderThickness="2"
                    Margin="14,5,4,10">
                        <Grid Margin="10">
                            <Grid.RowDefinitions>
                                <RowDefinition />
                                <RowDefinition />
                            </Grid.RowDefinitions>
                            <Grid.ColumnDefinitions>
                                <ColumnDefinition Width="100" />
                                <ColumnDefinition Width="*" />
                            </Grid.ColumnDefinitions>

                            <TextBlock
                                Text="{Binding ReceivedTime,
                                StringFormat='0:HH:mm:ss'}"
                                MaxWidth="100" />

                            <TextBlock Text="{Binding Text}"
                            Grid.Column="1"
                            TextWrapping="Wrap"
                            Style="{StaticResource PhoneTextSmallStyle}" />

                        </Grid>
                    </Border>
                </DataTemplate>
            </ListBox.ItemTemplate>
        </ListBox>
</Grid>
```

A `ProgressIndicator` is used to monitor the `Busy` property of the viewmodel and to display the viewmodel's `Message` text, as shown:

```
<shell:SystemTray.ProgressIndicator>
    <shell:ProgressIndicator IsIndeterminate="{Binding Busy}"
                             IsVisible="{Binding Busy}"
                             Text="{Binding Message}" />
</shell:SystemTray.ProgressIndicator>
```

When a result is received from the Twitter service it is displayed in the view as shown in Figure 26.5.

FIGURE 26.5   `TwitterTimelineView` page

Viewing a Local Database Schema

Visually exploring your database schema can help to reveal inadequacies in its structure. Missing indexes and foreign key relationships can be overlooked when relying solely on metadata in your code. In addition, having the ability to arbitrarily query your tables to see what is in your database can be useful during development.

Given that SQL CE database files usually reside in isolated storage, however, makes exploring the schema difficult.

This section looks at tools to retrieve your local database file from isolated storage and at using Visual Studio and SQL Server Management Studio to view the database on your desktop.

File Explorers for Isolated Storage

The Windows Phone 7.5 SDK comes with a tool that allows you to read and write to your app's isolated storage area via the command line. The first part of this section examines the Isolated Storage Explorer present in the Windows Phone SDK. The second part examines a free alternative third-party explorer named WP7 Isolated Storage Explorer.

Windows Phone 7.5 SDK Isolated Storage Explorer

Depending on your operating system, Isolated Storage Explorer is installed in one of following locations:

▶ Program Files\Microsoft SDKs\Windows
   Phone\v7.1\Tools\IsolatedStorageExplorerTool

▶ Program Files (x86)\Microsoft SDKs\Windows
   Phone\v7.1\Tools\IsolatedStorageExplorerTool

When using Isolated Storage Explorer, your app must be deployed to the device or emulator. The emulator or device must be running, but the app does not have to be running.

Isolated Storage Explorer uses the following syntax:

```
ISETool.exe <ts|rs|dir[:device-folder]> <xd|de> <Product GUID> [<desktop-path>]
```

Table 26.2 lists the command-line options for Isolated Storage Explorer.

TABLE 26.2   Isolated Storage Explorer Command-Line Options

Option	Description
ts	(Take snapshot) Copies the files and directories in isolated storage from the device or emulator to your computer.
rs	(Restore snapshot) Replaces the files and directories in isolated storage on the device or emulator with files and directories from your computer.
dir	Lists the files and directories in the specified directory of isolated storage. If a directory is not specified, the files and directories in the root are listed.
device-folder	Specifies the directory in isolated storage on the device or emulator that you want to target.
xd	Indicates to target the emulator.
de	Indicates to target a tethered device.
Product GUID	Specifies the ProductID from the WPAppManifest.xml file for the application you want to test.
desktop-path	Specifies the directory on your computer where isolated storage files are written to or copied from. A subdirectory named IsolatedStore is created in desktop-path when files are copied using the ts command. If the specified directory already exists, a ts command overwrites the contents of the directory with no warning.

Source: http://msdn.microsoft.com/en-us/library/hh286408(v=vs.92).aspx

To use the Isolated Storage Explorer, open a command window and navigate to the location of ISETool.exe. Retrieve the product GUID from the ProductID attribute of the App element in the project's WMAppManifest.xml file.

Listing the files and directories at the root directory of an app's isolated storage area can be done using the following command (replacing the GUID with your app's product GUID):

```
ISETool.exe dir xd 11111111-2222-3333-4444-555555555555
```

To copy all of the files from isolated storage to your computer, use the following command:

```
ISETool.exe ts xd 11111111-2222-3333-4444-555555555555 "C:\Phone"
```

This command creates a directory on your computer named C:\Phone\IsolatedStore and copies the files and directories in isolated storage into the directory.

> **CAUTION**
>
> If the IsolatedStore directory exists and the copy command is performed, the contents of the IsolatedStore directory are overwritten without any warning.

Use the following command to replace all the files in isolated storage with files from your computer:

```
SETool.exe rs xd 11111111-2222-3333-4444-555555555555 "C:\Phone\IsolatedStore"
```

WP7 Isolated Storage Explorer

A useful alternative to the built-in Isolated Storage Explorer is the WP7 Isolated Storage Explorer, which can be found at http://wp7explorer.codeplex.com/. This open source tool can be used to retrieve a local database from isolated storage, and works both on the emulator and a real device. The advantage of the WP7 Isolated Storage Explorer is that it comes with a GUI.

The tool can be used either as a standalone application or within Visual Studio and provides a dockable tool window that displays the contents of your app's isolated storage directory (see Figure 26.6).

FIGURE 26.6   WP7 Isolated Storage Explorer dockable window

WP7 Isolated Storage Explorer uses WCF service to communicate with your app.

After installing the tool, to use it in your project, add a reference to the `IsolatedStorageExplorer` assembly and then add some initialization code to your app's launching and activated events, as shown:

```
void Application_Launching(object sender, LaunchingEventArgs e)
{
    IsolatedStorageExplorer.Explorer.Start("localhost");
}

void Application_Activated(object sender, ActivatedEventArgs e)
{
    IsolatedStorageExplorer.Explorer.RestoreFromTombstone();
}
```

The ability to retrieve files from isolated storage and open them on your desktop is very useful, and being able to retrieve a local database from isolated storage means that it can then be loaded into Visual Studio or SQL Server Management Studio, allowing you to explore the schema and to verify the results of your mapping attributes. It is also possible to modify the structure of a database and use the SqlMetal tool to generate your data model, including its `DataContext` and entity classes. The database-first approach using SqlMetal is discussed in a later section.

Viewing and Modifying an SQL CE Database File

Once an SQL CE file has been retrieved from isolated storage, it can be opened in an application such as Visual Studio or Microsoft SQL Server Management Studio.

To open an .sdf file in Visual Studio, follow these steps:

1. Within Visual Studio, right-click on the Data Connections node in the Server Explorer and select Add Connection. The Add Connection dialog is displayed (see Figure 26.7).

2. Within the Add Connection dialog, set the Data Source to Microsoft SQL Server Compact 3.5.

3. Browse and locate the .sdf file using the Connection Properties section.

4. Select OK.

The Server Explorer pane allows you to explore and modify the database schema (see Figure 26.8), and to view table data by right-clicking on a table node and selecting Show Table Data.

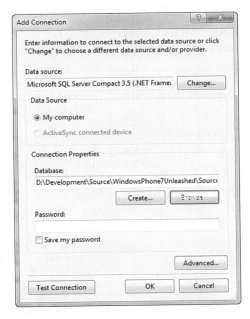

FIGURE 26.7   Visual Studio's Add Connection dialog

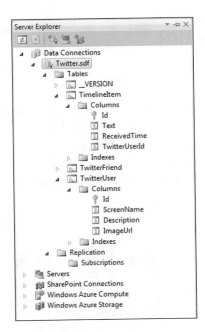

FIGURE 26.8   Server Explorer with the Twitter.sdf database connected

If you prefer to use a dedicated database management tool, such as Microsoft SQL Server Management Studio, you can. The 2008 version was used for this demonstration, but the 2005 version can also be used if it has at least service pack 2 installed.

To open an .sdf file in SQL Server Management Studio, follow these steps:

1. Within SQL Server Management Studio select File and then Connect Object Explorer (see Figure 26.9).

2. Within the Connect to Server dialog, set the Server Type to SQL Server Compact Edition.

3. Use the Database File combo box to browse to your .sdf file.

4. Select Connect.

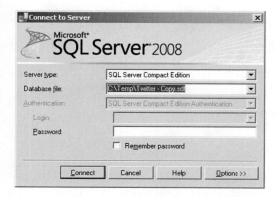

FIGURE 26.9   The SQL Server Management Studio Connect to Server dialog

Once connected, the database is displayed in the Object Explorer. You can write queries to explore the table data using the New Query button on the toolbar (see Figure 26.10).

The ability to visually explore your database schema is important during development. The next section looks at how to generate an entity model from a database using a database-first approach, allowing you to not only view the schema but to make changes to it also.

Database-First Using SqlMetal

So far, this chapter has focused on a code-first approach for generating a local database. To reiterate, code-first is the recommended approach for developing on the phone. The database-first approach, however, can also be used, though it is not fully supported.

SqlMetal is a command-line tool used to generate an entity model from a database. SqlMetal is not fully compatible with Windows Phone, as the code it generates does not compile until some minor alterations are made to it.

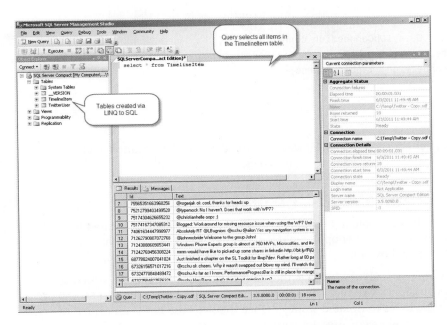

FIGURE 26.10   An .sdf file opened in SQL Server Management Studio

SqlMetal generates a `DataContext` derived class and entities representing database tables. Associations are inferred from the foreign key relationships in the database.

SqlMetal can be launched via a Visual Studio Command Prompt by selecting Microsoft Visual Studio 2010/Visual Studio Tools/Visual Studio Command Prompt (2010) in the Windows Start menu.

In the following example, the database file has been downloaded from isolated storage, using the WP7 Isolated Storage Explorer, and placed in a directory called C:\Unleashed. SqlMetal is provided with the database path, the name code file to output, and the name-space in which to place all generated classes (ignore line breaks):

```
C:\Unleashed>SqlMetal C:\Unleashed\Twitter.sdf
                /code:C:\Unleashed\TwitterDataModel.cs
                /namespace:DanielVaughan.WindowsPhone7Unleashed.Examples
```

Once the code file has been generated, it can be added to your project. But before it can be compiled, two constructors must be removed. The key to identifying the errant constructors is that they both accept an `IDbConnection` and resemble the methods shown in the following excerpt:

```
public Twitter(System.Data.IDbConnection connection)
    : base(connection, mappingSource)
{
    OnCreated();
}
```

```
public Twitter(
        System.Data.IDbConnection connection,
        System.Data.Linq.Mapping.MappingSource mappingSource) :
     base(connection, mappingSource)
{

    OnCreated();
}
```

An example of a generated code file is located in the downloadable sample code. The file is named TwitterDataModel_Generated_Unused.cs.

Deploying a Database to Isolated Storage

As stated earlier in this chapter, a local database is read-only when it is located in a XAP file. If you want to provide a prepopulated database that is writable from your app, the database must be copied by your app, from your XAP file, to isolated storage.

Like any other resource, such as an image file, an .sdf database file may be stored as content within your app's XAP file. The app then reads the database file as a Stream of bytes and writes the bytes to isolated storage. Once the database has been copied to isolated storage, it is ready to be used by your app.

> **NOTE**
>
> To prevent the size of your project's assembly from being unnecessarily increased by the inclusion of a database file, set the file's Build Action to Content in the Visual Studio Properties pane. This decreases your app's startup time because it takes less time for the CLR to load a smaller assembly. It does not, however, affect your project's XAP file size.

Listing 26.6 shows the custom IsolatedStorageUtility class, whose CopyApplicationResourceToIsolatedStorage method locates an application resource and copies it as a stream to a specified location in isolated storage.

LISTING 26.6   IsolatedStorageUtility Class (excerpt)

```
public class IsolatedStorageUtility : IIsolatedStorageUtility, ISettingsService
{
    public void CopyApplicationResourceToIsolatedStorage(
                    string inResourceName, string outFilename)
    {
        ArgumentValidator.AssertNotNull(inResourceName, "inResourceName");
        ArgumentValidator.AssertNotNullOrWhiteSpace(outFilename, "outFilename");

        Uri uri = new Uri(inResourceName, UriKind.Relative);
```

LISTING 26.6   Continued

```csharp
        string destination = outFilename;
        int seperatorIndex = destination.LastIndexOf("/");
        if (seperatorIndex == destination.Length - 1)
        {
            throw new InvalidOperationException(
                string.Format("Destination '{0}' should not end with '/'",
                            destination));
        }

        string directory = null;
        if (seperatorIndex != -1)
        {
            directory = destination.Substring(0, seperatorIndex);
        }

        using (Stream resourceStream = Application.GetResourceStream(uri).Stream)
        {
            using (IsolatedStorageFile isolatedStorageFile
                    = IsolatedStorageFile.GetUserStoreForApplication())
            {
                if (!string.IsNullOrWhiteSpace(directory)
                    && !isolatedStorageFile.DirectoryExists(directory))
                {
                    isolatedStorageFile.CreateDirectory(directory);
                }

                using (IsolatedStorageFileStream outStream
                    = isolatedStorageFile.OpenFile(
                                        destination, FileMode.Create))
                {
                    resourceStream.CopyTo(outStream);
                }
            }
        }
    }
...
}
```

26

A database file can then be copied from a XAP file to isolated storage in a single step:

```csharp
IsolatedStorageUtility.CopyApplicationResourceToIsolatedStorage(
        "/Subdirectory/XapDatabase.sdf",
        "/Subdirectory/IsolatedStorageDatabase.sdf");
```

This can be seen in action in the unit test class named `IsolatedStorageUtilityTests`, located in the downloadable sample code (see Listing 26.7). The `CopyDatabaseToIsolatedStorage` test method copies an .sdf file to isolated storage and then verifies that the bytes of both files are equivalent.

The `CollectionAssert.AreEquivalent` method compares the members of both collections. If all members match, the assert succeeds. The `CollectionAssert` class is a part of the Silverlight Unit Testing Framework, discussed in Chapter 22, "Unit Testing."

LISTING 26.7   IsolatedStorageUtilityTests.CopyDatabaseToIsolatedStorage Method

```
[TestMethod]
public void CopyDatabaseToIsolatedStorage()
{
    const string databaseName = "TestDatabase.sdf";
    IsolatedStorageUtility utility = new IsolatedStorageUtility();
    utility.CopyApplicationResourceToIsolatedStorage(databaseName, databaseName);

    Uri uri = new Uri(databaseName, UriKind.Relative);

    byte[] resourceBytes;

    using (Stream resourceStream = Application.GetResourceStream(uri).Stream)
    {
        resourceBytes = resourceStream.ReadAllBytes();
    }

    Assert.IsNotNull(resourceBytes, "Resource bytes in null");
    Assert.IsTrue(resourceBytes.Length > 0, "Resource bytes length <= 0.");

    using (IsolatedStorageFile isolatedStorageFile
                = IsolatedStorageFile.GetUserStoreForApplication())
    {
        using (IsolatedStorageFileStream outStream
            = isolatedStorageFile.OpenFile(databaseName, FileMode.Open))
        {
            byte[] isolatedStorageBytes = outStream.ReadAllBytes();
            Assert.IsNotNull(isolatedStorageBytes);
            Assert.IsTrue(isolatedStorageBytes.Length > 0);

            CollectionAssert.AreEquivalent(resourceBytes, isolatedStorageBytes);
        }
    }
}
```

Abstracting the Navigation Service

This section begins with a brief note about its inclusion. I did not intend to show the abstraction of the navigation service. When I began work on the sample for this chapter, however, and I reached the point of needing to navigate from the sign-in page to the timeline page, I felt that it would make for a nice demonstration of a custom testable navigation service.

The custom navigation service abstracts the navigation mechanism provided by the `System.Windows.Controls.Frame` component or the `System.Windows.Navigation.NavigationService` (available via the `NavigationService` property of the `Page` class).

A custom `INavigationService` interface is used to navigate in a UI technology agnostic manner and allows the class implementation of the interface to be replaced to enable unit testing of viewmodels. `INavigationService` contains the following three methods:

▶ **GoBack**—Navigates the application to the most recent entry in the back navigation history or raises an exception if no entry exists.

▶ **Navigate(Uri source)**—Navigates to the content specified by the uniform resource identifier (URI).

▶ **Navigate(string relativeUrl)**—Navigates to the content specified by the relative URL.

Included in the downloadable sample code are two implementations of the `INavigationService`, which are also present and maintained in the open-source project Calcium (http://calciumsdk.net). The first implementation, named `NavigationServiceWrapper`, leverages the `System.Windows.Navigation.NavigationService` of a `Page`. The second implementation, named `FrameNavigationService`, relies on the phone app's root `Frame` (see Listing 26.8). The `FrameNavigationService` is the implementation used in the sample for this chapter and is the recommended implementation for use on the phone.

LISTING 26.8   FrameNavigationService Class

```
public class FrameNavigationService : INavigationService
{
    Frame frameUseProperty;

    Frame Frame
    {
        get
        {
            if (frameUseProperty == null)
            {
                frameUseProperty = (Frame)Application.Current.RootVisual;
            }
```

LISTING 26.8 Continued

```
                return frameUseProperty;
        }
    }

    public FrameNavigationService(Frame frame)
    {
        frameUseProperty = ArgumentValidator.AssertNotNull(frame, "frame");
    }

    [InjectDependencies]
    public FrameNavigationService()
    {
        /* Intentionally left blank. */
    }

    public void GoBack()
    {
        Frame.GoBack();
    }

    public void Navigate(Uri source)
    {
        ArgumentValidator.AssertNotNull(source, "source");
        Frame.Navigate(source);
    }

    public void Navigate(string relativeUrl)
    {
        ArgumentValidator.AssertNotNull(relativeUrl, "relativeUrl");
        Frame.Navigate(new Uri(relativeUrl, UriKind.Relative));
    }
}
```

The INavigationService is placed in the IoC container in the App class's
InitializeContainer method, as shown:

```
void InitializeContainer()
{
    SimpleContainer container = new SimpleContainer();
    container.InitializeServiceLocator();
    ...
    Dependency.Register<INavigationService, FrameNavigationService>(true);
}
```

The `InjectDependencies` attribute on the `FrameNavigationService` parameterless constructor, indicates to the dependency injection system that it should use that particular constructor when instantiating the class.

In the Twitter timeline viewer sample for this chapter, the `TwitterSignInViewModel` class uses the `INavigationService` to navigate to the `TimelineView` page. `TwitterSignInViewModel` relies on a `UriMapping` to navigate to the page. The URI mapping is located in the App.xaml file of the project and causes the root frame of the app to direct to `TwitterTimelineView.xaml` whenever an attempt is made to navigate to a URI beginning with /TwitterTimeline/. See the following excerpt from the App.xaml file:

```
<phone:PhoneApplicationFrame.UriMapper>
    <navigation:UriMapper>
        <navigation:UriMapper.UriMappings>
            <navigation:UriMapping Uri="/TwitterTimeline/{name}"
                MappedUri="/DataDrivenApps/TwitterExample
                            /TwitterTimelineView.xaml?name={name}" />
        </navigation:UriMapper.UriMappings>
    </navigation:UriMapper>
</phone:PhoneApplicationFrame.UriMapper>
```

The screen name of the Twitter user is passed using a query string parameter called name.

By abstracting the `INavigationService`, you increase the reusability of your viewmodel code, and it enables you to coordinate navigation via viewmodel logic. This alleviates the logic fragmentation that can occur when relying on the view to perform navigation.

Observing LINQ to SQL Queries with a Custom Log

LINQ to SQL allows you to capture the generated SQL as it is being sent to a local database. This can be achieved by creating a custom `TextWriter` that outputs to the Visual Studio console window using `Debug.WriteLine`. An instance of the custom `TextWriter` is assigned to the `Log` property of the `DataContext` class.

John Gallardo demonstrates how to do this on his blog at http://bit.ly/mJYY74. The custom `TextWriter`, called `DebugStreamWriter`, is shown in Listing 26.9.

LISTING 26.9   `DebugStreamWriter` Class

```
public class DebugStreamWriter : TextWriter
{
    readonly int bufferSize = 256;
    readonly StringBuilder stringBuilder;

    public DebugStreamWriter(int bufferSize = 256)
    {
        this.bufferSize
            = ArgumentValidator.AssertGreaterThan(0, bufferSize, "bufferSize");
```

26

LISTING 26.9   Continued

```csharp
        stringBuilder = new StringBuilder(bufferSize);
    }

    public override Encoding Encoding
    {
        get
        {
            return Encoding.UTF8;
        }
    }

    public override void Write(char value)
    {
        stringBuilder.Append(value);
        if (stringBuilder.Length >= bufferSize)
        {
            Flush();
        }
    }

    public override void WriteLine(string value)
    {
        Flush();

        using (var reader = new StringReader(value))
        {
            string line;
            while ((line = reader.ReadLine()) != null)
            {
                Debug.WriteLine(line);
            }
        }
    }

    protected override void Dispose(bool disposing)
    {
        if (disposing)
        {
            Flush();
        }
    }

    public override void Flush()
    {
```

LISTING 26.9   Continued

```
        if (stringBuilder.Length > 0)
        {
            Debug.WriteLine(stringBuilder);
            stringBuilder.Clear();
        }
    }
}
```

To send all LINQ to SQL logging output to the `DebugStreamWriter`, it is assigned to the `Log` property of the `DataContext` class. I have chosen to do this in the `TwitterDataContext` class, as shown:

```
public class TwitterDataContext : DataContext
{
    public TwitterDataContext(string connection) : base(connection)
    {
        Log = new DebugStreamWriter();
    }
...
}
```

With this in place, we are able to view the activity of the `DataContext` via the Visual Studio Output pane (see Figure 26.11).

Observing the generated SQL can help you gain an understanding of how LINQ to SQL works, as well as giving you the opportunity to optimize query complexity.

Updating a Database Schema

It is almost inevitable that when updating your app, adding new features and so forth, you will want to make changes to your database schema. Fortunately, local database support on the phone includes the ability to perform additive changes to a database, such as adding tables, columns, indexes, or associations, while preserving the data in the database.

For more complex schema changes, however, such as dropping a column from a table, you need to create a new database and migrate the data to the new schema.

> **NOTE**
>
> Changes to your local database schema begin with changing the object model of the corresponding data context. Therefore, modify your entity classes first to reflect the desired state of the schema.

26

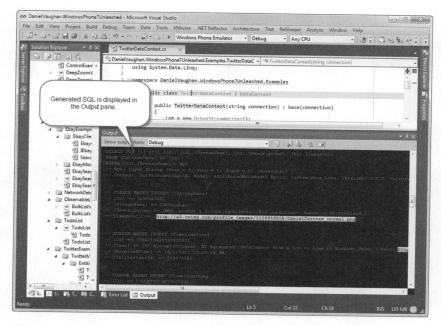

FIGURE 26.11   The Output pane displays the LINQ to SQL query.

The `Microsoft.Phone.Data.Linq.DatabaseSchemaUpdater` class provides four schema altering methods:

▶ `AddColumn<T>(string columnPropertyName)`

▶ `AddTable<T>()`

▶ `AddIndex<T>(string indexName)`

▶ `AddAssociation<T>(string associationPropertyName)`

The following sections discuss each of these methods in greater detail.

AddColumn

`AddColumn` allows you to add a new column to an existing table. For example, if you added a new property to the `TwitterUser` class to record the user's age, you would then need to use the `DatabaseSchemaUpdater` to create a new column to store the `Age` value. This could be achieved in the following manner:

```
using (DataContext dataContext
          = new TwitterDataContext("isostore:Twitter.sdf"))
{
    DatabaseSchemaUpdater updater
              = dataContext.CreateDatabaseSchemaUpdater();
```

```
    updater.AddColumn<TwitterUser>("Age");
    updater.Execute();
}
```

NOTE

The AddColumn method only allows columns to be added that can contain null values. Therefore, decorating a property with [Column(CanBeNull = false)] prevents the AddColumn method from succeeding and causes an SqlCeException to be raised when the DatabaseSchemaUpdater.Execute method is called.

The database does not change to reflect updates from the DatabaseSchemaUpdater until its Execute method is called, at which point all changes are submitted to the local database as a single transaction, which ensures the database maintains integrity if it is interrupted, such as when the user exits the app during an upgrade.

AddTable

Using the AddTable method allows you to create a new table for an entity class. On adding a new table, the DatabaseSchemaUpdater also applies the metadata associated with the entity class and creates any related indexes or foreign key constraints.

To add a new entity to the Twitter data model, we first create that entity and decorate it with Table and Column attributes. In the following example, the TwitterFriend class represents a Twitter user who happens to be a contact of another Twitter user (see Listing 26.10). TwitterFriend contains an Id and a ScreenName property. In addition, an index is declared for the ScreenName property.

LISTING 26.10   TwitterFriend Class

```
[Table]
[Index(Columns = "ScreenName")]
public class TwitterFriend : NotifyPropertyChangeBase
{
    string id;

    [Column(IsPrimaryKey = true)]
    public string Id
    {
        get
        {
            return id;
        }
        set
        {
```

LISTING 26.10   Continued

```
            Assign("Id", ref id, value);
        }
    }

    string screenName;

    [Column]
    public string ScreenName
    {
        get
        {
            return screenName;
        }
        set
        {
            Assign("ScreenName", ref screenName, value);
        }
    }
}
```

The following code is used to upgrade the schema to include a new table for storing TwitterFriend data:

```
using (DataContext dataContext
            = new TwitterDataContext("isostore:Twitter.sdf"))
{
    DatabaseSchemaUpdater updater
            = dataContext.CreateDatabaseSchemaUpdater();
    updater.AddTable<TwitterFriend>();
    updater.Execute();
}
```

It can be seen from Figure 26.12 that after execution, the Twitter database contains the new table, with a secondary index on the ScreenName column, as desired.

AddIndex

Suboptimal query performance is sometimes caused by table scans, where a query causes every row of a table to be examined. Depending on the kind of data in a column, bottlenecks of this nature can often be rectified by placing an index on the column.

The need for an index may be discovered after a table has been populated with a substantial number of records and after an app has been published to the marketplace, or the need may arise with the introduction of a new feature that causes the table to be queried in a different way. In both cases, adding an index to an existing table is done by decorating the entity class with an `Index` attribute and then by calling `DatabaseSchemaUpdater.AddIndex`.

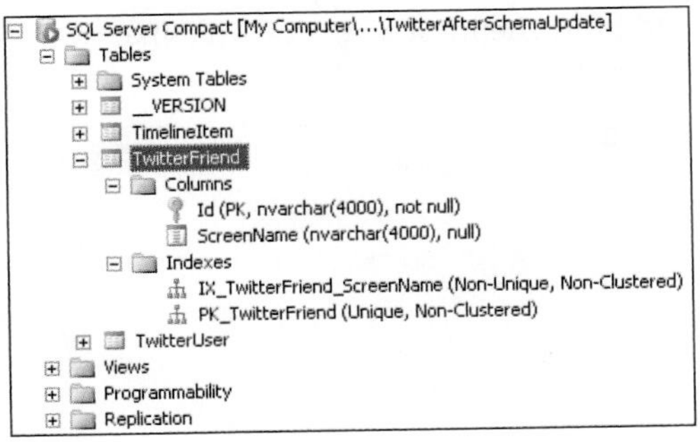

FIGURE 26.12   The `TwitterFriend` table has been added to the schema.

For example, if we add an `EmailAddress` property to the `TwitterFriend` class and later decide to add an index to improve query performance, we would first decorate the `TwitterFriend` class with an index attribute like so:

```
[Index(Name = "EmailAddressIndex",
       Columns = "EmailAddress", IsUnique = true)]
public class TwitterFriend : NotifyPropertyChangeBase
{
...
}
```

Once decorated with the `Index` attribute, the schema can be updated to include a new index for the column, as shown in the following excerpt:

```
using (DataContext dataContext
            = new TwitterDataContext("isostore:Twitter.sdf"))
{
    DatabaseSchemaUpdater updater
            = dataContext.CreateDatabaseSchemaUpdater();
    updater.AddIndex<TwitterFriend>("EmailAddressIndex");
    updater.Execute();
}
```

AddAssociation

`AddAssociation` allows you to add a one-to-many association between two entities. This method results in a foreign key constraint being added to the column that holds the primary key of the foreign table.

AddAssociation accepts a single parameter: associationPropertyName, which is the name of the entity member that holds the foreign key of another table.

To illustrate, if we were to add a new association between the TwitterUser and the TimelineItem classes that matches the existing association, we would first set about by adding a new property to the TimelineItem class to hold the id of a TwitterUser like so:

```
[Table]
public class TimelineItem : NotifyPropertyChangeBase
{
    string twitterUser2Id;

    [Column]
    public string TwitterUser2Id
    {
        get
        {
            return twitterUser2Id;
        }
        set
        {
            Assign("TwitterUser2Id", ref twitterUser2Id, value);
        }
    }


    EntityRef<TwitterUser> user2;

    [Association(Storage = "user2", ThisKey = "TwitterUser2Id",
                IsForeignKey = true, Name = "FK_TwitterUser2")]
    public TwitterUser TwitterUser2
    {
        get
        {
            return user2.Entity;
        }
        set
        {
            user2.Entity = value;
        }
    }
...
}
```

TIP

Explicitly providing a name for the foreign key constraint avoids collisions with existing constraint names, especially if similar associations have already been defined, as is the case with our `TwitterUser` property.

On the other side, the *one* side of the association, we would create a new `EntitySet` property for the new `TimelineItem` children, as shown:

```
[Table]
[Index(Columns = "ScreenName")]
public class TwitterUser : NotifyPropertyChangeBase
{
    readonly EntitySet<TimelineItem> timelineItems2;

    [Association(
        Storage = "timelineItems2",
        OtherKey = "TwitterUserId")]
    public EntitySet<TimelineItem> TimelineItems2
    {
        get
        {
            return timelineItems2;
        }
        set
        {
            timelineItems2.Assign(value);
        }
    }
    ...
}
```

To materialize the association in the database, we would then perform the following updates:

```
using (TwitterDataContext dataContext
                = twitterDatabaseUtility.CreateContext())
{
    DatabaseSchemaUpdater updater
                = dataContext.CreateDatabaseSchemaUpdater();
    updater.AddColumn<TimelineItem>("TwitterUser2Id");
    updater.AddAssociation<TimelineItem>("TwitterUser2");
    updater.Execute();
}
```

26

Schema Versioning

The DatabaseSchemaUpdater class provides a DatabaseSchemaVersion property that allows you to programmatically distinguish between different versions of your database.

When a local database is created with the DataContext.CreateDatabase method, a table named _Version is automatically created. This table holds the current DatabaseSchemaVersion number.

In the following example, the database version is used to determine what needs to be done to update the schema to the current version:

```
using (TwitterDataContext dataContext
                = twitterDatabaseUtility.CreateContext())
{
    DatabaseSchemaUpdater updater
                = dataContext.CreateDatabaseSchemaUpdater();
    int databaseVersion = updater.DatabaseSchemaVersion;

    if (databaseVersion < 2)
    {
        updater.AddColumn<TwitterUser>("Homepage");
        updater.DatabaseSchemaVersion = 2;
        updater.Execute();
    }

    if (databaseVersion < 3)
    {
        updater.AddColumn<TwitterUser>("Birthday");
        updater.DatabaseSchemaVersion = 3;
        updater.Execute();
    }
}
```

TIP

As you make changes to your schema, take note of them. This eases the burden of writing schema versioning code later.

Mapping an Inheritance Hierarchy

So far in this chapter, you have seen how LINQ to SQL has been used to map entity classes to database tables in a one-to-one fashion. There are times, however, when constraining an entity model to a flat hierarchy can feel too restrictive, and you may want to use inheritance in your entity model. This is possible with LINQ to SQL using single table inheritance.

When multiple classes of a hierarchy are stored within the same table, this is called single table inheritance. It works by dedicating a column within the table to represent the type of the particular entity class.

While this approach decreases the level of normalization in a database, it can be an effective approach for entity classes that have a small degree of variation in their storage needs.

The following example creates an entity model representing bank accounts. These bank account objects are stored using a single table in a local database.

The example code for this section is located in the /DataDrivenApps /LinqToSqlInheritanceMapping directory of the WindowsPhone7Unleashed.Examples project in the downloadable sample code.

At the base of the class hierarchy is the BankAccount class, and deriving from this are the three classes: SavingsAccount, CheckingAccount, and FixedDepositAccount (see Figure 26.13).

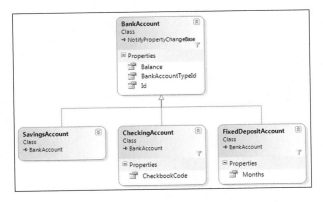

FIGURE 26.13   Bank account class hierarchy

The two primary elements for mapping an inheritance hierarchy are the InheritanceMapping attribute and the Column attribute's IsDiscriminator property.

Listing 26.11 shows that the BankAccount class declares each of its derived types using the InheritanceMapping attribute. The Code property of the InheritanceMapping attribute is the unique column value representing the derived type. The BankAccountTypeId is decorated with a Column attribute that has its IsDescriminator property set to true, indicating that it corresponds to the InheritanceMapping attribute's Code property.

Thus, if an entity is a SavingsAccount, then LINQ to SQL sets its BankAccountTypeId to 0. If the entity is a CheckingAccount, then BankAccountTypeId is set to 1. And so on.

LISTING 26.11   BankAccount Class

```
[Table]
[InheritanceMapping(Code = 0, Type = typeof(SavingsAccount), IsDefault = true)]
[InheritanceMapping(Code = 1, Type = typeof(CheckingAccount))]
[InheritanceMapping(Code = 2, Type = typeof(FixedDepositAccount))]
```

LISTING 26.11   Continued

```csharp
public class BankAccount : NotifyPropertyChangeBase
{
    int id;

    [Column(
        IsPrimaryKey = true,
        DbType = "INT IDENTITY NOT NULL",
        IsDbGenerated = true,
        UpdateCheck = UpdateCheck.Never)]
    public int Id
    {
        get
        {
            return id;
        }
        set
        {
            Assign("Id", ref id, value);
        }
    }

    int bankAccountTypeId;

    [Column(DbType = "Int NOT NULL", IsDiscriminator = true)]
    public int BankAccountTypeId
    {
        get
        {
            return bankAccountTypeId;
        }
        set
        {
            Assign("BankAccountTypeId", ref bankAccountTypeId, value);
        }
    }

    decimal balance;

    [Column]
    public decimal Balance
    {
        get
        {
            return balance;
```

LISTING 26.11   Continued

```
        }
        set
        {
            Assign("Balance", ref balance, value);
        }
    }
}
```

Only the base class is decorated with a Table attribute; entity subclasses are not. Members of the subclass that are to be stored in the database are decorated with a Column attribute (see Listing 26.12).

LISTING 26.12   CheckingAccount Class

```
[Index(Columns = "CheckbookCode")]
public class CheckingAccount : BankAccount
{
    string checkbookCode;

    [Column(DbType = "NCHAR(16)")]
    public string CheckbookCode
    {
        get
        {
            return checkbookCode;
        }
        set
        {
            Assign("CheckbookCode", ref checkbookCode, value);
        }
    }
}
```

The custom BankingDataContext class has a single BankAccounts property and is used in the same manner as the Twitter example earlier in this chapter (see Listing 26.13).

LISTING 26.13   BankingDataContext Class

```
public class BankingDataContext : DataContext
{
    public BankingDataContext(string connection) : base(connection)
    {
        Log = new DebugStreamWriter();
    }
```

LISTING 26.13   Continued

```
public Table<BankAccount> BankAccounts
{
    get
    {
        return GetTable<BankAccount>();
    }
}
}
```

The `BankingDataContextTests` class, in the WindowsPhone7Unleashed.Tests project, demonstrates storage and retrieval of various banking entity types. A custom `BankingDatabaseUtility` is used to initialize the database file. Two accounts are inserted into the database and then retrieved using LINQ to SQL. See the following excerpt:

```
[TestMethod]
[Tag("i1")]
public void ContextShouldReadAndWrite()
{
    using (BankingDataContext context = databaseUtility.CreateContext())
    {
        SavingsAccount savingsAccount = new SavingsAccount {Balance = 50};
        CheckingAccount checkingAccount = new CheckingAccount
                                        {
                                            Balance = 100,
                                            CheckbookCode = "12345"
                                        };
        context.BankAccounts.InsertAllOnSubmit(new List<BankAccount>
                                        {
                                            savingsAccount,
                                            checkingAccount
                                        });
        context.SubmitChanges();
    }

    using (BankingDataContext context = databaseUtility.CreateContext())
    {
        List<BankAccount> accounts = context.BankAccounts.ToList();
        Assert.IsTrue(accounts.Count > 2, "There should be two accounts.");

        IQueryable<SavingsAccount> savingsAccounts
            = context.BankAccounts.OfType<SavingsAccount>();
        Assert.IsTrue(savingsAccounts.Any());
```

```
        SavingsAccount account = savingsAccounts.First();
        Assert.IsTrue(account.Balance == 50, "Balance should be 50");
    }
}
```

Having support for mapping inheritance hierarchies in LINQ to SQL is a tolerable way of bridging the object relational divide.

Concurrency

LINQ to SQL has built-in support for optimistic concurrency; an entity is able to be retrieved and used in more than one operation at a time. When an entity is retrieved from the database, and then updated, if changes by another party occur in the interim, they are identified and a conflict is detected.

The mechanism supporting this feature is configured using two `Column` attribute properties: `IsVersion` and `UpdateCheck`.

`IsVersion` allows you to designate an entity class member to be used for optimistic concurrency control (OCC). Before committing a change to an entity, the data context verifies that no other transaction has modified its data. If the check reveals conflicting modifications, the committing transaction rolls back and an exception is raised.

> **NOTE**
>
> `IsVersion` is not required for conflict detection. When not specified, however, the data context must retain copies of the entity's member values and must compare the original values with the database values to detect conflicts, which is not terribly efficient.

LINQ to SQL supports multitier applications by allowing entities to be attached to a `DataContext`. Such an entity may have been retrieved using a different `DataContext` instance or deserialized after being sent over the wire from another tier via a web service.

In the following example you see that by adding a version property to the `BankAccount` class (presented in the previous section), you can prevent conflicting changes from being written to the database. `BankAccount` now contains a `DateVersion` property of type `byte[]`:

```
byte[] dataVersion;

[Column(
    IsVersion = true,
    IsDbGenerated = true,
    UpdateCheck = UpdateCheck.Never)]
public byte[] DataVersion
{
    get
    {
        return dataVersion;
```

```
    }
    set
    {
        Assign("DataVersion", ref dataVersion, value);
    }
}
```

The `DataVersion` value is materialized as a ROWVERSION field in the database (see Figure 26.14). The ROWVERSION data type causes the table field to be automatically updated whenever a row update occurs.

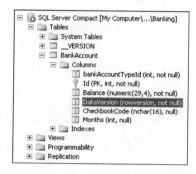

FIGURE 26.14   By default, the version member is materialized as a ROWVERSION column.

The `BankingDataContextTests` class contains a test method for demonstrating conflict detection. It creates a `CheckingAccount`, called `beforeAccount`, and inserts it into the database.

It then retrieves the same account, this time in the scope of a new `BankingDataContext`, sets its `CheckbookCode` to a new value, and then updates the database.

Finally, it attaches the `beforeAccount` instance to a new `DataContext` and attempts to update the `CheckbookCode` to a new value. See the following excerpt:

```
[TestMethod]
[Tag("i2")]
[ExpectedException(typeof(ChangeConflictException))]
public void ContextShouldEnforceUpdateChecking()
{
    CheckingAccount beforeAccount;

    using (BankingDataContext context = databaseUtility.CreateContext())
    {
        beforeAccount = new CheckingAccount
                        {
                                Balance = 100,
                                CheckbookCode = "11111"
```

```
                            };
        context.BankAccounts.InsertOnSubmit(beforeAccount);
        context.SubmitChanges();
    }

    using (BankingDataContext context = databaseUtility.CreateContext())
    {
        CheckingAccount afterAccount
            = (CheckingAccount)context.BankAccounts.Where(
                        x => x.Id == beforeAccount.Id).First();
        afterAccount.CheckbookCode = "22222";
        context.SubmitChanges();
    }

    using (BankingDataContext context = databaseUtility.CreateContext())
    {
        context.BankAccounts.Attach(beforeAccount);
        beforeAccount.CheckbookCode = "33333";
        context.SubmitChanges();
    }
}
```

When `context.SubmitChanges` is called, a conflict is detected because the `afterAccount` object, representing the same account, was updated in the database in the interim. This raises a `ChangeConflictException` (see Figure 26.15), which is defined as an expected exception, using the `ExpectedException` test attribute shown in the previous excerpt.

Providing a dedicated version property within your entity classes is good practice when enabling conflict detection. When not used, the data context relies solely on the `Column` attribute's `UpdateCheck` property for inferring conflict detection behavior.

ColumnAttribute.UpdateCheck

`UpdateCheck` informs the data context when to verify that a member value in the database has not changed since it was retrieved. The following is the list of valid `UpdateCheck` values:

- ▶ `Always`

- ▶ `Never`

- ▶ `WhenChanged`

When performing an update without the existence of a dedicated version member, LINQ to SQL generates an UPDATE statement with a WHERE clause that includes the original column values. If the values do not match those in the database, no update occurs, and a conflict is detected, raising an exception.

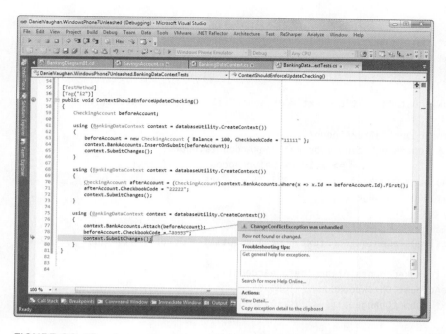

FIGURE 26.15   A `ChangeConflictException` is raised when a conflict is detected.

The default value of `UpdateCheck` is `UpdateCheck.Always`. If set to `UpdateCheck.Always`, conflict detection occurs even if the entity's member value has not changed.

If the `UpdateCheck` attribute property is set to `UpdateCheck.Never`, the member does not participate in conflict detection. You can use this value to effectively switch off conflict detection for a particular member.

If the `UpdateCheck` attribute property is set to `UpdateCheck.WhenChanged`, conflict detection for the member occurs only if the value has changed in the entity object.

Summary

This chapter began with an overview of how local databases are deployed to Windows Phone.

The chapter explored the code-first approach to data model creation and walked through a sample Twitter timeline viewer that caches data in a local database, during which you explored several facets of LINQ to SQL including entity creation, change tracking, and entity multiplicity.

The chapter then looked at the database-first approach to data model creation. You saw how to retrieve a local database file from isolated storage, and how to use the SqlMetal tool to generate a data model from a database.

The chapter then examined a custom navigation service that allows navigation from a viewmodel without reliance on the built-in navigation of the phone, which can increase the testability of viewmodel classes.

A technique for observing LINQ to SQL queries using a custom log was discussed. You saw how to upgrade a schema without losing data, and how to use version numbering to provide incremental updates to your database schema.

Finally, the chapter looked at mapping inheritance hierarchies using LINQ to SQL, and at concurrency and conflict detection.

26

Scheduled Actions

The need to perform background processing is not uncommon for Windows Phone apps. The transient nature of the app's life cycle makes performing some long-running or periodic tasks difficult.

One of Microsoft's goals with Windows Phone has been to forestall the battery life limitations present on other phone platforms. One way that it first did this was to limit the number of apps that could run simultaneously to just one app. This meant that using a cloud service and push notification was the only way to simulate background processing.

With the introduction of multitasking capabilities in the Windows Phone 7.5 (Mango) release, a limit of one foreground app in execution is still in place, yet now Microsoft has introduced a new way to run part of your app in the background.

This chapter looks at the scheduled notification system, which consists of a useful set of classes for setting reminders and alarms, which are able to present a message to the user at a predetermined time regardless of whether your app is running in the foreground.

The chapter then examines the scheduled task system, which extends the principles underpinning the notification system and offers the capability to run your own code in the background. You see how to create a todo list app that leverages a local database and updates live tiles from a background agent.

Finally, the chapter delves into a more advanced topic that explains how to use a `Mutex` to provide safe access to resources shared by your foreground app and your background agent.

Background Tasks

Background tasks refer collectively to actions that are registered with the phone OS to run in the background and that occupy the following four distinct areas of application functionality:

- ▶ Scheduled notifications
- ▶ Scheduled tasks
- ▶ Background file transfers
- ▶ Background audio

Of these, scheduled notifications are the simplest to use and understand. They are notifications that can be set from your app to display a message to the user at some time in the future.

Scheduled tasks allow you to register a class containing a method that is called periodically, even when your app is not running. They are multipurpose and offer the greatest utility for extending your app to perform background activities. Scheduled tasks may be used to perform some action periodically, such as querying a cloud service and updating a live tile, or they may be used to perform a less frequent resource intensive action, such as batch processing a set of images.

Transferring large files is difficult when your app may be tombstoned or closed at any time. The phone includes a background file transfer system that allows you to request a file to be downloaded from the Web to isolated storage or uploaded from isolated storage to a cloud service.

Windows Phone devices generally offer a rich multimedia experience for users. Users today are frequently forgoing a dedicated audio device and turning instead to the phone to play audio. Windows Phone allows you to build an audio app that can respond to the phone's built-in play controls even when your app is not running.

The following sections explore scheduled notification and scheduled tasks in detail. Background file transfers and background audio are discussed in subsequent chapters.

Scheduled Notifications

Sometimes an app may need to schedule a message to be displayed to the user at a future date. One way to achieve this, without relying on the user to have the app open to display the message, is to use a scheduled notification. Scheduled notifications present a dialog to the user at a predefined date and time that provides the user with the following three options:

- ▶ A snooze button allows the user to postpone the notification for several minutes. The snooze period can be set by the user when using a reminder.
- ▶ A dismiss button allows the user to close the notification.
- ▶ Tapping elsewhere within the notification dialog launches your app.

The Windows Phone notification system consists of two types of notifications: alarms and reminders. These provide a simple way to link back to your app and do not depend on your app being in the foreground. Figure 27.1 shows an alarm being displayed.

WP7U Background Agents

Alarm

test content

| snooze | dismiss |

FIGURE 27.1   An alarm may be snoozed or dismissed by the user.

> **NOTE**
>
> Tapping an alarm or reminder launches your app. If your app is in the foreground and the user taps the alarm, the alarm dialog is simply dismissed.

The two types of scheduled notifications are represented by the `Alarm` and `Reminder` classes. Both types may be set to be periodic, occurring every day for example, or they may be set to occur only once.

Registration of a notification is done using the `ScheduledActionService` class, which is demonstrated later in this section. `ScheduledActionService` handles the registration of both scheduled notifications and scheduled tasks.

> **NOTE**
>
> While scheduled notifications offer an effective and easy way to link back to your app, there is a limit to how many can be registered by your app. This limit is 50 alarms and reminders in total. Attempting to register more than this number raises an `InvalidOperationException`.

27

`Alarm` and `Reminder` classes are derived from the `ScheduleNotification` class, which contains a `Content` property and a `Title` property that are displayed to the user (see Figure 27.2).

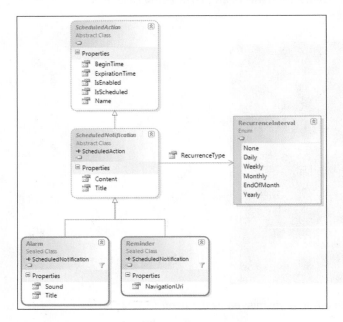

FIGURE 27.2   Scheduled notifications class diagram

NOTE

The `Title` property is supported only by the `Reminder` class and not by the `Alarm` class. `Alarm` overrides the `Title` property, and its setter raises a `NotSupportedException` if it is used. When the alarm notification is displayed, the title in the alarm dialog is always *Alarm*.

The most important distinction between alarms and reminders is that reminders allow you to deep link to your app. This means that a URI can be associated with the reminder so that when the user taps the reminder, your app is launched to a specific page and you can determine the course of action based on the URI's query string. While tapping an alarm also launches the app, it does not provide an equivalent URI property.

Another distinction between the `Alarm` and `Reminder` classes is that the `Alarm` class includes a `Sound` property, which allows you to specify the sound file to play when an alarm occurs, which the `Reminder` class does not.

The time and date of the notification are specified using the `ScheduledAction.BeginTime` property, which is of type `DateTime`. The date component of the `BeginTime` property is relevant only when using a `RecurrenceType` of `None`. `RecurrenceType` defines if, and for what period, scheduled notifications should be periodically presented to the user. If the value is None (the default), the notification is raised only once.

When setting the BeginTime property of a notification, the value must fall after the current time, or an InvalidOperationException ensues.

The ScheduledAction.ExpirationTime property is used to define the window for which the notification is raised; when the date and time on the phone occur after the ExpirationTime value, the notification schedule expires and the notification is no longer raised. If not specified, ExpirationTime is set to DateTime.MaxValue, resulting in it never expiring.

The following sections examine the use of each notification type in greater detail.

Alarm Registration

As previously stated, registering an alarm is done via the ScheduledActionService. When using the ScheduledActionService, each notification must be given a unique name, or an exception is raised when you try and add it to the service. In the following example, we avoid reregistering a notification by detecting whether a notification with the same name has already been registered. We then use the ScheduledActionService class's Add method to register the alarm, as shown:

```
Alarm alarm = new Alarm(alarmName)
{
    BeginTime = DateTime.Now.AddDays(1),
    Content = "A test alarm.",
    RecurrenceType = RecurrenceInterval.None,
    Sound = new Uri("/Sounds/Alarm.wma", UriKind.Relative),
};

if (ScheduledActionService.Find(alarm.Name) != null)
{
    ScheduledActionService.Remove(alarm.Name);
}

ScheduledActionService.Add(alarm);
```

The BeginTime property indicates when the alarm is due to occur. RecurrenceInterval.None specifies that the alarm is not recurring, which need not be specified as it is the default value.

The Alarm.wma audio file is located in the project and has its Build Action set to Content. When the alarm occurs, the audio file is played.

The Alarm class properties are examined in greater detail in the following section, where you explore the downloadable sample code for this section.

Alarm Sample

The sample code for this section includes a page that allows you to enter the details of a new alarm—including its name and begin time—and to set the alarm via an application bar button. The code is located in the Alarms directory of the WindowsPhone7Unleashed.BackgroundAgents project, in the BackgroundAgents solution.

Within the sample, the `AlarmViewModel` class contains various properties that correspond to the following properties of the `Alarm` class:

▶ **BeginTime**—A DateTime value indicating when the alarm should occur.

▶ **Name**—A unique string identifier for the alarm.

▶ **RecurrenceType**—A `RecurrenceInterval` enum value that specifies whether the alarm is a one-time alarm, or that it should recur every day or month.

▶ **ExpirationTime**—When the alarm is a recurring alarm, this value indicates when the alarm is to be deemed no longer valid, and removed by the OS.

▶ **Content**—A string that is presented in the alarm dialog when the alarm occurs.

▶ **Sound**—When the alarm occurs, a sound is played. This property is a relative URI to an audio file within the assembly, allowing you to change the default sound that is played to one of your choosing.

The viewmodel contains a single `ICommand` called `AlarmSetCommand`, which is initialized in the viewmodel's constructor, as shown:

```
public AlarmViewModel()
{
    alarmSetCommand = new DelegateCommand(obj => SetAlarm());
}
```

When executed, the command calls the `SetAlarm` method, which creates a new `Alarm` using the viewmodel's property values. The built-in `ScheduledActionService` is used to register the alarm, as shown in the following excerpt:

```
void SetAlarm()
{
    Alarm alarm = new Alarm(alarmName)
                    {
                        BeginTime = alarmBeginTime,
                        ExpirationTime = alarmExpirationTime,
                        Content = alarmContent,
                        RecurrenceType = alarmRecurrenceType,
                        Sound = alarmSound,
                        /* Alarm does not support setting the Title. */
                        // Title = alarmTitle
                    };
```

```
if (ScheduledActionService.Find(alarm.Name) != null)
{
    ScheduledActionService.Remove(alarm.Name);
}

ScheduledActionService.Add(alarm);

MessageService.ShowMessage("alarm set");
}
```

The `alarmSound` field of the viewmodel is set to a Content resource located in the project's Sounds directory, as shown:

```
readonly Uri alarmSound = new Uri("/Sounds/Alarm.wma", UriKind.Relative);
```

While nearly all of the viewmodel's properties are used merely as values for a new Alarm, one property, `RecurrenceIntervals`, allows the user to pick the recurrence type of the alarm using a Silverlight Toolkit `ListPicker` in the view. The `ListPicker` is bound to the `RecurrenceIntervals` property of the viewmodel.

Population of the `recurrenceIntervals` backing field is done using the custom `EnumUtility` class, presented in Chapter 6, "Text Elements." The `CreateEnumValueList` method retrieves the possible enum values using reflection. See the following excerpt:

```
readonly IEnumerable<RecurrenceInterval> recurrenceIntervals
            = EnumUtility.CreateEnumValueList<RecurrenceInterval>();

public IEnumerable<RecurrenceInterval> RecurrenceIntervals
{
    get
    {
        return recurrenceIntervals;
    }
}
```

By using reflection to retrieve the list of enum values, it means they do not have to be hard-coded into the viewmodel.

The view allows the user to set the properties of a new alarm. Silverlight Toolkit `TimePicker` and `DatePicker` controls are used to set the begin and expiration times of the alarm, as shown in the following excerpt:

```
<StackPanel Grid.Row="1" Margin="12,0,12,0">
    <TextBlock Text="name" />
    <TextBox Text="{Binding AlarmName, Mode=TwoWay}" />
    <TextBlock Text="content" />
    <TextBox Text="{Binding AlarmContent, Mode=TwoWay}" />
    <StackPanel Orientation="Horizontal">
```

27

```
        <StackPanel>
            <TextBlock Text="begin time" />
            <toolkit:TimePicker
                Value="{Binding AlarmBeginTime, Mode=TwoWay}" />
        </StackPanel>
        <StackPanel>
            <TextBlock Text="expires" />
            <toolkit:DatePicker
                Value="{Binding AlarmExpirationTime, Mode=TwoWay}" />
        </StackPanel>
    </StackPanel>
    <toolkit:ListPicker
        Header="recurrence interval"
        ItemsSource="{Binding RecurrenceIntervals}"
        SelectedItem="{Binding AlarmRecurrenceType, Mode=TwoWay}" />
</StackPanel>
```

The view also includes an `AppBar` with a button that is bound to the `AlarmSetCommand`, like so:

```
<u:AppBar>
    <u:AppBarIconButton
                Command="{Binding AlarmSetCommand}"
                Text="Set Alarm"
                IconUri="/Images/ApplicationBarIcons/Check.png" />
</u:AppBar>
```

The various viewmodel properties are initialized with default values. Figure 27.3 shows the set alarm view, which allows the user to enter the new alarm information.

When the set alarm button is tapped, the `AlarmSetCommand` is executed, registering the alarm with the OS. Once the begin time for the alarm comes around, the alarm dialog is displayed to the user.

Reminder Registration

Reminder registration is done in much the same way as for `Alarm` objects. The reminder is instantiated and then registered with the `ScheduledActionService`. With reminders, however, you are able to provide a URI that allows you to deep link back to a particular page within the app, as shown in the following excerpt:

```
Reminder reminder = new Reminder("ReminderName")
    {
        BeginTime = DateTime.Now.AddMinutes(5),
        ExpirationTime = DateTime.Now.AddDays(5),
        Content = "Your daily reminder.",
        RecurrenceType = RecurrenceInterval.Daily,
        NavigationUri = new Uri("/ReminderView.xaml?Id=ReminderName",
```

```
                        UriKind.Relative),
        Title = reminderTitle
    };

if (ScheduledActionService.Find(reminder.Name) != null)
{
    ScheduledActionService.Remove(reminder.Name);
}

ScheduledActionService.Add(reminder);
```

FIGURE 27.3   The set alarm view

The following section looks at creating a page that allows you to experiment with reminders.

Reminder Sample

The Reminder sample mirrors the alarm sample; however, the reminder sample demonstrates how to use the deep linking feature of reminders to allow editing of a reminder after it has been created.

The sample code for this section is located in the Reminders directory of the WindowsPhone7Unleashed.BackgroundAgents project in the BackgroundAgents solution.

Like the `Alarm` sample, the `ReminderView` page allows the user to enter the details of a new reminder and to set the reminder via an application bar button.

The `ReminderViewModel` class contains various properties that correspond to the `Reminder` class properties. Unlike the `Alarm` class, however, the `Reminder` class does not provide the ability to customize the sound effect of the notification.

The viewmodel contains two `ICommand` properties: one for registering a new reminder, the other for displaying an existing reminder after it has been navigated to via a deep link. The backing fields for both commands are initialized in the viewmodel constructor, like so:

```
public ReminderViewModel()
{
    reminderSetCommand = new DelegateCommand(obj => SetReminder());
    loadReminderCommand = new DelegateCommand<string>(LoadReminder);
}
```

When executed, the `ReminderSet` command calls the `SetReminder` method, which creates a new `Reminder` using the viewmodel's property values. In addition, we construct a `Uri` object that links back to the page if and when the user taps the reminder when it is displayed. See the following excerpt:

```
void SetReminder()
{
    const string reminderUrlFormat = "/Reminders/ReminderView.xaml?Id={0}";
    string navigationUrl = string.Format(reminderUrlFormat, ReminderName);
    Uri navigationUri = new Uri(navigationUrl, UriKind.Relative);

    Reminder reminder = new Reminder(ReminderName)
                    {
                        BeginTime = reminderBeginTime,
                        ExpirationTime = reminderExpirationTime,
                        Content = reminderContent,
                        RecurrenceType = reminderRecurrenceType,
                        NavigationUri = navigationUri,
                        Title = reminderTitle
                    };

    if (ScheduledActionService.Find(reminder.Name) != null)
    {
        ScheduledActionService.Remove(reminder.Name);
    }

    ScheduledActionService.Add(reminder);

    MessageService.ShowMessage("reminder set");
}
```

When the `LoadReminderCommand` executes, the `LoadReminder` method is called with the command parameter, which should be the name of a registered `Reminder`. The `ScheduledActionService` is used to retrieve the `Reminder` by name. If it is located, then the viewmodel's properties are populated with the `Reminder` values, as shown:

```
void LoadReminder(string name)
{
    Reminder reminder = ScheduledActionService.Find(name) as Reminder;
    if (reminder == null)
    {
        MessageService.ShowError("Reminder not found.");
        return;
    }

    ReminderBeginTime = reminder.BeginTime;
    ReminderContent = reminder.Content;
    ReminderName = reminder.Name;
    ReminderRecurrenceType = reminder.RecurrenceType;
    ReminderTitle = reminder.Title;
}
```

`LoadReminderCommand` is executed via the view's `OnNavigatedTo` method. When the user taps a reminder, the app starts with the `ReminderView` displayed. The `OnNavigatedTo` method extracts the `Reminder` name using a key exposed by the viewmodel (see Listing 27.1).

The command is prevented from being executed more than once using an `initialized` flag. `OnNavigatedTo` may be called more than once if the app was tombstoned or a back navigation took place.

LISTING 27.1   ReminderView Class

```
public partial class ReminderView : PhoneApplicationPage
{
    bool initialized;
    readonly ReminderViewModel viewModel;

    public ReminderView()
    {
        InitializeComponent();

        DataContext = viewModel = new ReminderViewModel();
    }

    protected override void OnNavigatedTo(NavigationEventArgs e)
    {
        base.OnNavigatedTo(e);
```

LISTING 27.1   Continued

```
        if (initialized)
        {
            return;
        }
        initialized = true;

        string reminderId;
        if (NavigationContext.QueryString.TryGetValue(
                ReminderViewModel.IdQueryKey, out reminderId))
        {
            viewModel.LoadReminderCommand.Execute(reminderId);
        }
    }
}
```

The root grid within the view XAML contains a custom AppBar that includes an
AppBarIconButton bound to the ReminderSetCommand, like so:

```
<u:AppBar>
    <u:AppBarIconButton
                Command="{Binding ReminderSetCommand}"
                Text="Set"
                IconUri="/Images/ApplicationBarIcons/Check.png" />
</u:AppBar>
```

The view allows the user to set the properties of a new Reminder or to edit the properties of
an existing Reminder.

```
<StackPanel Grid.Row="1" Margin="12,0,12,0">
    <TextBlock Text="name" />
    <TextBox Text="{Binding ReminderName, Mode=TwoWay}" />
    <TextBlock Text="title" />
    <TextBox Text="{Binding ReminderTitle, Mode=TwoWay}" />
    <TextBlock Text="content" />
    <TextBox Text="{Binding ReminderContent, Mode=TwoWay}" />
    <StackPanel Orientation="Horizontal">
        <StackPanel>
            <TextBlock Text="begin time" />
            <toolkit:TimePicker
                Value="{Binding ReminderBeginTime, Mode=TwoWay}" />
        </StackPanel>
        <StackPanel>
            <TextBlock Text="expires" />
            <toolkit:DatePicker
                Value="{Binding ReminderExpirationTime, Mode=TwoWay}" />
```

```
            </StackPanel>
        </StackPanel>
        <toolkit:ListPicker
            Header="recurrence interval"
            ItemsSource="{Binding RecurrenceIntervals}"
            SelectedItem="{Binding ReminderRecurrenceType, Mode=TwoWay}" />
</StackPanel>
```

Figure 27.4 shows the set reminder view, which allows the user to enter the new reminder information.

FIGURE 27.4   Set Reminder view

Once the reminder has been set and the begin time arrives, a dialog is presented to the user, displaying the reminder information (see Figure 27.5).

Tapping the reminder launches the app and automatically causes the app to navigate to the NavigateUri property of the Reminder, which allows the Reminder to be modified and reregistered.

Alarms and reminders offer a simple way to add notification support to your app. The next section looks at scheduled tasks and how they offer the ability to perform application logic in the background.

27

FIGURE 27.5   A reminder can be snoozed or dismissed by the user.

Scheduled Tasks

A scheduled task allows you to perform an activity in the background while your app is, or is not, running. A task can be used to query a cloud service and update the app's shell tiles and provides your users with the opportunity to respond to some event.

Scheduled tasks follow the same model as scheduled notifications, yet they add one other dimension: user-defined task agents. While scheduled notifications rely solely on built-in task agents for presenting notification dialogs, with scheduled tasks, you define your own.

Like scheduled notifications, scheduled tasks are registered with the ScheduledActionService when your app is running. Registration causes your task agent to run in the background at an indeterminate time and in a separate process.

Once a scheduled task is registered, it is persisted across reboots of the OS. The user can view and/or disable background tasks from the Settings screen by navigating to Settings/applications/background tasks (see Figure 27.6).

The scheduled task system consists of the following three components:

▶ A task registration service called ScheduledActionService, which is the same service used by the scheduled notification system (uses Alarms and Reminders).

▶ A background agent that derives from ScheduledTaskAgent, which is used to perform the background activity.

▶ The tasks themselves, which can be either of type `PeriodicTask` or `ResourceIntensiveTask`. Task objects allow you to pass information to your task agent from your app, determine how the task agent is executed, and when it expires.

FIGURE 27.6   The user can disable scheduled tasks via the background tasks screen.

Background Agent Types

Windows Phone supports three types of background agents: `ScheduledTaskAgent`, `AudioPlayerAgent`, and `AudioStreamingAgent` (see Figure 27.7).

Audio player agents are specialized agents used to retrieve audio files and coordinate the playback of background audio. `AudioPlayerAgent` and `AudioStreamingAgent` are explored in Chapter 29, "Background Audio."

`ScheduledTaskAgent` is an abstract class, which you subclass to provide your own logic to be performed whenever the OS chooses to invoke your agent. When invoked, the OS passes the registered task object to the task agent, which allows you to determine what kind of activity is to be performed.

`ScheduledTaskAgents` handle two kinds of tasks: periodic and resource intensive, which are represented by the `PeriodicTask` and `ResourceIntensiveTask` classes, respectively.

> **NOTE**
>
> An app may have only one periodic task and/or one resource intensive task. If an attempt is made to register more than one of either type, an `InvalidOperationException` is raised.

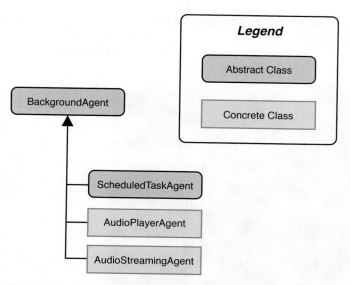

FIGURE 27.7 BackgroundAgent types

Scheduled tasks are registered in the same manner as ScheduledNotification objects: with the ScheduledActionService. At an indeterminate time after registration, the operating system instantiates your task agent and passes it the scheduled task (see Figure 27.8). The agent then performs any processing it needs to do in the background and then signals that it has either completed its work or that it is unable to complete.

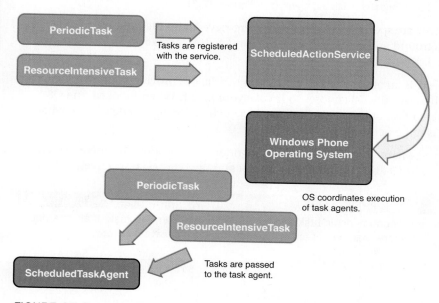

FIGURE 27.8 Periodic tasks are registered with the ScheduledActionService. The OS invokes the ScheduledTaskAgent, passing it the PeriodicTask object.

It is important to recognize the distinction between the roles of tasks and task agents. Tasks contain information that is passed to the task agent. Their purpose is to allow the `ScheduledActionService` to determine how and when to run the task agent. It is the task agent that performs the background activity, and it is there that you can place your code to be executed in the background.

`PeriodicTask` and `ResourceIntensiveTask` are analogous to the `ScheduledNotification` classes: `Alarm` and `Reminder`. `ScheduledTask` and `ScheduledNotification` both derive from `ScheduledAction`, which includes properties for the name and expiration date of the task (see Figure 27.9).

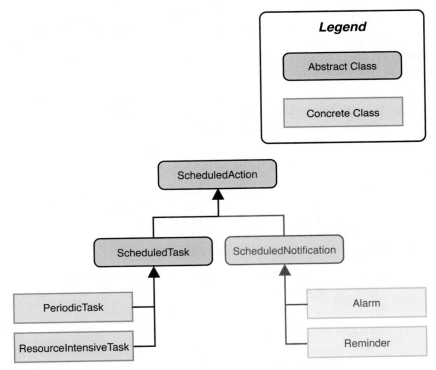

FIGURE 27.9   `ScheduledTask` is derived from `ScheduledAction`, the same base class for scheduled notifications.

The following sections examine the two `ScheduledTask` types, `PeriodicTask` and `ResourceIntensiveTask`, in greater detail.

Periodic Tasks

A periodic task is used to perform short operations and is allocated a 15-second window to complete its work. Periodic tasks run, at most, every 30 minutes. Typical scenarios for periodic tasks include performing small incremental data synchronization with a cloud service, using geographic location to track the location of the device, or polling a social network cloud service for new messages or status updates.

> **NOTE**
>
> When retrieving the geographic location of the device within a scheduled task (via a `GeoCoordinateWatcher`), a cached location value is used instead of real-time data. This helps to minimize the power consumption of background agents. It does, however, also introduce a lag for determining the location of the device, which may be problematic in some scenarios.

Periodic Task Invocation

There are no guarantees that a periodic task will ever run. To minimize resources, the phone OS launches all periodic tasks for all apps on the device at approximately the same time. This can mean that if a large number of periodic tasks are registered, not all will be invoked. Moreover, Battery Saver mode is an option that the user can enable on the device to indicate that battery life should be prioritized. If this mode is enabled, periodic agents may not run, even if the task interval has elapsed.

There is also a limit on the total number of periodic agents that can be scheduled on a device. This limit varies from device to device, but it can be as low as six. If this limit is approached, the user is warned that multiple background agents are running and that it may cause faster battery consumption.

Resource Intensive Tasks

Resource intensive tasks (also known as *on idle* tasks) are allocated a substantially longer execution time than periodic tasks. Resource intensive tasks, however, only run when the phone meets a minimum set of requirements relating to processor activity, power source, and network connection type (see Table 27.1). This task is typically used to synchronize large amounts of data to the phone during periods of inactivity.

Resource intensive tasks typically run for a maximum of 10 minutes. The runtime is cut short, however, if one or more of the requirements that determine eligibility to launch are no longer met.

TABLE 27.1   Run Eligibility Requirements for Resource Intensive Tasks

Requirement	Description
External power	The device must be connected to an external power supply.
Non-cellular connection	The device must have a network connection over Wi-Fi or through a connection to a PC.
Minimum battery power	The device's battery power must be greater than 90%.
Device screen lock	The device's screen must be locked.
No active phone call	A phone call cannot be under way.

Using Scheduled Tasks

Using scheduled tasks in your app involves creating an agent class and adding an XML fragment to your WMAppManifest.xml file. This process can be done manually or by using the Windows Phone Scheduled Task Agent project template that resides beneath the Silverlight for Windows Phone node of the Add New Project dialog (see Figure 27.10).

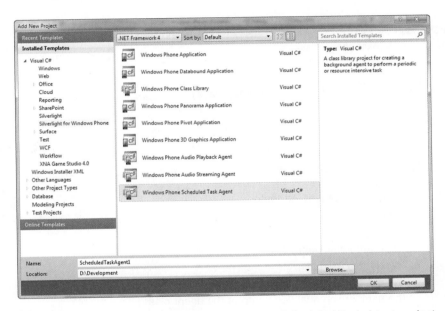

FIGURE 27.10   Adding a new Windows Phone Scheduled Task Agent project

The benefit of using the project template to create a scheduled task agent is seen when you reference that project from your primary phone project; a required XML fragment is automatically placed in the WMAppManifest.xml file.

In the samples for this chapter, I have chosen to place the background agent code within the same project as the main application, purely for the sake of convenience.

For more information on scheduled task limitations, see the section "Scheduled Task API Limitations" later in the chapter.

A secondary benefit that can arise from using a separate project for your agent is that it can help to minimize the size of the assembly that is loaded by the CLR when your agent is invoked, which may marginally improve the load time of your agent; the larger an assembly is, the longer it takes the CLR to load it.

The XML fragment placed in the WMAppManifest.xml file informs the OS of the agent class type, so that it can be resolved and invoked. The XML fragment resembles the following:

```
<Tasks>
    <DefaultTask  Name ="_default" NavigationPage="MainPage.xaml"/>
    <ExtendedTask Name="BackgroundTask">
        <BackgroundServiceAgent Specifier="ScheduledTaskAgent"
                                Name="[An identifier]"
                                Source="[Assembly Name]"
                                Type="[Class Name]" />
    </ExtendedTask>
</Tasks>
```

Table 27.2 provides descriptions of the attributes of the BackgroundServiceAgent element.

TABLE 27.2   BackgroundServiceAgent Attributes

Attribute	Description
Specifier	Indicates the kind of agent and can be AudioPlayerAgent, AudioStreamingAgent, or ScheduledTaskAgent
Name	An arbitrary identifier for the agent
Source	The assembly in which the agent class resides
Type	The namespace qualified name of the agent class

NOTE

If an attribute of the BackgroundServiceAgent element is incorrect—for example, the type is unresolvable or the Specifier is not a known value—then an InvalidOperationException is raised when the OS attempts to invoke the task agent, and not before.

Scheduled Task Agent

When using the Windows Phone Scheduled Task Agent project template, you begin with a class resembling the following:

```
public class ScheduledAgent : ScheduledTaskAgent
{
    protected override void OnInvoke(ScheduledTask task)
    {
        //TODO: Add code to perform your task in background

        NotifyComplete();
    }
}
```

Your agent's `OnInvoke` method is called by the OS. In this method, your app can determine the type of `ScheduledTask` that triggered the invocation of the agent and perform actions accordingly. The task passed to the `OnInvoke` method is either a `PeriodicTask` or a `ResourceIntensiveTask`. To branch according to the type of task, something like the following can be used:

```
if (task is PeriodicTask)
{
    ProcessPeriodicTask();
}
else
{
    ProcessResourceIntensiveTask();
}
```

The `NotifyComplete` method of the base class informs the background task system that your task has finished its activities and signals that it is okay for the process to be terminated.

NOTE

Only call `NotifyComplete` when your agent has finished everything it needs to do, or your agent may be terminated along with any child threads spawned along the way.

If your agent is unable to perform its work because of an unavailable resource, a cloud service for example, call the `Abort` method instead of the `NotifyComplete` method. `Abort` has the same effect on task termination, but causes the task's `IsScheduled` property to be set to false, which can then be detected and dealt with appropriately by your foreground app. If `IsScheduled` is false, you know that `Abort` was called.

NOTE

To maximize the number of dormant applications, each scheduled task agent is limited to 6MB of RAM. If your agent exceeds that amount, the agent is terminated. Two consecutive violations result in schedule suspension.

Be mindful, however, that this limitation is not enforced while debugging.

27

The amount of memory available to your agent can be measured like so:

```
long usedBytes
        = Microsoft.Phone.Info.DeviceStatus.ApplicationCurrentMemoryUsage;
long limitBytes
        = Microsoft.Phone.Info.DeviceStatus.ApplicationMemoryUsageLimit;
if ((usedBytes + 1048576) < limitBytes) // 1 048 576 = 1 MB
{
    /* Do work with 1 MB. */
}
```

Scheduled Task Registration

Registering a task is achieved from your foreground app.

> **NOTE**
>
> ScheduledAction objects can be registered only when your app is in the foreground and not from a background agent. Attempting to register ScheduledAction in a background agent raises an InvalidOperationException.

The following shows how to create a new PeriodicTask:

```
string taskName = "a unique name";
PeriodicTask periodicTask = new PeriodicTask(taskName)
    {
        /* Description is required. */
        Description = "A description for the task"
    };
```

All ScheduledAction objects added to the ScheduledActionService must be named uniquely. Therefore, you should test whether the task has already been added to the scheduled action service. The task may then be added to the service as shown:

```
if (ScheduledActionService.Find(taskName) != null)
{
    ScheduledActionService.Remove(taskName);
}

/* This can only be called when the application
 * is running in the foreground. */
ScheduledActionService.Add(periodicTask);
```

> **NOTE**
>
> Tasks expire after a maximum of 14 days. If the task's `ExpirationTime` property is not set, it defaults to 14 days.
>
> Tasks can be renewed by removing them, re-creating them, and then adding them back to the `ScheduledActionService`. This can, however, only be done from a foreground app, which means that if the user does not launch your app, you have no way to prevent your tasks from expiring after the default expiration period of 14 days.

The next section looks at putting periodic tasks into action.

Todo List Scheduled Task Sample

This section looks at creating a todo list app that uses periodic tasks in conjunction with a scheduled task agent. The app allows the user to enter a todo item, which is stored in a local database and which can be pinned as a live tile on the start experience. We look at using a periodic task to update the status of the todo item live tiles.

TodoItem

Todo items are represented by the `TodoItem` class, which contains three properties: `Id`, `Description`, and `DueDate`. `DueDate` is of type `DateTime` and indicates when the todo item should be considered overdue. `TodoItem` objects are persisted using LINQ to SQL. The `TodoItem` class is decorated with a `Table` attribute, and its properties with `Column` attributes (see Listing 27.2).

LISTING 27.2   TodoItem Class

```
[Table]
public class TodoItem : NotifyPropertyChangeBase
{
    int id;

    [Column(
        IsPrimaryKey = true,
        DbType = "INT IDENTITY NOT NULL",
        IsDbGenerated = true,
        UpdateCheck = UpdateCheck.Never)]
    public int Id
    {
        get
        {
            return id;
        }
        set
        {
            Assign("Id", ref id, value);
        }
```

LISTING 27.2   Continued

```
    }

    string description;

    [Column]
    public string Description
    {
        ...
    }

    DateTime dueDate;

    [Column]
    public DateTime DueDate
    {
        ...
    }
}
```

For more information on LINQ to SQL and using databases in Windows Phone, see Chapter 26, "Local Databases."

We now look briefly at the app's data layer before moving on to its viewmodels. Persistence of TodoItem objects is performed using a LINQ to SQL DataContext instance, and an intermediary service that decouples the data context from the app's viewmodels.

TodoDataContext

To retrieve and store TodoItem objects in a database, we use a custom DataContext class called TodoDataContext. This class allows TodoItem objects to be retrieved via its TodoItems property (see Listing 27.3).

LISTING 27.3   TodoDataContext Class

```
public class TodoDataContext : DataContext
{
    public TodoDataContext(string connection)
        : base(connection)
    {
    }

    public Table<TodoItem> TodoItems
    {
        get
        {
```

LISTING 27.3   Continued

```
            return GetTable<TodoItem>();
        }
    }
}
```

In the sample app, viewmodels do not directly interact with the TodoDataContext but rather perform all CRUD operations via a todo service. This decouples the data context from the viewmodels, allowing you to replace the todo service with an implementation that could, for example, use a cloud service rather than a local database. Decoupling the data context also means that you have the flexibility to unit test the code outside an emulator, perhaps on a build server.

TodoService

A custom service provides for all CRUD operations for the TodoItem objects. It serves as an intermediary between the LINQ to SQL DataContext for TodoItems and viewmodel logic.

When the TodoService is instantiated, a TodoDataContext is created. TodoItem objects can then be retrieved using the GetTodoItem method, shown in the following excerpt:

```
public TodoItem GetTodoItem(int itemId)
{
    TodoItem item = dataContext.TodoItems.Where(
                todoItem => todoItem.Id == itemId).FirstOrDefault();

    if (item == null)
    {
        throw new KeyNotFoundException(
            string.Format("Item with key '{0}' was not found.", itemId));
    }

    return item;
}
```

Conversely, inserting a new TodoItem into the database is done using the service's AddOrUpdateItem method.

If the TodoItem has an Id that is less than 1, it indicates that the TodoItem does not already exist in the database. If greater than 0, it is indicative of an update. See the following excerpt:

```
public void AddOrUpdateItem(TodoItem todoItem)
{
    ArgumentValidator.AssertNotNull(todoItem, "todoItem");

    if (todoItem.Id <= 0)
    {
```

27

```
        dataContext.TodoItems.InsertOnSubmit(todoItem);
    }
    dataContext.SubmitChanges();
}
```

The third method of the `TodoService` worth noting is `GetTodoItems`, which retrieves all `TodoItem` objects via the `TodoItems` property of the data context, like so:

```
public IEnumerable<TodoItem> GetTodoItems()
{
    return dataContext.TodoItems;
}
```

As you see in a moment, `GetTodoItems` is used by the `TodoListViewModel`.

With the `TodoService` in place, we now look at how the service is used by the app's view-models to display all todo items and to create new todo items.

TodoItemViewModel

The `TodoItemView` page retrieves all `TodoItem` objects for the user and displays them in a list. Its viewmodel relies on the todo service being passed as a constructor argument.

Retrieving the `TodoItem` objects is performed in the viewmodel's `PopulateItems` method. The todo service is used to retrieve the items, and then, using a LINQ expression, the items are grouped by the `TodoItem.DueDate` property. This allows the list to be bound to a Silverlight Toolkit `LongListSelector` in the view. See the following excerpt:

```
void PopulateItems()
{
    try
    {
        IEnumerable<TodoItem> items = todoService.GetTodoItems();

        IEnumerable<Grouping<TodoItem>> groups
                    = from todoItem in items
                      orderby todoItem.DueDate
                      group todoItem by todoItem.DueDate.Date
                      into grouping
                      select new Grouping<TodoItem>(
                                new DateGroupingKey(grouping.Key),
                                grouping.AsEnumerable());

        GroupedTodoItems = groups;
    }
    catch (Exception ex)
    {
```

```
        Message = "Unable to retrieve items.";
        Console.WriteLine(ex);
    }
}
```

TodoItems are grouped using a custom class called DateGroupingKey, which allows us to provide some additional logic to the item groupings, namely an Overdue property (see Listing 27.4). This allows you to change the background for the grouping header to red if the todo items in the group have due dates occurring in the past.

Alternatively, you may choose to use a value converter for determining whether the date is overdue. The example uses a custom key class, however, because it better encapsulates the date value and the logic for determining whether it is overdue.

LISTING 27.4   DateGroupingKey Class

```
public class DateGroupingKey
{
    public DateTime DateTime { get; private set; }

    public DateGroupingKey(DateTime dateTime)
    {
        DateTime = dateTime;
        Overdue = DateTime.Now > dateTime;
    }

    public bool Overdue { get; private set; }
}
```

The viewmodel's Load method commences population of the todo items asynchronously, using a thread from the thread pool. This prevents blocking the UI thread during a potentially long-running operation.

A PeriodicTask is registered with the ScheduledActionService. If the PeriodicTask has already been registered, it is first removed. This resets the task's expiration date. See the following excerpt:

```
public void Load()
{
    ThreadPool.QueueUserWorkItem(delegate { PopulateItems(); });

    PeriodicTask periodicTask = new PeriodicTask(agentName)
    {
        Description = "Updates a tile.",
        ExpirationTime = DateTime.Now.AddDays(14)
    };
```

27

```
    if (ScheduledActionService.Find(agentName) != null)
    {
        ScheduledActionService.Remove(agentName);
    }

    /* This can only be called when the app
     * is running in the foreground. */
    ScheduledActionService.Add(periodicTask);
}
```

The `TodoListViewModel` constructor calls its `Load` method after initializing various `ICommands` (see Listing 27.5). `NewItemCommand` uses the `ViewModelBase` class's `Navigate` method to open the `TodoItemView` page. `EditItemCommand` also navigates to the `TodoItemView` page, but passes the `Id` of the `TodoItem`; provided as a command argument.

LISTING 27.5   TodoListViewModel Constructor

```
public TodoListViewModel(
    ITodoService todoService, IDeviceProperties deviceProperties)
{
    this.todoService = ArgumentValidator.AssertNotNull(
                                     todoService, "todoService");
    this.deviceProperties = ArgumentValidator.AssertNotNull(
                 deviceProperties, "deviceProperties");

    editItemCommand = new DelegateCommand<int>(
        todoItemId => Navigate(todoItemViewUrl + "?TodoItemId=" + todoItemId));

    testAgentCommand = new DelegateCommand(
                        obj => ScheduledActionService.LaunchForTest(
                            agentName, TimeSpan.Zero));

    backupDatabaseCommand = new DelegateCommand(obj => BackupDatabase());
    restoreDatabaseCommand = new DelegateCommand(obj => RestoreDatabase());

    Load();
}
```

`BackupDatabaseCommand` and `RestoreDatabaseCommand` are discussed later in this chapter.

Debugging Scheduled Tasks

Debugging a task agent is done by calling the `ScheduledActionService.LaunchForTest` method. Calling `LaunchForTest` is a way of forcing the OS to run your task agent. `LaunchForTest` accepts two parameters: the name of the scheduled task and a `TimeSpan` that indicates the delay before the task agent is invoked. By specifying `TimeSpan.Zero`, the task agent is invoked immediately.

With the `TestAgentCommand` wired up to the UI you can instruct the OS to launch the task agent, allowing you to step into the task agent's `OnInvoke` method. The task agent for the sample is discussed later in this section.

The viewmodel relies on a custom `IDeviceProperties` interface, which allows the viewmodel to retrieve the Windows Live anonymous ID. Windows Live anonymous IDs are discussed further in Chapter 28, "Background File Transfers."

`TodoListView` XAML

The `TodoListView` XAML contains a `LongListSelector` that is bound to the `GroupedTodoItems` property of the viewmodel (see Listing 27.6). The `LongListSelector`'s `ItemTemplate` uses a `TextBlock` to display the `Description` property of each `TodoItem`. When the user taps the description, the `EditItemCommand` is executed, and the `Id` of the `TodoItem` is passed as a command parameter. This is done using the custom commanding infrastructure, introduced in Chapter 8, "Taming the Application Bar."

The `LongListSelector`'s `GroupHeaderTemplate` contains a `Border` whose background is determined by the `Overdue` property of the group key, which is a `DateGroupingKey` instance.

LISTING 27.6   `TodoListView.xaml` (excerpt)

```xaml
<StackPanel x:Name="ContentPanel" Grid.Row="1" Margin="12,0,12,0">
    <toolkit:LongListSelector
            ItemsSource="{Binding GroupedTodoItems}"
            Background="Transparent"
            Height="600">
        <toolkit:LongListSelector.ItemTemplate>
            <DataTemplate>
                <StackPanel Orientation="Horizontal">
                    <TextBlock Text="{Binding Description}"
                        Margin="12,10,0,10"
                        Style="{StaticResource PhoneTextLargeStyle}"
                        c:Commanding.Event="Tap"
                        c:Commanding.Command="{Binding DataContext.EditItemCommand,
                                            ElementName=page}"
                        c:Commanding.CommandParameter="{Binding Id}" />
                </StackPanel>
            </DataTemplate>
        </toolkit:LongListSelector.ItemTemplate>

        <toolkit:LongListSelector.GroupHeaderTemplate>
            <DataTemplate>
                <Border Background="Transparent">
                    <Border Background="{Binding Key.Overdue,
                        Converter={StaticResource BooleanToBrushConverter}}"
                            Padding="5"
                            HorizontalAlignment="Left"
```

27

LISTING 27.6   Continued

```
                              Margin="0,10,0,0">
                    <TextBlock
                        Text="{Binding Key.DateTime, StringFormat=\{0:d\}}"
                        Foreground="{StaticResource PhoneForegroundBrush}"
                        Style="{StaticResource PhoneTextLargeStyle}"
                        VerticalAlignment="Bottom" />
                </Border>
            </Border>
        </DataTemplate>
    </toolkit:LongListSelector.GroupHeaderTemplate>
  </toolkit:LongListSelector>
</StackPanel>
```

The custom `BooleanToBrushConverter` is used to transform the `Overdue` property of type `bool` to a brush. For more information about the `BooleanToBrushConverter`, see Chapter 9, "Silverlight Toolkit Controls."

The `BooleanToBrushConverter` is defined as a page resource as shown:

```
<phone:PhoneApplicationPage.Resources>
    <ValueConverters:BooleanToBrushConverter
            x:Name="BooleanToBrushConverter"
            BrushIfTrue="Red"
            BrushIfFalse="Blue" />
</phone:PhoneApplicationPage.Resources>
```

Overdue groups are shown with a red header, while regular groups have a blue header (see Figure 27.11).

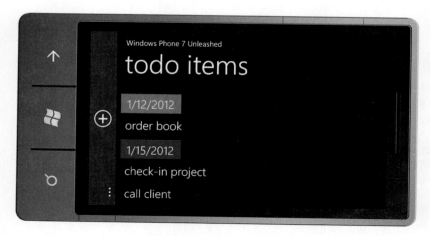

FIGURE 27.11   Todo items are grouped according to when they are due to expire.

The custom `AppBar` for the page includes an `AppBarHyperlinkButton`, which takes the user to the `TodoItemView` page and allows the user to create a new todo item. The other view-model commands are bound to `AppBarMenuItems`, as shown:

```xml
<u:AppBar>
    <u:AppBarHyperlinkButton
                NavigateUri="/TodoList/TodoItemView.xaml"
                Text="New"
                IconUri="/Images/ApplicationBarIcons/Add.png" />
    <u:AppBar.MenuItems>
        <u:AppBarMenuItem
                Command="{Binding BackupDatabaseCommand}"
                Text="Backup" />
        <u:AppBarMenuItem
                Command="{Binding RestoreDatabaseCommand}"
                Text="Restore" />
        <u:AppBarMenuItem
                Command="{Binding TestAgentCommand}"
                Text="test agent" />
    </u:AppBar.MenuItems>
</u:AppBar>
```

You have seen how the list of todo items is displayed, the next section examines how new todo items are created.

TodoItemView and ViewModel

The `TodoItemView` allows the user to perform the following three tasks:

▶ Create a new todo item.

▶ Update an existing todo item.

▶ Delete a todo item.

The `TodoItemViewModel` constructor receives the `ITodoService`, initializes commands, and registers persistent state, as shown:

```csharp
public TodoItemViewModel(ITodoService todoService)
{
    this.todoService = ArgumentValidator.AssertNotNull(
                                        todoService, "todoService");

    saveCommand = new DelegateCommand<bool>(SaveItem);
    loadItemCommand = new DelegateCommand<int>(LoadItem);
    deleteCommand = new DelegateCommand(obj => DeleteItem());
```

27

```
RegisterStatefulProperty(ApplicationStateType.Transient,
                    () => TodoDescription);
RegisterStatefulProperty(ApplicationStateType.Transient,
                    () => TodoDueDate);
}
```

The viewmodel contains a Description property and a DueDate property, which coincide with the properties of the TodoItem class. When the SaveCommand is executed, the SaveItem method is called. SaveItem uses the ITodoService to persist the TodoItem to the database and to optionally create a live tile representing the todo item.

Creating the Todo Item Shell Tile

To create a shell tile, you must pass a StandardTileData instance to the static ShellTile.Create method. Because this is performed in several places in the sample, the code for creating the StandardTileData has been placed into a class called TodoTileDataCreator (see Listing 27.7). This class uses the todo item's due date to determine the numeric icon shown on the tile. If it exceeds 99 days, it is not shown. The tile has a foreground and a background image and shows the description and due date of the todo item.

LISTING 27.7   TodoTileDataCreator Class

```
public static class TodoTileDataCreator
{
    public static StandardTileData CreateTile(
        string todoItemDescription, DateTime dueDate)
    {
        /* The Count property of the tile data is set
         * to the number of days remaining.
         * It must be between 0 and 99 inclusively. */
        int daysUntilDue = 0;
        bool overdue = DateTime.Now > dueDate;
        if (!overdue)
        {
            int temp = (int)(DateTime.Now - dueDate).TotalDays;
            if (temp < 100)
            {
                daysUntilDue = temp;
            }
        }

        const string tilesDirectory = "/TodoList/Images/Tiles/";

        string backgroundUrl = overdue
                                    ? tilesDirectory + "Overdue.jpg"
                                    : tilesDirectory + "Ok.jpg";
```

LISTING 27.7   Continued

```
        StandardTileData tileData = new StandardTileData
            {
                Title = todoItemDescription,
                BackgroundImage = new Uri(backgroundUrl, UriKind.Relative),
                Count = overdue ? 0 : daysUntilDue,

                BackTitle = dueDate.ToShortDateString(),
                BackContent = todoItemDescription,
                BackBackgroundImage = new Uri(
                    tilesDirectory + "Background.jpg", UriKind.Relative)
            };

        return tileData;
    }
}
```

Saving a Todo Item

Saving an item involves instantiating a new item and sending it to the ITodoService to be stored in the database (see Listing 27.8).

If a shell tile is created for the todo item, the NavigationUri of the tile is set to the TodoItemView page, and the Id of the TodoItem is placed in the query string of the URI, so that by tapping the tile, the user is brought back to the TodoItemView page, which allows editing or deletion of the todo item.

> **NOTE**
>
> Calling ShellTile.Create immediately deactivates your app.

The final task of the SaveItem method is to navigate the user back to the TodoItemList page.

LISTING 27.8   TodoItemViewModel SaveItem Method

```
void SaveItem(bool createTile)
{
    if (string.IsNullOrWhiteSpace(todoDescription))
    {
        MessageService.ShowError("Please enter a description.",
                                "Required Field Missing");

        return;
    }
```

27

LISTING 27.8   Continued

```
if (todoItem == null)
{
    todoItem = new TodoItem();
}

todoItem.Description = todoDescription;
todoItem.DueDate = todoDueDate;

todoService.AddOrUpdateItem(todoItem);

StandardTileData tileData = TodoTileDataCreator.CreateTile(
                            todoItem.Description, todoItem.DueDate);

string url = string.Format("/TodoList/TodoItemView.xaml?{0}={1}",
                            TaskScheduler.TodoItemIdQueryKey,
                            todoItem.Id);

if (createTile)
{
    /* Creating a shell tile takes the user to the start experience. */
    ShellTile.Create(new Uri(url, UriKind.Relative), tileData);
}
else
{
    ShellTile shellTile = ShellTile.ActiveTiles.Where(
      tile => tile.NavigationUri.ToString()
                .Contains(url)).FirstOrDefault();

    if (shellTile != null)
    {
        shellTile.Update(tileData);
    }

    Navigate(todoListUrl);
}
}
```

Editing an Existing Todo Item

The TodoItemViewModel can be in one of two modes: creation mode or edit mode. Either a
new item is to be created, or an existing todo item is being edited. This is indicated to the
view using a VisualState property, which is of type string. By default, the viewmodel is in
creation mode. When the user taps a todo shell tile or a todo item on the TodoListView
page, the view is placed in edit mode.

If in edit mode, the viewmodel's `LoadItem` method is used to retrieve the TodoItem with the specified `Id` from the `ITodoService`. The viewmodel's `TodoDescription` and `TodoDueDate` are populated using the retrieved item's values, as shown in the following excerpt:

```
TodoItem todoItem;

void LoadItem(int itemId)
{
    try
    {
        todoItem = todoService.GetTodoItem(itemId);
    }
    catch (KeyNotFoundException)
    {
        MessageService.ShowError("Item not found.");
    }

    TodoDescription = todoItem.Description;
    TodoDueDate = todoItem.DueDate;

    VisualState = "Update";
}
```

As you see later in this section, the `VisualState` property is used by the `TodoItemView` page to hide or reveal elements on the page.

When in edit mode, the user also has the ability to delete the todo item. The `DeleteItem` method uses the `ITodoService` to perform the data operation. Any shell tiles whose `NavigationUri` contains the query string corresponding to the todo item are also removed. See the following excerpt:

```
void DeleteItem()
{
    if (todoItem == null)
    {
        throw new InvalidOperationException("Not in edit mode.");
    }

    todoService.RemoveTodoItem(todoItem);

    string tileQueryString = string.Format("{0}={1}",
                                    TaskScheduler.TodoItemIdQueryKey,
                                    todoItem.Id);

    ShellTile tile = ShellTile.ActiveTiles.FirstOrDefault(
        x => x.NavigationUri.ToString().Contains(tileQueryString));
    if (tile != null)
```

27

```
    {
        tile.Delete();
    }

    Navigate(todoListUrl);
}
```

The `TodoItemView` page uses the IoC container to resolve the `ITodoService` instance. If it has not been defined in the container, a `TodoService` is instantiated.

For more information on IoC and IoC containers, see Chapter 22, "Unit Testing."

The following excerpt shows the `TodoItemView` constructor and fields:

```
readonly TodoItemViewModel viewModel;
bool initialized;

public TodoItemView()
{
    InitializeComponent();

    var todoService = Dependency.Resolve<ITodoService, TodoService>();
    DataContext = viewModel = new TodoItemViewModel(todoService);
}
```

The `Id` of the `TodoItem` is passed as a query string parameter, which causes the view to be placed in edit mode. This is determined in the `OnNavigatedTo` method of the view. If the `TodoItem Id` has been supplied, then the viewmodel's `LoadItemCommand` is executed.

When the `LoadItemCommand` completes, the visual state of the view is updated according to the `VisualState` property of the viewmodel, as shown in the following excerpt:

```
protected override void OnNavigatedTo(NavigationEventArgs e)
{
    base.OnNavigatedTo(e);

    if (initialized)
    {
        return;
    }
    initialized = true;

    string itemId;
    if (NavigationContext.QueryString.TryGetValue("TodoItemId", out itemId))
    {
        /* Custom commanding infrastructure performs automatic conversion
         * from a string to an int. */
        viewModel.LoadItemCommand.Execute(itemId);
```

```
        }
        VisualStateManager.GoToState(this, viewModel.VisualState, true);
}
```

The `TodoItemView` page contains a `TextBox` to edit the viewmodel's `TodoDescription` property and a Silverlight Toolkit `DatePicker` to edit the `TodoDueDate` property.

To force the `TextBox` to update the viewmodel when the text changes, the custom `UpdateSourceTriggerExtender` is used. This prevents changes to the description from being missed if the user taps an application bar item without first tapping elsewhere on the page to lose focus. See the following excerpt:

```xml
<StackPanel x:Name="ContentPanel" Grid.Row="1" Margin="12,0,12,0">
    <TextBlock Text="description"
               Style="{StaticResource PhoneTextNormalStyle}" />
    <!-- UpdateSourceTriggerExtended causes the value
         to be updated in the viewmodel as soon as the text changes. -->
    <TextBox Text="{Binding TodoDescription, Mode=TwoWay}"
             u:UpdateSourceTriggerExtender.UpdateSourceOnTextChanged="True" />
    <TextBlock Text="due"
               Style="{StaticResource PhoneTextNormalStyle}" />
    <toolkit:DatePicker Value="{Binding TodoDueDate, Mode=TwoWay}" />
</StackPanel>
```

For more information on the `UpdateSourceTriggerExtender`, see Chapter 23, "Input Validation."

The view contains an `AppBar` with an `AppBarHyperlinkButton` that links back to the `TodoListView` page and `AppBarIconButtons` that are bound to the various viewmodel commands, as shown:

```xml
<u:AppBar>
    <u:AppBarHyperlinkButton
            NavigateUri="/TodoList/TodoListView.xaml"
            Text="Items"
            IconUri="/Images/ApplicationBarIcons/List.png" />
    <u:AppBarIconButton
            x:Name="Button_Delete"
            Command="{Binding DeleteCommand}"
            Text="Delete"
            IconUri="/Images/ApplicationBarIcons/Delete.png" />
    <u:AppBarIconButton
            Command="{Binding SaveCommand}"
            CommandParameter="False"
            Text="Save"
            IconUri="/Images/ApplicationBarIcons/Save.png" />
    <u:AppBarIconButton
```

```
            Command="{Binding SaveCommand}"
            CommandParameter="True"
            Text="Save &amp; Pin"
            IconUri="/Images/ApplicationBarIcons/AddTile.png" />
</u:AppBar>
```

The visibility of the Delete button is determined by the `VisualState` property of the view-model. When the `VisualState` property is equal to Update, the Delete button is shown; if equal to Create, it is collapsed (see Figure 27.12). See the sample code if you are interested in the visual state group XAML.

FIGURE 27.12   Creating a new todo item

When tapping the Save & Pin button, the app is deactivated and the tile is displayed on the Start Experience (see Figure 27.13).

Tapping the tile returns the user to the `TodoItemView`, where the item can be edited or deleted.

When the tile is overdue, a different image is displayed. Changing the properties of the tile can be done from your foreground app or from a background agent, which is demonstrated in the following section.

Updating Tiles Using a Scheduled Task Agent

The background agent for the sample is the `TaskScheduler` class, which is a subclass of the `ScheduledTaskAgent` class. `TaskScheduler` is registered using the WMAppManifest.xml file.

As you saw earlier, a periodic task is registered in the `TodoItemViewModel` class. This causes the `TaskScheduler.OnInvoke` method to be called periodically. The `OnInvoke` method determines what kind of task is being launched by the OS, either periodic or resource intensive. For the todo sample, it is always a periodic task (see Listing 27.9).

FIGURE 27.13   Todo item shell tile is displayed on the Start Experience.

LISTING 27.9   TaskScheduler OnInvoke Method (excerpt)

```
protected override void OnInvoke(ScheduledTask task)
{
    /* Detect if the task is periodic or resource intensive. */
    if (task is PeriodicTask)
    {
        ProcessPeriodicTask();
    }
    else
    {
        ProcessResourceIntensiveTask();
    }
...
    NotifyComplete();
}
```

The main purpose of the TaskScheduler is to refresh the shell tiles on the Start Experience, updating the overdue status and changing the background image as required (see Listing 27.10).

The ProcessPeriodicTask method retrieves all tiles for the app containing the todo item query string parameter. Each tile is processed by extracting the Id of the todo item and then by retrieving the actual `TodoItem` object using the todo service. A new `StandardTileData` object is created for the `TodoItem` using the `TodoTileDataCreator`, and the tile is updated.

LISTING 27.10   TaskScheduler ProcessPeriodicTask Method

```
void ProcessPeriodicTask()
{
    TodoService todoService = new TodoService();

    string queryWithEquals = TodoItemIdQueryKey + "=";
    IEnumerable<ShellTile> tiles = ShellTile.ActiveTiles.Where(
            tile => tile.NavigationUri.ToString().Contains(queryWithEquals));

    foreach (var tile in tiles)
    {
        /* NavigationUri.Query raises an exception on relative URIs. */
        Dictionary<string, string> queryPairs
            = UrlUtility.ParseQueryString(tile.NavigationUri.ToString());

        string idString = queryPairs[TodoItemIdQueryKey];
        int todoItemId;
        if (!int.TryParse(idString, out todoItemId))
        {
            Debug.Assert(false, "Invalid id " + idString);
            continue;
        }

        TodoItem todoItem;
        if (!todoService.TryGetTodoItem(todoItemId, out todoItem))
        {
            Debug.Assert(false, "Unknown item " + idString);
            continue;
        }

        StandardTileData tileData = TodoTileDataCreator.CreateTile(
                                        todoItem.Description,
                                        todoItem.DueDate);
        tile.Update(tileData);
    }
}
```

Using a scheduled task agent to update shell tiles provides the means to engage with your users even when your app is not running. It should be remembered, however, that there is no guarantee that a scheduled task will run, and therefore it is wise not to depend solely on a background task for activities critical to the proper functioning of your app. Indeed, updating of shell tiles should also be done within your foreground app, which is not done in the sample.

Scheduled Task API Limitations

Scheduled task agents do not have access to the entire set of APIs that foreground apps do. There is a set of APIs that are off-limits, and using an API from the set either raises an `UnauthorizedAccessException` at runtime or causes the app to fail certification during submission to the Windows Phone Marketplace. For the list of unsupported APIs, see Table 27.3.

TABLE 27.3   Scheduled Task Agent Unsupported APIs

Namespace	Unsupported API
Microsoft.Devices	Camera.
Microsoft.Devices	VibrateController.
Microsoft.Devices	NowPlaying.
Microsoft.Devices.Radio	All APIs in this namespace are unsupported.
Microsoft.Devices.Sensors	All APIs in this namespace are unsupported.
Microsoft.Phone.BackgroundAudio	BackgroundAudioPlayer.
Microsoft.Phone.BackgroundTransfer	Add(BackgroundTransferRequest).
Microsoft.Phone.Controls	WebBrowser.
Microsoft.Phone.Info	IsKeyboardDeployed.
Microsoft.Phone.Notification	All APIs in this namespace are unsupported.
Microsoft.Phone.Scheduler	Add(ScheduledAction).
Microsoft.Phone.Shell	All APIs are unsupported except the following: ShellToast method of ShellToast class. Update(ShellTileData) method of ShellTile class. Delete() method of ShellTile class.
Microsoft.Phone.Tasks	All APIs in this namespace are unsupported.
Microsoft.Xna.*	All APIs in all XNA Framework namespaces are unsupported.
System.Windows	MessageBox.
System.Windows	Clipboard.
System.Windows.Controls	MediaElement.
System.Windows.Controls	MultiScaleImage.
System.Windows.Media	LicenseAcquirer.
System.Windows.Media	A/V Capture.
System.Windows.Navigation	All APIs in this namespace are unsupported.

Source: http://msdn.microsoft.com/en-us/library/hh202962(v=VS.92).aspx

One noteworthy limitation is the inability to display visual elements from a background agent. You see a workaround in the next section.

27

Providing Feedback to the User from an Agent

On occasion, your background agent may want to notify the user of some event. This is, however, not possible using custom UI nor with a Silverlight MessageBox.

A solution is to use a shell toast, which can provide immediate feedback to the user. A toast notification can be presented from within your task agent like so:

```
protected override void OnInvoke(ScheduledTask task)
{
    ShellToast toast = new ShellToast
                        {
                            Title = "Windows Phone 7 Unleashed",
                            Content = "Task Scheduler running..."
                        };
    toast.Show();

    /* ... */
}
```

If the user taps the toast notification, your app is launched in the foreground. By setting the NavigationUri property for the ShellToast, you can also provide a deep link with a query string, as was demonstrated for the todo item shell tiles.

Using a Mutex to Access Common Resources Safely

Your app's task agent may be invoked even when your app is in the foreground. It is, therefore, important to ensure that simultaneous access to shared resources, such as files in isolated storage, is controlled and performed safely.

A System.Threading.Mutex can be employed to synchronize critical sections of code—code that accesses a common resource—within your primary app and your background agent. A Mutex is a synchronization primitive. It is similar to the Monitor class but with a scope that allows you to achieve interprocess synchronization, allowing you to synchronize across your foreground app and your background agent.

Unlike Silverlight for the browser, a Mutex instance in Windows Phone must be named, and the scope of a Mutex is limited to your primary app and its background agent.

> **NOTE**
>
> A Mutex cannot be used to synchronize different apps, nor as a conduit for interapp communication.

Listing 27.11 shows an excerpt from the CommonResourceExample class in the downloadable sample code that demonstrates how to read and write to a file in isolated storage in a safe manner while preventing another thread, such as from your background agent, from accessing the file simultaneously.

When the `ReplaceFileContents` method is called, `WaitOne` is called on the `Mutex`, which blocks if the `Mutex` is owned by another thread in your foreground app or a background agent. If not owned, or when released by another thread, the contents of a file is read and then overwritten with a new content string. The result is returned to the caller. By using a `Mutex`, the result is guaranteed to be the content of the file immediately prior to writing the new content.

LISTING 27.11   CommonResourceExample Class (excerpt)

```
public class CommonResourceExample
{
    static readonly Mutex mutex = new Mutex(false, "CommonResourceExample");
    static readonly string fileName = "CommonResourceExample.txt";

    public string ReplaceFileContents(string fileContent)
    {
        try
        {
            mutex.WaitOne();
            string result = ReadFileCore();
            WriteFileCore(fileContent);
            return result;
        }
        finally
        {
            mutex.ReleaseMutex();
        }
    }

    void WriteFileCore(string fileContent)
    {
        using (IsolatedStorageFile isolatedStorageFile
                    = IsolatedStorageFile.GetUserStoreForApplication())
        {
            using (IsolatedStorageFileStream outStream
                    = isolatedStorageFile.OpenFile(
                            fileName, FileMode.Create))
            {
                using (StreamWriter writer = new StreamWriter(outStream))
                {
                    writer.Write(fileContent);
                }
            }
        }
    }
```

27

LISTING 27.11   Continued

```csharp
string ReadFileCore()
{
    using (IsolatedStorageFile isolatedStorageFile
                = IsolatedStorageFile.GetUserStoreForApplication())
    {
        if (!isolatedStorageFile.FileExists(fileName))
        {
            return string.Empty;
        }

        using (IsolatedStorageFileStream inStream
                    = isolatedStorageFile.OpenFile(
                            fileName, FileMode.Open))
        {
            using (StreamReader reader = new StreamReader(inStream))
            {
                return reader.ReadToEnd();
            }
        }
    }
}
```

It is important to ensure that your Mutex is released upon exiting from a critical section. This is done by wrapping the section in a try/finally block. If your foreground app or your background agent terminates while owning a mutex, the state of the mutex is set to signaled and the next waiting thread gets ownership.

To test whether the Mutex is owned, you can specify a timeout parameter to the WaitOne method (see Listing 27.12). This is an effective way to prevent your task agent from being terminated because it is blocked on a WaitOne call. Recall that a PeriodicTask has a maximum 15 seconds of execution time.

LISTING 27.12   Using WaitOne to Determine Whether a Mutex Is Owned

```csharp
bool mutexAcquired = false;
try
{
    mutexAcquired = mutex.WaitOne(10000);
    if (mutexAcquired)
    {
        /* Access common resource here. */
        Debug.WriteLine("mutex entered.");
    }
}
```

LISTING 27.12   Continued

```
finally
{
    if (mutexAcquired)
    {
        mutex.ReleaseMutex();
    }
}

if (!mutexAcquired)
{
    /* Unable to acquire ownership of mutex. */
    Debug.WriteLine("mutex timed out.");
}
```

> **TIP**
>
> To test whether a `Mutex` is owned, without blocking the calling thread, use a timeout value of 0 when calling `WaitOne`.

`Mutex` provides an effective way to synchronize critical sections of code and can assist in avoiding race conditions and other concurrency issues when accessing shared resources.

Summary

This chapter looked at the scheduled notification system, which consists of a useful set of classes for setting reminders and alarms that can present a message to the user at a predetermined time, whether or not your app is running in the foreground.

It then examined the scheduled task system, which extends the principles underpinning the notification system and offers the capability to run your own code in the background. You saw how to create a todo list app, which leverages a local database and updates live tiles from a background agent.

Finally, the chapter explained how to use a `Mutex` to provide safe access to resources shared by your foreground app and your background agent.

The next chapter continues with the todo list app and demonstrates how to use a background transfer service to back up the todo database to a cloud service.

Background File Transfers

When developing a phone app, your app may need to transfer files to or from a remote server. In some cases, your app may not be able to continue without having a certain file on hand. But in other cases, the file may not be required immediately and can be downloaded asynchronously using a background file transfer. Candidates for these kinds of file transfers include downloading large files (for example, music and video files) or backing up an app's local database.

Transferring files from a foreground app can be problematic due to the transient nature of an app's run cycle; if your app is tombstoned or terminated, any file transfers under way are interrupted. Background file transfers allow your app to download or upload files asynchronously and remain active even if your app is terminated, while still allowing your app to monitor the progress of the transfer.

The previous chapter looked at background actions and how a todo list app uses a local database to store todo item information. This chapter continues with the todo list sample, and you see how to back up and restore the todo list local database using a background transfer request. The chapter examines how to leverage the URL routing features of ASP.NET to pass arguments to a WCF service via a background transfer request, and you see how to retrieve the user's Windows Live anonymous ID. Finally the chapter looks at monitoring a background transfer using a progress indicator.

Background Transfer Requests

Transfer requests are represented by the BackgroundTransferRequest class. The BackgroundTransferService maintains a queue of background requests and is used to submit new background requests, remove requests from the queue, and retrieve active requests.

Submitting a background request can be done by creating an instance of the BackgroundTransferRequest class, specifying the request end points, and then adding the request to the BackgroundTransferService. The following excerpt shows a transfer request that downloads a file from a remote server to a location in isolated storage:

```
BackgroundTransferRequest request
    = new BackgroundTransferRequest(remoteUri, localUri)
    {
        TransferPreferences = TransferPreferences.AllowBattery,
        Method = "Get",
    };

BackgroundTransferService.Add(request);
```

> **NOTE**
>
> An app can have at most five requests queued at a given time. Attempting to add more than five raises an InvalidOperationException. It is the responsibility of the app to remove requests from the queue by using the BackgroundTransferService.Remove method after requests have completed.

By default, background transfer requests occur only when the device has a Wi-Fi connection and is connected to external power. By using the TransferPreferences property of the BackgroundTransferRequest class, you can override this behavior so that transfers occur when one or both of these conditions are not met. Table 28.1 describes the available TransferPreferences values.

> **NOTE**
>
> Setting the TransferPreferences property does not guarantee that transfers will occur under the preferred conditions. If the battery level is critical, for example, background transfers are suspended regardless of the TransferPreferences value.

TABLE 28.1   TransferPreferences Enum

Enumeration Value	Description
None	Allows transfers only when the device is using external power and has a Wi-Fi connection. This is the default setting.
AllowCellular	Allows transfers when the device is connected to external power and has a Wi-Fi or cellular connection.

TABLE 28.1   Continued

Enumeration Value	Description
AllowBattery	Allows transfers when there is a Wi-Fi connection and the device is using battery or external power.
AllowCellularAndBattery	Allows transfers when the device is using battery or external power and has a Wi-Fi or cellular connection.

> **CAUTION**
>
> Transferring files when the phone does not have a Wi-Fi connection can unduly consume the user's data plan. In addition, transferring files without an external power connection can rapidly drain the phone's battery. Both cases can potentially result in a poor experience for the user, and it is therefore recommended to leave the default value of TransferPresences as None.

BackgroundTransferRequest is bidirectional, allowing you to transfer files from and to the phone device. The BackgroundTransferRequest API is peculiar in that it determines the direction of the request based on which of its two constructors is used and whether its UploadLocation property has been set. The constructor to use when performing a download (from a remote server to isolated storage) has two parameters: the remote URI and the local (destination) URI. To perform an upload (from isolated storage to a remote server), its single parameter constructor is used in conjunction with its UploadLocation property. The following excerpt demonstrates the creation of an upload transfer request:

```
Uri remoteUri = new Uri(remoteUrl, UriKind.Absolute);

BackgroundTransferRequest request
    = new BackgroundTransferRequest(remoteUri)
        {
            Method = "POST",
            UploadLocation = new Uri(uploadPath, UriKind.Relative)
        };

BackgroundTransferService.Add(request);
```

By default, BackgroundTransferRequest uses the HTTP method GET.

> **NOTE**
>
> If you are performing an upload and fail to set the method to POST, an ArgumentNullException is raised because the BackgroundTransferRequest mistakes your request for a download and complains that the download URI was not supplied. Conversely, if Method is set to anything other than GET, BackgroundTransferRequest assumes the transfer is an upload and raises an ArgumentNullException if UploadLocation is not specified.
>
> It is another peculiar aspect of the API that an ArgumentNullException is raised rather than an InvalidOperationException.

28

A parameter indicating the direction and nature of the transfer would, in my view, make the BackgroundTransferRequest easier to use.

BackgroundTransferRequest provides the following two events for monitoring the progress and status of a background transfer:

► TransferProgressChanged

► TransferStatusChanged

Both events pass a BackgroundTransferEventArgs object that provides nothing apart from a reference to the associated BackgroundTransferRequest.

The TransferProgressChanged event, as its name implies, allows you to track the amount of data that has been transferred. The following excerpt shows a TransferProgressChanged event handler that determines the current progress of a transfer as a value between 0 and 1:

```
void HandleTransferProgressChanged(object sender,
                                    BackgroundTransferEventArgs e)
{
    if (e.Request.BytesSent > 0)
    {
        Progress = (double)e.Request.TotalBytesToSend / e.Request.BytesSent;
    }
    else
    {
        Progress = 0;
    }
}
```

The TransferStatusChanged event allows you to monitor the critical events of the transfer request and enables you to determine, for example, when the transfer has completed and whether an error has occurred, as shown:

```
void HandleTransferStatusChanged(object sender,
                                  BackgroundTransferEventArgs e)
{
    if (e.Request.TransferStatus == TransferStatus.Completed)
    {
        BackgroundTransferService.Remove(e.Request);

        if (e.Request.TransferError != null)
        {
            /* Handle the error. */
            return;
        }
    }
}
```

The `Request.TransferStatus` property identifies the request's current state. Table 28.2 describes each `TransferStatus` enum value.

TABLE 28.2   TransferStatus Enumeration

Enumeration Value	Description
None	The request has not yet been queued. This is the default value before the request is submitted to the `BackgroundTransferService`.
Transferring	The requested file is currently being transferred.
Waiting	The request is waiting in the background transfer service queue. This status can indicate that the request is queued and waiting for previous transfers to complete or that the service is retrying the request due to a network error.
WaitingForWiFi	The request is waiting in the background transfer service queue for a Wi-Fi connection.
WaitingForExternalPower	The request is waiting in the background transfer service queue for external power to be connected.
WaitingForExternalPower -DueToBatterySaverMode	The request is waiting for the device to be connected to external power because the user has enabled Battery Saver mode on the device.
WaitingForNonVoiceBlockingNetwork	The background transfer service does not run when the device is on a nonsimultaneous voice and data network, including 2G, EDGE, and standard GPRS. This status indicates the service is waiting for a supported network connection.
Paused	The request has been paused and waiting in the background transfer service queue.
Completed	The request has completed. This means that the request is no longer actionable by the background transfer service regardless of whether the transfer was completed successfully. To confirm that a transfer was successful, confirm that the `TransferError` property is null.
Unknown	The background transfer service could not retrieve the request status from the service. Once in this state, a `BackgroundTransferRequest` object is no longer useable. You may attempt to retrieve a new instance using the `Find(string)` method.

28

The role of the `TransferStatusChanged` event is discussed in greater detail later in the chapter.

Handling App Termination and Resubscription to Transfer Events

When a `BackgroundTransferRequest` has been added to the `BackgroundTransferService`, you can store the value of the request's `RequestId` property in isolated storage. This enables you to retrieve the request later if your app is terminated and to continue monitoring the progress of your background request by resubscribing to the request's `TransferStatusChanged` and `TransferProgressChanged` events.

The `BackgroundTransferService.Find` method is used to retrieve an existing request, like so:

```
BackgroundTransferRequest request
        = BackgroundTransferService.Find("request id string");
if (request != null)
{
    request.TransferStatusChanged += HandleUploadTransferStatusChanged;
    request.TransferProgressChanged += HandleTransferProgressChanged;
}
```

Background File Transfer Sample Code

The sample for this chapter continues from where we left off in Chapter 27, "Scheduled Actions." This chapter looks at backing up the todo items database to a remote server using WCF.

Within the BackgroundAgents solution in the downloadable sample code is a project named WindowsPhone7Unleashed.BackgroundAgents.Web. This project exposes a WCF service named BackupService, which allows the phone app to save files to the Backups directory on the server by way of its `SaveFile` method (see Listing 28.1). The `SaveFile` method accepts a Stream, which is written to a file on the server. The unique id of the user is also sent to the server to allow correct retrieval of the file at a later time.

LISTING 28.1   BackupService Class

```
[ServiceBehavior(InstanceContextMode = InstanceContextMode.PerCall)]
[AspNetCompatibilityRequirements(
    RequirementsMode = AspNetCompatibilityRequirementsMode.Allowed)]
public class BackupService : IBackupService
{
    public void SaveFile(string userId, string fileName, Stream fileStream)
    {
        string location = string.Format(
                            @"~\Backups\{0}_{1}", userId, fileName);
        var filepath = HttpContext.Current.Server.MapPath(location);
        using (Stream outputStream = File.OpenWrite(filepath))
```

LISTING 28.1   Continued

```
        {
            CopyStream(fileStream, outputStream);
        }
    }

    static void CopyStream(Stream input, Stream output)
    {
        var buffer = new byte[8 * 1024];
        int streamLength;

        while ((streamLength = input.Read(buffer, 0, buffer.Length)) > 0)
        {
            output.Write(buffer, 0, streamLength);
        }
    }
}
```

There is no retrieval method in the WCF service because an ordinary HTTP GET request is used to download the file.

The WindowsPhone7Unleashed.BackgroundAgents contains a web reference to the WindowsPhone7Unleashed.BackgroundAgents.Web project, and the service is consumed within the TodoListViewModel class.

Using URL Rerouting with a WCF Service

The Web Application project uses URL rerouting to allow the BackgroundTransferRequest to pass the user ID and filename to the service via the URL.

The routing system on the server is initialized in the RegisterRoutes method of the Global class in the Web Application project. The URL routing APIs reside in the System.Web. Routing namespace. A new ServiceRoute is added to the RouteTable, so that when a request for the URL BackupService arrives, the built-in WebServiceHostFactory creates an instance of the BackupService class to service the request. See the following excerpt:

```
public class Global : System.Web.HttpApplication
{
    protected void Application_Start(object sender, EventArgs e)
    {
        RegisterRoutes();
    }

    void RegisterRoutes()
    {
        RouteTable.Routes.Add(new ServiceRoute(
            "BackupService", new WebServiceHostFactory(),
```

28

```
            typeof(BackupService)));
    }
...
}
```

The service interface for the backup service defines a `UriTemplate` that maps the incoming request URL, which includes the user ID and filename, to the `SaveFile` method parameters. This means that we are able to translate the incoming URL and forward the call to the service method. See the following:

```
[ServiceContract(Namespace = "http://danielvaughan.org")]
public interface IBackupService
{
    [OperationContract, WebInvoke(
        Method = "POST", UriTemplate = "UploadFile/{userId}/{fileName}")]
    void SaveFile(string userId, string fileName, Stream fileStream);
}
```

URL rerouting is an elegant way of providing a WCF service with extra information, such as the user's ID, while still remaining compatible with the `BackgroundTransferRequest` and its simple `Uri UploadLocation` property.

Retrieving the User's Windows Live Anonymous ID

To associate a database file on the server with the user of the device, the app retrieves the user's Windows Live anonymous ID from the `Microsoft.Phone.Info.UserExtendedProperties` class. The Windows Live anonymous ID is a representation of the user's Windows Live ID that does not include any user identifiable information. When a user activates a device, he must provide a Windows Live ID. The Windows Live anonymous ID lets you identify the user by his Windows Live account, without actually seeing his details, and there is no way to correlate the anonymous ID with the Windows Live ID.

When retrieving the anonymous ID from `UserExtendedProperties` by way of the ANID key value (see Listing 28.2), the resulting string contains a series of name value pairs resembling a URL query string, like the following:

A=1E234A328BC18118DB64D915FFFFFFFF&E=a45&W=1

The anonymous ID is a GUID consisting of 32 characters. It is extracted by skipping the first two characters of the value, as these characters are the name part of a *name=value* pair.

LISTING 28.2   DeviceProperties Class

```
public class DeviceProperties : IDeviceProperties
{
    /// <summary>
    /// Gets the windows live anonymous id.
```

LISTING 28.2   Continued

```
/// This method requires ID_CAP_IDENTITY_USER
//  to be present in the capabilities of the WMAppManifest.
/// </summary>
/// <returns>The string id for the user.</returns>
static string GetWindowsLiveAnonymousId()
{
    const int idLength = 32;
    const int idOffset = 2;

    string result = string.Empty;
    object id;
    if (UserExtendedProperties.TryGetValue("ANID", out id))
    {
        string idString = id != null ? id.ToString() : null;
        if (idString != null && idString.Length >= (idLength + idOffset))
        {
            result = idString.Substring(idOffset, idLength);
        }
    }

    return result;
}

string windowsLiveAnonymousId;

public string WindowsLiveAnonymousId
{
    get
    {
        return windowsLiveAnonymousId
            ?? (windowsLiveAnonymousId = GetWindowsLiveAnonymousId());
    }
}
}
```

28

TIP

It is better to associate data with the user of the device rather than the device itself. By relying on the ID of the user, rather than the ID of the device, you can provide a greater level of assurance that if the phone changes ownership, the new user of the phone will not have access to previous owner's data.

Retrieving the anonymous ID from the UserExtendedProperties does not work on the emulator. For testing purposes, the IDeviceProperties implementation can be swapped with a mock implementation that retrieves a predefined anonymous ID.

TodoListViewModel

The TodoListViewModel constructor accepts an IDeviceProperties instance and an ITodoService instance, which, as you saw in Chapter 27, is used for storage and retrieval of todo items. See the following excerpt:

```
public TodoListViewModel(
    ITodoService todoService, IDeviceProperties deviceProperties)
{
...
    backupDatabaseCommand = new DelegateCommand(obj => BackupDatabase());
    restoreDatabaseCommand = new DelegateCommand(obj => RestoreDatabase());

    Load();
}
```

The viewmodel contains a method that leverages the IDeviceProperties instance to create a unique ID to use to identify itself to calls to a WCF service.

```
string GetUserId()
{
    string id = deviceProperties.WindowsLiveAnonymousId;
    if (string.IsNullOrWhiteSpace(id))
    {
        id = "Emulator";
    }
    return id;
}
```

The anonymous ID is passed to the WCF service when backing up the local database file and used as part of the URL when restoring it.

Backing Up the Local Database

To transfer the local database to the server, it must first be copied to a directory in isolated storage. This prevents the file from being modified by the SQL CE engine while the transfer is under way. The viewmodel's BackupDatabase method creates a temporary directory and then copies the local .sdf database file to the directory, as shown:

```
string uploadUrl = "http://localhost:60182/BackupService/UploadFile/";
const string localDatabaseName = "Todo.sdf";
const string transferDirectory = "/shared/transfers";

string uploadPath = transferDirectory + "/" + localDatabaseName;
```

```
using (IsolatedStorageFile isolatedStorageFile
            = IsolatedStorageFile.GetUserStoreForApplication())
{
    if (!isolatedStorageFile.FileExists(localDatabaseName))
    {
        throw new InvalidOperationException(
            "Database file does not exist in isolated storage.");
    }

    if (!isolatedStorageFile.DirectoryExists(transferDirectory))
    {
        isolatedStorageFile.CreateDirectory(transferDirectory);
    }

    isolatedStorageFile.CopyFile(localDatabaseName, uploadPath, true);
}
```

The `BackupDatabase` method then constructs a destination URL for the upload. The remote URL is constructed using the base URL of the upload file path on the server. This URL is rerouted when it arrives at the server, and its segments are passed as arguments to the `SaveFile` WCF service method. See the following excerpt:

```
string deviceId = GetUserId();

string remoteUrl = string.Format("{0}{1}/{2}",
                                  uploadUrl,
                                  deviceId,
                                  localDatabaseName);

Uri remoteUri = new Uri(remoteUrl, UriKind.Absolute);
```

A `BackgroundTransferRequest` is constructed, which causes the file to be uploaded to the server. Uploads use the HTTP POST method, as shown:

```
BackgroundTransferRequest request
    = new BackgroundTransferRequest(remoteUri)
            {
                TransferPreferences = TransferPreferences.AllowBattery,
                Method = "POST",
                UploadLocation = new Uri(uploadPath, UriKind.Relative)
            };
```

To monitor the progress of the transfer request, while the app is running in the foreground, we subscribe to the `TransferStatusChanged` and the `TransferProgressChanged` events. The transfer request is then added to the `BackgroundTransferService`, which queues the upload. See the following:

28

```
request.TransferStatusChanged += HandleUploadTransferStatusChanged;
request.TransferProgressChanged += HandleUploadTransferProgressChanged;

BackgroundTransferService.Add(request);
Message = "Backing up data to cloud.";
ProgressVisible = true;
```

When the viewmodel's `ProgressVisible` property is set to true, it causes a progress indicator to be displayed in the view. This occurs via a custom `ProgressIndicatorProxy` class, first discussed in Chapter 5, "Content Controls, Items Controls, and Range Controls." In addition, the progress indicator also displays the progress of the operation via the viewmodel's `Progress` property. The `Progress` property is updated whenever the `TransferProgressChanged` event is raised, as shown:

```
void HandleTransferProgressChanged(
        object sender, BackgroundTransferEventArgs e)
{
    if (e.Request.BytesSent > 0)
    {
        Progress = (double)e.Request.TotalBytesToSend / e.Request.BytesSent;
    }
    else
    {
        Progress = 0;
    }
}
```

When the request's `TransferStatusChanged` event is raised, if the request has completed, it is removed from the `BackgroundTransferStatus`, and the progress indicator is hidden.

> **NOTE**
>
> A `TransferStatus` of Completed does not necessarily mean that the transfer completed successfully, but rather that the operation has ended for whatever reason. It is therefore critical to test for the presence of an error contained in the `Request.TransferError` property.

The `ViewModelBase` class's `MessageService` is used to display the result to the user, as shown:

```
void HandleUploadTransferStatusChanged(
        object sender, BackgroundTransferEventArgs e)
{
    if (e.Request.TransferStatus == TransferStatus.Completed)
    {
        BackgroundTransferService.Remove(e.Request);
```

```
        ProgressVisible = false;

        if (e.Request.TransferError != null)
        {
            MessageService.ShowError("An error occured during backup.");
        }
        else
        {
            MessageService.ShowMessage("Backup successful.");
        }
    }
}
```

Once the local database file has been transferred to the server, the user can nominate to restore the database from the backup.

Restoring the Local Database

Restoring the local database involves submitting a background transfer request to download the previously uploaded file from the server. The file is downloaded to a temporary location in isolated storage, the existing local database is disconnected, and its file is replaced.

The RestoreDatabase method begins by creating a temporary directory where the downloaded .sdf file can be placed by the BackgroundTransferService:

```
const string downloadPath = transferDirectory + "/" + localDatabaseName;

using (IsolatedStorageFile isolatedStorageFile
            = IsolatedStorageFile.GetUserStoreForApplication())
{
    if (!isolatedStorageFile.DirectoryExists(transferDirectory))
    {
        isolatedStorageFile.CreateDirectory(transferDirectory);
    }
}
```

It then creates two Uri objects specifying the location of the .sdf file on the remote server, and the file's destination location in isolated storage, as shown:

```
string deviceId = GetUserId();

string remoteUrl = string.Format("{0}{1}_{2}",
                                downloadUrl,
                                deviceId,
                                localDatabaseName);
Uri remoteUri = new Uri(remoteUrl, UriKind.Absolute);
Uri localUri = new Uri(downloadPath, UriKind.Relative);
```

The BackgroundTransferRequest is constructed using the two Uri objects. The default HTTP method Get is used because we are downloading the file to the device. See the following excerpt:

```
BackgroundTransferRequest request
    = new BackgroundTransferRequest(remoteUri, localUri)
    {
        TransferPreferences = TransferPreferences.AllowBattery,
    };
```

Finally, we subscribe to the transfer request's status changed and progress changed events, and the request is added to the BackgroundTransferService. The progress indicator is displayed, and it is updated as the progress of the background transfer changes:

```
request.TransferStatusChanged += HandleDownloadTransferStatusChanged;
request.TransferProgressChanged += HandleDownloadTransferProgressChanged;

BackgroundTransferService.Add(request);
Message = "Restoring data from cloud.";
Progress = 0;
ProgressVisible = true;
```

When the background transfer completes the TransferStatusChanged event handler is called (see Listing 28.3). The downloaded file is copied to the location of the local database, which replaces the existing file. The ITodoService.Initialize method re-creates the connection to the database, and the viewmodel's GroupedTodoItems are re-created via a call to PopulateItems.

LISTING 28.3   HandleDownloadTransferStatusChanged Method

```
void HandleDownloadTransferStatusChanged(object sender,
                                         BackgroundTransferEventArgs e)
{
    if (e.Request.TransferStatus == TransferStatus.Completed)
    {
        BackgroundTransferService.Remove(e.Request);

        ProgressVisible = false;

        if (e.Request.TransferError != null)
        {
            MessageService.ShowError("An error occured during restore.");
            return;
        }
```

LISTING 28.3 Continued

```
    try
    {
        using (IsolatedStorageFile isolatedStorageFile
                    = IsolatedStorageFile.GetUserStoreForApplication())
        {
            string downloadedFile
                    = e.Request.DownloadLocation.OriginalString;
            isolatedStorageFile.CopyFile(downloadedFile,
                                    localDatabaseName, true);
        }

        todoService.Initialize();

        ClearPinnedItems();

        PopulateItems();
    }
    catch (Exception ex)
    {
        MessageService.ShowError("An error occured during restore.");
        return;
    }

    MessageService.ShowMessage("Restore successful.");
    }
}
```

Backup and restore operations are actuated by application bar menu items in the view. The view's AppBar menu items are bound to the BackupDatabaseCommand and the RestoreDatabaseCommand (see Figure 28.1).

Using a BackgroundTransferRequest is an effective way to back up your app's data because it does not rely on your foreground app being active. Be mindful, however, that the BackgroundTransferService does not guarantee that a transfer request will be serviced.

28

FIGURE 28.1   The `TodoListView` provides menu items for backing up and restoring the local database, and a progress indicator that shows the progress of the background transfer request.

Summary

In this chapter you saw how to back up and restore the todo list database using a background transfer request. The chapter examined how to leverage the URL routing features of ASP.NET to pass arguments to a WCF service via a background transfer request, and you saw how to retrieve the user's Windows Live anonymous id. Finally, the chapter looked at monitoring a background transfer using a progress indicator.

CHAPTER 29

Background Audio

Windows Phone allows you to create apps that respond to the Universal Volume Control (UVC) on the phone and, in conjunction with an onscreen menu, coordinate the playback of audio, even when your app is not running in the foreground.

This chapter begins with an overview of the background audio player and shows how it is used to control the playback of local or remote audio files. You look at how audio file information is represented by the AudioTrack class and examine the role of background audio agents, which are used to coordinate audio playback while your app is not running in the foreground.

The chapter then demonstrates how to build a UI that leverages the background audio agent for controlling playback while your app is in the foreground.

Finally, the chapter examines audio streaming agents and how they are used to provide custom streaming and decoding of audio files. You see how a custom audio streaming agent can be employed to play audio directly from an assembly resource, something that is not possible using the built-in streaming and decoding system of the phone.

Background Agent Recap

In Chapter 27, "Scheduled Actions," you learned that Windows Phone supports the following three types of BackgroundAgents:

▶ ScheduledTaskAgent (presented in Chapter 27)

▶ AudioPlayerAgent

▶ AudioStreamingAgent

Background agents are classes invoked by the OS at certain times to carry out activities in the background (from another process) while your app may not actually be running in the foreground.

This chapter examines the last two agent types: `AudioPlayerAgent` and `AudioStreamingAgent`.

Background Audio Overview

The following comprise the three main classes used for background audio, which are explored in this chapter:

- ▶ `BackgroundAudioPlayer`
- ▶ `AudioPlayerAgent`
- ▶ `AudioStreamingAgent`

`BackgroundAudioPlayer` is a class that allows you to specify an audio file for playback and to carry out playback activities such as play, pause, fast-forward, and rewind. `BackgroundAudioPlayer` allows you to specify track information, such as the title of the track and its location. The built-in playback capabilities of the `BackgroundAudioPlayer` allow audio files to be streamed from either a remote server or locally from isolated storage.

Out of the box, `BackgroundAudioPlayer` supports playback formats such as MP3, WMA, and WAV. For a complete list of supported audio formats see http://bit.ly/pnnT8C. `BackgroundAudioPlayer` offers little in the way of coordinating the playback of a list of audio tracks. This is the task of the `AudioPlayerAgent`.

`AudioPlayerAgent` classes are specialized agents used to retrieve audio files and coordinate the playback of background audio via the `BackgroundAudioPlayer`. `AudioPlayerAgent` provides a number of method callbacks that are automatically called by the OS based on user actions.

An `AudioStreamingAgent` can be used to customize how audio data is procured by your `BackgroundAudioPlayer`. You can supplant the `BackgroundAudioPlayer`'s media sourcing capabilities by providing your own logic to download and decode an audio file.

Background Audio Player

The `BackgroundAudioPlayer` class implements the singleton pattern. The single instance of the `BackgroundAudioPlayer` is accessed in your foreground app via its static `Instance` property, as shown:

```
BackgroundAudioPlayer.Instance.Track
    = new AudioTrack(
            new Uri("http://example.com/Audio.mp3", UriKind.Absolute),
            "Track Name", "Artist", "Album", null);
BackgroundAudioPlayer.Instance.Play();
```

The behavior of the BackgroundAudioPlayer changes depending on whether it is being used in your foreground app or from an AudioPlayerAgent. When the BackgroundAudioPlayer is used in your foreground app, all calls are relayed to your AudioPlayerAgent. When used from an AudioPlayerAgent, the BackgroundAudioPlayer affects the playback of audio directly. Without an AudioPlayerAgent, the BackgroundAudioPlayer does nothing.

This dual behavior can be best understood by looking at the internal workings of the BackgroundAudioPlayer. The BackgroundAudioPlayer is actually a proxy that relies on a native implementation of an internal IAudioPlaybackManager interface. When the BackgroundAudioPlayer is used in your foreground app, the IAudioPlaybackManager relays all audio requests to the app's AudioPlayerAgent. Conversely, when used from your AudioPlayerAgent, the IAudioPlaybackManager uses the native audio playback system instead.

BackgroundAudioPlayer contains several public methods that allow you to control the playback of audio (see Table 29.1).

TABLE 29.1   BackgroundAudioPlayer Audio Playback Related Methods

Method Name	Description
FastForward	Starts fast-forwarding through the current AudioTrack
Pause	Pauses playback at the current position
Play	Plays or resumes the current AudioTrack at its current position
Rewind	Starts rewinding through the current AudioTrack
SkipNext	Skips to the next track
SkipPrevious	Skips to the previous track
Stop	Stops and resets media to be played from the beginning

BackgroundAudioPlayer contains several public audio playback related properties, which are shown in Table 29.2.

TABLE 29.2   BackgroundAudioPlayer Audio Playback Related Properties

Property Name	Description
BufferingProgress	A double value representing the amount of buffering that is completed for the media content. This property is most relevant for streaming remote audio files.
CanPause	A bool value indicating whether the media can be paused when the Pause method is called.
CanSeek	A bool value indicating whether the media can be repositioned by setting the value of the Position property.
Error	The last Exception object, if any, to have occurred while playing the current AudioTrack.
PlayerState	Gets the current PlayState of the player.
Position	Gets or sets the current position within the current AudioTrack.
Track	Gets or sets the current audio track, whether it is playing or not.
Volume	The media's volume represented on a linear scale between 0 and 1. The default is 0.85.

29

BackgroundAudioPlayer contains a principle event, PlayStateChanged, which is used to detect, for example, when a track begins playing. You see later in the chapter how this event can be used to hide and show UI elements based on the current state of the player.

Representing Audio Files with the AudioTrack Class

The AudioTrack class includes information about the location of an audio file, as well as track metadata such as the track's title. Table 29.3 describes each of the AudioTrack properties.

TABLE 29.3   AudioTrack Properties

Property Name	Description
Album	The string name of the track's album.
AlbumArt	A Uri indicating the location of an image showing the album cover. Once set, this value can be used to show the album cover in your foreground app.
Artist	The string name of the artist.
Duration	A TimeSpan representing the length of the track.
PlayerControls	A Flags enum value that determines which playback controls are enabled in the system user interface. The current phone OS (7.5) supports All, None, SkipNext, SkipPrevious, and Pause. This property allows you to disable the next, previous, or pause button on the audio menu when the user presses the UVC.
Source	The URI path to the track.
Tag	An arbitrary string associated with this track, used to store application-specific state.
Title	Text to display as the track's title.

AudioTrack implements IEditableObject to enable batching of property change requests. Once an AudioTrack object has been instantiated, it cannot be changed without putting it in edit mode first. AudioTrack uses an IAudioTrack backing field, which links the managed AudioTrack object to the native audio system via Com Interop. To make changes to an AudioTrack object, its BeginEdit method must be called. Once all changes have been made, EndEdit should be called. This commits the property changes to the OS via the native IAudioTrack object.

Creating a Custom Audio Player Agent

An audio player agent can be created by selecting the Windows Phone Audio Playback Agent project type from the Visual Studio New Project dialog (see Figure 29.1). This produces a new project that includes a class that derives from AudioPlayerAgent.

FIGURE 29.1   Visual Studio Windows Phone agent projects

When you link to an Audio Player Agent project from your main project, a
`BackgroundServiceAgent` task definition is added to your main project's
WMAppManifest.xml file, resembling the following:

```
<Tasks>
  <DefaultTask  Name="_default" NavigationPage="MainPage.xaml" />
  <ExtendedTask Name="BackgroundTask">
      <BackgroundServiceAgent Specifier="AudioPlayerAgent"
          Name="<Unique name within the app>"
          Source="<Assembly>"
          Type="<Namespace.Class>" />
  </ExtendedTask>
</Tasks>
```

It is not necessary to use Visual Studio's Audio Player Agent project template to create a
custom background audio agent. You can create the class and add the task definition to
the WMAppManifest.xml file manually if you so choose.

AudioPlayerAgent Sample

The custom audio player agent for this section includes a simple playlist, which includes
both locally stored and remote audio files. The class is called `BackgroundAudioPlayerAgent`,
and it is located in the WindowsPhone7Unleashed.BackgroundAudio project, within the
BackgroundAudio solution in the downloadable sample code.

29

A static list of audio tracks defines the playlist, shown in the following excerpt:

```
static readonly List<AudioTrack> playList
    = new List<AudioTrack>
        {
            new AudioTrack(new Uri("AudioFiles/Audio01.wma",
                                UriKind.Relative),
                            "Ringtone 1",              // title
                            "Windows Phone",           // artist
                            "Windows Phone Ringtones", // album
                            null),
            /* ... */

            /* A remote URI. */
            new AudioTrack(new Uri("http://example.com/track.mp3",
                                UriKind.Absolute),
                            "Episode 29",
                            "Windows Phone Radio",
                            "Windows Phone Radio Podcast",
                            null)
        };
```

> **TIP**
>
> AudioPlayerAgents remain active during playback. This allows the creation of dynamic playlists. During playback, you could retrieve a playlist on a background thread from a remote server.

If providing playback of local media files, the files must be copied to isolated storage before they can be played by the background audio player. The IIsolatedStorageUtility is a custom interface that abstracts access to isolated storage. It is used by the BackgroundAudioPlayerAgent to detect whether the media files have already been written to isolated storage; if not, it is used to copy the sample files. The downloadable sample code contains all the code for the IIsolatedStorageUtility and its default implementation IsolatedStorageUtility. See the following excerpt:

```
internal static void CopyAudioToIsolatedStorage(
    IIsolatedStorageUtility isolatedStorageUtility)
{
    ArgumentValidator.AssertNotNull(
        isolatedStorageUtility, "isolatedStorageUtility");

    /* If a file exists, do not copy. */
    if (isolatedStorageUtility.FileExists("AudioFiles/Audio01.wma"))
    {
        return;
    }
}
```

```
string[] files = new[] { "Audio01.wma", "Audio02.wma", "Audio03.wma" };

var sourceToDestinations = from file in files
                    let path = "AudioFiles/" + file
                    select new KeyValuePair<string, string>(path, path);

isolatedStorageUtility.CopyApplicationResourcesToIsolatedStorage(
                                            sourceToDestinations);
}
```

The custom `BackgroundAudioPlayerAgent` keeps track of the current track number using a static `int` field. This is made possible because, unlike its `ScheduledTaskAgent` counterpart, the process for an `AudioPlayerAgent` is not terminated when `NotifyComplete` is called.

The track number field is used to select the correct track to play when the user requests the previous or next track, as shown:

```
void PlayNextTrack(BackgroundAudioPlayer player)
{
    if (++trackNumber >= playList.Count)
    {
        trackNumber = 0;
    }

    PlayTrack(player);
}

void PlayPreviousTrack(BackgroundAudioPlayer player)
{
    if (--trackNumber < 0)
    {
        trackNumber = playList.Count - 1;
    }

    PlayTrack(player);
}
```

A `PlayTrack` method is used to toggle the play state of the `BackgroundAudioPlayer`, as shown:

```
void PlayTrack(BackgroundAudioPlayer player)
{
    if (player.PlayerState == PlayState.Paused)
    {
        player.Play();
    }
    else
```

29

```
    {
        player.Track = playList[trackNumber];
    }
}
```

During playback, when the `BackgroundAudioPlayer.Track` property is set, the track does not begin immediate playback, but rather the `BackgroundAudioPlayer` is placed into a TrackReady state, and the `AudioPlayerAgent.OnPlayStateChanged` method is called. You see how this fits together in a moment.

AudioPlayerAgent Virtual Methods

`AudioPlayerAgent` has the following three virtual methods that can be overridden in your implementation:

▶ OnPlayStateChanged

▶ OnUserAction

▶ OnError

The following sections explore each method in detail.

AudioPlayerAgent.OnPlayStateChanged

`OnPlayStateChanged` allows you to respond to changes in the playback state of an audio track. For example, it allows you to transition the play state of a track once it has completed downloading or to move to the next track when a track finishes, as shown in the following excerpt:

```
protected override void OnPlayStateChanged(
    BackgroundAudioPlayer player, AudioTrack track, PlayState playState)
{
    switch (playState)
    {
        case PlayState.TrackReady:
            /* The track to play is set in the PlayTrack method. */
            player.Play();
            break;

        case PlayState.TrackEnded:
            PlayNextTrack(player);
            break;
    }

    NotifyComplete();
}
```

Table 29.4 describes the `PlayState` enum values that can be handled in the `OnPlayStateChanged` method.

TABLE 29.4   PlayState Enum

Enum Value	Description
BufferingStarted	The current track has started buffering.
BufferingStopped	The current track has stopped buffering.
Error	An error occurred.
FastForwarding	The current track is fast-forwarding.
Paused	Playback for the app is paused.
Playing	This app is currently playing a track.
Rewinding	The current track is rewinding.
Shutdown	The app has shut down.
Stopped	No playback is occurring in this application.
TrackEnded	The last track has ended and the app is currently changing tracks.
TrackReady	The current track is ready for playback.
Unknown	The current `Microsoft.Phone.BackgroundAudio.PlayState` is indeterminate. For example, a new `Microsoft.Phone.BackgroundAudio.AudioTrack` has been set, but playback has not been initiated.

NOTE

The `OnPlayStateChanged` method is used to respond to playback state changes, but not to errors that occur during playback. Use the `OnError` to respond to such errors.

AudioPlayerAgent.OnUserAction

The name of the `OnUserAction` method is somewhat misleading. The task of the `OnUserAction` method is to handle `BackgroundAudioPlayer` actions that occur in your foreground app.

Two actions cause the `AudioPlayerAgent.OnUserAction` method to be called. The first action occurs when the user presses the UVC and an onscreen menu is displayed allowing the user to play, pause, and skip forward and backward between tracks (see Figure 29.2). User actions do not directly affect the `BackgroundAudioPlayer`, but rather your `AudioPlayerAgent` is responsible for manipulating the player via the `OnUserAction` method.

The second action occurs when your app is in the foreground and it calls one of the playback related methods on the `BackgroundAudioPlayer.Instance` object, such as `Play`. This type of action may or may not have been directed by the user.

FIGURE 29.2   Tapping the onscreen menu background launches your app.

OnUserAction is passed a UserAction enum value that allows you to determine the behavior of the audio player agent. In some cases the player can be put into action immediately. See the following excerpt:

```
protected override void OnUserAction(
    BackgroundAudioPlayer player, AudioTrack track, UserAction action,
    object param)
{
    /* User actions can be initiated from the main application
     * or from the UVC (Universal Volume Control). */
    switch (action)
    {
        case UserAction.Play:
            PlayTrack(player);
            break;

        case UserAction.Pause:
            player.Pause();
            break;

        case UserAction.SkipPrevious:
            PlayPreviousTrack(player);
            break;
```

```
        case UserAction.SkipNext:
            PlayNextTrack(player);
            break;

        case UserAction.Stop:
            player.Stop();
            break;
    }

    NotifyComplete();
}
```

Table 29.5 lists the UserAction enum values that can be handled in the OnUserAction method.

The param object argument, of the OnUserAction method, is used only with the action argument UserAction.Seek, in which case the param argument is a TimeSpan that indicates the requested track position.

TABLE 29.5   UserAction Enum

Enum Value	Description
FastForward	Fast-forward the current track.
Pause	Pause playback.
Play	Play or resume playback.
Rewind	Rewind the current track.
Seek	Seek to a position within the current track.
SkipNext	Skip to the next track.
SkipPrevious	Skip to the previous track.
Stop	Stop playback.

AudioPlayerAgent.OnError

OnError is called when an Exception is raised during playback of an audio track. The method is generally called when the agent encounters a connection error when downloading an audio file from a remote server and offers the opportunity to transition to a different track, one that is potentially stored locally if the error is due to an absence of network connectivity.

In the following excerpt, you see that when an error is determined to be fatal, the Abort method is called, signaling to the OS that playback should be disabled. The method implementation is identical to the base class implementation and need not be implemented if you do not want to provide explicit error handling:

```
protected override void OnError(BackgroundAudioPlayer player,
                                AudioTrack track,
                                Exception error, bool isFatal)
{
    if (isFatal)
    {
        Abort();
    }
    else
    {
        NotifyComplete();
    }
}
```

Controlling Background Audio from Your Foreground App

Most apps employing background audio are going to want to provide an enhanced interface within the foreground app for controlling playback and displaying track information. This section looks at the `MainPage` and associated classes of the WindowsPhone7Unleashed.BackgroundAudio project. The page allows the user to play audio via the `BackgroundAudioPlayer` class. It provides application bar buttons for play and pause, stop, rewind, and forward, and several fields for displaying the current track information.

NOTE

It is a Windows Phone Marketplace certification requirement that when the user is already playing background music on the phone when your app is launched, your app must ask the user for consent to stop playing or to adjust the background music. This prompt must occur each time the app launches, unless there is an opt-in setting provided to the user, and the user has used this setting to opt-in.

A Testable `BackgroundAudioPlayer`

The `BackgroundAudioPlayer` class is inherently difficult to use in unit tests because of the cross process interaction with the `AudioPlayerAgent` and its dependence on native phone components. For this reason, I have provided a wrapper called `BackgroundAudioPlayerProxy`, which implements a custom `IBackgroundAudioPlayer` interface. In addition, there is a second implementation: `MockBackgroundAudioPlayer`, which allows you to test whether your code called the background audio player as expected; it allows you to test, for example, whether your code attempted to play a track.

The code for `IBackgroundAudioPlayer` and its associated class implementations is not shown in this chapter because it is lengthy, and the methods, properties, and events of the `IBackgroundAudioPlayer` coincide with those of the built-in `BackgroundAudioPlayer`. You can, of course, find the code in the downloadable sample code for the book.

MainPageViewModel

The viewmodel is declared as a field of the MainPage, as shown:

```
readonly MainPageViewModel viewModel = new MainPageViewModel(
                                    new BackgroundAudioPlayerProxy(),
                                    new IsolatedStorageUtility());
```

The `MainPageViewModel` class constructor accepts an `IBackgroundAudioPlayer` as well as an `IIsolatedStorageUtility` instance (see Listing 29.1). A subscription to the `PlayStateChanged` event of the background audio player allows the viewmodel to update various properties whenever the play state changes.

The viewmodel contains five commands for controlling the `BackgroundAudioPlayer` while the app is in the foreground, which provide for playing, pausing, stopping, and skipping between tracks.

The viewmodel's `Refresh` method is called to update the viewmodel, which relies on the state of the `BackgroundAudioPlayer`. A `Timer` is used to monitor the progress of the track while it is being played.

LISTING 29.1   MainPageViewModel Constructor

```
public MainPageViewModel(
    IBackgroundAudioPlayer backgroundAudioPlayer,
    IIsolatedStorageUtility isolatedStorageUtility)
{
    player = ArgumentValidator.AssertNotNull(
                backgroundAudioPlayer, "backgroundAudioPlayer");
    ArgumentValidator.AssertNotNull(
                isolatedStorageUtility, "isolatedStorageUtility");

    player.PlayStateChanged += HandlePlayStateChanged;
    BackgroundAudioPlayerAgent.CopyAudioToIsolatedStorage(isolatedStorageUtility);

    playCommand = new DelegateCommand(obj => player.Play());
    pauseCommand = new DelegateCommand(obj => player.Pause());
    stopCommand = new DelegateCommand(obj => player.Stop());
    previousTrackCommand = new DelegateCommand(obj => player.SkipPrevious());
    nextTrackCommand = new DelegateCommand(obj => player.SkipNext());

    Refresh(false);

    timer = new Timer(HandleTimerTick, null, 3000, 1000);
}
```

The viewmodel's `TrackArtist` and `TrackTitle` properties reflect the `Artist` and `Title` properties of the current `AudioTrack`.

The viewmodel's VisualState property, which is of type string, determines the visual state of the view and the visibility of various application bar buttons. The VisualState value is set to the PlayerState property of the BackgroundAudioPlayer, as shown:

```
void Refresh(bool setVisualState = true)
{
    switch (player.PlayerState)
    {
        case PlayState.Playing:
            CanPause = true;
            TrackArtist = player.Track.Artist;
            TrackTitle = player.Track.Title;
            break;
        case PlayState.Paused:
            CanPause = false;
            break;
    }

    BufferingProgress = player.BufferingProgress;

    if (setVisualState)
    {
        VisualState = player.PlayerState.ToString("G");
    }

    if (player.Error != null)
    {
        MessageService.ShowError("A problem occured:" + player.Error);
    }
}
```

When the viewmodel's VisualState property changes, the view responds by refreshing the VisualStateManager state. This is performed from the MainPage constructor, as shown:

```
public MainPage()
{
    InitializeComponent();

    DataContext = viewModel;

    viewModel.PropertyChanged
        += (sender, args) =>
            {
                if (args.PropertyName == "VisualState")
                {
                    SetVisualState();
                }
            };
}
```

The view's custom `AppBar` includes icon buttons bound to the viewmodel's commands, as shown:

```xml
<u:AppBar>
    <u:AppBarIconButton
            Command="{Binding PreviousTrackCommand}"
            Text="Previous"
            IconUri="/Images/ApplicationBarIcons/Previous.png" />

    <!-- A toggle button is used rather than visual state to avoid
         repopulating the app bar when the user taps play or pause. -->
    <u:AppBarToggleButton
            x:Name="Button_Play"
            Command1="{Binding PlayCommand}"
            Text1="Play"
            Icon1Uri="/Images/ApplicationBarIcons/Play.png"
            Command2="{Binding PauseCommand}"
            Text2="Pause"
            Icon2Uri="/Images/ApplicationBarIcons/Pause.png"
            Toggled="{Binding CanPause}"/>

    <u:AppBarIconButton
            x:Name="Button_Stop"
            Command="{Binding StopCommand}"
            Text="Stop"
            IconUri="/Images/ApplicationBarIcons/Stop.png" />

    <u:AppBarIconButton
            Command="{Binding NextTrackCommand}"
            Text="Previous"
            IconUri="/Images/ApplicationBarIcons/Next.png" />
</u:AppBar>
```

The viewmodel's `ViewState` property determines the visibility of each button. The XAML that defines the `VisualStateGroups` is not shown, but if you are interested, see the downloadable sample code.

Two `TextBlock` controls are used to display the viewmodel's `TrackArtist` and `TrackTitle` properties, like so:

```xml
<TextBlock Text="{Binding TrackArtist}"
           Style="{StaticResource PhoneTextTitle3Style}"
           TextWrapping="Wrap" />
<TextBlock Text="{Binding TrackTitle}"
           Style="{StaticResource PhoneTextTitle2Style}"
           TextWrapping="Wrap" />
```

Whenever the track changes, these fields are updated according to the new track.

Monitoring Playback Progress

The viewmodel contains a `Position` property that reflects the progress of the current `AudioTrack`. Because the `BackgroundAudioPlayer` does not have facility to monitor the progress of a track directly, the viewmodel uses a `Timer` to periodically raise a property changed event for the `Position` property. The tick handler is shown in the following excerpt:

```
void HandleTimerTick(object state)
{
    if (player.PlayerState == PlayState.Playing)
    {
        OnPropertyChanged(() => Position);
    }
}
```

When a `Position` property change is detected in the view, it prompts a `Slider` control to reread the property. The `Position` get accessor calculates the position value, which is returned as a value between 0 and 1, as shown:

```
public double Position
{
    get
    {
        if (player.Track == null || player.Track.Duration.TotalSeconds < 1)
        {
            return 0;
        }
        double result = player.Position.TotalSeconds
                            / player.Track.Duration.TotalSeconds;
        return result;
    }
    set
    {
        if (player.Track != null)
        {
            double newSeconds = player.Track.Duration.TotalSeconds * value;
            TimeSpan newPosition = TimeSpan.FromSeconds(newSeconds);
            player.Position = newPosition;
        }
        OnPropertyChanged(() => Position);
    }
}
```

Raising a property changed event for the Position property causes the Slider, which is bound to the property, to be updated. The Slider is defined like so:

```
<Slider Value="{Binding Position, Mode=TwoWay}" Minimum="0" Maximum="1" />
```

Figure 29.3 shows the MainPage with the slider indicating the progress of the current track and the application bar icon buttons for controlling playback.

FIGURE 29.3   A user interface to control the BackgroundAudioPlayer from a foreground app

There are numerous possibilities for extending an app such as this. For example, it could be extended to include a view for the playlist or an image for the album art—the sky's the limit!

Audio Streaming Agents

Audio streaming agents allow you to customize how audio files are downloaded and decoded by your app, and they enable you to support live streaming scenarios not natively supported by the phone.

An audio streaming agent can be created in the same manner as an audio player agent, by using the "Windows Phone Audio Streaming Agent" Visual Studio project template (shown previously in Figure 29.1).

29

The Visual Studio project template produces a class that derives from `AudioStreamingAgent`. The agent must then be registered with your main projects WMAppManifest.xml file, which is done automatically when linking to an Audio Streaming Agent project. The XML definition can be seen alongside the `AudioPlayerAgent`, as shown:

```xml
<Tasks>
  <DefaultTask  Name="_default" NavigationPage="MainPage.xaml"/>
    <ExtendedTask Name="BackgroundTask">
        <BackgroundServiceAgent Specifier="AudioPlayerAgent"
            Name="<Unique name within the app>"
            Source="<Assembly>"
            Type="<Namespace.Class>" />
        <BackgroundServiceAgent Specifier="AudioStreamingAgent"
            Name="<Unique name within the app>"
            Source="<Assembly>"
            Type="<Namespace.Class>" />
    </ExtendedTask>
</Tasks>
```

Registering a custom `AudioStreamingAgent` does not disable the built-in streaming and decoding of the phone. The OS determines whether to use the built-in audio streaming or your custom `AudioStreamingAgent`, based on the `AudioTrack`'s `Source` property, each time a new `AudioTrack` is played. To have your custom `AudioStreamingAgent` called for a particular track, assign the `Source` property of the `AudioTrack` to null, as shown in the following excerpt:

```
new AudioTrack(null, /* Uri is null so that it is sent
                      * to the AudioStreamingAgent
                      * called AssemblyAudioStreamingAgent. */
                      "Assembly Track!",
                      "Acquired using AudioStreamingAgent",
                      "Unleashed",
                      null,
                      "AudioFiles/Audio04.mp3", // Tag parameter.
                      EnabledPlayerControls.All),
```

If the `Uri` is not null, the OS performs all streaming and decoding. By using this technique, you can use a combination of both the inbuilt streaming and decoding for some tracks, and custom streaming and decoding for others.

The `AudioTrack` class contains a `Tag` property, which can be used to pass information to an `AudioStreamingAgent`. Notice from the previous excerpt that this property is set to the relative path of an audio file resource. You see, in the next section, how this value is used to resolve an audio file resource from the current assembly.

`AudioStreamingAgent` contains a virtual method named `OnBeginStreaming`, which is overridden to handle streaming and decoding of an audio track. The method has two parameters:

the AudioTrack and an AudioStreamer. The AudioStreamer allows you to attach your own MediaStreamSource. MediaStreamSource provides you with direct access to APIs for manipulating encoded elementary audio and video streams. It enables you to implement your own mechanism for processing the contents of a media file, enabling support beyond the native built-in media formats.

Creating a custom MediaStreamSource is a large topic and one that is outside the scope of this book. A good starting point for learning about the MediaStreamSource is the MSDN ManagedMediaHelpers project located at http://archive.msdn.microsoft.com/ ManagedMediaHelpers.

While not covering MediaStreamSource in detail, this section does, however, look at applying a specialized MediaStreamSource from the ManagedMediaHelpers project to enable the playback of audio files that are located in an app's assembly, something that is not supported by the phone's built-in streaming and decoding system.

Using a MediaStreamSource to Play Back an Assembly Resource

The built-in streaming and decoding system on the phone only supports playback of local audio files when they are located in isolated storage. This section looks at enabling the direct playback of audio files located within an app assembly.

The code for this section resides in the AssemblyAudioStreamingAgent class of the WindowsPhone7Unleashed.BackgroundAudio project in the downloadable sample code. AssemblyAudioStreamingAgent is a subclass of AudioStreamingAgent and overrides the base type's OnBeginStreaming method (see Listing 29.2). The custom IsolatedStorageUtility is used to retrieve the byte stream for an audio file whose location is specified by the AudioTrack.Tag property. An Mp3MediaStreamSource, from the ManagedMediaHelpers library, is created using the stream. The Mp3MediaStreamSource is then assigned to the AudioStreamer, which then relies on the Mp3MediaStreamSource to provide format-independent audio data.

LISTING 29.2   AssemblyAudioStreamingAgent.OnBeginStreaming Method

```
protected override void OnBeginStreaming(AudioTrack track, AudioStreamer streamer)
{
    IsolatedStorageUtility utility = new IsolatedStorageUtility();
    Uri uri = new Uri(track.Tag, UriKind.Relative);
    Stream stream = utility.GetApplicationResourceStream(uri);
    Mp3MediaStreamSource mediaStreamSource
            = new Mp3MediaStreamSource(stream, stream.Length);
    streamer.SetSource(mediaStreamSource);

    /* Not to be called. */
    //NotifyComplete();
}
```

> **NOTE**
>
> Do not call `NotifyComplete` within the `OnBeginStreaming` method. Doing so causes the process running the `AudioStreamingAgent` to be terminated, which halts playback of the file.

Having the ability to provide your own custom streaming means that you can support other third-party services or retrieve files from, for example, a WCF service, which is not supported natively by the OS.

Listing 29.3 demonstrates how to use a `WebRequest` to manually stream an audio file from the Web.

LISTING 29.3   OnBeginStreaming Method with `WebRequest`

```
protected override void OnBeginStreaming(AudioTrack track, AudioStreamer streamer)
{
    HttpWebRequest request
            = WebRequest.CreateHttp("http://localhost:4864/Audio.mp3");
    request.AllowReadStreamBuffering = true;
    request.BeginGetResponse(asyncResult =>
        {
            HttpWebResponse response
                = request.EndGetResponse(asyncResult) as HttpWebResponse;
            if (response != null)
            {
                Stream stream = response.GetResponseStream();
                mediaStreamSource = new Mp3MediaStreamSource(
                                    stream, response.ContentLength);
                streamer.SetSource(mediaStreamSource);
            }
        }, null);
}
```

While not something you will need every day, audio streaming agents provide the means to overcome any limitations imposed by the built-in streaming and decoding system on the phone.

Summary

This chapter began with an overview of the background audio player and showed how it is used to control the playback of local or remote audio files. You looked at how audio file information is represented by the `AudioTrack` class and examined the role of background audio agents, which are used to coordinate audio playback while your app is not running in the foreground. You saw that when used in the foreground, a `BackgroundAudioPlayer` forwards all calls to the registered `AudioPlayerAgent`. Conversely, when a `BackgroundAudioPlayer` is used in an `AudioPlayerAgent`, it directly affects playback on the device.

The chapter then demonstrated how to build a UI that leverages the background audio agent for controlling playback while your app is in the foreground.

Finally, the chapter examined audio streaming agents, and you saw how they are used to provide custom streaming and decoding of audio files. You also saw how a custom audio streaming agent can be employed to play audio directly from an assembly resource, something not possible using the built-in streaming and decoding system of the phone.

29

Bibliography

Chapter 2, "Fundamental Concepts in Silverlight Development for Windows Phone":

"Model-View-ViewModel," http://en.wikipedia.org/wiki/Model_View_ViewModel.

Smith, Josh, "WPF Apps with the Model-View-ViewModel Design Pattern," http://msdn.microsoft.com/en-us/magazine/dd419663.aspx.

Chapter 3, "Application Execution Model":

Rodriguez, Jaime, "Running a Windows Phone Application under the Lock Screen," http://blogs.msdn.com/b/jaimer/archive/2010/11/01/running-a-windows-phone-application-under-the-lock-screen.aspx.

Chapter 7, "Media and Web Elements":

Rodriguez, Jaime, "A deepzoom primer (explained and coded)," http://blogs.msdn.com/b/jaimer/archive/2008/03/31/a-deepzoom-primer-explained-and-coded.aspx.

Chapter 9, "Silverlight Toolkit Controls," and Chapter 14, "Sensors":

Sampson, Nigel, "Using LoopingSelector from the Silverlight Toolkit," http://compiledexperience.com/blog/posts/using-loopingselector-from-the-silverlight-toolkit.

Chapter 10, "Pivot and Panorama":

Vaughan, Katka, "Netflix Browser for Windows Phone 7—Part 1," http://www.codeproject.com/KB/windows-phone-7/NetflixBrowser.aspx.

Chapter 23, "Input Validation":

"Understanding Validation in Silverlight," *AJ's blog*, http://ajdotnet.wordpress.com/2010/02/28/understanding-validation-in-silverlight.

Chapter 24, "Network Services":

Dolhaig, "Zune Detection and Network Awareness," *The Code Project*, http://www.codeproject.com/KB/windows-phone-7/ZuneDetectAndNetworking.aspx.

Index

Symbols

B

How can we make this index more useful? Email us at indexes@samspublishing.com

How can we make this index more useful? Email us at indexes@samspublishing.com

O

obscurity characters, 178

OCC (optimistic concurrency control), 899

 conflict detection, 900-901

 entities, designating, 899

OData (Open Data Protocol), 792

 benefits, 797

 eBay search app

  eBay logo, displaying, 813

  EbayClient class, 804

  network connection changes, monitoring, 807

  OData wrappers, creating, 804-806

  records, retrieving, 807-808

  results, 808-812

  search queries, entering, 810

  view page, 809-813

  viewmodel, 806-809

 entity classes, extending, 816-817

 implementing, 797

 proxies, generating, 800

 queries, 802

  collections, populating, 802-803

  customizing, 802

  model class instance, creating, 802

  results, retrieving, 803

  service operation parameters, 802

  system, 801

  types, 800-802

 URI, 798-799

 website, 797

 wrappers, creating, 804-806

official fonts, 18

offline browsing, 221

 reading content, 225-226

 storing content, 223-225

OnBeginStreaming method, 984-985

OnError method, 977-978

OnErrorsChanged method, 775

OnInvoke method, 925, 942-943

OnNavigatedFrom method, 74, 78, 654

OnNavigatedTo method, 75, 78, 654, 686

OnNavigatingFrom method, 78

OnOrientationChanged method, 102

OnPlayStateChanged method, 974-975

onPropertyChanged method, 46

OnUserAction method, 975-977

opacity (AppBar), 239

Opacity property, 31, 230

Open Data Protocol. See OData

OpenFile method, 822

OptimallyFilteredAcceleration property, 502

optimistic concurrency control (OCC), 899-901

Organizer property, 447

orientation

 compass, 514-515

 page

  animations, 109-112

  determining, 104

  fades, 110

  forcing, 107

  layout visibility conversions, 104-106

  PhoneApplicationPage class, 101

  rotations, 110

  setting at runtime, 106-108

  switching, 102-104

  UI elements, 102, 108-109

  valid device orientations, 103

 PanoramaItems, 346

Orientation property, 101, 104-106, 153

OrientationChanged event, 102-104

OrientationChangedEventArgs class, 103

OrientationView.xaml, 108-109

OriginalFileName property, 434

OriginalSource argument, 360

Overdue property, 931

Owner attribute, 722

How can we make this index more useful? Email us at indexes@samspublishing.com

P

UNLEASHED

Unleashed takes you beyond the basics, providing an exhaustive, technically sophisticated reference for professionals who need to exploit a technology to its fullest potential. It's the best resource for practical advice from the experts and the most in-depth coverage of the latest technologies.

informit.com/unleashed

WPF 4 Unleashed
ISBN-13: 9780672331190

OTHER UNLEASHED TITLES

Microsoft Dynamics CRM 4 Integration Unleashed
ISBN-13: 9780672330544

Microsoft Exchange Server 2010 Unleashed
ISBN-13: 9780672330469

WPF Control Development Unleashed
ISBN-13: 9780672330339

Microsoft SQL Server 2008 Reporting Services Unleashed
ISBN-13: 9780672330261

ASP.NET MVC Framework Unleashed
ISBN-13: 9780672329982

SAP Implementation Unleashed
ISBN-13: 9780672330049

Microsoft XNA Game Studio 3.0 Unleashed
ISBN-13: 9780672330223

Microsoft SQL Server 2008 Integration Services Unleashed
ISBN-13: 9780672330322

IronRuby Unleashed
ISBN-13: 9780672330780

Microsoft SQL Server 2008 Integration Services Unleashed
ISBN-13: 9780672330322

Microsoft SQL Server 2008 Analysis Services Unleashed
ISBN-13: 9780672330018

ASP.NET 3.5 AJAX Unleashed
ISBN-13: 9780672329739

Windows PowerShell Unleashed
ISBN-13: 9780672329883

Windows Small Business Server 2008 Unleashed
ISBN-13: 9780672329579

Microsoft Visual Studio 2010 Unleashed
ISBN-13: 9780672330810

Visual Basic 2010 Unleashed
ISBN-13: 9780672331008

C# 4.0 Unleashed
ISBN-13: 9780672330797

ASP.NET 4.0 Unleashed
ISBN-13: 9780672331121

Silverlight 4 Unleashed
ISBN-13: 9780672333361

SAMS

informit.com/sams

SAMS

REGISTER

THIS PRODUCT

informit.com/register

Register the Addison-Wesley, Exam Cram, Prentice Hall, Que, and Sams products you own to unlock great benefits.

To begin the registration process, simply go to **informit.com/register** to sign in or create an account. You will then be prompted to enter the 10- or 13-digit ISBN that appears on the back cover of your product.

Registering your products can unlock the following benefits:

- Access to supplemental content, including bonus chapters, source code, or project files.
- A coupon to be used on your next purchase.

Registration benefits vary by product. Benefits will be listed on your Account page under Registered Products.

About InformIT — THE TRUSTED TECHNOLOGY LEARNING SOURCE

INFORMIT IS HOME TO THE LEADING TECHNOLOGY PUBLISHING IMPRINTS Addison-Wesley Professional, Cisco Press, Exam Cram, IBM Press, Prentice Hall Professional, Que, and Sams. Here you will gain access to quality and trusted content and resources from the authors, creators, innovators, and leaders of technology. Whether you're looking for a book on a new technology, a helpful article, timely newsletters, or access to the Safari Books Online digital library, InformIT has a solution for you.

informIT.com

THE TRUSTED TECHNOLOGY LEARNING SOURCE

Addison-Wesley | Cisco Press | Exam Cram
IBM Press | Que | Prentice Hall | Sams

SAFARI BOOKS ONLINE

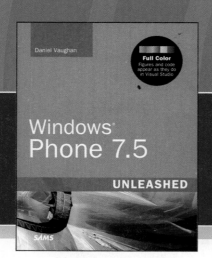

Windows® Phone 7.5 UNLEASHED

Daniel Vaughan

Full Color
Figures and code appear as they do in Visual Studio

FREE Online Edition

Your purchase of *Windows® Phone 7.5 Unleashed* includes access to a free online edition for 45 days through the **Safari Books Online** subscription service. Nearly every Sams book is available online through **Safari Books Online**, along with thousands of books and videos from publishers such as Addison-Wesley Professional, Cisco Press, Exam Cram, IBM Press, O'Reilly Media, Prentice Hall, Que, and VMware Press.

Safari Books Online is a digital library providing searchable, on-demand access to thousands of technology, digital media, and professional development books and videos from leading publishers. With one monthly or yearly subscription price, you get unlimited access to learning tools and information on topics including mobile app and software development, tips and tricks on using your favorite gadgets, networking, project management, graphic design, and much more.

Activate your FREE Online Edition at
informit.com/safarifree

STEP 1:   Enter the coupon code: EFEGFAA.

STEP 2:   New Safari users, complete the brief registration form.
Safari subscribers, just log in.

If you have difficulty registering on Safari or accessing the online edition,
please e-mail customer-service@safaribooksonline.com

  Adobe Press Cisco Press Press IBM Press  New Riders O'REILLY

 Peachpit Press PRENTICE HALL que Redbooks SAMS SAS vmware PRESS WILEY   wrox